100 Best Family Resorts in North America

"Unlike usual 'family' (mostly just tantrum-tolerant) guides, this gives equal time to grown up gimmes, miraculously pinpointing spots that combine kidstuff and capital 'C' Class."

—Pamela Robin Brandt
New York Daily News

"Are you tired of family vacations that offer limited activities? Bored with the usual tourist-trap destinations? Then pick up a copy of *The 100 Best Family Resorts in North America* . . . and start planning the best family vacation ever."

—*BCP Parent Pages*

"Gives parents scores of options for family travel . . . from charming country lodges and mountain getaways, to the big hotels. A great place to start when you're looking for the ultimate family destination."

—Felice H. Shapiro, Publisher
New York Family Publications

Help Us Keep This Guide Up to Date

Every effort has been made by the author and editors to make this guide as accurate and useful as possible. However, many things can change after a guide is published—establishments close, phone numbers change, hiking trails are rerouted, facilities come under new management, etc.

We would love to hear from you concerning your experiences with this guide and how you feel it could be made better and be kept up to date. While we may not be able to respond to all comments and suggestions, we'll take them to heart and we'll also make sure to share them with the author. Please send your comments and suggestions to the following address:

The Globe Pequot Press
Reader Response/Editorial Department
P.O. Box 833
Old Saybrook, CT 06475

Or you can e-mail us at:

editorial@globe-pequot.com

Thanks for your input, and happy travels!

DANA-FARBER
CANCER INSTITUTE

William J. Schaller
Director of Media Relations

Department of Communications

375 Longwood Avenue
Boston, Massachusetts 02215
617.632.5357 tel.
617.632.5520 fax
william_schaller@dfci.harvard.edu

Dr Bunnell,

there is a copy of the Channel 4 + 7 interviews

Thanks again for your time.

Bill

100 Best Resorts Series

100 Best Family Resorts in North America

•••••••••••••••••••

*100 Quality Resorts
with Leisure Activities
for Children and Adults*

Fourth Edition

by **Janet Tice**
and **Jane Wilford**

*Revised by
Becky Danley*

A Voyager Book

The Globe Pequot Press

Old Saybrook, Connecticut

Cover Photo Credits
Top left: Courtesy of Flathead Lake Lodge, Bigfork, Montana
Bottom left: Courtesy of Stratton Mountain Resort, Stratton Mountain, Vermont
Bottom right: Courtesy of The Tyler Place on Lake Champlain, Highgate Springs, Vermont

Cover Design by Saralyn D'Amato Twomey.

Library of Congress Cataloging-in-Publication Data

Tice, Janet, 1942-
  100 best family resorts in North America : 100 quality resorts with leisure activities for children and adults / by Janet Tice and Jane Wilford. — 4th ed.
      p. cm. — (100 best resorts series)
  "A voyager book."
  Includes index.
  ISBN 0-7627-0112-9
      1. United States—Guidebooks. 2. Resorts—United States—Guidebooks. 3. Family recreation—United States—Guidebooks. 4. Canada—Guidebooks. 5. Resorts—Canada—Guidebooks. 6. Family recreation—Canada—Guidebooks. I. Wilford, Jane, 1951- . II. Title. III. Series.
  E158.T53   1997
  917.304'929—dc21   97-29277
                                                                                CIP

Manufactured in the United States of America
Fourth Edition/First Printing

*To Fabiana and Sykes, who first provided
the inspiration, and to Paul and Sarah,
who continue to share the adventure.
Our wonderful children and
our best family travel critics!*

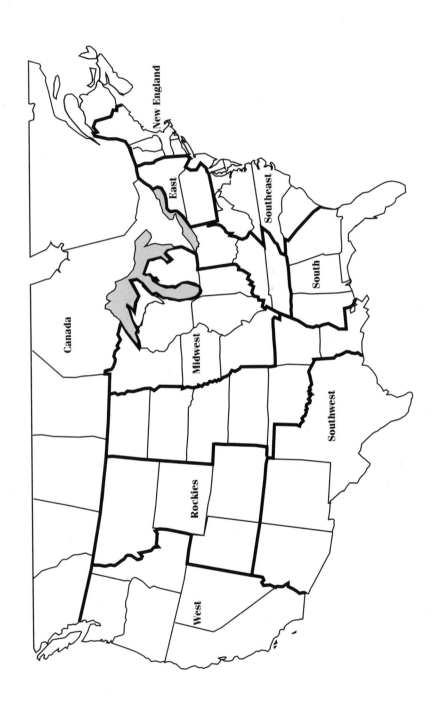

Contents

Preface

"Best" is a curious adjective, one that is entirely subjective. So let us define our sense of best—both what it does and what it doesn't mean.

Best is not necessarily the fanciest, the biggest, the most expensive.

Best is not always the sleekest, the poshest, or the newest.

Best, in the context of this book, is what is best for families.

Best is variety—in setting and atmosphere.

Best is variety in recreational interests and in prices.

Best is variety in geographical location. A broad selection allows you to have choices whether you want to travel far or near.

We searched for the most extensive children's programs, yet balanced this with an interest in presenting a good cross-section of North America. If we have overlooked your favorite, let us know. Please write to us in care of The Globe Pequot Press, P.O. Box 833, Old Saybrook, CT 06475.

Janet Tice
Jane Wilford

Acknowledgment

Many thanks to D. Sykes Wilford, who shared his travels and his travails during the production of this manuscript.

Introduction

Although traveling with children is not a new phenomenon, many Americans these days are viewing the traditional family vacation in a different light. In past decades family vacations have most frequently been determined by the needs and wants of the children. Planning the entire vacation around the kids often left Mom and Dad with the sense that they had not had a vacation at all but, rather, a trial by fire. The only option was to leave Junior behind in the care of grandparents or close family friends while the parents ventured off on their own. In an attempt to share experiences with their children, many parents, seeking middle ground, are adjusting the focus of their leisure-time plans.

Vacations these days often mean shorter and more frequent jaunts. Increasingly, they involve flying rather than loading up the family car and driving. Mini-vacations are becoming popular and are frequently planned to coincide with one or the other parent's business trips. On the philosophical side, current trends in child care emphasize the importance of a parent's presence, especially for the first three years, and many parents are reluctant to leave their infants and toddlers for extended periods.

The intent of this book is to identify those places where adults and children can enjoy interesting and age-appropriate activities. Babysitting services for infants, a ski school for three-year-olds, and a supervised recreational program for older children are some of the possibilities explored. In selecting resorts we have taken into consideration different styles, price ranges, and diverse geographic locations. It is a representative sampling rather than an all-inclusive listing. Often we have been limited by lack of space and lack of information. This book does not highlight every Disney World and Six Flags Over Somewhere establishment in the United States. While these certainly serve an important educational function in a pleasant and exciting atmosphere for children, therein lies the catch: They are directed primarily toward children. But parents deserve vacations, too—adult vacations with grown-up activities.

This is not, then, a book about vacations for kids. Rather, it is a book about vacations with kids, about family adventures in which adults can be adults and children can be children and in which there is common ground for sharing.

In general we are pleased with the progress we've noted in the resorts we have chosen from our previous editions. They are not resting on their laurels but seem to be enthusiastic and dedicated to making more and more improvements and providing better and better facilities and programs for families. In addition, new resorts developing exciting agendas are constantly entering this family-oriented market.

If we've left out your favorite family spot, or if you own a resort and feel slighted, please write to us in care of The Globe Pequot Press. We're always glad to know of places where families find special treatment.

The prices and rates listed in this guidebook were confirmed at press time. We recommend, however, that you call establishments to obtain current information before traveling.

Costs and Caveats

Prices are noted throughout the book in the accommodations section of each resort's description. They are current as of 1997. But, just like the new car that depreciates the minute you drive away from the showroom, prices have to be adjusted for inflation the minute they're stated. Keep this in mind if your travel plans do not materialize right away but instead are put on the back burner for a couple of years. Inflation takes its toll simultaneously and universally; however, the prices quoted here can serve as a basis for comparison among resorts regardless of the year in which you consult this guide.

The problem most commonly caused by prices is sorting out just what a given price includes. In the travel industry, various pricing schedules are frequently used to identify the relationship between lodging and meals. For example:

European plan means the rate quoted is for lodging only.

Modified American plan means two meals a day (usually breakfast and dinner) as well as lodging are included in the daily rate.

Full American plan means three meals a day and lodging are covered in the daily rate.

The extent of what else is included in the daily room rate, such as use of the recreational facilities, varies widely from one resort to another. Every effort has been made to identify the extras for which no additional charge is required. If "complimentary" or "free" is not clearly stated for a service or activity, you can safely assume that there is a fee.

Besides lodging and meals, prices are specifically noted for children's programs. As a well-seasoned traveler, you already have a ballpark idea of the prices of lift tickets for skiing and greens fees for golf. Emphasis here is on costs of the children's activities because now you're trying to become well seasoned as a traveling parent.

Planning Family Vacations

How This Book Can Help You

As your vacation rolls around, you start weighing the pros and cons of bringing the children along. You feel that you desperately need exclusive time for adult conversation with your spouse or other grown-ups. Yet you wonder if following through on that idea is fair to your kids. Vacations need not be an either–or proposition—either resigning yourself to a week or two of nonstop "Sesame Street" activities with no relief in sight or excluding the children from the few leisure weeks you have away from a demanding career. The former scenario almost always requires relinquishing your own interests, while the latter is complicated by worry and guilt over little Johnny or Susie left behind at Grandma's as you're off footloose and fancy-free. It is possible, however, to have a vacation that is fair to both you and your children.

So you're ready to plan a vacation with the kids. Though this sounds like what parents have been doing for generations, you're different from previous generations. You're better educated and fairly well traveled; you've delayed getting married and having children until your career was launched; and most likely you're older as you reach this phase of family life than were your parents. In addition, you probably have different expectations for both yourself and your children, expectations that influence how you want to spend your leisure time. While you're devoted to your children and conscious of the importance of your input into their intellectual, emotional, and social growth, you also realize that part of being a good parent is tending to your own physical and psychological well-being. You imagine that it must be feasible to share a pleasurable vacation experience with your children without denying your own interests and concerns. Well, it is!

When you've made the decision that the kids should come along this time and you know that one more carousel or one more pair of Mickey Mouse ears just might drive you crazy, then let this book help you discover the perfect vacation spot, where the whole family can be happy together.

Whether you are considering a few relaxing days at a country hideaway or a week of fun in the sun on a beach, rest assured that there are accommodations with facilities and activities that will delight you and your children. A family vacation doesn't have to mean settling for renting the same house at the nearest beach each season for the next several years or the proverbial visit to Grandma's house year after year. Variety can be found, and if you're itching for a good game of golf, you don't have to fret over whether your three-year-old can manage walking eighteen holes or what antics he'll perform along the way. These concerns can be resolved by choosing the proper surroundings and conditions.

When a young parent once inquired about children's activities at one resort, the staff member gave her a bottle of bubbles. That would last about thirty seconds, right? Thank goodness many resorts are more enlightened, and those you'll find here.

Explore in the following pages a selection of hotels, condominiums, and resorts that offer conveniences to accommodate the needs and wishes of both adults and children. So that you can gratify your diverse and periodically changing geographical interests, you will discover that this guide includes establishments throughout the United States, with a few in Canada. The United States is at the forefront of the new approach to family vacations.

In compiling this collection several criteria were considered: attractive surroundings; good dining facilities, including comfortable lounges and bars; babysitting services; and recreational activities for both parents and children. Needless to say, some of the establishments listed here meet more of the criteria or meet them better than others. But then, your wishes and requirements may vary from one trip to the next: One year you may need just a competent babysitter to stay in your hotel room with your infant while you enjoy an elegant, leisurely dinner, and the next year you may need a complete day-care center/nursery school for your energetic toddler while you spend the day out on the slopes. This book does not rank resorts on how well the criteria are met; it simply describes them and all their available services. You can then pick and choose according to your personal preferences and current needs.

To make it easier to find your ideal vacation spot, the descriptive entries are grouped by geographical location, then alphabetically within these divisions; addresses and telephone numbers are included in the descriptions.

Following the descriptions is a standard alphabetical index of resort names to help you pull out the perfect place that a friend recently mentioned at a dinner party, the location of which eludes your recollective powers. This arrangement should afford you easiest access to the required information regardless of your perspective when designing your vacation.

Finally, a special categories index is given that lists resorts by type, such as seaside resorts or resorts with skiing. A resort may appear under more than one heading—it may, for example, shine for its golf course as well as for its beach. Conversely, a resort will not appear under every heading for which it has attractions, only for those that particularly distinguish it.

While probably foremost in your mind for your next trip is simply to make that perfect match between your personal circumstances and the most suitable resort, you may occasionally feel a bit nervous about some of the practical logistics of traveling with kids. The section on helpful hints when traveling with children may forestall a few inconveniences that may arise when away from home; the chapter on medical information should allay some fears about illnesses and emergencies; and the segments on educating yourself and the advantages of a good travel agent may assist in ironing out the details of your vacation arrangements. In any case, they will stimulate you to analyze your own and your children's habits so that you can anticipate some of the problems and joys of traveling with youngsters.

So you're off. Good luck and happy vacation!

Helpful Hints for Traveling with Children

It can be a joy to travel with children. Sure, sometimes the preparations may seem exhausting and spurts of parental anxiety en route may be tiring as well, but the excitement and wonder of children as they encounter new experiences are worth the price of admission.

In the following pages you'll find some helpful hints for traveling with kids. Many of these suggestions may seem incredibly obvious, but stating the obvious is not always a disadvantage. And a little repetitive reinforcement may help you react more quickly or think better on your feet. An excellent resource book is *Trouble-free Travel with Children* (The Book Peddler, 1991), by Vicki Lansky, author of more than twenty books for new parents.

The first trick to traveling with kids is preparing them for the adventure. Talk to your child in advance; advise her where you're going and what you'll be doing. Infants (in spite of the mounds of disposable diapers you must tote) are very portable. Even toddlers whose whole world revolves around Mom and Dad are happy as long as familiar faces are near at hand. But as a child's world expands to include friends and a wider realm of belongings, verbal preparation becomes very important. Sometimes it's easy to assume that your youngster will pick up on things by osmosis, but children don't always assimilate information about vacation plans that floats around the house in chitchat. It's necessary to explain directly to them what is in store. Books and maps about your destination and route can be shared; even for very young children, maps translate the excitement of travel into a tangible form.

Besides detailing the fun of this new experience, reassure your child that you'll be returning home; that although your daughter may not bring along every Barbie doll and Raggedy Ann, her dolls will still be here when she gets back; and that even though your son may miss his best friends, they won't forget him. Even three- and four-year-olds can "write" postcards along the way as a means of staying connected with friends back home. As an experienced traveler, you know the ropes of appropriate packing for trips. As a conscientious parent, you are most familiar with what your child will want or need away from home. The standard rule of thumb—don't overpack—applies just as well for children as it does for adults. The length of the trip adjusted for the dirt factor of your own child (how many outfits can he go through in a day?) should give you a reasonable handle on the amount of clothes to pack. Laundromats are never that far away, many hotels have laundry services, and kids' clothes (just by virtue of their size) are fairly easy to hand wash in a hotel bathroom. And don't take along what your child isn't happy with. No matter how much time dear Aunt Josie spent crocheting that sweet little dress, if your daughter doesn't like it, if it's uncomfortable, it will be nothing more than an unnecessary bulge in your suitcase.

If your child uses a bottle, a trip may not be the best time to nudge him out of it; a bottle may provide a bit of security in unfamiliar surroundings. Just be sure to pack a bottle brush: If a bottle gets lost at the bottom of a travel bag for a day or two, mysterious molds blossom, dispelled only by a little scrubbing.

Toys, too, have to fall under the "don't overpack" rule. Remember that for children, seemingly mundane objects in new surroundings often provide considerable amusement. It's a good idea to stash away a couple of new attention-getters, but don't forget the tried and true. A cuddly doll, even if it is beginning to look somewhat old and ratty, or a special pillow is often very comforting for a little one sleeping in a strange bed for the first time. Age-adjusted, of course, books, a small ball, crayons, coloring books, scissors, construction paper, a bean bag (remember them from when you were a kid?), and small games such as a pint-size checkerboard are all packable items. Even blocks like Duplos or Legos, if arranged in one compact cube, can be packed fairly easily. Some parents cherish a Fisher-Price tape recorder or a Walkman (with earphones, please) as something akin to a gift from the gods. Terrifically totable and accompanied by a selection of tapes (anything from Walt Disney stories to old radio shows to historical accounts of George Washington and Benjamin Franklin are on the market now), a tape recorder can effectively hold a child's attention.

For the preschooler or older child, you may consider investing in a backpack. Set down the rules with your child when packing: He can bring along whatever fits in the pack, and he has to carry it. In this way you can give your child a sense of participating in the preparations and obviate the almost inevitable whine about something Mom didn't include. And practically unnoticed you can sneak in a little lesson in responsibility. A "surprise box" is also a fun way to generate excitement about a trip. Without divulging details, clue your child in to your preparations of the secrets and mysteries of this cache. Then watch the fun as he delves into the goodies (snacks and small toys) when the vacation adventure begins. A surprise box can entertain your youngster anywhere from two minutes to two hours; if you're particularly circumspect and shrewd, you'll be on the latter end of the spectrum.

When making plane reservations, try to secure seat assignments at the same time. Indicate the age of your young traveler, and request the bulkhead seats. These seats afford a little extra leg room and can be padded with blankets and pillows if your child decides to snooze (lucky you!). It may mean that your feet will be struck by paralysis if little Janie nestles down on her pillow and curls up on your toes, but it is an improvement over having her elbow in your drink. Also, without passengers in front of you in this seating arrangement, you won't fret over a rambunctious child's kicks disturbing other people.

If two parents are flying with a lap child, reserve an aisle seat and a window seat. Regular air travelers never request a center seat, so if the plane is not full, you'll wind up with that third seat in which to spread out; if a stranger does venture into your row, it's simple enough for one parent to move over a notch.

Many airlines stock on-board activity packs for children, and some even prepare special meals for their younger travelers. Sometimes airlines have a limited amount of baby food; usually you need to pack your own. Inquire about these services.

If you plan to rent a car during your vacation, be sure to request a car seat for a child four years old and younger. While many rental agencies take this in stride, the number of car seats is usually limited, so it's important to make a reservation for this accessory in advance of your arrival. Whether your mode of transportation is your own car or a rental, plan frequent stops. Cramped legs and fidgetiness set in fast for youngsters. These factors are not unknown in air travel either; even a walk down the aisle of the plane to the bathroom is a change of pace for a child.

Airplanes pose additional problems: Small children often have greater difficulty than adults in adjusting to altitude changes. During takeoffs and landings, infants should be encouraged to nurse or drink a bottle; the sucking action combats blocked ear and painful sinus problems. Older children can use the same techniques as adults—yawning and chewing gum.

In car travel, a small ice chest in the backseat can be a real boon. Filled with milk, juice, and fruit, it provides a source of ready refreshment and relieves frantic searches for a fast-food stop or a corner grocery. Even when traveling by air, if your luggage allotment permits, check a small ice chest (empty) along with your other bags. Once you arrive at your hotel, it can be filled with ice and drinks and can be taken along in a rental car on side trips. Many accommodations include small refrigerators in the rooms, and some are equipped with kitchens, but if not, you've solved a problem before it arises. It's much easier to dig into an ice chest for a drink than to track down juice somewhere in the hotel facilities at nine o'clock at night. But if this seems too cumbersome and your child desperately needs something late at night, remember the hotel bar—it is the best place to hit, for it always has orange juice (for Screwdrivers), tomato juice (for Bloody Marys), and milk (for White Russians). It may be more expensive, but can you really afford to count pennies when Johnny refuses to go to sleep without his nightly cup of milk? It's an investment in your peace of mind.

When stocking up on drinks, buy the variety in cardboard cartons. Since they are unbreakable and need no refrigeration, they can be squirreled away in a suitcase or even tossed into a purse. On an airplane, the flight attendants never seem to pass by soon enough or often enough to satisfy little ones.

For edibles, small boxes of raisins, granola bars, and individually wrapped cheese chunks such as La Vache qui Rit (what child can resist a silly laughing cow in a red net bag?) make good nourishing snacks. Good old clever Mom can rack up some kudos when she pulls one of these treats from her bag before Susie even thinks about getting antsy.

Once you arrive at your destination and settle into your hotel, turn over an area, even if just a corner, to your child. His own space filled with his own stuff may mean a lot to him in terms of a sense of belonging, and with a bit of prodding you may avoid having toys strewn all about.

Collecting souvenirs on a trip is at best a time-consuming process or maybe even a headache or two. Either Joey wants everything in sight or he chooses the most inappropriate piece of junk you've ever seen. Sure, certain limits on buying have to be set, but who cares if he chooses the made-in-Japan pencil sharpener in the shape of a cannon during a visit to Valley Forge? With a nod from Lady Luck, it will be lost before you're homeward bound. Just as a cookbook containing three wonderful meat-pie recipes from Nova Scotia or an artistic ceramic tile made in the Southwest is something that you can't possibly do without, there are special reminders of a trip that a child feels he needs. They're just different. A few neat rocks and a couple of sticks may be the only things he wants to show off to his best buddy back home. Or if your little girl wants to take home a shiny red coin purse to her best friend, she doesn't care (and neither does her friend) that the same item is on the shelves in every Woolworth across the country, so why should you? A smattering of understanding and patience can go a long way. Recreational activities in your new surroundings must be evaluated with a clear head and a sharp eye. All of the resorts included here offer organized children's activities or babysitting services, so it's not necessary to drag kids along on every adult event you want to investigate. Antiques hunting and museum visits are usually not first-rate attractions for members of the kiddie league. Plan on a babysitter or a group activity for an afternoon that you want to spend on a grown-up outing.

And for those days that are devoted entirely to being together, alternate grown-up pursuits with juvenile ones. Remember that a child's attention span is not as refined or sophisticated as an adult's; variety is more than the spice of life—it's the key to sanity in some cases. Climbing on the cannons at an old fort is much more fun for a child than reading every historical marker; a mixture of both keeps everyone happy. All day on the beach may be too much for a three- or four-year-old, and you can take ten-to-one odds that he won't be content following your lead to relax and soak up the sunshine. Bargain with your child: a run on the beach and a few splashes in the waves, then quiet time building a sand castle.

Many resorts have lodging with fully equipped kitchens so that you can cook family meals in a homelike setting. Many resort restaurants make an attentive effort to please children; a special dining hour for families or a clever children's menu certainly helps make life more pleasant. But when you grow weary of dining in restaurants, a picnic may be a reasonable alternative. Many hotels can prepare box lunches, or you can pick up some cold cuts at a small grocery for a do-it-yourself picnic. Ordering a meal through room service can be a special treat for a child.

As you skim the descriptive entries of the resorts, you'll realize that most are self-contained vacation spots. Each offers a place to sleep, a place to eat, and something to do. This is intentional, as children seem to function best staying in one place. Establishing a home base, exploring the setting, and taking afternoon side trips are often preferable to being on the road constantly. Besides negating all the packing and unpacking of a traditional road trip (remember, this is not the newest rock star promoting his latest album that you're traveling with!), having a home base helps a child develop a sense of security as the new surroundings become familiar.

With a few tricks up your sleeve and some understanding forethought, traveling with kids can be a fun-filled family adventure. Your well-considered plans make the whole process workable and buy a lot of happiness for both you and your child.

Medical Information

Unless you can take Doogie Howser or Marcus Welby with you, the best advice to follow is the old Girl Scout motto "Be Prepared." Keep in mind: (1) This adventure you're about to embark upon is not a trek along the shores of the East Siberian Sea, and (2) you are not the sole custodian of Band-Aids. As exciting as it may be, your vacation destination is a part of twentieth-century technology, and (this may be even more amazing to believe) doctors and pharmacies do exist out there in that twilight zone called family vacations.

Before starting your trip, consult your pediatrician for advice; she/he may even be able to supply names of colleagues where you'll be visiting. If you fear that your child is coming down with something as you depart on your vacation, or if she's particularly accident-prone, you can check with the resort staff upon arrival about the location of the nearest hospital and pharmacy and the availability of doctors and nurses (many resorts have medical personnel on call). Sometimes the best recommendations come from other parents, wherever you may find them. If the need is immediate, don't hesitate to ask a likely looking parent working in a car rental agency, a restaurant, a shop, or the airport. And without seeming alarmist, look up the telephone number of the local poison control center; anticipating the slim chance of ever needing it, you'll be gratified that it's handy should your child ingest a handful of your brightly colored vitamin pills.

Pack a medical/emergency kit and try to envision the unexpected. If your child scrapes a knee at a playground or develops an earache in the middle of the night, you won't want to take time tracking down a drugstore in order to relieve his discomfort. You can purchase a ready-made medical kit that fits compactly in a car's glove compartment or carry-on bag, or you may prefer the do-it-yourself variety. The following list is merely suggestive; review your own medicine cabinet to fill in the gaps.

standard vitamins and medications your child normally takes
a thermometer
children's aspirin or Tylenol
children's cough syrup
adhesive strips
nose drops (though most kids hate them)
a decongestant such as Dimetapp
an aspirator
ear drops
suppositories (change in water and altitude or sheer excitement can affect a child's system)

Desitin or A and D ointment
antibiotic ointment or spray such as Bacitracin or Bactine (for cuts and scrapes)
tweezers and a sterile needle (to remove splinters)
ipecac (to induce vomiting if your child overdoses on peculiar substances)
Q-Tips and cotton balls
sterile gauze pads (for applying direct pressure to cuts)
insect repellent

Though this list seems long, the items take up very little space in a suitcase. Remember, you don't have to pack a lifetime supply of any of these things. A small box of adhesive strips and a small bottle of cough medicine will meet the immediate need and buy you time to find the drugstore.

Knowing What Questions to Ask

There seem to be almost as many pricing schedules, package plans, and special programs as there are resorts. There are EP, MAP, FAP, golf and tennis packages, weekend specials, and midweek discounts. Depending on geographical location, high season is winter at one resort and summer at another. Even the seasons are defined arbitrarily. Summer may be the end of June through Labor Day or, perhaps, Memorial Day through Labor Day. Christmas season starts December 15 at some places and a week later at others. All the jargon and variations on a theme can make you feel like a babe in the woods when contacting a resort about your plans. To avoid arriving someplace and getting halfway through your stay only to find out that you should have taken advantage of some special offer, you have to be savvy in the possibilities and the vocabulary. Even if you aren't familiar with the latest buzzwords, just knowing that different vacation configurations exist puts you a leg up; you can at least ask, "Are there any family discounts or package plans for _____ [fill in the blank—golf, tennis, skiing, etc.]?"

At some resorts, you walk in and pay one price. At others, every hour on the tennis court or every bicycle ride around the block is charged separately. Both approaches have redeeming aspects. To some folks, it's downright annoying to have to reach constantly for a wallet. After all, this is a vacation and they don't want to be troubled with mundane monetary matters. On the other hand, some people would rather pay as they go, laying down the cash for only the services they use. If you've had aquaphobia since childhood and don't care to be within 10 feet of a lake, much less out in the middle rocking a canoe, free boating privileges are worthless. As long as you're in the know as to a resort's practices and policies beforehand, you'll suffer no surprises and no aggravation or disappointment during your visit.

Much of a resort's terminology is self-explanatory, and for the experienced traveler, even the acronyms are no mysteries. The most commonly used abbreviations are EP, for European plan, meaning lodging only; MAP, for modified American plan, which includes two meals a day in the room rate; and FAP, for full American plan, which includes three meals a day.

Knowing a resort's designation of low and high season is also crucial to your planning. If you're not absolutely wedded to certain dates and you can juggle your schedule on the home front, you might land in the low season simply by altering your plans by a week.

Moving to more detailed information, you may want to ask a resort certain specific questions. The questions outlined here can be used on the resorts described in this book for elaboration on particular points, or you can test them out on places that you discover on your own.

Lodging

Are the accommodations hotel rooms, condominium units, or cottages with kitchens?

If they are hotel rooms:
- Are there connecting rooms?
- Is there a refrigerator in the room? (This is handy for chilling juice and milk and keeping snacks fresh.)
- What is the range of prices, and is there a reduced rate for children?
- Is there a charge for a crib or rollaway bed?

Dining

What types of dining areas are there? Is there a spot to get Joey a hot dog and a place that tantalizes more refined taste buds?

Is there a dress requirement? (What a disappointment to venture into a tempting restaurant only to learn that gentlemen are required to wear jackets and you packed nothing but golf shirts!)

Is there a meal plan? Is it mandatory or optional?

Kids

Is there a supervised program for children?
- What are the planned activities, and what are the ages of the children who participate?

- When is it held—times of the year, days of the week, and hours of the day? (The level of specificity may seem a little overboard, but consider a Monday-through-Friday-morning program: It's not going to be much help if you pull in at 1:00 P.M. on Friday and leave at 10:00 A.M. Tuesday.)
- What is the daily or hourly fee?
- Is there a playground or game room? (Even if you're doing the supervision, if there's something amusing for the kids, they can release some energy and you can sit on the sidelines and read the newspaper.)

Are babysitting services available?

- Who makes the arrangements—you or the resort staff?
- What is the average rate? (You may linger a bit longer over that fine Cabernet if your babysitter receives $3.00 an hour rather than $6.00 an hour.)

And if you're skittish about your kid's health or proclivity toward disaster, inquire about local medical facilities.

- Is there a doctor or nurse in residence or on call?
- Where are the nearest hospital and pharmacy?

For You

If you're investigating a resort or have chosen it as a vacation destination, you no doubt have an inkling as to its recreational facilities. You're looking at it *because* of its beach, golf course, tennis center, or ski mountain. Besides its main attraction, you'll also want to know what secondary diversions are possible. You can't play golf sixteen hours a day—not even Jack Nicklaus does that. So ask:

- Is there a jogging path? parcours fitness trail? hiking trails?
- Is there a spa or exercise room? sauna, steam room, whirlpool?
- Does the tennis complex also house racquetball courts?
- For golf, tennis, and fishing—is it possible to rent equipment, or is it necessary to bring your own?
- Are there any concerts, lectures, and classes?

Your interests will determine which questions to ask. Once you get a handle on what to ask, you'll find planning a vacation a lot more fun and a lot less time-consuming. You don't have to have all the answers; just being able to pose a few intelligent questions sets the ball in motion and can generate maybe even more information than you thought you wanted. As a knowledgeable consumer, you can pursue plans on your own or you can work quite effectively with a travel agent. In either case, a little self-education can certainly enhance the preparation and the end product: your leisure time.

Using a Travel Agent

Going to a travel agent has certain overtones of the classic Dr. Jekyll and Mr. Hyde story. Almost everyone has a friend or relative in the travel business; almost everyone has at least one horror story. Working conscientiously with a competent travel agent minimizes the possibility of frightful tales and increases the chances of very positive experiences.

Why should you use a travel agent? The main reasons are three: (1) Agents have a knowledge and expertise that comes with training and experience (yours is not the only vacation ever planned); (2) they have access to comprehensive resources and services; and (3) it is convenient and economical, both in time and money.

Travel agents provide a service. They can book an airline flight, reserve a hotel room, and line up a rental car. There is generally no charge for this attention, as agents' commissions are paid by the supplier—either airlines, hotels, or car companies. An agent's success depends to a large extent on repeat business and referral, so pleasing the passenger is a top priority. Ideally, agents should be passenger advocates, defending "those who roam the world."

Travel, like so much else today, has become increasingly complicated. Since the deregulation of the airlines, the proliferation of air fares has been phenomenal. Any given pair of cities has up to sixty different fares, with as many rules and regulations. While this ultimately benefits the pleasure traveler, it also creates a certain amount of chaos. On a trip from New York to San Francisco, for example, the same seat in the airplane can cost anywhere between $299 and $750, depending on how far in advance you book, how long you're staying, and the promotional needs of the air carrier. When one adds other factors such as the day of the week, certain airports, one-stop versus nonstop flights, or whether you're wearing polka dots, more complications arise. While airlines generally give you their own lowest fares, they do not necessarily tell you about a competitor who may have even lower fares or more convenient flights.

This scenario supports all three reasons for using a travel agent. Save yourself time and money by turning over these problems to a travel agent. While you could spend literally days tracking down this information, a good travel agent with a talent for mysteries and a handy-dandy computer can accomplish miracles in anywhere from five minutes to an hour or so. Equipped with something called the "shoppers' fares," the computer allows a quick review of all the airlines that travel to a given destination and lists the fares beginning with the lowest. You can then work with the agent to figure out if saving $100 is really worth getting up at 3:00 A.M. Finally, you can capitalize on an agent's knowledge of the fares and facilities that each airline provides for children and of any special family-travel offers, such as "kids fly free" and discounts for spouses.

Even something as seemingly straightforward as a hotel reservation can be complicated by weekend specials, golf or tennis packages, seasons, midweek, and family offers. If there are many hotels on your agenda, it is a real pleasure to let the agent repeat sixteen times over the same information about your needs and desires. A good agent is a whiz at interpreting brochures and deciphering the fine print. "Ocean view" does not mean on the beach; in fact, you may have to hang over the balcony with a pair of binoculars to see the ocean. "Secluded" may mean private, or it may mean you have to go 10 miles to find any other signs of life. In the air or on the ground, the knowledgeable agent saves you time and converts elusive information into something concrete in your vacation plans.

This is the age of information overkill; managing this information, sorting through the myriad possibilities, can be mind-boggling. Working with a professional travel agent can add several dimensions to this information process. An agent is a bountiful source of books, brochures, and maps; but more important are the agent's personal experience, the client base that gives feedback on pros and cons of trips, and close contact with colleagues in the travel agency who have traveled extensively. A good agent can pull all of this together, analyze your needs, and help make your vacation dream become a coherent reality.

While the savings in time have been illustrated, let's not forget how enlisting the services of a travel agent can save you money as well. This is an advantage not to be overlooked, for it is the travel agent who can find the most economical way of doing what you want to do. A good agent with appropriate input from you can match alternatives with your particular budget demands.

Now that you are aware of the joys of using a travel agent, how do you find this wonderful person? Travel agents are dealers in dreams—in charge of that very precious event, your vacation. You should pick your travel agent as carefully as you would your doctor—or your car mechanic! It's very nice to go to your Aunt Nelly or your neighbor's first cousin, but a smart consumer considers more substantial factors. Most important of these are the accessibility and policies of the agency and the personality and qualifications of the agent.

Working from the general to the specific, look first at the agency itself. Is it a pleasant environment; are the people animated? What are their policies on service charges, refunds, payments? Are they an appointed agency of the airlines, Amtrak, and the cruise lines? Airline appointments indicate a certain basic financial investment and preparation and the ability to write airline tickets. Is the agency computerized? Most are nowadays and because of computerization have the capability to scan quickly for the best fares and most convenient flights, make seat assignments, and issue boarding passes. Another consideration is whether the agency is a member of the American Society of Travel Agents (ASTA). There are good agencies that may not be members, but affiliation with this professional organization of the travel industry indicates that an agency has been in operation for at least three years. ASTA also acts as a ready resource for problems and possible complaints.

The ability and personality of an individual agent are crucial factors in your selection. You should like and respect the person you entrust your pleasures to and have confidence in his/her ability and desire to look after your interests. A reliable, though subjective, way of choosing an agent is to ask friends whose opinion you trust and whose values you share. On a more objective level, you can check an agent's credentials. More and more agents are now becoming certified travel consultants, indicating at least five years' experience and completion of a two-year intensive study program. While this is a professional plus, it is not a requirement for a good agent. Personal compatibility, however, is of paramount importance. You should feel comfortable with the agent and able to ask questions—even the same one repeatedly or even the ones you're afraid may sound dumb.

The higher your level of involvement in planning, the more satisfaction you stand to gain from your trip. A good agent should be able to determine the broad outlines of your trip, to respond and listen to your ideas and needs, and to fill in with specific suggestions. The agent should have an idea of your lifestyle, your ideal vacation, and your budget. Your agent should ask, or you should volunteer, what seems to be personal information: How do you like to spend your days? Is shopping important to you? If you have a beach, are you happy? Will you die if you have no evening entertainment, or do you prefer a quiet stroll and a good book? What are your hobbies or special interests? Again, do not be afraid to discuss financial expectations. This can avoid a few nasty surprises—such as having to ransom one of the kids to pay for the trip! Also, be as specific as you can. "Sometime in August" does not get the same response and work as "one week, with a departure date between August 2 and August 8."

Even the best travel agent has a limited amount of time, and no one knows your expectations as well as you, so assume some of the legwork for detailed information yourself. Check with the tourist offices of the state or country you plan to visit for brochures and information on special events and attractions. The American Automobile Association (AAA), if you're a member and are driving for part or all of the trip, is an excellent resource for maps and detailed information. Travel books and articles are fun for the family and often have good advice on extras or little-known attractions in the area; check your local library for these. (Chinaberry Book Service, in San Diego, California, (800) 777–5205, has a catalogue of well-selected books and tapes for various ages and interests.) Also, talk to your friends who have been there for those real inside tips. In these ways, even if you're a do-it-yourselfer, you can comfortably join forces with a travel agent.

Several tour operators specialize in family travel, working with both travel agents and individual clients. Call them for their brochures. In Chevy Chase, Maryland, Grandtravel does escorted tours for grandparents and grandchildren, both in the United States and abroad (800–247–7651). In Durham, North Carolina, Families Welcome! offers families individually planned packages for travel in Europe as well as select destinations in the United States and Caribbean (800–326–0724). In San Francisco, California, Rascals in Paradise offers some resorts in the United States, some with their own personally directed children's programs during school holidays (800–U–RASCAL). Many local agencies are becoming aware of the family market and are beginning to specialize in this field; check your local parents' paper or the travel section of the local Sunday paper for these agencies in your area.

Finally, close your suitcase, lock the door, and take off—secure in the knowledge that your advance planning, plus professional help, will make this the best trip ever!

New England

Connecticut
Maine
Massachusetts
New Hampshire
Vermont

The BALSAMS Grand Resort Hotel

Dixville Notch, New Hampshire 03576
(603) 255–3400, (800) 255–0600, (800) 255–0800 (in New Hampshire)

In the fine tradition of grand old hotels, The BALSAMS has been graciously welcoming guests since 1866. The three main buildings are interconnected and quite impressive, with their white facades and red-tiled roofs. Two date from the late 1800s—the Dixville House and The BALSAMS Inn—and the newcomer, the Hampshire House, was added in 1917. At the foot of three very precipitous mountains—almost entirely surrounded by steep, 1,000-foot cliffs with the Notch Road the only way in or out—and overlooking Lake Gloriette, The BALSAMS offers a relaxed escape in a charming atmosphere. In summer Dixville Notch is a refreshing mountain retreat, in winter a delightful getaway for skiers.

The BALSAMS adds all the amenities for a fun-filled vacation in a worry-free atmosphere. Golf, tennis, swimming, lawn games, fine dining, and nightly entertainment are available and in keeping with an almost unique practice these days—no additional charges for use of any of the facilities. Your needs are tended to, your interests can be pursued, and your cares can be dispelled. The resort is open from the third week in December until early April, reopening for the summer season from late May to mid-October.

Accommodations: There are 209 rooms at The BALSAMS, many with views of the mountains or the lake. The family suites with two bedrooms offer ample space for youngsters; these are limited in number and quite popular. The Hampshire House is configured to provide convenient adjoining rooms for family accommodation. All the rooms have been restored, thus creating a comfortable ambience. Depending on the size of the room, its location and view, and the time of the year, prices range from $89 to $205 per person per night. Children's rates are on a graduated scale, calculated at $7.00 per day multiplied by the child's age, with a minimum charge of $28. So, infants to four-year-olds are $28 per day, five-years-olds are $35, and so on. These rates are based on a full American plan and include unlimited access to all the facilities. Cribs are provided.

Dining: The main dining room serves breakfast, lunch, and dinner during the summer season, breakfast and dinner only during the winter season. The summertime luncheon buffet is a sumptuous display of hot and cold entrees, cheeses, fruit, and desserts; you might sample the fried Maine shrimp or the Atlantic salmon. A menu luncheon is available at the Golf Clubhouse. The dinner menu offers an entirely different selection every evening, featuring seafood dishes as well as Long Island duckling, beef,

and chicken. At the dinner hour jackets for men are appropriate. Parents are advised to bring appropriate dinner clothes for older children as well.

The Cafe is open year-round, 10:00 A.M.–midnight, and is perfect for lighter meals (sandwiches and grilled items). In the summer you might try The PANORAMA Golf Clubhouse or the poolside bar for refreshments; both offer delightful views and a chance to soak up the beautiful scenery. In the winter warm up with a cup of cider or hot buttered rum in La Cave. Also in winter you'll be shuttling over to The BALSAMS/Wilderness Ski Area, where breakfast and lunch are served at the Base Lodge and an à la carte luncheon is served in the dining room. Evening entertainment means cocktails and floor shows in the Switzerland of America Ballroom or dancing in the Wilderness Lounge; both are in the hotel.

Children's World: The BALSAMS is interested in providing excellent service for its younger guests as well as its adult visitors. For children this translates into a busy schedule of fun activities. Camp Wind Whistle is available from the Fourth of July through Labor Day (seven days a week); here children ages five through thirteen meet with counselors in The BALSAMS Playroom for sports, games, picnics, swimming, nature walks, arts and crafts, fishing, farm visits, and movies. Outdoor activities are stressed. Children have lunch with their counselors and then, after linking up with Mom and Dad around 4:00 P.M. to share their day's experiences, they can rejoin their young group for dinner at 6:30 P.M. There is no charge for this service.

Age groups are divided as follows: five to seven years, eight to ten years, and eleven to thirteen years. Camp Wee Whistle is a special program for younger children, ages three and four, at no additional charge; call ahead for available dates. The outdoor children's area features a state-of-the art fiberglass and stainless-steel play structure. The indoor game room (supervised) has an array of board games, video games, and Ping-Pong and pool tables. Open daily from 9:00 A.M. to midnight, the game room is a popular spot for youngsters to gather and make friends during both summer and winter seasons.

In winter children ages three to five can enroll in the Wee Whistle Ski School. Older children have their own morning and afternoon lessons. The cost is approximately $25 for 2 hours. Wintertime room rates for children at The BALSAMS include ski privileges.

A nursery at the Base Lodge takes nonskiing youngsters under six (who are out of diapers) while you're on the slopes. The experienced staff amuses children with a selection of games and toys from 9:00 A.M. to 4:00 P.M.; parents should join their children for lunch. This service is provided gratis to children of hotel guests. Individual babysitters (usually off-duty hotel employees) can be arranged at reasonable rates; sitters should be reserved when lodging reservations are made.

Recreation: At The BALSAMS you can spend busy days of back-to-back events from morning to night or just relax, set an unhurried pace, and enjoy the peace and beauty of the mountains. Two golf courses await golfers. The eighteen-hole championship course was designed by Donald Ross, an architect famous during the early twentieth century; set in the mountains, the undulating terrain can be challenging and the views truly stunning. The nine-hole course is just right for beginners or those who haven't tested their clubs in a while. There are pro shops at each course, putting greens, a practice fairway, and a pro staff on hand to help you polish your swing. The Centennial Golf School operates from May through early July and features a PGA professional for every four students.

Tennis enthusiasts can choose to play on either red-clay courts (three) or all-weather courts (three). Sign up with the pro for group or private lessons, and stop by the tennis shop to pick up those indispensable accessories.

Swim a few laps in the Olympic-size heated swimming pool; overlooking Lake Gloriette, with the mountains in the background, this is an idyllic spot for sunbathing. You might try a refreshing dip in the lake or a relaxing excursion in a paddleboat, canoe, or rowboat. Fish in a crystal-clear mountain stream, hike in the wilderness (solo or with a guided group), or take a nature walk with the staff naturalist. The hotel's natural-history program combines tours, hikes, and discussions in a good introduction to the flora and fauna of the area.

Lawn sports include badminton, horseshoes, croquet, volleyball, and shuffleboard; when you head indoors, there are billiards, Ping-Pong, bingo, an aerobic exercise room, and a movie theater. Take to the library/card room to snuggle up with a good book or play a few hands of bridge. To track down that essential souvenir, drop in at the gift shop, craft shop, gallery, balloon store, and fashion boutique.

In the wintertime this wonderland is draped in snow, and The BAL-SAMS/Wilderness Ski Area (located on the property) is just a short shuttle ride from the hotel. There are thirteen downhill trails and 45 miles of wilderness trails for cross-country techniques. Wintertime also means ice skating, tobogganing, snowshoeing on dedicated trails, and riding in horse-drawn sleighs. Whether you're seeking an escape from city crowds or want an active sports-oriented vacation, The BALSAMS offers the attention and service to make it all possible.

Bolton Valley Ski and Summer Resort

Bolton, Vermont 05477
(802) 434–2131, (800) 451–3220

Bolton Valley Resort in central Vermont is truly a family-oriented resort. Bolton Valley focuses on downhill and cross-country skiing in winter, hiking and mountain biking in summer. Literally *in* the Green Mountains, Bolton boasts a 2,150-foot base elevation, the highest in the East. The resort is fashioned after the concept of a European ski village, with easy access to all facilities. Nineteen miles west of Burlington, Bolton is the closest ski area to the Burlington airport. The resort is open from November to late April and from late May to late October.

Accommodations: Here you may choose your style of accommodations, with on-slope lodging for 1,400 people in a 150-room hotel, more than 100 condominiums, and a small New England–style inn. The Bolton Valley Lodge, in the center of most activities, is designed to complement the countryside and is decorated in a Vermont country theme, including locally made, handcrafted furniture and country quilts. Amenities located in the lodge are four restaurants, the ski shop, and a deli. You may prefer the privacy and convenience of the Trailside Condominiums—each with its own deck or patio and firewood for the fireplace. The Black Bear Inn, 2,000 feet above the valley on the mountainside, offers traditional inn-style rooms, some with views.

Lift tickets and accommodation for three days in the lodge run $240 per person, double occupancy. A one-bedroom condominium unit is $450 for a three-night stay. At the Black Bear Inn, the rate is $150 per person for three nights, breakfast included. More economical winter packages, as well as summertime specials, are available. Some of the condominiums are ski-in/ski-out, and cross-country trails start at the front door of the inn. For the really adventurous an overnight hike to two rustic backwoods cabins is a great experience.

Dining: You can refuel at more than half a dozen places. The Fireside Restaurant serves hearty breakfasts and full-course dinners; it is the main dining room of the lodge. If you stay at the lodge, you can participate in the modified American plan at this dining room. Special menus for the young group include smaller portions of the things that kids really like to eat. Also in the lodge is a cafeteria—open all day, for all tastes. Enjoy an Italian meal or great pizza from Cafe Lortina, in a cozy environment. At Lindsay's Restaurant you can enjoy an elegant gourmet dinner in a facility overlooking the mountains.

The Sports Club Lounge is suitable for light meals and quick snacks. The Club always has something to entertain the kids. The James Moore Tavern is a bit more sedate, with music and dancing for evening entertainment. It is a favorite for après-ski, but lunches are also served. And last but not least are the great Vermont country meals served at the rustic Black Bear Inn.

Children's World: Bolton Valley has an extensive year-round program for kids. The nursery, a fully licensed day-care center, is located in the lodge. The fee for the supervised indoor and outdoor play is $34 a day for infants and $30 a day for toddlers.

In the winter things really swing into action, with the Honey Bear Nursery, Bolton Bears and Cubs program, and Bolton Mountain Explorers. Morning and afternoon snacks and lunch are provided; formula, food and feeding utensils, and diapers for infants must be supplied by the parents. The nursery is open daily from 8:45 A.M. to 4:30 P.M., and the usual games, books, toys, crafts, and nap times are on the agenda.

The evening program is from 5:30 to 9:00 P.M. Tuesday, Thursday, and Saturday nights. It is a special dinner followed by quiet games, crafts, or movies. The cost is $18, including dinner; $16 for each additional child. For teens the Sports Center with its teen nights is a popular attraction.

Recreation: Bolton Valley offers lots of skiing. Try Alpine skiing on fifty-one trails connected by six lifts, with a summit elevation of 3,400 feet and a 1,600-foot vertical drop. Skiing lessons and programs are designed for all ages and abilities. All of Bolton's trails end at the base lodges (nice in case you lose your friends or instructor on the slopes), and it's one of the few places in Vermont to offer night skiing. Snowmaking capabilities now cover 75 percent of the most popular trails. Cross-country skiing is given more credit here than many places. There are more than 60 miles of trails, including Norpine skiing. Ride the chairlift up for a 5-mile descent on mixed Nordic/Alpine terrain. The cross-country skiing center offers ski lessons, packages, camping, mountaineering, and, on special request, winter survival courses. Because of its elevation, Bolton usually has a very long cross-country ski season.

Enjoy the eight outdoor tennis courts and the two indoor courts at the Sports Club. Also enjoy one inside and one outside swimming pool. Golf is the one thing off-premises, but fees are included in golf packages. Located in West Bolton, about 10 miles away, the eighteen-hole course has a typical New England background.

The package plans for skiing and golf include membership in the million-dollar Sports Club—a complex that encompasses two indoor tennis courts, a Jacuzzi, a sauna, tanning rooms, an indoor pool, and exercise classes. Having access to this facility makes the packages particularly good values.

Highland Lodge

Caspian Lake
RR 1, Box 1290
Greensboro, Vermont 05841
(802) 533–2647

Cross-country skiing in Vermont—it sounds so romantic and wholesome. You almost expect to see Bing Crosby round the corner of the inn. A lovely old white-frame building with a comfortable front porch, the lodge is set on 160 acres bordering Caspian Lake. Open from Christmas to mid-March, the lodge facilities make it easy to enjoy wintertime sports; open again from Memorial Day weekend until mid-October, the lodge is a perfect spot for enjoying the fall foliage colors or for enjoying a summer trip of swimming and boating.

Accommodations: Choose a guest room in the lodge or one of the cottages just behind the main building. Tastefully decorated with nice furnishings (some rooms have brass beds) and old-fashioned wallpaper, these accommodations can house approximately sixty guests. The cottages feature a living room, porch, bath, and one to three bedrooms; nine cottages include kitchenettes. Cribs are provided for little ones. Based on a modified American plan and double occupancy, rates are $95 to $115 per person per night. Children sharing a room or cottage with their parents are charged according to their ages, $20 to $65 a day.

Dining: Two connecting dining rooms in the lodge serve breakfast, lunch, and dinner. For entrees you may select fresh fish, lamb, duck, veal, or prime rib with vegetables from a local farm, and sample the homemade soups and breads, but be sure to save room for what the staff boasts are sinful desserts. You might sit near the fireplace in the dining room or by the large windows to take in the view; weather permitting, dining tables are set up on the porch. A full American meal plan is offered, and there are children's portions and special items for youngsters.

Children's World: A swing set and a sandbox stocked with toys attract little ones. There are tennis and hiking for older children. For children of all ages, swimming at the supervised private beach is a great way to spend the afternoon. After a busy day kids may settle into the children's library, where they'll find books, games, and puzzles. In the mornings during July and August, youngsters ages four to nine link up with the Play Lady, who devises programs of crafts, swimming, and nature hikes; this is free of charge to guests. In addition, the staff can make arrangements for individual babysitters ($4.50 an hour).

Recreation: Thirty miles of groomed cross-country ski trails meander through fields and forests and across frozen lakes. You can line up a

Photo courtesy of Highland Lodge

guided tour or pick up a little instruction. Bring your own equipment or rent the necessary paraphernalia at the ski shop.

In warmer weather hike or jog in the adjoining Barr Hill Nature Preserve, walk the Lodge's nature trail, or take to the water; swim at the beach or head out on the lake in a canoe, sailboat, or paddleboat provided by the lodge. The lake also means good fishing, particularly in early summer and fall; set your line for salmon, trout, or perch.

Back on land, challenge another guest to a tennis match on the clay court and then round up a game of badminton, volleyball, or croquet on the lawn. The nearby Green Mountains and White Mountains lure guests into afternoon driving excursions.

Jay Peak Ski Resort

Jay, Vermont 05859
(802) 988–2611, (800) 451–4449

Way up in northern Vermont, just about 10 miles from the Canadian border, is the Jay Peak Ski Area. In a friendly, comfortable atmosphere, skiing Montrealers who drift down this way add a bit of an international flair to Jay. The resort encompasses more than 300 acres of skiable terrain, sometimes plummeting and sometimes meandering down from a 4,000-foot summit. With a ski season that lasts from November to late April or early May, a 325-inch average annual snowfall, and snowmaking on more than 80 percent of skiable terrain, skiing is serious business in this area of Vermont. Eighteen glade and tree areas add to the uniqueness of skiing here.

Though primarily a winter holiday destination, many of the accommodations in Jay are open year-round and can serve as a home base while you go off fishing, hiking, picking wildflowers, and enjoying the clean mountain air. Plans are under way for the creation of a four-season recreational resort village designed with a deep commitment to environmental harmony.

Accommodations: Hotel Jay, located at the mountain base, has rooms with private balconies and also houses a restaurant and a lounge. Rates start at $189 per person for a two-night stay, including lifts, breakfast, and one dinner. When sharing a room with parents during the regular ski season, children under age six stay and ski free; juniors fourteen and under stay free.

At Slopeside condominiums, enjoy the convenience of ski-in/ski-out and the comfort of one to three bedrooms with balconies, kitchen, living room, and fireplace. The newest townhouses, whose number is limited, feature two floors of elegant space, with huge picture windows to enjoy the mountains. Jay has a variety of lodging; choose from small inns, lodges, and townhouses. Inglenook Lodge, located about a mile from the slopes, begins at $98 per night. Children ages five to sixteen pay $15; those under age five stay free. Inglenook has the only indoor swimming pool in the area, a big plus for kids. Call the 800 number listed above for information on packages and lodging.

Dining: The dining room at Hotel Jay features international fare. The Inglenook Lodge and Jay Village Inn also have restaurants. Some evening you may wish to seek out the charm of an old country inn such as the Black Lantern.

Children's World: The Jay Peak Child Care Center provides indoor fun and games for two- to seven-year-olds from 9:00 A.M. to 4:00 P.M. at the Kinderschool, and from 4:00 to 9:00 P.M. at the Hotel Jay Family Room, with supervised dinner at 5:30 P.M. This service is free to guests of Jay Peak Condominiums or Hotel Jay; otherwise, the cost is $20 full-day and $10 half-day. For infants under age two, private care is available for $4.00 per hour, with a minimum of three hours. The Kinderschool Ski program is a special half-day morning ski program, followed by afternoon rest and activities; the cost is $20 for guests, $30 for nonguests. SKIwee, a nationally acclaimed children's program using fun and games to teach skiing skills, is an all-day program for children ages five to twelve. The cost is $40 for one day, $95 for three days, or $115 for five days. SKIwee kids have access to the Mountain Adventureland, a no-adult area in the woods with a snow hut and obstacle course for the more accomplished, and their own room with kid-size spaces and indoor ramp for a warmer practice. Older children, ten to sixteen years, can join the Mountain Adventurers and sample not only downhill skiing but also snowboarding, snowshoeing, cross-country skiing, or assisting the instructors with the smaller children and other snow activities. The cost of $125 for three days or $160 for five days includes rental of all equipment except downhill skis.

Preregistration is required for all programs. A large activity room in the base lodge gives kids a place to meet and play video games, pool, or Ping-Pong. Movies are shown regularly in the spacious family room, and families visiting during midweek can enjoy such unique activities as a visit to a working dairy farm, night sledding and marshmallow roasts, and ice skating.

In the summertime Jay Peak offers a children's swim program and day camp. Activities include swimming instruction, arts and crafts, hiking, and more.

Recreation: The center of the wintertime attention and activity is Jay Peak, with its 2,100 vertical feet and thirty-five downhill runs. The aerial tram reaches from Hotel Jay up to the summit, and five other lifts keep skiers on the move. Lessons are offered at the ski school for all levels, from barely beginners to advanced trying perfect mogul skiing. The 20 kilometers of groomed trails lead cross-country skiers over the hills and through the woods. Instruction is also available in cross-country techniques and telemarking—ever wonder how people do it? Here's your chance to find out.

While skiing is the reason for a winter holiday here, you may find yourself quite taken with the new Jacuzzi and sauna facilities at Hotel Jay, especially after a tough day skiing (use is complimentary for Hotel Jay guests). The Inglenook has a sauna, an indoor swimming pool, and racquetball courts.

In the summer the emphasis is on relaxation and clean country living. Fishing and hiking in the mountains are favorite pastimes. Hotel Jay has an outdoor swimming pool and Har-Tru tennis courts (free for guests of the hotel). And to really appreciate the mountain scenery, take a ride on the aerial tram; on a clear day, views extend for 150 miles.

Killington Ski and Summer Resort

Killington Road
Killington, Vermont 05751
(802) 773-1330, (800) 621-MTNS

Killington is the largest ski area in the eastern United States, and its vital statistics are indeed impressive: 212 runs on six interconnected mountains, plus Pico Mountain at Killington; more than 3,000 vertical feet; and a ski season that starts in mid-October and continues to June. Killington boasts an average annual snowfall of 250 inches. To ensure its earliest opening date and latest closing date in the East, sophisticated snowmaking techniques assist Mother Nature. Thirty-three lifts, including a new, eight-passenger heated gondola, get you quickly to the top.

A year-round resort, Killington is cradled in the Green Mountains of central Vermont, a setting whose beauty does not wane with the melting snow; in the late spring and summer, the lush green landscape is the backdrop for tennis and golf holidays; in autumn the fall foliage colors take over.

Accommodations: There are almost 200 properties at Killington, ranging from small inns and lodges to condominium complexes. Killington Travel Services (800–621–6867) lists more than 115 of these and publishes helpful, descriptive information clearly outlining the many package plans

available. Ski-in locations include Trailside Lodge, with standard rooms/bunk beds, and Trailside Village, Sunrise Village, and Spruce Glen condos. Rates are lower in summer and higher at holiday periods. Call for the latest rates.

Killington Resort Villages (800–343–0762) offers hotel-style and one-, two-, and three-bedroom condos, some within walking distance of the slopes, plus several other condominium complexes. The Villager nightly rates range from $52 to $92 in summer, $49 to $196 in winter. Condo summer rates are $89 to $240, rising to $112 to $688 in winter. Condominiums not within walking distance but right at the base of Killington Mountain include Edgemont, Whiffletree, Highridge, Mountain Green, and Pinnacle. Studio to four-bedroom units have fully equipped kitchens and fireplaces. Some condominiums have special features such as indoor pools or spa/exercise facilities (if you don't get enough on the slopes!).

Dining: In addition to the half dozen cafeterias at the bases of and on the mountains, The Clubhouse Grill is located across from Snowshed Base Lodge. In the area you'll find Italian, Chinese, Mexican, and German restaurants, or perhaps you'll sample French country dinners at the Red Clover Inn, typical New England dishes at the Vermont Inn, or continental cuisine at the Pittsfield Inn. Pubs and nightclubs provide late-evening entertainment.

Children's World: Whether your child is six weeks old or twelve years old, a first-time skier or a veteran, he or she will find a niche at Killington's Children's Center. Open daily from 8:00 A.M. to 4:30 P.M., the staff orchestrates indoor and outdoor play for infants to six-year-olds. First Tracks Ski School, for four- to five-year-olds, includes ski lessons as well as supervised play; and the Superstars Ski Program groups six- to twelve-year-olds by ability for a full day of ski and play. Full-day fees include lunch; half-day sessions are available for the nonskiing and introductory skiing groups. For teenagers there's a weekly under-twenty-one disco with DJ or live bands, soda, and pizza. In December and March special weeks for teens are scheduled as well.

The Alpine Adventure Summer Camp offers age-grouped activities for youngsters six weeks to six years. The child-care ratio is four to one. Call for current cost of youth activities.

Recreation: Start your visit with a Meet the Mountain tour; skiers are grouped by ability and guided through a complimentary two-hour introduction to Killington's mountains. All seven mountains are accessed by the same lift ticket. All have beginner runs from their summits so that even novices can enjoy top-of-the-mountain views. From long lazy runs (one beginner's trail is 10 miles long) to steeply pitched expert terrain, every skier finds the appropriate challenge. This goes for ski clinics, too, from classes for the newest beginner to workshops in racing for the advanced skier.

Après-ski activities include sleigh rides in the country and movies in the village, but maybe most appropriate for the end of an active day is a quiet rest in a sauna.

Summertime brings golf on an eighteen-hole course; tennis at the Killington School for Tennis; fishing, hiking, mountain biking, and horseback riding (Sunrise Stables) in the mountains.

The Lighthouse Inn

Lighthouse Road
West Dennis, Massachusetts 02670
(508) 398–2444

An old-fashioned country inn, The Lighthouse Inn sits on the shores of Nantucket Sound. The core of the main building is aptly named as the historic Bass River Lighthouse. The inn recalls an easier pace of past times. The classic Cape Cod–style main house provides a beautiful view of the ocean; sprawling out behind are nine secluded acres comprised of additional accommodations and recreational facilities.

Accommodations: The main house offers individual rooms and suites. Alternatively, you might choose one of the cottages with one to three bedrooms. Prices are $184 a night (including breakfast) in the summer season, $134 a night (including breakfast) in the spring and fall. Children sharing a room or cottage with their parents are charged a graduated rate depending on their ages: ages three to five years, $25 a day; ages six to eight, $30 a day; nine to twelve, $40 a day; and thirteen-year-olds and older, $50 a day. For children the daily rate includes breakfast. Rates that include dinner are available.

Dining: The dining room in the main house entices guests with fresh fish and lobster dinners and lovely views over the water. Outdoors, the oceanside deck is the setting for lunch. A snack bar adjoins the pool. Once a week a poolside cookout is planned.

Children's World: Games, swimming, arts and crafts, sand-castle building, kite flying, miniature golf, and nature walks fill the days for InnKids. Three- and four-year-olds participate from 9:30 A.M. to noon, while children ages five and older carry on until 3:00 P.M. In the evening both groups are invited to get together from 5:30 to 8:30 P.M. for dinner and entertainment, perhaps a movie or a magician's show. The InnKids program runs from late June through August and is included in the fees for children noted above. Individual babysitting costs $5.00 an hour.

Recreation: Enjoying the soft ocean breezes may be all the activity you want during your first couple of days at Lighthouse Inn. Renewed and refreshed, you can then jump into the swimming pool, splash in the gentle waters of Nantucket Sound, and stroll along the beach. The outdoor tennis court awaits you when you turn energetic, and fishing can be a pleasant morning outing. You can also play Ping-Pong, pool, and shuffleboard or pursue quieter interests in the library/game room.

Mount Snow/Haystack Ski Area

Mount Snow, Vermont 05356
(802) 464-8501, (800) 245-7669

A very popular New England ski resort, Mount Snow/Haystack is situated in the beautiful Green Mountains of southern Vermont. Much of its popularity is, no doubt, due to its accessibility and proximity to major Northeast metropolitan areas; a four-and-one-half-hour drive from New York, two-and-one-half hours from Boston, make this a very manageable weekend trip for residents of these cities. But Mount Snow's size and variety also account for its appeal. From gentle beginner and broad intermediate slopes to some of the steepest expert runs in the Northeast, 127 trails in all drop down from a 3,600-foot summit for 1,700 vertical feet. The average annual snowfall is about 150 inches. It is supplemented by sophisticated snowmaking that covers 80 percent of the skiable terrain; the ski season runs from about early November to early May.

Accommodations: Lodging, in atmosphere, style, prices, and location, runs the gamut of possibilities. From modern condominium complexes to quaint country inns, more than 50 options are within 10 miles of the mountain base. The lodging bureau issues descriptive booklets to help you choose the right spot, and various package plans for lodging and lift tickets are offered.

A full-service hotel at the edge of a small lake, Snow Lake Lodge is very close to the base of the mountain; with its own restaurant, game room, and spa, a two-day weekend rate is $225 per adult in a double room, on a modified American plan; reduced rates apply for children. Seasons and Snow Mountain Village are condominiums near the base, where two-bedroom units start at $640 for a two-day weekend. These units have kitchens and fireplaces; some have balconies and mountain views.

The many country inns around the area can add a distinctly New England flavor to a ski holiday. The charming Hermitage Inn, 3 miles from Mount Snow, maintains 40 miles of cross-country ski trails; a two-day weekend is $200 per adult.

Photo by David Brownell, courtesy of Mount Snow

Dining: At the base of Mount Snow are four cafeterias, four lounges, and a restaurant; at the Summit Lodge, views over the mountains complement cafeteria-style lunches. Also near the base is the Lakeside restaurant in the Snow Lake Lodge. Most of the inns and lodges of the area have their own restaurants and feature a variety, from hearty home-style cooking to the continental cuisine typical of the Hermitage and the White House of Wilmington.

Children's World: Throughout the ski season kids from babies (six weeks old and up) to twelve-year-olds have a place at Mount Snow. The Pumpkin Patch Nursery takes infants and toddlers for primarily indoor supervised play of exercise, games, and stories and some outdoor activities in a daily 9:00 A.M.–4:00 P.M. program; the fee with lunch for a two-day package is $88.

Children three to twelve years old can join instructors for lessons and supervised skiing and play daily. The fee is $131 for two days of lifts, lessons, and lunch. The teaching slope for children is reserved just for youngsters, providing them with a controlled environment in which to learn. During special Teddy Bear weeks, in January and March, kids twelve and under ski free all day, all week—if they bring a teddy bear with them. Teddy-related festivities, including a parade, an ice-cream sundae party, and a magic show, round out the fun.

A list of babysitters is available through the nursery. A supervised children's activities program operates in July and August.

Recreation: Almost 75 percent of the runs at Mount Snow are ranked intermediate. The rest just about evenly split between beginner and expert. The Main Mountain has forty beginner and intermediate trails, the North Face with its steeper terrain and moguls attracts advanced skiers, and the Sunbrook area with sunny southern exposure supports a couple of long lazy runs. The teaching staff is prepared to show you the way to improved techniques, and you have your pick of packages for various combinations of lifts, lessons, and equipment.

For cross-country skiers, four touring centers are within 10 miles of Mount Snow at the Hermitage, Sitzmark, Timber Creek, and White House. Also within this distance are three stables—Beaver Brook, Flames, and Adam's Farm—where you can arrange sleigh rides.

When these mountains turn green, the big event is the Golf School, held on the championship Geoffrey Cornish course. Other warm-weather activities include swimming, fishing, hiking, biking, and horseback riding.

The Mount Washington Hotel & Resort

Route 302
Bretton Woods, New Hampshire 03575
(603) 278–1000, (800) 258–0330

Majestic Mount Washington presides over this resort, a massive complex of lodging, dining, and recreational facilities, on 2,600 acres of wooded New Hampshire countryside in the White Mountains. Recently voted a *Better Homes and Gardens* "Favorite Family Resort," the architectural gem of this New England resort and the summertime focal point is the gracious and stately hotel. Built in 1902 by the industrialist and railroad tycoon Joseph Stickney, the hotel began welcoming visitors to a lifestyle of classic elegance and soon claimed its status among prime vacation retreats of the Northeast.

International fame came to Bretton Woods in 1944 when the hotel hosted financiers from forty-four countries who created the World Bank and the International Monetary Fund and set the gold standard at $35 an ounce (ah—the good old days). In 1978 this fine old structure—with its glimmering white facade topped by red-tiled roofs, its wonderfully spacious veranda furnished with white wicker chairs and settees, and its 150-foot-long lobby—was added to the National Register of Historic Places. Since 1986 it has held the distinction of being a National Historic Landmark.

Although the Grand Hotel is closed mid-October to mid-May, wintertime activities and accommodations are available at The Bretton Arms Country Inn, The Bretton Woods Motor Inn, and The Townhomes at Bretton Woods.

Accommodations: The 200-room hotel offers standard to deluxe lodging with a number of two-bedroom family suites. Nearly all have views of Mount Washington, the Willey-Rosebrook Mountain range, or the well-tended gardens. All guests in the hotel participate in a modified American plan, and prices range from $185 to $445 for double occupancy. Children under age four are free; ages five to twelve are $30; and over twelve are $60. A family chamber costs $320–$375 a night and accommodates up to four persons. The hotel is open mid-May to mid-October. The Bretton Arms, also a National Historic Landmark, offers accommodations in the atmosphere of an English country home. Guests here enjoy all the facilities of the main hotel. Based on a European plan, prices range from $90 to $189 per night. The Bretton Arms is open year-round.

Photo courtesy of The Mount Washington Hotel & Resort

Also open year-round, The Bretton Woods Motor Inn, located across from the hotel's entrance, offers contemporary accommodations at rates of $70 to $129 per night.

For an economical alternative, The Townhomes at Bretton Woods provide ample space for parties of two to twelve people; situated on the mountainside, these one- to five-bedroom units (with full kitchens) run from $129 to $369 per night, depending on the size of the unit and the season. All guests have access to all resort recreational facilities at established guest rates. Cribs and cots are available at $10 a night. Inquire also about special packages.

Dining: With all the different dining arrangements, your biggest problem will be deciding where to pick up your napkin. From casual, light meals to gracious, formal dinners, it just depends on how the spirit moves you. The main dining room of The Mount Washington Hotel is a large octagonal space (heaven forbid anyone should be relegated to a corner!) glimmering with crystal chandeliers and stained-glass windows. The menu changes nightly and features continental cuisine and regional American dishes. In this elegant setting, with views of Mount Washington, guests are invited to regard dinner as a dress-up affair; jackets are required for men, and ladies and children should dress appropriately. Sumptuous breakfasts are also served in the dining room.

The Bretton Arms dining room is also open for breakfast and dinner; here the evening meal features classic New England cuisine. For lunch Stickney's Restaurant (located on the lower concourse of the hotel) has a cafe atmosphere and specializes in light lunches—salads, sandwiches, and light entrees; afternoon cocktails are also served here. Darby's Restaurant in the Motor Inn serves breakfast and dinner; here guests enjoy continental cuisine, along with scenic views of the mountains and the hotel. For sandwiches, Italian fare, and seafood, Fabyans Station is open for lunch and dinner. A restored railroad depot from the Victorian era, Fabyans is near the base of the ski area about a mile from the hotel. The base lodge at the ski area offers quick breakfasts and lunches cafeteria-style for those eager to hit the slopes. The midmountain Top O' Quad restaurant serves lunch and dinner, with spectacular mountain views in winter and summer.

For sipping cocktails, you may want to linger at Stickney's, Darby's, or Fabyans. Or perhaps you'll discover the Cave Lounge; located in the lower lobby of the hotel, the speakeasy atmosphere and nightly live entertainment transport you to the days of Prohibition. The elegant Princess Lounge is perfect for before- and after-dinner cocktails. The Pool Bar offers refreshments on warm summer days.

Children's World: Mid-June through Labor Day, and on weekends in spring and fall, the hotel sponsors the King of the Mountain Kids Kamp for children five to twelve. Enroll your child for a full- or half-day program with adventures like hiking in the woods, treks to the stables, swimming, tennis, "Cooking with the Chef," "Putting with the Pro," and crafts sessions. The program is from 9:00 A.M. to noon and from 1:00 to 4:30 P.M. The cost is $10.00 full-day, $7.00 half-day. Lunch is available for $7.25. There's also an evening program ($5.00) from 7:00 to 9:00 P.M. so that parents can dine quietly. Guests not on the modified American plan pay an additional $10.00 for dinner. Babysitting can be arranged for $4.50 per hour, plus 50 cents for each additional child.

In the wintertime, the nursery at the ski area lodge takes children from two months to five years for an indoor program costing $30 full-day or $20 half-day. Children ages three to twelve participate in the Hobbit Children's Ski School. Rates for lifts, lessons, equipment, and lunch are $49 a day. Those children under age five who are new to the slopes can join a snow play and ski-readiness program, also $49 a day.

Recreation: You'll never be at a loss for things to do at Bretton Woods; your only dilemma may be trying to fit in all the activities. You may start your day jogging on one of the many marked trails ranging from 1 to 11 miles in length and graded by levels of difficulty.

Then stroll over to the first tee for a match on the eighteen-hole Donald Ross–designed championship golf course or challenging nine-hole course and take in the rolling terrain and mountain views, or sharpen your skills on the putting green and driving range. The Golf Club Pro Shop can meet all your needs for equipment and accessories (including attire) and can assist in scheduling lessons.

There are two heated pools at the hotel (one outdoor and a smaller one indoors) and another indoor heated pool at the Motor Inn; both locations have a sauna, and the lodge facility includes a Jacuzzi as well.

Tennis buffs can head over to one of twelve well-groomed, red-clay courts or join the tennis program for instruction (group and private lessons) at all levels of expertise.

The horseback-riding stables mean good fun for those who want their exercise sitting down. Set in an old Victorian building, the stables offer lessons and guided trail rides on the 50 miles of picturesque trails in the woods and fields. The woods are captivating whether you choose horseback riding or hiking (maybe you'll link up with a guided tour or a nature walk).

If fishing is your pleasure, some mighty fine trout are found in the Ammonoosuc River, which winds its way through the hotel grounds.

For other diversions you might consider a game of badminton, croquet, volleyball, or horseshoes; an afternoon of bicycling; or an hour in the game room for billiards, Ping-Pong, and video games (particularly big with the seven- to fourteen-year-old group). Your interests may take you to a night at the movies, a fashion show, an aerobics class, a bridge tournament, or a presentation of fine culinary techniques (these often include a bit of wine, sampling a dish, and a tour of the kitchen). The activities staff is on hand full-time to plan interesting and varied events. For some private, quiet time, wander into the library or relax under the nimble fingers of an expert masseur.

Music is special at Mount Washington. Chamber-music recitals are held frequently in the Conservatory; live music is featured in the Cave Lounge; the Mount Washington Orchestra will dance you off your toes nightly during dinner.

Kids love an excursion on the Mount Washington Cog Railway, the original "little train that could." Built in 1869, it was the world's first mountain-climbing cog railroad, and it remains the only one still powered entirely by steam. The (breathtaking!) round trip takes about three hours, and you can visit the mile-high park and observation center at the top.

Stickney Street, in the lower concourse of the hotel, is an array of shops featuring gifts, crafts, fashions, ice-cream delights, flowers, and the hotel's own post office.

Wintertime explodes in skiing events at Bretton Woods. The Bretton Woods Touring Center, housed in a Victorian-style building, is one of the finest cross-country skiing complexes in the East. There are approximately 100 kilometers of beautifully groomed trails among the firs and birches of the scenic countryside; three different trail systems are ranked in difficulty. Head out on your own, enroll for instruction, or join a daytime guided tour or a moonlight trek. Alpine skiers are delighted with the expansion done in the past decade. This once pleasant ski area of 1,100-foot vertical drop has added 400 vertical feet and now boasts thirty-two trails serviced by five lifts. The ski season lasts from mid-December to early April; the average annual snowfall is 180 inches, and 98 percent of the trails are covered by snowmaking equipment to assist Mother Nature. In addition to the children's ski school, instruction for the more advanced is also available, accommodating all skiing levels in your family.

Smugglers' Notch Resort

Route 108
Smugglers' Notch, Vermont 05464
(802) 644–8851, (800) 451–8752

The Green Mountains of Vermont are not just beautiful foliage colors in the autumn and skiing fun in the winter. Smugglers' Notch Resort makes sure there's much more all year long. Tucked in the rolling hills and mountains of northern Vermont, Smugglers' Notch is a self-contained resort village with sports facilities and getaway relaxation potential for the whole family. In winter, when Mother Nature blankets the region in snow, skiing on the three interconnected mountains is the primary activity. Tennis, swimming, and horseback riding are favorite pastimes when the weather warms. Any time of year one can explore the natural beauty and charm surrounding this mountain village and experience family fun—guaranteed! (Yes, the resort guarantees families will have fun or it refunds the activity portion of their stay.)

Accommodations: Approximately 415 condominium units are arranged in clusters of 2- and 3-story, modern but rustic buildings. From these all the amenities of the village are accessible on foot. Most of the units have fireplaces and private balconies, and all have completely equipped kitchens or kitchenettes. Size varies from studios to five-bedroom apartments.

The Club Smugglers' package plans cover lodging and most of the recreational activities. For example, the summertime FamilyFest program for five days and five nights includes accommodation in a one-bedroom condo (which sleeps four), the children's day camp, guided walks and hikes, swimming and water sliding, and family game nights, from $1,095 (rates based on dates of stay and size of accommodation). A winter five-day package for a family of four in the same type of lodging runs about $1,615; this includes lift tickets, lessons (Nordic, Alpine, snowboard, and parabolic),

Photo courtesy of Smugglers' Notch Resort

outdoor ice skating, limited tennis, parties, swimming pool, sauna, and après-ski activities. A crib or extra futon cot for two- to seven-year-olds can be provided for $20 for the entire stay.

Dining: Though you may opt to cook in your condo, there are several restaurants in the village when dining out seems better than facing a skillet. In winter The Green Mountain Cafe and Bakery serves home-baked breakfast treats and hot lunches with fresh-roasted specialty coffees. The Mountain Grille is open for all three meals, including light fare available well into the evening and a special buffet for children. At the Hearth & Candle parents enjoy nouveau cuisine, and at the Snowsnake Pizzeria all ages savor the ever-popular Italian favorites—pizza, calzones, salads, and beverages—to eat in or have delivered to their condo. For summertime ice-cream treats, there's the Village Creamery, or choose refreshing drinks at the Sports Bar, with its big-screen TV.

The Poolside Cafe and Mountainside Cabana are relaxing summertime spots for lunch and cocktails. And teenagers even have their own clubhouse, Teen Central, open daily from 4:00 P.M. to midnight, serving juice and soda. For extras and snacks stop by the Village Grocery, with Deli and Wine Shop.

Children's World: The Little Smugglers' Discovery Ski School and Camp operates from mid-December to the beginning of April. Three- to five-year-olds join their ski host for morning and afternoon ski lessons, sleigh rides, movies, and arts and crafts. Skiers and boarders ages six to twelve meet with the Smugglers' Adventure Ski Camp for lessons, snow soccer, and races. Après-ski activities include a daily bonfire at 3:30 P.M. with storytelling and hot chocolate for parents and children. With lunch included, the daily rate for these programs, 9:30 A.M.–4:00 P.M., is $52. The program, however, is included in the FamilyFest packages.

For teens ages thirteen to seventeen, the Explorer Ski Program offers challenging instruction and techniques, racing development, and a great way to make new friends. A full-day program is included in the package. With the Teen Central Clubhouse and scheduled daily activities at 5:00 and 7:00 P.M., teenagers have plenty to do.

For younger, nonskiing children (newborn to six years), Alice's Wonderland is just that. Located in a quiet, sunlit corner of the resort, Alice's is 6,900 square feet or ten rooms of real state-of-the-art facilities. There are kid-size bathrooms, a complete kitchen, an infant "crawler room" equipped with mirrors and soft-sculpture gym, a separate crib room for naps, a closet of costumes, and an indoor jungle gym—one could go on and on. Open from 9:00 A.M. to 4:00 P.M. (8:30 A.M. to 4:30 P.M. during ski season), staffed with professionals, and boasting a ratio of one to four, it's a steal at $10 an hour ($49 for a full day).

During the summer season, from the end of June through Labor Day, the Discovery and Adventure Day Camps offer daily activities for three- to twelve-year-olds. Fun events include outdoor games, fishing, arts and crafts, hiking, treasure hunts, and swimming. At the playground are swings, climbing equipment, and a sandbox. Tennis, movies, hayrides, dances, and scavenger hunts/overnight hikes are scheduled for teenagers. The day camp is included in the price of the family vacation. For the really wee ones, individual babysitters can be booked for $6.00 an hour. A really nice feature is Parents Night Out, when children ages three to twelve are invited to dinner and a fun evening from 6:00 to 10:00 P.M. The cost is $15 per child. A similar program is free with the FamilyFest program.

Recreation: A network of sixty runs on three interconnected mountains is the focus of wintertime play. The ski season runs from mid-December to early April, and the average annual snowfall of 286 inches is supplemented by snowmaking equipment. The three mountains fall more or less into novice, intermediate, and advanced runs, but each mountain offers skiing for all levels of expertise. The total vertical drop is just over 2,600 feet. For the cross-country skier, 14 miles of trails roam through the mountains. Lessons in cross-country skiing, downhill skiing, and snowboarding can help you learn as a beginner or improve your skills. You might also try ice skating with the kids or a sleigh-ride adventure.

Turning indoors, you can enjoy the benefits of The Tub Club; with an exercise room and whirlpool and sauna facilities, you learn the proper regimen for a spa experience. With the resort's two indoor courts, tennis can be a wintertime sport; also in winter the large, heated swimming pool is covered with a bubble, so pack your swimsuit along with your ski sweater. In summer the bubble comes down. There's a water slide, called the Flume; a baby wading pool; and a seventeen-person outdoor Jacuzzi. Free swimming instruction is provided as part of the day-camp program, and adults can join the Aqua Aerobics for a good workout.

The Family Water Playground is a second, separate water facility that includes a turtle slide (for children ages three to eight years), the Little Smugglers' Lagoon (a large splash pool with waterfall, tunnels, fountains, and a lazy river ride), a lap pool, and every mother's delight, the Giant Rapid River Ride—306 feet of twists and thrills on an inner tube beginning 26 feet up in the air. Bathhouse, snack bar, and lounging deck with gorgeous mountain views help one recover.

Also a favorite with families is Rum Runner's Hideaway, a beautiful swimming lake tucked in the mountains, a short hike or hay-wagon ride away from the Village. Access is free to resort guests for swimming, fishing, picnicking, and relaxing; canoes and paddleboats are available for rent. It's a great way to relive the old days and introduce your kids to the joys of summer days at the ole swimmin' hole.

In addition to the two indoor courts, there are eight outdoor clay courts; six are lighted for evening play. The Ten Pro Tennis School, which has videotape review, just about guarantees improvement in your game. Hiking and biking are popular ways to enjoy the mountain countryside, or try jogging on one of the cross-country trails. Head to a mountain stream for perch, pike, and trout fishing. Outdoor lawn games include softball, volleyball, soccer, and shuffleboard. And reserve time for a session in the spa or a horseback ride at the Vermont Horse Park (services here are not included in the package plans). For those who can't possibly leave home without their golf clubs, courses in nearby Stowe and Morrisville are open to Smugglers' guests.

Stratton Mountain Resort

Stratton Mountain, Vermont 05155
(802) 297-4137, (800) 843-6867 or (800) STRATTON

Lessons, lessons, lessons! At Stratton Mountain Resort you can have instruction and training in several major sports. Whether your interests lead you to golf, tennis, swimming, racquetball, cross-country skiing, downhill skiing, telemark skiing, snowboarding, or snowshoeing, you can participate in classes for an introduction to a new sport or for polishing existing skills and techniques.

And where could you find a better place to get into shape and sharpen your sports expertise than in southern Vermont? Stratton Mountain Resort is set on 4,000 acres in the beautiful Green Mountains of Vermont. Since its opening in 1961, the resort has expanded a number of times to enhance the facilities and to attract sports-minded visitors to return again and again. Stratton Mountain is open year-round.

Accommodations: Choose a resort hotel, an alpine lodge, or your own villa. The Stratton Mountain Inn has 125 rooms and suites and also houses a restaurant, lounge, pool, sauna, and tennis courts. Stratton Village Lodge has ninety-one rooms and is in the heart of the village, just a few steps away from shops, and is considered ski-in/ski-out. The Birkenhaus and the Liftline Lodge offer more traditional accommodations, and each has its own restaurant. Winter rates at the Stratton Mountain Inn or Stratton Valley Lodge range from $119 to $169 a night; the Liftline Lodge is $85 to $135; the Birkenhaus, $99 to $149. Rates vary depending on date, midweek or weekend, packages, and so on. The Mountain Villas are one- to four-bedroom condominium apartments with fully equipped kitchens; many have fireplaces and private balconies. One-bedroom condos cost $90 to

$230 per night, two bedrooms are $130 to $320, and three bedrooms are $170 to $400.

Two- to five-day/night Lifts and Lodging packages are available, from $49 to $99 based on a per person, per night rate. The popular Family Ski Week package includes five days' skiing and five nights' lodging, midweek (nonholiday), in a two-bedroom Valleyside condominium for families consisting of two adults and two children, all for $65 per person per night, and children between the ages of four and twelve receive free KidsKamp. Call ahead for other available packages.

Summer rates at Mountain Villas range from $59 to $79 for hotel rooms, $90 to $150 for one-bedroom villas, and $110 to $170 for two-bedroom villas. Again, check for special-interest packages.

Dining: The Sage Hill Restaurant at the Stratton Mountain Inn serves hearty breakfasts, lunches, and New England cuisine dinners; savor cranberry duck or rack of lamb and pick up the recipe for your favorite dish, graciously shared by the chef. Also at the inn is The Tavern, a cozy spot to sip a hot toddy or your favorite cocktail. Tenderloins is the restaurant and lounge at the Clubhouse on the golf course.

In the winter start your day with breakfast at the Base Lodge, also fine for a quick lunch; the Mid-Mountain Restaurant (at 2,700 feet) is perfect for those who don't want to be off their skis long. Also at the mountain are the Birkenhaus Restaurant and the Liftline Lodge, which offer an old-world European atmosphere and cuisine, and the Partridge in a Pantry deli. Mulligan's Tavern is a great spot for families, with a good kids' menu, fireplaces, and live music. For terrific entertainment head back to the Base Lodge for live music at The Roost, a new bar/restaurant.

Children's World: The ski season lasts from mid-November into April, and during this period youngsters are well cared for and find lots of entertainment. Seven- to twelve-year-olds join the Big Cub group for full-day supervision, lunch, and ski lessons, at $66 a day. Little Cubs take in ages four to six years for indoor games and fun as well as ski lessons (9:00 A.M.–3:45 P.M. daily); the fee is $56 a day, including lunch; a half-day is $30. And real tiny tots gather at the Stratton Childcare Center, a certified day-care facility for children six weeks to three years old. It operates year-round from 8:30 A.M. until 4:30 P.M. and offers indoor and outdoor activities. The cost is $45 a day in winter. The Stratton offers night skiing trails and extended nighttime childcare. Contact the resort for details.

The fun continues in summer with day-camp programs offered seven days a week during July and August. Kids between six and twelve years old spend from 8:30 A.M. to 4:00 P.M. busily engaged in art classes, swim and gymnastics lessons, group games, and field trips. The cost is $37 a day. The child-care center entertains ages six weeks to five years during the same hours for $40, including lunch. An intensive tennis camp for ages seven to seventeen focuses on lessons and tournaments but breaks up the day with hikes, games, and swim time. Its cost is $60 per day.

Recreation: Skiing at Stratton Mountain is a big event. Thirty-seven miles of trails add up to ninety-two runs for all levels of downhill skiers. Mother Nature drops an average annual 170 inches of snow on this mountain, at 3,875 feet the highest peak in southern Vermont, and is nudged along by rather sophisticated snowmaking equipment, covering 80 percent of the skiable terrain.

The Stratton Ski School holds classes for every level of ability. It prides itself on a full-day learning experience—five hours with an instructor. The Stratton Touring Center offers instruction in cross-country skiing for treks through the tall evergreens and across quiet meadows. Ice skating is another favorite winter sport.

If you're more inclined to warm-weather sports, enroll in the Stratton Golf School. Meet fellow students and your PGA instructors in a twenty-two-acre outdoor classroom where all playing conditions can be simulated, then head to the Stratton Mountain Country Club for a round on the twenty-seven-hole championship course.

Attend the Stratton Tennis School for private lessons or a group clinic. There are nineteen indoor and outdoor tennis courts at the Stratton Sports Center and two courts at the inn.

At the Sports Center are classes in swimming and aquacise in the 75-

foot indoor pool, aerobics classes, Nautilus exercise, tennis, and three racquetball courts. During a recess from classes, sneak into the steam room or the whirlpool for some solitary relaxation. In addition, an outdoor pool, a sauna, and three whirlpools are located at the inn. And don't forget to poke around the beautiful Vermont countryside. Hike in the hills and breathe that fresh clean air, jog or bicycle (rentals available) down country roads along fields of wildflowers, horseback ride on mountain trails, or try mountain biking from the summit. When you've had your fill of exercise, join bargain hunters at a local antiques auction or crafts fair. At the Stratton Arts Festival, in September and early October, you'll discover the fine wares of Vermont artists and craftspeople. Stratton Mountain Village, with the flair of an Alpine village, has lots of quaint shops, so finding the right memento of your trip will be an easy task.

Sugarloaf/USA

RR 1, Box 5000
Carrabassett Valley, Maine 04947
(207) 237–2000, (800) THE–LOAF
E-mail: lodging@sugarloaf.com

Traditional New England reserve seems to be missing at Sugarloaf/USA. The prevailing attitude is friendly, upbeat, casually welcoming. While mainly associated with skiing and winter, Sugarloaf is fast becoming a four-season destination. All access is via Portland or Bangor, and once in western Maine, just about all roads lead to Sugarloaf. Route 27 is the main road to the ski area, and from the Carrabassett Valley, Sugarloaf literally stands out. You can distinguish the peak from 20 to 40 miles away, and once you leave the valley floor and start to climb, the panorama just gets better and better. Locals and repeat visitors have dubbed one particular spot "Oh-my-gosh corner," because it is so stunning as you round the corner and suddenly see the front of this impressive mountain with its seventy trails and an Alpine village set on the slope.

Accommodations: Sugarloaf has the capacity to sleep approximately 7,000 people on the mountainside. Condominiums, 912 of them, are set in various clusters of two to twenty-eight units and offer a wide selection of design. Styles include hotel rooms, studios, lofts, and up to five-bedroom, three-bath complexes. The thirty-six room Sugarloaf Inn and the Sugarloaf Mountain Hotel complete the lodging options. Custom-made packages are planned for each family's needs. Packages always include a health club pass, and a complimentary shuttle system gets you around the resort with ease.

Rates range from $100 to $220 for a hotel room, from $153 to $241 for a one-bedroom unit, and from $292 to $447 for a four-bedroom condominium. Cribs and rollaway beds are provided at a daily charge of $5.00.

Sugarloaf was one of the first ski areas to introduce the ski-in/ski-out concept; in fact, every accommodation is ski-in/ski-out. This is great for older children, as it gives them a sense of independence and it gives everyone a sense of freedom. If you want to sleep late or linger over coffee, others in your party need not delay their skiing. Gondola Village is the largest condominium and the heart of the development, and here you will find the nursery.

Dining: Dining in the Sugarloaf area is a fun adventure that is taken quite seriously. With fourteen on-mountain restaurants, you can have everything from burgers to bouillabaisse to haute cuisine.

Gepetto's is a slopeside restaurant with a greenhouse addition and a gourmet menu for lunch or dinner. The Seasons Restaurant at the Sugarloaf Inn offers innovative American cuisine in a relaxed atmosphere. A highlight of the Seasons' menu is fresh Maine lobster. For après-ski the Widowmaker Lounge advertises "comfort with class," cocktails, and music you can hear yourself talk over. Upstairs at the base lodge, Avalanche provides a nonalcoholic teen center with lots of action. One of the more recent additions to Sugarloaf/USA is the Shipyard Brewhaus, located just at the base of the Birches slope. It serves fine Maine microbrews on tap, lunch daily, and pub fare after 2:00 P.M. During the summer six restaurants remain open, so there's still a wide choice.

Children's World: Sugarloaf has a terrific child-care program. A state-licensed child-care center at the base of the mountain accepts children from six weeks to six years of age. Hours are from 8:30 A.M. to 4:00 P.M. Advance reservations are a must. The charges are $42 a full-day or $27 a half-day. The night nursery is available from 6:00 to 9:00 P.M. on Thursday and Saturday for $15, $10 per additional sibling. Reservations are required. A fenced-in outdoor play area adds to winter fun, and inside are toys, movies, storytime, circletime, arts, and crafts—a developmentally appropriate program provided by caring professionals. The nap area is separate, with individual cribs, cots, and mats. A hot lunch is served, and snacks are given during the day. Introduction to skiing lessons for three-year-olds originate from the child-care center. For $54 a full-day or $39 a half-day, your child has the option of a thirty- to forty-minute private lesson or two-hour group experience. Price includes lifts, rental equipment, and all the components of the child-care program.

Evenings offer free supervised activities for five- to twelve-year-olds, six nights a week. Included in the offerings are game nights, Movie Night, Wild Card Night, and Turbo-tubing. Reservations are required.

Mountain Magic teaches skiing to children ages four to six years and stresses independence, safety, and fun. The system teaches walking on skis, side-stepping, wedge stops and turns, falling, and, of course, getting up. Mountain Adventure is a program for ages seven to sixteen, where skills are perfected. These programs run from 8:30 A.M. to 3:00 P.M.; the costs start at $54 a day and include lift ticket, lessons, lunch, and equipment rentals.

Summertime brings flowers and traditional July and August day camps. A five-week program provided by Carrabassett Valley begins in the second week in July. Kids ages four to fourteen enjoy lessons in swimming, tennis, golf, and fly fishing, and an extensive arts program. At $65 a week, with daily rates also available, it's a great deal. On the mountain, Sugarloaf now offers summer child-care for little ones, six weeks to six years. The facility is open daily from 8:00 A.M. to 5:00 P.M., and the cost is $40 a day. Reservations are required.

Recreation: The most impressive aspect of skiing Sugarloaf is that you are skiing a big mountain. It is a traditional mountain, in that it begins gently, goes to intermediate in the middle, and gets "durn hard at the top," as a local might say. Sugarloaf has the greatest vertical drop in the East. It is possible to come almost straight down the 2,820-foot vertical drop (and even do it in an upright position if you're good) having taken only two lifts. A good beginner or low intermediate skier can take Tote Road, a 3-mile trail from the top that follows the ridge and comes safely to the base, but gives that exciting feeling of skiing at the top of the world and surviving it. Cross-country skiers can explore 59 miles of trails, including some lighted for night skiing. Other winter fun includes ice skating, snowshoeing, and cross-country skiing, with some scheduled night tours. The three Family Theme weeks offer additional family activities, and Holiday Weeks are chock-full of entertainment opportunities. Come summer, when there is no snow on the ground, the Sugarloaf Golf Club opens. Designed by Robert Trent Jones, Jr., this course is one of the best for wilderness golf and is rated the #23 golf course in the country by *Golf Magazine*. Every tee has a spectacular view, and the mountain air is always cool. Tennis is limited to outside play, with two courts on the mountain and four in the town. The village has indoor racquetball courts, a sauna, hot tubs, a steam room, tanning beds, a climbing wall, and two swimming pools. But probably the most exciting summer sport is whitewater rafting on the Kennebeck River. Sugarloaf also has a concentrated mountain-biking program.

Sunrise Resort

Moodus, Connecticut 06469
(860) 873–8681, (800) 225–9033 (limited)

If cities or grand resorts aren't your style and you have fond memories of your own summer-camp days, Sunrise Resort may be just the place for you. This is a summer place for the whole family, in the rolling hills of rural Connecticut, on the banks of the Salmon River. It is open Memorial and Father's Day weekends, and the season is in full operation from late June through Labor Day. The office is open year-round; people are encouraged to call or visit ahead of the season. And since it's not open in winter, Sunrise schedules a "Christmas in July" weekend, complete with Santa and Rudolph. Activities go from 8:00 A.M. to midnight, and there's something for everyone in the family.

Accommodations: A wide variety of accommodations occupy the 200 acres. Across the river is another, undeveloped, 200 acres. All the 160 accommodations have names, and the style and number of beds vary in each—we recommend calling for a map and descriptions to help you decide between the Waterfront cottages, the Rustic or Cabana rooms, and the Motel rooms. Rates are $77 to $98 per person per day, $385 to $490 per week. There are five-day (stay five days, pay for only four) and weekend special rates as well. Children ages five to fourteen pay two-thirds of the adult rate; children under four pay one-third the adult rate. Meals and activities are included in these rates. For $47 per person per day, you can even bring your own recreational vehicle.

Dining: Described "as American as apple pie," meals are hearty. Select from five choices of entrees, three appetizers, and four or five desserts—and the menu changes daily. Three times per week dinner is served outdoors, with live music. The seven dining areas include two indoors and five outdoors, or partially outdoors. Children can choose from a menu especially geared to them.

Children's World: Outdoor fun is supervised from 9:30 A.M. to 5:00 P.M. in the fenced play area. Several areas, such as the School House, Playscape, and Western Village, complement the wading pool, swings, slides, and other playground equipment. The Merry-Go-Round Room is an enclosed area for when weather dictates, as well as for the 8:00 to 11:00 P.M. Fun Room activities. For younger children (under six), counselors are generally added as needed for the size of the group. For older children (either on their own or with Mom and Dad watching, participating, or taking pictures), activities are scheduled at various times throughout the day. Times change each day, perhaps beginning at 8:00 A.M. Tuesday with a paddle breakfast at the beach, or maybe at 2:30 P.M. Thursday for a scavenger hunt. A weekly activity schedule is given to everyone, and the participation is up to each family member.

Such things as fire engine rides, diving for pennies, canoe races, a lollipop hunt, and rubber ducky games in the pool create a lot of laughter. There are family field events, softball and volleyball games, and dance lessons—aerobic, ballroom, and line dancing. A separate counselor for teens helps them plan activities they like, such as watching the movie *Jaws* while swimming (uh-oh), night hikes, and various sports and games (sometimes with kids challenging the parents).

Recreation: The opportunities for recreation form a long and familiar list, just like summer camp. The two main areas of activity are the pool and clubhouse at the top of the hill, and the waterfront at the Salmon River. There are canoes, rowboats, and watercycles on the river; and a children's pool, hot tubs, sauna, and exercise equipment on the hillside. Tennis and tennis lessons are free; this is a great chance to improve your game or get your child interested. Sports include softball, volleyball, shuffleboard, basketball, horseshoes, bocce, and, of course, Ping-Pong. A game room and two arcades provide a more sedentary, but not necessarily quieter, kind of action, and nearby are six golf courses for the enthusiast. Excursions in the area include Gillette's Castle, Essex Steam Train and Riverboat Ride, Lyman Orchard, two casinos, and Broadway musicals at Goodspeed Opera House.

The Tyler Place on Lake Champlain

P.O. Box 66, Old Dock Road
Highgate Springs, Vermont 05460
(802) 868–4000, Fax (802) 868–7602
E-mail: tyler@together.net; Website: http://www.tylerplace.com

Tucked away in the northwestern corner of Vermont, just minutes away from the Canadian border, Tyler Place boasts of its beautiful setting and family-friendly atmosphere. The Tyler Place was one of the first resorts to devote itself entirely to families. The original owners, Mr. and Mrs. Edward Tyler, developed a concept that includes family time and time for parents to rejuvenate as a couple. The Tyler family (second and third generation) continues to carry on the resort's family philosophy. Open from late-May to mid-September, it's the kind of place that families return to again and again.

Accommodations: The Inn is the hub of activity, with its recreation rooms, main dining room, fireside lounge, deck, and glass-enclosed porches for visiting, relaxing, cocktails, and candlelight dining. Guest rooms—some are studios, some suites—are located in a separate wing. In addition, twenty-seven cottages, most with a fireplace in the living room and two or more bedrooms, are situated on and near the lake; these have kitchenettes and can sleep up to eight people. Many of the rooms include sleeping lofts or bunk beds; with these special attractions, it may not be difficult at all to get a youngster to go to sleep in a strange place. Cribs and high chairs for infants and toddlers are available at no extra charge.

In total, Tyler Place accommodates approximately fifty families. Based on a full American plan, the daily per person rate for each of the first two lodgers in a unit is $114 to $183 during July and August. Depending on the child's age, a reduced rate of $67 to $78 a day applies; this covers lodging, meals, sports, and the activities program. Rates are 15 to 30 percent lower in May, June, and September; the resort is closed the rest of the year.

Dining: The main dining room in the Inn serves a semibuffet breakfast, lunch, and dinner. New American country cuisine is the kitchen's specialty, and as a full American plan is in effect, you have only to decide which delicious entree to sample. Children have earlier dining hours with their counselors, allowing parents to relax over meals. A family breakfast room and family picnic lunch baskets are available.

Children's World: During the entire season there's an extensive program of events geared to seven different age groups, plus infant care. From the youngest Toddlers (eighteen months to two and one-half-year-olds) to Senior Teens (fourteen- to sixteen-year-olds), children are well entertained, with morning and evening activities led by energetic and enthusiastic college students. Children take meals with their group leaders, and the hours between breakfast and lunch and after supper are filled with arts and crafts, nature walks, songs, games, storytime, volleyball, swimming, hayrides, fishing, movies, treasure hunts, sailing, tennis, sailboarding, kayaking, indoor pool parties—one gets out of breath just listing the activities! Busy and active, your child will no doubt be happy as well, with no chance of being "kid-starved." Afternoons are devoted to individual family time, with activities available if desired. If you can drag the kids away from friends and counselors, the staff will help you plan a day of sightseeing or fishing and send you off with a picnic lunch.

For the very young (newborns to two and one-half years), the resort features a one-on-one "Parents' Helper," a full-time sitter (from high-school-age to mature adult), who will care for your child and even prepare meals. The standard fee is $3.00 to $6.00 per hour. This is a real vacation for Mom and Dad, a break from wet diapers and baby food.

Recreation: Beautiful Lake Champlain is the source of much of the recreation and relaxation of Tyler Place. Take off in one of the resort's sailboats, canoes, kayaks, or sailboards. Try a little waterskiing, with instruction. Or bait your fishing line for bass and pike. The outdoor and indoor heated pools and Jacuzzi on the lakeshore provide hours of fun.

On land, six tennis courts and a fleet of bikes (one-speed, mountain, children's, tricycle, and child seats, all with helmets) are at your disposal, and the nature trails beckon hikers and joggers. For a change of pace, challenge another guest to an old-fashioned game of horseshoes, or try your hand at archery. Maybe you'll join a soccer game or start up a tennis round-robin with the folks in the neighboring cottage. Golf privileges are available at three golf courses within a fifteen- to forty-five-minute drive of the resort. Recreation fees are applied only for golf, outboard motors for fishing, waterskiing, lake cruises, and mountain bikes.

Nighttime brings other events, from dances and live jazz to guitar sing-alongs, and Monte Carlo nights—pick your pleasure. What many guests like most is the hospitable atmosphere of the many and varied activities, with never any pressure to participate.

Whitney's Inn

Box 822
Jackson, New Hampshire 03846
(603) 383-6886, (800) 677-5737

A holiday at a classic country inn does as much for the mind as for the body, and Whitney's Inn seems equally capable of repairing the spirit and rejuvenating the body. Located in the beautiful White Mountains of New Hampshire, the inn sits at the base of Black Mountain on fourteen acres of open fields and wooded hills, with a mountain pond and a brook. Drive into town across an old covered bridge, point your car toward the mountain, and at the end of the road, you'll find the welcoming charm of Whitney's Inn. Open year-round, this is a family operation, and the owners, the Bowmans, appreciate the special interests of families.

Accommodations: Standard and deluxe rooms are in the main inn, and family suites, particularly suited to parties with children, are close by in a separate building. The rate structure is a little complicated, as you have a choice between bed and breakfast or a modified American plan, with breakfast and gourmet dinner. Few standard rooms will accommodate families. B&B in deluxe rooms and family suites (more motel than inn style, but with more space also) cost $42 to $63 per person, double occupancy; children under twelve are $12 to $15, and older kids are $20. MAP rates are $62 to $83 per person; children are $17 to $25 midweek, $40 weekends. A good deal, and very popular, is one of the freestanding cottages (there are only two, so reserve early) with fireplace and two bedrooms: $124 to $165 per night, including breakfast. Weekend and holiday times are the higher rates. Children twelve and under stay and eat free during summer months in a Family Suite.

Dining: Breakfast and dinners will satisfy the best appetites. Breakfasts are hearty fare, preparing you for an outdoor, athletic day. Dinners are relaxing affairs where you'll find such tasty items on the menu as smoked trout and roast turkey with an herb-sausage stuffing. The children's table at dinner offers grown-ups their much-needed quiet time and youngsters their favorite dishes, such as pizza, fried chicken, and fried fish. Try The Shovel Handle for lunch fare of salads, sandwiches, and hearty soups. Or stop by at the end of the day for a little après-ski.

Children's World: On weekends and during school vacations, six- to twelve-year-olds can participate in organized skiing at Black Mountain. The program runs daily from 8:30 A.M. to 3:00 P.M. The First Mountain Division is for experienced juniors; the $45 fee includes mountain skiing, instruction, snow sports, and lunch. The Second Mountain Division is for entry-level juniors; priced at $38, it includes the same activities, but surface lifts only. On weekends and holidays, half-days are available. Penguin Peak is for children ages three to five years and is a skiing-nursery program with one-on-one instruction. Open 9:00 A.M. to 4:00 P.M.; call (800) 475–4669 for details.

Recreation: Skiing at the Inn's back door is the primary wintertime activity. Of the twenty downhill trails, 34 percent are ranked intermediate. The vertical drop on this sunny side of Black Mountain is 1,100 feet. From the summit, skiers look out to Mount Washington and across picturesque New England farms. Snowmaking facilities on 98 percent of the mountain complement Mother Nature's efforts.

In 1994 a new trail, named in honor of longtime resident Betty Whitney, was added. The Betty, as it's called, provides a 2-kilometer groomed loop connecting Whitney's Inn and Black Mountain Ski Area. This is a great starting point for families who ski both cross-country and downhill.

For cross-country skiers, the Jackson Ski Touring Center is located just 2 miles from the Inn; some of its 150 kilometers of trails crisscross the inn's property. Also on the wintertime calendar, the Inn has sledding, ice-skating parties, sleigh rides, and movies. The activities room offers games for the whole family, and the library is a peaceful hideaway.

In the summer, mountain biking, hiking, and jogging in these beautiful mountains are favorite activities. You can also fish, swim, join a cookout, and play a bit of tennis, badminton, croquet, volleyball, and shuffleboard.

East

New York
Pennsylvania

Concord Resort Hotel

Kiamesha Lake, New York 12751
(914) 794-4000, (800) 431-3850

The Concord is a year-round mountain resort on Lake Kiamesha in the scenic Catskill Mountains, two hours from New York City. The sheer size of the Concord seems more suited to Texas than to upstate New York, and the hotel delights in enormous numbers—forty tennis courts, 180 babysitters, the ability to serve dinner to 3,500 people at a single sitting, and a cabaret that accommodates 3,000 guests. However, the very size helps provide vacation activities to please families of all ages and sizes.

Accommodations: A large, modern, high-rise complex set on 2,000 wooded acres, the Concord has 1,250 rooms, including forty suites. Two hundred of these rooms are in an 11-story addition called the Towers. Full American plan rates are available upon request. There are special rates for children who share their parents' room. Rates are higher during holiday periods, and family packages are offered throughout the year. Cribs and rollaway beds are available at no charge.

Photo courtesy of Concord Resort Hotel

Dining: Six dining rooms serve strictly kosher dishes. While dining hours are set for lunch and dinner (one hour each), breakfast is a little more flexible, from 8:30 to 10:15 A.M., with coffee from 6:30 A.M. in the Main Lobby and continental breakfast until noon. A coffee shop makes snacks available from 10:00 A.M. to 6:00 P.M. and from 9:00 P.M. to 3:00 A.M., and during the summer you may have lunch on the outside patio near the pool. The Golf Club House serves breakfast and lunch, but it is limited to registered golfers and guests staying at the Club House. Jackets are required for gentlemen at dinner; casual attire is appropriate at other meals. Children have their own dining room, the Empire Room, and special earlier meal hours. Their mealtimes are supervised and specially planned for younger tastes. The gourmet restaurant, Raymond's, offers continental, nonkosher cuisine and is also open to the public. It is not included on the full meal plan.

Children's World: A formal day camp operates daily year-round, from 8:30 A.M. to 4:30 P.M. and from 6:00 to 8:30 P.M. The ratio of counselors to kids varies with the different age groups, the younger children receiving the closest attention. The four age groups break down into three- to five-year-olds, six- to nine-year-olds, ten- to thirteen-year-olds, and teens.

While the indoor location consists of two rather small rooms, the program utilizes all the hotel facilities. A kiddie pool is open in the summer only, and a fantastic playground structure can amuse up to eighty-five children at one time. An extensive complement of musical instruments, books, records, toys, and crafts projects are well used in a day's events. Entertainment varies with the season, the number of children in the program, and their ages. Magic shows, sports events (swimming, golf, tennis, horseback riding, ice skating), an amusement park, carnival rides, talent shows, and cookouts are scheduled.

The Camp for Tots accepts children from six weeks to three years from 9:30 A.M. to noon and 1:00 to 4:00 P.M. and entertains them with puzzles, stories, and games. Both camps are free, and preregistration is requested.

Babysitting is done by off-duty staff or an approved list of local residents. All sitters must have security clearance and be at least fifteen years old. Rates are $15.00 for the first three hours or less and $5.00 an hour after that; rates are based on the number of children. "Mother's helpers" may be requested at a usual charge of $35.00 a day (morning to evening).

The Teen Club schedules a variety of activities, such as sports, games, contests, and dances, to give teens an opportunity to meet and mingle.

Recreation: Suffice it to say that activities are as plentiful as everything else at the Concord. One of the three golf courses is known as the Monster; perhaps a few warm-up rounds on the nine-hole Challenger International course and the other eighteen-hole course are in order before tackling this one. Driving ranges, putting greens, and pro shops complete the picture for the golfer.

Tennis players never experience waiting time, as forty courts (sixteen indoor and twenty-four outdoor) can handle lots of traffic. Court time is free on all outdoor courts and from 2:00 to 8:30 A.M. on the indoor courts, if you're inclined instead of reclined during those hours. Indoor and outdoor swimming pools, steam rooms, and saunas make exercise a breeze. And joggers can choose one of the courses, ranging from half a mile to 5 miles, that are recommended in a special brochure for joggers. Other outdoor interests may lead you to archery, boating on Lake Kiamesha, horseback riding, and hiking on the wooded trails in the Catskills. And don't forget bicycling, Ping-Pong, baseball games, and horseshoes. In winter the Concord offers gentle downhill skiing (a 200-foot vertical drop), cross-country skiing, ice skating on indoor and outdoor rinks, and tobogganing.

The Concord is as proud of its sports facilities as it is of its entertainment. The Imperial Room, a 3,000-seat cabaret, is host to such big-name entertainers as Joan Rivers, Tom Jones, and Rita Moreno. Several sports stars also visit the Concord for seminars, exhibitions, and just plain relaxation. The hotel publishes a list of activities; it encompasses ninety-six items ranging from aerobics to zen (well, actually . . . volleyball).

Places of interest in the area include river rafting on the Delaware River; Basha Kill, a 2,000-acre wetland that's unique in this area and great for hiking, canoeing, and fishing; Hudson River cruises; and West Point, which is only an hour away. If shopping is your sport, two outlet malls are in the vicinity. And finally, for those of you who remember the first one, in 1969, the site of Woodstock is nearby for reminiscing.

Golden Acres Farm and Ranch

South Gilboa Road
Gilboa, New York 12076
(607) 588–7329, (800) 847–2151, (800) 252–7787 (in New York)

"Old MacDonald had a farm, ee-i-ee-i-oh. And on that farm he had a cow." Well, the Gauthiers have a farm also, with at least as wide a variety of animals as Old Mac did—horses, goats, sheep, ducks, chickens, and a number of baby animals for cuddling and petting. If you like, you can begin your day by milking a cow, collecting eggs from the henhouse, or feeding the animals. The farm has always been family oriented and prides itself on a genuine "down-on-the-farm" experience with modern comforts.

This 800-acre farm/resort is located on top of a 2,000-foot-high knoll in the Catskill Mountains and is open Memorial Day to Labor Day only. Local sites of interest include Howe Caverns, Secret Caves, Hunter Mountain, game farms, and bird sanctuaries. Cooperstown, home of the Baseball Hall of Fame, is nearby, as is the Oneonta Soccer Hall of Fame. Golden Acres is in the center of numerous auction barns, flea markets, and roadside vegetable stands.

Accommodations: In the main house are the dining room, the nursery, an indoor playroom, and a teen lounge. Next door is a motel complex connected to game rooms, lounges, and the indoor pool and hot tub. Across the road (a short city block away) is Gilboa Ridge, with a farmhouse and farm cottage. There are ten connecting rooms and suites. Most rooms contain a double bed and a single bed, with space for rollaways or cribs ($25 per week per crib). Also at Gilboa Ridge are twenty-six "you cook" vacation apartments with kitchenettes and a campground area with water and electric hookups. The farm pays particular attention to single parents and has nondiscriminatory rates based on one adult traveling with a child. Rates are $60–$110 daily, with children paying $20–$35, depending on their age.

Dining: A modified American plan is optional and includes two meals for adults and three for children. Children and adults have a joint menu and dining room for breakfast and dinner, but no adults are allowed at lunch; then the children and teens and their counselors eat all those things that are so dear to their hearts—pizza and hamburgers, along with a few fruits and vegetables. Jewish dietary laws are observed. Two snacks daily are included for the young set, and the selection at the Snack Bar hits the spot between meals. Food is fresh and hearty, and you can eat all you wish. The evening menu includes appetizer, salad, soup, choice of two meats or one fish entree, side dishes, and desserts. All breads and pastries are freshly baked daily in the farm bakery.

Evening activities center on the Skylite Room and the Ragtime Lounge and include happy hour, bands, and entertainment; folk and square dancing; night at the races; and other activities—some for everyone, some for adults only, and a teen lounge for special programs. After the early evening entertainment, live music and dancing continue in the Ragtime Lounge.

Children's World: The program for children varies by age, takes advantage of the farm surroundings, and is offered from the end of May through the first week of September. For the under four-year-old set, a complete nursery service is scheduled from 10:00 A.M. to noon, 1:30 to 5:00 P.M., and 6:30 to 7:45 P.M. Parents collect their children for mealtimes.

For the four- to twelve-year-olds, it is nonstop action throughout the day. For the teens informal activities emphasize meeting others and sharing things while maintaining freedom of action. The rec room, with its jukebox and video games, is popular with this group. Experienced and enthusiastic counselors (most of whom are studying to be teachers) supervise the events. The staff is international, with thirty-eight countries represented. It's great exposure for the children, who learn games and activities from around the world.

A typical day starts at 10:00 A.M., with a tour to feed the animals, collect eggs, or visit the gardens. Then come horseback riding (teaching beginners is a specialty here), swimming, lunch, and a rest period. Afternoon activities are geared to the children's interests—berry picking, frog hunts, hayrides, crafts, games, and perhaps an excursion to the caves or a hike and cookout in the woods. A snack of milk and cookies is followed by rounding up the cows for milking.

After a break for dinner and a quick hello to the parents, evening activities such as bonfires, talent shows, or cartoons start at 7:45 P.M. Kids have another snack, then head for bed about 9:00 P.M.—and well deserved it is! If parents want, they can go out, as a night patrol is on duty from 9:00 P.M. to 1:00 A.M., with a sign-in sheet on each room door. If you prefer, you can take a babysitter from either the staff or local listings at approximately $4.50 an hour, with a three-hour minimum.

Recreation: There is no charge for any of the activities. After catching your limit of fish, you might take off to one of the two tennis courts, the archery field, either of the two swimming pools, or the exercise room. The boats and floating docks at the lake make for a relaxing afternoon, or join a group for softball or volleyball. And grown-ups, too, can partake in the farm activities—feeding the animals, horseback riding, hopping aboard a hayride. A less active afternoon might include a class in macramé, copper enameling, pottery, or stained glass, or a stop by one of the recreation rooms for Ping-Pong and pool. If the weather is uncooperative, there's an indoor riding arena, five playrooms for rainy-day activities, and a complete workout room for adults. One nice feature at the Golden Acres is the policy of allowing an early check-in and late use of the facilities when checking out.

Mohonk Mountain House

New Paltz, New York 12561
(914) 255–1000, (800) 772–6646

The wholesome peace and serenity of the Mohonk Mountain House are not merely by-products of its setting in 2,200 acres of the Shawangunk Mountains, 90 miles north of New York City. The resort was founded in 1869 by twin brothers, Albert and Alfred Smiley, who, following their

Quaker upbringing, regarded drinking, dancing, smoking, and card playing as unacceptable habits. Rather, they emphasized spiritual renewal as evidenced by the nature walks or prayer meetings planned for their proper clientele.

The times have indeed changed, but the gracious, quieter way of life of a bygone era still prevails at Mohonk. No discos swing until dawn here, and, in fact, no bar is on the premises, though guests may order cocktails with the midday and evening meals. Instead, you'll find cozy conversation lounges furnished with Victorian antiques, verandas lined with rocking chairs, miles of hiking trails, and extensive gardens. Open year-round, the rambling wood-and-stone Victorian structure appears almost like a castle, complete with turrets and towers, and sits on the edge of a clear mountain lake a half mile long.

Accommodations: The 261 guest rooms are spacious and tastefully and simply decorated with period furnishings. Most have private balconies overlooking the lake or looking across the valley to the mountains. Many have fireplaces. Some connecting rooms share a bath. On a full American plan (mandatory), daily rates are from $280 to $390 for a standard double guest room. The special Victorian and tower rooms command higher rates. For children occupying a room with their parents, the charge is $100 a day for those over twelve and $63 a day for four- to twelve-year-olds; children under age four are accommodated free. There

Photo by Matthew Seaman, courtesy of Mohonk Mountain House

is no charge for cribs or rollaway beds. Weekly rates and package plans are available. Ask about the "kids stay free" events held throughout the year.

Dining: The main dining room where breakfast, lunch, and dinner are served is a large and elegantly simple room with highly polished woodwork and paneling rising 30 to 40 feet. The kitchen specializes in good American cuisine, from blueberry pancakes to fried chicken, steaks, fish, vegetarian dishes, and homemade breads and pastries. Jackets are standard attire for gentlemen at the evening meal. Cookouts and clambakes are occasionally planned. Afternoon tea is served daily at 4:00 P.M. Refreshments are also available in the Ice Cream Parlor and Soda Fountain and the Tee Room on the golf course.

Children's World: On weekends and holidays throughout the year and daily from mid-June through Labor Day, children are divided into four age groups: two- to four-year-olds, five- to six-year-olds, seven- to eight-year-olds, and nine- to twelve-year-olds. All groups have daily activities in the morning and, after lunch with the family, again in the afternoon. Typical events on the agenda are hikes, nature walks, scavenger hunts, shuffleboard contests, swimming, pony rides, rock scrambles, and frog hunts. Movies, square dances, and campfires are frequently planned for evenings. This is a complimentary service for hotel guests. Babysitters can be hired for younger children, with advance notice.

Recreation: Discovering nature's beauty is at the core of many of Mohonk's recreational activities. More than 85 miles of hiking trails wind through the woods and along the lake; dotting the paths are one hundred gazebos where you can sit to take in the views. Explore the grounds on horseback (Western and English style) or in a horse-drawn carriage ride, and leisurely meander through the award-winning gardens. Mohonk Lake has a small sandy beach at the west end and is stocked with trout; it is the location of swimming, fishing, and boating.

Traditional sports are tennis (lessons available) on the six courts (four clay, two Har-Tru) and the two platform tennis courts and golfing on the nine-hole Scottish-design course and the eighteen-hole putting green. There are tennis and golf pro shops for equipment and apparel. The fitness center offers exercise equipment, saunas, and spa services. Lawn games include shuffleboard, croquet, and lawn bowling.

During the winter months horse-drawn sleigh rides are popular, and when the lake freezes, ice skating is a favorite sport. And Mohonk maintains more than 35 miles of marked trails for cross-country skiing.

Throughout the year lectures, concerts, and slide shows are scheduled in the evening. Several three-day to weeklong programs are planned, covering topics such as bird-watching and identification, gardening, photography, foreign languages, cooking, music, mystery and sleuthing, and stargazing; professionals in the respective fields conduct these programs.

The Mountain Laurel Resort Hotel & Golf Club

White Haven, Pennsylvania 18661
(717) 443–8411, (800) 458–5921
Website: http://www.mountainlaurelresort.com

The Pocono Mountains embrace all four seasons, and whether covered with snow, spring flowers, or the vibrant colors of fall, nature is in its glory here. Mountain Laurel capitalizes on its location in this private part of the mountains. Relax, breathe the fresh air, enjoy a stroll down one of the nature trails. Nominated as one of the top family resorts in America by *Family Circle* and *People* magazines, the Mountain Laurel offers something for everyone.

Accommodations: Nestled in the mountains, the 4-story hotel has 250 guest rooms, executive suites, and hospitality suites. All have two double beds and either a balcony or a patio. Rates are either per room, $110 to $130; or $78 to $99 per person for a modified American plan; call ahead for children's rates as well as Holiday and special packages. The Mountain Laurel Resort Hotel has completed numerous renovations to its property, including new TVs in all its rooms, along with Nintendo game features. The 12,000-square-foot Laurel Ballroom is fully redecorated, and state-of-the-art sound and lighting systems have been added for meetings, weddings, and other social events.

Dining: A Touch of Vanilla is the Michelin three-star restaurant, classic in every sense of the word. Treetops is a combination grill and outdoor garden-terrace restaurant. It is, however, enclosed, and has a wonderful 210-degree view of the mountains; it also has a children's menu. Molly Maguire's Soda Emporium features sandwiches and ice cream, and the Victorian-style Clubhouse on the golf course has breakfast and luncheon menus. The Mountainview Lounge offers weekend evening entertainment, and the bilevel Tavern on the Terrace offers drinks and evening entertainment.

Children's World: "Leave the Kids to Us" is an integral part of the resort. It operates daily from 9:00 A.M. to 9:00 P.M., July 1 through Labor Day and on weekends and holidays throughout the year. For younger children a Playmates Nursery is packed with toys, games, and crafts, and offers a separate crib room with changing tables and monitor system. Kidtraks Kubs, for three- to five-year-olds, and Kidtraks Krew, for ages six and over, have a $12 membership fee, which includes a T-shirt for identification purposes.

Some kids even plan their own reunions with newfound friends! Children have a nice mix of indoor and outdoor activities, from the daily "Everybody's Birthday Party," with homemade ice cream, to creek stomping—for you city slickers, that's walking along a tree-shaded stream turning over rocks, finding salamanders, letting feet and minds free. McDoogles Farm is a great spot to see, pet, and hold the many farm animals.

Children's dinner hour is at 5:00 P.M., which they take with the staff, and evening activities include cartoons, pinball, stories, and music. Weekend programs run Friday from 6:00 to 9:00 P.M., Saturday from 1:00 to 4:30 P.M. and again from 6:00 to 9:00 P.M., and Sunday from 9:30 A.M. to 12:30 P.M.

Recreation: From archery to cross-country skiing (350 acres of trails), there's lots to do here. The Mountain Laurel Golf Club, an eighteen-hole championship golf course with shuttle service and club storage provided, was rated highest among Pocono Resort Golf Clubs by *Golf Digest's 1997 Places to Play*. Golfers will now enjoy PROLINK, the #1 electronic course caddie in the industry. The Mountain Laurel Golf Club is the only course in Pennsylvania with this premier yardage and information system for golfers. Three lighted all-weather tennis courts, an Olympic-size outdoor pool, a fully heated indoor pool, a sauna, a whirlpool, and a fitness center could take most of your time. Divide the rest between old-fashioned favorites like badminton, horseshoes, and miniature golf or the latest video games and mountain bikes. Hike on a twenty-station, self-guided nature walk, or rent a horse nearby, and let him walk! Go on a hayride.

Beyond the resort, the unspoiled Pocono Mountains are the main attraction. Located on 300 wooded acres nearby is Hickory Run State Park, with an elaborate 30-mile hiking-trail system; swimming, canoeing, hunting, and fishing; and weekend campfires and nature walks led by park naturalists. White-water raft or canoe on the Lehigh or Delaware rivers. Day trips for the non-sports-minded include outlet shopping, horse racing, and car races at the Pocono Raceway.

The usual winter sports are also here; sledding, ice skating, more cross-country skiing, and seven downhill ski areas are within 25 miles of the resort. A fast, free shuttle goes to Jack Frost and Big Boulder ski areas.

The Pines

South Fallsburg, New York 12779
(914) 434–6000, (800) 367–4637 (in the U.S.)

Located just ninety minutes from New York City in the lovely Catskill Mountains is The Pines, an all-season, all-family resort. One of the more el-

egant hotels in the region, The Pines has a reputation for being both traditional and innovative. The 450-acre resort is a self-contained complex set in a meadow amid the gentle mountains. A generous number of evergreen and pine trees justify the name, and the best part of all just may be The Pines's approach to a family holiday.

Accommodations: The Pines is one of those rare places where all of the 422 rooms are connecting—a delight for those with small children. All rooms have two double beds. Refrigerators are available on request, and a crib can be added to your room at no charge. Daily rates range from $89 to $129 per room.

Dining: At The Pines eating is itself a special activity, and you can select the meal plan that best suits your needs. Choose a full breakfast, a full-course luncheon, an elegant full-course dinner, or The Pines American Plan, which includes all three! Prices range from $13.00 to $50.00 for adults and from $7.00 to $26.00 for children three to thirteen years of age. Children under three eat free on all dining room plans. All dining room plans are optional; à la carte menu dining is available. Seven or eight entrees are usually featured each evening; these may include steak, roast beef, and fish. The menu changes daily, so there's not much chance of getting bored. In addition to the main dining room, the coffee shop is available. The children's dining room is totally separate, with child-size furniture and a menu geared to the somewhat peculiar tastes of the two- to twelve-year-old set. After dinner you can find amusement in the disco until the wee small hours or in the nightclub, which features name entertainment. Game nights and laser karaoke add to the fun.

Children's World: The children's program is extensive and is divided into prenursery, day camp, preteen, and a teen program. All programs are free of charge, and within the main groups, further divisions are made by age. A nice aspect of the prenursery program is that The Pines provides a private "mother's helper" for a child under age two for $20 a day. The mother's helper feeds and changes your baby, supervises play, and even stays in your room while the child naps.

Prenursery hours are 8:00 A.M. to 3:45 P.M., the same as the day camp. The program is New York State certified and licensed.

The day camp is taken quite seriously. Continuity during the child's visit is stressed, and toward this goal the resort requests that parents not visit in the dining room or interrupt group activities unless absolutely necessary. A typical day begins with breakfast, followed by games, arts and crafts, a swim in the indoor pool, or perhaps ice skating. After lunch afternoons continue with a quiet rest period, followed by more active pursuits such as pony riding or a talent-show rehearsal. After a couple of hours with Mom and Dad and a chance to change for the evening, children have dinner at 6:00 P.M. Movies, clown and magic shows, tournaments, or campfires amuse them until 8:30 P.M. At 9:00 P.M. the night patrol begins its routine room checks at half-hour intervals for children whose parents are out for the evening. Babysitting is available if you prefer someone in the room; rates start at a $20 minimum for three hours.

The teen program, while equally active, is more loosely structured. A daily schedule, posted each morning, lists events such as swimming, hiking, hayrides, tennis, and horseback riding. Dinner reservations may be made in a special teen area of the dining room. While the programs are free, nominal fees are charged for skate rentals, pony rides, and ski equipment. The resort suggests a gratuity for group counselors and mother's helpers.

Recreation: The Pines packs a lot of recreation into its sports facilities, which are all within walking distance of the rooms. The golf course is only nine holes, but it was designed by a master—Robert Trent Jones. Fishing in the little lake may not break a world record, but it does provide pleasant hours. The swimming pool and tennis courts are indoors for year-round enjoyment, and ice skating in winter is also indoors. Take to the nature trails, the outdoor swimming pool, jogging paths, and exercise rooms; and if you still have energy, sign up for horseback riding, a hayride, or dance lessons. Have your pick of board games, organized games such as bingo and video games, or just relax in the sauna or Jacuzzi.

In the winter The Pines adds tobogganing, sleigh rides, and cross-country and downhill skiing. The ski area, Holiday Mountain, is reached by a shuttle bus. While the 400-foot vertical drop does not excite the good intermediate or expert skier, this is a fine spot for a family to learn to ski. With fifteen slopes, eight lifts, and a kinderski program, lift tickets are a bargain at $12.

Rocking Horse Ranch

Highland, New York 12528
(914) 691–2927, (800) 647–2624

"Giddy-up, ole paint" and, with a tip of your ten-gallon hat, off you ride into the sunset. Located only 75 miles from New York City and recently awarded a three-diamond rating by AAA, Rocking Horse Ranch has been owned and managed by the Turk family for years. They take pride in treating their guests as family; in fact, over 80 percent of the guests are repeat clients. The 500 acres easily accommodate up to 350 guests while permitting a feeling of "wide open spaces." With a stable of 120 horses, mainly quarterhorse stock, Rocking Horse stakes a claim to being one of the best dude ranches around.

Accommodations: Rooms (120 in all) are located in either the Main Lodge or the Oklahoma Annex (motel-style units). The twenty-four con-

Photo courtesy of Rocking Horse Ranch

necting rooms and the ranchettes may be appropriate for large parties. The latter are similar to mini-suites, with sitting areas and convertible sofa beds. Eighteen rooms have refrigerators. Daily rates based on double occupancy and a modified American plan are $65 to $150 per adult; children are charged at 50 percent of the adult rate, and weekly stays offer savings. In some package plans children stay free and are charged only for meals ($30 a day).

Dining: A modified American plan is mandatory at the resort and includes two meals for adults but three full meals for children. The three dining areas are the main dining room, an indoor snack bar, and, during the summer, an outdoor snack area by the pool. Meals are five to six courses, prepared by graduate chefs from the nearby Culinary Institute of America. Dinner selections include roast prime ribs, barbecued steaks, or fillet of sole brought in fresh from a local market, complemented by a huge salad bar. At the dessert bar the chocolate blackout cake is not to be missed. The Round-Up Room Nightclub has floor shows and a live band. Two other cocktail lounges, each with a fireplace and a conversation area, are also quite inviting.

Children's World: The Fort Wilderness playground area, with swings and climbing equipment and the animal farm where Tony the Llama lives, is a favorite with kids. All year round children have a planned, supervised program seven days a week. The 9:00 A.M.–5:00 P.M. schedule is filled with horseback riding, swimming, waterskiing, crafts, and games. In the evening fun continues with pizza parties, dances, and cookouts. On weekends during the winter, kids turn to skiing, tobogganing, and snowtubing.

There is no charge for the day's events, which include lunch and snacks with the counselors, or for the "nite patrol," set up to make rounds of corridors and, upon request, to check inside the room when parents are out. Babysitting can be arranged at $5.00 per hour.

Recreation: You might start your day with an early-morning horseback ride; invigorated by the sweet mountain air, lead your horse down a quiet trail through the woods. You can try both English- and Western-style riding. If you're a novice, you can link up with the experienced ranch staff for some basic instruction.

The rest of your day may be filled with waterskiing (instruction is free), enjoying more than 150 feet of waterslide, swimming, fishing, and boating (paddleboats and rowboats) on the ten-acre lake. Play a game of tennis and hike or jog along the nature trails. A relaxing swim in one of three heated pools (two are outdoors—with one just for kids) can revive your spirits for a workout in the exercise room or a rousing game of volleyball, softball, basketball, or badminton. For an easier pace try a round of croquet, shuffleboard, or horseshoes. An archery field and an indoor shooting range are available for aspiring marksmen, and the eighteen holes of miniature golf are fun for kids and their parents.

In the fall the social director plans apple-picking trips, hayrides, and cookouts. In winter add cross-country skiing, tobogganing, snowtubing, and horseback riding in the snow; the 300-foot vertical ski slope is modest but has two new trails. At Rocking Horse all activities are free; the horseback riding, the use of all the sports equipment and facilities, and the entertainment are covered in the lodging rates.

The Sagamore

Lake George at Bolton Landing, New York 12814
(518) 644–9400, (800) 358–3585

The notion of an island hideaway usually involves images of thatch-roofed huts or oceanside condominiums, palm trees waving in a gentle breeze, miles of sandy beach, and golf, tennis, sailing, and swimming. The Sagamore will take you by surprise, for it is an island resort, and it grants its guests opportunities for golf, tennis, sailing, and swimming—and then it deviates from the image. You see, The Sagamore is on a seventy-acre island in Lake George in upstate New York. Surrounded by clear lake waters and the Adirondack Mountains, the tall evergreen trees and the clean mountain air set the stage here.

The Sagamore itself is different. It is part of another era, the gracious and elegant turn of the century. The Sagamore originally opened in 1883. The main hotel building dates from 1930 and is listed in the National Register of Historic Places. After an extensive multimillion-dollar renovation, The Sagamore reopened as a year-round resort in June 1985 and is now an Omni Classic resort. The wings radiate from the main lobby and its semicircular, white-columned porch and seem to embrace the lawns, gardens, and lake views. Down the wings are more porches for sitting, strolling, and catching a different view of the lake. In the center, topping off this Victorian showplace, is the bell tower.

Accommodations: Of the 350 rooms and suites, 100 are in the main hotel and another 240 are distributed among the island's seven modern lodges (don't worry, modern does not denote a disturbance to The Sagamore's ambience). The remaining ten suites are part of a business executive complex. You will find attention to detail and historical accuracy in the decoration of the rooms and throughout the hotel. You'll think "charming, quaint, elegant, reserved" when you see Adirondack-stick or American-country furniture. Perhaps your room will be in mahogany and you'll draw a Queen Anne–style chair up to the desk when writing postcards. Rocking chairs and quilted bedspreads complete the picture in some rooms. In others fireplaces or balconies capture a guest's eye. Even the bathrooms are special and true to a grand era, with their pedestal-base sinks and mahogany towel bars.

During the summer season, May 1–October 31, rates range from $150 for a lodge bedroom to $410 for a lake-view suite in the hotel. Children under age seventeen stay free in the room, but everyone pays the $4.00 per person, per day service charge. In July and August and on holiday weekends (except Thanksgiving), the hotel requires a three-night minimum stay. Holiday room rates are higher by approximately $10 a room. From November through April rates are lower: $95 to $155 per room. Cribs are available, and a modified American meal plan costs $42 for adults, $24 for children six to seventeen, and is free for kids under five.

Dining: For a casual afternoon by the pool, you can have a light lunch and beverages at the Terrace. For a truly elegant and memorable dinner, the Trillium can transport you back through time in style (coats and ties required for gentlemen). Recipes for this restaurant have been carefully researched so that you can have an adventure in history as well as in dining. In between these options are the Sagamore Dining Room, where regional favorites are served at breakfast, lunch, and dinner, and the Club Grill on the mainland, where views stretch out over the golf course and the lake. At the Verandah, in the lobby, guests can have continental breakfast in the morning, tea and finger sandwiches in the afternoon, and nightcaps before retiring. Mr. Brown's is a cafe on the lake that serves light dishes, snacks, and pastries throughout the day and at night magically becomes Italian and very family oriented. The yacht *Morgan* cruises the lake during lunch and dinner, offering its diners constantly changing scenic views.

Children's World: Under the cheerful and watchful direction of the activities counselor, Sagamore kids take swimming lessons, play lawn games, dance, do face painting, go on boat rides, see clown shows, and unveil their hidden talents in crafts classes. In this one area The Sagamore does not follow nineteenth-century practices, which were somewhat restrictive when it came to children. Instead, in keeping with modern philosophies, The Sagamore wants its energized children to have a fun, athletic, and creative visit. They've added an authentic 22-foot tepee, giving the program a new name: The Teepee Club. It runs from 8:00 A.M. to 4:00 P.M. daily during the summer and on major holidays and winter weekends for ages three to thirteen. The cost is $20 for the first child, $15 for the second, including lunch. From 4:00 until 9:00 P.M., six- to thirteen-year-olds can have dinner, play, or enjoy dress-ups and clown parties. A game room includes a Ping-Pong table, a pool table, video games, and a television. For children under age three, babysitting is offered at $7.50 an hour, with a three-hour minimum. Children ages three to five can join the evening program with a babysitter for $10.00.

Recreation: Just across the bridge from The Sagamore's island, Donald Ross designed an eighteen-hole championship golf course in the Adirondack foothills near the lake's edge, complemented by the restaurant and pro shop facilities at the course's attractive Tudor-style clubhouse.

The indoor swimming pool, tennis courts, and racquetball courts help guests stay busy and active year-round. The complete health spa offers its own form of indoor workout with its Nautilus equipment and then pampers with saunas, whirlpools, and massages. Spa packages include special diets, herbal wraps, and aromatherapy.

In warm weather swim in the beautiful, clean, freshwater lake; skim across its surface sailing, waterskiing, and sailboarding; or gently stroke the waters in a rowboat or fishing boat. Jog on the trails around the island or hike the foothills around the golf course. Take a horse out for an hour-long jaunt or stay close to home for a Sunday afternoon concert on the lawn.

In the wintertime Lake George freezes; hearty souls go ice fishing while others snuggle together during a horse-drawn sleigh ride. Ice skate over the frozen lake or go tobogganing and cross-country skiing on the snow-covered golf course. Downhill skiers can take advantage of nearby Gore Mountain and West Mountain, ski areas to which The Sagamore provides free bus transportation.

Saratoga is about 30 miles away and in summer shares its Performing Arts Center with interested visitors.

Skytop Lodge

Skytop, Pennsylvania 18357
(717) 595-7401, (800) 345-7759

The Pocono Mountains have long had a reputation as a romantic honeymoon destination. While this is certainly warranted, the Skytop Lodge will convince you that this area of northeast Pennsylvania is just right for a family vacation as well. Set on 5,500 acres of rolling hills, lakes, and rivers, the lodge is a large, rambling, stone building with a welcoming circular drive. Just 100 miles from either New York or Philadelphia, Skytop attracts many visitors with its relaxed atmosphere, hospitable charm, and recreational activities. It is open year-round.

Accommodations: Most of the rooms have views of the gardens and grounds; some will accommodate a family of four. If a large-enough room is not available, or if parents prefer, children are given their own room at $100 off the regular rate. Based on double occupancy, full American plan high-season (May through October) rates are $300–$425 weekends and $285–$375 Sunday through Thursday. Children under seventeen sharing the parents' room pay $20. November to April has special off-season rates and packages available; weekend and holiday rates, however, are more comparable to those in summer.

Dining: All meals are served in the main dining room, where gentlemen are requested to wear jackets in the evening. The Tea Room serves light fare such as soups and sandwiches, and the seasonal Golf Shop Grill is an alternate luncheon spot in warm weather. The Pine Room, an elegant and inviting area of the lobby with floor to ceiling windows, is the site of afternoon musical entertainment in the summer and cozy gatherings near the fireplace in the winter. The Tap Room serves cocktails and features dancing several nights a week.

Children's World: Camp-in-the-Clouds is in session for three- to twelve-year-olds, daily from July 1 to Labor Day. The morning program runs from 9:30 A.M. to noon, the afternoon program from 2:00 to 5:00 P.M. Each session is $18, or $25 for the full day, and covers a program of swimming, boating, hiking, games, and crafts. Young children also enjoy the playground and the kiddie pool, while the older ones make the most of pool, Ping-Pong, and video games in the Recreation Room. The weekly Saturday night "Grand March" has become a tradition at Skytop. A combination parade, quadrille, and snake dance, it becomes hilarious at times, and guests and staff alike anticipate the fun. At holiday times during the rest of the year, the activities staff plans dinners and movies for children. Individual babysitters can be arranged for evenings only at $5.00 an hour.

Recreation: The Poconos make a lovely setting for sports activities. The eighteen-hole championship golf course is a combination of lush fairways and beautiful old trees on a rolling terrain. Putting greens and a pro shop round out the golfing facility. Tennis players are invigorated by the clean mountain air; of the seven outdoor courts, five are Har-Tru and two are an all-weather surface. Private lessons and clinics are offered.

Fishermen like the trout-filled stream and the three lakes full of bass and pickerel; novices will appreciate the fly-fishing instruction. Others take to these waters for swimming, boating, and canoeing. There's an outdoor swimming pool, and in cool weather swimmers enjoy the large indoor pool in its solarium setting.

You can work out in the exercise room, but outdoors you can have beautiful scenery *and* all the exercise you want. Try lawn bowling on well-tended greens (tournaments are held during the summer), or practice more conventional sports like badminton, croquet, archery, shuffleboard, softball, and miniature golf. The trails through the woods are perfect for hiking, biking, and jogging, and the gardens are suitable for relaxing strolls. Naturalists conduct tours of the local wildlife and vegetation. In the evening you might find a bridge game, play a little pool or billiards, take in a movie, or relax in the library.

In the winter Skytop has a few gentle slopes for downhill skiing; two poma lifts and seven trails with a vertical drop of just 275 feet make it ideal for learning. A ski pro can help with lessons. Several well-groomed trails cover acres of attractive territory for cross-country skiing. Rental equipment is available for both types of skiing, and larger ski areas are nearby at Alpine Mountain (8 miles) and Camelback (15 miles). Tobogganing, sledding, and ice skating are also wintertime favorites.

Southeast

North Carolina
South Carolina
Virginia
West Virginia

Fairfield Sapphire Valley

4000 Highway 64 West
Sapphire, North Carolina 28774
(704) 743–3441, (800) 533–8268

The rolling foothills of the Blue Ridge Mountains provide the backdrop for Fairfield Sapphire Valley, a year-round resort community. The 5,700 acres, filled with the scent of pines and fresh mountain air, encompass three lakes, a golf course, a horseback-riding stable, and picturesque scenery for nature lovers and hikers. The serenity of a canoe ride on the lake, a relaxing afternoon fishing from the dock, or the rigors of a tennis clinic attract vacationers to this mountain setting tucked in the southwestern corner of North Carolina.

Accommodations: Hotel rooms, efficiencies, and one- to three-bedroom condominiums are found in attractive villas, both modern and rustic, that are clustered near the lakes or nestled among tall pines near the tennis center. Most of these lodgings have kitchens, and many have sundecks or balconies where you can sit to watch the sunset. Rates begin at $85 for a room and go to $225 for a deluxe three-bedroom with view. Off-season (November–March) rates are $10 to $35 less.

Photo courtesy of Fairfield Sapphire Valley

Dining: Many families prepare meals in their villas, but if your idea of a vacation does not include cooking, the restaurants can relieve you of this chore. The Library Restaurant offers fine dining in a casual atmosphere, while Mica's Restaurant has an old-world charm and serves lunch and dinner daily. The club for the Holly Forest Golf Course also houses a restaurant, which is open for lunch. There's no meal plan, so you're free to pick and choose as you please. The resort is located in a dry township; while no liquor, beer, or wine can be purchased, brown bagging is permitted and setups are available in the restaurants.

Children's World: The children's program operates Monday through Friday from 9:00 A.M. to 5:00 P.M., June 1 through mid-August. Enroll your child for a full- or half-day session of events supervised by an enthusiastic staff. A full-day with lunch is $20, a half-day with lunch is $15, and a half-day without lunch is $12. The program is offered for ages six to twelve.

Swimming, boat rides, tennis, nature walks, fishing, and arts-and-crafts classes are on the agenda, as are an occasional puppet show and scavenger hunt. Video games are offered for the young computer whiz in your group. The recreation staff assists in making individual babysitting arrangements.

Recreation: The Holly Forest Golf Course is an eighteen-hole championship course; views of the beautiful Blue Ridge Mountains provide ample diversion if your game is not up to snuff. Water hazards on nine holes, including a waterfall, make it a memorable experience. If you're really serious about your performance, you can seek private instruction at the pro shop, which also accommodates your fashion and equipment needs.

Tennis enthusiasts enjoy the Tennis Center, which includes eight Har-Tru courts and two all-weather courts (two lighted for evening play), as well as a well-stocked pro shop. The resident pro can assist in improving your swing in either private lessons or clinic programs.

For hikers and nature lovers, several trails wind around the lakes and through the woods; along the Fairfield Lake Trail, information plaques describe the plants and wildlife of the area. At the Equestrian Center you can engage a mount for a solo adventure or join a group for an escorted trail ride.

For an unusual afternoon outing, you might consider gem mining. In the late 1800s the land was mined quite successfully, and while you probably won't bring home a sapphire or a ruby, you'll no doubt have a good excursion. Check with the Recreation Department for mining tips and equipment.

Swimmers can opt for a dip in one of the lakes or in the outdoor heated pool located at the Recreation Center. Lake Fairfield is also the setting for boating expeditions; canoes, paddleboats, rowboats, and fishing boats can be acquired on a rental basis. Fishermen head to the lakes or a quiet mountain stream for fine trout fishing. At the Recreation Center you'll also find basketball, volleyball, Ping-Pong, miniature golf, the swimming pool, a weight room, Jacuzzi, and a sauna. In the winter the Recreation Center becomes the focus of ski activities; three main trails are covered by snowmaking and lighted for evening skiing; group and private lessons are taught at the ski school. Many visitors reserve time for sightseeing in the area. The Biltmore House and Gardens, along with its winery, certainly warrant a side trip. Local mountain crafts can be purchased in Cashiers and Highlands.

The Greenbrier

300 West Main Street
White Sulphur Springs, West Virginia 24986
(304) 536–1110, (800) 624–6070

The Greenbrier is a 6,500-acre estate in the beautiful Allegheny Mountains. Its history dates back to just after the Revolutionary War, when early settlers discovered the sulfur springs of this area. The grand Georgian architecture of The Greenbrier with its white columned porticos, elaborate formal gardens, and friendly atmosphere set the scene for a memorable experience of fine dining, recreation, and relaxation.

The only problem at The Greenbrier may be deciding what to do first. With a list of recreational and social activities a mile long, you may need a personal secretary to help you get organized. When planning events for your stay, though, save time for an escape to discover nature's charms along the enticing woodland trails, well marked for joggers and walkers alike. And pause among the twelve acres of formal gardens, tended meticulously from spring through fall. With a reputation that has attracted presidents and royalty, The Greenbrier provides a level of elegant service and comfort that ensures an unforgettable vacation. It is open year-round.

Accommodations: With rooms and suites in the hotel as well as guest houses and cottages, you have a wide choice of accommodations. The rooms are large and bright, with comfortable, elegant furnishings. Based on a modified American plan, daily rates for a standard room start at $154 to $194 (depending on the season) per person, double occupancy; larger rooms and prime locations command slightly higher

Photo courtesy of The Greenbrier

rates. There is no charge for children occupying the same room as their parents. The guest cottages include one to four bedrooms, a living room, and a porch or patio; many have fireplaces. The daily per person rate, based on an occupancy of two to eight people, is $206–$349, modified American plan. The Creekside Cottages are available to guests visiting for a minimum of one week. Golf, tennis, and family package plans are offered. Cribs are provided at no extra charge.

Dining: The Greenbrier boasts exciting culinary experiences. Regional Southern specialties, such as spoon bread and fresh trout from the nearby mountain streams, as well as continental dishes, make dining a special part of a visit here. The sumptuous breakfasts, featuring homemade biscuits and country ham, are a real treat. A modified American plan is required for all guests. A coat and tie are standard attire for gentlemen at dinner.

The main dining room serves breakfast and six-course dinners; for à la carte dining April through October, the Tavern Room and Lounge provides a sophisticated setting. Sam Snead's at the Golf Club and Slammin' Sammy offer dining and entertainment during the summer season. At these spots diners enjoy views of the beautiful golf courses. Drapers Cafe—especially popular for its homemade ice cream—is convenient for light meals, snacks, and pastries throughout the day.

Afternoon tea is served daily with musical accompaniment. In the elegant and warm Old White Club, guests gather at 5:00 P.M. for cocktails and complimentary hors d'oeuvres and later for music and dancing until closing.

Children's World: From Memorial Day through Labor Day and at the holiday times of Thanksgiving, Christmas, and Easter, the children's program more than fills the days of three- to twelve-year-olds. During the summer experienced counselors direct arts and crafts, picnics, nature hikes, croquet, shuffleboard, swimming, and games. The older children (six to twelve years) have tennis and golf instruction as well. The fee is $30 a day (10:00 A.M.–4:00 P.M.) for your first child and $20 a day for each additional child.

From 6:30 to 10:00 P.M., children ages six to twelve years old can join their counselors for dinner and an evening bowling or at the movies. So it's possible for grown-ups to arrange an evening or two for wining and dining. Babysitting services for younger children are also available at an average hourly rate of $5.00.

Recreation: Avid golf and tennis players are well satisfied at The Greenbrier. The Allegheny hills provide the beauty and the challenge of three eighteen-hole championship golf courses, one of which was redesigned in 1979 by Jack Nicklaus. Refine your stroke on the driving range and the putting green, or schedule lessons through the pro shop.

Of the twenty tennis courts, fifteen are outdoors and five are indoors. The staff at the tennis pro shop can assist in finding partners. You may also confront the idiosyncrasies of your swing during instructional videotaped replays of your performance.

Kate's Mountain is the picturesque site of the Gun Club, with its four trap and skeet fields. Group tournaments can be organized, or perhaps you'll take in the action from the sidelines in the Clubhouse lounge.

Fishing enthusiasts head for the well-stocked streams and lakes, while swimmers can work out in the indoor or outdoor pool or relax at poolside. An exercise room is adjacent to the indoor swimming pool. The bowling center (eight lanes), table tennis, horseback riding, shuffleboard, horseshoes, croquet, bicycling, carriage rides, and movies offer additional diversions. The five hiking trails are graded by length and rise in elevation. One of the two jogging trails features twelve exercise stations. Winter sports include cross-country skiing, ice skating, and sleigh rides. Downhill skiing is ninety minutes away at the Snowshoe Ski Resort.

And when the body wearies and the spirits droop, the only respectable place to be is the Spa, which pampers guests with mineral baths, massage, steam, and sauna facilities—it was the sulfur water with its medicinal and recuperative powers that first attracted visitors to this region. For shoppers a fine selection of fashions, jewelry, handcrafts, and gifts is presented in the Gallery of Shops.

The Grove Park Inn Resort

290 Macon Avenue
Asheville, North Carolina 28804-3799
(704) 252–2711, (800) 438–5800

The scenery and climate of the Blue Ridge Mountains have long attracted visitors to Asheville. The Grove Park Inn, located on the western slope of Sunset Mountain, opened its doors to guests in 1913 and gives a feeling of pure country in the midst of the city, with grand vistas of mountains and green golf courses. Built of granite from the nearby mountains and dedicated to preserving a gracious turn-of-the-century atmosphere, the inn was named to the National Register of Historic

Photo courtesy of The Grove Park Inn Resort

Places in 1973. Its guest list over the years reads somewhat like a *Who's Who:* Thomas Edison, Henry Ford, Woodrow Wilson, Enrico Caruso, Béla Bartók, and President and Mrs. Franklin Roosevelt. History buffs will have a fine time wondering which room General Pershing slept in or if F. Scott Fitzgerald sat by the fireplace in the Great Hall sipping an after-dinner brandy. A fireplace there, by the way, is so huge that an adult can walk into it! The resort's country club (originally the Swannanoa Hunt Club, begun in 1893) and the Inn were renovated from 1984 to 1988. Two wings, which complement the architectural style and materials of the main building, were added. The four-diamond, four-star Grove Park Inn is open yea-round.

Accommodations: Both the historic main inn and the wings house guest rooms; those offering panoramic mountain views enchant many a guest. There are twelve suites and an exclusive club floor if your entourage warrants the space or additional amenities. In the regular rooms you can request a small refrigerator to keep children's drinks and snacks chilled and close at hand. During the low season, from January to April, the deluxe room rate is $149 a night in the main inn and $159 in the wings per double room. In the high season a deluxe double room is $200 in the main inn and $220 in the wings per night. Children under sixteen stay free in their parents' room; cribs and rollaway beds are available at no cost.

Dining: A full range of refreshments, from snacks and sandwiches to full-course meals, is offered. In the Blue Ridge Dining Room, buffet and table d'hôte meals are served. At the Sunset Terrace enjoy mountain views from the veranda along with fine continental cuisine. The Carolina Cafe fills the bill for early lunches or late-afternoon snacks; it, too, attracts guests with its lovely views. For a change of pace, sample the gourmet cuisine at Horizons, a four-diamond-rated restaurant. In the evening you can enjoy your favorite beverage in the Great Hall Bar or take in the entertainment at Elaine's Nightclub (weekends).

Children's World: The Inn organizes children's activities throughout the year, tailor-made to the number of children visiting the hotel, for ages three to twelve years. The program is most active from Memorial Day to Labor Day, when a large number of families are vacationing at The Grove Park Inn.

From May through Labor Day, the resort offers Operation Kid-Nap, Monday through Saturday from 9:00 A.M. to 4:00 P.M. Saturday Operation Kid-Nap is offered year-round. The $27 fee includes lunch and a snack plus activities such as sports, arts and crafts, nature hikes, and swimming (yes, there is an indoor pool). From Monday to Thursday,

6:00–9:00 P.M. during the summer, a Dinner Club offers dinner and great activities for kids (and a chance for Mom and Dad to dine alone) for only $20. Kid's Night Out is a year-round program, held on Friday and Saturday nights from 6:00 to 10:30 P.M., which costs $25. If you prefer, the concierge desk will provide a list of individual babysitters, with varying fees.

Recreation: An eighteen-hole Donald Ross championship golf course meanders down the gentle mountain slope. Practice your backhand on one of the nine tennis courts (six outdoors, three indoors). The staff in the tennis and golf pro shops can assist you with your playing and fashion needs. An indoor Sports Center has raquetball, squash, and tennis courts; whirlpool; weight and exercise rooms; saunas; massages; and a fully equipped aerobics room with professionally taught classes. There are also indoor and outdoor pools available for hotel guests. But don't forget to take a walk down the garden paths and nature trails (also suitable when the urge to jog hits you).

Nearby you can explore the lake or try your hand at fishing, horseback riding, cycling, mountain biking, white-water rafting, ballooning, or llama trekking. In the winter a day of skiing (cross-country and downhill) is a popular excursion. For souvenirs you'll discover the six gift shops at the resort as well as many crafts shops and potteries in the area. The Biltmore Estate is only 8 miles from the inn; an afternoon can be well spent discovering the art, antiques, winery, and formal gardens of this magnificent old estate.

High Hampton Inn and Country Club

Highway 107
Cashiers, North Carolina 28717
(704) 743–2411, (800) 334–2551

The verdant Blue Ridge Mountains provide a beautiful setting, and High Hampton, located in the Cashiers Valley at an altitude of 3,600 feet, allows its guests an escape to clean, crisp air, clear mountain lakes, and tall pine trees. Some people like the ambience of a country inn—quiet, friendly, with rustic accommodations and good home cooking. Others like the atmosphere of a resort, with lots of activities and events and busy days and nights. Happily, High Hampton has managed to blend the best of both these worlds. Roam over the 2,300 acres and explore the beauties of nature in the southwest corner of North Carolina. Dating from the mid-nineteenth century, High Hamp-

Photo copyright © 1991 by Lavidge & Associates, courtesy of High Hampton Inn and Country Club

ton was once the summer home of Confederate General Wade Hampton and remained in the Hampton family until the 1920s.

For the past seventy years, under the continuing ownership of the McKee family, the inn has welcomed guests to an informal atmosphere for golf, tennis, swimming, fishing, horseback riding, and simple relaxing. The architecture of the inn is charming and rustic, blending with the natural surroundings. The wide porches filled with plants and the lobby's stone chimney with four fireplaces hint at the warmth and friendly spirit within. The inn is open only from mid-April to mid-November, with a famous Thanksgiving Houseparty to close the season.

Accommodations: The 130 rooms at the inn (some of which are suites) are simple, warm, and rustic; the knotty pine walls and mountain-style furniture echo the landscape and the crafts of the region. Many of the rooms have very pleasant views of the grounds. Based on a full American plan, daily rates are $69 to $81 per person midweek, $75 to $88 on Friday and Saturday; children under six are $40, while older children are $49. Cribs are available for infants and toddlers at no charge. A number of privately owned homes are also available; these are fully equipped, with fireplace, deck, laundry, and kitchen. Choose from two to four bedrooms with no meals, but with daily maid service, for $184 to $334 a day. If you choose not to cook, a full American plan is available for $31 per person per day, or $20 for children under six years. Golf package plans are offered as well.

Dining: The one dining room at the Inn specializes in regional Southern cooking, and service is buffet style. Imagine down-home favorites like country ham, cream of peanut soup, homemade biscuits, and vegetables fresh from the garden. Afternoon tea is served daily in the lobby. Coats and ties are standard attire for men in the evening, as High Hampton is one of the few resorts to cling to its traditional ways.

Wine and beer only are served in the dining room, but mixed drinks are now served at the Rock Mountain Tavern, a popular spot to gather, listen to music, meet other guests, and line up partners for bridge or tennis. Movies, lobby games, dancing, and mountain hay rides fill the evening. Small groups of guests may gather on porches to compare notes, sip their own drinks, and talk about the day.

Children's World: Kids have their own building at High Hampton, called Noah's Ark, where youngsters ages five to twelve meet with counselors for daily activities such as arts and crafts, games, tennis, nature studies, and hiking. Offered from June 1 through Labor Day, the program runs from 9:00 A.M. to 2:00 P.M. and includes lunch. After a free afternoon children can rejoin their group at 6:00 P.M. for dinner (sometimes a hayride and cookout!) and games, movies, and stories until 9:00 P.M. The fee is $2.00 an hour per child. For wee ones and the hours after 9:00 P.M., babysitters are available.

The Play Group, for ages two, three, and four, is a fun experience where little ones do donkey-cart rides, bubble blowing, games, and crafts. The ratio of children to counselors is small, with lots of attention for each child.

While there's no swimming pool, a restricted, shallow area of the lake with a sandy beach is especially designed for young children. The area includes a toddlers' playhouse, swings, seesaw, and jungle gym, keeping the little ones amused for hours.

Rather than a teen club, High Hampton has The Gathering Place for Young Adults. Here, the next generation can gather to socialize and enjoy the pool table, Ping-Pong, and video games. Outdoor activities such as volleyball games, boating excursions, and picnics or mountain hikes are planned and enjoyed by all.

Recreation: The mountain terrain and picturesque scenery make golf a challenge and a pleasure. The eighteen-hole course, designed by George Cobb, is carved on a gently rolling plateau, skirting lakes and weaving through white pine and hemlock. There are two putting greens and a practice range; lessons are available. A new dining facility, The Overlook Cafe, is above the pro shop. It features light lunches and snacks, with continental breakfast for early birds.

The tennis center encompasses five outdoor courts, a pro shop, and an indoor practice area; clinics and private lessons are offered. You pay court fees and green fees unless you are on a four- or seven-day golf or tennis package.

There are three mountain lakes for swimming and boating, but the thirty-five-acre Hampton Lake is the center of activity, where paddleboats, canoes, rowboats, and sailboats can be rented. But these clear waters are not just for invigorating swims and peaceful excursions. When the fishing mood strikes, you'll be happy to know that one of the lakes is stocked with rainbow and brook trout; bass and bream can also be lured from the waters.

Discover the rich natural beauty of these surroundings on one of the eight hiking trails. Or take to the mountain trails—in one and one-half hours you can climb to the 4,618-foot summit of Chimney Rock for absolutely spectacular views. Take the ten-station Fitness Trail to the base of Rock Mountain. In a more leisurely manner, lawn sports such as badminton, croquet, shuffleboard, and archery may attract you, or maybe you'll be drawn to the gardens for a stroll among the dahlias, dogwoods, and azaleas.

The inn occasionally holds workshops in such diverse areas as bridge, fly fishing, quilting, watercolor painting, and investments—what a pleasant way to glean helpful hints on a variety of topics! While proud of its facilities, the High Hampton Inn mostly boasts of its friendly atmosphere, its low-key pace, and the serenity and beauty of its natural setting. It is also proud that High Hampton "is not for everyone." But those who stay return year after year, and their children bring their own children. It's that kind of place.

The Homestead

Hot Springs, Virginia 24445
(540) 839–1766, (800) 838–1766

A few classic institutions in the United States have captured the attention of vacationers for many years. With all its charm and grace, The Homestead ranks as one of these. Its fascinating history has roots in the 1700s, yet The Homestead has moved into the twentieth century with style, preserving an atmosphere of friendly elegance. As with several fine old resorts in this country, the medicinal quality of mineral springs first attracted people to the site of The Homestead. While the Spa is still a captivating diversion of many guests, many recreational facilities have been developed over the years, with golf being the premier sport here.

The current hotel was built in 1902, with additions continuing into the late 1920s. Despite those three decades of construction, The Homestead is a cohesive, majestic structure of red brick and white columns in Georgian style. At 2,300 feet, the estate sprawls over 15,000 acres (yes—15,000!) of the Allegheny Mountains in western Virginia. It is open year-round.

Accommodations: The Homestead boasts more than 500 bright and spacious rooms. Sizes vary from traditional rooms to parlor rooms and suites; the rate is determined by the size of the room and its location. Based on a modified American plan, the rate for a double room during the April through October season is $166–$213 per person per day. From November through March the rates are slightly lower, except during the Christmas holidays, which more or less follow the high-season price schedule. The rates for children sharing a room with their parents are $34 for children ages five to twelve, and $55 for children thirteen and older. There is no charge for children under five and no additional charge for cribs and rollaways. The modified American plan rates include the room, two meals a day, swimming, afternoon tea, evening movies, and use of the supervised children's playground. Separate fees are charged for all other activities.

Photo courtesy of The Homestead

Dining: Dining at The Homestead is special. Executive chef Albert Schnarwyler ensures that every meal is a memorable experience. Imagine baked apples and kippered herring for breakfast; consider lunches and dinners that feature local favorites such as Smithfield ham, rainbow trout from nearby mountain streams, and fresh turnip greens, as well as fine international cuisine. A selection that includes bluepoint oysters, grilled Dover sole with almonds, roast baby pheasant, and tournedos Rossini makes for difficult decisions; it's almost necessary to spend extended time at The Homestead just to sample the specialties. And the sublime creations of pastries, sorbets, and fresh fruit tarts should not be missed.

The dining room is open year-round. During the April through October season, The Homestead Grille serves dinner. Golfers enjoy lunch at the Cascades Club restaurant, and Sam Snead's Tavern is yet another alternative for dinner. Casual resort wear is expected for lunch in the dining room, and coats and ties are required for gentlemen in the evening. Picnic lunches can also be prepared if you choose to spend the day outdoors in the wooded mountains.

A time-honored custom at The Homestead is high tea, served daily at 4:00 P.M. in the Great Hall. In an elegant setting graced by chandeliers and Corinthian columns, you can relax to soft piano music while sipping tea.

Children's World: Although The Homestead has traditionally catered to an older set, supervised children's activities are now offered year-round. Children are divided into groups—ages three to twelve years—to enjoy an active sports program of swimming, tennis, fishing, nature walks, and visits to the stables. The outdoor playground has been completely renovated, and children have their own fishing pond—great for kids of all ages. If bad weather precludes outdoor play, children move inside the Children's Cottage for creative endeavors, stories, and educational games. The program operates Monday to Saturday from 9:00 A.M. to 4:00 P.M., and Sundays from 9:00 A.M. to 1:00 P.M. The cost is $39 for a full day with lunch; $26 half-day.

During the winter children can learn to ski on The Homestead trails. The Homestead Kids Club (supervised children's program) operates seven days a week year-round. Individual babysitters can be arranged at any time (with proper advance notice); the rate is $6.00 an hour for one child; $1.00 more for each additional child.

Recreation: Even golf and tennis have hundred-year-old histories at The Homestead. There are three eighteen-hole golf courses, and the fact that native son Sam Snead started his golfing career here adds a certain panache to the atmosphere and lends credence to the caliber of play. The first course was opened in 1892 and revamped in the 1920s when a second course, the Cascades, was added. Robert Trent Jones designed the third course, the Lower Cascades, which opened in 1963. All three courses weave through picturesque wooded landscape. With a putting green, a practice fairway, a pro shop, and lessons available, you have all the necessary ingredients to improve your game.

Tennis also got under way here in 1892; it has since expanded to seven courts. Lessons in tennis can be scheduled, and the tennis shop is well equipped.

The facilities at the Spa (also known as the Bath House) include massage, mineral baths, aerobic classes, and indoor and outdoor swimming pools. There may be no proven miraculous powers of the famous mineral waters, but the benefits of a spa regimen to both body and spirit are not questioned.

For fans of trap and skeet, there are four fields; instruction is offered so that even novices can try this sport. Other outdoor sports include horseback riding in the wooded countryside, trout fishing in the Cascades Stream, and hiking in the mountains. Or you may prefer to enjoy the scenery during a carriage ride. You might take your skills indoors to the eight bowling lanes. Or you might opt for Ping-Pong, billiards, or card and board games. In the evenings go dancing or take in the movies.

Winter sports are limited, but The Homestead does have its own small downhill ski area, open mid-December through March. With only nine runs and a vertical drop of just 700 feet, it cannot offer the diversity and challenge that a good skier seeks, but it may be a fun place for kids to learn, and it does provide an added dimension to a winter vacation. Near the lodge, which houses a restaurant, the ski school, and ski shops, is an Olympic-size skating rink; lessons are offered in ice skating. And cross-country skiers can explore acres of mountain meadows and trails, weather permitting, of course.

Kiawah Island

12 Kiawah Beach Drive
Kiawah Island, South Carolina 29455
(803) 768–2121, (800) 845–2471 (South Carolina), (800) 654–2924

In climate and scenery, the islands off the coast of the Carolinas offer some of the finest resort living. At Kiawah Island the beauty of the natural setting has been carefully respected, while man-made

amenities have been added to provide visitors with the best in comfort, relaxation, recreation, and fun. An island with 10 miles of beach on the Atlantic Ocean, Kiawah is actually two resort villages, each with its own lodging and recreational facilities; a shuttle-bus connects the villages.

West Beach Village (which dates from 1976) consists of the Kiawah Island Inn, condominiums, restaurants, a racquet club, shops, pools, and a golf course. At East Beach Village (the younger by five years), there are condominiums, restaurants, shops, a golf course, a tennis club, and Night Heron Park, a twenty-one-acre recreation area that encompasses a pool, lake, playgrounds, and picnic sites.

All these conveniences and amenities, and yet you still have the opportunity to feel close to nature, as only half the land will ever be developed. The sound ecological planning at Kiawah has preserved the lagoons and marshes and ensured homes for deer, raccoon, egret, and the brown pelican; you might even get to see a loggerhead sea turtle, alligators, dolphins, or perhaps an eagle. If you drive from Charleston (about a forty-five-minute ride from the airport), you'll be given at the main gates to Kiawah a car registration pass that reads "Please respect the wildlife that inhabits Kiawah Island. Alligators are potentially dangerous and extremely fast. They should never be fed or teased in any way." When you see alligators plying the lagoon waters, you'll understand the seriousness of this warning.

Accommodations: The Kiawah Island Inn, located in West Beach village, is the right choice for those who want to be pampered. The 150 rooms, distributed among four lodges, all have private balconies over-looking the ocean, pools, lagoons, or picturesque wooded areas; the services and conveniences are typical of a fine resort hotel.

The condominium villas, cedar-shingled or natural-wood frame structures, are dispersed throughout the island in different settings appealing to all different interests. You may choose one with an ocean view or one next door to the tennis courts, one alongside the lush green fairways of a golf course, one on a lake, or one nestled among oaks and hickories and sweet gum trees. These one- to four-bedroom units have well-equipped kitchens, and most of them have sundecks or screened porches—terrific spots for having breakfast or just taking in the views. One- to five-bedroom luxury homes are also available.

Peak-season (mid-March to the end of April and mid-June to mid-August) rates range from $155 to $205 for an inn room; $175 to $295 for a one-bedroom villa; and $270 to $395 for two bedrooms. Low-season rates are $95 to $135 for inn rooms, $105 to $250 for villas. Weekly rates, shoulder-season rates, and special family packages are also available. Cribs are free at the inn, $15 per day in the villas; rollaways are $15 at the inn and $25 in the villas.

Dining: You'll never have a problem here; there are enough restaurants to meet varied moods and tastes. For South Carolina low-country specialties and continental fare, you might choose the Jasmine Porch (at the Inn), which serves a buffet breakfast (mmm—French pastries and eggs Benedict), lunch, and dinner. Warm weather lures diners to the veranda to enjoy lovely views along with delightful meals.

The Sweetgrass Cafe is a casual dining spot in the Straw Market of West Beach Village; it's open for lunch and dinner and features tempting focaccia-crust pizzas and sandwiches to please any palate. Nearby is Scooper's, where the ice cream and pastries are hard to resist (who can pass up an ice cream flavor called Mississippi Mud?). Beside the inn's pool, Sundancer's serves salads, burgers, and other light fare for lunch and supper. At East Beach Village the restaurant is the Indigo House, an "island bistro" featuring Mediterranean, Caribbean, and the new Florida cuisine. In Night Heron Park (at East Beach Village), two elegant yet casual clubhouses, located at the golf courses, serve breakfast, lunch, and cocktails.

On Monday evenings families head to Mingo Point on the Kiawah River for an outdoor barbecue and oyster roast, followed by the down-home music of a bluegrass band. For evening cocktails and musical entertainment, try the Topsider Lounge at the Inn or Sundancer's, popular places to sip an old favorite or an exotic tropical drink. A casual food court is located in East Beach, offering a variety of quick meals.

Children's World: From early May through September and at Thanksgiving, Christmas, New Year's, and Easter, children and parents alike find Kiawah the perfect destination for a family vacation. Energetic college students with training in sports and recreation supervise young visitors in four different age groups in activities designed to ensure happy, fun-filled days. In fact, there's much more to do than we have room to outline. In summer Kamp Kiawah is in swing from 9:00 A.M. to 4:30 P.M. Monday through Friday. The cost is $21.00 (half-days are available); lunch is an extra $5.00. Divided into three groups— three to four years, five to seven years, and eight to twelve years—the kids enjoy swimming, treasure hunts, crabbing, storytime, and crafts. Kids Nature Club is a special program for eight- to fourteen-year-olds that is limited to twelve participants. Twice-weekly three-hour excursions with a staff naturalist allow them to have a hands-on, fun experience with nature ($14). More painless learning is provided by Kiawah Kollege, an award-winning program for all ages that allows exploration of Kiawah's ever-changing ecosystem. Ocean seining with a huge 40-foot net, canoe trips through the marshes, pond exploration, night walks on the beach, bird-watching—with more than 10,000 acres of marshland and five staff naturalists, the possibilities go on and on. Costs range from $3.00 to $15.00.

Discovery Series, a free weekly program, features speakers accompanied by live snakes or alligators, storytellers, and more. Kiawah has found a successful blend of activities that includes teenagers' favorite things: sports, music, food, and loose structure. Volleyball and basketball tournaments, "teen splash" (pool time only for them), T-shirt graffiti, and a Friday-night dance with DJ are just a sample of the options. There is also a River Cruise with teens from nearby islands, exploring the Kiawah River, maybe even sighting dolphins; limited to twenty kids, the cost is $25.

Children also enjoy the playgrounds filled with wooden climbing equipment, swings, and slides; the largest one at Night Heron Park is built in and among the trees, hardly disturbing the natural vegetation. The Heron Park Center features video games, live animals, and nature wear and gear, as well as a recreation concierge.

When you want to be together and join other families, afternoon and evening hours are filled with bingo, games, nature films, family movies, and cookouts; most of these activities are free. Particularly fun is the "dive-in movie"—movies shown at the pool, with swimming allowed. Babysitters are available when you want to indulge in a strictly grown-up evening.

Recreation: With four excellent eighteen-hole championship golf courses, golfers think they've discovered a little bit of paradise at Kiawah. Host site of the 1991 Ryder Cup and 1997 World Cup of Golf, The Ocean Course, designed by Pete Dyre, is known worldwide. The Cougar Point Golf Course was designed by Gary Player, the Turtle Point Golf Course by Jack Nicklaus, and the Osprey Point Golf Course by Tom Fazio; talent like this ensures challenge in a beautiful natural setting. You can enroll in group or private lessons or in a clinic, then practice newly acquired skills on the driving ranges and putting greens. The pro shops are well stocked with equipment, apparel, and accessories to enhance your game.

For tennis enthusiasts the West Beach Racquet Club offers sixteen courts, while the East Beach Tennis Club has twelve courts and a ball machine. Add a practice alley, resident pros, clinics, and group and private lessons and you have every opportunity to improve your game. Kiawah has been rated the third-best tennis resort in the nation by *Tennis* magazine. It offers free tennis clinics and one hour of free tennis daily to guests.

Swimmers take to the ocean from April through October or dip into one of the three pools at the Inn (one for adults only, one for the family, and one a children's pool). Two 25-meter pools are located in Night Heron Park and Turtle Point. You can sign up for swimming lessons for yourself or your child (even an infant). Other water sports, such as sailing, canoeing, and sailboarding, are also popular.

Bicyclists have more than 20 miles of hard-packed beach and paved trails to explore (rentals, many with baby seats, are available). Joggers find a good workout on the 1.1-mile parcours fitness trail with twenty exercise stations. Try your luck fishing in the lake or creek and surf casting in the ocean, or introduce your child to the fun of crabbing, where an old chicken neck can net beautiful blue-legged crabs. Adult exercise classes (aerobics and water exercise) are offered weekdays during the summer. Nature lovers can participate in numerous expeditions into wilderness areas and river tours for a close look at the lowcountry wildlife and vegetation.

If shopping entices you, the Straw Market at West Beach Village and the Town Center at East Beach Village have stores offering clothing, books, stationery, games, toys, jewelry, and gifts. And nearby Charleston (only 21 miles away) can charm you with historic tours and antiques shopping. With all it places at your disposal, Kiawah may tempt you back for many return visits.

Palmetto Dunes Resort

P.O. Box 5606
Hilton Head Island, South Carolina 29938
(803) 785–7300, (800) 845–6130

Hilton Head Island, the second-largest barrier island on the East Coast, lies at the southern tip of South Carolina, in a semitropical setting. Trees, birds, and wildlife abound, and winters are generally mild. First settled in the mid-1500s, it is steeped in history and renowned now as a resort destination.

Hilton Head is also famous for fine golfing. Palmetto Dunes offers some of the finest golfing in the country (backed by names like Robert Trent Jones and George Fazio) along with an array of other sports and activities. Whether your interests lead you to poolside sunning, a rigorous game of tennis, leisurely strolls on the beach, boating, or fine dining, you'll enjoy the lively variety and relaxed setting, which are designed to please all members of your family.

Palmetto Dunes encompasses 2,000 acres of Hilton Head Island with 3 miles of white sandy beaches on the Atlantic Ocean. Give in to the warm sunshine and gentle sound of the waves and you'll soon forget your regular workday routine. Broad Creek is west of Palmetto Dunes, and 10 miles of man-made lagoons weave through the property; water sports abound. From April through October daytime temperatures are in the seventies and eighties; through the rest of the year, you'll need only sweaters and jackets. Winter and early spring are known as "value season," spring and fall are for golf, and summer is for everything.

Accommodations: Five hundred one- to four-bedroom villas are located on the ocean, along the fairways, overlooking peaceful lagoons, and at Shelter Cove on Broad Creek. With tasteful decor, fully equipped kitchen, and private balcony, patio, or deck, you're surrounded by comfort and convenience. In the low season (November through March), daily villa rates are $106–$331; during the fall (September and October), $126–$361; and in the high season (April through August), $126–$451; size and location determine the rental fee. A minimum stay of two nights is required; the rates drop for four nights or more. A wide variety of packages are offered, so be sure to check. Maid service and cribs are also available, for an extra charge. In addition to the villas, some private homes can be rented.

Dining: Cooking in your villa is quite convenient and economical, but the many restaurants at Palmetto Dunes will no doubt lure you for delightful meals. Sample the breakfast buffet at The Cafe (in the Hyatt) or the Palmetto Cafe (in the Hilton). Golfers on the go can get breakfast and sandwiches at the grill found at each of the three pro shops on the golf courses; Scott's is casual dining at the harbor for lunch or dinner, with popular croissant sandwiches. Patti Arbuckle's Restaurant and Bar has great food, live entertainment, and the island's largest selection of appetizers. Sit on the patio and watch a spectacular sunset on the marsh. Alexander's, with excellent seafood in a beautiful setting overlooking the lagoon and canals, is open for dinner only.

At Shelter Cove there are four restaurants: Little Venice (lunch and dinner) for Northern Italian dishes; Harbourmaster's (dinner), which combines great seafood and beautiful views of the harbor; Kingfisher, for informal seafood dinners; and San Miguel's, for a taste of Mexico. P.J.'s Incredible Edibles offers New York deli–style foods of gourmet quality. Eat in, take out, or have it delivered. And this is only at Palmetto Dunes. On Hilton Head Island itself, more than 200 restaurants vie for your gastronomic attention—indeed, deciding on a restaurant could become the evening's entertainment! For nighttime entertainment you might try Club Indigo or Scarlett's.

Children's World: There's a playground at the Hilton where children can burn off energy; additional ones are being planned as more and more families vacation here. Palmetto Dunes Activities Center includes children in many activities, both free and with a small charge, with and without parents. Water balloon contests, sand castles, canoeing, crabbing, and arts and crafts are scheduled throughout the day. From June through August, however, the real fun for ages four to twelve is at Vacation Station at the Hilton, which is open Monday through Friday from 9:00 A.M. to 3:30 P.M. and on weekends during the winter. Full-days ($25 guest/$35 nonguest) or half-days ($20 guest/$25 nonguest) provide children with a wealth of activities: swimming, crabbing, fishing, beach games, face painting, and dolphin watching, just to mention a few. Kids are enthusiastic about their adventures and new friends, and their stories will no doubt amuse you at day's end. From 6:30 to 11:00 P.M. on weekends, pizza, movies, games, and stories occupy their time while parents enjoy an evening out.

Awesome Adventures is a sports camp for nine to sixteen year olds and provides an awesome amount of fun. Owner Jim Slagle is an experienced and highly motivated leader of youth sports and a parent himself. The program accommodates all skill levels and combines island history and ecology, learning a new sport (or perfecting an old one), and plain old outdoor, active fun. Activities featured include mountain biking, scuba diving, sailing, canoeing, sailboarding, sea kayaking, horseback riding, and much, much more. The $85 per day fee includes lunch, all extras, equipment, and instruction.

While there's nothing structured for teenagers, there's plenty of activities that they like; beach games and sports provide opportunities to meet other teens and socialize or maybe take a walk to Harbor Town.

For younger children and for evenings when you want a grown-up dinner, you may request a copy of a list of local babysitters. There are professional child-care centers on the island; the resort staff will be happy to share this information with you.

Recreation: Golfing at Palmetto Dunes is like a dream come true for most players. There are three eighteen-hole golf courses, one designed by Robert Trent Jones, one by George Fazio, and the newest by Arthur Hills. Filled with challenge, finesse, and beauty, the courses range over gently rolling grounds and often skirt lagoons; the views of the Atlantic are a real bonus. Two other championship courses are in Palmetto Hall Plantation, about 4 miles north of the resort. To hone your skills, sign up for some instructional classes or practice on the driving ranges and putting greens. The pro shops can meet all your needs in equipment, fashions, and accessories.

The Palmetto Dunes Tennis Center will snare the tennis buffs in your party. The nineteen clay courts and two hard-surface courts (six of which are lighted for evening play) provide more than sufficient opportunity to test your game. You may want to try one of the four Supergrasse courts; the play is quick and challenging on a combination of artificial grass and sand. Serious players join clinics or lessons, and less active enthusiasts enjoy weekly exhibition matches by the pros. For appropriate apparel and equipment, you'll find the pro shops can accommodate you. Villa guests enjoy free tennis.

There are twenty-seven swimming pools at Palmetto Dunes—yes, twenty-seven. The possibility of a quick swim always seems just steps away, as all the pools are nestled among the clusters of villas. Swimmers also enjoy a refreshing dip in the ocean after sunbathing or collecting seashells on the beach.

Bicycling (rentals available) is a fun and relaxing way to explore the beautiful grounds of the resort; the tree-lined paths are often used by joggers, too. In-line skating is a popular mode of travel as well. Rental canoes, paddleboats, catamarans, and sailboats are on hand when you want to spend an afternoon on the water, but if you'd rather leave the work to someone else's hand, sign up for a narrated tour of Broad Creek or a dinner cruise in the moonlight. Sailing and fishing charters can be arranged. Palmetto Dunes is also home to the largest sailboarding school on the East Coast.

For those in your family (like teen-age girls) who consider shopping as recreation, the Low Country Factory Outlet Village just at the gateway to Hilton Head Island offers good stores and better prices.

Shelter Cove is a fifteen-and-one-half-acre deep-water harbor and a Mediterranean-style seaside village. Besides restaurants and villas, Shelter Cove has a collection of shops and boutiques, where you'll find interesting gifts to take home.

Awesome Expeditions offers two-hour guided salt marsh tours by kayak for $30, where you'll encounter local wildlife, and perhaps even a dolphin. And Captain Jim on the "Crabber J" gives the kids a fun experience in crabbing—and good lessons in ecology as the crabs are returned to the water unharmed after some games.

Seabrook Island Resort

1002 Landfall Way
John's Island, South Carolina 29455
(803) 768–1000, (800) 845–2475
E-mail: Resort@Charleston.Net; Website: http://www.seabrookresort.com

Sunshine and sandy beaches; lazy strolls under moss-draped oaks, palmettos waving in the breeze; enough fresh crabs, shrimp, and oys-

ters to make your mouth water; golf, tennis, and water sports—is this a little bit of paradise? Visitors to Seabrook believe so. All this is only about forty-five minutes from beautiful old Charleston; it almost seems like you can have your cake and eat it too. A vacation at Seabrook is not exclusively a golfing trip or just an opportunity to develop a spectacular tan. You can go crabbing, ride horses, or join an exercise class in the morning, then discover the history and charm of Charleston in the afternoon. Take a house tour, visit nearby plantations, or go shopping, then return to the resort for an evening of dining and entertainment. Activities and events for every member of the family support Seabrook's "something-for-everyone" philosophy. The resort is open year-round.

Accommodations: The one- to three-bedroom villas—all with fully equipped kitchens, many with sundecks or balconies—are distributed throughout the 2,000 acres of property. Some are oceanside, with expansive views of the Atlantic and close to the Beach Club, some line the scenic fairways of the golf course, and some overlook the marshlands and woods near the Racquet Club. Rates depend on size, location, and time of year. During low season, from November through mid-March, villa rates are $90–$195; mid-March to mid-August is high season, at $155–$460; and mid-August to early November, $120–$320.

Rates are for accommodations only; most recreational activities have separate charges. Weekly rates (for five to seven nights) provide a savings, as do tennis, golf, or equestrian packages. A family recreation package during June, July, and August is a good value, as it gives 20 percent discounts on most things, including golf.

Dining: With three restaurants, you'll have no trouble finding the cuisine and atmosphere to satisfy your taste and whim. The Island House Restaurant is elegant and offers traditional Southern cuisine and tempting seafood specialties. Here you might choose a sweet-potato soufflé or prawns stuffed with crabmeat. Bohickets Restaurant is next door, with equally good food in a more casual atmosphere. For steak and seafood and an ocean view, head to the Seaview Restaurant, more informal than the Island House and more family oriented. At Cap'n Sams you can pick up quick take-out orders (great for picnics or snacking in your villa), or stop at the Village Market for groceries and a deli sandwich. A friendly atmosphere in which to sip a drink and discuss the day's events is provided at the Pelican Nest and Bohickets Lounge. Island House and Bohickets are open year-round; the others are seasonal.

Children's World: From Memorial Day to Labor Day, kids and teens have their own Monday-to-Friday recreation program. Children ages three to eleven meet from 9:00 A.M. to 3:00 P.M. in the Escapades, where activities include swimming, treasure hunts, nature hikes, puppet shows, and storytelling. The cost is $27 a full-day, or $15 per half-day. Full-day includes lunch.

Older children from twelve to nineteen are invited to the Recreation Pavilion every night from 8:00 to 11:00 P.M. This is their own time for beach volleyball, water basketball, and Gameroom Gala—video games, Ping-Pong, and socializing. Special theme parties, teen casino night, and even teen cruises are planned. Game nights are also planned for the entire family at a small cost—Win, Lose, or Draw; Bingo, and Ice Cream Socials.

The fun keeps on rolling at holiday times like Christmas and Easter. Added to the regular activities may be Christmas caroling and a visit from Santa or an Easter decorations crafts class and an Easter egg hunt. A day of Tom Sawyer adventures like hoop rolling, leapfrog, stickball, and fishing will give your child fond memories for years to come. With all of this, normal babysitters may seem a bit of a letdown, but they are available.

Recreation: Golfing's fine in the Carolinas, and Seabrook has put together a nice setup. There are two beautifully manicured courses. Crooked Oaks was designed by Robert Trent Jones; it struts past majestic oaks and dips along the sea marshes. Ocean Winds, designed by

Willard Byrd, catches some of the tricky ocean breezes that make the play interesting. A fine teaching staff can help you smooth out the rough spots of your game, and the pro shop can fill in the gaps for clothing, equipment, and accessories.

Enjoy one of thirteen Har-Tru tennis courts at the Raquet Club across the island. The Raquet Club offers a pro shop and a staff of pros that can do wonders for your backhand in either private lessons or group clinics.

With 3½ miles of glorious ocean beach, you might suspect that water sports tempt many visitors here. There are sunbathing, swimming, ocean fishing, and shelling. Canter along the beach at the edge of the surf or take a leisurely ride through the forests—both are possible at Seabrook, one of the few resorts with an on-site Equestrian Center. The center offers trained instructors who can give you tips to improve your technique. Six swimming pools more than accommodate serious swimmers. With their palm trees, gardens, and lovely surroundings, they also charm serious loungers in for just a quick splash. Perhaps you don't want to sing for your supper, but if you want to *catch* your supper, try fishing (in the ocean or the creeks) or crabbing and shrimping in the tidal marshes. Bicycle along the island's 10 miles of roads—many rental bikes come equipped with baby seats—or join the current craze for in-line skating.

The Recreation Pavilion takes care of a lot of your needs (rental bikes, fishing and crabbing equipment) and is the focus of the Family Fun Program—activities that all the family members can enjoy together, like nature walks, family games, cookouts, bingo, and water volleyball. You may even challenge your child to an evening of video games.

Within 1 mile of Seabrook's gate, enjoy the Bohicket Marina for chartered deep-sea fishing, creek fishing, and three family-style restaurants and shops. For the essentials and the fun of shopping, Seabrook has a few stores: Village Spirits for wine and liquor, the Village Market for groceries, and the Seabrook Shoppe for gifts, souvenirs, and sundries.

The Tides Inn

Irvington, Virginia 22480
(804) 438–5000, (800) TIDESINN

In eastern Virginia peninsulas of land reach out like fingers between the many rivers heading into the Chesapeake. It is a region steeped in history, from the early seventeenth-century settlements of

Jamestown and Yorktown to the family homestead of Robert E. Lee. Its people have always had close ties to the water, originally for commerce and travel and today for recreation. The northernmost of these peninsulas, bounded by the Potomac River and the Rappahannock River, is known as the Northern Neck. On its southern shore, on one of the Rappahannock's inlets, sits The Tides Inn. The hotel is surrounded on three sides by water, and yachts literally dock in the front yard. A sense of happiness and pride permeates the resort. The Tides is small and very much a family affair. It emphasizes uncrowded luxury and informal elegance in a leisurely atmosphere that supports its motto: "The place where nice people meet."

Accommodations: With 134 rooms, you might choose a room in the main building or a semisuite (some with balconies) in the Windsor House or the Lancaster House. Cribs are available, and room rates are per person, modified American plan. Rates range from $140 per person, double occupancy (includes breakfast and dinner) in the main building to $400 for an executive suite. Children under ten are free, while children ten to fifteen pay a $48 meal charge. A surcharge is applied when staying only Friday and/or Saturday. The high season at The Tides Inn is May to October; the Inn is closed from January 2 to mid-March.

Dining: Breakfast and dinner are served in the main dining room. Breakfast is from 7:30 to 9:30 A.M., with an "early bird" continental breakfast or a "sleepyhead" breakfast later in the morning. Lunch can be taken in the main dining room, at the poolside Commodore's, at Captain B's on the Golden Eagle Golf Course, and on many days aboard one of the yachts. Imagine your fun and pleasure as you cruise the coves and waterways while enjoying a gourmet meal. Captain B's is a popular spot even with nongolfers, as the 400 rolling acres with lovely lakes and unspoiled woodlands add an extra dimension of pleasure to your dining. Adjacent to the main dining room is the Chesapeake Club, where expansive views, music, and dancing can relax and entertain you. Dress is casual during the day, with coat required in public rooms during the evening.

Children's World: In addition to the beach and swimming pool, a grassy playground with slides, swings, climbing bars, and Chesapeake Bay Lighthouse attracts young guests. From Memorial Day to Labor Day, The Crab Net Kids, a complimentary youth program, is in session Monday through Sunday, from 10:00 A.M. to 4:00 P.M., with lunch ($6.00) at the pool and swimming twice a day. Crafts and games, scavenger hunts, sand sculpting, bicycling, boating, and crabbing keep youngsters from four to twelve years old busy. On Wednesday, Friday, and Saturday evenings from 6:00 to 9:00 P.M., children meet as a group for a "coketails and pizza party," followed by a movie. Babysitting is available at $5.00 an hour for one child; add $1.00 an hour for each additional child.

Recreation: With water on practically all sides of the inn, boating is a natural sport here. You can take off in a small craft like a sailboat, canoe, or paddleboat or check out the yacht program and cruise the creek, the river, and the bay. The weekly routine schedules varied yachts for luncheon cruises, cove cruises, and bayshore picnics. No additional fees are charged for use of the sailboats, paddleboats, and canoes, or for the yacht program. In fact, rates include almost all activities—tennis, nine-hole par three golf course, bicycles to explore scenic Irvington, evening music and dancing, the fitness and health facility, oyster roasts in season, and nightly parties.

The Tides Lodge, located just 200 yards across Carter's Creek, is connected to the inn by gondola service. While legally separate, it is used as another service and facility of the inn. For example, the three tennis courts at the lodge, one of which is lighted, supplement the four at the inn. Three golf courses (forty-five holes) skirt the waterways and dip back into the trees. A nine-hole executive course is on the inn's property; the eighteen-hole Tartan Course is across the creek at the lodge; and the most challenging course with more hilly terrain is the championship Golden Eagle, 2½ miles from the inn.

Many of the ponds along the golf courses are well stocked for the fisherman who may also, in search of a saltwater catch, line up a trip with the dockmaster. A saltwater pool overlooks a small sandy beach, and Ping-Pong, pool table, video arcade, croquet, and shuffleboard are available in the activities cottage. For your evening entertainment enjoy dancing, movies, bingo, or a pleasant stroll.

Nearby sightseeing excursions lead to Stratford Hall Plantation (the birthplace of Robert E. Lee), Christ Church, and Epping Forest, where George Washington's mother lived. Colonial Williamsburg is just one and one-quarter hours away and makes a nice day excursion.

Wild Dunes

5757 Palm Boulevard
Isle of Palms, South Carolina, 29451
(803) 886–6000, (800) 845–8880

Have you ever seen a three-year-old scamper across a sandy beach to the ocean? A biker pedal down paths through the marshes? A fishing boat return to harbor after a successful day's mission? A sailboat catch the sun and the wind in one skillful motion? An ace serve zing across the net? Or a golf ball soar over the fairway and over grand oaks on its way to a perfectly manicured green? Wild Dunes can package all of these images into quite a family vacation for you.

Wild Dunes has garnered some of the best features of the Carolina coastal islands and wrapped them up into a fine year-round resort. It is recognized by *Better Homes and Gardens* as one of thirty "Favorite Family Resorts." This relaxed and gracious community occupies 1,600 acres of the northern part of the Isle of Palms, just thirty minutes from historic Charleston. Bounded by the Atlantic Ocean on the east and the Intracoastal Waterway on the west, Wild Dunes delights in mild temperatures, soft ocean breezes, and fresh salt air. Relax and rejuvenate your spirits here in South Carolina's low country.

Accommodations: The one-, two-, and three-bedroom villas are grouped in two- to five-story buildings. Many are arranged along the beach, some border the tennis center, others look out on the fairways of the golf course, and still more enjoy the seclusion of the woods and marshland scenery. Inside decor ranges from dramatic, bold interiors to soft pastel furnishings that reflect nature's seaside colors; a fully equipped kitchen is standard in every unit. Cribs can be provided for infants and toddlers.

The high season at Wild Dunes is from mid-March through the end of October. Until mid-June and after Labor Day, daily rates for a one-bedroom unit are $130–$180, $180–$255 for a three-bedroom. From mid-June until Labor Day, rentals are on a weekly basis only, ranging from $900 (one bedroom near beach) to $1,800 (three-bedroom beachfront). Wintertime (November to mid-March) nightly rates are $90–$115 for a one-bedroom unit and $105–$200 for a three-bedroom. Private homes are also available. The location of a villa is a big determinant of price; an oceanfront location commands the highest rate. Special family vacation plans as well as golf and tennis packages are available.

Dining: Not surprisingly, seafood is highlighted on the menus of Wild Dune's restaurants; gumbo and she-crab soup are favorite low-country dishes. But beefeaters can find tasty tender selections here, too. Edgar's is the main dining location, serving breakfast, lunch, and dinner. Southern regional cuisine is the specialty, with a children's menu available. The Grand Pavilion, open only in summer, has turn-of-the-century architecture, an old-fashioned boardwalk, Coney Island–style food, and an airy gazebo. If you have a hunger attack on either golf course, you're in luck. Hot dogs, sandwiches, and drinks are to be found at both the Half-Way House, on the Links, and at the 19th Hole, on the Harbor Course, during the summer only. The Dunes Deli & Pizzeria features light fare for breakfast and lunch, as well as grocery items. At least twelve restaurants offer a variety of dining on nearby Sullivan's Island and the Isle of Palms.

Children's World: Wild Dunes's summer program for kids runs from the end of May through Labor Day and is complimentary for guests. Toddler Time provides structured morning (9:00 A.M.–noon) and afternoon (1:00–4:00 P.M.) sessions with two full-time staff members. Parents are welcome to drop in, as kids enjoy tumbling, storytime, and arts and crafts. On Tuesday mornings they can have "Breakfast with Barney" (oh boy!) and make their own creations at the pancake and waffle bar. Babysitting is also available by the hour or day for a fee. Older children, from five to twelve years, are part of the Wild Adventure Club, held Monday to Friday from 9:00 A.M. to 4:00 P.M. Kids enjoy beach games, swimming, crabbing, scavenger hunts, putt-putt golf, and other "wild" adventures.

Li'l Dune Bug Club allows the kids (ages five to twelve) to leave the parents at home for a night out to play games, watch movies, and munch goodies. These sessions are held Monday to Saturday evenings from 6:00 to 10:00 P.M., the cost is $12.00 for the first child (the second is only $8.00), and kids get a T-shirt to wear and keep. A special version of this program, Parents' Night Out, allows parents who dine at Edgar's Restaurant to leave their children ages two to twelve upon presentation of receipt. Space is limited, so reserve in advance.

Activities for teens include beach volleyball, psychedelic tie-dye, dances, pizza parties, and cookouts. There is generally a $7.00 to $10.00 fee for materials, food, and so on. Video movies and special pool games allow teens to socialize and "hang out."

Recreation: A day of golf can begin on one of the two eighteen-hole golf courses designed by Tom Fazio. The older course, the Wild Dunes Links, is on the resort's ocean side and provides interesting play, with its many water holes. Two holes edge by the sand dunes of the beach and are dramatically beautiful as well as challenging. The newer Harbor Course is across the island, surrounding the marina and harbor, and has its own fair share of demanding water holes. A practice range, professional instruction, and a pro shop can help you over the hurdles with improved style and equipment.

A tennis fan starts the day at the Tennis Center on one of the seventeen Har-Tru courts; four of these are lighted for play at night. Tennis instruction can take the form of private or group lessons, clinics, and camps for a week, a weekend, or an intensive one-day session. Along with its well-stocked pro shop, this tennis facility leaves you very few excuses for not improving your game.

The marina at the Yacht Harbor has 200 boat slips. Here you can dock your own vessel or rent a boat for fishing in the Gulf Stream. Join a charter if you need an experienced captain's guidance in snagging the big ones, or finish off a day with a cruise in Charleston's harbor. Besides taking deep-sea excursions, fishermen can cast their lines in the ocean's surf, the creek, and the lagoons.

Swimmers have pools at most of the villa complexes, the main pool at the Swim Center, and, of course, the beautiful Atlantic Ocean. Joggers and bikers share the nature trails, where pine, oak, and magnolia trees grow; the hard-packed sand beach is also suitable for running and biking. Along the 2½-mile stretch of beach, you'll find sunbathers, strollers, and seashell collectors, and just offshore, sailors and sailboarders. At the beachfront picnic area, the kids' playground consists of natural-wood climbing equipment under the trees. For a close look at the egrets, herons, and pelicans of Wild Dunes, take the canoe trip through the creeks and marshes.

Many family events, such as a sailing class, bingo, and an afternoon ice-cream party, are planned each week. Be aware, however, that there are charges for most of the activities. And when you decide to take a break from the fun and recreation, don't forget how close Charleston is. In a day of sightseeing, you can enjoy a historic Charleston tour of antebellum houses, fine restaurants, and shopping for antiques or at more modern boutiques.

Nighttime comes alive at Wild Dunes. On Sunday start the week with a Welcome Party. There are also repertory theater two nights a week, line dancing, Casino Night, and Blues on the Beach. And finally to bed, replete with the sun, sea air, and all those activities.

South

Alabama
Florida
Georgia

Amelia Island Plantation

Amelia Island, Florida 32034
(904) 261–6161, (800) 874–6878

Like many of its counterparts along the coasts of the Carolinas, Amelia Island Plantation is a well-planned and carefully executed development that combines resort living with an appreciation for natural beauty. Similarity to its sisters is no surprise, for this land was purchased in the late 1960s by Charles Fraser of Sea Pines in Hilton Head, one of the first resorts to blend nature's beauties with gracious amenities. In many ways Sea Pines set the standard for resort communities that followed.

Amelia Island Plantation, which opened in 1972, occupies 1,330 acres of the southernmost island in the Golden Isle chain along the Eastern Seaboard of the United States. Open year-round, it is just off the coast of northeast Florida, about a forty-five-minute drive from Jacksonville. Besides palmettos and oak trees, a 4-mile sandy beach, marshlands, and lagoons, this corner of paradise is blessed with mild temperatures year-round and

Photo courtesy of Amelia Island Plantation

balmy ocean breezes. Amelia Island Resort is a two-time winner of *Family Circle* magazine's "Best Family Beach Resort" award.

Accommodations: You can lodge in oceanfront hotel rooms—many with private decks or balconies—or in a villa overlooking the ocean or a lagoon, bordering the tennis complex or one of the fairways of the golf course. These one- to four-bedroom apartments have complete kitchens; many have private patios, balconies, or screened porches. Architecturally, the multilevel accommodation buildings arranged throughout the property are of various contemporary styles, with stucco or natural-wood facades.

Rates depend on the size and location of the unit and on the number of people occupying it. For four people in a two-bedroom ocean-view villa, rates vary between $273 in winter, $459 in spring, and $408 in summer and fall. The off-ocean price range is $219 (winter), $358 (spring), and $309 (summer/fall). Cribs are provided for little ones at $10 per night or $40 per week (four to seven days). Weekly rates are available, and package plans such as six-day/five-night family vacations are offered. All lodgings are connected to the recreational and dining facilities via a complimentary shuttle bus.

Dining: When cooking in your villa seems just too strenuous after a day of sunbathing, gather the family at the Verandah in Racquet Park. Located in a building tucked among old oak trees, the dining room has large windows overlooking the tennis courts. Sample such fresh seafood from the Atlantic as oysters, flounder, shrimp, and crab in the family-style atmosphere.

More elegant dining will be available in spring 1998, when the new Amelia Inn opens. With expansive views of the ocean, this restaurant will feature escargots, quail, and roast duck and desserts like Southern pecan pie. In addition to dinner, breakfast and a sumptuous brunch on Sundays will be offered.

The Coop is a come-as-you-are breakfast and lunch spot where the menu includes salads and sandwiches, hamburgers and hot dogs. Also appropriate for breakfast and lunch is the Golf Shop Bar and Restaurant at Amelia Links, or the Longpoint Clubhouse. At the Beach Club Seaside Sports Bar, burgers, wings, and ribs plus TVs and electronic games add action to a meal. Seaside Sweets, at the poolside (seasonally), will satisfy your sweet tooth, while the Dunes Club Bar serves light lunches and tropical drinks poolside between Sea and Turtle Dunes.

Children's World: Kids cAMpELIA children's program entertains kids year-round. Activities include swimming, crabbing, and arts and crafts. Take nature walks and enjoy many activities with the resident naturalist. As additional activities are too numerous to mention, contact the resort directly for age, cost, and time specifications.

At Aury Island, a tree house and a dock for fishing and crabbing are reserved just for the twelve-and-under set. At the Beach Club little ones have their own wading pool and a playground filled with wooden climbing equipment. To find a babysitter, you can pick up a list of names and numbers at the main registration desk.

Recreation: The Amelia Links, twenty-seven holes of golf designed by Pete Dye, offer variety in play, as each of the nines has its own personality. One nine-hole course weaves through groves of oak and palmetto trees, another course challenges with play through the marshlands, and the third skirts the ocean, with three holes along the sand dunes and sea oats of the beach. An additional nine holes will be completed by the fall of 1998, bringing the total of Amelia Island Plantation's golf holes to fifty-four. The eighteen-hole Long Point Golf Course, designed by Tom Fazio, opened in 1987. Lessons can be arranged through the pro shop, where you will also find equipment and fashions.

Racquet Park is well situated among beautiful live oaks, a lovely setting for twenty-one courts. Some are lighted for evening play. The site of the Bausch and Lomb Women's International Tennis Association Championships, this tennis complex offers adult and junior clinics, ball machines for solo practice, and a pro shop for equipment and apparel.

Also part of Racquet Park is the Health and Fitness Center. Complete with racquetball, indoor heated lap pool, exercise equipment, steam room, sauna and whirlpool facilities, aerobics classes, and the soothing techniques of a masseuse, it fills the bill for a good workout or relaxing rejuvenation.

Swimmers can choose the ocean or pools for their hours of fun in the sun. In addition to the Olympic-size pool at the Beach Club, each of the groups of villas (except the Lagoon Villas) has a swimming pool—twenty-one pools in all.

Along the 4-mile beach, you can collect shells, sunbathe, play volleyball, ride horseback (the Seashore Stables are just 2 miles away), and fish in the surf for whiting, sea trout, and bluefish. Surrounding the island in bays and sounds and the Gulf Stream are tarpon, marlin, swordfish, flounder, trout, redfish, red snapper, and king mackerel. The waters in this area give up some beautiful prizes, and for advice, insider's hints, tackle, and information on charters, head to the Amelia Angler.

Bicycle along 7 miles of trails (rental bikes with baby seats and children's bikes are available), take a paddleboat out to explore the lagoons (maybe you'll spy an alligator or a white heron), jog along the wooded paths and down the beach, or maybe even challenge the kids to a half hour of video games at the Beach Club Game Room.

For an outing of a different sort, you may browse through the shops of Amelia Village or discover the Victorian district of Fernandina Beach at the north end of the island. The Amelia monthly calendar is worth checking upon your arrival; here you'll learn of classes, movies, hayrides, and cook-outs.

Bluewater Bay Resort

P.O. Box 247
1950 Bluewater Boulevard
Niceville, Florida 32578
(904) 897–3613, (800) 874–2128

Imagine the serenity of a safe harbor, a lush wooded landscape bordering clear blue waters, a sunset over the bay, and a blue glow that settles over still waters and docked boats at dusk. You feel light-years away from the office, staff meetings, and business lunches. In northwest Florida, Bluewater Bay is nestled on the northern shore of Choctawhatchee Bay and can certainly provide that get-away-from-it-all feeling. You'll relax in the peaceful surroundings of Bluewater Bay, but you'll never be bored. The resort is open year-round.

Accommodations: The hotel accommodations overlook the marina at Ward's Cove and include one- and two-bedroom suites as well as the more standard single and double rooms. At the other end of the spectrum are the Villas of St. Andrews, freestanding homes with two and three bedrooms, tucked in among oak and magnolia trees. The name itself alludes to the fine old golf course in Scotland, so it's no surprise that from these homesites you have lovely views of the golf course.

In between these extremes, you may choose a Mediterranean-style townhouse on the water or surrounded by gardens, a bayside villa featuring one- and two-bedroom apartments, one of the golf villas bordering the first and second fairways, or a two- to three-bedroom patio home near the swim and tennis center.

Cribs are available for a nominal charge, and the rooms have refrigerators for your toddler's milk and juice as well as your own refreshments. Rates range from $65 to $165 a night during the low season (November through February) and from $85 to $225 a night in the high season. Weekly and monthly rates are also available.

Dining: The new Clubhouse Restaurant serves breakfast, lunch, and dinner. Seafood from the local waters is always a good choice from the varied menu. Children have a special menu.

Children's World: From Memorial Day to Labor Day, children ages three to twelve don their Bluewater Day Camp T-shirts and join the summer youth program. In this program, which operates Monday through Friday, 9:00 A.M. to 4:00 P.M., kids find adventure and fun under the direction of trained counselors. Junior golf, sailing and tennis clinics, arts-and-crafts classes, swimming instruction, nature hikes, and treasure hunts are typical elements of the program. Six- to twelve-year-olds can enroll for a full-day for $16, while the three- to five-year-olds participate in the mornings for $10 a session. Teens are rounded up three days a week for excursions to an amusement park, a canoe ride, a bowling party, or a miniature golf tournament. There's an occasional kids' dinner and movie night. Individual babysitters, drawn from among the resort staff and local people, are available for younger children and in the evenings; the hotel staff will make the arrangements for you.

Recreation: Although the atmosphere is relaxing and laid-back, you'll never be wanting for something to do. The thirty-six-hole championship golf course shows the imprint of its designers, Tom Fazio and Jerry Pate. Respecting the natural setting, they've brought nature and the golfer together in a congenial blend. At the tennis center twelve of the nineteen courts are lighted for nighttime play. Investigate the tennis and golf pro shops for your equipment and fashion needs.

And if water sports are your true love, there are oh, so many to entice you. Swim in one of four Olympic-size pools, or splash in the waters of the bay. The 120-slip marina provides full services for your days on the water. Bring your own boat, or rent a catamaran, sailboard, or powerboat. Line up a sport-fishing charter to the nearby Gulf of Mexico, leisurely fish in the bay, join a canoe trip down the Blackwater River, or take in a round of shuffleboard. Whether you're active or relaxed, Bluewater Bay accommodates everyone from the young to the young at heart.

The Breakers

South County Road
Palm Beach, Florida 33480
(561) 655–6611, (888) BREAKERS

In the 1880s Henry Flagler, a railroad magnate and cofounder of Standard Oil, was advised to spend time in Florida for his health. From this happenstance evolved a world-class luxury resort. Flagler discovered the warm climate of the Atlantic Coast, was captivated by the scenery, expanded railroad lines down the Eastern Seaboard, and set into motion the development of Palm Beach as a winter playground of the wealthy.

The original Palm Beach Inn, built in 1896, was destroyed by fire in

1903. A second hotel, The Breakers, also succumbed to fire, in 1925. Efforts to rebuild were begun immediately, and the new facility was opened at the end of 1926. The project was inspired by buildings of the Italian Renaissance; the era's artistic influence is evident in the loggias, courtyards, and hand-painted, vaulted ceilings that adorn The Breakers. Open year-round, the hotel has completed a $75 million renovation and was recently awarded the AAA five-diamond status. The grand beauty of this sparkling structure is perhaps met only by its natural setting on 140 acres of lush semitropical landscape bordering the blue-green waters of the Atlantic Ocean.

Accommodations: The 572 well-appointed and recently renovated guest rooms and 88 suites have views of the ocean, the well-tended formal gardens, or the golf course. During the summer (low season), from May 27 to September 30, rates for a double room are $140–$335 a day; there is no charge for children under seventeen sharing a room with parents. Cribs and rollaways are provided at no charge. Rates are about 20 percent higher during the fall and spring; and during the high season, from January to the end of April, rates range from $295 to $500 per day. Some of the package plans eliminate the need for individual fees for golf and tennis.

For those who enjoy more privacy is the Flagler Club, located on the top two floors, with restricted access and additional guest services and amenities. Rates here are $325–$525 per night.

Dining: Dining at The Breakers can be as formal or casual as one desires. Breakfast is served in the lavishly elegant Circle Dining Room, and the best of the Mediterranean can be found in the romantic Florentine Dining Room. Fresh seafood (lobster, red snapper, oysters) is abundant in the Seafood Bar. To say that the wine list is exceptional is an understatement; more than 400 vintages are represented in the wine cellar. In the evenings jackets are recommended for gentlemen. During dinner The Breakers provides music for entertainment and dancing. More casual luncheon dining is enjoyed at Henry's Place, the Beach Club, and the Beach Club Patio. Flagler's Steak House has the finest USDA prime-grade meats available and features mouth-watering steaks and chops. The Tapestry Bar is a favorite spot for afternoon tea as well as for cocktails into the wee small hours.

At The Breakers restaurants, the under-elevens have their own menus. Children under three eat free, and everyone gets a special coloring book.

Children's World: With its broad spectrum of amenities, creative recreational programs and activities, and pervasive family-friendly mindset, The Breakers was deemed worthy of the "Premier Property Award" recently bestowed by the Resort and Commercial Recreation Association (RCRA). The resort has formed a Kids' Advisory Board, composed of

eight young people, ages five to twelve, who meet quarterly to advise the resort on children's wants and needs. In response to this advice, there is a year-round children's program called Coconut Crew Camp for ages three to twelve, where kids enjoy a full day (9:00 A.M. to 3:00 P.M.) of active sports, contests, crafts, pool and beach games, and field trips (the latter may have an extra charge), at a cost of $35, including lunch. For a weekly fee, the Summer Coconut Crew Camp is for those kids who want a little more excitement in their vacation. Each week has a different topic, such as Ocean Life or Theater Week, and the focus is on action, wildlife adventures, exploration, and field trips, as well as golf, tennis, snorkeling, and more!

The agenda for all programs is relaxed and flexible, so your child has the freedom to choose only specific events or to stay with the group for longer periods. Babysitting is also available, even on a twenty-four-hour basis.

Specialty one-week camps offer real-life lessons. Culinary Camp lets budding chefs work side by side with the culinary staff—a real hands-on approach. Etiquette Camp, covering all aspects of proper etiquette and dining, gives preteens or young teenagers the confidence to handle situations with ease. And finally, the Money Management Camp teaches twelve- to seventeen-year-olds how to earn, save, spend, and invest money wisely. The cost is $775 (not including lodging) for each camp.

Recreation: Allow yourself to be pampered; a staff of 1,500 people is dedicated to making a stay here quite memorable. Stroll through the beautiful gardens or the half mile of private beach, linger under the palm trees, or relax in a patio surrounding a fountain.

There are two eighteen-hole golf courses—the Ocean Course, Florida's oldest eighteen-hole golf course, and the newer Breakers West Course, in West Palm Beach. With water hazards and stately coconut palms at many holes, play can be challenging as well as incredibly scenic. The Golf Club houses a restaurant and a pro shop; a resident pro is available to assist you in your game.

With twenty-one Har-Tru tennis courts, eleven of them lighted, you shouldn't have to wait to play. Two pro shops and private lessons or clinics can provide inspiration to improve your game. A junior tennis program begins with peewees, ages three to seven, and continues on through junior academy/tournament training.

The large, outdoor, freshwater swimming pool is right on the ocean, at the Beach Club. Sunbathe beside the beautiful Atlantic, or sip a tall cool cocktail on the patio or at the Reef Bar. Join a deep-sea fishing or fly-fishing excursion for an offshore adventure, go snorkeling, or sign up for scuba instruction.

Bicycle (rentals available) or jog on the paths through the gardens and around the property, or head to the new fitness center for a good workout or massage. For periods when you're not feeling so energetic, there are shuffleboard, croquet, horseshoes, bridge, and backgammon. Other events scheduled throughout the week include water aerobics classes, family movies, and shopping expeditions to famous Worth Avenue. Add lectures, crafts, garden tours, concerts, and cooking demonstrations and you'll have to stretch your vacation to fit it all in.

Callaway Gardens

Pine Mountain, Georgia 31822
(404) 663–2281, (800) 282–8181

Cason Callaway was a textile industrialist in Georgia. In the 1930s he became so enamored of the countryside around Pine Mountain that his life began to change. He turned from industry first to farming and then to gardening. He learned that the plumleaf azalea was peculiar to this area of Georgia, and he was determined to nurture it and share its beauty with others. He established the Callaway Foundation, in honor of his mother, and opened his gardens to the public in 1952. While the gardens remain the focal point of the setting, the resort has grown to include gracious lodging, pleasant restaurants, and sports activities ranging from golf and tennis to swimming and fishing. This naturally wooded and carefully cultivated land—14,000 acres of lakes, woodlands, and gardens—is located 70 miles south of Atlanta, in the Appalachian Mountain foothills of west Georgia.

Accommodations: The Callaway Gardens Inn, near the entrance to the gardens, is a 350-room hotel, which also houses restaurants, lounges, and the Fitness Center. From mid-April through November a double room starts at $100 a night ($96 a night during the winter months, and suites are $200–$300 a night).

Next door to the inn is the Tennis and Racquetball Club; next to that are the Mountain Creek Villas: one- to four-bedroom units with fireplace, screened porch or patio, and fully equipped kitchen. Nightly rates for a two-bedroom villa are $264–$292, depending on the season. The weekly rate during the summer is approximately $2,500. The rates for inn rooms and villas include admissions to the gardens and to Robin Lake Beach.

Many families opt for one of the Country Cottages, which are arranged in small clusters amid tall trees near Robin Lake. All have well-equipped kitchens; some have fireplace, screened porch, deck, or outdoor grill. Daily rates for a two-bedroom cottage range from $240 to $268. During the summer the weekly rate for a two-bedroom cottage is $1,840. The weekly rate includes admissions to the gardens and to the beach at Robin Lake and participation in the summer recreation program for families. Modified and full American meal plans are offered, and golf and tennis packages are featured. Cribs are provided at no charge; rollaway beds are charged at a $15 daily rate in the Inn only.

Dining: In the Inn are the Plantation Room, known for its buffets—particularly the Friday-night seafood buffet—and the Georgia Room, featuring fine Southern cuisine enhanced by candlelight and flowers. While the former is open for breakfast, lunch, and dinner, the latter serves dinner only (dress code).

With red-checked tablecloths supporting the atmosphere that its name connotes, the Country Kitchen, located in the Country Store, serves breakfast, lunch, and dinner in a friendly, family-style setting. It's famous for its muscadine bread and country bacon. The Gardens Restaurant, where lunch and dinner are available, and the Veranda, for dinner only, are at the edge of Mountain Creek Lake; both are open seasonally. Sandwiches and snacks are available in the Champions Restaurant. The latest addition to Callaway dining is the Flower Mill Restaurant near the cottages.

The Vineyard Green Lounge is a great spot for an evening cocktail, with live entertainment nightly.

Children's World: For thirty-six summers Florida State University's Flying High Circus has performed at Callaway Gardens. With the big top pitched at Robin Lake Beach, this area becomes the focus of the Summer

Family Adventure Program, June through mid-August. If daily circus performances are not enough to charm youngsters, the performers also act as counselors, directing kids in games and sports and teaching them a few juggling tricks and circus acts, too. In addition, kids go sailing, swimming, waterskiing, rollerskating, and biking. They take riverboat rides, attend golf and tennis instruction, and grow imaginative in crafts classes. Kids ages three to twenty can participate. The Summer Discovery Program provides an informal look at the animals, plants, and ecology at Callaway Gardens. Family events, such as barbecues, square dances, and movies, are also planned.

These are one-week programs (Saturday to Saturday) with special introduction and orientation for which there is no charge when renting a cottage on a weekly basis. If, however, you cannot schedule a full week in a family cottage and are staying a couple of days at the inn, you can enroll your child on a daily basis, for $35 a day. Besides the program, there are children's playgrounds at the inn and at the cottage area.

Recreation: The gardens are a continuous source of beauty, pleasure, peace, and serenity. This is a place to enjoy, to reflect, and to learn. The colorful, changing displays of begonias, snapdragons, geraniums, zinnias, pansies, tulips, marigolds, chrysanthemums—the list seems endless—are presented in the outdoor garden of the Sibley Horticultural Center. Visitors who explore the walking trails are treated to mountain laurel, hydrangea, narcissus, magnolias, dogwoods, crabapples, hollies, wild flowers, and 700 varieties of azaleas (the famous plumleaf blooms during the summer). At Mr. Cason's Vegetable Garden, you can wander through row after row of more than 400 different types of fruits and vegetables. Workshops on topics like flower arranging and bonsai techniques are available year-round. The John A. Sibley Horticultural Center, which opened in 1984, is a five-acre, innovative greenhouse design that is an architectural as well as a horticultural feat. The resort's newest addition is the Day Butterfly Center, which houses up to 1,000 butterflies (representing more than fifty species) in a lush tropical setting.

Besides its magnificent gardens, the resort also offers more traditional diversions. Four golf courses (three eighteen-hole courses and one nine-hole course) unroll past forests and lakes. The names of the courses are descriptive of their surroundings—Mountain View (the most challenging), Gardens View, Lake View (the most picturesque), and Sky View. A driving range, two pro shops, and a year-round instructional program complete the golfing facilities.

The Pete Sampras in your party has ten lighted tennis courts from which to choose. Eight clay and two Plexipave courts are at the Tennis and Racquetball Club, which also houses two racquetball courts and the pro shop. The instructional program includes videotape analysis, or you can practice on your own with a ball machine.

Robin Lake is the center of lots of summer fun, from paddleboat rides and circus performances to swimming and sunbathing along the mile-long sandy beach. Besides the lake, swimmers can enjoy the pools at the inn, at the Mountain Creek Villas, and at the cottage area.

On the shores of Mountain Creek Lake is a boathouse where you can rent a motorboat and fishing tackle—the lake is stocked with bass and bream—or a Sunfish sailboat, paddleboat, or canoe. You can discover the lakes from their shores as you bicycle along the trails and paths.

You may want to spend an afternoon at an organ concert (daily during the summer) in the chapel on Falls Creek Lake. For indoor exercise the Fitness Center offers equipment for unwinding. For an afternoon of history, you can take the 15-mile trip to Warm Springs and Franklin Roosevelt's Little White House.

Cheeca Lodge

Islamorada, Florida 33036
(305) 664-4651, (800) 327-2888

Stretching over 150 miles south from Miami, the Florida Keys enjoy a subtropical climate and a friendly, laid-back philosophy. Just getting there is an adventure. As you travel along U.S. Highway 1, you get the feeling that you're the string connecting a necklace of islands. And sometimes there are no islands—just a narrow ribbon of concrete in the middle of a very wide ocean—or two! The Atlantic Ocean and the Gulf of Mexico both border this strip of islands. Islamorada is just 75 miles from Miami, but really it is another world.

Accommodations: Cheeca Lodge is a twenty-seven-acre luxury oceanfront resort (AAA four diamond), with more than 1,000 feet of palm-lined beach, not often found in the Keys. A variety of accommodations—154 villa rooms or suites and forty-nine rooms in the main lodge—are spread throughout the landscaped grounds. Generous in size, all guest rooms are air conditioned and also have ceiling fans, and most have a private balcony. Sixty-four villa suites feature kitchen, screened-in porch, living room, and one or two bedrooms. Mid-December to May rates are the highest, when standard rooms range from $240 to $610 and one-bedroom suites are $315 to $1,100. In summer the rates drop to $100–$250 for rooms, $200–$325 for one-bedroom suites. Children under sixteen stay free in their parents' room. Specials and packages are offered year-round.

Dining: Savor fine dinners at The Atlantic's Edge, a plantation-style restaurant with lovely panoramic views of the ocean. Dine inside or outside next to the free-form swimming pool at the Ocean Terrace Grill, sampling the local specialty, stone-crab claws, or soups and sandwiches; here there is a special children's menu. Another indoor/outdoor dining option is the Light Tackle Lounge, great for snacks, cocktails, and piano entertainment in the evenings.

Children's World: Award-winning Camp Cheeca has a purpose: learning about the environment while having fun. Children ages six to twelve are busy from 9:00 A.M. to 4:00 P.M., Tuesday through Sunday, in the summer, weekends year-round, and for special holiday weeks. Full-day costs $26; half-day is $14. Learning to snorkel and fish, doing nature art or sand sculpture, feeding the fish or exploring the beach—everything has an ecological approach that kids really respond to. There's a good mix of activities, with field trips, scavenger hunts, arts and crafts, and Saturday Sundae (everyone's favorite). Thursday and Saturday "Movie Nights" are from 7:00 to 9:00 P.M. The charge is $5.00, which includes movies, snacks, and games. When three children or fewer are present, camp will be open only for the morning session. Families with three or more children receive a reduced rate of $22.00 full-day, $12.00 half-day. Box lunches are available for $5.50. Babysitting is $8.00 an hour, with a three-hour minimum.

Recreation: You can be on the go from dawn to dusk, or make the most strenuous activity of the day deciding between a hammock, chaise longue, or tiki hut on the beach. Consider renting a paddleboat, catamaran, or kayak; a beach cruiser bicycle; or parasailing—or maybe just a pool float is your speed. The three pools are all very different—a free-form swimming pool, a lap pool, and a saltwater lagoon keep boredom at bay. Play tennis on one of the six courts, or try the executive golf course. Take a self-guided walk along Cheeca's Nature Trail, or watch the sunrise from the pier. Or maybe the sunset.

It's a fisherman's paradise here, with more than 600 species of marine life and a calendar of what's running each month that fills a page. No wonder Islamorada is known as the sports-fishing capital of the world. A nice touch is that the chef will, on request, prepare your hard-won catch. Cheeca has its own Dive Center, with equipment and instruction. The Cheeca View doubles as a dive boat twice a day, then does sunset and moonlight cruises. The biggest problem is trying to fit all the options in.

Theater of the Sea, the world's second-oldest marine park, is a natural lagoon where humans and marine animals interact (kids love getting kissed by a sea lion!). They've gone beyond a glass-bottom boat—here they have a bottomless boat. Hmm, neat trick. If you want to range farther afield, the concierge can help arrange a swim with the dolphins, or a trip to either Key West, the southernmost U.S. city, or Pennekamp State Park, the first underwater state park. Combine a visit to Miccosukee Indian Reservation with an airboat ride through the Everglades.

The Cloister

Sea Island, Georgia 31561
(912) 638–3611, (800) SEA–ISLAND

Charming, gracious, and so civilized—The Cloister brings all this to mind. Family holidays at this fine old resort are fun-filled, but the elegance of a bygone era prevails. The Cloister boasts that here children learn manners as well as golf, tennis, and swimming. The dress-for-dinner standard and the children's weekly dances reinforce this philosophy.

Sea Island's rich history dates back to the antebellum days of the Old South, when a large cotton plantation was active on what is now the Sea Island Golf Club. The ruins of a slave hospital standing near the Clubhouse recall this period. Early in this century the property was acquired by Howard Coffin, an automobile engineer who had visions of creating a resort on this lovely 900-acre island, with its warm temperate climate and ocean breezes. His dreams were realized in the construction of The Cloister. Designed by Addison Mizner, who is known primarily for his work in Palm Beach, this "friendly little hotel" (as Coffin described it) opened its doors in October 1928. It successfully weathered the Depression and over the years has warmly greeted guests from the rich and famous to the mere plebeian of good taste. Ivy-covered walls, gently swaying palm trees, impeccable gardens, and wide verandas set the stage for a memorable vacation. The resort is open year-round.

Accommodations: Accommodations are provided in the main building (the original hotel) set back a couple of hundred yards from the beach, in the River House fronting on the Black Banks River, and in guest and beach houses. The original structure has a Mediterranean style with red-tiled roofs and courtyards. The architecture of the newer buildings and the gardens complement this style and maintain the flavor of a gracious island retreat. Rooms range from standard, tastefully decorated bedrooms and baths to superior rooms and oceanfront suites.

Based on a full American plan, daily rates per person (double occupancy) are $154–$305 depending on the type of room, mid-March through November and Christmastime. From December through February (with the exception of Christmastime), rates are slightly lower. In addition to three full

Photo courtesy of The Cloister

meals a day, these rates include most recreational activities except golf, tennis, spa, shooting school, and horseback riding.

Children sharing a room with their parents are charged for meals only, $18–$72 a day, determined by the age of the child. For most of July and all of August, they're not even charged for meals. In addition, the eighteen-and-under group is exempt from golf and tennis fees (playing times may be restricted). Cribs are provided at no charge. Credit cards are not accepted.

Dining: Dining is elegant as well as very appetizing and sumptuous. In the dining rooms of The Cloister (including the Patio, the Georgian, and the South Georgian), gentlemen wear coats and ties for evening dinners. On Wednesday and Saturday evenings, ladies frequently choose to wear cocktail dresses, while men wear dinner jackets. More casual attire is appropriate at the Beach Club (open for breakfast, lunch, and seafood dinner buffets) and at the golf clubhouses for luncheon and dinner.

American and continental cuisines are featured. Given the oceanside location of the resort, it's no surprise that fresh seafood specialties are prominent on the menus. Whether you choose the gracious setting of the dining rooms, with fresh flowers on the tables and lovely views of the gardens, or the casual atmosphere of the clubhouses, you'll find that the careful attention to preparation makes meals a visual delight as well as a culinary treat.

For light refreshments during spring and summer, there's a snack bar near the swimming pools at the Beach Club, and high tea is served afternoons during cooler months in the Spanish Lounge. Special evenings are frequently scheduled, such as a Polynesian luau or a supper at Rainbow Island.

Children's World: The junior staff will charm your child with active days. During the summer, from June through Labor Day, and during Thanksgiving and Christmas holidays, energetic, friendly counselors provide daily supervised play for youngsters ages three (no pull-ups or diapers, please) through twelve, from 9:30 A.M. to 3 P.M. (9:00 A.M.–1:00 P.M. for the three- and four-year-olds) at no charge. Activities include swimming, fishing, crabbing, art sessions, games, and nature walks, just to mention a few.

During the summer months children ages four through eleven can even join their counselors for dinner from 6:00 to 9:00 P.M. (Sundays and Family Beach Supper nights excluded), allowing parents dinners at leisure. For younger children babysitters are available .

It's essential to check the weekly calendar for additional events, because the junior staff also plans various activities for different age groups. Teen dances and pool parties, Ping-Pong tournaments, swimming and hamburger parties, and crabbing parties frequently appear on the agenda.

Recreation: Whether you choose a leisurely stroll along the 5 miles of sandy beach, a rigorous game of tennis, a round of golf, or a refreshing dip in the pool, your vacation stay can be as relaxing or active as you wish. The Racquet Club offers seventeen well-maintained clay courts, an automated practice court, and instruction by a professional teaching staff. Even a little criticism of your backhand is easy to take in a setting graced by oak trees and azaleas. At the pro shop you can pick up equipment and new tennis togs and sign up for a tournament.

The Sea Island Golf Club is located not on Sea Island but on neighboring St. Simons Island; it's just a short drive over the small bridge spanning the Black Banks River. Once you arrive you'll be charmed by the Avenue of Oaks—majestic moss-draped oak trees leading up to the clubhouse. There are thirty-six championship holes; each of the four nine-hole courses has a different personality, whether it's oceanside, along the marshes, or past beds of flowering azaleas and dogwoods. Also operated by The Cloister is the St. Simons Island Club, with another fine eighteen holes providing lots of variety for avid golfers. Each location has its own clubhouse with dining facilities, a well-stocked pro shop, and excellent teaching pros for private lessons and clinics. The Golf Learning Center, a joint venture of Sea Island and *Golf Digest,* offers state-of-the-art practice and learning facilities. There's a driving range at each club, and back on Sea Island you'll find a putting green and a chip 'n' putt area when you want to work in some extra practice time. And if you're a real devotee, rest assured that golfing interests do not fade with the setting sun; join the discussions with the pros at golf seminars two evenings a week.

The Beach Club overlooks the Atlantic, so you can choose an ocean swim or a few laps in one of the two pools. Besides a dining room and a snack bar, the Beach Club offers Ping-Pong, volleyball, shuffleboard, and a terrific soak-up-the-sun atmosphere. Other water sports include sailboarding and sailing in the ocean, snorkeling and scuba diving, and boating and fishing in the river. After excursions through the waterways, you might try exploring the grounds as you jog, bike, or ride horseback. Many folks enjoy a horseback ride along the beach, or you may contact the stables about moonlight supper rides. At the Shooting School you'll find instruction in sporting clays, trap, and skeet shooting as well as all the equipment necessary to learn these sports. And after golf, tennis, swimming, sailing, and skeet-shooting lessons, if you're still dying to try something new or brush up on dusty skills, sign up for dance instruction. After a couple of sessions, you'll no doubt be a hit dancing nightly to the hotel's Sea Island Orchestra.

The Sea Island Spa offers a full range of services. You can join an exercise class, develop an individualized program, consult a nutritionist, have a massage, and relax with a facial.

Special programs are planned throughout the year; they may be just the thing to schedule a family vacation around. Food and wine seminars, bridge festivals, a garden series, and a personal financial-planning seminar are standard events at The Cloister. At any time of the year, it's important to check the weekly calendar. You might want to see a movie, play bingo, listen to a classical piano concert, head to an exercise workout, join a nature walk, or take in a lecture on the local wildlife. But don't crowd your schedule too much, for one of the nicest pleasures at The Cloister is strolling through the gardens and discovering the camellias, gardenias, wisteria, geraniums, and petunias.

Club Med/Sandpiper, Florida
Port St. Lucie, Florida

40 West 57th Street
New York, New York 10019
(800) CLUB MED
Website: http://www.clubmed.com

Club Med is practically synonymous with a carefree, fun-in-the-sun holiday, a tradition going back more than forty years. The only warm-weather village that Club Med operates in the United States is Sandpiper, and it's not only a mini-club but a baby club as well. Located in Port St. Lucie, Florida, about an hour's drive north of Palm Beach, the Club Med village spreads out over 400 beautifully landscaped acres along the St. Lucie River. The verdant green landscape and the clear blue waters make an attractive setting for a fun-filled, sun-filled vacation.

Accommodations: Sandpiper is one of the most luxurious Club Med properties, termed the "Finest." It seems more like a deluxe hotel, boasting brick-colored tile floors covered with kilim carpet, original artwork by local artists, and a separate dressing area, with large closets. Unlike most Club Med villages, the rooms here have telephone, TV, and mini-fridge. Each room has a private balcony or terrace and is located in one of several 3-story buildings near the river.

Weekly rates for adults range from $1,000 (summer/fall) to $1,150 (winter/spring); Christmas, Presidents' Week, and Easter are higher. Children's rates are from $700 to $800. During many weeks a baby age four to twenty-three months or a child age two to five years is free with a full-paying adult; check with the Club for these dates. Sandpiper is one of the few Club Meds with daily rates; these range from $145 to $170 for adults and $100 to $115 for children ages four months to eleven years.

A Club Med membership is required; this is a one-time fee of $30 per family plus an annual membership fee of $50 per adult, $20 per child. The rates include accommodations, all meals, the children's program, and most of the activities, with instruction.

Dining: The main dining room is informal, serving breakfast, lunch, and dinner buffets. Dining at Club Med is a bountiful experience, with selections of American, French, and continental delicacies. (It's also a good chance to meet people and socialize.) The Club has its own baker and pastry-maker—yum. No fewer than twelve different fresh-baked breads are served at every meal. But not to worry, there are enough activities daily to work off any calories from overindulging. A special kid-friendly menu is served to children early at lunch and dinner. Parents may join their children while they eat, and the G.O.s (*gentils organisateurs*—French for "gracious organizers") supervise as well. Highchairs and booster seats make life easier for the little ones. After their early dinner kids return to the mini-club. Mom and Dad, meanwhile, savor a superb and blissfully quiet dinner, perhaps in one of the two specialty restaurants—beautifully decorated, smaller and more intimate, table service is the order of the day here. Choose La Fontana, with the freshest of fish, or The Riverside, which offers fine French dishes. Complimentary wine is served with lunch and dinner, thanks to the French heritage of the Club.

Children's World: Kids are thoroughly entertained at Club Med. In fact, you may almost have to make an appointment to see your little one. The Baby Club is available for infants ages four to twenty-three months. Strollers, baby phones, bassinets—all the necessary equipment can be borrowed; and a pediatrician is either in the village or on call, plus one registered nurse. Each baby gets her own crib, and there's even a special Baby Chef, who prepares the food using only natural ingredients. Lunch is handled by the G.O.s, but parents are on duty for dinner. Need juice or milk in the middle of the night? No problem; just go to the twenty-four-hour convenience room. Depending on their ages, babies are changed, fed, napped, and played with in the adjacent garden, with swings and toys. The more mobile go on walks or play on the beach. A new service available only at this Baby Crib is "Twilight Care." Babies are brought back to the Baby Club at 7:00 P.M., in their pajamas, and can sleep there while parents take in a show or stroll along the river.

The Petit Club is for two- to three-year-olds, the Mini Club is for four- to seven-year-olds, and the Kids Club entertains eight- to eleven-year-olds. Each has its own area, its own G.O.s, and an unbelievable number of activities. In addition to all the usual activities of children's programs, Club Med also offers circus workshops, with real trampolines, trapeze and low-wire work, juggling, trick bikes, and clowns. At the end of the week, the entire group puts on a show under the Big Top for adoring parents. It's really terrific, and the kids are so proud of themselves. Children also rave about the scuba experience in the swimming pool, with kid-size masks, fins, and tanks. In one-on-one instruction, even four-year-olds get to breathe under water—what a thrill! There's intensive tennis for kids eight and older, and soccer, softball, in-line skating, sailing, waterskiing—and much more, all included in the one price.

Recreation: The sun is warm, the water inviting. You have five swimming pools to choose from and a little sandy beach where you can splash in the river. A shuttle leaves hourly for the twenty-minute ride to the Atlantic for ocean swimming. In the calm water of the river, you can glide along on a sailboat and later have a go at waterskiing. Tennis clinics are held daily on the nineteen courts; after intensive two-and-one-half-hour sessions, you will surely find improvement in your game. A normal program with one-hour daily lessons at all levels is another option. Aerobics classes, calisthenics, and volleyball games always pop up on the agenda. Perhaps you prefer a routine in the fitness center or biking and jogging along the paths through the property. Maybe you can sneak in a trial swing on the trapeze—it's scary, but very safe.

Speaking of swings, unique to Sandpiper is a concentrated golf program, including two eighteen-hole championship golf courses designed by Mark Mahannah, called Saints and Sinners; a driving range; a free nine-hole par three; an enclosed driving range, with free lessons at all levels; two putting greens; a chipping green; and a practice sandtrap. For serious golfers the Golf Academy provides two and one-half hours daily of instruction and course play at an additional cost.

The Mini Clubs run from 9:00 A.M. to 9:00 P.M. Afterward the whole family can enjoy the evening entertainment, usually a show or participatory fun. After the kids finally fall into bed, the nightclub continues into the night.

If you have time, which we doubt, Club Med offers a mind-boggling array of excursions. You may not want to mention it to the kids, but Disney World is only two hours away. Also nearby are the Kennedy Space Center, hot-air ballooning, and deep-sea fishing. Palm Beach shopping is also within close striking distance.

Hawk's Cay Resort and Marina

Mile Marker 61
Duck Key, Florida 33050
(305) 743–7000, (800) 432–2242

In a flight of fancy, you might dream of a tropical island paradise—coconut palms and banyan trees, sandy beaches, clear blue waters, warm temperatures, and balmy ocean breezes. You don't have to go halfway around the world to a deserted island in the South Pacific for this atmosphere: Hawk's Cay combines all this natural beauty with the comforts and conveniences of a fine resort. Located in the middle of the Florida Keys, Hawk's Cay is a secluded sixty-acre island. The resort was built in the late 1950s and has hosted numerous presidents and film stars. Recently refurbished, the rambling West Indies–style hotel sets the tone for the relaxed, elegant atmosphere that you'll find here. Ceiling fans, indoor plants, wicker furniture, and French doors in the lobbies and lounges echo the easygoing pace. The temperatures are mild, averaging in the low eighties in the summer and the low seventies in the winter, and the water stays warm year-round. Water sports—from fishing and sailing to swimming and waterskiing—are, naturally, the main focus in an island resort. The only living coral reef in the continental United States is just offshore; guests can snorkel and scuba dive, indulging in the adventure and beauty of the underwater world. A unique program of scuba instruction for the physically challenged has been very well received.

Accommodations: This comfortable, rambling inn has an ambience of the timeless graciousness of an old estate home. Most of the 176 rooms and sixteen suites have views of the Atlantic Ocean or the Gulf of Mexico; each has a private balcony, separate dressing and seating areas, and a mini-refrigerator. Suites boast a sleeping alcove, one or two bedrooms, and a living area. Room rates are $150–$250 (May to mid-December is low season) and $210–$325 (December to April); children under sixteen are free. Suites begin at $245 (low season) and range to a high of $850. During summer a family package for four is $317 for two nights and includes breakfast, two hours of tennis and tiki boats, and other discounts.

Dining: If you like fresh seafood, you'll find dining here a treat. Selected fresh each morning, the harvests of the local waters grace every luncheon and dinner menu. But start the day with a breakfast buffet ($8.95 for adults, $4.95 for children). Presented in the Palm Terrace, this buffet opens at 7:00 A.M. for early birds and continues to 10:30 A.M. for late risers.

For casual lunches and dinners, the Cantina at poolside features croissant sandwiches and conch chowder (since the shellfish conch is typical fare in this part of the word, you *must* try it) as well as exotic rum concoctions recalling the island's history as a stopover for Prohibition rum-runners. The Ship's Galley, dockside at the Marina, specializes in seafood fried or broiled over mesquite.

For dinner Porto Cayo features Italian specialties, accompanied by the elegant sounds of an international pianist, while the Pub serves steak and fresh-off-the-boat seafood, dockside at the Marina. The adjacent Ship's Pub

Photo courtesy of Hawk's Cay Resort and Marina

is a lively disco where you can dance the night away.

Children's World: A natural-wood jungle gym is located near the swimming pool, and the kids' game room is stocked with board games, TV, video games, and Ping-Pong.

The Island Pirate's Club is available for children ages five to eleven, daily from early June to early September. The program runs from 10:00 A.M. to 3:00 P.M. and costs $25, including lunch and a T-shirt. Daily activities include tiki-boat races, field trips, scavenger hunts, fishing, and ecology tours. Every Wednesday has a theme, such as Earth Day, Dolphin Day, or Health Day; and the "No Parents Allowed" parties are very popular. The program is offered on weekends and major holidays throughout the year. In addition, on Friday and Saturday evenings, from 6:30 to 9:00 P.M., pizza movies are offered for $12 a child. Babysitting services can be arranged for younger children or during the evening hours; the average rate is $8.00 an hour.

Recreation: The water tempts, entices, and captures the heart of visitors. It establishes the mood and is the setting for most of the recreation. Swim in the pool or the saltwater lagoon; stretch out beneath the tropical sun or soak in one of the two Jacuzzis on the pool deck.

Discover the mysteries and wonder of undersea life. The coral reef offshore is home to a colorful array of tropical fish and is one of the best spots in the country for snorkeling and scuba diving (rental equipment is available).

Fishing here puts you in the big leagues, and it's exciting. Just offshore you'll find red snapper and mackerel; farther out in Gulf Stream waters are marlin, dolphin, and tuna; and in Florida Bay tarpon ply the waters. There are amazing fish stories told in this part of Florida and some fine captains at Hawk's Cay to guide you in your expeditions. Charter a vessel at the Marina for a full- or half-day excursion; you can even rent fishing equipment. Also at the sixty-slip Marina, you can join a small group in an oceangoing sailboat for a full-day trip or a sunset cruise, or you can rent a boat and be your own captain. It's at the Marina, too, that you'll find the dive boats that will take you to the reef for snorkeling and scuba diving. The local marine life is described during raft cruise tours of the sea flats and glass-bottom boat tours of the reef. If you are among the adventurous, don't forget parasailing.

Explore the island by bicycle (rentals available), test the parcours fitness trail, or take a self-guided walking tour to learn about the indigenous vegetation and tropical birds such as the brown pelican and the blue heron. Ecology Tours provide "hands-on" excursions to a secluded back-country island.

Of the eight tennis courts, two are composition-clay and six are hard-surface courts; two are lighted for evening play. Enjoy eighteen-hole golf at nearby Sombrero Country Club, or just relax indoors, in the Game Room or Library.

Unique to Hawk's Cay is the Chicago Zoological Society's Dolphin Connection, a program designed to study, protect, and increase public interest in dolphin biology and ecosystems. Training sessions at 10:00 A.M., 1:00 P.M., and 4:00 P.M. daily are complimentary and open to guests.

Indian River Plantation Marriott Resort

555 Northeast Ocean Boulevard
Hutchinson Island
Stuart, Florida 34996
(407) 225–3700, (800) 444–3389

Hutchinson Island, off the east coast of Florida, is a preserve for the giant loggerhead turtle (some weigh up to 450 pounds!). During the nesting season, from May through August, these huge turtles come ashore to lay their eggs in the island's sandy beach. Indian River Plantation Marriott Resort, on the southern end of this island, has been planned to coexist harmoniously with these survivors of a prehistoric age. Careful attention in design ensures that man-made fixtures (such as artificial lighting) do not intrude on the ocean side of the sand dunes and its natural inhabitants. Behind the sand dunes, however, Indian River caters to human guests. Among palm trees and ocean breezes, golf and tennis fans can enjoy a carefree holiday.

Accommodations: The new hotel offers rooms and suites ranging from $109 a night, June through September, to $399 in February and March. One- and two-bedroom apartments overlook the water or the golf course. Each has a fully equipped kitchen and private balcony. Daily rates, depending on the size, are $199–$249 in the low season (June through September) and $329–$399 in February and March. The other months of the year fall between these two sets of rates. Check on the tennis and golf packages and long-summer-weekend specials. Cribs are provided at an additional daily charge of $5.00.

Dining: The four restaurants at Indian River range from very informal to dressy. The Emporium is a casual ice-cream parlor and restaurant open all day, and the 19th Hole in the golf clubhouse on the lake serves lunch; two poolside bars serve snacks and cocktails. Scalawags, the flagship restaurant, overlooks the marina and offers such tempting choices as salmon with watercress sauce and pasta with wild mushrooms. The resort

features two poolside Tiki bars that offer sandwiches and snacks for lunch and dinner.

Children's World: Whenever weather permits (which is almost non-stop in sunny Florida), you find kids at the playground on the natural-wood jungle gym equipment. From Memorial Day to Labor Day, the Pineapple Bunch Children's Camp corrals youngsters ages three to fourteen and directs their energy in swimming, golf and tennis lessons, bowling, arts and crafts, beach games, and fishing. All ages can participate in a half-day program, from 8:30 A.M. to 2:00 P.M., at $20 a session. Six- to fourteen-year-olds can join the full-day program, from 8:30 A.M. to 5:00 P.M., at $25 a day. Full-day agendas are offered Monday through Friday, half-days only on Saturday.

From September through May a 9:00 A.M. to 2:00 P.M. schedule is offered Monday, Wednesday, Friday, and Saturday each week.

Throughout the year movies, pizza parties, bicycling, field games, and get-togethers frequently appear on the calendar for tots to teens. A licensed service provides babysitters.

Recreation: The plantation seems replete with blue waters and lush green lawns. With the Atlantic Ocean to the east, Indian River to the west, and lakes throughout the property, you can sail, waterski, snorkel, and fish for pompano and snapper. Head over to the seventy-seven-slip marina to join a deep-sea-fishing group searching for marlin and sailfish or to board the *Island Princess* for a sightseeing cruise. Stroll along the private beach through the surf, or swim in one of the four pools. The lush lawns are the fairways and greens of an eighteen-hole executive golf course. Join a golf clinic, practice on the driving range and putting green, then sign up for a tournament. The tennis facilities include thirteen courts; seven are lighted for evening play. At the pro shop you can enroll in a clinic or line up a date with the ball machine. You can rent a bicycle or work out in an aerobics class. Be sure, though, to set aside time for turtle watching; tours are arranged in season.

Innisbrook Hilton Resort

P.O. Box 1088
Tarpon Springs, Florida 34688
(813) 942–2000, (800) 456–2000

Sunshine athletes and summertime jocks may shrink from the rigors of a real sports resort, but determined enthusiasts find Innisbrook the appropriate place for honing skills. Located near Tarpon Springs, Florida, where tall pines, azaleas, and hibiscus flourish, Innisbrook sprawls over 1,000 acres and is one of the finest golf and tennis resorts in the country. Attuned to the ecology of western Florida, the resort encompasses a wildlife sanctuary that black swans, herons, egrets, and mallards call home. Its sixty-three golf holes may be the most challenging you'll ever play, and its instructional program can help you tackle them in style. A bus service connects lodging and recreational facilities. Innisbrook is convenient to all of central Florida's attractions, such as Disney World, Busch Gardens, Sea World, and the nearby Gulf of Mexico beaches. The resort is open year-round.

Accommodations: Twenty-eight lodges containing 1,000 guest suites are located throughout the property. All suites have a fully equipped kitchen and a balcony or patio. Depending on the season (the highest rates prevail January through April, the lowest in June through August), the rates are $86–$364 a day. Children under eighteen stay free in their parents' room. For an additional fee you can participate in a full or modified American meal plan. Cribs are available at no charge.

Various golf, tennis, and holiday package plans are available throughout the year. The most popular package is Preferred Golf; its rates are $135–$195 per person, and it boasts many special features. A tennis program with instructors is also available (call for custom packages).

Dining: The three golf clubhouses are the centers of a variety of dining arrangements, from the Northern Italian ambience of Toscana to the

Photo courtesy of Innisbrook Hilton Resort

more casual atmosphere of Hacker's Pub. The Copperhead Grille is an American steakhouse, and the Sandpiper Restaurant serves fresh regional seafood in a tropical atmosphere. The Island Clubhouse serves a champagne brunch on Sundays. Evening entertainment and dancing take place in the clubhouse lounges. There are snack bars at all three of the golf courses.

Children's World: Zoo Crew, a professionally supervised program for four- to twelve-year-olds, bursts into action every day of the year from 7:30 A.M. to 5:00 P.M. Activities include arts and crafts, swimming, volleyball, basketball, bicycling, miniature golf, nature tours, story hour, film festivals, and fishing contests. The daily fee is $26, including lunch. Tennis and golf instruction is available for older children. For the under-four set, babysitting services can be easily arranged.

Recreation: Innisbrook is famous for its golf and tennis institutes, which provide organized instructional programs utilizing modern audiovisual equipment and individualized small-group teaching sessions. Sixty-three holes of golf undulate over gently rolling terrain and skirt flowerbeds, tall pines, groves of orange trees, and sparkling lakes. The Copperhead is an eighteen-hole course and the most challenging of Innisbrook's three courses. The other two, the Island and the twenty-seven-hole Sandpiper, are very scenic as well, but not quite so demanding. The Innisbrook Golf Institute offers daily clinics, private lessons, and three- to five-day programs year-round.

The Tennis and Racquetball Center, in a grove of grapefruit trees (this *is*

Florida, right?), is a spacious complex that consists of three racquetball courts, a tennis shop, and the headquarters for the year-round tennis clinics. The thirteen courts are outdoors; seven of these are lighted for evening play. A 6-mile jogging trail can test your stamina. For an indoor workout the Fitness Center provides exercise equipment, supervised fitness programs, a sauna, and a massage therapist (thank goodness!). There are six swimming pools, sunny poolside patios to ensure that you go home with a good Florida tan, and bass fishing in the many ponds and lakes. Bicycling, basketball, volleyball, and miniature golf are additional recreational diversions. Since Innisbrook is set inland from the Gulf, guests are shuttled by bus to the nearby beaches.

Marriott's Grand Hotel

Point Clear, Alabama 36564
(334) 928–9201, (800) 544–9933

The charm and graciousness of the Old South has not faded in southern Alabama. The Grand Hotel preserves its rich tradition of almost 150 years of elegant service as a premier resort. Known as the Queen of Southern Resorts, the hotel is set on 550 acres at Point Clear, a peninsula in Mobile Bay. In this secluded location the quiet lagoons, majestic oak trees draped in hanging Spanish moss, and beautiful gardens can make you forget the worries and concerns of the workaday world. Leave your troubles and anxieties on the doorstep and enter this vacation retreat, where your biggest dilemma will be whether to play a round of golf, ride horseback in the peaceful landscape, stroll along the sandy beach, or sip a mint julep while watching the sun set over the bay.

The fascinating legacy of the Grand Hotel captures the heart of many a history buff. First discovered as an ideal location for a resort retreat in 1847, the hotel was the site of lively antebellum social events in its early years. Then, during the days of the Civil War (or as some folks down here still call it, the War of Northern Aggression), it served as a hospital for Confederate soldiers. After the war the hotel resumed its original function and once again became the center for leisure activities. A fire in 1869 and a hurricane in 1893 destroyed some of the old facilities, but rebuilding efforts and expansion were frequently undertaken in order to maintain accommodations for guests. Today's main hotel building was constructed in 1941. In 1967 the Bay House was added, and 1983 witnessed a restoration of the existing rooms and the addition of two new buildings—the North Bay House and the Marina House.

Accommodations: The main building has been described as rustic, but don't be deceived; this is rustic in a grand old manner. The lobby here is a charming octagonal structure that focuses on a massive fireplace. From its wide planks of pine flooring to its cypress-beamed ceiling, visitors immediately sense a warm, hospitable atmosphere. There are a total of 306 guest rooms in the different buildings and the cottages. Many rooms are decorated with white cypress paneling and ceiling fans (maintained primarily for ambience, but also to capture the bay breezes; modern-day air conditioning relieves the sultriness of summer days). Open year-round, the hotel has several rate structures. In the winter season daily room-only rates range from $89 to $149 midweek, $119 to $179 weekends. Special rates that include breakfast for two are just $10 more, and children under five can dine from the special children's buffet. Daily rates based on breakfast and dinner for two are $179 to $188; here children under age five are free, ages five to eleven are $14 a day, and those ages twelve and up are $48. Summer rates are higher: for example, for the breakfast-for-two plan it would be $159 to $179 weekdays or $179 to $199 weekend days. There is no charge for cribs and rollaways.

Dining: The main dining room offers an elegant atmosphere for lunch and dinner. An orchestra performs nightly here during dinner and afterward for dancing. Since the hotel is located on Mobile Bay and so close to the Gulf, many of the house specialties rely on the fresh local seafood. Oysters, red snapper stuffed with crabmeat, and seafood gumbo are a few of the selections. The hearty-meat-and-potatoes fan will find excellent prime rib of beef. The gourmet will be enticed by the elegant Bayview Room, for intimate and scenic dining.

For early risers coffee is available in the lobby and in every room; for a sumptuous buffet breakfast, try the Grand Buffet in the Grand Dining Room, where you may sit in a gazebo area with a bay view. Lunch is served not only in the main dining room but also in the restaurant at the Lakewood Golf Club, which is set in a wooded landscape. While soaking up the sunshine, you may choose the Poolside Grill and Snack Bar for a light lunch. The Birdcage Lounge provides delightful cocktails and beautiful views for leisurely enjoyment. A special dinner hour is reserved for children.

Children's World: The Grand Fun Camp is in operation from Memorial Day to Labor Day and on all major holidays. Every day but Sunday a group of friendly hostesses coordinates fun-filled activities. Five- to twelve-year-olds frolic from 10:00 A.M. to 4:00 P.M. and from 6:00 P.M. for dinner until 10:00 P.M. Swimming, shuffleboard, putt-putt golf, arts and crafts, video games, fishing, and sandcastle building entertain children, who will no doubt entertain their parents as they recount a day's adventures. Special events include movies and puppet shows. Individual babysitters are also available on an hourly basis ($3.00–$4.00 an hour).

Recreation: In the old days of the resort, two favorite spots were the wharves—one for men and one for women, because sunbathing and swimming in mixed company were unacceptable. Having come a long way since then, the Grand now offers innumerable popular activities for its guests. Given this prime location and mild climate, water sports attract many visitors. After a little warm-up fishing at the pier or in the bay, you might take on the challenges of deep-sea fishing. Your catch may be your evening's dinner, prepared especially for you by the hotel chefs. Reserve a sailboat or paddleboat for an afternoon's outing, or bring your own boat to the forty-slip marina. Splash in the waters of the bay along the sandy beach, or take a dip in the beautiful large pool, the largest pool on the Gulf Coast, in fact.

If you're more of a landlubber, the championship thirty-six holes of golf are a suitable diversion. Regardless of their level of play, all golfers appreciate the rolling, wooded setting of oak and pine. The facilities of the club abound—instructors, carts, putting greens, a sauna, and locker room.

Photo courtesy of Marriott's Grand Hotel

The ten Rubico tennis courts lure many ace players, and novices can enroll for lessons with one of the pros. And no day of golf or tennis is complete without the requisite stop at the pro shops; there's always that extra bit of new equipment to pick up. Head to the stables for horseback riding around the picturesque lakes and lagoons, or jog or bicycle (rentals available) through the gardens and along the boardwalk.

Slower-paced activities include croquet, putting green, and video games, or you may want to wind up the day in the hot tub. In the 1930s The Grand Hotel advertised itself as the place of "Every Creature Comfort." Many visitors today feel that reputation has withstood the test of time.

The Resort at Longboat Key Club

301 Gulf of Mexico Drive
P.O. Box 15000
Longboat Key, Florida 34228
(813) 383–8821, (800) 237–8821

An island retreat, The Resort at Longboat Key Club specializes in relaxation and recreation for golfers and tennis players. Located on a barrier island in the Gulf of Mexico just west of Sarasota, it doesn't short-change swimmers and sun worshippers either. The Resort enjoys a lush, tropical setting between the Gulf and Sarasota Bay that seems worlds away from your regular routine, yet it is only fifteen minutes away from the Sarasota Airport.

Accommodations: Seven modern buildings, 4 to 10 stories high, are arranged throughout the property to afford guests magnificent views of the Gulf, the bay, and the golf course fairways. Of the 232 accommodations (each with its own balcony), the majority (220) are suites, each with a king-size bed, a sleeper sofa, and a fully equipped kitchen. Summer is the low season, when guest rooms range from $115 to $225 a night and suites start at $155 a night; the deluxe two-bedroom suites command $285 to $435 a night. During the high season (Christmas and February through late April), a guest room is $205 to $325 a night, while suites cost $305 to $715 a night. During the rest of the year, prices fall between these parameters. Up to two children (seventeen and younger) can stay in a suite with their parents at no additional charge.

Dining: Dining can be as elegant or as casual as you choose. On the sophisticated side is the Orchids. Tempting fresh seafood dishes are frequently featured on its menus. For more casual dining drop by Spike 'n' Tees, and for truly relaxed mealtimes, saunter over to Barefoots, at poolside.

Children's World: The Kids' Klub operates daily from Presidents' Day weekend through Labor Day and on holiday weekends throughout the year. Experienced counselors direct youngsters ages five to twelve in a full 9:00 A.M.–3:00 P.M. program. Swimming, beach fun, volleyball, basketball, field trips, and arts and crafts are all part of the schedule. The program is complimentary, though fees may be charged for special field trips. The average cost of individual babysitting is $6.00 an hour, with a four-hour minimum.

Recreation: The Islandside Golf Course has eighteen holes, and the Harborside Course has twenty-seven holes. With palm trees and quiet lagoons throughout these courses, who can have a bad game? Two complete pro shops, a golf school, and professionals to guide players in private lessons and tournaments round out the picture for golfers.

Thirty-eight Har-Tru tennis courts await your ace serves and graceful lobs. Six of these are lighted for night play. Tennis play is complimentary. Two tennis shops, ball machines, a videotaped game analysis, and a professional staff will urge you on to better play.

Swimming in the outdoor pool or the gentle waters of the Gulf may top off your day. Bicycle along the nature trails, stroll on the snow-white beach, or spend an afternoon snorkeling or sailing. You can even organize a deep-sea fishing expedition through the concierge.

The Resort's newest recreational amenity is a 4,000-square-foot Fitness Centre, which features weight-training and cardiovascular equipment as well as instructor-led aerobics classes. Fitness Centre equipment is available to guests on a complimentary basis. For soothing life's daily stress and the ultimate in personal pampering, neuromuscular, sports, and Swedish massage is also available.

Sandestin

Highway 98 East
Destin, Florida 32541
(904) 267–8000, (800) 277–0800

Maximizing an unusual setting in the panhandle of Florida, Sandestin focuses on water for both recreational activities and picture-postcard vistas. Its 2,400 acres, dotted with lakes, are bounded by the Gulf of Mexico on the south and the Choctawhatchee Bay on the north. Many of the quiet lagoons sport warnings that read DO NOT FEED THE ALLIGATORS. Seeing a gator's nose just above the waterline, you realize that these are not just decorative signs. The alligators turn these water hazards into tricky play for golfers. The grounds and facilities straddle U.S. 98, but a tunnel underneath the roadway obviates traffic hassles, especially for youngsters and for golfers using carts. A small bus winds through the property if too much sunbathing or a fast-paced game of tennis has sapped your energy and you need a lift to your next activity. The resort is open year-round.

Accommodations: The 175-room Inn at Sandestin (each room with kitchenette) overlooks the Choctawhatchee. In addition, privately owned condominiums and villas can be rented on a short-term basis. Beachside I and Beachside II are high-rise condominiums with views along the sandy coastline. Many of the two- and three-bedroom villas are arranged along the lakes and fairways. Rates range from $55–$150 a night (hotel room) to $45–$600 a night (condominium or villa), depending on the season and the type of accommodation selected. Cribs and rollaway beds are provided at no charge.

Dining: The Sunset Bay Cafe is a family grille. Featuring steaks, seafood, burgers, pasta, and pizza, it easily pleases every member of the family. On weekends live entertainment takes over Taylor's Tiki Deck, which overlooks the bay.

For casually elegant dining overlooking the Gulf, try the Elephant Walk. Fresh local seafood dominates the imaginative menu here.

Children's World: From Memorial Day to Labor Day, children can participate in supervised activity programs, called Sand Pals, Monday through Saturday. A half-day tot's program (8:30 A.M.–noon) is designed for four- to six-year-olds; older children, seven to twelve years old, are busy in the youth program from 8:30 A.M. to 3:00 P.M. Activities include swimming, crabbing, treasure hunts, games, songs, nature walks, and crafts classes. Children in the older group can participate in golf and tennis clinics as well. The morning program for tots is $17 a session, and the full-day program for older children is $28 a day including lunch or $23 without lunch. A program for teens (ages thirteen to seventeen) operates in the afternoons and evenings and includes golf and sports clinics. For individual service Sandestin recommends Nanny's Babysitting.

Recreation: For golfers there are a total of sixty-three holes. The Sandestin Links, an eighteen-hole championship course, is a good challenge. Watch those water hazards and their alligator residents! The Baytowne Golf Club has a twenty-seven-hole layout to occupy golfers well. Also available is the eighteen-hole, Rees Jones–designed Burnt Pine Course. Courses feature pro shops and driving ranges.

Tennis buffs can choose from two playing surfaces: somewhat rare grass courts or very nice hydrogrid clay courts. All ten courts (four of which are lighted for evening play) are located at the new Bayside Tennis Center. Large pro shops meet the clothing and equipment requirements of golf and tennis enthusiasts.

A ninety-eight-slip marina and brand-new ship's store on the bay ac-

commodates powerboats and sailboats. Rentals are available, and daytime and evening sails are scheduled frequently. Lots of good fresh- and saltwater fishing goes on in the Destin area; the resort staff can help you arrange a deep-sea charter for bonita and amberjack.

Absolutely beautiful sand—very fine and almost snow white—tickles your toes during strolls along the half-mile of private beach, and the warm, gentle waters of the Gulf are so enticing. One swimming pool and a wading pool are at the inn, and another is at the Elephant Walk. Several of the accommodation areas have their own pools.

After a relaxing swim, you can rent a bike, play a game of volleyball (three courts), jog the 2-mile course, work out in the Health Club, or enjoy the full-service salon/spa—complete with professional counselors.

South Seas Plantation Resort and Yacht Harbour

P.O. Box 194
Captiva Island, Florida 33924
(800) CAPTIVA
Website: http://www.ssrc.com

Located at the northern tip of Captiva Island in the Gulf of Mexico,

3 miles off Florida's southwest coast, Captiva Island is connected to the mainland via Sanibel Island and the Sanibel Causeway. South Seas Plantation is approximately 30 miles from the Southwest Florida International Airport in Fort Myers.

Dubbed "Florida's Tahiti" for its subtropical climate and lush foliage indigenous to the Southern Hemisphere, Captiva Island—famous for its shell-covered beaches—was recently rated one of America's most romantic beaches. South Seas Plantation is a 330-acre island resort with 2½ miles of beach, a full-service yacht harbor and marina, recreational options from golf and tennis to island excursion cruises and water sports, fine restaurants, shopping, children's programs, and a complimentary open-air trolley transportation system.

Accommodations: The South Seas Plantation Resort and Yacht Harbour boasts more than 600 luxurious units, ranging from deluxe hotel rooms and villa suites to three-bedroom beach homes and cottages. Contact South Seas Plantation Resort for additional accommodation information and costs.

Dining: The resort's legendary New King's Crown Restaurant recently reopened, after a $1.2 million renovation. Preserving its rich legacy, King's Crown features exquisite architecture and an award-winning culinary team. Discover fine dining in an elegant, waterfront setting where New American cuisine is graciously served, traditions of yesterday are preserved, and new traditions are created. *Florida Living Magazine* readers recently honored King's Crown with the distinction of "Best Restaurant with a View." Chadwick's Restaurant features casual dining in a tropical setting. It is open for breakfast seasonally, and lunch and dinner menus feature daily breakfast and lunch buffet, Sunday Champagne Brunch, and evening theme buffets, including Caribbean Celebration Buffet, Bourbon Street Bash, Key West Clambake, and Seafood Extravaganza.

Dine indoors or in the open air at Cap'n Al's Dockside Grille overlooking the Yacht Harbour. Cap'n Al's serves breakfast, lunch, and dinner daily. Enjoy Mama Rosa's Pizzeria, offering eat-in or take-out dining; the convenience of delivery is provided after 5:00 P.M. Choose from mouth-watering pizza, garden-fresh salads, and delicious subs. Fresh dough is made daily on the premises. Uncle Bob's Ice Cream Emporium serves delicious, old-fashioned soda fountain and ice-cream treats and tempting candies, and sells educational toys and kites. Pelican Pete's Pool Bar offers a full-service bar specializing in tropical libations, and poolside dining at the north end features grilled sandwiches, snacks, and more.

For dining entertainment the King's Crown Lounge, located in the

King's Crown Restaurant, offers cocktails and live, easy-listening entertainment. Chadwick's Lounge has a full bar and live entertainment
nightly. A steel drum band is featured Tuesday evenings and a jazz
quartet during dinner on Thursday evenings. The tropical sounds of an
island favorite—The Danny Morgan Band—light up the lounge Sunday
through Wednesday with lively island-style music.

Children's World: Activities for all ages are available. A professional staff organizes daily itineraries of recreational and educational activities. Explorer Kids' Club, for children ages three to eleven, includes
activities such as Nature Camp, Pirate Mania, Circus at South Seas, and
Dinner Theatre. Supervised social events for teens, such as parasailing,
waterskiing, volleyball tournaments, pool parties, canoeing, kayaking,
and Frisbee golf are sure to provide hours of enjoyment.

Recreation: Dozens of recreational activities are available to guests
of South Seas Plantation, including a par thirty-six, regulation nine-hole
golf course; tennis on twenty-one courts; biking; and water sports, including game fishing, sailboarding, snorkeling, sailing, and excursion
cruises to nearby islands.

Family activities and workshops also feature aerobic exercise
classes, canoe excursions, sailing clinics, guided shelling excursions,
family fishing, shell art, and more. A variety of nature activities for the
whole family include Dolphin and Manatee Awareness, Shells of Captiva, Wildlife Refuge Trips, and Birds of Captiva. *The Explorer Bulletin,*
a current schedule of activities, is given to guests upon check-in. Preregistration is required for all activities.

Shopping at South Seas includes quality boutiques, gift shops, pro
shops, grocery store and gourmet deli, ship's store, and full-service
beauty salon.

Midwest

Illinois
Indiana
Michigan
Minnesota
Missouri
Wisconsin

Eagle Ridge Inn and Resort

U.S. Route 20
Box 777
Galena, Illinois 61036
(815) 777-2444, (800) 892-2269

With 6,800 acres of rolling, wooded terrain and sixty-three challenging holes of golf, Eagle Ridge is a major Midwest resort. When you're not on the links, you'll find that 220-acre Lake Galena is the focus of most resort activities. Located in northwest Illinois just minutes from historic Galena, with its well-preserved nineteenth-century architecture, Eagle Ridge is only 150 miles from Chicago.

Accommodations: The Eagle Ridge Inn, with its eighty rooms, sits at the edge of the lake. In addition, resort homes are scattered throughout the hills and consist of one- to five-bedroom accommodations. During the peak season, from May 1 to late October, and around New Year's, Inn rooms are $195–$255 a night (children sharing a room with parents are free); the resort homes are $220–$515 a night. The resort homes are also available for weekly rental, and many different packages are offered.

Dining: The elegant dining spot is the Woodlands Restaurant in the Inn, where you'll enjoy steaks, pastas, and seafood along with beautiful views of the lake. Next door is the Woodlands Lounge, for cocktails and more casual dining. Also located in the Inn is Scoops Ice Cream Parlor. Each golf course has its own snack bar and tavern. The Clubhouse Bar and Grill offers great views of Eagle Ridge's newest golf course, The General, and a casual dining menu of appetizers, soups, salads, sandwiches, and wonderful entrees. When stocking up on provisions, stop by the General Store for delicious deli selections and freshly baked pastries.

Children's World: The Kids Klub is in operation from Memorial Day through Labor Day as well as weekends and holiday times throughout the year; it is designed for three- to twelve-year-olds. The 9:00 A.M.–4:00 P.M. day is filled with swimming, hiking, boating, games, and arts and crafts; the fee of $28 a day includes lunch. A half-day with lunch is $23; a half-day without lunch is $20. On three nights a week, dinner, movies, and games entertain children from 7:00 to 10:00 P.M. ($20 an evening). Teens have a Saturday-evening event from 6:00 to 11:00 P.M. ($20) that might include a volleyball game, bowling, Alpine slide, or movie outing—all with dinner at a local pizza parlor. Individual babysitting is available at $4.00 an hour.

Recreation: The North and South Golf courses are eighteen holes each over rolling hills and wooded countryside. The East Course provides nine holes of play. The latest addition, The General, is a challenging layout that opened in May 1997. For serious instruction the fourteen professionals of the Eagle Ridge Golf Academy can guide you in everything from the basics to business golf. One-, two-, and three-day programs are offered.

On Lake Galena fishermen go in search of bass, walleye, and crappie, and boaters head out in paddleboats, canoes, and pontoons. Swimmers can take a dip at the indoor pool adjacent to the fitness center in the Inn. Horseback riding along 40 miles of trails begins at the Shenandoah Riding Center. Rent a mountain bike, or hike the trails to seek out native plants and wildlife. For a solitary excursion the fitness trail has twenty-one exercise stations, or round up the whole family for a volleyball game (two courts) or a tennis match (four courts). From the end of July to mid-August, you can combine an Eagle Ridge holiday with watching the Chicago Bears in summer practice at nearby Platterville.

In the winter sportslovers turn to tobogganing, sledding, and ice skating. Forty miles of cross-country ski trails are carefully groomed. Nearby Chestnut Mountain offers downhill skiing on seventeen runs.

French Lick Springs Resort

French Lick, Indiana 47432
(812) 936–9300, (800) 457–4042

French Lick Springs is a curious name with an interesting history behind it. This area of southwest Indiana was settled by French traders more than 200 years ago. Subsequently, mineral springs were discovered, and, because animals lapped the waters from the wet rocks, locals dubbed it "The Lick." The British moved in during the early nineteenth century, and by the 1830s the first hotel was built on this site because visitors were attracted to the healing powers of the mineral waters.

At the end of the century, fire destroyed the original buildings, but the property was purchased and the facilities reconstructed and expanded by Thomas Taggert, then mayor of Indianapolis. Under Taggert's guidance French Lick Springs developed into a first-class resort, with restaurants, golf courses, and a spa. The turn-of-the-century elegance and the devotion to health and recreation were maintained for the next thirty years. Popularity waxed and waned through the Depression, World War II, and the postwar years. For nearly four decades restoration has again been emphasized; today French Lick Springs encompasses 2,600 acres of the rolling foothills of the Cumberland Mountain range and is dedicated to making the "Golden Days" of the Taggert era an ongoing reality. It is open year-round.

Accommodations: The rambling main building and its adjacent wings house almost 500 rooms and suites. The large and gracious front porch hints at the relaxed pace that prevails here. Rates for accommodations vary depending on the size, location, and view of a room; they range from $79 to $99 per day, based on double occupancy. Children under age seventeen are free; cribs are $10 a day. Package plans are available for golf, tennis, holiday weekends, and the Spa's health and fitness programs.

A modified American plan is available (breakfast and dinner). The cost is $30 per day per adult, $20 per day for ages six to twelve years, and free for children under five.

Dining: Dining possibilities are many and varied. Chez James is the right choice for an intimate, gourmet dinner, while Le Bistro is a casual steak-and-sandwich restaurant open for lunch and dinner. Combine pizza and bowling at the family-oriented Pizzeria in the Recreation Center, and don't forget to stop at Double Scoops for ice cream. The Country Club Restaurant overlooks the golf course, and the Hoosier Dining Room serves Sunday brunches and international buffet dinners. Sip cocktails in the Derby Bar, the Country Club Lounge, or Le Bistro Bar.

Children's World: The Pluto Club, for five- to twelve-year-olds, starts Memorial Day weekend and runs through Labor Day. Counselors guide kids in arts and crafts, swimming, hiking, and games. The fee is $1.00 an hour. Younger children (three to five years old) have a less rigorous program, for which the fee is $2.00 an hour. Lunch is available for $3.50. From September to May children's activities are offered Saturday afternoons. At the Christmas and Easter holidays, more elaborate programs are planned.

The unsupervised outdoor playground, filled with swings, slides, monkey bars, teeter-totters, a merry-go-round, and a sandbox, is also a big hit with youngsters.

Children's Tennis Clinics and "Horse Sense" programs are also available for a fee. These supervised activities last about an hour and include instruction. Teen events such as mini-golf tournaments, horseback rides, and scavenger hunts are organized by the Social Staff but are not supervised.

Daily family and social activities are open to children accompanied by an adult; these include hayrides, cookouts, bingo, treasure hunts, lawn sports, and card games.

Recreation: You may not be able to shine in sports quite like Boston Celtic whiz Larry Bird, a native son of French Lick, but at least you have the facilities here where you can focus on improvement. On the gentle, wooded hills, through stands of butternut and oak trees, you can play golf from mid-March to mid-November on two eighteen-hole courses, one of which was designed by Donald Ross. The golf clinics offered April through September put you through the paces in improving your swing, grip, and stance and provide guidance in scrutinizing a course with a bit of strategy.

The tennis complex includes eight indoor courts and ten outdoor lighted courts. Tennis players, too, can have workouts in clinics that cover analyzing a stroke and planning a strategic performance in doubles.

Choose a mount from among thirty horses (lessons available) and head for the trails through the hills; take to the hilly terrain on foot, hiking along the many paths; or hop a surrey to see the scenery. Try out the skeet and trap range, or go for a warm lazy swim in the indoor or outdoor pool. Stroll through the gardens and challenge other guests to lawn games like shuffleboard, volleyball, croquet, badminton, and horseshoes. Rent a bicycle, go bowling (six lanes), play pool, or hit the video games in the Recreation Center. During the winter, cross-country skiing, horse-drawn sleigh rides, and ice skating draw attention.

Don't forget the tradition of the magical quality of the mineral waters. At the Spa you can have mineral baths and massages. Work out in the exercise room, soak in the whirlpool, and block out the rest of the world while sitting in the sauna; a total fitness program can be designed for you.

Nearby activities include the restored Pioneer Village at Spring Mill Park, Marengo Caves, skating at the Roller Dome, and a train ride at the Railway Museum.

Grand Geneva Resort & Spa

Highway 50 East at Highway 12
7036 Grand Geneva Way
Lake Geneva, Wisconsin 53147
(414) 248–8811, (800) 558–3417

Tucked into the southeastern corner of Wisconsin, between Milwaukee and Chicago, are Lake Geneva and the Grand Geneva Resort. Less than a day's drive from 9 states and 60 million people, the resort sits in the midst of 1,300 acres and has as its stated goal "to be a destination for relaxation and pleasure." Built originally in the 1960s as a Playboy Club, it has been completely renovated. It reopened in June 1994 with a brand-new image. The town of Lake Geneva has been called "the Newport of the Midwest," and that flavor is cultivated here.

Accommodations: A total of 357 rooms and suites overlook the rolling green hills and clear blue lake (some also overlook the parking lot, so be careful when you book). Decor is that of an elegant and comfortable vacation home. In summer courtside rooms are $179–$199, while lakeside rooms are $199–$219; in winter the same types of rooms are $99–$119 and $119–$139. Suites range from $169 to $269 in winter and from $249 to $349 in summer. One- to three-bedroom villas are available on-site; summer rates are $239–$369 and winter rates are $159–$289.

Dining: Almost everyone likes Italian food, so the upscale Ristorante Brissago is sure to please. Open for dinner only, the pastas are homemade, and the atmosphere is special without being stuffy. Another restaurant choice, The Newport Grill, puts the kitchen right on display, so you get the full effect of sight and aroma as well as the taste of typical Midwestern dishes such as grilled steak; it is open for lunch and dinner. The Grand Cafe offers American cuisine, with a children's menu; it's open for breakfast, lunch, dinner, and a special Sunday buffet. Snacks and sandwiches are available in the Pro Shop at the Golf Course, and the Spa and Sports Center has a full menu of healthful food and beverages. For evening cocktails or live entertainment, stop by the Cabaret nightclub.

Children's World: The Grand Adventure Club operates year-round on weekends and holidays, daily from Memorial Day through Labor Day, for ages four to twelve years. The morning session is from 10:00 A.M. to noon ($15); the afternoon session is from 1:00 to 5:00 P.M. ($30); the full-day session includes lunch ($40). Evening movies and popcorn are free. A daily newsletter gives the specifics of the day's activities, but generally, the schedule is arts and crafts in the morning, and one hour of arts and crafts and three hours of outside activity such as pony rides, paddleboating, or hiking in the afternoon. Kids get to make the choice of what they want to do within this framework.

Recreation: All the amenities for a resort vacation are here. Two PGA championship golf courses lure golfers. The Highlands, one of the first Scottish-design courses in the United States, was designed by Jack Nicklaus and Pete Dye. The other course, Brute, is one of the longest courses in the United States, measuring 6,997 yards. Putting greens, driving ranges, and scrupulous attention to grooming keep golfers happy. Pick up a tennis game on one of the four indoor or five outdoor courts, or play racquetball. A private lake provides boating opportunities—exercise your arms with a rowboat or your legs with a paddleboat—or just relax and cruise beautiful Lake Geneva on one of the excursion boats, like the *Lady of the Lake,* a modern reproduction of a Mississippi paddle-wheel steamer. More water opportunities present themselves at the indoor and outdoor pools or with some serious swimming in the lap pool. Jogging, biking, and fitness trails wind through the property, taking advantage of the natural beauty.

You may want to spend the entire day in the Spa. Day membership is $10 for guests and includes use of the whirlpool, sauna, steam, and robes. Fitness classes, therapeutic baths, herbal wraps, antistress facials and massages, and a variety of body masks are just a few of the treatments guaranteed to make you feel like a new person. Enjoy them à la carte or preplanned, for example, an antistress day ($104) or custom spa day ($98).

In the wintertime Grand Geneva has its own mountain for skiing. Even if there is no snow in Wisconsin, with snowmaking, there will be snow at the resort. Twelve slopes descend from the top elevation of 1,086 feet, with a 211-foot vertical drop. Night skiing, 10 kilometers of cross-country skiing, and a special area for snowboards ensure winter fun for everyone. The Ski School uses Station Teaching to allow individuals to progress at their own rate, mastering each "station," then moving on.

Grand Traverse Resort

Acme, Michigan 49610
(800) 748–0303

Long known as the Cherry Capital, this area of northwest lower Michigan has a lot more to offer visitors than just its beautiful orchards and fine fruit. Besides providing memories of Ernest Hemingway, who spent many summers here and used this area as the setting for several short stories, Grand Traverse Resort offers guests golf, swimming, sailing, cross-country skiing, and a complete sports complex and health club. Set on 1,400 acres

of forests and orchards with ½ mile of shoreline on East Grand Traverse Bay, the year-round resort boasts fine golf courses designed by Jack Nicklaus and Gary Player.

Accommodations: The resort hotel, which houses 238 rooms, is adjacent to the Traverse Pavilion, the site of summertime barbecues and wintertime ice skating. The 310 condominium units are spread throughout eight clusters of buildings. Some overlook the bay, and some skirt the golf courses; many have a fireplace. A shuttle service connects the condominiums with the other resort facilities. Rates range from $90 a night (hotel room, low season) to $380 a night (three-bedroom condo, summer). The deluxe Tower opened in 1986, encompassing 186 suites, two lounges, a restaurant, and twenty boutiques. This is consummate luxury, with a private two-person whirlpool in each bathroom. Children under eighteen sleep free when sharing a room with their parents. Be sure to inquire about the many package plans. Cribs are available at no charge; rollaway beds are provided at a daily charge of $15.

Dining: Sweetwater Cafe features an open kitchen in the center of the restaurant and serves American fare plus select pasta dishes; it is open seven days a week for breakfast, lunch, and dinner. The Trillium Restaurant, located in the Tower, serves regional American dishes. The Sandtrap Restaurant and Lounge offers relaxed dining with views of the golf course. A children's menu is available in most restaurants. The Club

Deli, in the Village Health Club also provides an informal setting for dining and cocktails. Besides the Sandtrap and Club bars, there are Jack's Lounge, the Trillium Nightclub for dancing and nightly entertainment, and the Shores Beach Club, on the bay.

Children's World: For seven- to twelve-year-olds, a day camp is scheduled half-days and full-days, Monday through Sunday in the summer, and weekends the rest of the year. Activities include arts and crafts, games, swimming, exercise classes, and hiking; fees may be charged for some events. For younger children day care is available in the Cub House, a 2,000-square-foot children's center. During the summer tennis and golf lessons are available, for $10 and $15, respectively. During the winter cross-country ski instruction is offered. Each event through the day is geared to a specific age group; you must register in advance for each event. An adventure playground near the Village Health Club also keeps youngsters well entertained, and the electronic game room may keep them mesmerized. Individual babysitters can be scheduled with the assistance of the health club staff.

Recreation: The pride of Grand Traverse Resort is The Bear. Designed by Jack Nicklaus, this golf course meanders through cherry and apple orchards, with plenty of hardwood forest areas for contrast; it is quite scenic as well as challenging. The older course, Spruce Run, also offers championship play. The resort's third course, Northern Knight, scheduled to open in 1998, will be a championship course designed by Gary Player. The Northern Knight will be complete with a state-of-the-art, 17,000-square-foot Clubhouse. Future plans are to also build a Lee Trevino–designed golf course. The CompuSport Golf School program provides three-day sessions in the summer months.

The Village Health Club is a championship setup, too. With four outdoor and five indoor tennis courts (instruction available), four racquetball courts, indoor and outdoor swimming pools, and an exercise/weight room, you'll get quite a workout. Afterward you'll probably head straight to the saunas. In the Tower, a full-service spa and salon provides all the pampering you need. Mountain bikes and in-line skates are available for rent.

If water sports capture your interest, try swimming, sailing, or sailboarding, or take an evening cruise or a charter fishing trip on the bay. Fishermen seek out the many lakes and streams for trout and salmon. Hike or jog through the hills and past the orchards; the scenery is so good for the soul that you may not notice you're also helping your body.

But don't be deceived; Grand Traverse is not just a summertime resort. In the fall trees burst into autumn colors and make a beautiful backdrop for horse-drawn hayrides and trips to nearby wineries for sampling and festivals. In the winter cross-country skiing takes over; Nordic trails weave through the forests and gently rolling hills. Private lessons and group clinics are offered at the Village Nordic Center. Take a sleigh ride through the woods, or go ice skating in the Traverse Pavilion. And remember, while working out at The Village Health Club, you'll never know how low the temperature dips outside. In the spring, when the weather is warm enough for you to want to pick up a golf club, the cherry orchards come to life. The white blossoms of the trees blanket the hillsides for more than half the month of May.

Grand View Lodge

134 Nokomis
Nisswa, Minnesota 56468
(800) 432–3788

Nestled among the Norway pines on the north shore of Gull Lake is Grand View Lodge, the focal point of this 900-acre resort. Built in 1918 of native cedar logs and now a National Historic Site, the lodge welcomes guests during its May-to-October season. In addition to the lodge, sixty-five

Photo courtesy of Grand View Lodge

cottages border the lake. Located 142 miles northwest of Minneapolis, the Lodge is within a fifteen-minute drive of seven golf courses, Paul Bunyan Center, animal parks, and Indian mounds and museums.

Accommodations: The twelve rooms in the lodge are comfortable for couples, while a cottage is the right choice for a family. Since these range in size from one to eight bedrooms, owner Fred Boos explains that they "try to fit the cabin to the family." Some cabins feature a kitchenette and living room; all have decks as well as large picture windows and views of the lake. Daily maid service is provided for both the lodge and the cabins. Reservations are accepted on a daily as well as weekly basis. Rates from $95 to $140 per person per day include two meals a day, golf, tennis, and the children's program. For children the charge is $10–$55 a night, American plan, depending on the age of the child.

Dining: There are several dining rooms: main dining room in the historic lodge, Freddy's in the Pines Clubhouse, The Preserve Steak House in the Preserve Clubhouse, Sherwood Forest (also a historic building), and new Italian Gardens. Dress is casual. Barbecues on the beach are often planned. Children may dine with their parents or their counselors. A special menu for children features fresh fish, steaks, chicken, and ribs. Cocktails are served on the large, three-level redwood deck or in the North Woods Lounge, where you'll hear live music nightly. The smorgasbord is a traditional Sunday event—great fun and all you can eat.

Children's World: From Memorial weekend to Labor Day weekend, Grand View has three separate and very well-organized programs, for children ages three to six, six to ten, and ten to thirteen. There is a wonderful wooden playhouse in the woods with slides and climbing equipment, a well-stocked play area, and the beach along Gull Lake. The programs run from 9:00 A.M. to 3:00 P.M. and from 5:30 to 8:00 P.M., Monday through Saturday. The schedule includes arts and games, storytime, movement activities, exercise, swimming, peanut hunts, hayrides, and visits to a game farm. A talent show is held on Friday, and Saturday is carnival night for everyone.

The staff is college age and generally has past experience with children. The program is free except for special tours and trips. For those under age three, the front desk can arrange babysitting ($3.00 to $5.00 per hour) with either an off-duty staff member or selected local persons.

Recreation: The lake attracts swimmers, fishermen, sailors, and sunbathers. Here you can also venture out in a pontoon or kayak or practice some waterskiing. An eighteen-hole championship golf course is aptly named, given its setting: The Pines. The nine-hole Garden Course depends more on floral configurations in the layout of the holes. A championship golf course, The Preserve, is located 10 miles north of The Pines.

A tennis complex with eleven Laykold courts is set among tall trees.

Court time is free. The tennis pro teaches guests in private lessons, organizes tournaments, and conducts free group lessons for children eight to nineteen years old. Two hitting walls and an automatic ball machine allow for extra practice before a good match. The staff horticulturist conducts tours of the newly developed gardens, introducing guests to the extensive collection of flowers and shrubs.

The Homestead

Wood Ridge Road
Glen Arbor, Michigan 49636
(616) 334–5000

The Great Lakes are truly great—and not just in size. While Lake Michigan's 22,400-square-mile area is indeed impressive, imagine the possibilities it affords in recreation and relaxation: swimming, boating, and fishing in the water, and on land, hiking and biking the wooded trails beyond the lake's sandy beach. At The Homestead all this great potential is realized, combined with tennis facilities, variety in dining, and comfortable, attractive

Photo courtesy of The Homestead

lodging. When the weather cools the swimmers give way to skiers, who discover nature's wintertime beauty. The Homestead is located on the northwest shore of lower Michigan. Its 500 acres embrace gently rolling land covered with pine trees, aspens, and oaks; 1 mile of sandy beach on Lake Michigan; and 6 miles of shoreline along the banks of Crystal River. Surrounding the resort is the Sleeping Bear Dunes National Lakeshore; besides ensuring The Homestead's secluded position, this national preserve opens up additional opportunities for nature explorers. The resort is closed in April and November.

Accommodations: The village is the center of most activities, as accommodations, restaurants, shops, and a heated swimming pool are located here. The Lodge in the village offers standard and deluxe rooms overlooking the pond. One- to four-bedroom condominiums, each with a full kitchen, are located on the beach, along Crystal River, on a ridge overlooking the shoreline, and in the village. Crystal River cuts through the hills and runs more or less parallel to the lakeshore a short way before emptying into the lake. Where the river and the lake merge is another center of activity, the Beach Club.

Lodge rooms are $96–$175 a night during the summer and approximately 20 to 30 percent less during the rest of the year. A one-bedroom condominium unit ranges between $150 and $335 a night, depending on the location you choose; lakefront and lakeview units are the most expensive. The rates for larger units graduate to $517 a night for a four-bedroom home/condominium. These rates are applied during the summer and on weekends through the year; package plans are also available. Cribs are provided at no charge; children are free when staying in their parents' room.

Dining: At the Beach Club the Cafe Manitou draws diners to its ideal location on the beach; open daily in the summer only, its setting and attire are casual.

Around the bend in the village, Nonna's boasts a bountiful breakfast and Italian dinners, and Whiskers attracts pizza and burger fans. Also in the village, at Cavanaugh's you can pick up groceries or deli sandwiches for lunch and snacks all day long. In the winter skiers gather in CQ's Cabin for its cozy atmosphere and friendly conversation.

Children's World: The children's summer program runs from late June through late August and entertains guests from toddlers to teenagers.

Daily from half- to full-days, five- to twelve-year-olds are busy with soccer and volleyball games, hiking, fishing, exercising to music, and arts and crafts. The Kids Kamp cost is $25 for half-days and $40 for full-days. Activities for this group and for teens are published in a weekly calendar. Kids can also join junior golf or tennis programs.

Teenagers enjoy a loose schedule that focuses on meeting other teens during canoe races, volleyball games, tennis matches, and pizza parties. Like the events for the younger group, some are free, while others require a fee. Private swimming lessons can be arranged, and tennis clinics are offered for young adults ages twelve to seventeen and juniors ages six to eleven.

In the winter the children's program teaches five- to twelve-year-olds fun-in-the-snow activities with ski lessons. It is offered for two and one-half hours twice a day, Fridays through Sundays and holidays, from mid-December through March, and the fee is $25 for a half-day or $65 for a full-day with lunch.

Any time of year, individual babysitters can be hired, at approximately $5.00 per hour. The resort staff assists in making the arrangements.

Recreation: The clear waters of Lake Michigan are fine for sailing, boating (rentals available), fishing, and swimming. Maybe still a little nippy in June, the lake's temperature averages sixty-five to seventy degrees by July and August, and its sandy bottom is particularly attractive to young swimmers. The river waters tend to be warmer, and both the Beach Club and the village have a heated pool and a hot tub, so guests have their pick of swimming conditions. Fishing is good sport in the river as well as in the lake, and canoeing up the river allows you to investigate the local wildlife. Hike, jog, and bicycle (children's bikes and bikes with children's seats are available for rent) on the 24 miles of wooded trails; a self-guided nature tour can introduce you to the area's flora and fauna. Or just take a relaxing stroll along the beach at sunset.

For tennis players the Beach Club, with its five clay courts, is the site of many exciting matches. Here you can join a clinic, take private lessons, and watch real talent during professional exhibitions. If you're still looking for things to do, drop by the aerobics exercise class; work out on the fitness trail, with twenty exercise stations; head to the playground at River Park; or throw your hat into a volleyball tournament. You can also enjoy the new pool and spa at the Beach Club. Now here's ingenuity in utilizing space: In 1995 a new, nine-hole par three golf course opened—built in part on the downhill ski slopes! Visit the nearby Sleeping Bear Dunes National Park, take a ferryboat ride to the islands in Lake Michigan, and sample the wines of local vineyards.

In the winter 36 kilometers of trails attract cross-country skiers to The Homestead's wooded hills, and the frozen ponds are ideal for ice skating. Downhill skiing is modest, with fourteen runs and 350 vertical feet, but the view down a snowy slope to whitecaps on the lake is an uncommon juxtaposition you'll long remember. All runs benefit from artificial snowmaking, and those lighted for nighttime skiing add another dimension to a winter holiday.

The Lodge of Four Seasons Championship Golf Resort & Spa

State Road HH
Lake Ozark, Missouri 65049
(573) 365-3000, (800) THE-LAKE

Lake of the Ozarks, a man-made lake developed in the 1930s, has provided scenic and recreational diversion for the residents of central Missouri for sixty years. Overlooking the lake, in the wooded gentle hills of the Ozarks, is The Lodge of Four Seasons. Opened in 1964, The Lodge has grown over the years into a major, year-round resort with extensive recreational facilities and fine dining. Today it is a convenient escape from city cares for the residents of St. Louis and Kansas City and is sought as a vacation spot for visitors from farther afield as well.

Accommodations: In addition to the rooms in The Lodge (more than 300), accommodations include two- and three-bedroom condominiums frequently more suitable for families. The Four Seasons Racquet and Fitness Club is built in Mediterranean style and is perfect for vacationers who want to be in the midst of athletic and fitness facilities. Treetop Village is a group of secluded villas nestled in the heavily wooded area along the lakeshore. Also on the water is Water's Edge; although it is not as private as Treetop Village, it offers beautiful views of the lake. Condominium prices range from $179 to $299 a night, March to November; the rates are $89 to $179 in The Lodge. Lower rates prevail during the rest of the year. Children under eighteen share their parents' room and Fun Pass at no extra charge; complimentary cribs are available. The Fun Pass gives access to the Executive Nine-Hole Golf Course, movies, and scenic cruise. The cost is $10 per person.

Dining: Toledo's offers a unique combination of great dining and live entertainment. Toledo's menu features a variety of fresh selections incorporating specialties indigenous to the area. The menu changes monthly, depending upon the availability of fresh items. Toledo's also features a Tapas Bar, offering a variety of appetizers. Enjoy the finest cuts of certified Angus beef (or turkey steak if you prefer) at HK's Steak House, located on the golf course; it features a custom-designed, elevated charcoal grill. Have breakfast or lunch at Roseberry's Cafe, in a casual family-style setting. The Atrium Cafe is the place for baked goods hot from the oven, and for tasty deli sandwiches, stop at the Country Deli. In the evening relax with cocktails in the Lobby Bar and watch the world go by, or listen to live jazz in Toledo's. Studios Entertainment and Dance Club is the place for dancing and live entertainment.

Children's World: From June through August the Youth Program accommodates four- to twelve-year-olds in a medley of fun activities. Monday through Saturday, from 9:00 A.M. to 4:00 P.M. and 6:00 to 9:00 P.M., this group enjoys swimming, boating, nature walks, games, movies, arts and crafts, and cookouts. Staffed by college seniors working on recreation/hotel management degrees, the Youth Program crew knows how to keep kids happy. Lunch is provided in the full-day program. There is a daily charge for each child. Check with the hotel for any changes in the program.

Recreation: The sports enthusiast will be well satisfied at The Lodge of Four Seasons, named one of the "Top 50 Golf Resorts" by *Condé Nast Traveler*. One championship eighteen-hole golf course was designed by Robert Trent Jones, Sr., and interests players with its narrow undulating fairways and glimpses of the lake's blue waters. A second eighteen-hole championship golf course, Seasons Ridge, is carved into the rolling Ozark terrain, where multiple tee boxes accommodate golfers of all skill levels. Golf instruction is offered at both of these courses. In addition, golfers can turn to the nine-hole course and the indoor driving range to sharpen their skills. Equipment and attire can be purchased at the pro shop, if you've forgotten anything.

The tennis facilities are extensive—twenty-three courts in all, indoor, outdoor, hard-surface, clay—take your pick! Seventeen of the courts are at the Racquet Club; the remaining six are at The Lodge. The Pro Shop can meet your equipment and fashion needs with style and ease. Among the resort's many tennis awards is the Midwest's only "Top 50 Tennis Resorts," as rated by *Tennis* magazine.

Dennis Van der Meer's Tennis University runs weekend clinics year-round for adults as well as daily programs. For juniors ages nine to sixteen, a weeklong junior camp is offered in June, July, and August. In addition to intensive tennis, a number of off-court activities are planned. The cost is $325 with meals and lodging, or $165 for tennis only.

If water sports are your life's love, you certainly won't feel slighted here. Swimming pools are indoor and outdoor, Olympic-size and kiddie-size. And swimmers can also move on out into the lake or sunbathe on the private beach. The lake is a favorite of sailors. The full-service marina can handle more than 200 boats and is the base for lake activities—from boat rentals and waterskiing to fishing hints and parasailing. The Lodge excursion boat, *The Seasons Queen,* takes guests on a smooth journey around the lake.

The Racquet Club houses the fitness center, a state-of-the-art facility that can really put you through your paces. Besides appreciating all the high-tech equipment and aerobics classes, you can rely comfortably on the professional guidance of the staff. After a super workout you may want to melt into a sauna, a whirlpool, or a massage at the Spa.

If you have any energy left, wander over to the stables, from which trail rides leave daily, bike or hike along wooded paths, and try your hand at trapshooting. Racquetball, volleyball, basketball, bowling, and Ping-Pong are even more options to fit into a busy schedule. At the end of a very full day, you may choose to relax at the movies, dance at Studios Entertainment and Dance Club, or retire early for a well-deserved repose.

Ludlow's Island Lodge

P.O. Box 1146
Cook, Minnesota 55723
(218) 666–5407, (800) 537–5308
Website: http://www.ludlowsresort.com

Minnesota has a reputation as the land of 10,000 lakes (ever wonder who counted them all?), and Ludlow's Island Lodge is well situated on one of these—picturesque Lake Vermilion. The resort facilities are located on Ludlow's Island and on the north and south shores of the lake. A boat shuttle connects the three areas. Water-related activities are the primary recre-

Photo courtesy of Ludlow's Island Lodge

ation at this wooded resort. Fishing, swimming, sailing, and exploring among 365 islands provide wonderful experiences. The seclusion among the pines and birches, with the lake practically at your front door, makes this retreat a real back-to-nature experience. The resort is open from May through September.

Accommodations: Eighteen cabins with enchanting names like Stardust, Evergreen, and Twilite are located on the island and the shores. Designed with knotty pine or cedar interiors, all have a fireplace and outdoor deck; most have a screened porch. They range from one- to five-bedroom cottages with a fully equipped kitchen (yes, even a dishwasher and microwave). Daily rates start at $165 for two adults and $30 for each child. Summer weekly rates start at $1,350 for two people.

Dining: Ludlow's offers full menu choices for evening meals delivered to your cabin. Each cabin has a menu with items ranging from $9.50 to $17.50. Pizza and burgers are also available. The order is placed with the lodge by 5:00 P.M. and delivered to your cabin by 7:00 P.M., to be served on cabin dishes.

Children's World: Planned activities just for children are scheduled only an hour or two each day, Monday through Friday. Boat rides, nature hikes, and fishing derbies introduce kids to the surrounding woods and waters. Movies are shown in the afternoons. The two-story tree house and a small camping island for overnight trips are probably the biggest attractions for the younger set, but the swings, the lake (with a section roped off for children's safety), and the sandy beach are good play areas, too. Kids also enjoy the video-game room, Ping-Pong, and exploring the trails in the forest, just like Paul Bunyan of Minnesota lore. The recreation complex on the south shore has a children's play area. The Ludlows help in arrangements for babysitters ($5.00 an hour).

Recreation: Fishing buffs relish this bit of paradise on the south shores of Lake Vermilion. Walleye, bass, and crappie lure fishermen to these waters. Each cabin is provided with a 16-foot aluminum boat. And there's no excuse for not landing the big one; a fishing clinic is held every week, and a guide is available for private excursions. The staff at the lodge will fillet and freeze your catch. Besides fishing boats, the lodge has canoes, kayaks, paddleboats, and a sailboat for guests' use.

The recreation center houses an indoor raquetball court, two tru-flex tennis courts, and an exercise area. After a good workout there, you may enjoy a leisurely swim or a relaxing sauna. Along the north shore you can take a stroll down the mile-and-a-half hiking trail. There are also many miles of hiking and biking trails in the area.

Marriott's Tan-Tar-A Resort and Golf Club

State Road KK
Osage Beach, Missouri 65065
(314) 348-3131

Located in central Missouri, Marriott's Tan-Tar-A Resort rests comfortably in the foothills of the Ozark Mountains. The resort complex covers 420 acres and sprawls along the shores of the scenic Lake of the Ozarks. The hilly terrain and lakeside exposure provide a lovely backdrop for the many recreational activities. Tan-Tar-A is only a three-hour drive from either St. Louis or Kansas City.

Accommodations: The 930 guest rooms and suites are in the main resort buildings and in smaller two-story accommodations bordering the lake and the golf course. Some have a fireplace and a deck or patio. The high season is mid-May to mid-September, when rates are $99–$165 a night. During the low season (November to mid-March) prices drop to $65–$110 a night. In the remaining months the rates are $89–$145 a night.

Dining: The casual family-style restaurant, the Cliff Room, has a large deck for outdoor dining. Here, between 5:00 and 7:00 P.M., children eight years old and younger eat free. For a fancier evening try Windrose on the Water, where you'll enjoy luscious steaks and fresh seafood. If all you want is a quick bite, there are fast food facilities nearby. At the golf course The Oaks serves breakfast and lunch, overlooking the course.

For liquid refreshment The Landing is a daytime pub, The Jetty Bar is adjacent to the Arrowhead Pool, and Tradewinds is near the Tradewinds Pool. Mr. D's also serves cocktails, and The Nightwinds Lounge offers live music for dancing in the evening.

Children's World: Camp Tan-Tar-A, for children ages five to ten years, is in session Monday through Friday, from early June through mid-August and at holiday times the rest of the year. The fee for the 9:30 A.M.–4:00 P.M. schedule is $25 for the first day and $20 for each additional day. Activities include swimming, beach games, races, treasure hunts, and crafts. Also, kids ages seven to ten can join a guided fishing tour for two hours ($25 per child).

A less structured routine is found at the Children's Playhouse, which is open to four- to ten-year-olds, Saturday from 9:00 A.M. to 5:00 P.M. and Monday through Saturday evenings from 6:30 to 11:00 P.M. Here counselors supervise children as they play with the array of toys, board games, puzzles, and books. During the spring, fall, and winter, the schedule at the

Playhouse is limited to all day Saturday and Friday and Saturday evenings. The fee is $4.00 an hour for the first child and only 50 cents an hour for each additional child. These same rates apply for individual babysitters.

Recreation: The lake is the venue for boating fun for everyone. You can rent ski boats (waterskiing instruction available), sailboats, paddleboats, kayaks, fishing boats, and waverunners. You can even try parasailing. Though there's a small sandy beach nice for sunbathing, the lake is primarily the domain of boaters and fishermen. Swimmers usually opt for time at one of the five pools (four outdoors, one indoors).

Golfers can take on the challenges of The Oaks (an eighteen-hole course) or Hidden Lakes (nine holes). The Racquet Club houses tennis and racquetball courts as well as billiards. Outdoors and adjacent to the club are basketball and volleyball courts. Tennis buffs can also try the indoor or outdoor tennis courts near the Racquet Club.

At the fitness center you can use the exercise room as well as the indoor pool, and you can indulge in the many programs at the Windjammer Spa. Facials, massages, aromatherapy, and detoxification treatments are just some of the pleasures from which to choose.

Back in the great outdoors, find a good horse at the stables for a nice trail ride, rent a mountain bike, jog along the paths around the property, test your skill at the trap range, or challenge the kids to a round of miniature golf. If you still have time and energy, try bowling, shuffleboard, horseshoes, and Ping-Pong. Even the shoppers in your family will have plenty of fun in the dozen shops, featuring jewelry, toys, fashions, and country crafts. And be sure to take an evening cruise on the lake; the *Ozark Princess* sails four nights a week during the summer season.

In the winter ice skating is available for both adults and children.

Ruttger's Bay Lake Lodge

Box 400
Deerwood, Minnesota 56444
(218) 678–2885, (800) 450–4545

If you have ever entertained thoughts of owning your own lakefront cottage in the land of 10,000 lakes, Ruttger's Bay Lake Lodge may satisfy your yearning. Set on 400 acres directly on Bay Lake, in north-central Minnesota, the Lodge emphasizes relaxed outdoor recreation in surroundings of clear lake waters, tall trees, and pine-scented air. Open from May 1 to

October 31, it is family run and family oriented. With its tradition of old-fashioned hospitality, the lodge allows you a well-deserved escape to the peace and serenity of the North Woods.

Accommodations: For years the lakefront cottages and the Lodge rooms have been favorites among vacationers. To these have been added condominiums, villas, and townhouses. Many have views of the lake, and all include a refrigerator. Rates are $66–$134 per person per day, modified American plan. Children under three are free, while the rate for four- to eight-year-olds is one-third the adult rate and for nine- to fifteen-year-olds is one-half the adult rate. Cribs are provided at no additional charge with a weekly package plan.

Dining: The modified American plan is mandatory for cottage guests, and the homemade pastries are practically a requirement. The main dining room is an inviting setting, with natural logs, an open-beamed ceiling, and a stone fireplace. Lunches are also served on the deck overlooking the lake at the Pro Shop Grill or Auntie M's Kafferhaus. You may cook lunch for yourself in the condos or townhouses. The Terrace Cocktail Lounge has picture windows that are great for viewing the North Woods while sipping a cool drink.

Children's World: Kids' Kamp is a supervised and complimentary program for children in operation from mid-June until Labor Day, every day except Sundays, on the modified American plan. Beginning at age four, kids join their counselors from 9:00 A.M. to 2:00 P.M. The counselors organize the day for fishing, swimming, crafts, treasure hunts, nature programs, and talent shows. A playground is equipped with swings, sandboxes, a merry-go-round, ropes, slides, and seesaws. Three times a week the children can join a dinner and movie evening from 5:30 to 8:30 P.M. Babysitting can be arranged by the staff for approximately $3.50 per hour.

Recreation: With such a beautiful lake, you might find yourself drawn to the water almost continuously through the day—for sunning, swimming, waterskiing, fishing, and boating, and for building sand castles along the beach. Swimmers also enjoy the indoor and outdoor pools, and tennis fans turn to the two Omni-turf and three Laykold courts. Round up a game of volleyball, basketball, or horseshoes; play Ping-Pong and shuffleboard; or go walking through the woods. Practice on the putting green, and plan a round of golf on the eighteen-hole championship course or the Lodge Nine. And treat yourself to relaxation in the card room or TV room, the whirlpool, or the sauna. The staff naturalist directs programs introducing visitors to the loon, osprey, and bald eagle. Waterskiing, sailboats, motorboats, pontoon boats, and fishing boats are available.

Shanty Creek

1 Shanty Creek Road
Bellaire, Michigan 49615
(800) 678–4111
E-mail: info@shantycreek.com; Website: http://www.shantycreek.com

Shanty Creek, located in northern Michigan, is actually two resorts in one, which translates into a bit of variety for guests. Summit Village is elegant and contemporary, while Schuss Village is modeled on an Alpine village. Together they encompass 4,000 acres of rolling woodlands on the shores of Lake Bellaire. In the summertime golfing is the favorite activity; in winter skiing is the preferred sport.

Accommodations: Lodging choices are innumerable: guest rooms, studios, condominiums, and chalets. Some are equipped with a fireplace or whirlpool; others have a deck. You might have a view of the lake, the forests, a fairway, or the Alpine village. Rates start at $84 a night for a guest room and rise to $340 a night for a deluxe two-bedroom condominium. Children ages seventeen and under stay free when occupying a room with their parents. Cribs can be added to your accommodation for a fee of $5.00 a day. The many package plans offer good savings.

Dining: The Lakeview Dining Room is an elegant restaurant at Summit Village. At Schuss Village a European atmosphere prevails at the more casual Ivanhof. For light meals and easy dining, try La Bodega Deli and Arnie's at The Legend Pro Shop. The Beach Club, right on the shores of Lake Bellaire, also provides refreshments.

Children's World: When the weather warms up, just as the golf season begins, infants to ten-year-olds can be accommodated in a daily child-care program. From 9:00 A.M. to 5:00 P.M., children join together in storytime, movies, arts and crafts, and music. The fee is $22 full-day, $15 half-day. Lunch is $5.00 extra.

From early June through Labor Day, Kid's Korner explodes with summertime fun: nature hikes, basketball, volleyball, scavenger hunts, shuffleboard, and swimming. This program is designed for children ages six and older. The fees and hours are the same as above.

When the ski season starts, in November, the daily child-care program applies to infants to six-year-olds. In addition to stories, movies, and indoor play, the older children discover the excitement of outdoor play in a winter wonderland. The same fees as above are charged for this program.

Young skiers, ages three to five, combine indoor play with sledding and ski instruction in their 9:30 A.M.–3:30 P.M. schedule. The fee is $45 a day and includes ski rental and lunch.

Kid's Academy, for older children (ages five to eleven), runs from 10:00 A.M. to 4:00 P.M. daily. This is more serious instruction but still doesn't lose sight of the fun of skiing. The fee is $35 full-day, $30 half-day with lunch, and $25 half-day without lunch. Ski rentals are not included in these fees. At any time of the year, babysitting can be booked through the concierge for $5.00 an hour.

Recreation: Golfers experience a bit of a dream come true here. The resort's original golf course is the eighteen-hole Shanty Creek Course. Another championship eighteen holes comprise the beautiful Schuss Mountain Course. And the crowning gem is The Legend, an exciting eighteen-hole course designed by Arnold Palmer. With the carefully maintained courses complemented by an experienced teaching staff, all golfers will surely improve their games here.

Other summertime activities include tennis, with eight courts and a pro staff available for lessons; biking on the mountain trails; and boating. At the Fitness Center work out on the Nautilus equipment, head to the racquetball courts, hit the steam room or sauna, and wind up the day with a massage. With indoor swimming pools and a heated pool outdoors, swimmers are satisfied whatever the season.

The ski season starts in November and carries through late March or early April, depending on how generous Mother Nature has been. There are forty-one runs for downhill skiers, almost 20 miles of groomed trails for cross-country skiers, and a new snow park for snowboarders. When you're not on skis, pile the whole family into a horse-drawn sleigh for an old-fashioned ride in the woods.

Southwest

Arizona
New Mexico
Texas

Angel Fire Resort

Drawer B
Angel Fire, New Mexico 87710
(505) 377–2301, (800) 633–7463

Impressed by the pink glow on the mountains, Indians named this area "the land of Angel Fire." This year-round resort in the ancient Sangre de Cristo Mountain range of northern New Mexico allows for escape, renewal, and rejuvenation. Angel Fire encompasses 20,000 acres of mountain scenery and beauty and extends its southwestern ambience with a warm, neighborly feeling in spite of its size.

Accommodations: Angel Fire can accommodate approximately 4,000 guests in a variety of lodges and condominiums scattered through the village area. At first glance so many guests conjures up images of crowds, but remember that this still leaves five acres of land per person! In addition, the Starfire Lodge and Angel Fire Resort hotel offer rooms and suites, so you may take your choice of accommodation styles. Prices range from $80 for a room up to $250 for a three-bedroom unit. Cribs are provided at a nominal nightly fee.

Photo courtesy of Ben Blakenburg and Angel Fire Resort

Dining: Hungry? The resort has eleven dining areas. Choose from a variety of foods including Italian, Mexican, or steakhouse specialties. Dress is casual, and selected restaurants cater to children with special menus for them. For relaxing with drinks, most of the restaurants and clubs have lounges, many with inviting fireplaces. The Angel Fire Country Club matches up spectacular mountain views with tasty breakfasts, lunches, and dinners. Live entertainment enlivens weekends at Angel Fire.

Children's World: The Angel Fire resort area offers children's programs in both summer and winter.

During the winter, from Thanksgiving to Easter, the focus is on skiing. Young skiers ages three to twelve can join the Children's Ski and Snowboard Center, which runs from 8:30 A.M. to 4:00 P.M.; a $70-a-day fee covers lessons, lift tickets, rentals, and lunch. And in case you do not believe your eyes, indeed a Disneylike "Snow Bear" does ski with the children.

Very young or nonskiing children can participate in daily activities at the Angel Fire Day Camp. Children six weeks to twelve years old can join the fun on an hourly basis from 8:00 A.M. to 5:00 P.M. daily. These sessions are a combination of indoor play—such as games, treasure hunts, and crafts—and outdoor play that emphasizes fun in the snow—such as "snowercise" and snow sculpture. The fee is $6.00 per hour, $45 for a full-day, or $30 for a half-day. Parents must supply diapers, bottles, formula, and other supplies. Lunch is provided for $3.00 extra.

Recreation: The primary diversion in winter is skiing. Angel Fire has hosted the World Cup Freestyle Competition, but don't be intimidated. Over two-thirds of the trails are for beginners and intermediates. The vertical drop is 2,050 feet, and the longest trail is a cruising 3.2 miles long. Six chairlifts cover 30 miles of trails, two ski shops are ready to rent or sell equipment and accessories, and lessons are available. The Nordic skier can enjoy unlimited trails at the Angel Fire Resort Golf Course. In varying levels of difficulty, these trek through aspen, spruce, and ponderosa pine groves. Sleigh rides, snowmobiles, and snowboards round out the wintertime fun.

Once the snow melts, these same trails offer fantastic opportunities for mountain biking, hiking, backpacking, and horseback riding. Catching a trout from the annually stocked lake can be an exhilarating experience, but if fishing is not your sport, you can canoe and sail in these waters. Have a swim in the pool, play tennis, or bicycle on the paths around the village. At an elevation of 8,600 feet, the eighteen-hole golf course weaves through a wooded terrain. Practice also on the driving range and putting green, or enlist the expert advice of the golf pro. Summer Adventures offers such things as white-water rafting or gold panning for a fee. Whatever your activity, the crisp mountain air enhances it.

The Arizona Biltmore

24th Street and Missouri
Phoenix, Arizona 85016
(602) 955-6600, (800) 950-0086

The Arizona Biltmore is often referred to as the "jewel of the desert." At the entrance to the grounds, Main Drive is lined with lovely private homes and landscaped with citrus trees and flowering oleander, petunias, and pansies. The main structure at the end of this drive is an architectural masterpiece. Inspired by Frank Lloyd Wright and constructed of Biltmore blocktile, the buildings reflect the gracious charm and innovative spirit of the 1920s. Exploring the thirty-nine acres of this fine establishment is an adventure in architectural history and a delightful experience in imaginative landscaping. Stroll along the beautifully manicured lawns and gardens for visual delights in carefully tended beds of yellow pansies or pink petunias or multicolored snapdragons. In dining, shopping, and recreational activities, The Biltmore has consistently maintained its reputation as a world-class resort. It is open year-round.

Accommodations: There are 600 well-appointed rooms and suites, approximately 100 of which are located in the main building. The others are arranged in several buildings and cottages bordering flower beds. Many rooms have mountain or garden views, and all rooms have been recently remodeled. Standard rooms cost $130 in the summer, $280 September to December, and $395 January 1 to April 30. Resort rooms are more spacious with extra-large bathrooms and private balcony or terrace. Those rates are $170, $315, and $435 for the above dates. Children under eighteen can stay free in the same room with their parents. Cribs are provided at no extra charge.

Dining: For dining, modified and full American meal plans are available. Enjoy regional and American cuisine for breakfast, lunch, and dinner in the casual atmosphere of the Biltmore Grill and Patio. A children's menu is available. Or you can experience the award-winning New American specialties at Wright's, where the striking architecture enhances the enjoyment of the food. Wright's serves breakfast, lunch, and dinner. Private wine tastings can be arranged—the Biltmore has one of the most extensive wine lists in the region. If you're near the waterslide and new pool, try the Cabana Club Restaurant and Bar for sandwiches and cool drinks during the day and cocktails and entertainment in the evening. The grand atmosphere of the lobby also provides several grand options for the tummy. Traditional tea is served from 3:00 to 4:30 P.M. The Squaw Peak Lounge allows you to sit either indoors or outdoors, listen to music, and savor the view of the mountain along with your drinks and hors d'oeuvres. For the morning

Photo courtesy of The Arizona Biltmore

hours, Coffee Art is just that—the art of espresso, cappuccino, imported coffees, and delicious pastries served for your satisfaction. The Gift Shop is a nostalgic soda fountain for small gifts, breakfast, lunch, snacks, and, of course, ice-cream sodas.

Children's World: "Kids Kabana—A Learning Center" is a well-planned activity center where children ages four to twelve can enjoy a variety of activities—crafts and computers as well as outdoor activities such as swimming, croquet, putting, or cycling. It is open daily year-round from 8:00 A.M. to 6:00 P.M.; the cost is $7.00 per hour (two-hour minimum), $25 for a half-day, and $50 for a full-day. Children under four may visit the center at the same rates if accompanied by a responsible adult.

Recreation: Merely the setting of The Biltmore could charm you for days on end, but once the inner spirit is renewed, try your hand at some of the many recreational activities. Eight lighted tennis courts attract tennis enthusiasts; schedule yourself for a tennis clinic or private lessons.

The avid golfer can take on one of the two eighteen-hole PGA courses or refine a technique on the putting greens and driving ranges. At the pro shop you can seek out the guidance of the teaching staff, pick up some vital accessories, or rent equipment.

The five swimming pools can mean either invigorating laps or a relaxing dip. One of the twenty-three cabanas will protect you from the desert sun, and the new, 92-foot waterslide is guaranteed to get a "wow!" To check out the scenery and still test your athletic abilities, rent a bicycle or jog along the trails flanking the Salt River Canal. You might spend a session in the exercise salon, which offers group classes, individual instruction, and skin consultation. The steam room, saunas, whirlpools, and a masseuse or masseur at the resort's new spa (opened December 1997) can do wonders for overworked muscles. Or perhaps you will alternate rigorous athletics with less demanding games of croquet, lawn chess, and volleyball.

If shopping is your interest, discover a varied and extensive line of merchandise in the hotel shops: jewelry, silver, regionally crafted products, both Southwest and Native American artists; and tennis, golf, and swimming clothes and accessories. Adjacent to the grounds is the Biltmore Fashion Park, filled with more shops and restaurants and reached by a shuttle bus.

The Bishop's Lodge

P.O. Box 2367
Santa Fe, New Mexico 87504-2367
(505) 983–6377
Website: http://www.bishopslodge.com

Just a five-minute drive north of Santa Fe, 1,000 acres of the foothills of the Sangre de Cristo Mountains comprise the range of The Bishop's Lodge. At 7,200 feet, this area of north central New Mexico shares its warm sunny days with cool crisp nights. The clean mountain air, the setting, and the atmosphere of the lodge combine to emit the flavor and tradition of the old Southwest. The adobe architecture reminiscent of a Spanish and Native American heritage and the friendly spirit of the resident wranglers give The Bishop's Lodge its true Western flair.

In the nineteenth century, the ranch was the home of Archbishop Jean Baptiste Lamy, a pioneering French cleric who became the Southwest's first Catholic bishop. His life was the inspiration for Willa Cather's novel *Death Comes for the Archbishop* (good background reading for an introduction to the history and topography of the region). The property was bought by the newspaper publisher Joseph Pulitzer and then acquired in 1918 by James Thorpe. Since then, the Thorpe family has operated the lodge as a vacation resort and since 1994, it is open year-round. The facilities have undergone expansion and renovation during the years, but the private chapel built by the archbishop still stands, a sentinel to the lodge's history.

Accommodations: The lodge's eighty-eight rooms and suites are grouped in several adobe buildings nestled among fruit trees and flower

Photo courtesy of The Bishop's Lodge

beds. The North and South lodges are the oldest, both having been grand summer homes before World War I; the newest one, "Chamisa" (added in July 1994), contains fourteen deluxe accommodations above the banks of the Tesuque Creek. Many of the rooms are decorated in warm earth colors, with a Southwestern flair—deluxe rooms include fireplaces and many have outdoor sitting areas. European plan is available year-round; based on two adults, daily standard rooms are $95 in winter, $145 spring and fall, and $165 to $205 from late May to early September. Deluxe room rates for the same periods are $150, $220, and $250 to $295. Children under three stay at no charge; others pay $15 per day. Cribs and rollaways are available on request. In summer, Modified American Plan rates are offered for $241 to $281 standard, and $326 to $371 deluxe; additional person in the room is either $10 (under three) or $53. Besides lodging and two meals, these rates include the supervised children's program. Special packages are offered throughout the year.

Dining: New American and Southwestern cuisine are featured in the main dining room; jackets for gentlemen are suggested at the evening meal. The decor is classic Santa Fe: beamed ceilings, Navajo rugs, Spanish chandeliers, and four life-size murals done in the 1920s by W. E. Rollins. You can also have a box lunch prepared and enjoy your own picnic. For cocktails and snacks there's El Rincon, a delightful corner bar opening onto the Firelight Terrace, which offers sunsets, stars, and firelight as accompaniments to Mexican margaritas.

Children's World: During the summer months, kids four to twelve years old can participate in full-day programs (8:00 A.M.–4:00 P.M. and 6:00–9:00 P.M.) of supervised activities, such as swimming, tennis lessons, pony rides, picnics, games, and fishing. Children can even have meals with their counselors in their own dining room or at picnics, pool parties, and cookouts. In addition, a pond stocked with trout and an outdoor play area of swings, a slide, and a sandbox translate into active fun for kids. Included with the Modified American Plan, the program is also available to European Plan guests in day ($40 per child, meals included) and evening ($30) sessions.

Recreation: Recreation at The Bishop's Lodge starts with horseback riding in the wide open country. Experienced cowboys match you and your ability with the appropriate steed from a stable of more than seventy horses and then guide you on trail rides throughout the lodge's 1,000 acres. The cost is $30, children must be over eight years and 4 feet tall, and the maximum weight is 225 pounds. Free pony rides are offered for the little ones at 11:30 A.M. daily. A memorable experience is the Sunrise Ride through the canyons and foothills of the Sangre de Cristo Mountains followed by a hearty "cooked-on-the-range" breakfast of eggs, pancakes, and biscuits. The

Santa Fe National Forest is adjacent to the grounds of the lodge and provides more opportunities to explore the scenery on horseback. But if you're a little skittish about mounting a horse, you can fill your days with lots of other recreational fun: Hike on the trails through the foothills, fish the mountain streams for trout, swim in the pool, and bask in the sunshine. At the Tennis Center, you can play on one of four courts, have a lesson with the resident pro, and purchase some new accessories at the pro shop. On the skeet- and trapshooting ranges, experts offer instruction, and rental equipment is provided. Play a game of Ping-Pong or treat your sore muscles to a relaxing hour in the whirlpool and sauna. The nearby country clubs of Santa Fe, Cochiti Lake, and Los Alamos grant lodge guests golfing privileges on their eighteen-hole courses. Be sure to take at least a day to discover the narrow streets, interesting adobe architecture, quaint shops, and art galleries of old Santa Fe. Open-air performances of the Santa Fe Summer Opera Festival are a special attraction for summertime visitors. Pueblo Indians show their jewelry and pottery on blankets around the Palace of the Governors or the famous Indian Market, and visitors are welcome to the colorful ceremonies at nearby pueblos.

Flying L Guest Ranch

P.O. Box 1959
Bandera, Texas 78003
(210) 460–3001, (800) 292–5134

Bandera, 45 miles northwest of San Antonio, claims to have invented dude ranching during the Depression when an enterprising rancher decided to take in "dudes" for extra money. So now, with true Texan style, they have laid claim to being the "Cowboy Capital of the World." Seven rodeo world champions have hailed from here, however, so there may be something to it. Set in the midst of the beautiful Texas Hill Country, this is not the Texas of the movies. Here there are verdant green hills, oak and maple trees, wildflowers and flowing rivers, not sagebrush and sand.

The Flying L Ranch was first settled in 1874. It became a dude ranch in 1946 when Jack Lapham, a retired Air Corps colonel, started to realize his dream of a place where "a modern person can go and find himself in the midst of yesterday." (OK, who can figure out the name of the ranch based on this story? You already did? Good!) The ranch became a favorite "watering hole" for celebrities, and the television program *The Cisco Kid* was filmed here.

Accommodations: You can bunk in style here—all are two-room suites with bath, real Texas-style lodging with room to spread out. The forty-one guest suites are in guest houses either with a Hill Country view or along the golf course and are geared toward comfort, with refrigerator, microwave, coffee pot, and color TV. Daily rates in low season are $75 to $90 per adult; high season (summer and holidays) rates are $95 to $105 per adult. Children twelve to seventeen are two-thirds of the adult rate, and ages three to eleven are half of the adult rate. Children under three stay free, but there are no special facilities for them. Discount rates are given for five nights or more.

Dining: Two full meals are included in the rate and are hearty samples of Texas barbecue, mesquite grill, and Mexican specialties. Seven days a week, at 7:00 A.M. sharp, start your day with a continental breakfast. Then, four days every week enjoy a breakfast buffet in the Main House dining room, and on the other three days, feel like a real cowpoke as you head down to the river on a haywagon for a creekside breakfast hot off the coals. Lunch is on your own, with burger and fries at the pro shop or an afternoon picnic from your refrigerator. Dinner is from 5:30 to 7:00 P.M., either in the Main House dining room or creekside. Vegetarians beware—this is Texas, with meat every night! At 4:00 P.M. the Branding Iron Saloon opens, and there's family entertainment every night—cowboy music, dancing, tricycle roping, gun slinging, or a rodeo, usually topped off with a marshmallow roast and s'mor making. Do the kids love that!

Children's World: Children are divided into two groups, ages three to five and six to twelve. Program runs from 9:30 A.M. to 12:30 P.M. and from 2:00 to 4:30 P.M., but the first half hour of both sessions is considered free time—for those 'ole slowpokes.' Activities include feeding animals, nature walks, scavenger hunts, sports, fishing, and crafts, such as leather bracelets and vest making. Golf and tennis clinics are included for the older children along with trail rides with the grown-ups, while the little ones can take pony rides at the Kids Korral every day. The program runs Monday through Saturday during summer, spring break (March–April), and holidays. And, as they say at the Flying L, "there ain't no nickel and dimein' here," it's all included in the rates.

Recreation: The only activity not included in your price is golf. When they say pack your shootin' irons, they mean golf clubs, pardner. Drive, chip, and putt on the par seventy-two, fully-irrigated course. A driving range lets you perfect your skills if you don't get distracted by the beautiful view; private lessons are also available. Try the outdoor swimming pool or venture off the "Ranch" to the Medina River for a little inner tubing or canoeing. Tennis, hayrides, rodeo events, a playground, and a seasonal petting corral add to the fun. Riding lessons are available for the 'young-uns,' as are instructions in horse grooming, saddling, and roping.

In the Bandera area, fish in the crystal waters of Medina Lake, tour a working Longhorn ranch, visit the Cowboy Artists Museum in Kerrville, tour the World War II Nimitz Museum, or enjoy antiquing in the German town of Fredericksburg. On Bandera's Main Street there's a working blacksmith shop. Nearby excursions include San Antonio (the Alamo, Market Square, and the River Walk) and various theme parks such as SeaWorld, Fiesta Texas, Pear Apple County Fair, and Splashtown. Visit natural wonders such as the caverns or tour the Lone Star Brewing Company to see how beer is made. All in all, the "Ranch" promises "a rootin', tootin' time."

Hyatt Regency Hill Country Resort

9800 Hyatt Resort Drive
San Antonio, Texas 78251
(210) 647–1234, (800) 233–1234

The Texas Hill Country is as much a state of mind as it is a region. It certainly doesn't look like Texas—its green rolling hills, abundance of water, and variety of trees surprise the first-time visitor. San Antonio calls itself "a big city with small town charm," and, as the #1 tourist destination in Texas, has a multitude of attractions for families to enjoy—including the famous Alamo, centerpiece of Texas history, and the River Walk, lined with shops and restaurants along the tree-shaded banks of the San Antonio River.

Twenty minutes from downtown, a scenic drive meanders through the landscape, culminating at the lobby entrance, reminiscent of a Texas ranch house and complete with fireplaces and overstuffed furniture—even a shady back porch. In fact, the resort's 200 acres are a part of the Rogers–Wiseman Ranch, honored for being in continuous agricultural production at the hands of one family for one hundred years or more. Hyatt has successfully adapted a full-scale destination resort into this casual, laid-back lifestyle; the results are downright pleasurable. Enjoy a championship golf course, nature trails, a health club, and a wonderful four-acre water park featuring the 950-foot-long Ramblin' River—the centerpiece of the property and the greatest place to get into an inner tube, kick back, and just relax.

Accommodations: Traditional Hill Country, German-style architecture with native limestone and decorative wood exterior, the two- and four-story hotel has nine guest-room wings, housing 500 rooms. A stand-alone, 2-story luxurious guest house styled after a ranch house is in the courtyard—there's even an authentic windmill! As usual with Hyatt, the rooms are large and

Photo courtesy of Hyatt Regency Hill Country Resort

well decorated, ranging from standard to Regency Club level, with no-smoking rooms and suites available. Room rates are from $190 to $315; suites from $295 to $2,250. Children under eighteen are free in the room. Packages are a good value and may include golf, the children's program, or other family excursions. Be sure to ask.

Dining: The flavor is definitely Tex-Mex, so expect tortillas even for breakfast, but you have lots of options here. The Springhouse Cafe features regional specialties, a large buffet and salad bar, and Sunday brunch. A wood-burning oven makes great pizzas. In the clubhouse, The Antlers Lodge has the ambience of a country lodge and puts the accent on regional Southwestern cuisine of steak, chicken, and seafood. Many entrees are mesquite-grilled and accompanied by a spicy Tex-Mex sauce. Also here, golfers will find sandwiches and light snacks in the Cactus Oak Tavern at the halfway point in the golf course. The General Store offers hamburgers, deli sandwiches, and home-baked cookies as well as licorice sticks, wine, sodas, fresh coffee, and muffins. In the evening, relax at Aunt Mary's Porch, an open-air bar just off the lobby, or kick up your heels at Charlie's Long Bar, an old-fashioned Texas saloon complete with tin ceiling and a 56-foot copper-top bar. Yes, they have the tequila with the worm. Pool, shuffle-board, backgammon, and chess enhance the bar.

Children's World: Camp Hyatt, developed in 1989, offers not only supervised programs but children's menus and an opportunity to buy a second room for the kids at half-price. Custom tailored for ages three to twelve, Camp Hyatt operates during holidays, weekends, and daily throughout the summer. The program runs from 9:00 A.M. to noon and from 1:00 to 4:00 P.M. and keeps the kids busy with games and activities. There is a special Camp Hyatt room with a different schedule for every day of the week. The cost is $18 for a half-day; $30 for a full-day (lunch included for $5.00 additional), or $26 for the Friday and Saturday evening sessions from 5:00 to 9:00 P.M.

Recreation: Golfers enjoy the Arthur Hills–designed course with its 170 acres of rolling, scenic terrain. It truly blends into the countryside and has been recognized as one of the premier courses in the United States. Tennis is available on three courts, with a pro on hand. Walking, jogging, and biking paths crisscross the property, and the health club features aerobics classes and all the latest equipment—and, of course, a massage to help you recover from your workout.

By far the most popular spot, though, is the Ramblin' River, modeled after all those Hill Country river experiences. Pick up an inner tube, drop your cares, and let the lazy current carry you away. The journey varies from brisk to slow and allows riders to swim, walk, or take detours into two swimming pools, a cascading waterfall, or even a little sand beach.

Day excursions to Sea World, Six Flags, Fiesta Texas, Splashtown water park, or many of the nearby Hill towns, each with its own personality and charm, can pleasurably fill your days or evenings. Visit the Natural Bridge Caverns, with active formations more than 140 million years old, or stroll through Bandera, the self-proclaimed "cowboy capital." The Alamo is a must, and the IMAX production, *Alamo—the Price of Freedom,* does help in understanding the role of the Alamo and in bringing it to life (although it's pretty violent at times). Missions, museums, and Market Square, which feels like shopping in Mexico, are all nearby.

Hyatt Regency Scottsdale at Gainey Ranch

7500 East Doubletree Ranch Road
Scottsdale, Arizona 85258
(602) 991–3388, (800) 233–1234

Entering the private road that leads to this resort does not prepare you for the beauty of this lush and luxurious oasis in the midst of the Arizona desert. Water surrounds, cascades, falls, bubbles, flows, even sprays from the air; water and flowers are everywhere. You feel as though you are part of the landscape, not separated from it. Twenty-eight fountains, forty-seven waterfalls, and hundreds of palms, fir trees, and flowers create a twenty-seven-acre garden, part of the 560-acre Gainey Ranch, a planned residential complex that includes golf, parks and lakes, private homes, and businesses.

Accommodations: The double "H" shape of the 4-story resort provides five courtyards and four glass-enclosed atriums, with a movable 820-square-foot glass wall at the center of the lobby that allows a panoramic view of the McDowell Mountains and Sonoran Desert. The main building, inspired by the desert work of Frank Lloyd Wright, houses 493 rooms and suites; on either side are seven two- and four-bedroom freestanding casitas with fireplaces and terraced balconies overlooking the lake. The decor blends with the desert setting, using natural textures and artifacts. Children under eighteen stay free in existing bed space of parents' rooms, and every room has the Disney channel. Rates vary according to season: High season (February to May), rooms are $345; $435 in the Regency Club, which offers VIP service, complimentary breakfast, beverages, and evening hors d'oeuvres. January and fall season is approximately $20 lower, and June to early September is the lowest season, with rates from $155 to $195. Casitas range from $950 to $2,055 per night.

Dining: The Golden Swan is the hotel's specialty restaurant, named one of the best in the world by *Travel/Holiday* magazine and one of the

top five in the Southwest by *Condé Nast Traveler*. One can dine indoors or out, in a charming gazebo nestled inside a lagoon with black swans. A special Sunday buffet, the "Chef's Brunch," is served right in the kitchen, where you can watch and talk with the chefs, making sure your food is hot and fresh. The Squash Blossom restaurant is open for breakfast, lunch, and dinner, with a warm Southwestern ambience and regional specialties (try the Arizona toast or a wide variety of salads and sandwiches or fajitas). Ristorante Sandolo is a casual Italian bistro, overlooking the pool, where the servers serenade you. After you dine, enjoy a Venice-style gondola ride on the resort's waterways. Again, a *sandolier* will sing to you. (You can enjoy the gondola ride for $4.00 even if you don't eat.) Both restaurants have indoor/outdoor seating with very clever "air-conditioning." A very fine, invisible mist cools and moisturizes the air above you, making it comfortable year-round. Poolside, you'll find two bars, the Waterfall Juice Bar, and the Water Garden Cafe, serving snacks, lunch, yogurt, and fruit drinks. In the evening, watch the cascading fountains and listen to classical guitar or perhaps a marimba band as you relax in the Lobby Bar.

Children's World: Camp Hyatt Kachina, designed in 1989, is the prototype children's program for all Hyatt resorts. It operates daily year-round and offers three- to twelve-year-olds a well-balanced program of activities. A specially appointed Camp room has all the crafts and games children like best, and the playground, Fort Kachina, has lots of climbing and "imagination areas." And don't forget the ten swimming pools, one complete with white sand beach and a 3-story water slide. Each day has a different theme, such as Rootin' Tootin' Reptiles, Wading in the Wetlands, Don't Bug Me, or Feathered Friends. Age groups are three to five and six to twelve. The morning session, from 9:00 A.M. to noon, is $21, and the afternoon session, from 1:00 to 5:00 P.M., is $28. Lunch, from noon to 1:00 P.M., can be added to either session for $11. The full-day costs $54, including lunch, and $32 per evening session from 5:00 to 9:00 P.M., including dinner. If you have an active child who loves the program, the best deal is all day (9:00 A.M. to 9:00 P.M.) and all meals for $80. Kids even have their own frequent traveler program for Camp Hyatt merchandise. During holidays the resort offers "destination specific" activities designed for the entire family, from cowboy roping, cowboy guitarists, and Native American storytelling to family fun sing-alongs round the campfire.

Recreation: Where do we start? With the twenty-seven-hole championship golf course at Gainey Ranch Golf Club? Actually, it's composed of three separate, individually designed courses—the Dunes; the Lakes, with five lakes and lots of water hazards; and the Arroyo, the most difficult. Or with the eight tennis courts or 3 miles of jogging and cycling trails? Or the Regency Spa, with state-of-the-art equipment, classes, sauna, and massage? Let's start with the water playground—most impressive in this dry, desert area. The design is a combination of Roman, Greek, and art deco and is truly spectacular. Zip down the 30-foot waterslide, stroll over an aqueduct connecting six of the ten pools, swim around (or through!) the "Big Gun," a 5-foot-wide waterfall, or "thunderfall" as the hotel terms it, at the end of the aqueduct. Relax in the Grecian temple with 16-foot hot tub and four 'cold plunges' in each corner. Water comes from all directions—from fountains, trailing down tall glass columns, and from water spouts along the roof. Build sand castles on the beach at one end or play volleyball at the other. Kids never want to leave this watery fantasyland.

Phoenix attractions include a zoo, a desert botanical garden, and stately old homes; in Scottsdale, find an IMAX theater, the world's highest fountain, and shopping on Fifth Avenue. View large cats in the wild at Out of Africa; experience a re-creation of the Old West at WestWorld or Rawhide, Arizona's largest Western-themed attraction. Pick up a copy of *GUEST* for lots more ideas. If you have time to venture farther, the concierge will help you plan excursions to the Grand Canyon (five hours away) or Montezuma Castle, a 600-year-old Pueblo Indian cliff dwelling only ninety minutes away. Who knew the desert could be like this?

Inn of the Mountain Gods

P.O. Box 269
Mescalero, New Mexico 88340
(505) 257–5141, (800) 545–9011

Not many families can boast a vacation on an Indian reservation. At the Inn of the Mountain Gods, your family can enjoy all the amenities of a full resort while learning some of the history and customs of the Mescalero Apache tribe. They are a proud people with infinite respect for the land and an eagerness to introduce you to the natural beauties of a setting believed to have been home to the Apache gods. Whether horseback riding or big-game hunting, Indian guides navigate excursions over the rugged terrain of this 460,000-acre reservation. The reservation, established over a hundred years ago, sprawls through the Sacramento Mountains of south-central New Mexico. Open year-round, the Inn sits on the shores of the 140-acre Lake Mescalero. The clear blue waters of the lake provide the setting for many water-sports enthusiasts (fishermen and boaters) and the picturesque backdrop for golfers and tennis players. Views of nearby Sierra Blanca (12,000 feet) complete the scenic ambience.

Accommodations: The 253 guest rooms (including twenty suites) are located in lakeside buildings adjacent to the main lodge. Each has a private balcony, which allows impressive views of the lake and the mountains. Prices range from $90 to $130 a night for a double room depending on the time of the year; July through September is the high season. Slightly higher rates are applied for suite accommodations. There is no charge for children twelve years and under sharing a room with adults (each room has two double beds), but a rollaway carries a $14-per-night fee. Package plans are arranged for golf, tennis, skiing, and hunting.

Dining: The lobby of the main building greets guests with a massive, copper-sheathed fireplace; this is a popular gathering spot for afternoon and evening cocktails. The Gas Kan Lounge also serves refreshments in the piano bar, which provides evening entertainment, and on the sundeck, which affords views over the lake.

The Dan Li Ka in the main building serves a buffet breakfast, casual lunches, and more formal dinners. Specializing in American and continental cuisine, the menu offers steak, veal, seafood, and chicken dishes and many tempting desserts. The Apache Tee Bar and Cafe is adjacent to the golf pro shop; it is open year-round for breakfast, lunch, and dinner. Top O' The Inn Deli features sandwiches made fresh while you wait, salads, and desserts; it's open from 11:00 A.M. until late for the night owl. A snack bar is located at the swimming pool.

Children's World: Children's events are low-key. The Tee Pee Arcade is open for children eight to ten years of age and up. There is no supervised play; for younger children an adult is a must. Children twelve and up can meet guides for horseback riding without parental supervision. For infants and toddlers, individual babysitters can be arranged.

In the wintertime kids six years and up can learn how to ski in the ski school of nearby Ski Apache Ski Area.

Recreation: The most unusual sport offered at the Inn is big-game hunting on the reservation. Because of a conscientious wildlife preservation program, elk, deer, antelope, bear, wild turkey, and quail are plentiful. Apache guides lead expeditions into the heavily wooded mountain terrain. Package plans are available for hunters during the season from mid-September through December; these include facilities for processing and packaging game. You can also enlist the services of a taxidermist for trophy preparation.

More traditional sports include golfing on an eighteen-hole championship course designed by Ted Robinson. This well-maintained course on rolling terrain skirts the lake and winds through tall pines and aspen. A resident pro is on hand for lessons, and there's a well-stocked pro shop. For tennis players, six outdoor courts are located on the lake. You can arrange private lessons or enroll in a clinic through the tennis pro shop.

On Lake Mescalero water sports are popular. Canoes, rowboats, and paddleboats can be rented at the boat dock. The lake's good stock of rainbow and cutthroat trout adds up to fine fishing. Swimmers and sunbathers are found at the heated outdoor pool and adjacent whirlpool overlooking the lake. There's a wading pool, too. The stables, a couple of miles from the Inn, maintain twenty to twenty-five horses. You can take half- or full-day trail rides with a guide. Combining exercise and solitary scenic enjoyment, some visitors take to the jogging and hiking trail around the lake or rent bicycles. Equipment is available for several lawn games such as horseshoes, badminton, volleyball, and soccer. Casino Apache provides lively indoor entertainment. After a full day of activities, you might enjoy wandering through the gift shop, where you'll find lovely Indian jewelry, weaving, and pottery.

Wintertime brings skiing at the nearby Ski Apache Resort. Snowmaking equipment aiding Mother Nature translates into a ski season from Thanksgiving to Easter. Owned and operated by the Mescalero Apache Indians, the ski area includes in its services lessons for all levels of skiers, restaurants, a lounge, and a ski rental and repair shop. Guests at the inn are shuttled daily to the mountain, where they find thirty-two designated groomed trails and a vertical drop of 1,700 feet.

At the inn there are recreational fees for many of the activities (golf, tennis, and horseback riding). Package plans for golf, tennis, and skiing, for example, eliminate the need for additional assessment.

Los Abrigados Resort & Spa

160 Portal Lane
Sedona, Arizona 86336
(602) 282–1777, (800) 521–3131

Close to the Grand Canyon and just two hours from Phoenix, Sedona is noted for its spectacular red rock formations and scenic canyons. For centuries, it has been a sacred place to The People, the earliest inhabitants, and legend holds that the Grandmother Spirit of the World still lives here. There is a magic quality in the air that many attribute to the energy points that converge here. At the least, the light, color, and awe-inspiring rocks combine with the many artisans living here to create something special.

Accommodations: Los Abrigados, Spanish for "the shelters," is in the heart of the small town of Sedona but stands in the midst of twenty-two acres of private ranchland/park and feels secluded. All of the 175 guest suites have oversize living rooms and separate bedrooms plus a balcony or private patio. Many feature a private whirlpool and fireplace. The plazas, walkways, and bridges connect the suites and main hotel area. Suites range from $210 to $275; $240 reserves one with spectacular views of the red rocks. Children under fifteen are free in the room with parents. During the summer, Family Fun packages are offered midweek. For $210 per day families receive accommodation, Spa passes for the adults, and full-day passes to Fun Club, the children's program.

Dining: The Celebrity, for casually elegant dining with a Southwestern flavor, is the domain of award-winning chef Scott Uehlein. Enjoy indoor or patio dining for breakfast and dinner. Imaginative dishes with an accent upon indigenous ingredients make dining an adventure. Do try the "Armadillo Eggs"; they're wonderful! Also available here is the "spa cuisine," healthful and lighter versions of many favorites. Redecorated in 1994, The On the Rocks Bar & Grill serves lunch, snacks, and dinner in a casual atmosphere and features nightly live entertainment. Steaks and Six offers dinners of grilled specialties in a billiard club atmosphere. And of course, suite service is available if no one wants to budge from the room. The Celebrity Dining Room and On the Rocks both feature children's menus. On The Rocks goes a bit further—instead of plates, they serve kids meals on a Frisbee! More restaurants are right next door at Tlaquepaque Village, a re-created Mexican village/plaza with tiled courtyards, fountains, and many craft shops.

Children's World: Children five to twelve years old enjoy the Fun Club, an innovative program that operates from Memorial Day through Labor Day as well as other major holidays. A changing schedule of daily projects may include kite flying, karate lessons, hiking, tumbling, drama, and arts and crafts. Outdoor activities are often held along the banks of the creek that wanders through the property, and swimming is supervised. Special theme days include Circus, Christmas in July, and Island Days. Fun Club is open from 8:30 A.M. to 4:00 P.M. and costs $28, including lunch and a snack. Half-days are available for $16, and on Saturday evenings a special program runs from 6:00 to 10:00 P.M. for $20.

Recreation: After a game of tennis or volleyball, relax at the heated outdoor pool and chat with other guests. Enjoy the jogging and walking trails or just sit by the creek and dream. The centerpiece of activities here is the Sedona Health Spa—10,000 square feet of state-of-the-art equipment and professional services providing a combination of fitness and relaxation. Massage, full body treatments and masks, facials and fitness classes/personal training contribute to physical and mental well-being. Nearby are two championship golf courses, designed by Robert Trent Jones and Gary Panks. Hiking, fishing streams, horseback riding, and jeep tours can also be arranged. The Grand Canyon is a two-hour drive, and closer is Oak Creek Canyon, with Slide Rock State Park, aptly named for the stretch of slippery creek bottom that forms a natural slide. For Southwestern art at its best, Tlaquepaque demands a visit (see Dining).

Red Rock Fantasy is the West's largest holiday light display, with over

Photo courtesy of Los Abrigados Resort & Spa

half-a-million lights. From late November until mid-January it transforms Los Abrigados into a fairyland.

Sheraton El Conquistador Resort and Country Club

10000 North Oracle Road
Tucson, Arizona 85737
(520) 544–5000, (800) 325–7832

The Arizona desert climate is perfect sporting weather practically year-round. The sun shines warmly and the humidity is low, just the right combination for the world-famous saguaro cacti that seem to be everywhere. It's also the perfect combination for nudging that golf ball farther down the links or sending an ace across the tennis court. El Conquistador wraps up tennis, golf, horseback riding, and terrific sunshine together for a holiday present for you. It sits among imported palm trees and native cacti with stark mountains towering behind it. The golden tan stucco facades and the red-tiled roofs of the low-rise buildings blend well with the colors nature has given the surrounding landscape.

Accommodations: More than 400 rooms and suites are decorated with modern contemporary-style furnishings. The use of Mexican tiles and brick in ornamental designs adds to the Southwestern ambience. All the rooms have balconies or patios that open up to the mountains, the golf course, or a flower-filled courtyard, and each room has a mini-bar. During the high season from January through April, a double room is $230–$310 a night and in the low season (June through Labor Day), $100–$125 a night; autumn and spring rates are $165–$240 a night. No charge is applied for children (seventeen and younger) staying in their parents' room or for cribs and rollaways. Golf and tennis packages are offered.

Dining: Innovative Southwestern cuisine is served in the informal, but elegant White Dove. For a fun evening of Western fare, head to the Last Territory for thick, juicy steaks broiled over a mesquite fire, barbecued ribs, and chicken. The Sundance Cafe is a casual, patio restaurant for breakfast and lunch. Around the pool, sip a bit of cool refreshment from the Desert Spring, and indoors have your favorite cocktail at the Lobby Lounge. Dos Locos Cantina serves spicy Southwestern food in the evening; mariachi musicians serenade diners here. At the Country Club, La Vista offers continental cuisine at lunch and dinner.

Children's World: Camp Conquistador offers daily summer activities for kids six to twelve years old. In an 8:00 A.M. to 3:00 P.M. schedule youngsters take nature walks, play tennis, volleyball, and basketball; show off artistic talents in crafts classes; and swim. The fee is $40 and includes lunch. Children's movies are shown Wednesday and Friday nights. Individual babysitting arrangements at $6.00 per hour can be made through the hotel staff.

Recreation: Tee up for the nine-hole or either of the two eighteen-hole golf courses, and watch your shot soar a bit farther in the clean desert air. Even taking lessons is no chore when the setting is so beautiful. Play tennis day or night on any of the thirty-one lighted courts. Lessons are available, too, for tennis and for racquetball (seven courts).

At the stables, choose a horse for a breakfast ride or a sunset champagne trail ride. Jog on one of the four designated trails ranging from 1½ to 7 miles in length. Fitness centers are located at the main hotel and at the country club; join an exercise class, then wind down in the whirlpool or sauna and pamper yourself with a massage. Take a dip in one of the four swimming pools. Rent a bike or get the whole family into a game of horseshoes, badminton, or volleyball. Explore the exciting possibility of a balloon ride, or poke around the Arizona terrain during a desert jeep ride.

Photo courtesy of Sheraton El Conquistador Resort and Country Club

Tanque Verde Guest Ranch

14301 East Speedway Boulevard
Tucson, Arizona 85748
(520) 296–6275, (800) 234–3833

In the Arizona desert, 2,800 feet high in the foothills of three mountain ranges, Tanque Verde Guest Ranch has been serving travelers for more than one hundred years. Once merely a stagecoach stop, today it is a year-round resort. The area is rich in the history of Native Americans and Spanish settlers who dubbed the area Tanque Verde—immortalizing the deep pools of artesian water found here. Located 12 miles outside Tucson, it borders Saguaro National Park. The saguaro cactus is immediately recognizable to anyone who has seen a western movie or a picture of the desert. They stand quite tall, with "arms" curving up toward the sky. From here visitors can take side trips to Tucson, to old Spanish missions, and to Mexico, which is about a one-and-a-half-hour drive away.

Accommodations: The seventy-one guest rooms and suites are located in the main ranch house and in individual cottages called "casitas"; most of the casitas have patios and corner fireplaces The decorative motif is Native American, and antiques and original art are carefully arranged to lend a warmth to the inn. Cribs are available, and there are refrigerators in the rooms. During the high season (mid-December through April) full American plan rates for a double room are $250–$340 per day; from May to mid-December, $175–$250 per day. Rates increase with the number of people; anyone over three is considered "people," and therefore pays the full rate. Triples range from $375 to $445 in winter, $310 to $345 in summer, and quads are $450 to $530 and $375 to $410, respectively. These prices include not just meals and lodging, but also riding, ranch activities, tennis, and the children's program.

Dining: Everyone eats at long tables in the one main dining room, encouraging an informal friendly atmosphere. Dress is casual and appetites are generally big due to the desert air and the exercise. American and continental dishes are standard fare, and, as expected, Spanish and Mexican specialties also appear on the menu. A separate children's dining room is reserved for youngsters and their counselors, who can take all meals together. Children are also welcome to dine with their parents. Many guests look forward to outdoor dining, enjoying hearty Western meals either on the range or at poolside.

Children's World: The Ranch offers a year-round, seven-day-per-week, fully supervised program for four- to eleven-year-olds. Horseback riding forms the core of the program and is adjusted to fit the ability and interest of the youngsters. Children under twelve must ride with the children's program; adults may join their children on these rides.

Besides riding, children are offered tennis lessons, nature programs, hikes, swimming, and some evening activities. The program is from 8:00 A.M. to 3:30 P.M., and 6:00 to 8:15 P.M. The cost is included in the daily rates. For infants and toddlers, babysitters can be hired for $5.00 to $6.00 per hour.

Recreation: Active relaxation is the byword at Tanque Verde. The clear desert air and low humidity, coupled with abundant sunshine, make all the activities pleasant. Horseback riding is the major part of the program. Whether you're interested in a slow-moving trail ride or a spirited sprint, the right mount can be found from a string of one hundred horses.

Early morning and late afternoons are perfect for strenuous outdoor activities such as tennis (five courts). In the middle of the day, seek out one of the two swimming pools or perhaps the lake for a cool dip. Numerous guided nature walks introducing visitors to the Arizona desert ecology are conducted along trails throughout the 25,000 acres. Some 200 species of birds have been identified in the area, making the ranch very popular with avid bird-watchers. The final touch to the active relaxation concept is the El Sonora Spa, well equipped with its swimming pool, sauna, whirlpool, exercise room, and lounge. In nearby Tucson, six championship golf courses grant playing privileges to ranch guests.

Taos Ski Valley

P.O. Box 90
Taos Ski Valley, New Mexico 87525
(505) 776–2291, (800) 776–1111

Nine hundred years ago the Pueblo Indians settled the area around Taos. They were followed in the sixteenth century by the Spanish and in the nineteenth century by fur traders. In the early 1950s, Ernie Blake searched carefully for just the right spot for a ski resort and rediscovered this bit of northern New Mexico. Since then, skiers have been coming to Taos Ski Valley for the incredible powder snow and the glorious sunshine. Several ski magazines are calling Taos one of the hottest places to ski, citing the steep, challenging terrain and trails for all abilities so all levels may ski together. Once again, Taos has the #1 ski school in North America, featuring the Ski-Better-Week. Grouped according to ability, each group remains with the same instructor, developing new, close friendships and improving skills.

A three-hour drive from Albuquerque, Taos Ski Valley combines lodging, restaurants, shops, and a beautiful mountain. The town of Taos is only 18 miles away and, with its Indian and Spanish heritage, is an interesting alternative for dining, shopping, and entertainment. The Ski Valley operates during the ski season only, which generally runs from Thanksgiving through mid-April.

Accommodations: Although there are inns and hotels in the town of Taos, every skier's dream is to be on the mountain. The Taos Valley Resort Association (800 number above) represents more than 95 percent of all lodging in and around Taos. For lodges right near the slopes—such as Hotel Edelweiss, Hotel St. Bernard, and the Thunderbird Lodge—rates for a one-week package run $1,320 per person double occupancy; besides your room, this package includes meals, lifts, and morning lessons. Condominiums right at the slopes charge $758–$1,105 per person for a one-week package; based on four people in a two-bedroom unit, this fee covers lodging, lifts, and morning lessons. All facilities offer a nightly rate, but the week package, known as a Ski-BETTER-Week, is good value for your money.

Dining: Whatever your dining mood, you'll be satisfied in Taos with more than fifty restaurants to choose from. On the mountain there are quick and easy stops like the Phoenix Restaurant and the Whistlestop Cafe serving hamburgers, sandwiches, and pizza. At the base, you can go really casual at the Snack Bar or delightfully international at the restaurant in the Thunderbird Lodge or very family-style at the nearby Amizette Inn. In the town of Taos, try Cajun and Creole at Carl's French Quarter, seafood at Casa Cordova, or Mexican at Casa De Valdez. And of course there's always your own fine cooking in your condominium!

Children's World: The Kinderkäfig takes children ages three to six. The five- and six-year-olds ski two hours in the morning and two hours in the afternoon. The three- and four-year-olds ski at least an hour in the morning and in the afternoon and have lunch, enjoy crafts, and play games indoors. A full-day is $55; a half-day is $30. The Junior Elite group covers ages seven to twelve and provides morning lessons and supervised afternoon skiing; the fee is also $55 a day. For your hot-shot teenager, the Teen group offers a lot of action for $54 a day, $30 per half-day including a bit of Nastar racing in the two-hour morning lessons. All of these rates include lift tickets. Taos Ski Valley also provides a KinderKare facility for one- and two-year-olds. Open daily from 8:30 A.M. to 4:00 P.M., the center provides indoor and outdoor play, stories, games, naps, and lunch for $45 per day, $30 per half-day. BébéCare nurtures infants from six weeks to one year for the same rate, or $10 per hour. All these programs are located in the 18,000-square-foot children's center, which includes ski rentals, ac-

Photo by Caven/Alpine, courtesy of Taos Ski Valley

cessories, cafeteria, and information center, all at the base of the Rueggli Lift.

Recreation: Partially located in the Carson National Forest, the Taos ski area is in the Sangre de Cristo Mountains, the southernmost part of the Rockies. The base village sits at 9,207 feet, and the peak towers above at 11,819 feet, affording skiers over 2,600 feet of vertical drop down seventy-two different slopes. This is a challenging mountain with just over 50 percent of its runs classified as expert; however, even the novice can feel that classic mountaintop high, since some beginners' runs descend directly from the peak. In a ski season that lasts from about Thanksgiving to Easter, the average annual snowfall is over 320 inches, plus snowmaking on more than 93 percent of beginner and intermediate terrain.

When you can pull yourself away from the open bowls, dramatic chutes, and lazy meandering-down trails lined with spruce and aspen, you might consider cross-country skiing, a sleigh ride, or an evening skier's seminar on such topics as avalanches and adjusting to the altitude. Skiers in January experience the added pleasures of Taos's jazz festival.

Late spring and summer brings great white-water rafting, trout fishing, mountain bikes and hikers, horseback riding, and golf. Six museums, art galleries, and music festivals entertain those less athletically inclined, and the Taos Chamber of Commerce (800–732–8267) even publishes a *Kid's Guide* with advice from local children.

Rockies

Colorado
Montana
Utah

Aspen Chamber Resort Association

425 Rio Grande Place
Aspen, Colorado 81611
(970) 925–1940 for guest information; (970) 925–9000 and
(800) 262–7736 for reservations

Big Sky of Montana

P.O. Box 160001
Big Sky, Montana 59716
(406) 995–5000, (800) 548–4486

The sky isn't really bigger in Montana—not by scientific measurements, that is. But don't tell the folks around here that. These die-hard Westerners believe they've got the market cornered on the best, biggest, bluest sky ever; and if you don't watch out, by the end of a visit here, you'll be a believer, too.

In the wintertime, skiing Lone Mountain (summit elevation 11,166 feet) can make you feel like it's almost possible to touch that beautiful, clear sky. Lone Mountain and adjacent Andesite Mountain are carved with seventy-five runs that add up to fine skiing at Big Sky. During the summer, these mountains and their evergreens, the sunshine and clean mountain air make the perfect setting for hiking, horseback riding, white-water rafting, and fishing as well as golf and tennis.

Open year-round, Big Sky is located in southwestern Montana just north of Yellowstone and is surrounded by rivers and national forests.

Accommodations: Huntley Lodge is at the base of Lone Mountain; the Explorer chairlift is right out the back door. The lodge has more than 200 rooms, some with views straight up the mountain, and an outdoor heated swimming pool, sauna, and Jacuzzi. Huntley is the hub of Big Sky, since events are posted in the lobby. Its dining areas and lounges also draw visitors.

Regular season rates are in effect from the beginning of February through the end of March and range from $177 to $218 per night for a double room. During the rest of the ski season (except Christmas), rates are reduced 15 to 20 percent. The larger loft rooms are more expensive, and children under ten stay free in their parents' room. Cribs and rollaways are $15. Summer rates at the lodge are $125–$145 a night for a double.

At the area's condominiums, the studios and one- to three-bedroom units have kitchens and fireplaces. While all the complexes (Stillwater, Skycrest, Lake Hill, Arrowhead, Beaverhead) are at the base of the mountain, the Arrowhead is closest to the lifts. During the regular winter ski season, rates are $135–$700 a night, depending on the unit's size. During the low ski season, rates are discounted 20 percent. In the summer, the condominium rates range from $97–$497. Some complexes feature heated swimming pools, saunas, and Jacuzzis.

Dining: If you are staying in Huntley Lodge or just cannot face cooking after a busy day, you can dine at the Huntley in the large dining room. In the winter, take the sleigh ride up into the mountains for dinner in a log cabin, and in the summer, join an outdoor Western barbecue. Next door to Huntley Lodge is a collection of shops, restaurants, and bars in the Mountain Village Mall. Here you'll find casual spots for pizzas, deli sandwiches, and delicious ice-cream sundaes. In the evening, Chet's Bar in Huntley Lodge is popular for its warm atmosphere, nightly entertainment, and regular game of poker.

Children's World: During the ski season, the Handprints on the Mountain Daycare Center in the Mountain Village Mall is open every day from 8:30 A.M. to 4:00 P.M. for children six months and older. Little ones enjoy a combination of indoor and outdoor play: sledding, stories, songs, and arts and crafts. The fee is $55 a day for eighteen months and older, and $65 for six- to eighteen-months old. The four- through six-year-olds at the center have ski lessons two hours a day in addition to their indoor activities. The daily rate for this group is $80. Older children six to fourteen years can enroll in the Ski Day Camp. The daily fee is $53 for an active 9:45 A.M. to 3:00 P.M. program.

The game room in Huntley Lodge, open from 10:00 A.M. to 10:00 P.M., offers video games and television. No special activities are organized for children during the summer, but any time of the year babysitting arrangements can be made through the activities desk at Huntley Lodge. The average rate is $8.00 per hour.

Recreation: The 4,180-vertical-foot-drop takes you through open bowls and tree-lined trails. The average annual snowfall is an amazing over-400 inches. Skiing starts mid-November (an opening guaranteed by snowmaking if Mother Nature is skimpy with her supply) and continues on into April. Whatever your level of skiing, you can join lessons at the ski school. Cross-country skiers enjoy treks over broad meadows and through stands of pine trees. Just 5 miles from Huntley Lodge, the Lone Mountain Guest Ranch maintains 45 miles of cross-country trails. When you're not on skis, swim in one of the heated pools or take a trip to Yellowstone for snowmobiling and sightseeing.

When the weather warms up, the mountains are terrific for hiking and backpacking. For horseback riding you can link up with Big Sky Stables through the activities desk in Huntley Lodge. You may prefer adventures in white-water rafting or the quiet solitude of fishing for prize-winning trout in the mountain streams.

The eighteen-hole golf course was designed by Arnold Palmer and is well situated in the mountain meadows. Play tennis (six courts, two of which are at the lodge) and volleyball, or relax with a Swedish massage or a leisurely guided nature walk, learning the wildflowers of Big Sky.

Breckenridge Ski Resort

Box 1058
Breckenridge, Colorado 80424
(303) 453–2918, (800) 789–SNOW
Website: http://www.ski-breckenridge.com

The town of Breckenridge is more than 130 years old, and skiing at Breckenridge is more than 30 years old. Quite a good combination! An old gold and silver mining camp proud of its history, Breckenridge is a charming town with carefully restored buildings that attest to its Victorian-era heyday. And the years of skiing have resulted in the development of 2,031 acres of skiing territory on four beautiful mountain peaks. All this skiing in a historic setting is a one-and-one-half-hour drive west of Denver—not so close that it is inundated by locals, yet close enough that once you land at Denver International Airport, your ski holiday begins with a scenic tour through the Arapahoe National Forest on your way to Breckenridge.

Like every Western mining town turned ski resort, Breckenridge has numerous hotels, vacation homes, and condominiums that can be investigated through the Breckenridge Resort Chamber (800–221–1091). Best known as a winter recreation area, Breckenridge is in fact open year-round. Beaver Run Resort (800–525–2253) and the Village at Breckenridge (800–800–7829) warrant special attention because of their locations and amenities. With lifts just steps away from either one, these self-contained resorts make life just a little bit easier for families. Besides their own restaurants and shops, each resort houses a child-care center.

Accommodations: Beaver Run is an attractive complex of granite and wood buildings just skirted by the Country Boy trail and is home to a high-speed quad chairlift. The hotel rooms are spacious, and condominium units have from one to four bedrooms. Fireplaces and private balconies are features of all the condominium units; the condominiums have fully equipped kitchens. Children twelve and under are free when staying with their parents, and cribs for infants and toddlers are provided without charge.

During the high ski season, February 1 through the first week of April, a double hotel room is $205 and a one-bedroom/one-bath condominium that sleeps four is $270 a night. During the rest of the ski season, rates are lower, with the exception of the holiday period at the end of December when higher rates are in effect. In the summer season, from late April to mid-November, the rate for a double room is $90 a night and $125 a night for a one-bedroom/one-bath condominium.

The Village at Breckenridge is a Western-style resort with 347 units, ranging from hotel rooms to condos; the Liftside Inn building features studio apartments; and Plazas I, II, and III house one- to three-bedroom condominium units. Most of the accommodations have kitchens, fireplaces, and balconies with views of the mountains or Maggie Pond, the ice-skating center. Children twelve years and under sharing a room with their parents are free; crib rental is available upon request.

The village defines the ski season as mid-December through March; during this time a double hotel room is $120–$195, studios are $175–$210, and a one-bedroom/one-bath condominium is $210–$290. Rates are lower during early and late weeks of the season and higher at holiday time. During the summer a double room is $100–$120 a night, and a one-bedroom/one-bath condominium is $130–$160 a night.

Dining: Elegant dining at Beaver Run takes place at Spencer's Steaks and Spirits Restaurant in a warm setting enhanced by oak and cane furnishings. Menu offerings include a selection of USDA choice beef entrees, seafood favorites, and other specialties like the "all you can eat" prime rib. The Copper Top Cafeteria and Bar are open winters only for skiers, but the deli is good for snacks year-round, and two bars provide evening and nighttime amusement.

For elegant dining in The Village at Breckenridge, try the Breckenridge Cattle Company, which features steak, game, and prime rib. The Maggie Restaurant and Cafe Breckenridge are casual spots open for breakfast, lunch, and snacks. Enjoy Italian food at The Village Pasta Company and casual pub fare at The Village Pub. Jake T. Pounders and Red River Billiards are ready to quench your thirst after that last, long run of the day.

In town more than five dozen restaurants and saloons (out West bars are called saloons—don't forget that!) offer atmospheres from quiet to lively and cuisines that run all over the globe—Mexican, Italian, Greek, German. A popular spot for steak and seafood is the Whale's Tail on Main Street. The ice-cream shop, also on Main Street, makes for a nice break during an evening walk.

Children's World: Breckenridge's children's centers offer kids ages three to seventeen a frolicking good time while they learn the joys of skiing in programs designed for specific age groups. Children's centers are located at both the Peak 8 and Peak 9 base areas. Parents must provide ski equipment, and lunch is provided for children enrolled in full-day programs. Reservations are recommended for children five and younger. Snowboarding instruction is also available. During the 1996–97 ski season, full-day lessons for three- to five-year-olds were $60, lessons for six- to twelve-year-olds were $55, and teen (thirteen to seventeen years old) classes were $45.

For children too young to ski or who don't ski, Breckenridge provides fun and nurturing environments. Children's centers are conveniently located at base areas: The Peak 8 Children's Center accepts children two months through five years and the Peak 9 Children's Center cares for children three to five years of age. Both centers include facilities that have everything kids need to enjoy their day: cribs, toys, art supplies, lunch facilities, and loving trained personnel. These popular programs fill up quickly, so make a reservation (required) by calling (800) 789–7669.

Recreation: If you said to some skiers that you'd found 138 trails, an average annual snowfall of more than 250 inches, a season from mid-November to mid-April, and a vertical drop of more than 3,398 feet, they might think you'd died and gone to heaven. Breckenridge gives you all this on its four interconnected mountains—Peak 7 is the latest addition in skiable terrain, while Peak 10 boasts the highest elevation, at nearly 13,000 feet. It also gives outstanding views over Summit County, 60 percent expert runs, 26 percent intermediate runs, 14 percent beginner runs, bowl skiing, above-the-timberline skiing, and lots of famous Rocky Mountain powder. You can line up a free guided tour of the mountains or plunge right away into group or private instruction.

Cross-country enthusiasts head to the Breckenridge Nordic Center, where more than 40 kilometers of groomed trails open up. Try snowmobiling at Tiger Run Tours; ice skating on Maggie Pond, at the base of Peak 9; and a horse-drawn sleigh ride to a steak-and-baked-potato supper in heated tents on the mountain.

At both the Village at Breckenridge and Beaver Run, you can jump into the indoor/outdoor pools, relax in one of the many outdoor hot tubs, or, if your muscles weren't tested enough on the slopes, finish up in the exercise rooms. An additional Beaver Run attraction is an indoor miniature golf course, where you can count on a fun family evening.

During warm-weather months venture out from the resorts and go biking through town, hiking in the woods, fishing in mountain streams, sailing on Lake Dillon, horseback riding on trails bordered by wildflowers, and white-water rafting on the Arkansas and Blue rivers. Breckenridge's eighteen-hole championship golf course, designed by Jack Nicklaus, opened in 1986. And during July and August, the mountains ring with classical and jazz music from the Breckenridge Music Institute.

The Broadmoor

P.O. Box 1439
Colorado Springs, Colorado 80901
(719) 634–7711, (800) 634–7711

As majestic as the neighboring Rocky Mountains, The Broadmoor reigns over Broadmoor Lake and 3,000 surrounding acres. The original hotel, known today as Broadmoor Main, was built in 1918 by Spencer Penrose, an enterprising man who made his fortune in gold mining in Cripple Creek (less than 20 miles from Colorado Springs) and copper mining in Utah. He dreamed of fashioning a Colorado resort along the lines of the grand European hotels that he had seen. The Mediterranean-style structure, with its pink-stucco facade, almost glimmers in the sunshine. Inside the Italian Renaissance trappings include wood-beamed ceilings, crystal chandeliers, gilt-framed mirrors, and hand-painted wall and ceiling decoration. Penrose's dream was realized—The Broadmoor fared well indeed when compared to its European counterparts. And the guests who followed were as impressive as the hotel, from royalty and presidents to movie stars and millionaires.

Over the years facilities and buildings were added to the original complex. Broadmoor South stands next to Broadmoor Main and is architecturally compatible with the original, because its design utilizes light-colored stucco for the exterior walls. Across the lake is Broadmoor West. A modern structure, it nonetheless blends well within the context of the resort as a whole. In May 1995, 150 new guest rooms were completed. The most luxurious accommodations on the property, the architecture of the new wing is reminiscent of Broadmoor Main. The newer structures reveal precise attention to architectural design, aesthetic decoration, and fine art. The resort is open year-round.

Accommodations: Some 700 rooms and suites are divided among the three Broadmoors. All are handsomely decorated and look out at either the clear blue Cheyenne Lake or the dramatic Colorado mountains; it's a tough task to find a view less than terrific. Broadmoor West features many rooms with private balconies. During the high season, from the first of May to mid-October, the European plan is $265–$355 a night. Suites are higher. Cribs are provided at no additional charge. For an extra $15 a night, a rollaway bed can be added to your room. Rates are lower during the remaining six months of the year, and are based on one to four persons.

Dining: On the top floor of Broadmoor South, The Penrose Room is an elegantly formal restaurant, with traditional menu, superb views, dinner music, dancing, and an Edwardian decor, with emphasis on elaborate styling. Charles Court, in the west building, offers fine dining without the formalities, yet still with wonderful lake views. One of the world's most extensive wine lists (more than 600 choices, with prices ranging from $12 to $1,300 a bottle!) complement such entrees as Colorado elk with lingonberry compote, Colorado striped trout, and black-diamond rattlesnake quesadilla.

Also at Broadmoor Main are the Tavern, exquisitely adorned with Toulouse-Lautrec lithographs, and the Lake Terrace Dining Room, opening onto the Sun Lounge, with palms, ficus trees, and a tiered Italian fountain. Sunday brunches here are an extravaganza featuring more than seventy items. Julie's, a sidewalk cafe along the west bank of Cheyenne Lake, offers a relaxed shirtsleeves-and-shorts atmosphere for sandwiches, salads, and burgers; while Espresso is a favorite stopping place for cappuccino, pastries, quiche, and eclairs. One of the merriest dining spots is the Golden Bee, an authentic English pub located behind and below the International Center; it is open for lunch and dinner and until the wee hours, with live ragtime and sing-alongs. The Golf Club Dining Room, in the new spa complex, is open for breakfast, lunch, and dinner and boasts "cuisine vivant" along with classic clubhouse favorites. Relax and find entertainment in any of six different lounges including the new Stars' Club and Cigar Bar. From piano music to full orchestra dancing to sports on the big-screen TV, it's all there for your enjoyment.

Children's World: Children ages three to twelve are revved up for active pursuits Monday through Saturday, mid-June to mid-August, Christmas and Easter, in the Bee Bunch Program. From 9:00 A.M. to 5:00 P.M., kids swim in one of the pools, explore the lake in a paddleboat, join games at the playground, and visit the zoo. And just wait until your child tells you about feeding the ducks! Golf, tennis, and cooking lessons or horseback riding provide more thrills, while games and crafts are quieter fun.

The youngsters meet again for dinner and games or a movie from 6:00 to 10:00 P.M. (summers only), granting their parents opportunities to sample the gourmet creations of the Broadmoor chefs. The children's meals are planned to ensure cleaned-up plates; the pizza, fried chicken, and hamburger dinners are favorites among the younger set and are included in the program cost of $40 daytime and $35 evening (for those five to twelve years old). The Toddler Bee Bunch Program is available 9:00 A.M.–2:00 P.M. for three-year-olds, at a cost of $25. Babysitting is available for $6.00 per hour, with a three-hour minimum.

Recreation: Golfing at The Broadmoor began when the original hotel opened in 1918. Donald Ross designed that first course and was followed by Robert Trent Jones, who added nine holes in 1950 and another nine in 1965. The Ed Seay course was completed in 1976. Once avid golfers discover the challenging variety of these fifty-four holes, the incredibly scenic setting, the high-quality equipment and accessories of the golf shops, and instruction with the resident pro, they may never explore the rest of The Broadmoor—and that would be a pity.

Twelve Plexipave tennis courts are located at the Golf Club; two of these are bubble-enclosed, allowing tennis play to continue through the winter. Both golf clubs include tennis shops, where you can purchase new equipment and attire or investigate classes and clinics.

An afternoon can be spent swimming at any one of three heated swimming pools at Broadmoor Main, Broadmoor West, and the Golf Club. Rent a paddleboat for a spin on the lake or a bicycle for a tour around the lake. Test a steady hand and a careful eye on the two skeet and three trap ranges, or stroll along One Lake Avenue to enjoy the twenty-plus shops.

The new Broadmoor Spa, Golf and Tennis Club is more than 90,000 square feet of luxury: state-of-the-art fitness facility, full-service spa, and private locker rooms with all amenities, including fireplaces!

A nonstop itinerary of off-property activities includes white-water rafting, hot-air ballooning, skiing, fly fishing, mountain biking, and hunting expeditions. Or perhaps you'll opt to take the famous cogwheel up to Pike's Peak. Check *The Broadmoor This Week* to stay abreast of the many resort activities.

C Lazy U Ranch

P.O. Box 379
Granby, Colorado 80446
(970) 887–3344

Ride 'em, cowboy! With a little time at C Lazy U Ranch, you could live up to this label. Experienced wranglers match you with just the right horse for you to call your own during a vacation stay, and they guide you through trail rides in the Colorado high country. Sitting at an elevation of 8,300 feet, the ranch sprawls over 2,500 acres, less than a two-hour drive west of Denver. A lot of territory to roam combines with warm sunny days that give way to cool nights—quite a setting for learning Western ways. For more than seventy years, C Lazy U has operated as a guest ranch. That adds up to a lot of experience, not only in riding and roping but also in welcoming and entertaining visitors. This working ranch is open for vacationers from mid-June to mid-October and mid-December through March.

Accommodations: About forty comfortable rooms and suites are in the Lodge and the guests' cottages that surround it. Seventy-five percent of these have a fireplace. During the summer and mid-December through New Year's, vacation stays are scheduled by the week, Sunday to Sunday. Guests can make reservations on a daily basis during the rest of the season.

Summer weekly rates per person are $1,200 to $1,650; Christmas weekly rates average $1,525 per person. Winter daily rates are $115 to $195 per person, and children receive a 20 to 40 percent discount. Children ages three to five are charged $200 a week less than the standard rate. These rates cover virtually everything you'll want or need during your visit: lodging, three meals a day, use of a horse, trail rides, use of the recreational facilities, and the supervised children's program.

Dining: At C Lazy U you'll get the hearty meals that you need to maintain an energy level consistent with the fresh air and outdoor fun. The warm, rustic dining room is in the Lodge, the main building of the ranch. Here guests sit at tables set for ten—a good way to make friends—for relaxed family-style dining. But don't expect baked beans and coffee in a tin pot. More likely, you'll have Black Angus prime rib or jalapeño-stuffed mountain trout, for this five-star, five-diamond resort has outstanding menus. Children and teens eat earlier with their counselors, and after dinner families regroup for the evening activities. Buffet lunches are often served near the swimming pool, and evening cookouts are frequently planned. The Lodge also houses a comfortable living room and bar, where drinks and hors d'oeuvres are served nightly at 6:30 P.M. Another bar is located in the Patio House, the recreation center adjacent to the swimming

Photo courtesy of C Lazy U Ranch

pool; enjoy an evening cocktail and swap tall tales with other guests about a day's adventure.

Children's World: The way they take to things so easily, the kids may turn into wranglers before you do. And with C Lazy U's special attention to youngsters, they've got a good shot at calling themselves cowpokes by the time they head home.

Starting at age three (the ranch does not provide care for younger children), kids get a good introduction to life out West. They learn how to ride (at age six they can go out on trail rides) and a little of how to care for and feed horses, and they go swimming and fishing—all under the watchful eye of trained counselors. Everyone is assigned a horse for the entire week, based on individual ability; and children are divided into three groups: three- to five-year-olds, six- to twelve-year-olds, and teenagers. The Kids Corral is a comfortable indoor children's place for reading, art projects, and napping. A Game Room offers billiards, Ping-Pong, and Foosball. Teens, as they much prefer, have their own separate program of riding, hayrides, and cookouts. The children's program is available from early June to Labor Day and from mid-December through March. The last week of August is Baby Week, when children under three years are accepted.

Recreation: Naturally, the main attraction of a ranch is horseback riding. From a string of 165 horses, you'll be assigned a mount that suits your ability. With experienced wranglers you'll ride the high country across mountain meadows, through tall evergreens, along Willow Creek. But there's a lot more to this ranch than just horses. Between trail rides sneak in a little fishing in the lake near the Lodge or at a secluded spot along Willow Creek, and have the trout for breakfast! Go hiking or spend an afternoon on the skeet range (the only activity not covered in the package rates), swim in the heated pool, or simply laze about nearby in the sunshine. Play tennis on two Laykold courts and racquetball.

For less strenuous activities you may seek out The Patio House, the principal recreation center, which includes exercise equipment, locker rooms, complimentary laundry facilities, game room, bar, TV room (good news—there's no television or phone in the rooms!), and a large, all-purpose activity room with fireplace. And when you fear that saddle sores and tennis elbow may set in, retire to the whirlpool and saunas. In the evenings you'll join in on campfire sing-alongs, square dancing, and rodeos, just so you don't forget you're out West.

During the winter season guests take to skiing—cross-country on the 15 miles of trails maintained by the ranch and downhill at Winter Park and Silver Creek ski resorts, 25 miles away and accessible via the ranch's complimentary shuttle service.

But winter activities don't stop there. Enjoy horseback riding in the snow or in the new, heated, 10,000-foot riding arena; or take a sleigh ride on an old-fashioned cutter and a world-class, ½-mile sled run; or try dog-sledding. Ride an inner tube down the tubing hill or behind a speeding snowmobile, and ice skate or play hockey or broomball on the groomed skating pond. Then snuggle in for hot drinks, the fireplace, Western dancing, and cowboy songs. Yippee-ay-a!

Club Med/Copper Mountain, Colorado

40 West 57th Street
New York, New York 10019
(800) CLUB MED
Website: http://www.clubmed.com

Club Med's village in Copper Mountain, Colorado, is in Summit County, famous for terrific downhill skiing and its Rocky Mountain powder. Seventy-five miles west of Denver, the village is surrounded by the Arapahoe National Forest, sits at 9,600 feet, and looks up to a glorious mountain with a summit elevation of 12,360 feet. Copper Mountain is open from early December to mid-April.

You might be thinking "Club Med and kids? It has a nice ring, but is this for real?" Yes, at certain Club Med destinations, the swinging singles image has been shed and whole families can partake in the attentive yet carefree spirit of a Club Med vacation. Mini-Clubs cater to the younger set and support the Club Med policy of "The children, don't leave home without them."

Accommodations: In four interconnecting buildings, five to seven stories high, lodging is provided in cozy rooms with twin beds. The views of the mountains and the valleys are truly beautiful. Club Med's "pay one price" philosophy relieves you of many hassles, including repeated searches for your wallet. A one-week stay runs $970–$1,280 per person, depending on the season; for children three to twelve, there's a 25 to 40 percent discount. This price covers accommodations, meals, the children's program, ski lessons, and lift tickets. There is no extra charge for cribs or rollaway beds. It's necessary to have a Club Med membership to vacation here. Annual dues are $50 per adult, $20 per child, and a one-time family fee of $30.

Dining: The main dining room, with its floor-to-ceiling windows (you don't want to miss those mountain views), is the setting for breakfast and lunch buffets and multicourse, table-service dinners. There's a more intimate restaurant on the lower level. The cuisine is French and is as elegantly presented as it is carefully prepared. Wine is served at lunch and dinner (free of charge). Located near the dining room is a large bar as well as a cozy fireplace where après-ski begins. For evening entertainment see the nightly show, drop by the disco, or perhaps find a good bridge game in the card room.

Children's World: The Mini-Club, directed by an experienced staff, offers organized activities for three- to twelve-year-olds. This optional, free program is available 9:00 A.M. to 9:00 P.M., Monday through Saturday during the ski season. Children can join the group or their parents at any time, depending on family plans.

Besides two hours of ski classes in the morning and the afternoon, kids go ice skating and sledding and have snow sculpture contests and arts-and-crafts classes. Don't worry about lunch and dinner; your child can enjoy the company of the counselors and other children at early mealtimes.

Recreation: Skiing at Copper Mountain just may lead to Rocky Mountain fever; with a 2,760-foot vertical drop, an average annual snowfall between 250 and 300 inches, and a season from early December to mid-April, it's not difficult to hit a skier's high. Fourteen chairlifts and seventy-six trails mean that long lift lines and crowded slopes are virtually unknown. The terrain offers beginner, intermediate, and expert runs, and Club Med's own ski school (two-hour classes mornings and afternoons) will guide you to

improved downhill techniques whatever your level of ability. Classes are frequently videotaped, so be prepared for review and analysis with your instructor in the evening. For cross-country skiers, there are 16 miles of marked trails; however, no instruction or equipment is provided. Ice skating nearby on an outdoor pond is another favorite wintertime sport, as is snowboarding, with lessons for beginners.

Other activities include aerobics and stretch classes, jogging, and hiking. When the body grows weary, it may be time for pure relaxation in one of the Jacuzzis or saunas. The Copper Mountain organization has developed an athletic facility outside the Club Med property; for a small daily fee, Club Med guests have access to the tennis and racquetball courts, exercise equipment, swimming pool, saunas, and steam rooms there.

Deer Valley Resort

P.O. Box 1525
Park City, Utah 84060
(801) 649–1000, (800) 424–3337
Website: http://www.deervalley.com

Skiing for most folks means a little bit of the rugged outdoors—windburned cheeks, the raw natural beauty of mountain vistas, fresh tracks through pristine powder. Deer Valley has redefined skiing somewhat. It's all of the above but with an added twist. Instead of the Western flair you'd expect in Utah, there's a more sophisticated European atmosphere at Deer Valley. This is warm hospitality with a heavy dose of pampering—from the valets who help you unload your skis to the quite comfortable chairlifts to the Gourmet Market in Snow Park Lodge.

Deer Valley, less than an hour's drive east of Salt Lake City, is actually three mountains: Bald Eagle Mountain, whose summit is 8,500 feet, Bald Mountain, which rises to 9,400 feet, and Flagstaff Mountain, with the summit at 9,100 feet. The hubs of activity are Snow Park Lodge at the base of Bald Eagle Mountain and Silver Lake Lodge at mid-mountain. Silver Lake Village is in effect the mid-mountain point, for it is from here that lifts ascend to Bald Mountain's summit. Snow Park Lodge houses a restaurant and lounge, the ski school, the ski rental shop, the children's center, and a well-stocked ski shop. Silver Lake Lodge has three restaurants and a smaller ski shop.

Both lodges are very tastefully designed; inside the columns are natural tree trunks at least 2 feet in diameter, and wood accoutrements abound—from the handrails to the ceiling beams, from the facial tissue dispensers to the trash cans. You'll find no plastic chairs and Formica-topped tables in the dining areas here—no indeed! Understated elegance and tasteful attention to detail are hallmarks of Deer Valley. The Deer Valley Club, the first country club for skiers, is already in its sixth season.

Accommodations: The Stein Eriksen Lodge, located at mid-mountain, is a Norwegian-style hotel built of stone and wood. There are 130 luxurious rooms and suites, starting at $450 a night in the winter and $175 in the summer. Shops, restaurants, a swimming pool, and a health club complement this lodge.

In addition, there are more than 500 units at the base of the mountain, along the trails, and near Silver Lake Lodge. The condominiums range from one- to five-bedroom units with fully equipped kitchens and living areas with fireplaces. Most have private Jacuzzis and individual decks or balconies; some include saunas and some feature ski-in, ski-out access. Daily maid service is available. There are substantial savings during value seasons, typically early December and early January, while rates increase during holiday periods. During the summer months rates range from $150 a night for a one-bedroom unit to $525 a night for a four-bedroom unit, with a minimum two-night stay. Contact Deer Valley Central Reservations for complete customized vacation planning.

Dining: Dining at Deer Valley is a gourmet experience. The Glitretind at the Stein Eriksen Lodge heads the list in elegance. The Snow Park Lodge and the Silver Lake Restaurant in the Silver Lake Lodge are "cafeterias."

What misnomers! Though they're self-service, the lavish lunchtime displays (homemade breads and pastries, salads, quiches, deli sandwiches) are hardly typical of the standard quick bite between ski runs. In the evening The Seafood Buffet is offered at the Snow Park Lodge (mmm—iced shrimp and raw oysters on the half shell). The Mariposa at Silver Lake Lodge features table service for an elegant candlelight dinner. All these provide interesting alternatives to gourmet cooking in your condo.

Children's World: Deer Valley's Children's Center is a state-licensed facility providing indoor supervision and activities for nonskiing children. Located on the main level of the Snow Park Lodge, the center is open daily 8:30 A.M.–4:30 P.M. during the ski season and can accommodate infants as young as two months of age. Prices for enrollment are as follows: two- to twenty-four-month-olds, $68 for full-day (with lunch) and $55 for half-day; two- to twelve-year-olds, $55 for full-day (with lunch) and $45 for half-day.

Recreation: There are seventy-three downhill runs, fifteen chairlifts, and a vertical drop of 2,200 feet. Combine these with well-groomed trails and a restricted number of skiers on a daily basis—what more could a skier ask for? The mountains are beautiful, and the attention to them and to the skiers is high quality. Full- and half-day private and group lessons are avail-

Photo courtesy of Deer Valley Resort

able. Cross-country ski lessons are also offered nearby; trails roll over broad open expanses and through aspen and evergreens. If you don't have a sufficient workout on the slopes, maybe the exercise rooms will test your limits. Then relax your weary muscles in one of the saunas or Jacuzzis. Though primarily a winter wonderland, Deer Valley operates year-round. In warmer weather guests enjoy 45 miles of lift-served mountain biking, scenic chairlift rides, the Utah Symphony Series, and the Deer Valley Summer Adventure Camp.

Flathead Lake Lodge

Box 248
Bigfork, Montana 59911
(406) 837–4391, Fax (406) 837–6977
E-mail: fll@digisys.net

Mix some city slickers with a few expert wranglers out in Montana horse country, toss in beautiful scenery and clear blue skies, and come up with quite a different vacation experience at Flathead Lake Lodge. On 2,000 acres in northwest Montana, just south of Glacier National Park, this dude ranch specializes in water sports and just about anything that has to do with horses, from riding them to shoeing them. The lodge is situated on the shores of Flathead Lake (15 miles wide by 30 miles long), and the surrounding timberland stretches up into the Rocky Mountains. The ranch is open from May 1 to October 1, and one- or two-week visits are standard.

Accommodations: The main lodge is the focus of activities and dining; in a warm and rustic setting, the old stone fireplace lures many guests to gather for cozy chats. There are guest rooms here and in the south lodge; some families find the two- and three-bedroom cottages particularly attractive. Many of the lodge rooms and the guest cottages have views of the lake. The weekly rate for an adult is $1,694; for a teenager, $1,253; for six- to twelve-year-olds, $1,064; for three- to five-year-olds, $833; and for infants and toddlers, $96. These fees include lodging, three meals a day, horseback riding, tennis, and use of the boats and sports equipment. Cribs are available at no additional charge.

Dining: Dining is a family affair, with good home cooking. Guests gather at the long tables in the lodge dining room or at the picnic tables out on the patio overlooking the lake. Everyone may sample buffalo or roast pig at an outdoor barbecue and homemade breads and pies. Children eat together before their parents, allowing grown-ups time to get acquainted and plan the next day's events. Sometimes adults meet in the Saddle Sore Saloon.

Children's World: The friendly staff—mostly energetic college students who can keep up with excited youngsters—guide children through the day's activities. They can swim, lend a hand with the daily chores, and learn to ride horses. Arts-and-crafts classes are offered from 10:00 A.M. to noon most weekdays. Children six years and older can join cowboys on the horseback-riding trails in the mountains. You might want to bring along a sleeping bag for your child; there's a campout in tepees near the ranch. Babysitting is also available.

Recreation: The great outdoors awaits you. Horses are a way of life here; ride 'em, rope 'em, or test your nerve and verve in competition. Take an early-morning breakfast ride to work up a good appetite, then enjoy a breakfast cookout amidst the tall pines. Old-fashioned Western rodeos are part of the evening activities.

Take a dip in the large swimming pool or the crystal clear waters of the lake. Sailing, canoe races, and waterskiing may fill your afternoons. Cruises on the lake are organized several times a week. Fish in the lake or the nearby streams, and add a trout to a cookout dinner or spin a good story about the one that got away.

It's easy to find partners for a game of tennis (four courts) and to organize Ping-Pong or volleyball. You might take a stroll along the wooded trails and pick berries. You can schedule full- or half-day excursions for white-water rafting, river tubing, and wilderness fishing. The National Bison Range, only an hour away, attracts many visitors; seeing real live buffalo is a highlight for kids—and parents, too.

Keystone Resort

Box 38
Keystone, Colorado 80435
(970) 468–2316, (800) 468–5004
Website: http://www.ski-keystone.com

Like many fine Western ski resorts, Keystone first attracted settlers in search of the rich minerals in its mountains. Today visitors flock here seeking light powdery snow and the mountain high for which the Rockies are known. At the base of Loveland Pass, 70 miles west of Denver, Keystone has ninety-one runs on three interconnecting ski mountains and a vertical drop of over 2,300 feet. The resort remains open year-round, so many folks, when summer rolls around, hang up their skis and head for Keystone's golf course, designed by Robert Trent Jones Jr., the Keystone Tennis Center, and the Keystone Music Festival.

Accommodations: River Run Village at Keystone Resort is the largest ski area development project in North America. When finished, Keystone will have an estimated 4,560 residential units and lodge rooms. To date, two new buildings have been constructed in River Run: Jackpine Lodge and Black Bear. Both buildings have ground-floor shops and restaurants, with three upper levels of mountain condominium homes. Upper-floor residential units total 61. A third building, Arapahoe Lodge, includes 36 upper-floor condominium homes. Rentals are available. Prices are yet to be determined.

The Keystone Lodge is an elegant resort hotel with more than 150 rooms offering mountain views, most with a private balcony. Facilities here include an indoor/outdoor swimming pool, sauna, Jacuzzi, and three restaurants. Nightly rates during the summer are $190–$230 for two people; during the ski season rates are $170–$236 a night.

The Inn at Keystone is a 6-story hotel with 160 rooms, just 200 yards from the lift. Rooms here are $130–$170 during summer, $135–$215 during ski season (from the end of November to the beginning of April). Children twelve and under stay free in the same room with their parents. Cribs are available.

In addition to River Run, 850 condominium units are arranged near the slopes, in the village, and bordering the lake; these studios to four-bedroom units have a fully equipped kitchen, and most have a fireplace. All complexes have a heated swimming pool, a sauna, or a Jacuzzi. In the summer one-bedroom units are $135–$195 a night, and a four-bedroom unit for eight people is $265–$360 a night. Winter rates are $140–$360 for a one-bedroom and $370–$960 for a four-bedroom unit. Package plans are offered for skiing, golf, tennis, and music festival vacations. A shuttle-bus service winds through the village and connects the mountain bases.

Dining: From romantic gourmet dinners in a mountaintop restaurant more than 2 miles high to family picnic lunches carried by llamas, unique and award-winning dining choices set Keystone Resort apart from other mountain resorts. The resort features more than a dozen dining options that range from gourmet six-course meals to a Western family-style cookout and include Summit County's only AAA four-diamond-rated restaurants—The Alpenglow Stube and Keystone Ranch.

At the Keystone Lodge, the Garden Room features continental cuisine and a Sunday brunch; the Edgewater is a casual restaurant open for breakfast and lunch. Among the numerous restaurants in the village,

you'll find Pizza on the Plaza; Idabelle's, for Mexican fare; and Out of Bounds, for a sports bar/nightclub atmosphere. Lunch and dinner are served at both the Keystone Ranch and Alpenglow Stube. In summer you can hop a hayride to Soda Creek Homestead—in winter a sleigh ride takes you there—for a juicy steak dinner.

Children's World: At Keystone youngsters start skiing at age three. The Mini-Minor's Camp is a program of introductory skiing and sledding and indoor activities for four- to five-year-olds. Graduating from this, a child joins the Minor's Camp for six- to eight-year-olds; more ski instruction is integrated into the fully supervised day. The fee for all day, 8:30 A.M. to 4:00 P.M., is $72, including lunch.

The Children's Center is located at the Mountain House base area of the mountain and provides nursery care for little ones as young as two months. The fees for the day-care centers are $46 a day.

During the summer Keystone's Children's Center provides attention for children two months to twelve years, 8:00 A.M.–5:00 P.M., in age-appropriate activities. Little ones are amused with a stock of toys; preschoolers enjoy nature walks, picnics, pony rides, and arts and crafts; and older children go swimming, boating, hiking, horseback riding, fishing, and take rides in the gondola. The daily charge for the program is $54; lunch is included except where baby food and formula are required. Babysitting services are also available, at an hourly rate of $8.00.

Recreation: With three interconnected mountains—Keystone Mountain, North Peak, and The Outback—Keystone offers terrain for skiers and snowboarders of all levels. Keystone Mountain offers mainly beginner and intermediate terrain, with night-skiing operations that keep the mountain open until 9:00 P.M. North Peak challenges guests with more intermediate slopes and runs that plunge down mogul-filled terrain. The Outback features only intermediate and expert runs. Some of Summit County's best tree skiing is found on The Outback. Skiers can find deep powder in open bowls adjacent The Outback. And the newly developed twenty-acre snowboard terrain park features two half-pipes. Nighttime lighting makes Keystone's terrain garden the largest night-snowboarding operation in Colorado.

The ski season opens at Keystone in mid-October (Colorado's earliest opening date), and the season continues into early May. Whether you're trying to figure out what a snowplow is or you're looking for perfection in powder skiing, the more than 350 ski and snowboarding instructors can guide you through the 1,749 acres of skiable terrain.

Other winter sports at Keystone are ice skating at the Skating Center in the village, cross-country skiing from the Keystone Cross-Country Center into Arapahoe National Forest (cross-country and telemark lessons are offered), snowmobile tours into the back country, sleigh rides, and indoor tennis.

Summertime at Keystone means golfing on the masterfully designed Robert Trent Jones, Jr., course; eighteen holes with a Scottish flair respect the woodlands, meadows, and a nine-acre lake. The course is open from June to mid-October; golf pros offer private lessons and clinics.

Keystone is a haven for mountain-bike enthusiasts. The resort offers a special program called Dirt Camp, which provides intense riding retreats for "mud studs" and "wannabes." Dirt Camp is a series of instructional mountain-bike camps. Even if you're a beginner and conquering single-track, Dirt Camp helps you hone your mountain-biking skills.

Another important summertime attraction here is the Music Festival. Ranging from classical to pop, the National Repertory Orchestra and the Summit Brass carry the season from June through Labor Day.

At the Keystone Tennis Center, two indoor courts permit year-round play, and an additional twelve outdoor courts expand summertime possibilities. Ball machines, video analysis, and group and private lessons aid the tennis player in his game.

Fishermen take to the local haunts for rainbow trout; boaters sail on

Lake Dillon (5 miles west of Keystone) or skim across Keystone Lake in a paddleboat or kayak. Bicyclists ride the paths along Snake River, and hikers plod along the trails through wildflowers and aspens into the national forest. Horseback ride from the Keystone Stables through the Snake River Valley (breakfast rides are specialties), tour the high country of the Arapahoe National Forest by jeep, go white-water rafting down the Colorado and Arkansas rivers, be treated to a lunch of rattlesnake meat and buffalo, or enjoy the great outdoors and mountain scenery on a gondola ride to Keystone Mountain's summit.

Reservations and more information on these activities (including dining at Keystone's award-winning restaurants) can be arranged by the Keystone Activities and Dining Center well before a guest arrives, so that everything is already in place at vacation's start. The number to call is (800) 354–4FUN.

Mountain Sky Guest Ranch

P.O. Box 1128
Bozeman, Montana 59715
(406) 587–1244, (800) 548–3392

"Just turn me loose, let me straddle my own saddle underneath the Western sky." At Mountain Sky each guest (ages seven and over) is assigned her own special horse. Careful matching of horse and rider according to the latter's age and skills ensures a compatible duo during a vacation stay. Under the guidance of experienced wranglers, you'll be swaggering like a Montana cowboy before the week is out.

Mountain Sky Guest Ranch has a rich history dating back to the mid-nineteenth century. This is no modern mock-up of Old West ranching. It was an active operation during the days of cattle empires and witnessed the excitement of the gold mining era. With its genuine Western flavor, Mountain Sky offers visitors a combination of "wide open spaces" and modern conveniences and comforts. Located just 30 miles north of Yellowstone National Park, Mountain Sky sits in Paradise Valley, in southwestern Montana. Surrounded by national forest and wilderness areas, the wooded mountainous landscape of Montana's high country is a beautiful vacation setting.

Accommodations: Guests are lodged in rustic but modern cabins; all have a refrigerator. Rates are $1,925–$2,345 a week for an adult, $1,680–$1,890 for a child seven to twelve years old, and $1,330–$1,505 for a younger child. These prices include accommodations, all meals, use of all recreational facilities, and a horse for each guest (except those six and under). Cribs are available at no charge. During the summer the vacation week runs from Sunday to Sunday; within a couple of days, you'll make friends not only with your horse but also with the other guests.

Dining: Meals are served in the dining room of the main lodge and at barbecue cookouts. Understanding that the atmosphere of the great outdoors can generate healthy appetites, the chefs often prepare hearty as well as gourmet meals. Rugged attire (jeans, boots) is standard most of the time; Tuesday- and Saturday-night dinners are a bit more formal. For good conversation and evening cocktails, drop by the Mountain View Lounge.

Children's World: In summer trained counselors guide children of all ages in a program of activities. The youth schedule includes arts and crafts, nature walks, and swimming. There's even a small fishing pond reserved for children. Children ages seven and older learn horseback-riding skills with the Children's Wrangler. With the exception of family cookouts, children can stay with their friends and counselors for evening meals. The game room for teens features Ping-Pong, a jukebox, and a pool table. There is no additional charge for these activities; the supervised children's program is part of the weekly rate. For children not old enough to participate, babysitting arrangements can be made.

Recreation: Horseback riding is the primary sport at the ranch. Mount-

Photo courtesy of Mountain Sky Guest Ranch

ing your own horse and exploring hundreds of miles of trails can be as invigorating or relaxing as you want to make it. Besides morning and afternoon excursions, guests enjoy evening dinner rides. In between take a dip in the heated swimming pool, play a game of tennis (two courts), or hike in the woods. Ping-Pong, volleyball, softball, and horseshoes are also popular games at the ranch. Anglers head to the mountain streams, where rainbow and brown trout are in plentiful supply. After active adventures, unwind in the hot tub or sauna. Capping off a fun-filled day, evening Western dances and campfire sing-alongs are frequently planned.

Park City Mountain Resort

P.O. Box 39
Park City, Utah 84060
(801) 649–8111; (800) 222–7275 for lodging information

Park City was originally a mining camp, in the nineteenth century. From the late 1860s to the 1930s, the wealth of silver in the mountains attracted miners with dreams of great fortunes. Today people flock to Park City not for the silver but for the incredible Utah snow.

As one local said, "Skiing is almost a religion here. People talk about when it snowed, how much it snowed, and what kind of snow it snowed when it snowed!" In the 1940s the potential of this snow was realized and the first runs were opened. By the 1960s the development known today as the Park City Mountain Resort had begun.

The town is at 6,400 feet, and summits rise to 10,000 feet. Just thirty-five minutes from Salt Lake City's airport and surrounded by the Wasatch Range of the Rocky Mountains, Park City is more than a mountain and luxury condominiums. The historic Main Street is lined with Victorian architecture containing shops, restaurants, and galleries and gives you a sense of what the Old West was all about. With a little imagination, you can just picture an old miner swaggering into a Main Street restaurant (it would have been a saloon in the old days), ready to make friends with some pretty dance-hall girl. The resort area is open year-round. A summertime calendar of events and activities can be obtained from the Park City Chamber of Commerce.

Accommodations: There are approximately 3,000 hotel rooms and condominium units in Park City at the mountain base, a couple of blocks from the runs, and throughout town. Prices vary depending on the proximity to the slopes and the amenities offered. The Park City Chamber of Commerce garners complete listings of accommodations in the area; call (801) 649–6100. A free bus connects all points in the town.

The Resort Center Lodge and Inn is at the base of the ski area and feature ski-in, ski-out convenience. Surrounding the ice-skating rink and above the many shops and restaurants of the resort center, the accommodations range from studios at $239 a night to four-bedroom units up to $999 a night during the regular season (late January to early April). Package plans that include lift tickets are offered.

The Silvertown Lodge offers one- to four-bedroom condominiums, each with a fireplace and kitchen. It is a couple of blocks from the slopes, and prices range from $134 to $215 a night for a one-bedroom to $240 to $399 a night for a four-bedroom unit, depending on the season.

Dining: With a well-developed resort village at the mountain base and a historic Main Street, the dining facilities are numerous, to say the least. Though most people lodging in condominiums find cooking at home convenient, the many eating establishments will probably entice you for a few meals out.

At the resort center are several refreshment spots, from the Cookie Bear, with delicious peanut butter–chocolate chip cookies, to the Rocky Mountain Chocolate Factory, with luscious bonbons and fudge, to Baja

Photo by Hughes Martin, courtesy of Park City Ski Area

Cantina, with its generous portions of Mexican dishes. Moose's serves burgers, and Food for Thought has deli sandwiches and pastries.

Three restaurants are on the mountain, one of which, the Mid Mountain Lodge, was built about 1898 and is one of the top twelve mountain restaurants in North America (as rated by *Ski* magazine). Enjoy a variety of entrees and sandwiches, either inside or out on the 10,000-square-foot deck. Summit House, at the top of the gondola, has lighter fare. Steeps, in the gondola building, is the largest. The private club on the second floor offers table-service lunch and live entertainment for après-ski along with full bar service. Enjoy the grill on the outside deck or homemade soups from the first-floor cafeteria.

Main Street opens up another realm of dining establishments: the Claimjumper, for steaks and prime rib; Cisero's, for chicken, seafood, and pasta dishes; and Texas Red's Pit Barbecue, for spareribs and beef brisket. At Prospector's Square the Grub Steak Restaurant features prime rib, steak, and seafood.

Children's World: Park City Mountain Camp is provided for five- to twelve-year-olds throughout the summertime. The day camp focuses on outdoor activities of all types, including hiking, mountain biking, swimming, tennis, and golf, plus additional activities involving arts and crafts.

The Kinderschule at the resort center entertains youngsters three to six years old in a variety of indoor and outdoor supervised play. The friendly bears painted on the walls of the entrance to the school greet children in the morning at 8:30 A.M. and hint at the fun that lies within. The friendly staff guides them in arts and crafts and games in between their one and one-half-hour morning and afternoon ski lessons. The fee for a full day of activities (until 4:30 P.M.), including snacks and a hot lunch, is $79. You receive daily reports on your child so that you can track his progress as a skier. Morning and afternoon ski lessons only (one-and-one-half hours each) are $43. The all-day mountain adventure, for older skiers, includes two hours of morning and afternoon lessons, plus lift ticket, for $89.

Children seven years and older can join group ski lessons; a five-day package plan that includes lessons and lunch is $355.

For younger children (eighteen months through kindergarten), Miss Billie's Kid's Kampus, a licensed child-care facility in Park City, is the logical alternative. Open year-round, Monday–Friday, 7:45 A.M. to 6:00 P.M., it also provides a "latch key" program for children up to nine years. Drop-ins are welcome. The cost is $55 for children up to three years, $50 for ages three and over, and includes lunch and a program of age- and season-appropriate activities. Call (801) 649–5437.

Recreation: With an annual average snowfall of 350 inches, a ski season from mid-November to the end of April, and 2,200 acres of skiable terrain, including ninety-three runs and bowls, fourteen chairlifts, and 3,100 vertical feet, Park City is one of the largest Rocky Mountain ski resorts. Whether you ride the new six-passenger high-speed chair, Silverlode, or the chairs up to Jupiter Bowl, you'll find runs to meet your whim and your expertise. Whether you ramble down gentle slopes past old mining buildings, take on the moguls between groves of aspen, or get knee-deep in powder, plenty of variety will keep you happy. There's even night skiing and riding, if you just can't bear to leave the slopes. Park City now allows snowboarding, too! Wolf Mountain is another whole mountain just down the road, and Deer Valley (see separate entry) is Park City's newest development. The ski school accommodates all ages and abilities in group and private lessons. Lessons are also available for cross-country skiers on a private basis.

Ice skating is another fun wintertime sport, and with the rink, rentals, and lessons available in the resort village, it's a convenient diversion. The resort village, which includes several restaurants, is also the center for many shops: ski rental and repair, fashions and ski accessories, gifts, T-shirts, toys, and handcrafted items.

Though primarily a wintertime resort area, Park City is a destination for summertime vacations as well. The clean mountain air, the plentiful wildflowers, and the great outdoors beckon you. Hiking, horseback riding, tennis and racquetball (at specific condominium properties, the Athletic Club, and the Racquet Club), golf, and bicycling are favorite warm-weather activities.

Snowbird Ski and Summer Resort

P.O. Box 929000
Snowbird, Utah 84092
(801) 742–2222; (800) 453–3000 for lodging and air reservations

Snowbird's diverse terrain includes some of the most challenging skiing in the world. Yet surprisingly, the size of its intermediate, novice, and beginner areas is greater than the total terrain of many notable resorts. Every night more than half the slopes and trails are groomed, paving the way for beginner and intermediate skiers, while leaving the rest for those who seek the light, dry Utah powder. Whatever your proficiency and desire, Snowbird accommodates you with more than 2,500 acres of wide-open bowls, gladed tree runs, steep chutes, nightly groomed trails, and cruising boulevards. From the new "snowcat skiing" in Mineral Basin to the terrific novice and intermediate terrain off the Thunder Chair, you'll be amazed by the sheer excitement of skiing the "Bird."

Here are a few facts about Snowbird: vertical rise of 3,240 continuously skiable feet; 2,500-plus skiable acreage; average annual snowfall of 500 inches; many lifts, including one aerial tramway, seven double chairlifts, one high-speed detachable quad, and snowcats; a ski season extending from mid-November through late-May; the longest descent, Gad Valley, at 3.5 miles; the longest designated run, Chip's Run, at 2.5 miles.

Snowbird enjoys one of the finest ski seasons in the world. Beginning in mid-November, the ski season regularly extends 200 days. In fact, skiers have even been known to celebrate the Fourth of July on the slopes.

Accommodations: A cozy slopeside pedestrian village, Snowbird harmonizes fittingly with the rugged, natural beauty of Little Cottonwood Canyon. Yet here you'll find all the services necessary to complete the perfect vacation. And everything at the resort—accommodations, restaurants, shops, skiing, and activities—is within easy walking distance.

Snowbird has three distinctive condominium properties: The Inn, The Lodge at Snowbird, and the Iron Blosam Lodge. Each offers homelike features, such as fireplaces and kitchens, with several different floor plans to suit your family's needs. Pools, saunas, exercise facilities, and other services are included or easily accessible. Snowbird's flagship accommodation, the Cliff Lodge, offers easy ski-in/ski-out access, fullservice child care, shops, and a business center. It is adorned with the decorative luxury of North America's foremost Persian and Oriental rug collection. Three restaurants, two lounges, and the world-class Cliff Spa and Salon make it the perfect place to retire after an exhilarating day on the slopes.

Snowbird's 57,000-square-foot conference center includes fourteen meeting rooms and a 7,800-square-foot ballroom. These facilities, uncompromising services, and a professional staff are the reasons Snowbird has been awarded one of the industry's highest honors, *Meetings & Conventions* magazine's Gold Key Award.

Dining: The dining at Snowbird is diverse. With many restaurants and lounges to please a variety of tastes and styles, Snowbird dining offers everything from Niçoise-Style Striped Sea Bass to Mountain-Grilled Burgers to Coconut Beer-Battered Shrimp. Live entertainment and other après-ski activities also complement Snowbird's winter season.

Children's World: Snowbird offers ideal family vacations. According to *Skiing* magazine, "Snowbird has come up with what might be the best family ski value at a major ski area." The resort was recently awarded the Family Channel's Seal of Quality. From family ski zones to the Kids Park Mining Town replica, Snowbird is certain to please young skiers. So don't bring the kids just because they ski for free; bring them because Snowbird is one vacation they'll always remember.

Camp Snowbird, located in the Cliff Lodge, provides state-licensed infant and toddler care. Available services at Camp Snowbird include daytime supervision, meals, ski lessons, and, most of all, a good time. In-room babysitting is also available to lodging guests. Make reservations two weeks in advance.

Recreation: Snowbird's Mountain Host program offers free guided skiing tours every day to acquaint guests with the runs and lifts best suited to their skiing abilities. All you need is a lift ticket and a smile to join the group and get better acquainted with the incredible mountain.

Almost as famous as the snow, and every bit as great, is the ski school. More than 200 professional instructors offer all-day or by-the-hour private and group lessons. Or, if you want to take your vacation to new heights, try one of Snowbird's specialized seminars that address the specific interests and needs of women, seniors, snowboarders, and experts.

Photo courtesy of Snowbird Ski and Summer Resort

The Cliff Lodge and the Snowbird Center house shops and boutiques specializing in products unique to Snowbird. From children's clothing to jewelry, from a general store to a pharmacy, and from ski rentals to Snowbird's own signature clothing line, you're certain to find what you're looking for.

Snowmass Resort Association

Box 5566
Snowmass Village, Colorado 81615
(970) 923–2000 for guest information;
(800) 598–2004 for reservations

Aspen is one heck of a fine mountain. With over 3,300 feet of vertical drop and exciting, challenging runs, it attracts very skillful skiers. But when talking Aspen skiing, you've actually got four mountains to consider: Aspen Mountain (sometimes called Ajax); Snowmass, 12 miles away; and Aspen Highlands and Buttermilk in between. A combined skiable terrain that totals over 3,000 acres provides more runs and variety than you could possibly test in a two-week ski vacation. Lift passes are valid for all four mountains. Aspen is chic and supports an active night life; Snowmass is devoted to its motto "A Mountain of Family Fun." But who splits hairs when the best of both worlds is all within 12 miles? Though best known for skiing, both resort areas are open year-round.

Aspen's origins are rooted in the silver boom of the early 1880s. Many of the charming Victorian structures have been preserved and renovated; today they house boutiques, art galleries, hotels, and restaurants. Skiing in Aspen started in the 1930s and really took hold after World War II during conscientious development of the area as a winter resort. Aspen is just waiting to tempt you. Folks here boast that 70 percent of their visitors return every year and more than 90 percent come back sooner or later. So if you give it a shot, you may just have to plan on being hooked.

Accommodations: Whatever your preference in lodging, you should have no problem finding the perfect place to hang your hat in the Aspen and Snowmass area. From moderate to expensive, from quaint to modern, all the possibilities seem to be here. For the most part, lodgings in Aspen are in the village; at Snowmass they're slopeside with immediate access to trails. This is not, however, a hard and fast rule, and because shuttle buses always cruise the roads, there's no problem getting to the lifts and from one mountain to another.

The Aspen Club Lodge is at the base of Aspen Mountain and includes a swimming pool, Jacuzzi, saunas, and restaurant ($170–$425 a night, higher for suites). Just across from the Little Nell Lift is Aspen Square, a complex of about one hundred condominium units that features a swimming pool and saunas; nightly rates range from $139 to $429, with a seven-night minimum for most of the season. The Hotel Jerome located on Main Street is a Victorian building more than one hundred years old; room rates are $255–$725 a night.

The Snowmass Lodge and Club in Snowmass Village combines hotel and condominium accommodations on 120 acres at the base of the mountain. The amenities include a restaurant and bar, indoor tennis courts (two), exercise equipment, swimming pools, and, for summer and fall holidays, eleven outdoor tennis courts and an eighteen-hole golf course. Double rooms start at $139 a night, going to $659 for a three-bedroom unit. They have a three-night minimum. Other hotels in Snowmass are the Wildwood Lodge, the Stonebridge Inn, the Pokolodi Lodge, the Mountain Chalet, and the Silvertree; among the more than twenty condominium complexes are Aspenwood, Shadowbrook, Crestwood, and Timberline. With close to one hundred hotels, lodges, inns, and condominiums in the Aspen area, it is indeed fortunate that the resort associations publish descriptive lists to help you sort through the possibilities. Inquire carefully about various pricing packages—five- or seven-day packages that include lifts and lessons, low-season rates, and family plans.

Dining: As with lodging arrangements, the possibilities in dining seem almost limitless. Whether you've got a hankering for pizza, quiche, fresh veggies and salads, a juicy steak, spicy Szechuan or Northern Italian cuisine, you'll find the right spot among the more than one hundred restaurants in and around Aspen. La Cocina Su Casa and the Cantina serve Mexican dishes, and steaks and prime rib are typical fare at the Steak Pit. And, of course, restaurants and refreshment stops are at the mountain bases and on the mountains. For sweets, you can stop by the Paradise Bakery or Pour La France.

Among the seventeen restaurants in Snowmass are The Stew Pot, featuring wholesome family fare; the Mountain Dragon, featuring Chinese food; and the premier restaurants La Bohème and Cowboys.

Children's World: Even the youngest traveling companion will not keep you from days on the slopes. From 8:30 A.M. to 4:00 P.M., Snow Cubs entertains eighteen-month to three-year-old children in a play program filled with puppet shows, stories, arts and crafts, snowman building, some skiing, and sledding; four- to six-year-olds participate in ski lessons as well as indoor and other outdoor activities in the Big Burn Bears program. The program is $78 daily or $360 for five full-days and includes lunch and lift tickets. Late-afternoon and evening babysitters are also available through Snowmass Ski School.

Powder Pandas is Buttermilk Mountain's ski school for three- to six-year-olds, 8:30 A.M.–4:00 P.M. Snowpuppies Ski School is Aspen Highlands' version of ski lessons and fun for three-and-one-half- to six-year-olds, 9:30 A.M.–3:30 P.M. The daytime programs include lunch and snacks at each of these locations and cost $72 at the Highlands and $78 at Buttermilk.

The children's classes at the Snowmass Ski School organize seven- to twelve-year-old skiers from 9:30 A.M. to 3:15 P.M.; the cost is $65 per day. Also at the Snowmass Ski School, a special teen program is designed to bring together by age and ability skiers thirteen to nineteen years old; besides skiing, picnics, races, and sled parties are planned. The cost is $60 per day.

Operating a summer program (June through August) for five- to twelve-year-olds, Camp Snowmass emphasizes a healthy, active outdoor schedule of fishing, hiking, swimming, nature walks, horseback riding, visits to the nature preserve, and picnics. Overnights are planned during the season. For a day's events from 7:45 A.M. to 4:00 P.M., Monday through Friday, the fee is $50 (lunch is provided for an additional $5.00). Five- and ten-day packages are available for additional savings.

Recreation: From the end of November to mid-April, skiing is on everyone's mind, and regardless of your skiing ability you'll have plenty of runs to schuss down. Aspen's reputation as a mecca for advanced skiers is well earned, with 30 percent of the runs down Ajax ranked as expert, 35 percent advanced, and the remaining 35 percent intermediate. But beginners and intermediates should not grow faint in the face of overwhelming ventures, for the other mountains accommodate the not quite so adept. Aspen Highlands is 50 percent intermediate and 25 percent each in expert and beginner categories; the total vertical drop is 3,635 feet. The vertical rise at Snowmass is almost 4,400 feet, and more than 60 percent of the runs are intermediate. Buttermilk with 2,000 vertical feet caters more to novices, with almost half of its runs designated for beginners. A teaching staff that totals more than 1,000 ski professionals can introduce a beginner to the slopes (except at Aspen Mountain) as well as help an expert perfect techniques in mogul skiing, snowboarding, and telemarking. At Buttermilk and Snowmass, look for special three-day, first-time-on-skis or -snowboard packages.

Wintertime fun continues with ice skating at the Aspen Ice Gardens and the Silver Circle, dogsled rides at Krabloonik Kennels, snowshoe tours, cross-country skiing, sleigh rides at Snowmass Stables and T Lazy 7 Ranch, snowmobiling, and hot-air ballooning (yes, even in winter!). Many of the lodging complexes have swimming pools and exercise equipment. The tennis and athletic clubs also provide opportunities for indoor workouts. Evening entertainment includes films, concerts, plays at the Wheeler Opera House, and classical music at Harris Hall.

Though skiing is practically synonymous with Aspen, this place does not turn into a ghost town when the snow melts. During the summer, the hills are alive with cultural events. The Aspen Music Festival, nearly fifty years old, runs from the end of June to the end of August and is complemented by the Aspen Community Theater, the Dance Aspen Festival, and the Snowmass Theater Festival. The Anderson Ranch Arts Center in Snowmass has a summer program of classes in photography, ceramics, painting, and printmaking.

You can just about have your pick of outdoor activities: horseback riding, hiking, jogging, rafting, kayaking, fishing, hot-air ballooning, and jeep tours. There is also lift-served mountain biking at Snowmass Ski Area. An eighteen-hole golf course is located on the west perimeter of Aspen; another is in Snowmass. Tennis courts at condominiums and racquet clubs dot the valley. But even in summer you have to take at least one gondola ride—to the top of Aspen Mountain for a spectacular view of this bit of the Rockies.

Vail Valley Tourism and Convention Bureau

100 East Meadow Drive
Vail, Colorado 81657
(970) 476–1000; (800) 525–3875 (outside Colorado)

Vail/Beaver Creek Central Reservations

P.O. Box 7
Vail, Colorado 81658
(800) 525–2257

Lots of folks talk of Vail and Aspen in practically the same breath. Usually these are people who have never visited either one. Granted, several similarities between the two come to mind: Both rank right at the top in excellent skiing, both are high in the Rockies west of Denver, both are chic and sophisticated, and to both have been appended newer developments that are more upscale and remote—Beaver Creek at Vail and Snowmass at Aspen.

Unlike Aspen's history as an old mining town, Vail grew up in the 1960s. The modern-day careful planning and systematic development give Vail its atmosphere; it is a well-laid-out, Alpine-style village designed with the pedestrian in mind (it's so nice that so few cars spoil the scenery). Actually, there are three village areas at the base of Vail Mountain—Vail Village, Golden Peak, and Lionshead—each with its own lodging, restaurants, and facilities, and each within walking distance of base lifts. In practical terms, though, since each abuts the next, most folks think of the tripartite as one friendly town. While Vail is 100 miles west of Denver, Beaver Creek is just 10 miles farther down the road. Opened in 1980, Beaver Creek, too, has been planned around a pedestrian village; in addition to the accommodations in the village, some lodges and condominiums are tucked among the grand spruce trees on the mountain. Shuttle-bus lines service the Vail Valley, within each village and between mountain bases. A year-round resort area, the Vail Valley also boasts of its summer beauty and offers art and music festivals, hiking, mountain biking, and more from April through October.

Accommodations: Lodging at Vail can be right at the mountain base a couple of skips from the chairlift and dripping with amenities, or back a couple of paces and not so overloaded with extras. Of course, the options

Photo by Jack Affleck, courtesy of Vail Associates, Inc.

are reflected in the rates. The Lodge at Vail, just steps from two chairlifts, has a heated swimming pool and a sauna, and some of its rooms feature a fireplace, balcony, and kitchen; daily rates for a one-bedroom condominium during the regular season, early February to early April, are $730–$775 per night. At the Lion Square Lodge, located at the lower terminus of the gondola, a one-bedroom condominium (regular season) is $395 to $445 a night; this complex has a heated swimming pool, sauna, and whirlpool and some accommodations include a kitchen, fireplace, and balcony. The Landmark faces the pedestrian area at Lionshead and rents a two-bedroom condo for $375 to $695 a night; the facilities include two outdoor hot tubs and a heated outdoor pool, and the rooms have a balcony, fireplace, and kitchen.

Within walking distance of Beaver Creek Village is the Charter at Beaver Creek, a ski-in/ski-out lodge and condominium property with balconies and indoor pool; daily rates range from $195 to $340. Beaver Creek Lodge is slopeside and the only all-suite property in Vail Valley; its rates are $285–$365. The Hyatt Regency at Beaver Creek is also ski in-and-out; in addition, it offers the Camp Hyatt children's program for ages three to thirteen. Rates are $380 to $470 and $290 to $355 in the summer. The cost of the children's program is $7.00 an hour; winter hours are Monday to Sunday, 9:00 A.M.–10:00 P.M.; summer hours are 9:00 A.M.–4:00 P.M. Sunday through Wednesday and 9:00 A.M.–10:00 P.M. Thursday though Saturday.

The rates quoted are in effect during the regular season (early February to early April); Christmastime rates are higher. Summer rates can be as much as 50 percent lower than the winter rates. The January value season represents approximately a 20 percent savings over regular rates; during late November to the third week of December and in April, further savings can be realized. Discounts for children are just about universal. Some package plans include lodging, lift tickets, and group lessons. The options are numerous, and fortunately, the resort associations at Vail and Beaver Creek publish detailed, descriptive accounts of their accommodations and packages. Cribs are available at most facilities upon request.

Dining: Hungry for a hamburger? Eager to savor a juicy steak? Or is Mexican fare your idea of the perfect après-ski dinner? In the Vail Valley all this is possible, plus Italian, Chinese, French, and German food. With more than 110 restaurants and bars, there is lots of variety. Many restaurants are right in the lodges, such as the Lodge at Vail, Lion Square Lodge, the Landmark, and the Charter at Beaver Creek. Others, like McCoy's and the Coyote Cafe, are in the villages at the base of the lifts or in the pedestrian areas.

More are on the mountains: Cook Shack at Vail and Spruce Saddle and Rafters at Beaver Creek. These are not just quick, cafeteria-style mountainside rest stops; some hit gourmet standards. Whenever weather permits, outdoor barbecues are planned at the mid-mountain points. Many of the restaurants have children's menus—just ask.

Children's World: Even a two-month-old can comfortably visit Vail Valley. At Beaver Creek and at Golden Peak in Vail, the Small World Play School entertains little ones two months to six years old from 8:00 A.M. to 4:30 P.M. daily. The toddlers and preschoolers enjoy games, songs, crafts, and indoor and outdoor play in a schoolhouse atmosphere. Separate playrooms for ages two to eighteen months, nineteen to thirty months, and preschoolers offer closer supervision. The cost is $57 a day.

The Children's Skiing Center operates out of three locations—Lionshead, Golden Peak, and the Village Hall at Beaver Creek (so convenient no matter where you're staying!)—and divides children into two groups (three- to six-year-olds and six- to twelve-year-olds) for daily lessons from 8:00 A.M. to 4:30 P.M. Both groups have some indoor activities as well as skiing; the older children's schedule concentrates more on skiing. These programs average $75 a day, including lunch.

In summer from early June to late August, five- to ten-year-olds can join Camp Vail, sponsored by the Town of Vail Recreation Department. On weekdays from 8:00 A.M. to 5:00 P.M., kids gather for mountain hiking, gymnastics, swimming, arts and crafts, films, and nature studies. The daily fee is $38 a child. More information is available by calling (970) 479–2292.

Recreation: The name of the game is skiing, and the Vail Valley has all the ingredients for an excellent ski holiday. In the middle of the White River National Forest, Vail Mountain rises to 11,250 feet; at Beaver Creek the summit is 11,440 feet. The vertical drop is more than 3,150 feet at Vail and close to 3,350 feet at Beaver Creek. An average annual snowfall between 300 and 350 inches (and an artificial snowmaking system) accounts for a season lasting from late November to mid-April.

Vail and Beaver Creek skiable terrain totaling 5,641 acres (lift tickets for the two mountains are interchangeable) provides variety for all levels of skiers, from gentle beginner slopes to challenging intermediates to exciting mogul and bowl skiing. At Vail the runs are ranked 32 percent beginner, 36 intermediate, and 32 percent advanced; at Beaver Creek the breakdown is 19 percent beginner, 43 intermediate, and 38 percent advanced.

So that you can cut tracks through the Rocky Mountain powder in style, a very large ski school (1,200 instructors!) can assist you. In addition to the typical group and private lessons for all ability levels, the Vail/Beaver Creek Ski School offers free Meet the Mountain introductory tours: a morning of skiing with guest services staff who acquaint you with the area's history and topography, classes with videotaped analysis, and high-powered workshops in mogul and powder skiing. Or enroll in lessons in cross-country skiing, which is so refined here that distinctions are made between back-country skiing, telemark skiing, and track skiing.

Other wintertime sports include ice skating at Dobson Ice Arena or Nottingham Lake, snowmobiling at Piney Lake, and ice fishing. An evening outing in a horse-drawn sleigh may be the right way to finish off a perfect day. Indoor evening entertainment includes nightclubs and movie theaters; favorite haunts for kids are the video arcades and the Vail Youth Center.

Even after the last skier comes down the mountain in late spring, fun in the Vail Valley continues. As in the winter, summertime activities focus on the beautiful outdoors. Hiking through stands of aspens along the trail systems up Vail Mountain and Beaver Creek Mountain, biking on paths through wildflowers, and fishing in mountain streams get you back to nature. Ride horseback at four Eagle Ranch, Beaver Creek Stables, and Piney River Ranch, or muster up your courage for river rafting with Timberline Tours or Nova Guides.

Of the five eighteen-hole championship golf courses in the valley, one was designed by Jack Nicklaus and one (the Beaver Creek Course) by Robert Trent Jones, Jr.; the clear mountain air and spectacular scenery lead to invigorating play. In Vail the twenty tennis courts, where clinics and lessons are scheduled, are located near Lionshead and Gold Peak; another twenty courts are scattered throughout the valley. And for purely taking in the scenery, ride the gondola or a chairlift.

West

California
Idaho
Nevada
Oregon
Washington

The Alisal Guest Ranch

1054 Alisal Road
Solvang, California 93463
(805) 688–6411, (800) 4–ALISAL, Fax (805) 688–2510

In the Santa Ynez Valley of southern California is a real working cattle ranch—The Alisal (from the Spanish word meaning "grove of sycamores"). Some things just don't change—cattle have been grazing here for almost 200 years. Fifty years ago the current owner's father, a cattleman himself, decided to open the ranch to guests. Today visitors enjoy the atmosphere of an active ranch and the facilities of a good resort on this 10,000-acre spread. Only forty minutes from Santa Barbara and two hours from Los Angeles, The Alisal is a welcome haven to harried city-dwellers. It is open year-round.

Accommodations: Decorated in classic California ranch design, seventy-three cottages accommodating up to 200 guests are clustered near the swimming pool and tennis courts or overlooking the golf course. All have a wood-burning fireplace; some have an outside patio. Based on a modified American plan, rates range from $325 to $400 a night, double occupancy; children three through five years are $40, and those ages six and older are $65 a night. Three-bedroom bungalows are available for larger families; these start at $500 a night for four people.

Dining: The Ranch Room serves breakfast (a lavish buffet or à la carte) and dinner. Jackets are required for men at the evening meal, ladies must dress appropriately, and children are discouraged from wearing jeans, shorts, T-shirts, or tennis shoes. Parents with small children are encouraged to have dinner at 6:30 P.M., before the peak hours of 7:15 to 8:15 P.M. Lunch (not included in the room rate) can also be taken at the Chuckwagon Grill poolside snack bar and at the Ranch Course Grill (open from 8:00 A.M. to 3:00 P.M.) on the golf course. The River Grill is open daily from 7:00 A.M. to 8:00 P.M. for all meals. Maybe once in a while you'll saddle up early for a breakfast ride or join a poolside steak fry. The Oak Room Lounge, an inviting room with a large fireplace, is decorated in warm rustic colors and Indian-style rugs. Cocktails and complimentary appetizers are served here, and stories are shared. It's adults only after 8:00 P.M., with entertainment and dancing beginning at 6:30 P.M. During the summer and holidays, The Waggin' Tongue Lounge, by the pool, is open daily from 11:30 A.M. to 5:00 P.M.

Children's World: At holiday times and all summer long, counselors lead children four to twelve years old in an active schedule of hikes, scavenger hunts, arts and crafts, volleyball, and croquet.

From age seven children can participate in horseback riding on the trail rides or in private lessons. Younger children get lead-around corral rides, riding, and equestrian-care lessons. Everyone learns more about ranch animals at the Petting Zoo. Children love the lake, and even though swimming is not allowed, fishing, boating, and canoeing are. Evening campfires with sing-alongs and stories are even nicer by a lake. A kids' Mini-Rodeo is staged weekly in summer—this is every kid's dream of being a cowboy come true, and after watching the wranglers perform, they get to participate in branding (leather or wood), roping, and rodeo games; a Western barbecue completes the evening. In the summer the children's program (no charge) runs seven days a week, all day. Evening events may include a movie, storytelling, or a talent show. During the winter supervised arts and activities go from 10:00 A.M. to 2:00 P.M., with golf, tennis, and horseback-riding lessons filling in the other times. While the program itself is free, some things, like lessons and horseback riding, do have a charge. Check the daily program.

Now there are weekend activities for teens, generally involving their favorite things: eating, music, and sports.

Recreation: Saunter over to the barn and stables to be matched with the perfect mount for the twice-daily trail rides and occasional breakfast rides ($50 per ride). Thirty different trails meander through oak and sycamore groves on the rolling hills and along the lake. Wranglers are happy to share a bit of advice and maybe some tall tales along the way.

But the fun doesn't stop at the end of a ride. The gently rolling fairways of two eighteen-hole golf courses are graced with eucalyptus as well as oak and sycamore trees and sometimes a grazing deer or two. Each of the two championship golf courses, The River Course and The Ranch Course, has distinct characteristics shaped by its unique terrain. Driving range, putting green, and practice trap can keep you so busy you'll ride off into the sunset on a golf cart rather than a horse! The resident pro and the pro shop can help with anything from lessons to new equipment. On the tennis courts (seven in all), you're likely to find a good game from 8:00 A.M. to 5:30 P.M. or the resident pro conducting lessons (private and groups).

If your interests are more wet-and-wild, you might swim in the large outdoor heated pool or head to the lake and hop aboard a sailboat, rowboat, or canoes. Even beginners find lots of enjoyment in the sailing and fishing lessons offered. The lake—man-made, but mature and more than ninety acres in size—is stocked with bass, bluegill, and catfish, much to the delight of every fisherman.

After riding, golfing, playing tennis, swimming, sailing, and fishing, you can always jog; join a guided nature walk; or play volleyball, badminton, horseshoes, shuffleboard, croquet, and archery. Tired yet? Indoors you might play pool or Ping-Pong in the recreation room or relax in the library with a good book or a board game by the fire. Be sure to save energy for the evenings, filled with square dancing, cookouts, and movies.

Coffee Creek Ranch

HC 2, Box 4940
Trinity Center, California 96091
(916) 266-3343

Coffee Creek Ranch is located in northern California, approximately 300 miles north of San Francisco. Surrounded by the Klamath and Shasta National Forests, the ranch covers 127 acres along Coffee Creek and is home to wranglers and dudes alike. Whether you are an old pro at horseback riding or a greenhorn mounting up for the first time, the ranch hands will ensure that your horse and your excursion match your abilities. You can roam this territory all day long or ease into your new cowboy lifestyle more slowly with a half-hour lesson or a two-hour trail ride.

Accommodations: The fifteen cozy, secluded cottages (one or two bedrooms) are scattered among the trees. Weekly rates during the summer are $740–$760 for an adult, $720–$740 for a teenager, $620–$640 for a three- to twelve-year-old child, and $250 for little ones under three. Rates are approximately $95 less per person the rest of the year. Cribs, playpens, and high chairs are provided at no extra charge. Besides lodging, these prices include three meals a day and all recreational activities. Horseback riding is priced separately for the summer but is included in the lower rates for spring and fall.

Dining: Recognizing the healthy appetites that fresh air and exercise can generate, the main dining room serves up hearty, nutritious meals with fresh fruit and vegetables, Black Angus beef, and homemade bread. Outdoor barbecues and poolside cookouts are friendly evening events. Beer and wine are served in the Pony Room.

Children's World: In the summer months the youth program, a complimentary service operating 9:00 A.M. to 5:00 P.M., Sunday through Thursday, attracts children ages three to seventeen. On its fun-filled schedule are pony rides, archery, nature walks, canoeing, gold panning, games, and crafts. For children under three the weekly rate includes babysitting while you're out on the trail. If additional babysitting is required, you can make arrangements for $3.00 to $4.00 an hour.

Recreation: Saddle up and head into the wilderness for an all-day ride or a two-hour ride. You'll venture up into the mountains and go through the wooded landscape along a clear fresh stream; maybe you'll spot a deer or a bear. Even novice cowpokes with a few lessons soon experience the friendly spirit of a trail ride.

When taking a break from riding, you might swim in the pool or in the creek; play volleyball, Ping-Pong, badminton, shuffleboard, and horseshoes; or hop aboard a hayride. Locals say that Coffee Creek yields up some mighty fine trout, so an afternoon with rod and reel may turn into a fresh fish supper. Perhaps you'll test your keen eye at the archery range, the rifle range, and the trapshoot, or save your energy for evening square dancing.

The Inn of the Seventh Mountain

18575 Southwest Century Drive
Bend, Oregon 97702
(541) 382–8711, (888) 466–7686

A vacation in the woods and mountains of the great Pacific Northwest, the serenity of hiking in the forest, and the excitement of exploring the De-schutes River whisk you away from city life and everyday routines. The Inn of the Seventh Mountain, located in the Cascade mountain range of central Oregon, is a year-round family resort that boasts a cool forest setting and warm hospitality. The recreation department at the inn plans activities for every member of the family, concentrating on water sports, swimming, ten-nis, and raft trips on the river in the summer and ice skating, cross-country skiing, and sleigh rides in the winter. Wintertime also means the thrill of downhill skiing at nearby Mount Bachelor (only 14 miles from the inn).

Accommodations: You can choose from a variety of accommoda-tions, from a lodge room to a full condominium apartment, depending on the size of your group. Most of the lodge rooms have a private balcony; the condominium units have one to three bedrooms, fireplace, kitchen, and balcony. Some of these units can sleep up to ten people. The architecture is modern and rustic, the natural-wood facades blending well with the wooded landscape. Prices range from $59 to $299 a night, depending on the size of the accommodation and the season (summer and fall are slightly higher than winter and spring). Cribs are available at no extra charge.

Dining: The Poppy Seed Cafe serves homestyle breakfasts, lunches, and suppers. Josiah's, open for dinner only, features seafood specialties and Northwest cuisine. For a light lunch or dinner, pick up a sandwich or salad at the Mountain Market. The lounge is open every night.

Children's World: In addition to individual babysitting, which the staff can help you arrange, events are scheduled all day long for your child's en-

joyment. In summer and winter the recreation office publishes a flyer, *This Week at the Inn,* to help you keep track of all the activities. At Camp 7, a supervised play program for children ages four to eleven, a daily charge of $25 buys lunch, arts-and-crafts classes, movies, and more from 9:00 A.M. to 4:00 P.M. each day. Your child might also participate in a tennis clinic, take a hayride or a sleigh ride, search out treasures on a scavenger hunt, or hop aboard the children's storybook train. For some events, no fees are charged; others are priced individually (for example, $6.00 for a half-hour swimming lesson). There are also two playgrounds and a wading pool.

In season the Mount Bachelor Ski School (541–382–2607) offers lessons for youngsters. The Children's Ski School, called Mountain Masters, is for ages four to twelve. Divided by age (four to six and seven to twelve) and also by level of ability, several options are available. Full-day, including lunch, is $45 for the younger children, $55 for the older group. Rentals are $5.00 extra. Morning or afternoon sessions (two and one-half hours each) cost $32 for ages four to six years and $42 to $47 for ages seven to twelve. Teens join the adult lessons for $30 to $40. Reservations are recommended.

The West Village Main Lodge, at the base of the mountain, has a day-care center for little ones six weeks to six years old; activities are planned from 8:30 A.M. to 4:30 P.M. The fee is $31.00 a day or $7.50 an hour. Lunch is an additional $5.00. Sunrise Lodge now has child care available. Rates and hours are the same.

Recreation: In summer you just have to discover the beauty of the Deschutes River. Take a relaxing canoe ride and get back to nature, or join a moonlight raft trip. For the more daring souls, there are guided white-water raft trips through the rapids. If you prefer to take in the scenic river from land, horseback riding is a great alternative; group trail rides run along the river and into the Deschutes National Forest. The National Forest is also a picturesque haven for hikers and joggers. For the fisherman the recreation office arranges trips to the favorite spots with a naturalist guide. Spend an afternoon in sailboarding or waterskiing classes.

Back at the Inn take a dip in one of the two pools, rent a bicycle, play a good game of tennis on one of the four Plexipave courts (group clinics and private lessons are offered), work out in an aerobic exercise class, try your talents in an arts-and-crafts class, go rollerskating, or get lucky in a bingo game. The rec office organizes all sorts of ball games—softball, volleyball, football, lacrosse, and soccer. Join a hayride, complete with a stop for a marshmallow roast, play Ping-Pong, take in a poolside movie, or head to the video-game room. Then relax in the sauna or one of the hot whirlpool baths.

The Oregon High Desert Museum, just 6 miles south of Bend, discloses the natural and cultural history of this region. The museum makes for a fun as well as educational afternoon.

This part of Oregon experiences beautiful Indian summers, so activities continue well into the fall. During the winter months the inn's special events include ice skating, sleigh rides, cross-country skiing (with lessons for novices), and horseback riding in the snow-covered landscape.

The Inn is the closest lodging facility to the Mount Bachelor ski resort and provides daily transportation to the mountain base. With 3,100 vertical feet, 40 runs, double and triple chairlifts, and plenty of dry powder, Mount Bachelor means excellent downhill skiing for all levels of ability. The five lodges at the mountain have restaurants for breakfast, lunch, snacks, and cocktails; ski shops; and the ski school, which offers group lessons for all ranges of expertise as well as private lessons. The season lasts long here, attracting many visitors late into spring. The summit season even extends into the summer.

Konocti Harbor Resort and Spa

8727 Soda Bay Road
Kelseyville, California 95451
(707) 279–4281, (800) 660–LAKE

Konocti Harbor Resort and Spa is a lakeside resort in northern California, approximately two and one-half hours from San Francisco. If you're driving from the city or other points south, your vacation begins with a tour of the Napa Valley wine country on your way to Konocti. Open year-round, the inn sits beneath the 4,300-foot peak of Mount Konocti (an extinct volcano) on the southern shore of Clear Lake, which stretches 25 miles by 8 miles. All this clear blue water of California's largest lake provides the setting for much of Konocti's recreation: swimming, boating, and fishing. Although today you'll find just happy, active visitors heading to the water, a romantic Indian legend tells of a saddened princess whose many tears formed the lake.

Accommodations: Hotel rooms, apartments, and beach cottages comprise the 266 guest units at the Konocti. All have different features, but families like the beach cottages for their convenient location and kitchen, open-air porch, and space. Some rooms include a private balcony, and most afford views of the lake. The location of some make the marina easily accessible, while others are near the tennis courts. Sixteen deluxe apartments, opened in 1989, are situated near the spa. The apartments and cottages have a complete kitchen and living room, and many have been recently renovated.

During the high season (May through October), a double room is $49–$85 a night, and the apartments and cottages for four are $135–$175 a night. Lower rates are in effect the rest of the year. Children eighteen years and under staying in their parents' room are accommodated free of charge. Rollaway beds and cribs are available for $10 a night. Tennis, fishing, spa, and golf package plans are offered.

Dining: For a relaxing evening meal, try the Classic Rock Cafe, which is open for breakfast, lunch, and dinner. Adjacent to the two pool areas are snack bars so that you don't have to interrupt a lazy day of sunning for refreshments. For evening entertainment The Full Moon Saloon beckons.

Children's World: Kids at Konocti practically live in the water, with hours spent on the lake swimming, boating, and fishing. They also take hikes and nature walks, play horseshoes, and putt around the eighteen holes of peewee golf. The events start at 10:00 A.M. Monday through Friday, break at 4:00 P.M., only to pick up again from 5:00 to 10:00 P.M. for a night camp. The children's programs are open only in the summer and the fee is $15 for each session. Little ones particularly like the two wading pools and the playground equipped with a slide, swings, and monkey bars, while those a bit older head to the recreation center for Ping-Pong, pool, and video games. Babysitting in the evening runs about $5.00 an hour.

Recreation: With Konocti's full-service marina, you can take your pick of water sports. Dock your own boat here or rent a paddleboat, waverunner, motorboat, or sailboat for an adventure on the lake. Go fishing in these waters where the rewards are many: largemouth bass, trout, crappie, and catfish. There's even a bass-fishing pro to advise you. Waterski across the lake, or board the *Konocti Princess,* a nostalgic paddle wheeler, for an afternoon excursion. Swim in the lake waters from the small sandy beach, or do laps in one of the two Olympic-size pools overlooking the lake. The new Dancing Springs Health Spa is designed to pamper you a bit. This facility features an indoor pool and capable personnel who will help you relax with a massage, facial, or herbal body wrap. Take a fitness class or work out with free weights or cardiovascular equipment if you're feeling more energetic.

The eight tennis courts are lighted for evening play, and lessons with the tennis pro are available. After a good practice session with a ball machine, reward yourself with a new accessory from the tennis shop.

Five area golf courses, all within 20 miles, honor Konocti's golf packages. Round up a fast-paced game of softball, basketball, volleyball, or Ping-Pong, or slow down to a more relaxing tempo with horseshoes and shuffleboard. While jogging and hiking, explore the scenic, hilly terrain that borders the lake.

La Costa Resort and Spa

Costa del Mar Road
Carlsbad, California 92009
(619) 438–9111, (800) 854–5000

La Costa is a luxurious resort and a serious spa. In fact, it was the first establishment to revive the spa regimen as Americans became more health-conscious in the 1960s. Today you can pursue a program of exercise and sound nutrition, redefining your lifestyle after years of sedentary executive matters; or you can indulge in a program of sheer pampering, relieving the stress and tensions of the business world.

Located in Carlsbad, just thirty minutes north of San Diego and ninety minutes south of Los Angeles, La Costa enjoys lovely southern California weather and a picturesque setting of rolling hills.

Accommodations: Rooms, suites, and private homes number 478. They are situated around courtyards, near the tennis facilities, adjacent to the spa, and along the golf courses. Room rates are $250–$440 a night; one- and two-bedroom suites are $500–$2,200 a night, and the commodious two- to five-bedroom executive homes are $1,150–$1,650 a night. Children under eighteen staying in their parents' room are free; cribs are provided without charge. Be sure to inquire about the spa, golf, and tennis package plans.

Dining: La Costa's four restaurants offer variety in cuisine and ambience. For a casual atmosphere Brasserie La Costa is open for breakfast, lunch, and dinner. Besides tempting fare such as eggs Benedict and grilled veal chops, the Brasserie has a selection of spa-menu items, just as tasty but low in calories and fat. The Center Court Restaurant at the Racquet Club serves light meals for breakfast and lunch. For more elegant dining Pisces specializes in fresh seafood, and Ristorante Figaro is devoted to Northern Italian cuisine. Both are open for dinner only.

Children's World: Camp La Costa is active year-round and operates from 10:00 A.M. to 5:00 P.M. daily. For five- to thirteen-year-olds, the fun includes golf and tennis lessons, swimming, kite flying, and arts and crafts. The fee is $40 a day and includes lunch. In the evenings Camp La Costa Nightclub takes over with dinner and entertainment from 6:30 to 9:30 P.M.; the fee is $30 a night. Individual babysitting can be requested through the concierge; the fee is $28.00 for the first three hours and $8.00 an hour thereafter.

Recreation: The spa programs and facilities are extensive. Facials from deep cleansing to mud packs, massages of the shiatsu and reiki variety, herbal wraps, body scrubs, exfoliation, and hydrotherapy baths are just some of the methods utilized to revive weary guests. Exercise facilities include swimming pools, a weight room, a cardiovascular room, and a jogging track. You can join one of the many exercise classes offered throughout the day or, with an exercise physiologist, you can devise a personalized fitness program. Individualized analysis also extends to dietary counseling and menu planning. Classes with psychologists cover topics such as stress reduction and relaxation.

Golf enthusiasts find their exercise on the two eighteen-hole championship courses. At the Golf School the latest technology is used to scrutinize and improve your game. Tennis players have twenty-one courts at their disposal and can choose grass, clay, or hard-court surface. Clinics are held daily, and private instruction is easily arranged. The golf and tennis pro shops offer a wide range of equipment and apparel. Five heated swimming pools complete the picture of exercise potential at La Costa.

MGM Grand Hotel/Casino
3799 Las Vegas Boulevard South
Las Vegas, Nevada 89109
(702) 891–7777, (800) 929–1111

Take the children to Las Vegas?! Are they out of their minds? Well, no. Surprisingly enough, about one in every twelve visitors is accompanied by a minor, and the number of children is increasing rapidly as Las Vegas consciously markets itself as a family destination, a unique entertainment capital. Where else can you see so many lights; watch a circus; experience Camelot with King Arthur and Merlin; have a taste of ancient Egypt, with a canal "Nile River" boat ride around a 30-story-high pyramid and a visit to King Tut's Tomb; or watch while pirates attack and sink a tall sailing ship (six times a day!)? The only problem is that you may need a vacation to recover from your Las Vegas vacation!

Accommodations: The MGM Grand opened in 1993, at a cost of $1 billion. Whatever words one uses to describe it, you just keep coming back to "grand." With 5,005 rooms (751 suites), it is the self-proclaimed "City of Entertainment." Rooms are set in the four emerald-green hotel towers and are decorated in "Oz," "Hollywood," "Southern," and "Casablanca" motifs.

Typical guest rooms are 446 square feet in size, with Italian marble bathrooms and sunken tub. Las Vegas is a gambling town, and this seems to apply to the rate structure as well. Rates change daily, based on number of rooms available. The range for double occupancy is $69–$399; up to three children under age twelve are free, with $25 per extra person per day.

Dining: With seven restaurants and a Food Court to choose from, you don't ever have to dine in the same place twice. The Oz Buffet serves brunch and dinner, while the Studio Cafe is a twenty-four-hour coffee shop. The fare at The Brown Derby, Tre Visi and La Scala, Emenl Lagasse's New Orleans Fish House, and Gatsby's is pretty obvious, but the Dragon Court and Wolfgang Puck's Cafe need exploring. Coyote Cafe serves up Southwestern specialties a la acclaimed chef Mark Miller, and twenty-six types of tequila at the "Tequila Bar." For evening entertainment select from two show rooms and five lounges/bars.

Children's World: Many hotels in Las Vegas have fun things or themes for children, but the MGM is the only one with a full children's program. The Youth Activity Center consists of four rooms of pretty much nonstop supervised activities. The preschool room, for three- to six-year-olds, has playhouse, tumbling mats, puppets, puzzles, and more. Seven- to twelve-year-olds have Foosball, Ping-Pong, board games, and mini-pool. An arts-and-crafts room is shared by all ages, and materials are plentiful, so there's no limit to what the kids dream up. The lounge area has bean-bag chairs, large-screen TV/VCR, and—what else—SuperNintendo.

Excursions to the Grand Adventures Theme Park (with behind-the-scenes learning), the Grand Oasis swimming complex, and other unique hotel areas are planned for children ages six to sixteen years. The center is equipped with its own snack bar for meals and snacks.

For hotel guests the center is open seven days a week, year-round, with varying hours. Children can stay for a maximum of five hours at a time, with a two-hour break required. The cost is $6.00 per hour during the day and $7.00 per hour in the evening after 5:00 P.M. (While the center is available to nonguests of the hotel from 8:00 A.M. until predetermined times, the rules and costs are different.) Always subject to availability.

Recreation: The four-acre Grand Oasis swimming complex has a huge pool, complete with sandy beach, luxury cabanas, and Sand Bar. Play day or night tennis on the four courts; or if all this gets to be too much, relax and rejuvenate at the Grand Spa, where you can be pampered with facials, body wraps, seaweed treatments, massage, even eyelash tinting. Rates are reasonable, and the spa is open from 6:30 A.M. to 7:30 P.M.

In the same grand scale as everything else, there's not just one casino area here, but four. The gaming area, larger than four football fields, spans more than 170,000 square feet.

MGM Grand Adventures, a theme park adjacent to the hotel, has rides, theater, entertainment, food, and retail shops to provide hours of fun. The newest attraction, SkyScreamer, is the world's tallest skycoaster. This dual-design skycoaster lifts one to three flyers to heights of approximately 220 feet off the ground. Flyers are instructed to pull their own ripcord to set into motion a free fall at speeds of up to 70 miles per hour.

Stroll along "The Strip" and marvel, but don't think that glitz and neon are all there is to Las Vegas. When you tire of all this concrete and fantasy, take a trek into nature and visit some of the scenic wonders nearby. Hoover Dam, more than 70 feet high, is considered one of the seven man-made wonders of the world; tours explain the dam and the generation of the electricity for all those Las Vegas lights. Lake Mead, next to the dam, offers boating activities; and about 50 miles north is the Valley of Fire State Park, named for the red and orange rock formations. Only about 20 miles west of Las Vegas is Red Rock Canyon, with scenic drives; and Old Nevada, a re-creation of a nineteenth-century town, with saloon, cowboys, and Wild West action.

Northstar-at-Tahoe

P.O. Box 129
Truckee, California 96160
(916) 562–1010, (800) GO–NORTH (466–6784)

Tahoe has long been known for the clear deep waters of a 200-square-mile lake, the majestic mountain peaks of the Sierra Nevada range, and its proximity to the entertainment and nightlife of Nevada casinos. Northstar-at-Tahoe enables vacationers to partake of all of these. Open year-round, it is a 2,500-acre mountain resort just 6 miles from Lake Tahoe that offers winter and summer family sports activities. With the Nevada stateline only 7 miles away, side trips to gambling casinos are manageable excursions for grown-ups.

Accommodations: The lodging facilities include hotel-type rooms, condominiums ranging in size from studios to four-bedroom units, and three- and four-bedroom homes. With the exception of the lodge rooms, all have a fully equipped kitchen and fireplace; many units have a private balcony overlooking the wooded landscape and the mountains. The wooden facades and rustic designs of the buildings blend well with the natural setting.

Prices range from $99 a night in the summer and $159 a night in the winter for a hotel room to $329 a night, summer, and $454 a night, winter, for a four-bedroom, two-bath condominium. Package plans are available throughout the year. The on-site transportation system is complimentary for Northstar guests. Cribs are provided at a daily charge of $5.00.

Dining: The six restaurants at Northstar mean time off for the family cook. Timbercreek Restaurant serves dinner in the winter and summer. The Basque Club specializes in traditional Basque cuisine, while Pedro's Pizza

Photo courtesy of Northstar-at-Tahoe

Parlor is a casual spot for lunch and dinner; the Basque and Pedro's are open only in winter. The two restaurants on the mountain are the Big Springs Day Lodge, open for breakfast and lunch, and the Summit Deck and Grill, open for lunch. Each offers an informal atmosphere and allows skiers to get back on the slopes quickly. The Clubhouse offers breakfast and lunch, indoors or outdoors, in summer only. The Village Food Company, in the Village Mall, is open year-round; with a deli, gourmet groceries, espresso bar, and video rentals, it also provides the supplies for a picnic or snacking in your condo.

Children's World: The Minors' Camp Child-Care Center is fully licensed and accepts children as young as two years old (must be toilet trained). In the winter it is open daily from 8:30 A.M. to 4:30 P.M. Under the guidance of an experienced staff, two- to six-year-olds paint, learn songs, listen to stories, play in the snow, and take walks; with snacks and a hot lunch, the full-day fee is $48.

At three years little ones can join the Ski Cubs Program; in addition to the nonskiing activities, these children receive one and one-half hours of ski instruction during the day. The fee for child care plus skiing (equipment included) is $58 a day. Four- to six-year-old Super Cubs receive two and one-half hours of ski instruction in addition to indoor activities at a daily rate of $68. When she's not with the other Cubs, a child under five years skis free with a ticketed adult.

The Star Kids Program is designed for five- to twelve-year-olds. The $60 daily fee covers three hours of lessons, lifts, and lunch.

The highlights of the summer program (mid-June to Labor Day) for children ages two (must be toilet trained) to ten are swimming lessons, nature walks, tennis, arts and crafts, and horseback riding. Day camp is in session Monday through Saturday, 9:00 A.M.–5:00 P.M. You can reserve a slot for your child for $24 per half-day or $42 all day (includes lunch). A free half-day is provided with more than two nights' lodging.

Recreation: For downhill skiing at Tahoe, you can look forward to 2,200 vertical feet. The Northstar Village is at the base of Mount Pluto, which rises to a summit of 8,600 feet. There are sixty-three runs and nine lifts, and locals boast of sunshine 80 percent of the season. The ski school, with its 180 instructors, offers lessons for beginners through experts to help all visitors meet the variety of this mountain. Forty miles of groomed trails attract cross-country skiers; lessons, guided tours, and snowshoe rentals are available at the Cross-Country Center.

Après-ski activities may mean taking a sleigh ride or a trip to the Swim and Raquet Club, where you'll find saunas, spas, an adult lap pool, a fitness center, and a teen center, or enjoying a stroll through the Village Mall, which houses shops, restaurants, and bars.

During the summer other activities lure visitors outdoors to the sunshine and clean mountain air. Enjoy golf on an eighteen-hole course that wanders over meadows, past mountain streams, and through groves of tall pines and aspen. The Golf Course Clubhouse includes a pro shop and a restaurant. To work on improving your game, check with the resident pro for tips, or practice solo on the driving range and putting green.

Play tennis on one of the ten courts, take a swim in the adult lap pool or junior Olympic-size pool, or just soak up the sunshine on the poolside deck. The Northstar stables provide well-groomed horses for riding the mountain trails and offer lessons and guided trail rides. Hiking and biking are also favorite sports in High Sierra country. For adventures in boating and fishing, the clear blue waters of Lake Tahoe await you. And music fills the air every summer Sunday afternoon with free outdoor concerts.

The Rancho Bernardo Inn

17550 Bernardo Oaks Drive
San Diego, California 92128
(619) 487–1611, (800) 542–6096

Listen up, weary travelers. It is still possible to vacation in the classic style and relaxed atmosphere of an old California ranch. Set in the San Pasqual Mountains of Southern California, The Rancho Bernardo Inn is just thirty minutes north of San Diego. Here, on 265 acres, the Inn revives the elegance and charm of the early rancheros' way of life, capitalizes on the California sunshine and balmy weather, and adds fine sporting facilities as well—all to provide the perfect holiday for you. The Inn is open year-round.

Accommodations: As you might expect of an old Southwestern ranch, the architecture reveals a Spanish influence reminiscent of the area's heritage. The eight red-tiled haciendas house 287 rooms and suites. These are decorated in warm earth tones, highly polished wood, and local art. The high season is January through March and October through December, when a double room is $185–$215 a night. From April through September double rooms are $135–$180 Sunday through Thursday, $185–$215 on weekends. Children under twelve stay free; those over twelve pay $15. Ask about family packages that include some meals and admission to attractions. Cribs are provided at no charge.

Dining: El Bizcocho is the elegant French restaurant of the Inn. This mission-style dining room is open for evening dinner and Sunday brunch, for which gentlemen should wear jackets. Of the many tempting menu selections here, you might try the roast duckling in Calvados. More casual and open for breakfast, lunch, and dinner, the Veranda Room will lure you with its fresh seafood dishes, such as tiger shrimp provençale. The Sports Grill serves sandwiches and snacks on its patio, near the ninth hole. Tea, tasty sandwiches, and pastries in the Music Room make a perfect afternoon interlude to tide you over between a lovely lunch and a delicious dinner. For evening entertainment La Taberna features a piano soloist, and La Bodega offers dancing.

Children's World: An active, fun-filled Children's Camp is on the docket for some holidays and the month of August. Daily from 9:00 A.M. to 9:00 P.M., children ages five to eleven play tennis and miniature golf, swim, bake cookies, make kites, and go on scavenger hunts. Arts-and-crafts classes, croquet, movies, track meets, and cookouts are also on the schedule. A child can join the group for one or two activities a day or stay at camp all day long if he's got the energy. Older children, to age seventeen, have tennis, golf, basketball, swimming, and biking activities. An evening event for this group might be a luau or a carnival. The cost is $15 per half-day; $20 for full-day. Second and third children in the family have reduced rates.

Recreation: Golf and tennis players are well cared for at Rancho Bernardo. Three nine-hole executive courses will whet your appetite for the eighteen-hole championship golf course. Planted with sycamore, eucalyptus, pine, and olive trees, the lush green fairways roll down the foothills to the valley. With five resident pros, individual and group lessons, clinics, tournaments, a driving range, and a well-stocked pro shop, you've got every chance in the world of polishing your game.

Tennis players are found on the twelve outdoor courts, four of which are lighted for nighttime play. The Tennis College has a twenty-plus-year history of providing programs to players of all skill levels. Stroke development, teamwork, and strategy are just some of the topics covered in the two- to five-day sessions. Private instruction is also available.

With some energy still left, you can head to the workout room in the Fitness Center, then unwind with a massage or a few minutes in the steam or sauna room. Have a pleasant dip in one of the two swimming pools, or bicycle and jog around the carefully tended grounds. Because of the sunny southern California weather, these sports continue year-round.

All of San Diego's attractions are twenty to thirty minutes away. The famous San Diego Zoo, Sea World, the Aerospace Museum, and a Wild Animal Park beckon. Enjoy a picnic in Balboa Park, or shop at Horton Plaza, a fabulous "mall" like no other. You can even take a quick trip to Mexico—it's an easy forty-five-minute train ride from downtown San Diego to Tijuana—for great bargains.

Port Ludlow Resort and Conference Center

200 Olympic Place
Port Ludlow, Washington 98365
(206) 437-2222, (800) 732-1239

Salmon fishing and timber from the hardwood forests first drew settlers to this area of the Northwest. Today visitors are lured by the clear deep waters of Puget Sound and the spectacular scenery presided over by the majestic mountains of the Cascade and Olympic ranges. Open year-round, the Resort at Port Ludlow is situated on a bit of land jutting out into Puget Sound, and with this prime location it's no wonder that water sports are favored here. The Olympic National Park and National Forest are practically in Port Ludlow's backyard (less than 15 miles away), which makes this a good spot for those who want the peace and serenity of a back-to-nature vacation. The weather here is mild, so many outdoor activities (such as golf) continue through the winter.

Accommodations: For lodging you may choose a traditional bedroom/bath combination (many with lovely views) or a one- to four-bedroom condominium, depending on the size of your party. The condominiums have living room, kitchen, fireplace, private deck, and water views. Sit on your balcony at night to catch a whiff of the clean, pine-scented air. There are 185 units in all, arranged in nineteen wooden townhouse structures; surrounded by beautifully landscaped grounds and bordering on wooded areas, these accommodations afford a sense of being close to nature.

Rates for a room alone start at $90 a night. A condominium starts at about $135 a night. Children twelve and under staying in their parents' room are free; cribs are available at no charge. Rates are lower in fall, winter, and spring.

Dining: The Harbormaster Restaurant, which serves breakfast, lunch, and dinner, overlooks Puget Sound and grants visitors views of sun-sparkling waters and sailboats tacking in the breeze. The house specialties are steak and fresh seafood; maybe you'll have the Ludlow clam chowder, followed by a tasty crab or shrimp entree. The children's menu features fried chicken and fish and chips. Two snack bars provide quick, light meals like hamburgers, sandwiches, and salads. The Wreckroom Lounge offers thirst quenchers, nightly entertainment, and views of the marina.

Children's World: During summer months, the recreation department plans daily supervised activities for children ages five through twelve years. Three two-hour sessions are provided Tuesday through Saturday at a cost of $15 per session per child. Scheduled events include nature walks, crafts classes, and beachcombing. The playground area, with jungle gym equipment, is located near the main building.

Recreation: The twenty-seven-hole championship golf course, designed by Robert Muir Graves, dips past ponds and edges around tall fir trees; during a challenging game you're rewarded with beautiful views of the water. For practice sessions head to the driving range and the putting greens. The pro shop can meet your needs for equipment, accessories, and clothing. If you don't want to bring along your own clubs, rentals are available and the golf pro is on hand to give you pointers on your swing.

For tennis enthusiasts, seven Plexipave courts are located near the Beach Club. The Beach Club also houses the squash court, year-round swimming pool, sauna, and game room with Ping-Pong and pool tables. The Recreation Department can set you up for games of softball, volleyball, basketball, or horseshoes.

Beautiful Puget Sound is the focal point of many activities. The 300-slip marina handles both power- and sailboats. If you sail your own boat up the coast, this is the perfect place to dock. If not, you might want to rent a powerboat or sailboat and go exploring, join a charter fishing craft and go off in search of salmon, reserve a spot on an evening champagne cruise, or take a daytime sightseeing adventure. Clamming, crabbing, and beachcombing along the shore are favorite pastimes here. With bicycling (rentals available) and hiking, you can get your exercise and see the scenery, too.

Nearby Port Townsend, a fine example of a Victorian seacoast town, is a great diversion for a day. You can join a guided tour, which includes entrance into a few of the old homes, or you can discover the restaurants, shops, and interesting architecture on your own.

San Ysidro Ranch

900 San Ysidro Lane
Montecito, California 93108
(805) 969–5046, (800) 368–6788

Elegant yet rustic is the best way to describe San Ysidro. A quiet charm pervades the property. From the many lovely gardens—the Citrus Garden, the Herb and Vegetable Garden, the Hacienda Garden, the Wedding Garden—to the trails into the Los Padres National Forest, a respect and appreciation for nature are apparent. One comes here to relax, to rejuvenate the soul as well as the body.

Once a waystation for Franciscan monks as they conducted their missionary work in the late 1700s, San Ysidro Ranch opened as a resort just over one hundred years ago. Today guests discover 550 acres of wooded countryside in the foothills of Montecito. Views extend into the Santa Ynez Mountains and down to the Pacific Ocean. San Ysidro Ranch is 8 miles south of Santa Barbara and just a one-and-one-half-hour drive north of Los Angeles.

Accommodations: Thirty-seven rooms and suites are arranged in twenty-one cottages. Each has a wood-burning fireplace and a private terrace; some have a Jacuzzi. The cottages have been christened delightful names, such as Creek, Outlook, Eucalyptus, and Acacia, each evoking the special milieu of its position. Room rates range from $325 to $399 a night; one- and two-bedroom suites are $499 to $1,250 a night.

Dining: The Stonehouse Restaurant is developing a reputation as one of the finest in the Santa Barbara area. With culinary creations such as tortilla soup, lobster mushrooms in huckleberry vinaigrette, and salmon in chive sauce, it's easy to understand the appeal. Even the low-calorie spa dishes are hard to resist. Casual dinners and live jazz are the offerings of the Plow and Angel Pub, which dates from the time of the original resort (it was built in 1893). Outdoor dining at poolside is yet another option.

Children's World: Summertime (June through August) at San Ysidro is filled with horseback riding, hiking, picnics, face painting, and treasure hunts. The full-day program, which rounds up kids at the treehouse at about 9:00 A.M., goes until 3:00 P.M., seven days a week. It is complimentary for guests ages five to twelve. Special activities and children's programs are planned at the major holidays. Babysitting on an individual basis can be arranged at $8.00 an hour, with a four-hour minimum.

Recreation: Hiking on this terrain is a favorite among guests. The tennis courts (two) are situated on the highest plateau of the grounds; enjoy a rousing match along with panoramic views of the mountains and the ocean. Private instruction is available with the tennis pro. Work out at the health facility, with its cardiovascular and weights equipment; you might even schedule an appointment with a personal fitness trainer in order to devise a personal regimen. Or take your exercise in the outdoor heated pool.

The full spa and beauty treatments may be the highlights of your visit here. Aromatherapy facials, massages, herbal body wraps, reflexology, and stress-relieving treatments will add up to a new you. Some programs are combined with yoga lessons or tranquil excursions on horseback to maximize your revitalization at the Ranch.

Schweitzer Mountain Resort

P.O. Box 815
Sandpoint, Idaho 83864
(208) 263–9555, (800) 831–8810

Way up in the northern part of Idaho's panhandle, just 60 miles from the Canadian border, is Schweitzer Mountain Resort. Set high in the rugged Selkirk Mountains, the skiing terrain sprawls over 2,400 acres. As it is a one-and-one-half-hour drive from Spokane and seven hours from Seattle, Schweitzer may not be the easiest resort to get to, but you rarely have to worry about the crowds. It is open year-round.

Accommodations: The Green Gables Lodge is at the base, and numerous condominiums supply ski-in/ski-out access. Rates range from $95 to $165 a night for hotel rooms; one- to three-bedroom condo units are $180 to $300; summer rates are lower. Additional condominiums are a bit of a walk to the lifts, and still other lodging facilities are in Sandpoint, 10 miles from Schweitzer. Many properties offer a "children ski and stay free" program, which applies to children twelve years and younger. Cribs are available at no charge.

Dining: Jean's Northwest Grill and Jimmies Bar serve Northwest cuisine for relaxing meals. But if you can't bear to take out much time from skiing, stop in the Outback or the Cafe for a quick lunch. Or you can rustle up meals in your condo, stocking up on supplies at the Plaza Mercantile near Sandpoint.

Children's World: The Mogul Mice program delights young skiers from five to eleven years. Skiing and lunching with new friends and an instructor fill the hours from 10:00 A.M. to 3:00 P.M. The fee is $40 a day. Kinderkamp, a day-care center, is a suitable alternative for nonskiers (infants to six-year-olds). In the summer months children and their parents can rent mountain bikes, take chairlift rides, and enjoy Western-style barbecues, picnics, and horse rides, too.

Recreation: Schweitzer has a lot of skiing terrain and a lot of variety from the open bowls, demanding good performance of advanced skiers, to gentle beginner runs. Two expansive bowls and fifty-five runs with 2,350 skiable acres ensure that you won't get bored. Add to this 2,400 feet of vertical drop and more than 300 inches of snowfall annually and you've got the full picture. The season starts up at the end of November and continues to early April. After skiing you might take a sleigh ride through the woods.

During the summer months visitors to Schweitzer turn to hiking along the mountain trails, getting a real feeling for Idaho's back country. You may even be able to take a llama to carry your pack.

Squaw Valley USA

P.O. Box 2007
Olympic Valley, California 96146
(916) 583-6985, (800) 545-4350

Squaw Valley—the name itself is synonymous with skiing. From the earliest days (would you believe 1949?), the sunny California weather combined with six mountains and 8,300 acres of skiable terrain have made this a world-class ski area. Mother Nature deposits an average of 450 inches of snow between mid-November and April. The Sierra Mountains and Lake Tahoe provide a spectacular backdrop, and the vastness of the area contributes to a wide variety of skiing.

Open year-round, Squaw Valley is located near the north end of Lake Tahoe.

Accommodations: A central reservation office (800-545-4350) will work with you to find the most appropriate lodging for your family and your needs. Hotels, motels, lodges, and condominiums all have various rates and package plans. Among the closest to the slopes are Squaw Valley Lodge, a deluxe ski-in/ski-out condominium ($190–$220), and the Squaw Valley Inn ($145–$185), located next to the tram, with sixty rooms. The Resort at Squaw Creek is the newest development, a deluxe conference center with an elaborate swimming complex and its own lift ($198–$270), plus a Robert Trent Jones, Jr., golf course.

The deluxe Olympic Village Inn is a European-style condominium complex about 2 blocks from the lift ($165–$195). Each property has its own policy regarding children.

Dining: You will find many fast-food locations offering pastry, ice cream, cookies, pizza—even tacos. Some of these, such as Dave's Deli, Mother Barkleys, Salsa Bar and Grill, Le Chamois, and The Sundeck, are found at the base facility, the Olympic Plaza.

Up on the mountain head to Alexander's for panoramic views and light lunches of soups and salads. In the evening the vistas take on a different glow and the dining becomes more sophisticated. At the Resort at Squaw Creek, Glissandi is an elegant restaurant featuring French cuisine, while the Cascades Restaurant offers regional American fare. And the Poolside Cafe is a casual, friendly dining spot.

The casinos and showrooms of Nevada are readily accessible for dining and evening pleasures. If you want to stay in the neighborhood, however, try the après-ski at Bar One, Le Chamois, or the Plaza Bar, where you'll find entertainment even after a strenuous day of skiing.

Children's World: Toddler Care is a program for children ages two to three years. Open from 8:00 A.M. to 4:30 P.M., the center offers a full-day of care and activity for $60 and a half-day for $40. Three- to twelve-year-olds take to the joys of skiing in the Children's World. The same hours and prices as above apply to this program, which focuses all efforts on teaching children to love skiing. Lessons as well as other fun-in-the-snow activities keep this group well occupied.

The Resort at Squaw Creek runs its own summer activities for children. Mountain Buddies, designed for three- to thirteen-year-olds, concentrates on sports, nature hikes, and arts and crafts. Teens join forces in the Mountain Adventure program.

Recreation: The definite wintertime focus of Squaw Valley is skiing. Imagine yourself on an uncrowded run. The sun is shining and you kick up some powder as you stop to check out the scenery. Take off your goggles and look out over glistening white snow to the blue waters of Lake Tahoe. More than 70 percent of the runs are for beginner/intermediate skiers. Moreover, Squaw Valley is one of those rare places where this group is not confined to the lower elevations but can ski all day above 8,000 feet in the sunny, sheltered bowls. The vertical drop is 2,850 feet, and challenging slopes for expert skiers are not lacking. In fact, the 1960 Winter Olympics were held here. Squaw's six mountains are interconnected by twenty-seven lifts that include a 150-passenger cable car, a six-passenger gondola, and four high-speed detachable quads. The ski school organizes classes and clinics for all levels, from beginners to racing competition. A coin-operated race course allows skiers to perfect their racing styles (and keeps them off the regular slopes!). Cross-country skiing augments the snow diversions of Squaw Valley.

In the summertime the cable car operates for scenic tours, and the surrounding hotels focus on tennis, fishing, biking, horseback riding, and nature trails. Golf is top notch here, with an eighteen-hole Robert Trent Jones, Jr., course that weaves its way through mountains and meadows. Swimming pools, exercise spas, and racquetball/squash courts round out the pleasures.

Sunriver Resort

Sunriver, Oregon 97707
(503) 593–1000, (800) 547–3922

Nestled in the pines along the beautiful Deschutes River and boasting more than 260 days of sunshine a year, Sunriver is an outdoorsman's delight. Whether it's tennis, golf, swimming, horseback riding, or boating that entices you, the great outdoors, with its clean pine-scented air and blue skies, awaits you at Sunriver. Set on 3,300 acres of central Oregon at an elevation of 4,000 feet, the year-round resort encompasses both well-developed land and wilderness areas. Coddle yourself in the amenities, or head to the back country for a real escape. Bordering on the Cascade Mountain range, Sunriver is only twenty minutes from Mount Bachelor. With lots of powder, plenty of sunshine, and a long season (into late spring and even into the summer on the summit), this impressive mountain means paradise for many skiers.

Accommodations: Accommodations at Sunriver Resort include deluxe rooms and suites. All have a stone fireplace and private deck; the suites accommodate two to six people and have a kitchen and dining/living room. Rates are $58–$195 a night, depending on the size and the season of the year. Cribs are provided at a daily charge of $2.00.

Also, approximately 250 private homes and condominiums can be rented on a short-term basis. With one to five bedrooms, these can easily sleep up to ten people comfortably. All include a well-equipped kitchen, living and dining areas, and alluring fireplace and private deck. They are strategically located along the golf course, tucked in among the trees, facing the Cascade Mountains, or overlooking the Deschutes River. Prices range from $130 to $274 a night, size and season being the determining factors; summer and Christmas are high season here. The architecture is warm and rustic, modern yet compatible with the surroundings.

Dining: The Meadows in the lodge specializes in Northwest cuisine and very tempting desserts; it is open for breakfast, lunch, and dinner daily. During the summer months the Par Patio or McDivot's Café offers refreshment after a good game of golf.

In addition, more than a dozen restaurants are in Sunriver's Village Mall. Whether you cook in your condo or dine out, the variety from quick sandwiches to gourmet fare satisfies almost any mood. For late-night amusement the Owl's Nest offers cocktails every night except Sunday.

Children's World: Youngsters enjoy the children's play area, filled with swings, slides, teeter-totters, and a small fort—imagine the great pretend games here! The resident naturalists at the Sunriver Nature Center introduce children to the magic and mystery of the local environment and animals. Summers also mean bicycle riding, swimming lessons, canoe rides, games, and tennis combined in a daily Kids Club program. Sunriver's activities, offered mid-June to Labor Day and Thanksgiving through February, are developed to enhance children's social, physical, and mental growth while they enjoy themselves. Kids Klub is offered daily all summer long for three- to ten-year-olds from 9:00 A.M. to 4:00 P.M. at a cost of $30. Evening programs are available for the same age group from 5:00 to

9:00 P.M. for $20, with dinner, or from 6:00 to 9:00 P.M. at a cost of $14, without dinner. Guided Adventures for eleven- to fifteen-year-olds is offered Monday through Friday, mid-June through Labor Day, from 9:30 A.M. to 3:30 P.M., at a cost of $25; lunch is not included. All youth program sessions are based on a theme and include nature study, adventure, crafts, and games. Reservations are required for all youth programs.

In the winter the rink at the Sunriver Village Mall makes a great spot for ice skating. Wintertime also means that all the services of Mount Bachelor open up to you.

Recreation: Sunriver is a beautiful setting for golf; snowcapped Mount Bachelor provides a dramatic backdrop year-round for the pleasure of both strong players and high handicappers alike. The Woodlands was designed by Robert Trent Jones, Jr.; the hilly terrain, the tree-lined fairways, the seven lakes, and the strategically placed sand traps reveal the talented crafting of this fine architect. The Meadows meanders over more level terrain and skirts mountain meadows. A great new course, Crosswater, designed by Robert Cup, offers play exclusively for resort guests and homeowners. Each course has a well-stocked pro shop, a driving range, a putting green, and PGA pros to guide you through group or private lessons and clinics.

With twenty-eight Plexipaved tennis courts, rimmed by tall pines and with blue skies overhead, who could possibly have a bad game of tennis? But if your swing does need some polishing, you can always sign up for lessons. Tennis camps from two to seven days are scheduled for both adults and children from age ten. Drills, competitions, tennis for tots (ages four to six years), and weekly clinics are also offered.

Two swimming centers each have a heated Olympic-size pool, a diving pool, and a wading pool—plenty of variety. Adjacent to the south swimming pavilion are hot tubs. Also available are the Lodge Village pool and three new outdoor spas.

The Deschutes River provides hours of enjoyment for fishermen who snag brookies, rainbows, and German browns. The Sunriver Marina offers canoe, raft, and kayak float trips down the scenic and calm Deschutes. Marina staff will pick you up downriver and bring you back to the marina; the trips are offered mid-April to mid-October, weather permitting.

For landlubbers in your party, rental bikes are available for excursions on the 35 miles of paved paths; guides at the Sunriver stables are ready to show off the scenery in rides along the river; the wilderness beckons interested backpackers. Trails past meadows and through the woods await joggers and nature lovers. The Sunriver is located within the Deschutes National Forest, offering additional opportunity for back-to-nature serenity and elbow room. The Sunriver Nature Center, now in its twenty-fifth year, has an extremely comprehensive, very reasonably priced program. Many nature walks, lectures, and campfires are free; there are also archaeology tours, combined bicycle/bird-watching, spelunking in Lava River Cave, and more, more, more.

The Sunriver Racquet Club is a nearby sports facility whose name belies its services. In addition to five racquetball courts, the club has three indoor tennis courts, a swimming pool, an exercise room, a spa, and saunas. Use of these facilities is $5.00 for lodge guests, or free with some private homes, so check when you're making reservations.

Sunriver Village has restaurants and interesting shops, boutiques, and an art gallery. The Sunriver Music Festival takes place in August; orchestral programs are presented in the Great Hall, originally constructed as an officers' club when what is now Sunriver Resort was Camp Abbot, a U.S. Army Engineer Replacement Training Center for the Corps of Engineers during World War II. The Great Hall is composed of 511 logs, totaling 150,000 board feet of lumber. Completely restored to its original beauty, it serves as Sunriver's most popular ballroom and can accommodate approximately 350 people for dinner or meetings.

The Oregon High Desert Museum (8 miles from the lodge) is a terrific educational introduction to the cultural and natural history of the Northwest, and it is a big attraction for kids and grown-ups alike. The otter pond, where you can watch playful otters preparing their food, is a favorite highlight, as is watching the birds of prey in action.

At Sunriver you'll find a dozen ways to enjoy winter. Mount Bachelor is one of the West's top-rated ski areas. You'll find breathtaking views, plenty of deep powder, and slopes to challenge skiers of all abilities—from beginners to Olympic champions. You can head cross-country on miles of groomed forest trails or break your own path through snowy meadows. Trek the mountain outback by snowmobile or take a leisurely tour in a horse-drawn sleigh. And at day's end slip into a steaming outdoor spa for a relaxing soak.

Sun Valley

Sun Valley, Idaho 83353
(208) 622–4111, (800) 635–8261

Just the name Sun Valley calls to mind fantastic downhill skiing, beautiful powder, and gorgeous sunshine. Located in south-central Idaho, Sun Valley is a Tyrolean-style village perched on 2,054 acres of skiable terrain high in the Sawtooth Mountains. With a ski season that runs from late November to early May, spectacular scenery, and mountain air, Sun Valley is indeed a skier's paradise. Founded as a ski resort in 1936 by W. Averell Harriman, then chairman of the board of Union Pacific Railroad, to draw rail travel west, Sun Valley immediately became the playground of Hollywood stars, introduced the world's first chairlift, and began the long-running affair between Americans and skiing. Winter holds forth with downhill and cross-country skiing, ice skating, and sleigh rides. In summer tennis, golf, hiking, and fishing move to center stage. The village, whose hub is the Sun Valley Lodge, supplements these activities with restaurants, lounges, shops, movies, a game room, saunas, and a playschool for children.

Accommodations: The Sun Valley Lodge is a full-service hotel with accommodations from standard and deluxe rooms to suites. The lodge also houses restaurants, a glass-enclosed swimming pool, a game room, massage facilities, and a sauna. Nearby is the Sun Valley Inn, another hotel, with its own restaurants and glass-enclosed swimming pool. In addition, there are 575 condominium units scattered in clusters about the village. They are studios and one- to four-bedroom units with kitchen; many have a wood-burning fireplace and private balcony. They may be near the tennis courts, the lake, the riding center, or the golf course.

Nightly rates at the lodge and the inn start at $110 and run to $285 for a deluxe suite. In the condominiums studio rates are $110 a night, and four-bedroom units (sleeping up to eight people) are $280 a night (graduated prices in between for one-, two-, and three-bedroom apartments). Package plans are available except from mid-December through January 1. Summertime rates are $75–$175 a night in the lodge and the inn, $100 a night for a studio, and up to $220 a night for a four-bedroom condominium. Children under fifteen ski and stay free, except during certain weeks of the year. There is no additional charge for cribs.

Dining: Twelve restaurants in the village please almost any mood from fancy to family style. Though many families cook meals in their condominium units, occasional nights dining out mean a real vacation for the family chef, too!

Open for breakfast, lunch, and dinner, Gretchen's, in the lodge, is a family restaurant featuring an American menu; the Konditorei, in the village, specializes in sandwiches, pastries, and ice cream; and the Continental Cafe, in the inn, is a cafeteria. Also at the inn, the Ram Dining Room (open evenings only) serves steak, seafood, and cheese and chocolate fondues.

For an unusual adventure in dining, take a horse-drawn sleigh ride to a rustic cabin nestled in the woods; at the Trail Creek Cabin, enjoy prime rib or Idaho trout near a warm fire. Or you can spend an elegant evening at

the Lodge Dining Room sampling French cuisine. On Sunday the dining room also serves a sumptuous buffet brunch of omelets, crepes, fresh fruit, and pastries. For après-ski refreshment or a nightcap, try the Ram Bar or the Duchin Room, where you'll find evening entertainment.

Skiers intent on not losing time on the slopes can stop in for meals and snacks at one of the four mountainside restaurants. They serve soup, salads, and sandwiches cafeteria style.

Children's World: While Mom and Dad are schussing down Bald and Dollar mountains, children are not left out of the fun in this winter wonderland. The Sun Valley Ski School starts three- and four-year-olds in introductory classes at $22 an hour. Five- to twelve-year-olds enjoy a full day of activity (8:30 A.M.–4:00 P.M.), which includes four hours of lessons. The fee is $64 a day.

The Sun Valley Playschool entertains nonskiing little ones six years old and younger (even infants). The school is equipped with games and toys and a nap room for tots who grow weary of all the excitement. There are opportunities for ice skating and an outdoor playground for romping in the snow. The basic fee for the school is $48 a day per child; $55 a day for toddlers; and $75 a day for infants six months to one year.

In summertime school activities for the six-and-under group turn to swimming, hiking, arts and crafts, boating, and hayrides; the same fees are charged in summer as in winter. The Sun Valley Day Camp is designed for six- to fourteen-year-olds. Horseback riding, tennis, golf, fishing, and backpacking are scheduled for these age groups. The fee is $50 a day, excluding lunch.

Recreation: Suitable terrain for all levels of skiers is provided at Sun Valley. With its wide open spaces and gentle trails, Dollar Mountain is favored by beginners and those who want a few warm-up runs. Bald Mountain is a challenge and caters to intermediate and expert skiers. Combined, these mountains offer seventy-eight runs, seventeen chairlifts, and 3,400 vertical feet. Sun Valley prides itself on lots of good skiing from well-groomed terrain to unpacked powder and short lift lines—the combination every downhill skier seeks. A complimentary bus service (operating continuously throughout the day) shuttles guests to the base of both mountains.

The Nordic Ski Center grooms 40 kilometers of well-marked trails for cross-country skiers through aspen trees, along the creek, and over sloping meadows. New in 1988, and first in the United States, is Nordic skiing specifically for children. Machine-set tracks designed for a child's stride cover 3 miles of the Nordic Ski Center and in some places parallel adult tracks, allowing an easy family cross-country-skiing experience. Backcountry skiers can tour the mountain from yurt to yurt (Siberian-style huts), finding a warm, welcoming meal and bed at each.

Private and group lessons are available in both downhill and cross-country skiing at beginner, intermediate, and advanced levels. At the ski shops you can rent equipment or purchase all the accessories necessary for either undertaking. Another favorite wintertime sport has become a year-round one here. Ice skates can be rented, and just behind the lodge is an Olympic-size skating rink where such greats as Sonja Henie, Peggy Fleming, and Dorothy Hamill have practiced. Saturday night ice shows are presented throughtout the summer.

Another year-round activity is swimming; there are two indoor heated pools (one at the lodge and one at the inn) and one outdoor Olympic-size pool. Relax in the sauna or the Jacuzzi, or make an appointment with the masseur in the lodge to ease your overworked muscles. The game room in the lodge offers pool tables, video games, and bowling alleys; or perhaps you'd like to take in a movie at the Opera House. The shops in the village might tempt you with their selections of books, gifts, fashions, jewelry, pottery, and toys.

Summer brings music festivals, parades, antiques and crafts fairs, motorcycle races, and much more. Tennis and golf enthusiasts are in their heyday, for there are sixty outdoor tennis courts and clinics and private lessons with videotaped analysis. An eighteen-hole championship golf course, redesigned by Robert Trent Jones, Jr., rolls over gently sloping terrain. Two nine-hole courses provide another option. At the pro shop, you can arrange for lessons and pick up extras in equipment and clothing.

Fishing in Silver Creek makes a pleasant afternoon for novice fishermen as well as experienced anglers; Sun Valley Lake is stocked with trout. The mountain trails are open to you for horseback riding and hiking in the wooded wilderness. Archery and trap and skeet shooting (instruction available) are also popular with summer visitors. Take a rowboat or paddleboat out on the lake, line up rentals at the bike shop, or plan a white-water raft trip. Whether winter or summer sports beckon you, you'll be captivated by the majestic mountains and the warm, friendly atmosphere of Sun Valley.

The Westin Mission Hills Resort

71333 Dinah Shore Drive
Rancho Mirage, California 92270
(760) 328–5955, (800) WESTIN–1

Palm Springs is synonymous with elegance and celebrities. The lush landscaping, verdant golf courses, and abundance of water belie its desert location, but the surrounding mountains and canyons, which reflect the sun and shadow and the clear starry nights, do not. The 360-acre Westin Mission Hills Resort (located in the Palm Springs vicinity) is adjacent to the Mission Hills Country Club—of course, Palm Springs is also synonymous with world-class golf.

Accommodations: Southwestern adobe mixed with classic Moroccan design provides a distinctive architectural achievement. Blue domes reflect the cloudless skies; warm brown arches repeat themselves down a long pathway, framing the desert palms and mountains. The 512 guest rooms are scattered in sixteen low-rise pavilions interspersed with meandering walks, gardens, lagoons, and waterfalls. Guest rooms are of generous size, and most feature a private patio. January to May is the high season, when rooms range from $260 to $310; from end of June through September, the rates drop to $129 to $160. The remaining months are a mid-range of $189 to $259. Children under eighteen stay free in their parents' room.

Dining: Bella Vista features California cuisine for breakfast, lunch, dinner, and Sunday brunch. Typically Californian, it blends a sunlit atrium with palm trees. Indoor/outdoor dining is available. Another interesting juxtaposition is La Concha, which specializes in "Pacific Rim cuisine"—Asian and Pacific ingredients and spices blended with European cooking techniques. La Concha is open for dinner in season, with entertainment on weekends. Each of the three swimming pools has a cabana serving breakfast, lunch, snacks, and cool beverages; you need never leave the sun. For evening cocktails the elegantly casual Lobby Lounge offers drinks and hors d'oeuvres, or relax and imbibe poolside at Las Brisas if you can't tear yourself or the kids out of the water. Westin has prepared a nice list of family restaurants in the area for those who want to venture out.

Children's World: Westin Kids Club is a basic program at all Westin resort properties, designed to make family travel safe, convenient, and enjoyable. Children get special age-appropriate gifts upon check-in; parents get a safety kit, if desired (electric-outlet covers, adhesive strips, ID bracelets, and local emergency numbers); and the room is ready with cribs, potty seats, or bed rails if needed. Jogging strollers, highchairs, and bottle warmers are complimentary, meals can be ordered in advance from a children's menu so that they are ready upon arrival at the restaurant, and a lot of information about local things of interest to families is available. It's a really comprehensive approach, and during the summer special rates and "Kids Eat Free" promotions are generally available.

The Cactus Kids program at Mission Hills bills itself as "the coolest thing in the desert." Operating daily year-round from 8:00 A.M. to 5:00 P.M., it costs $20.00 per four-hour session or $5.00 per hour. Lunch is additional, and a second-child rate is only $15.00 per day or $2.00 per hour. Reservations are requested at least one day in advance, and the program will be run for even one or two children. Activities include arts and crafts, volleyball, lawn games, movies, nature walks, and bicycle riding.

Recreation: Two championship golf courses, two practice ranges, and six greens and sand traps keep golfers happy. The Pete Dye Resort Course has his trademark deep bunkers and undulating fairways, while the Gary Player Signature Course is a mosaic of waterfalls, ravines, and lakes. Take lessons from the resident pros, or sign up at the Golf Academy with Joey Pickavance. Play tennis in the cool of the evening on the seven lighted tennis courts, or join the Reed Anderson Tennis School. Forget something? The pro shops have everything you need. Las Brisas is the largest of the three swimming pools; it was made to resemble the surrounding canyons and has a 60-foot waterslide, two whirlpools, and spacious sundecks. Treat yourself to massage, herbal wraps, and facials at the Aida Grey Salon; work out at the fitness club; or follow a more leisurely pace with traditional lawn games such as croquet and shuffleboard.

If you need more action, Oasis Waterpark is nearby as well as Camelot Park, where you can play miniature golf, action bumper boats, go-carts, or batting cages. Take the Palm Springs Aerial Tramway 8,516 feet to the Mountain Station for a bird's-eye view, and hike through Mt. San Jacinto

Wilderness State Park. Weather permitting (meaning there is snow), Nordic skiing operates from November to April. At the opposite end of the environmental spectrum, explore the desert by jeep with experienced guides who can show you the secret life of the desert, or have a real Old West experience in a two-hour covered-wagon tour. As a contrast to all this nature, any teenagers in your party might gravitate toward the Palm Desert Town Center, the area's largest indoor shopping mall.

Canada

Alberta
British Columbia
Ontario
Quebec

Auberge Villa Bellevue

**Lac Ouimet, Mont-Tremblant
Quebec, Canada J0T 1Z0
(819) 425–2734, (800) 567–6763**

Villa Bellevue occupies thirty acres on the shore of Lac Ouimet, just 3 miles from Mont-Tremblant, the highest peak in the Laurentian Mountains. Under the direction of the Dubois family, the inn began welcoming visitors in 1920; the third generation of this family continues to share its warm enthusiasm and hospitality with its guests today. In the wintertime more than half of the inn's clientele comes from the United States, so at the Villa Bellevue you'll find folks who know Americans well—not to mention a bit of Québécois flair.

Accommodations: Lodging varies from standard and deluxe rooms in the main lodge to rooms in the adjacent building (laid out more along the lines of a motel) to condominiums and apartments, each with kitchen and two or three bedrooms. During the regular season (early February almost to mid-March), rates for a five-day package range from $425 to $550 (U.S. dollars) per person, based on double occupancy and a modified American plan; besides lodging, breakfast, and dinner, this fee includes a six-day lift ticket. Children's fees run from $155 to $300 for the package, depending on age. Christmas week and a March holiday week command a higher rate, but nonholiday times (late November through January) are less expensive. If you don't wish to participate in a meal plan, the condominiums and chalets can be arranged on a European-plan basis. Weekend packages during the winter are also available.

Summer rates are $291 to $461 per person for a five-night package, based on a modified American plan and double occupancy. Children fourteen years and under sharing a room with their parents are charged only for two meals a day—$75 to $175, depending on age. A European plan is available during the summer, with rates for the hotel rooms at $215 to $443 per person for a five-night package.

Dining: In the main dining room and the banquet hall, lobster, shrimp, and filet mignon evolve into continental and French dishes. With two seatings for dinner, families may find the earlier slot more convenient. If parents wish to dine alone, children can join their instructors/counselors for dinner. For après-ski and après-dinner entertainment, La Musicale can fill the bill.

Children's World: During holiday times—Christmas and New Year's, President's Week in February, and the Ontario school break in March—Villa Bellevue organizes its Childrens Ski Weeks for youngsters ages five and older. The schedule includes four hours a day of ski instruction; in the evening children often eat with their classes, after which movies, games, and sleigh rides are planned. A five-day package is $104. At other times in the season, children participate in the ski classes at the mountain; this program also accommodates three- to five-year-olds in skiing and snow-play activities. At the Mont-Tremblant ski center, the fee is $70 a day for youngsters' events. For babies and young children, inquire about the agencies in the village (approximately $35 a day).

In July and August children and their counselors stay busy with swimming, beach games, volleyball, and badminton and frequent excursions for mini-golf, horseback riding, and hiking. The children are divided into three groups (five to seven years, eight to eleven, and twelve and over), which enables a child to find buddies his own age. Operating Monday to Friday, 1:00–4:30 P.M. and 5:30–9:00 P.M., the program is free.

Recreation: The ski season at Mont-Tremblant lasts from about Thanksgiving to mid-April. A short shuttle-bus ride from Villa Bellevue brings you to the mountain base. The summit rises to 3,000 feet and affords skiers more than 2,100 feet of vertical drop. Thirty-four runs add up to 65 miles of skiing, 65 percent of which are suitable for beginners and intermediates. Cross-country skiers head to the 55-mile network of ground trails. Instruction in downhill and cross-country skiing is available and encouraged.

The new Spa-Santé sports complex allows you to have an indoor workout; its facilities include a lap pool, exercise room, whirlpool, and sauna.

When you've had enough of real physical activity, turn to chess and checkers or head to the game room for Ping-Pong and pool. In the evening maybe you'll relax at a fondue party or go dancing.

Summer activities focus on the lake for swimming, sailboarding, waterskiing, boat tours, canoeing, and sailing. But tennis fans are not left out: Four clay courts and an instruction program await them. Keep your energy level up, because you may also want to bike, hike, or jog; play badminton, volleyball, or archery; or sign up for an aerobics class. For a slower pace you might participate in a hayride and a cookout dinner.

Château Montebello

392 rue Notre-Dame
Montebello
Quebec, Canada J0V 1L0
(819) 423–6341, (800) 441–1414

You don't have to travel all the way to Europe for a vacation in a French château. Château Montebello is a luxury resort in a peaceful woodland setting located on the shores of the Ottawa River between Montréal and Ottawa.

Built of massive cedar logs by a team of craftsmen in 1930, Château Montebello served as an exclusive private club for forty years. In 1970 it became a resort open to the public year-round. Today the Château's old-world charm and contemporary elegance come together as a lovely holiday destination, with the distinction of being the world's largest log structure.

Accommodations: The Château has four wings radiating from the center, affording the guest rooms outlooks to the river and the forests. For the 210 well-appointed rooms, rates begin at $121 (U.S. dollars) a night, including breakfast. The summertime family package starts at

Photo courtesy of Château Montebello

$104 per adult per night, based on double occupancy; it includes break-fast and dinner, pontoon riverboat cruise (one hour), bicycle rental (three hours), canoeing (half-day), and various other sports. With this package, two children under twelve stay and eat free when occupying a room with their parents. Each additional child age thirteen to seventeen is $45.

Dining: Aux Chantignoles is the elegant gourmet dining room of the resort. This is also the venue for Sunday brunch. The Golf Club House is popular for lunch; the Igloo is an outdoor barbecue restaurant, ideal for lunch or dinner. Light snacks and refreshments are served at the Golf Terrace and the Excalibur Bar.

Children's World: The Kid's Centre, presided over by Monte the Beaver, is open from 10:00 A.M. to 5:00 P.M. daily from July to September, and weekends year-round. For children ages three and up, the cost ranges from $12 to $18 per day, depending on the hours and activities. Toys, games, and arts and crafts are mixed with outdoor activities such as swimming, hiking, and group games based on the ages and number of children in the program. While the Centre is open all day, activities are not necessarily nonstop for the entire time. The hotel often arranges special things such as treasure hunts. Special events for children and families are usually planned for holiday periods and weekends throughout the year.

Recreation: The Château offers something for everyone. The eighteen-hole golf course, originally built in 1929, was totally renovated in 1989, resulting in a more challenging and more scenic course. The golf school provides lessons and organizes clinics. The course is rated "Platinum" by *Canada's Golf Course Ranking Magazine.*

Dale Power, a former member of the Canadian Davis Cup Team, runs the tennis operation.

At the Health Club and Sports Complex, you can work out in the exercise room, play squash or tennis, swim laps in the indoor pool, or relax at the Spa in the saunas or whirlpools. The outdoor pool is a beautiful setting for relaxing, sunning, and swimming. Referee the kids in volleyball and badminton games, then round up the whole crew for bike riding or mini-putt.

The Spa offers professional services, including full-body massage, facials, body wraps of mud or algae, body exfoliation and polishing, and therapeutic bath using either relaxing pine and rosemary milk or stimulating mineral salts. What a treat after a full day of activity! Other activities include water sports, cruises, jet skiing, and horseback riding.

The whole family can discover the beauties of Kenauk, a 100-square-mile plant and wildlife preserve within 6 miles of the Château, with scores of activities—bird-watching, picnics, hikes with or without a naturalist, mountain biking, or fishing. Explore White Fish Lake by rowboat or canoe, float down the Kinonge River, or rent a motorboat at the Marina. It's a great place to laze away summer days enjoying nature. Omega Park provides a slightly different approach to nature. Drive along a 10-kilometer road through 1,500 acres of a woodland corral where native animals small (raccoons, wild boar, and deer) and large (bison, black bear, and wild sheep) roam free.

Snow brings enchantment to the woods and hills and is the focus of wintertime fun. The familiar activities of ice skating, ice fishing, sleigh rides, and snowmobiling vie with the more exotic: dogsledding, curling, snowshoeing, broomball, and deck hockey. More than 100 kilometers of cross-country ski trails beckon, or you may prefer just a walk in the snow and curling up with a good book in front of the huge six-sided fireplace in the Château.

Deerhurst Resort

Canadian Pacific Hotels
1235 Deerhurst Drive
Huntsville
Ontario, Canada P1H 2E8
(705) 789–6411, (800) 461–4393

The Muskoka region is Ontario's most popular holiday area. With its clear lakes and beautiful woodlands, it attracts visitors both summer and winter. Deerhurst Resort encompasses 900 acres on the shores of Peninsula Lake and allows guests to experience all the beauty of the area.

The original lodge at Deerhurst was opened in 1896 by Charles Waterhouse, with just eighteen guest rooms. Three generations of Waterhouses oversaw the expansion of the property over the years. Since 1990, it has been managed by Canadian Pacific Hotels and today is one of the largest resort complexes in Canada.

Deerhurst is two and one-half hours by car north of Toronto, or only 40 minutes by air from Toronto to the resort's private airstrip.

Accommodations: Today's accommodations are a far cry from the lodge rooms (without baths) of the early days. The 350 guest rooms and suites are well appointed and comfortable and are grouped in condominium-style buildings with views of the lake, woods, pools, and golf course. Autumn and winter rates range from $73 (U.S. dollars) a night for a standard room to $402 a night for the finest three-bedroom

Photo courtesy of Deerhurst Resort

suite. Christmastime is slightly higher. Children under eighteen stay free when occupying their parents' room. For an extra $40 per person per night, you can add a modified American plan meal package. Summer rates range from $116 to $475.

Dining: In the Lodge Dining Room, the chef displays his talents with regional bounty; venison, fresh fish, wild mushrooms, and wild berries are featured in his creative dishes. The Lodge Dining Room is open for breakfast as well as dinner. The Pub in the Pavilion is casual and well suited for families; soups, sandwiches, pastas, and salads are typical fare here. Steamers Restaurant has a Southwestern menu during the summer season and an Alpine-inspired cuisine in the winter. The Poolside Deck, with views of the lake, serves barbecue favorites in the summer. Evening entertainment at the resort is lively, with a critically acclaimed musical stage show as well as dancing in the Cypress Lounge.

Children's World: Daily through the summer season, during school holiday periods, and on weekends throughout the year, Deer Club operates from 9:00 A.M. to 5:00 P.M. Children ages four to twelve swim, hike, make crafts, and enjoy the playground. The fee for a full-day, including lunch, is $18 and $13 for a half-day. Younger children, ages six months to three years, join the Bambi Club, which has its own premises especially suited to little ones. The cost is $29 full-days and $15 half-days.

Recreation: The eighteen-hole Lakeside Golf Course was built in 1966 and redesigned in 1988 with many enhancements. Built in 1991, the top-rated Deerhurst Highlands is a magnificent eighteen-hole course winding atop of a ridge above the lake, resulting in a combination of challenging play and beautiful scenery. A driving range, practice tees, and target greens comprise the seven-and-one-half-acre instructional facility. A team of professionals direct private lessons and group clinics. Also on the agenda are junior golf clinics utilizing clubs customized for children.

The Pavilion is a complete sports complex consisting of four indoor tennis courts, a racquetball court, three squash courts, a fitness room, a pool, a whirlpool, and a hot tub. Also housed here is a health and beauty spa, where you can relax in the steam and sauna rooms or schedule a massage, facial, body wrap, or hairstyling service.

If you prefer to exercise in the open air, three more swimming pools await you, and eight more tennis courts are outdoors (tennis lessons are available). Water sports on the lake abound: sailing, water-skiing, kayaking, fishing, and sailboarding. And don't forget to hike and jog along the nature trails in the beautiful Muskoka woods. Or try one of the resort's unique 4-by-4 off-road driving adventures.

In the winter guests turn their energies to cross-country skiing, ice skating, snowmobiling, and dogsledding (quite an unusual sport!).

Gray Rocks Resort

Mont-Tremblant
Quebec, Canada J0T 1Z0
(800) 567–6767, Fax (819) 425–3474
E-mail:grayrocks@tremblant.com; http://www.grayrocks.com

Just 75 miles Northwest of Montreal in the Laurentian Mountains, you will find a charming four season lakeside family resort with a French flavor. Though right in the middle of French-speaking Canada, Gray Rocks welcomes American visitors and English is spoken here routinely. You might choose to take the opportunity to brush up on your French, but rest assured that your interests uttered in English in the dining room, on the tennis courts, or during a ski lesson will be well received with warm French-Canadian hospitality.

Since its beginning in 1906, Gray Rocks has developed into a renowned ski, golf, and tennis resort with hotel and condominium accommodations for all tastes. The hotel, with dining room, fitness center, convention center, and bar, sits on the shores of Lac Ouimet. Gray Rocks' own ski mountain, Sugar Peak, rises right behind the hotel; beautiful views of Mont-Tremblant are also impossible to miss. Golf was the first sport in this area, followed by skiing. Today recreational pastimes also include tennis, water sports, horseback riding, mountain biking, or nature hikes.

Accommodations: Lakeside rooms with a private balcony are available in the hotel's Pavilion and Chalet Suisse. Fifty-six one- to three-bedroom condominiums are tucked in among the trees ¾ mile from the hotel. In summer hotel packages include accommodation, buffet breakfast and gourmet dinner, access to Le Spa fitness center, the private beach and marina, daily activities, nightly entertainment, Kids Club, supervised morning activities, and gratuities. Rates vary from $80 in regular season, superior room, to $114 in high season for a Pavilion room with private balcony; per person, per night, with double occupancy. A full American plan is available. One-bedroom, four-person condominium rates start at $132 per unit per night. A meal plan is also offered to condominium guests.

In winter guests enjoy a getaway, similar to the summer hotel package, with free skiing at Gray Rocks or nearby sister resort Mont Blanc.

The most popular winter package is the ski week. For approximately $733 per person, you will enjoy six nights of lodging; nineteen full-course meals; twenty-two hours of instruction with renowned Snow Eagle Ski School; video ski critique; free skiing during seven days; races; awards presentation; complete social program for adults, teens, and children; access to Le Spa, and much more—Gray Rocks' ski week is considered one of the best ski vacation values in North America. Other options: the ski week with condominium accommodation (no meals), at approximately $513 per adult; the ski week with a Snow Eagle instructor at nearby Mont-Tremblant ski area; and the American Thanksgiving Holiday package. A children-stay-for-less plan makes Gray Rocks family friendly in summer as well as in winter.

Dining: The main dining room located at the hotel, with its fireplace and picture windows overlooking the scenic landscape, provides a pleasant ambience during meals. Continental and French-Canadian cuisines are featured. Cozy lounges with fireplaces and lake views are perfect to relax and mix with old and new friends. There's also a cafeteria at the ski chalet, located mid-mountain and accessible by car, shuttle bus, or skis.

Children's World: In summer during regular and high seasons, the children's activity program is in high gear. Youngsters join other children their own ages for supervised morning and afternoon events. Preschoolers ages three to five head to the playground, go on treasure hunts and hayrides, or frolic on the private beach. Kids ages six to nine go swimming, horseback riding, try their talents in arts and crafts, and join hayrides. Preteens (ten to twelve) and teens (thirteen and over) enjoy volleyball, tennis, hiking, canoeing, sailboarding, fishing, and various excursions.

For the aspiring tennis or golf pro, there's a famous junior camp. Gray Rocks' Matchpoint Junior Tennis Camp or Eagle Junior Golf Camp offer a great program for eleven- to sixteen-year-olds. Two-week sessions include lakeside accommodations, all meals and snacks, five hours of instruction per day, round-the-clock supervision, and a complete social program for approximately $1,099 per child.

In the winter Gray Rocks' philosophy is to put children on skis as much as possible. Given that the resort's own gentle mountain is just out the back door, this philosophy is easily practiced. The children's ski classes are divided along age lines as well as ability; heaven forbid your first-time thirteen-year-old skier should be in a class with four-year-olds! Camaraderie in a peer group is important in the learning experience. Children and teens can also meet their friends in a variety of après-ski activities, such as cookie baking, face painting, treasure hunts, arts and

crafts, Ping-Pong tournaments, parties, movies, water polo, and sleigh rides or bingo with Mom and Dad. You want to have some fun with your kids, too!

Day-care service is available for six-month- to two-year-olds as well as private babysitting. In winter, a Ski 'n' Play program combines day care and one hour of ski instruction per day for three- to five-year-olds. The rate is $183 per child, with the hotel package free.

Recreation: Think of Gray Rocks as a university for sports. Its qualified ski, golf, and tennis instructors combine expertise with a sincere enthusiasm for teaching. Improvement of skills and self-confidence go hand in hand, and both are better achieved with ample doses of encouragement and humor.

The Snow Eagle Ski School has a fine reputation and more than fifty years of experience. Skiing is a major wintertime activity. The resort boasts of third-generation families who have learned to ski on these slopes and continue to return for their winter holidays. Though Gray Rocks has a modest 620-foot vertical drop, there's variety, and, if not long, then challenging runs. Snowmaking facilities cover 95 percent of the slopes, ensuring a ski season from Thanksgiving through early April. Mont-Tremblant ski resort is less than 5 miles from Gray Rocks, so intermediate and advanced skiers can seek out additional challenges there. The ski boutique can meet your needs for rentals, repairs, fashions, and accessories. Cross-country skiing is a growing favorite at Gray Rocks.

Nearby Domaine St. Bernard offers well-maintained trails through the woods, next to the river. A tour around the area is a lovely way to spend a winter morning, and a sleigh ride with the kids caps off a perfect day.

Summertime opens up another whole realm of outdoor sports and activities. There's a private sandy beach along a section of the lake. This is Canada, but summers are hot, so swimmers will be happy. The complete marina near the beach offers opportunity for canoeing, sailboarding, sailing, taking out a paddleboat, or enjoying an afternoon of fishing.

A championship eighteen-hole golf course will take you through lush fairways over diverse terrain framed by the rugged beauty of the Laurentians. Three new learning holes are now reserved for Eagle Golf Academy players. The combination of time-proven teaching strategies and small class ratios helps players take strokes off their game and turns newcomers on to the joys of the sport. Tennis buffs enjoy the twenty-two Har-Tru courts (ten near the hotel and twelve at the golf club). Tennis lessons with videotaping can help you isolate the improvements necessary for a good game. Gray Rocks' golf and tennis academies offer acclaimed two-, three-, and five-day clinics.

Jogging along the lake or hiking and horseback riding in the hills are excellent ways to explore the countryside and revel in the clean mountain air. You can enjoy a nice afternoon next to the beach playing lawn games, or get in shape at Le Spa fitness center. Le Spa features an indoor swimming pool, an exercise room, hot tubs, a sauna, and a professional massage service. Many activities are offered free of charge; some, such as golf, tennis, and horseback riding, carry additional fees.

Gray Rocks provides the area's only resort-based pet kennel. You can now travel with the entire family!

Inn on the Park

1100 Eglinton Avenue East
Toronto
Ontario, Canada M3C 1H8
(416) 444–2561, (800) 332–3442 (United States),
(800) 268–6282 (Canada)

If you're in the mood for a slightly different vacation experience from that offered by most of the resorts we've listed, this is the place. Inn on the Park has the distinction of being a city hotel in a resort setting: Situated on 500 acres of parkland, it's right in the middle of Toronto, one of Canada's liveliest cities. It's the best of both worlds, with shopping, art galleries, and museums offset by the green grandeur of the surrounding park.

Accommodations: A twenty-two-story high-rise with 268 rooms in one tower allows views of the city, the park, or the inner courtyard. Nonsmoking floors, twice-daily maid service, complimentary parking, shoe polishing, and terry cloth robes are some of the amenities offered, and the hotel prides itself on excellent service. Guest rooms are classified deluxe ($110–$155, U.S. dollars per night); differences in size, location, and view determine the rating. Some superior rooms have a patio leading directly to the pool area. Deluxe rooms overlook the city and park. If you like more space, one-bedroom suites are $200–$220. Children under nineteen stay free in their parents' room.

Dining: The Harvest Restaurant is casual, with a children's menu of those all-time favorites—grilled cheese sandwiches, hamburgers, and spaghetti. During the summer months the Cabana serves light snacks by the pool. The Terrace Lounge has buffet or à la carte lunches and late-night snacks, when you can also enjoy a piano bar. And what child doesn't adore room service? Here it's available daily. And, all the wonderful restaurants of Toronto are at your doorstep, waiting to be discovered.

Children's World: Innkidz is a very popular and highly organized program that is complimentary for hotel guests. Geared to children ages five to twelve, the program is available from 9:30 A.M. to 4:00 P.M. daily during the summer. Children gather at the Innkidz Centre on the first floor of the Tower for such activities as puppet making, outdoor games and swimming, and making sundaes or clay art. Special treats are a picnic on the helicopter pad and making cookies with the chef in the hotel kitchen. Counselors are art students and teachers, so the experience is very creative. At the end of every afternoon is Snak 'n' Yak, which provides a nice closure for the "kidz." Children under five are welcome if parents remain with them. Lunch can be ordered from the Harvest Room menu and charged to the room. Cribs, strollers, and high chairs are available, and the hotel will even provide diapers, powders, or thermometers if needed.

Recreation: At the hotel you can play a game of tennis, squash, or racquetball; work out in the fully equipped health club and then relax those muscles in the sauna or whirlpool; or try your hand at badminton, volleyball, or shuffleboard. Decide between the indoor and outdoor pools, then decide between swimming and lounging. Window shop the boutiques and gift shop, get your hair fixed, or stop by the games room.

Toronto holds many treats for families. Kids like to wander through

Ontario Place, by the harbor. Shops, eateries, an IMAX theater, and changing exhibits of dinosaurs or gemstones intrigue everyone. Go to the top of the C.N. Tower, the largest freestanding tower in the world; or check out the planetarium at the Royal Ontario Museum. Let the kids pick out a postcard in the gift shop, then try to find the original in the museum. The Ontario Science Museum has a lot of hands-on exhibits, and the Toronto Zoo is a nice excursion on a pretty day.

Severn Lodge

Box 250
Port Severn
Ontario, Canada L0K 1S0
(705) 756–2722, (800) 461–5817

Severn Lodge is beautifully located in the midst of the Georgian Lakelands of Ontario, only 90 miles from Toronto. Georgia Bay forms the northeastern part of Lake Huron and is named in honor of England's George IV. The area's piney woods, fine fishing, and clear waters attract many vacationers. And the Severn Lodge, on the shores of Gloucester Pool, adds to the natural features with its warm pride of being "owned and operated by the same family for families since 1937." The Lodge is open from mid-May to mid-October only.

Accommodations: Severn Lodge dates back to the late 1800s. Its turn-of-the-century ambience remains preserved in the many white clapboard buildings, log crisscross railings, and cobblestone sidewalks. All accommodations and facilities, however, are very modern.

Grouped in about a dozen individual buildings set among the trees and along the lake, the accommodations feature small living rooms, large windows for enjoying the lake views, and ample space for a crib or rollaway bed (for which there is no charge). Rates range from $69 to $88 (U.S. dollars) a day per person, double occupancy, and include three meals a day and all the planned activities and recreational facilities (except motorboats) of the lodge. When children share a room with their parents, they are free if under two years; two to five years are charged $37; six to twelve, $42; and thirteen to eighteen, $47. Two- to seven-day package plans are offered. During special family weeks in the summer season, rates for children twelve and under are reduced 50 percent or more. Several housekeeping cottages are available nearby, and they share some of the facilities of the Lodge.

Dining: The charming, elegantly rustic dining room has a wood-beamed ceiling and many large windows that capture the views. The Canadian cuisine is accompanied by freshly baked breads and pastries. Picnic lunches can be prepared for guests who are off hiking or canoeing during the midday meal.

Children's World: The activities program for children, which runs from mid-June to Labor Day, includes hikes, crafts, volleyball and baseball games, swimming, diving and boating lessons, picnics, and movies. Add waterskiing, Indian Night, Talent Night, a Fish Derby, corn roasts, and bonfire sing-alongs and you know you have happy kids. No additional charges are applied for these events, and children of all ages are welcome to participate.

Every effort is made to include even very young guests, but when your little one is just not able to keep up with the group, a supervised toddler activity program will provide pint-size fun. Specially designed indoor and outdoor play areas for two- to five-year-olds are open daily from 10:00 A.M. to noon and from 4:00 to 8:00 P.M. The program is complimentary and includes arts and crafts, sandcastle building, and other beach and playground activities. The lodge staff can also arrange an individual babysitter for an extra cost. Favorites among the younger set are the sandy beach; the playground, with its swings, slide, sandbox, and climbing equipment; and the dock, for "just fishin'."

Recreation: Water sports are an important part of Severn Lodge. Wonderful swimming can be had either in the lake or in the heated swimming pool; perhaps you'd like to try the whirlpool spa at the deep-water dock. Maybe you would prefer to stay on top of the water in a fishing boat reeling in walleye, bass, muskie, and northern pike. Also on top of the water (with any luck, you will stay on top) is the complimentary waterskiing instruction offered several times a week. Free use of the Lodge's sailboats, sailboards, paddleboats, kayaks, and canoes can make an afternoon lazy or exciting, depending upon your skill. The resort has a unique collection of antique runabouts and motor launches. Rental fees are charged on a daily or weekly basis for outboard boats and motors; the Lodge offers free cruises.

On land you can jog or hike on the trails around the Lodge's one hundred acres or play a game of tennis. The recreation building, with its library and large stone fireplace, is quite inviting if relaxing is a favorite pastime; here you will find Ping-Pong; a wide-screen TV; card and board games; and a pool table. Nearby sightseeing (15 to 20 miles) takes you back in history; Sainte-Marie among the Hurons, a Jesuit Mission, and the Huron Indian Village are reconstructions of seventeenth-century settlements.

Sunshine Village

Box 1510
Banff
Alberta, Canada T0L 0C0
(403) 762–6500, (800) 661–1676
Website: http://www.skibanff.com

High in the Canadian Rockies in Banff National Park is Sunshine Village, one of the best ski destinations in Canada. Perched along the Continental Divide, the peak elevation at Sunshine is 9,200 feet. Located only 85 miles west of Calgary and just 10 miles from the town of Banff, Sunshine is a three-mountain ski resort. More than $9 million in improvements await you at Sunshine, Banff's most visited ski resort..

Accommodations: The only accommodation on the mountain is the Sunshine Inn. A three-story complex consisting of eighty-five rooms and suites, the inn affords its guests ski-in/ski-out access. Rates start at $65 (U.S. dollars) per person per night. A five-night package, including lodging, lift ticket, and daily ski lessons, costs $350 (U.S. dollars) per person, based on double occupancy during the value season (November to mid-December, from the second week of January to mid-February, and from late April to closing). The powder season is defined as the week before Christmas, the week after New Year's, and mid-February to late April, when the package costs $450 (U.S. dollars). During Christmas week this package is $500 (U.S. dollars).

Dining: The Inn's dining room, the Eagle's Nest, offers fine dining, from rack of lamb to fantastic sirloin steak. The Chimney Corner is a lounge offering cocktails and entertainment in the evenings. In the Daylodge, the Deli and the Cafeteria offer soup and sandwiches; the new Mad Trappers Saloon, located in the original 1928 Sunshine Lodge, is the place to go for drinks and burgers.

Children's World: For young skiers and snowboarders, Wee Angels (ages three to six) and Young Devils (ages six to twelve) provide a great time, with snow games, skiing, and other fun activities. Divided not only by age but also by ability, the kids set the pace for the day—how much they want to ski, and where. The 10:00 A.M.–3:00 P.M. program costs $26 and includes lift ticket, lunch, and lessons. A day-care center, Sunshine Kids Kampus, is open from 8:00 A.M. to 5:00 P.M. for children nineteen months to six years. Full-day cost is $23, and half-day is only $15.

Recreation: Sunshine Village is located on the Continental Divide, where you can ski the provinces of both British Columbia and Alberta off the same run. The top elevation at Sunshine is more than 9,000 feet and the base elevation is 5,440 feet, yielding skiers more than 3,500 vertical feet. Mother Nature drops more than 360 inches of snow here each year, which results in good skiing from mid-November through the end of May. Of the eighty-nine runs currently open, 50 percent are intermediate; the remainder are split evenly between beginner and expert, with Goat's Eye Mountain (elevation 9,200 feet) offering extreme-expert-only (Double Black) chutes and glades. Many of the runs are above the treeline, giving skiers that top-of-the-world feeling. Sunshine Village boasts North America's largest new ski terrain with the opening of Goat's Eye Mountain, the last major new ski terrain in Banff National Park.

When not skiing, you may want to pursue less rigorous activities in the family games room or relax your weary muscles in the sauna or the Sunshine Inn's giant outdoor hot pool, rated Canada's best by *Ski Canada* magazine.

Whistler/Blackcomb

Whistler Resort Association
4010 Whistler Way
Whistler
British Columbia, Canada V0N 1B4
(604) 932–4222, (800) 944–7853

If you're lucky enough to hear the whistling call of the indigenous marmots, you'll easily recognize how Whistler Mountain got its current name. Originally known as London Mountain, on the old Caribou Gold Rush Trail, this area saw its first settlers in 1914, an adventurous couple who built a fishing lodge on the shores of Alta Lake. Though still attracting fishermen in the summer, Whistler is famous today as an outstanding ski destination.

Skiers first schussed these slopes in the mid-1960s, and the early 1980s witnessed considerable expansion and development, primarily the opening of Blackcomb Mountain. The two mountains, Whistler and Blackcomb, are serviced by three base facilities. In the Coastal Mountains, Whistler/Blackcomb is just 75 miles north of Vancouver.

Accommodations: Hotels and condominiums are found throughout Whistler Resort. The larger facilities are the Canadian Pacific Château Whistler at the base of Blackcomb, with 343 units, plus a 200-room expansion new in the spring of 1997, indoor and outdoor swimming pools, a health club, and indoor tennis courts; the Delta Mountain

Inn in Whistler Village, with 300 units, an outdoor pool, and indoor tennis courts; and the Crystal Lodge, also in the Village, with 137 units and an outdoor pool. But a smaller complex, such as the Hearthstone Lodge, Powderview, Whistler Resort and Club, or Whiski Jack Condos, might also be the perfect choice for your family. The Marriott Residence Inn, with 186 units, has recently opened slopeside on Blackcomb Mountain. Contacting Central Reservations at (800) 944–7853 is the first step in sorting out all these choices. A seven-night package, which includes lodging, lift tickets, and transportation to and from Vancouver Airport, starts at $722 (U.S. dollars) per person during the regular season (late January to late March). The value season is late November to mid-December and late March onward, when a seven-night package starts at $494 (U.S. dollars) per person. Christmastime commands higher rates than the regular season, and stays during the month of January cost slightly lower than the regular season.

Dining: With more than sixty restaurants and cafes, you'll never have trouble indulging your palate's whim, whether you crave French, Italian, Japanese, Mexican, or Greek cuisine. Three restaurants on Whistler and six on Blackcomb serve hearty soups and stews, burgers, pizza, and pasta to skiers reluctant to leave the slopes for very long. Some of the restaurants favored by families are Black's Restaurant, The Old Spaghetti Factory, and Hard Rock Cafe in the Village; Monk's at Blackcomb; and Hoz's Cafe, Boston Pizza, and Dusty's at Whistler Creek.

Children's World: Skiing starts young here. Wee Scamps on Whistler and Wee Wizards on Blackcomb take two- and three-year-olds from 8:30 A.M. to 3:30 P.M. for a combination of morning skiing and afternoon crafts, indoor activities, and storytime. More serious skiing carries on for four- to twelve-year-olds with Ski Scamps on Whistler and Super Kids on Blackcomb. Young skiers who are particularly proficient can join Red Star Scamps (six- to twelve-year-olds) on Whistler, and Mini Masters (seven- to ten-year-olds) and Superstars (ten- to thirteen-year-olds) on Blackcomb. For hot-shot teenagers, Whistler offers Club Free, and Blackcomb has Team Devo. The cost for these programs ranges from $37 to $41 for a full day including lunch, and groups are divided by ability as well as age. Special prices are available for half-day, three-day, and five-day programs. For nonskiing wee ones (ages eighteen months to three years), Blackcomb offers a program of indoor and outdoor play. Called Childminding, it runs from 9:00 A.M. to 3:00 P.M. and costs $34 for a full-day, including lunch; $25 for half-day. Individual babysitting rates are $6.00 to $8.00 an hour.

While neither Whistler nor Blackcomb has a formal summertime program, there's lots going on. Blackcomb Mountain can also provide contacts for privately run ski and snowboarding camps offered in June and July. The Community Recreation Center has an indoor swimming pool as well as an ice rink for those who miss winter. And with glacier skiing, winter sports lasts through August, side by side with hiking, biking, and swimming.

Recreation: Two amazing mountains—get introduced to them in a morning or afternoon guided tour (free) and you'll begin to appreciate their 6,900 acres of skiable terrain and 5,200 feet of vertical drop. More than 200 trails, 10 bowls, and 3 glaciers provide all the variety any skier could hope for. Choose chutes filled with powder, steep runs through trees, broad trails perfectly groomed, or mogul monsters. The average annual snowfall of 360 inches is complemented by sophisticated snow-making capabilities. Both mountains open in late November, and skiing continues to late April on Whistler and late May on Blackcomb. Blackcomb opens again in mid-June for glacier skiing through August. You can book private and group lessons or join a camp specializing in skiing bumps or powder.

When taking a break from skiing, try ice skating and snowmobiling, or organize a sleigh ride. Cross-country skiers take to the 14 miles of track set trails through the forest and valley. For less strenuous exercise stroll through the village to discover its eighty shops or hit Whistler Wonderland for air hockey and mini-golf.

In the summer golf is the premier sport, with three eighteen-hole courses, each with fine credentials. The Whistler Golf Course was designed by Arnold Palmer, and the Château Whistler Course was designed by Robert Trent Jones, Jr. Jack Nicklaus was responsible for the newest course, Nicklaus North, which opened in 1994.

Hiking and biking across the Alpine terrain are favorites with summertime visitors. And the five lakes provide fishermen, swimmers, and boaters with ample fun. Summer is also the season of music; the Country and Blues Festival takes place in July, whereas classical music is on the agenda in August. And if you can stretch your summer into September, stick around for the Jazz Festival.

Indexes

Alphabetical Index to Resorts

Classic Resorts

Country Inn Resorts

Resorts with Golf

Resorts with Horseback Riding

Lakeside Resorts

Seaside Resorts

Spa Resorts

Resorts with Skiing

Resorts with Tennis

Amelia Island Plantation Amelia Island, Florida, 106
Callaway Gardens Pine Mountain, Georgia, 113
Club Med/Sandpiper, Florida Port St. Lucie, Florida, 122
Gray Rocks Resort Mont-Tremblant, Quebec, Canada, 271
Innisbrook Hilton Resort Tarpon Springs, Florida, 130
Kiawah Island Kiawah Island, South Carolina, 87
La Costa Resort and Spa Carlsbad, California, 239
The Lodge of Four Seasons Championship Golf Resort & Spa
        Lake Ozark, Missouri, 155
Palmetto Dunes Resort Hilton Head Island, South Carolina, 92
The Rancho Bernardo Inn San Diego, California, 245
The Resort at Longboat Key Club Longboat Key, Florida, 135
Sheraton El Conquistador Resort and Country Club Tucson, Arizona, 186
South Seas Plantation Resort and Yacht Harbour Captiva Island, Florida, 138
Stratton Mountain Resort Stratton Mountain, Vermont, 41
Sun Valley Sun Valley, Idaho, 255
Wild Dunes Isle of Palms, South Carolina, 100

About the Authors

Janet Tice grew up in Oklahoma City and lived for twenty years in New York City. She earned an M.S. in Psychiatry from New York University, owned a travel agency for many years, and, in 1986, founded Families Welcome!, a tour company specializing in family travel. She currently resides in Chapel Hill, North Carolina, with her daughter, Fabiana, and travels extensively, "but never enough!"

Jane Wilford was born and reared in New Orleans, Louisiana. She earned a B.A. in Art History and History from Duke University and an M.S. in Library Service from Columbia University. In 1986 she moved to London, where she currently resides with her husband, D. Sykes Wilford, and sons, Sykes and Paul, and daughter, Sarah. The Wilford family has traveled extensively throughout the United States and Europe.

Other titles in the *100 Best Resorts* series:

The 100 Best Honeymoon Resorts of the World
The 100 Best Resorts of the Caribbean

Available from your bookstore or directly from the publisher. For a catalogue or to place an order, call toll-free 24 hours a day (800) 243-0495 or write to The Globe Pequot Press, P.O. Box 833, Old Say-brook, Connecticut 06475-0833.

The Struggle for Equality

The Struggle for Equality

ABOLITIONISTS

AND THE NEGRO IN

THE CIVIL WAR AND

RECONSTRUCTION

James M. McPherson

PRINCETON UNIVERSITY PRESS

PRINCETON, NEW JERSEY

1964

Published by Princeton University Press, 41 William Street,
Princeton, New Jersey 08540
In the United Kingdom by Princeton University Press, Chichester, West Sussex
Copyright © 1964 by Princeton University Press; copyright renewed
© 1992 by Princeton University Press

All Rights Reserved

Library of Congress Card 63-23411

Second edition paperback printing, with a new preface by the author, 1995

Princeton University Press books are printed on acid-free paper and meet the guidelines
for permanence and durability of the Committee on Production Guidelines for Book
Longevity of the Council on Library Resources

Printed in the United States of America

10 9 8 7 6 5 4 3 2 1

*This book is dedicated
to all those
who are working to achieve
the abolitionist goal
of equal rights for all men*

Contents

Preface to the 1995 Edition

PEOPLE OFTEN ASK ME how I became interested in the Civil War. *The Struggle for Equality* provides an answer. The book grew out of my Johns Hopkins doctoral dissertation, completed in 1963 almost simultaneously with the march on Washington led by Martin Luther King, Jr. My graduate-school years coincided with the sit-ins and freedom-rides phase of the civil-rights movement. During those years I was struck by the parallels between the events of my time and those of exactly a century earlier: confrontation between North and South, "massive resistance" to national law by Southern states, physical as well as rhetorical violence against blacks and whites trying to change Southern race relations, federal troops going into the South to enforce the freedom and civil rights of black people. These parallels spurred me to study the origins in the 1860s of what I witnessed and experienced in the 1960s. In particular, I wanted to know what part the civil-rights activists of the Civil War era—the abolitionists—played in the great drama of war and reconstruction that freed the slaves and pledged the nation to the promise of equal rights that activists in the 1960s were trying to force Americans to fulfill a century later. My dissertation, therefore, was my entrée into the endlessly fascinating subject of the American Civil War.

The perspective of this book is thus a product of the time in which it was written. That is true, I think, of most historical studies. As we tell our students, history is what historians say about the past. No two historians will view that past in precisely the same way. Indeed, the same historian will hold different perspectives at different stages in his own life cycle. In graduate school I read a number of books written a generation earlier and reissued in new editions. Their authors were still alive and active but they made no revisions in these reissued books, explaining in their prefaces that to do so would destroy the unity and integrity of perspective and interpretation particular to a time and place. I did not understand that then; I do now. This second edition of *The Struggle for Equality*, therefore, is unchanged from the first edition published thirty years ago.

The reader, however, is entitled to know some of the things I might change if I were writing the book today. One important change would be the perspective on Abraham Lincoln. Most abolitionists were sharply critical of Lincoln because they considered him too slow to act against slavery; once he had embraced emancipation as a war aim, they condemned him as too conservative on the issue of equal rights for freed slaves. Because I sympathized with the abolitionists' position on these questions, I tended to adopt their attitude toward Lincoln. Over the past thirty years my deepening understanding of the complexity and difficulty of the problems Lincoln faced has changed my perspective. If he had done precisely what abolitionists demanded when they demanded it, he would have lost the essential support of a large part of the Northern constituency for the Union war effort. There would thus have been no Union victory—and no Thirteenth, Fourteenth, and Fifteenth Amendments to the Constitution to free the slaves and grant them the equal civil and political rights for which the abolitionists fought. Lincoln's extraordinary skills of leadership and his sense of timing moved the country in the direction that abolitionists wanted to go more effectively than they recognized.

A second change I would make if I were writing this book today would be to emphasize more strongly the importance of the Union army in accomplishing these revolutionary changes in race relations. On "the progress of our arms," said Lincoln in his second inaugural address, "all else chiefly depends." That "all else" included the abolition of slavery. *The Struggle for Equality* focuses mainly on the home front—on the activities of abolitionists in the forum of public opinion and politics through their newspapers, speeches, and political activities in the North. But there were many abolitionists in the army, and while the great majority of Northern soldiers were by no means abolitionists when the war began, their experiences abolitionized many of them as the war went on. In the postwar years, the activities of abolitionists in the South as teachers, Freedmen's Bureau agents, and Reconstruction political leaders were of considerable importance. These matters probably deserve more attention than I gave them.

Nevertheless, the framework and core of this book would remain the same if I were writing it today. I still believe that abolitionists played an important and constructive part in achieving their lifelong goals of freedom and equal rights for the slaves during the Civil War and Reconstruction. Their movement did not fade away when emancipation was accomplished, as historians once thought. Abolitionists remained active as civil-rights advocates and educators of the freed slaves for years, indeed decades, after the Civil War. That is the story told by this book, a story as noteworthy today as when it was first published a generation ago.

James M. McPherson

Princeton, New Jersey
September 6, 1994

PREFACE

MOST historians have paid little attention to the abolitionist
movement after 1860. Yet it was in the 1860's that the
abolitionist crusade reached the height of its power and saw the
achievement of most of its objectives. After the outbreak of the
Civil War, abolitionists were transformed almost overnight from
despised fanatics to influential and respected spokesmen for the
radical wing of the Republican party. Early in the war, abolitionists outlined a broad program of emancipation, employment of
Negro soldiers in the Union Army, creation of a Freedmen's
Bureau, government assistance for the education of the freedmen,
civil and political equality for all black men, and grants of
confiscated land to the freed slaves. Under the military pressures
of war and the political pressures of reconstruction, the Republican party adopted all of these policies except the wholesale confiscation of southern plantations. True, the North retreated from
radicalism after 1870 and failed to enforce the provisions of Reconstruction after 1877, but the equalitarian achievements of the
Civil War and Reconstruction remained in the Constitution and
the statute books, where they constitute today the legal basis for
the "Second Reconstruction" of the South.

Despite the prominence of abolitionists during the war and
reconstruction years, standard historical treatments of the anti-
slavery movement virtually ignore the period after 1860. The
implicit assumption is that abolitionism merged itself with the
Republican party during the war and therefore no longer possessed a separate identity or purpose. Garrison's willingness to
cease publication of his *Liberator* and to dissolve the antislavery
societies in 1865 is deemed proof that abolitionists considered the
Thirteenth Amendment the consummation of their crusade and
were little concerned with the Negro after emancipation. Nothing
could be more misleading. It is true that for the first time in their
lives, abolitionists marched in step with a major political party
after 1861. But they marched far in advance of the Republican
party, and frequently the party refused to follow them as fast
as they desired. At such times they would chastise the Republicans
with old-time vigor and abandon. Throughout the 1860's most

abolitionists preserved their separate identity, and cooperated with the Republican party only when that party was marching in the direction they wanted to go. Abolitionists showed a greater concern for the plight of the Negro after 1865 than anyone else except the Negro himself. The American Anti-Slavery Society and its auxiliaries remained in existence after the war to wage battle for the full civil and political equality of the Negro. Even Garrison, despite his withdrawal from the antislavery societies in 1865, did not consider his crusade ended when the slave was freed. Along with many other abolitionists, he was active in the movement to educate the freedmen, and his denunciations of racial discrimination were no less militant after 1865 than before.

This book is an effort to trace the history of the abolitionist movement during the Civil War and Reconstructon, to evaluate the contribution of abolitionists to the efforts to solve the race problem in those years, and to view America's greatest social and political revolution through the eyes of the nation's foremost equalitarians. No claim will be made that the abolitionists were primarily responsible for the gains of the Negro in the war and reconstruction. Abolitionists did not forge or control events; but neither was their influence negligible. In many respects the abolitionists served as the conscience of the radical Republicans. They provided an idealistic-moral-humanitarian justification for the policies of the Republican party—policies which were undertaken primarily for military or political reasons. The ideas, activities, and responses of abolitionists during a period when their movement reached its climax are not without historical interest.

I am indebted to the following library staffs: the American Antiquarian Society, Worcester, Massachusetts; the Boston Public Library; the Columbia University Library; the Concord Public Library, Concord, Massachusetts; the Cornell University Library; the Frederick Douglass Memorial Home, Anacostia Heights, Washington, D.C.; the Essex Institute Library, Salem, Massachusetts; the Houghton Library, Harvard University; the Johns Hopkins University Library, especially the interlibrary loan division; the Library of Congress; the Massachusetts Historical Society; the New York Historical Society; the New York Public Library; the Pierpont Morgan Library, New York City; the Radcliffe Women's Archives, Radcliffe College; the Rochester

University Library; the Smith College Library; the Syracuse University Library; the Vermont Historical Society, Montpelier, Vermont; the Wayland Historical Society, Wayland, Massachusetts; and the Worcester Historical Society, Worcester, Massachusetts. They were very kind and I wish to thank them for assistance in locating materials and for permission to quote from manuscripts in their possession.

I owe a special debt of gratitude to Professor C. Vann Woodward, whose advice and counsel proved valuable at every stage of this work. I wish also to thank Professor David Donald, Professor Martin Duberman, and Mrs. Willie Rose, all of whom read the entire manuscript and made helpful suggestions. The encouragement and assistance of my wife, Patricia McPherson, has been inestimable from the first conception of this project to its final completion.

James M. McPherson

Department of History
Princeton University
Princeton, New Jersey

KEY TO ABBREVIATIONS

The following symbols are used in the footnotes to designate repositories of manuscript collections:

AAS . . . . . American Antiquarian Society, Worcester, Massachusetts

BPL . . . . . Boston Public Library

CU . . . . . Columbia University Library

Cornell . . . Cornell University Library

HU . . . . . Houghton Library, Harvard University

LC . . . . . Library of Congress

MHS . . . . Massachusetts Historical Society

NYHS . . . . New York Historical Society

NYPL . . . . New York Public Library

PML . . . . Pierpont Morgan Library, New York City

RU . . . . . Rochester University Library

SC . . . . . Smith College Library

SU . . . . . Syracuse University Library

VHS . . . . . Vermont Historical Society, Montpelier

The following abbreviation is used in the footnotes to designate the *National Anti-Slavery Standard*, organ of the American Anti-Slavery Society: *N.A.S. Standard*.

The Struggle for Equality

INTRODUCTION

IN this study the term "abolitionist" will be applied to those Americans who before the Civil War had agitated for immediate, unconditional, and universal abolition of slavery in the United States. Contemporaries of the antislavery movement and later historians have sometimes mistakenly used the word "abolitionist" to describe adherents of the whole spectrum of antislavery sentiment. Members of the Free Soil and Republican parties have often been called abolitionists, even though these parties were pledged officially before 1861 only to the limitation of slavery, not to its extirpation. It is a moot question whether such radical antislavery leaders as Charles Sumner, John Andrew, George Julian, Thaddeus Stevens, or Owen Lovejoy were genuine "abolitionists." In their hearts they probably desired an immediate end to slavery as fervently as did William Lloyd Garrison. But they were committed publicly by political affiliation and party responsibility to a set of principles that fell short of genuine abolitionism. The names of Sumner, Julian, and other radical Republicans will crop up frequently in this book, for they were closely connected with the activities of abolitionists during the Civil War and Reconstruction. No attempt will be made, however, to settle the question whether Sumner, for example, was an authentic abolitionist. The focus of this study will be upon those men and women who made no apologies for their radicalism and who crusaded militantly for immediate, unconditional, and universal emancipation.

In 1860 there were three loosely defined and somewhat interrelated abolitionist groups in the North. First and most prominent in the eyes of the public were the Garrisonians—the members of the American Anti-Slavery Society and its auxiliaries. The Garrisonians had a more cohesive and active organization than any of the other genuine abolitionist groups, and many of the ablest writers and speakers in the movement were affiliated with them. William Lloyd Garrison was widely regarded as the pioneer and leader of the militant abolitionist crusade. Wendell Phillips was universally acknowledged to be one of the finest platform speakers in the nation. In addition the American Anti-Slavery Society

3

contained a host of lesser luminaries who were fairly well known to the antislavery public: Lydia Maria Child, Theodore Tilton, Edmund Quincy, Parker Pillsbury, Oliver Johnson, Abby and Stephen S. Foster, Elizabeth Cady Stanton, Susan B. Anthony, Sydney Howard Gay, James and Lucretia Mott, Samuel J. May, Robert Purvis, James Miller McKim, and many others.

The Garrisonians were small in number, but their influence and their impact on public opinion cannot be measured by size alone. The radicalism of their doctrines, the vehemence of their language, and the prominence of their leaders gave them an audience and a notoriety far out of proportion to their numbers. This small army of talented and articulate reformers was active primarily in the eastern states. New England, of course, was the center of Garrisonian abolitionism. The *Liberator* was published in Boston. Eleven of the twelve members of the American Anti-Slavery Society's executive committee were from New England (the twelfth was from New York). The Massachusetts Anti-Slavery Society was the most vigorous auxiliary of the national organization. But there were pockets of Garrisonian strength elsewhere. Oliver Johnson, Theodore Tilton, and Sydney Howard Gay formed the core of a small group of Garrisonians in New York City. Johnson edited there the *National Anti-Slavery Standard*, organ of the American Anti-Slavery Society. In Philadelphia there were two Garrisonian organizations: the Pennsylvania Anti-Slavery Society, led by J. Miller McKim, James and Lucretia Mott, and Robert Purvis; and the Philadelphia Female Anti-Slavery Society, dominated by Mary Grew and Sarah Pugh. Scattered through parts of upstate New York were several active Garrisonians who constituted the leadership of the New York Anti-Slavery Society: Samuel J. May, Aaron M. Powell, Elizabeth Cady Stanton, and Susan B. Anthony. Finally, in the Western Reserve of Ohio there existed another outpost of Garrisonianism: Marius Robinson edited there the *Anti-Slavery Bugle*, organ of the near-moribund Western Anti-Slavery Society, and Giles B. Stebbins and Josephine S. Griffing headed the lecture corps of these western Garrisonians.

The second group of abolitionists active in 1860 is more difficult to delineate. Roughly it consisted of those who, for one reason or another, had broken with Garrison in 1840, but who had

4

nevertheless refused to submerge their abolitionist identity in the Free Soil or Republican parties. Of the men who had founded the Liberty party in 1840, some had died and many had been absorbed by the Republican party, but an indomitable remnant of political abolitionists had refused to adulterate their beliefs with the pale antislavery doctrines of the Republican party, and had kept the Liberty party alive through the 1850's. In 1860 they called their organization the Radical Abolitionist party. They proclaimed the constitutional right and duty of the federal government to abolish slavery in the states. Leaders of this party were Gerrit Smith, William Goodell, and Frederick Douglass. The center of their strength was in upstate New York, and the party organ, the *Principia*, was edited in New York City by Goodell.

Closely allied with the Radical Abolitionists was the Church Anti-Slavery Society, successor of Lewis Tappan's American and Foreign Anti-Slavery Society which had died a quiet death in the 1850's. The Church Anti-Slavery Society was founded in 1859 by a Connecticut Congregationalist minister, Henry Cheever, and his more famous brother, George Cheever, pastor of the Church of the Puritans in New York City. The Cheever brothers hoped to convert the northern Protestant clergy to the doctrine of immediate and unconditional emancipation, but the radicalism of the Society, and its insistence that slaveholding as well as slavery was a sin, alienated most of the northern clergy. No more than a few hundred members, mostly Congregational and Presbyterian ministers in New England, New York, and the upper tier of western states, ever belonged to the Society, and its influence was limited. Many members of the Society were also adherents of the Radical Abolitionist party, and Goodell's *Principia* doubled as an unofficial organ of the Church Anti-Slavery Society.

Another abolitionist-controlled organization, informally associated with the Radical Abolitionist party and the Church Anti-Slavery Society, was the American Missionary Association. Organized by Lewis Tappan, George Whipple, and Simeon S. Jocelyn in 1846, the A.M.A. was ostensibly nonsectarian, but in reality it was dominated by Congregationalists. It organized antislavery churches in the West and in Kentucky, carried on mission work in Africa, and in 1855 founded Berea College in Kentucky.

In 1860 the A.M.A. was small, with its major work of freedmen's education still in the future.

The third major grouping of abolitionists is almost impossible to define precisely. Speaking broadly, one might say that it consisted of all those who advocated the immediate, unconditional, and universal abolition of slavery, but who did not belong to any of the formal abolitionist organizations described in the preceding paragraphs. This included a majority of the old Liberty party stalwarts who had followed Henry B. Stanton, Joshua Leavitt, and Elizur Wright into the Free Soil party in 1848 and ultimately into the Republican party. Most of the western political abolitionists had pursued this course and had almost completely submerged their abolitionist identity in the weaker antislavery principles of the Republican party. Yet they remained militant and uncompromising in their basic abolitionist beliefs.

A subgrouping of abolitionists who do not fall readily within any organizational framework were the supporters of John Brown. The most famous members of this group were the "Secret Six" who had subsidized Brown's campaigns in Kansas and his abortive invasion of Virginia. Of these six, Theodore Parker had died and Gerrit Smith has been classified with another group, but the other four remained very much alive and were destined to play important roles in the drama of the Civil War: George L. Stearns, wealthy Boston lead-pipe manufacturer; Samuel Gridley Howe, world-famous for his work with the blind; and the young, romantic intellectuals, Thomas Wentworth Higginson and Frank Sanborn. All four were from Massachusetts. James Redpath and Richard J. Hinton, British-born radicals who had known John Brown in Kansas and who later published biographies of Old Ossawatomie, also lived in the Bay State.

In fact, Massachusetts was by far the most radical antislavery state in the Union. In addition to being the center of Garrisonian activity, Massachusetts was the home of many of the prominent non-Garrisonian abolitionists, and the state boasted two of the strongest antislavery senators in Congress, Charles Sumner and Henry Wilson. The center of this antislavery political power was a small, informal organization known as the Bird Club. The Bird Club originated about 1850 when a group of radical leaders of the Massachusetts Free Soil party began meeting together in

Boston on Saturday afternoons for dinner and long, confidential political discussions. Host on these occasions was Frank Bird, an East Walpole paper manufacturer and radical Free Soiler. Sumner, Wilson, and John Andrew, the famous war governor of Massachusetts, were members of this club, and as the decade progressed it became more and more powerful until by 1860 it virtually controlled the state's Republican party. For the next twelve years the Bird Club ruled Massachusetts politics. A majority of the men in the Club were probably not abolitionists according to the definition of that term used in this study, but a number of genuine abolitionists *did* belong to the Club. Stearns, Howe, Sanborn, Charles W. Slack, and other abolitionists were members, and exerted a strong influence on the Club's policies. Frank Bird himself presided over a disunion convention in 1857 organized by Garrisonians. Elizur Wright, who had served as secretary of the American Anti-Slavery Society in the 1830's and had helped found the Liberty party in 1840, was a member of the Bird Club. The line between abolitionist and Free Soiler was often blurred and indistinct in Massachusetts. If the Bird Club was not a formal abolitionist organization, it was the next thing to it.

There were also many abolitionists who did not belong to any definite antislavery organization, but who were nevertheless well known and influential in their communities and states: Dr. Henry I. Bowditch, Boston physician; James Freeman Clarke, Boston Unitarian minister; Levi Coffin, the Quaker "President" of the Underground Railroad in Cincinnati; Octavius B. Frothingham, liberal Unitarian minister and Transcendentalist intellectual of New York City; Gilbert Haven, a Massachusetts Methodist preacher and militant abolitionist; John Jay, wealthy grandson of the first chief justice; Samuel Sewall, Boston lawyer; John G. Whittier, beloved Quaker poet of Amesbury, Massachusetts; and Samuel Johnson of Lynn, Massachusetts, Unitarian minister and expert on Oriental religions. These were only a few of the scores of prominent men throughout the North who refused to identify themselves formally with any antislavery society, but who frequently appeared on abolitionist platforms and bore powerful testimony for freedom in their daily callings.

These various groups of abolitionists often differed on points of procedure or emphasis, but on the main objectives of the abolitionist crusade they were united. The crisis of the Civil War obscured most of their old academic disputes and caused them to close ranks, at least for a time, in the struggle for the freedom and equality of the Negro. The chapters that follow are the story of that struggle.

I ✦ THE ELECTION OF 1860

THE election of 1860 confronted Garrisonian abolitionists with a dilemma. For the first time an avowedly antislavery party had an excellent chance of winning the presidency. This intoxicating prospect was too much for some Garrisonians, especially those of the younger generation, who forsook the antipolitical traditions of the movement and gave positive support to Abraham Lincoln. A majority of Garrisonians, however, remained true to their principles, refused to give an explicit endorsement to the Republican party (though hoping for its victory), and criticized the party sharply for its antislavery shortcomings.

Garrisonians had always taken an ambivalent attitude toward antislavery political parties. In the 1840's Garrison and Phillips were not entirely displeased by the growth of the free soil coalition. "We look upon the Free Soil movement as the unavoidable result of our principles and agitation," declared Phillips in 1849, "and hail it so far as its formation gives proof of a wider spread of a degree of antislavery feeling in the community." But it remained nevertheless a *free soil* and not an abolitionist party, unworthy of genuine abolitionist support because it was not "pledged to trample underfoot the compromises of the Constitution."[1]

In 1856 many Garrisonians expressed sympathy for the Republican party and its dashing presidential candidate, John C. Frémont. From 1856 to 1860 there was a growing debate within the American Anti-Slavery Society over the attitude abolitionists should take toward the Republican party. Some Garrisonians became outright Republicans. Most of them, however, continued to shun politics, watching the course of the Republicans critically but sympathetically. In 1859 Garrison accused the Republican party of being a "timeserving, a temporizing, a cowardly party," but found some hope in the fact that it possessed "materials for growth."[2]

[1] *Liberator*, Feb. 2, 1849. See also William Lloyd Garrison to Henry Wilson, May 2, 1872, Garrison Papers, BPL.

[2] *Liberator*, Feb. 4, 1859. For a discussion of Garrison's attitude toward the rise of antislavery political parties, see John L. Thomas, *The Liberator: William Lloyd Garrison* (Boston, 1963), 325-26, 342-43, 388-89; and Walter M. Merrill, *Against Wind and Tide: A Biography of William Lloyd Garrison* (Cambridge, Mass., 1963), 212-14, 273-74.

In the left wing of the Society there was a group of contentious radicals, led by Parker Pillsbury, Stephen S. Foster, and his wife Abby Kelley Foster, who insisted on condemning the Republican party as no better than any other party. They considered Republicans "the greatest obstacles to the spread of anti-slavery" because the party stood for little more than the exclusion of slavery from the sparsely populated territories. Pillsbury charged that the weak-kneed policy of the party made it *"really* more dangerous to the cause of liberty . . . than any other party ever formed since the foundations of government were laid."[3]

Garrisonians carried their love-hate complex toward the Republican party into the 1860 presidential campaign. Prior to the Chicago convention it appeared that 1860 might be a year of abolitionist-Republican cooperation. William H. Seward seemed to have the nomination in hand, and for a decade Seward had been one of the brightest stars on the antislavery political horizon. A

Masthead of the *Liberator*.

week before the Republican convention Wendell Phillips declared that "the Republican party, so far as it has a heart, means to grapple slavery, and to strangle it. . . . When William H. Seward enters the Presidential chair, he means that his portrait . . . shall be painted with one hand upon the American eagle, and the other on the jugular vein of the slave system."[4]

---

[3] *Liberator*, Mar. 28, 1856, June 5, 1857. See also Abby K. Foster to Wendell Phillips, June 24, 1859, Foster Papers, AAS; and Maria W. Chapman to Sydney H. Gay, n.d., but probably written sometime in 1859, Sydney H. Gay Papers, CU.

[4] *Liberator*, May 18, 1860.

But to the surprise and disappointment of most eastern anti-slavery men, Seward was shunted aside for a relatively obscure politician from the Illinois prairies. Eastern abolitionists knew little about Lincoln, and as they searched his record they found little to commend. In his 1854 speech at Peoria, Lincoln had made a revealing statement on the subject of slavery: "If all earthly power were given me, I should not know what to do, as to the existing institution. My first impulse would be to free all the slaves, and send them to Liberia,—to their own native land. But . . . [this] is impossible. . . . What then? Free them, and make them politically and socially, our equals? My own feelings will not admit of this; and if mine would, we well know that those of the great mass of white people will not." In his debates with Stephen Douglas in 1858, Lincoln proclaimed that "I have no purpose directly or indirectly to interfere with the institution of slavery in the States where it exists. I believe I have no lawful right to do so, and I have no inclination to do so." He reasserted his opposition to the unconditional repeal of the fugitive slave law and to immediate and unconditional emancipation in the District of Columbia.[5]

Such sentiments could hardly endear Lincoln to abolitionists. But antislavery Republicans could also point to statements by Lincoln revealing a deep-rooted moral abhorrence of slavery. In 1858 he had branded the institution as "a moral, social and political wrong . . . an unqualified evil to the negro, to the white man, to the soil, and to the State." In his famous "House Divided" speech Lincoln expressed the belief that "this Government cannot endure, permanently half *slave* and half *free*." He hoped that "the *opponents* of slavery, will arrest the further spread of it, and place it where the public mind shall rest in the belief that it is in the course of ultimate extinction."[6]

Abolitionists were understandably perplexed about this man Lincoln. He was plainly *against* slavery, but he was just as plainly not *for* its immediate and total abolition. The *Annual Report* of the American Anti-Slavery Society considered Lincoln "a good enough Republican for the party's purposes, but far from being

[5] Roy P. Basler, ed., *The Collected Works of Abraham Lincoln* (9 vols., New Brunswick, N.J., 1955), II, 255-56, III, 16, 41-42.
[6] *ibid.*, III, 92, II, 461.

11

the man for the country's need." He was "a sort of bland, respectable middle-man, between a very modest Right and the most arrogant and exacting Wrong; a convenient hook whereon to hang appeals at once to a *moderate* anti-slavery feeling and to a timid conservatism."[7]

"Who is this huckster in politics?" asked Wendell Phillips a few days after Lincoln's nomination. "Who is this county court advocate? Who is this who does not know whether he has got any opinions?" The *National Anti-Slavery Standard*, official organ of the American Anti-Slavery Society, warned abolitionists that they could not "without utter self-stultification, vote for a man who is opposed to allowing the negro the rights of citizenship . . . and opposed to the unqualified abolition of Slavery in the District of Columbia." Edmund Quincy, the urbane, witty associate editor of the *Standard*, remarked acidly in June 1860, that for the next few months the country would be flooded with political oratory, mass meetings, tons of campaign pamphlets, and when it was all over the result would be "the election of a new administration pledged to the support of slavery in our Southern States, and this equally, whether success be to the Democrats or the Republicans."[8]

The Republican party made careful efforts to dissociate itself from public identification with the abolitionists and their doctrines. During the campaign Republicans frequently declared themselves the true "white man's party." Horace Greeley proclaimed that the Republican party "contemplates PRIMARILY the interest of Free White Labor, for which it struggles to secure the unoccupied territory of the Union." Democratic orators charged that Republicans intended to abolish slavery as soon as they had a chance. "That is not so," roared Greeley. "Never on earth did the Republican Party propose to abolish Slavery. . . . Its object with respect to Slavery is simply, nakedly, avowedly, its restriction to the existing states."[9]

Little wonder that abolitionists were sometimes disgusted with Republicans. "The Republican party means to do nothing, can

[7] *Twenty-Eighth Annual Report of the American Anti-Slavery Society, for the Year Ending May 1, 1861* (New York, 1861), 30-31.

[8] *Liberator*, June 8, 1860; *N.A.S. Standard*, June 2, 1860.

[9] *Liberator*, Oct. 5, 1860; *New York Tribune*, Sept. 7, 1860. See also Emerson D. Fite, *The Presidential Campaign of 1860* (New York, 1911), 124-25.

do nothing, for the abolition of slavery in the slave states," said Garrison. "The Republican party stands on a level with the Fugitive Slave law." Josephine Griffing complained that Republican leaders were covertly trying to discourage abolitionists from holding meetings during the campaign, for they feared such meetings might jeopardize Republican success. "Their great effort," wrote Mrs. Griffing, "is to convince the public mind that they are not Abolitionists, and the Abolitionists, that they *hate* slavery as much as they do. 'For by their sorceries were all nations deceived.' "[10]

The Pillsbury-Foster faction, traditionally hostile to Republicanism, attacked the party even more aggressively than did Garrison and Phillips. Under Pillsbury's influence the Western Anti-Slavery Society, meeting at Salem, Ohio, in late September, resolved that the Republicans were "committed to every constitutional compromise for slavery ever claimed by Calhoun or conceded by Webster . . . they are [unfit] to be entrusted with the interests of humanity and liberty."[11] In his attacks on Republicans, Pillsbury reasserted the conventional Garrisonian disunion views, but Stephen S. Foster went further and tried to organize an out-and-out abolitionist political party. Gadfly of the Garrisonians, Foster had for several years considered the disunion doctrine barren of promise for the slave. In 1860 Foster and John Pierpont, a Liberty party veteran, issued a call for a political abolitionist convention in Worcester, Massachusetts, in mid-September. The convention organized a new party to be known as "The Union Democratic Party" and adopted resolutions affirming that the Constitution, fairly interpreted, prohibited slavery in the *states* and gave the federal government ample power for its abolition therein. The new party made no nominations, but at Frederick Douglass' suggestion it extended "earnest sympathy and hearty Godspeed" to the Radical Abolitionist party and its presidential candidate, Gerrit Smith.[12]

[10] *Liberator*, July 20, 1860; Josephine S. Griffing to Parker Pillsbury, Aug. 22, 1860, published in *Liberator*, Aug. 31. See also the resolutions adopted by the Vermont Anti-Slavery Society at its convention of October 17, 1860, in *Liberator*, Nov. 2, 1860.

[11] *N.A.S. Standard*, Oct. 13, 20, 1860.

[12] Stephen S. Foster to Elizabeth Cady Stanton, Aug. 21, 1860, E. C. Stanton Papers, LC; *Liberator*, Aug. 31, Sept. 28, Oct. 5, 1860.

Rejecting both the nonpolitical stance of Garrison and the political abolitionism of Foster, a number of Garrisonians actively campaigned and voted for Lincoln in 1860. These Republican Garrisonians included some of the ablest men in the Society: Theodore Tilton, vice president of the New York City Anti-Slavery Society and member of the editorial staff of the *New York Independent*; Sydney Howard Gay, the only non-Massachusetts member of the American Anti-Slavery Society's executive committee and editorial writer for the *New York Tribune*; David Lee Child, husband of Lydia Maria Child and an expert on the legal aspects of slavery; and Moncure D. Conway, Virginia-born abolitionist who in 1860 held a Unitarian pastorate in Cincinnati and edited a Unitarian-Transcendentalist magazine, *The Dial*. These four and several other prominent Garrisonians voted for Lincoln in 1860 on the ground that a Republican triumph would be indirectly a victory for the abolitionist cause.[13]

In Massachusetts, the Republican party gave abolitionists something to cheer about by nominating John A. Andrew for governor. Andrew was one of the most steadfast antislavery men in politics. He had helped raise money for John Brown's legal defense, and at a meeting in Boston a month after the Harper's Ferry raid, Andrew had said that he did not know whether John Brown's enterprise in Virginia was wise or foolish, right or wrong; "I only know that . . . JOHN BROWN HIMSELF IS RIGHT. (Applause) I sympathize with the man, I sympathize with the idea, because I sympathize with and believe in the eternal right."[14] Conservative Republicans in Massachusetts were opposed to Andrew, but the powerful Bird Club secured his nomination. Samuel Bowles, editor of the conservative *Springfield Republican*, groaned at the news of Andrew's nomination. "His John Brown sympathies and speeches, his Garrisonian affiliations, his negro-training predilections and all that sort of extreme anti-slaveryism, with which his record abounds, will be trumpeted far and wide in the state

---

[13] Theodore Tilton to William H. Seward, Oct. 10, 1860, Seward Papers, RU; *New York Tribune*, Oct. 30, 1860; Oliver Johnson to Samuel May, Jr., Aug. 18, 1860, Samuel May, Jr. Papers, BPL; David Lee Child to Gerrit Smith, July 23, 1864, Smith Papers, SU; Mary E. Burtis, *Moncure Conway* (New Brunswick, N.J., 1952), 76.

[14] *Liberator*, Sept. 21, 1860; Henry G. Pearson, *The Life of John A. Andrew* (2 vols., Boston, 1904), I, 100-101.

to injure him, [and] out of it to harm Lincoln," wrote Bowles.[15]

Andrew toned down his antislavery utterances during the campaign to make them conform with the Republican platform, but Garrisonians were nevertheless delighted by his nomination. Garrison declared that Andrew "represents the highest phase of political anti-slavery feeling as yet developed." One Massachusetts Republican appealed directly to Samuel May, Jr., general agent of the American Anti-Slavery Society, for Garrisonian support of Andrew. Abolitionists should vote for Andrew, he wrote, because many conservative Republicans would not, and it would look bad if Andrew ran behind Lincoln in Massachusetts. "If the Anti Slavery men of Mass. do not do this, they will surely lose all the sympathy they had outside of their immediate body, which I assure you is no small am[oun]t. Andrew has done everything he could for them, & the cause of John Brown, and they will be the most ungrateful of men" if they do not give him hearty support at the polls. May responded enthusiastically, and it is probable that many Garrisonians voted for Andrew.[16]

As the campaign progressed the Garrisonians' critical attitude toward Lincoln and the Republicans seemed to soften. In August, Garrison had written privately that "the election of Lincoln seems more and more probable. He will do nothing to offend the South." Seven weeks later, however, Garrison declared in the *Liberator* that because the Republican party stood for the exclusion of slavery from the territories, "it will do no slight service to the cause of freedom; and to that extent, and for that reason, it has our sympathies and best wishes." The *Annual Report* of the American Anti-Slavery Society was severe in its strictures of Republican shortcomings, but pointed out the other side of the coin as well. "It would be injustice to the party not to say," commented the *Report*, "that all through the campaign its presses and its speakers uttered many noble sentiments; exposed, with many words of earnest reprobation, the folly and the wrong of slavery. . . . So that, with all its serious defects, the canvass hardly can have failed to do good service to the cause of freedom."[17]

[15] *Springfield Republican*, Aug. 30, 1860.

[16] *Liberator*, Sept. 7, 1860; W. G. Weld to Samuel May, Jr., Oct. 24, 1860, May to Richard Webb, Nov. 6, 1860, Samuel May, Jr. Papers, BPL. Andrew ran about one thousand votes behind Lincoln in Massachusetts.

[17] Garrison to Oliver Johnson, Aug. 9, 1860, Garrison Papers, BPL; *Liberator*,

15

The attitude of moderate Garrisonians toward the election was best illustrated by Oliver Johnson, editor of the *Anti-Slavery Standard*. Johnson thought that the Western Anti-Slavery Society had been crippled by Parker Pillsbury's fulminations against all Republicans. "Instead of allowing a fair margin for honest differences of opinion, and thus keeping on good terms with the better portion of the Republicans," wrote Johnson, the Western Society "has selected for special denunciation such men as Sumner, and thereby reduced itself needlessly & recklessly to a small faction of growlers." Despite the deficiencies of the Republican party, Johnson regarded its success "as the beginning of a new and better era. Let Stephen Foster and his sympathizers say what they will, to me it seems utterly preposterous to deny that Lincoln's election will indicate growth in the right direction."[18]

✦

Hostility toward the Republicans was greater within the Radical Abolitionist party than among Garrisonians. When invited in 1855 to join the antislavery coalition that was soon to blossom into the Republican party, Gerrit Smith scornfully replied: "I wish to have nothing to do with such trash as an anti-Nebraska party. If a disease is raging at my vitals I'd not wish a physician called to attend to a scratch on my little finger."[19] In 1856 the Radical Abolitionists nominated Smith for president on a platform calling for abolition of slavery in the states. Politically it was a forlorn gesture: Smith polled only 165 votes in the entire state of New York. But the Radical Abolitionists did not expect to win elections; they nominated candidates in order to keep their organization alive and to spread knowledge of their principles.[20]

One of the most prominent Radical Abolitionists was Frederick Douglass. In 1856, however, Douglass had dismayed his fellow party members by coming out publicly for Frémont. In 1860 there was little point in nominating Radical Abolitionist candidates unless Douglass could be persuaded to endorse the ticket, for without the support of New York's Negro voters the Radical

Sept. 28, 1860; *Twenty-Eighth Annual Report of the American Anti-Slavery Society*, 33-34.

18 Johnson to J. Miller McKim, Nov. 8, Oct. 11, 1860, McKim Papers, Cornell.

19 Gerrit Smith to W. D. Phillips, Mar. 23, 1855, Gerrit Smith Papers, NYHS.

20 Benjamin Quarles, *Frederick Douglass* (Washington, 1948), 159-63.

Abolitionist party would amount to almost nothing. Gerrit Smith, William Goodell, and other white Radical Abolitionists watched anxiously for Douglass' reaction to Lincoln's nomination. Initially that reaction was favorable. A week after the nomination Douglass described Lincoln as "a man of unblemished private character; . . . one of the most frank, honest men in political life." Douglass would have liked the Republican party to inscribe upon its banners "Death to Slavery" instead of "No more Slave States." But "in the absence of all hope of rearing up the standard of such a party for the coming campaign, we can but desire the success of the Republican candidates."[21]

William Goodell immediately mounted an attack on the Republican party in the columns of the *Principia*, the official organ of the Radical Abolitionist party. Goodell summarized Lincoln's policy statements on slavery and the Negro, and commented: "If any abolitionist or free-soiler, professing to remain such," could read these statements "and then give his vote for Mr. Lincoln, we can only say that we know not how to vindicate the sincerity of his professions, except by entertaining a less elevated conception of his intelligence." A prominent Ohio Radical Abolitionist declared that Lincoln "ignores all the principles of humanity in the colored race, both free and slave; and as abolitionists claim the right to freedom of the one class, and political equality to the other, how can they be consistent, to say nothing of honest, in supporting such a man?"[22]

Such criticism from his associates caused Douglass to moderate his enthusiasm for the Republican party, and he asked his friend Gerrit Smith for advice on the duty of abolitionists in the election. "I cannot support Lincoln," wrote Douglass, "but whether there is life enough in the Abolitionists to name a candidate, I cannot say: I shall look to your letter for light on the pathway of duty." Smith replied in a letter that was published as a broadside and circulated widely among political abolitionists. He asserted that abolitionists should vote only for those candidates who favored the entire abolition of slavery. The "low condition of the anti-slavery cause," wrote Smith, had been caused by the exodus of Liberty

---

[21] *Douglass' Monthly*, June 1860.
[22] *Principia*, June 2, 1860; W. A. Hunter to William Goodell, June 13, 1860, published in *Principia*, July 21, 1860.

party men into the Republican party. "The mass of those who were once intent on abolishing slavery every where, do not go now for its abolition any where. The calculating policy of non-extension has taken the place of the uncompromising principle of abolition."[23]

Two weeks after publication of this letter Douglass assailed the Republican party for its timidity. In a speech on August 1, he charged that by taking a limited defensive position against slavery the Republicans had allowed their opponents to choose the battleground. "Instead of basing ourselves firmly and immovably on the principle of immediate, unconditional emancipation . . . and being the aggressors, we have been defending outposts and allowing [the South] to be the aggressors. . . . The whole abolition . . . *train* . . . has been switched off the abolition track to that of non-extension." Douglass censured the old Liberty party men for allowing themselves to be weakened and absorbed by the Free Soil party. From 1848 to 1860 the antislavery element in the Free Soil and Republican parties had been diluted to the point where Douglass was hard put "to find *even a fibre*, to say nothing of a plank of abolition in the platform adopted at Chicago." Douglass declared his intention to act with the Radical Abolitionist party in the 1860 election.[24]

In a bellicose mood, Radical Abolitionists gathered in Syracuse on August 29 for a combined national and New York state convention. Gerrit Smith was nominated for president and William Goodell for governor of New York. The convention resolved that "the sole legitimate end of all true government is the protection of human rights, the execution of equal and exact justice between a man and his neighbor," and denounced all the major political parties for their eagerness "to assure slaveholders, who trample on all human rights, that they will protect them in so doing."[25]

Garrison expressed his respect for "the motives and aims" of the Radical Abolitionists, but pronounced "the act of making the nominations aforesaid extremely farcical." The Republican press paid little attention to the Radical Abolitionist convention. The

23 Douglass to Smith, July 2, 1860, Smith Papers, su; *Gerrit Smith to Frederick Douglass*, July 13, 1860 (Peterboro, 1860).
24 *Douglass' Monthly*, Sept. 1860.
25 *Principia*, Sept. 8, 15, 1860.

New York Tribune ridiculed the whole affair. Frederick Douglass countered with an attack on the Republican party. "It is simply opposed to allowing slavery to go where it is not at all likely to go," he wrote angrily. "It promises to be about as good a Southern party as either wing of the old Democratic party." Douglass declared that ten thousand votes for Gerrit Smith would do more for the abolition of slavery than two million for Lincoln "or any man who stands pledged before the world against all interference with slavery in the slave states and who is not opposed to making free states a hunting ground for men under the Fugitive Slave Law."[26]

In spite of Douglass' outburst, many political abolitionists voted for Lincoln. Their reasons for doing so were probably similar to those of Edward Gilbert, a New York lawyer and member of the Church Anti-Slavery Society. In June, Gilbert had complained: "How heretical our Republican Party is getting! Every where political leaders teach the people that it is for *white* men and *free soil.* . . . What political Atheism, what infidelity is this!" By October, however, Gilbert was hoping for Republican victory. He wrote to an abolitionist friend: "I quite agree with you as to the Republican party, though I ardently hope that Lincoln will be elected. He will disappoint us no doubt with a conservative administration, yet it will be *one step* and one which will place the hand of Freedom on the jugular & carotid of the slave oligarchy. . . . I am laboring with the Republicans. . . . There is a pulse in the rank and file of the party not to be controlled by the Chicago platform, a pulse impelled by the spirit of God's truth."[27]

Gerrit Smith did not take his own candidacy very seriously. In a letter accepting the nomination he wrote that the purpose of his party was not to win a victory at the polls, but to give abolitionists who believed in the duty of voting an opportunity to vote for a

---

[26] *Liberator*, Sept. 7, 1860; *New York Tribune*, Oct. 2, 1860; *Douglass' Monthly*, Oct. 1860.

[27] Edward Gilbert to Charles Sumner, June 9, 1860, Sumner Papers, HU; Gilbert to George Cheever, Oct. 17, 1860, Cheever Papers, AAS. Henry Cheever, Lewis Tappan, and Simeon S. Jocelyn were tempted to vote for Lincoln, but they rejected the temptation and voted for Smith instead. See William Goodell to George Cheever, Oct. 13, 1860, Cheever Papers, AAS; and Beriah Green to Gerrit Smith, Mar. 20, 1861, Smith Papers, SU.

genuine abolitionist candidate.[28] There is no record of the number of votes cast for Smith in 1860, but it seems unlikely that it was greater than two or three thousand, and it may have been less.

✦

Members of the third major group of abolitionists—those unaffiliated with any formal abolitionist organization—nearly all voted for Lincoln in 1860. Many of them contributed importantly to the Republican effort. Richard Hinton, for example, wrote the first campaign biography of Lincoln. He published it anonymously, for his connection with John Brown made it necessary to conceal his authorship if the book was to help Lincoln. In the biography Hinton went to great lengths to emphasize Lincoln's antislavery sentiments. In actual fact, however, Hinton was not very enthusiastically in favor of Lincoln because he considered him too conservative on the slavery question. Hinton had supported Seward for the nomination. Antislavery Republicans were so confident of Seward's nomination that Hinton had actually written a campaign biography of the New York senator prior to the convention. In any event, Hinton's hastily prepared biography of Lincoln did good service during the campaign. Ten thousand copies were sold inside of two weeks, and the book went through three editions in all.[29]

Two other abolitionists performed an important service for the Republicans by publishing collections of campaign songs. Ever since the famous Harrison-Van Buren campaign of 1840, songs had been a vital part of every presidential election. In 1860 the huge Republican rallies and spectacular "Wide-Awake" parades demanded more songs than ever before, and John Wallace Hutchinson and William H. Burleigh supplied them. John Hutchinson was a member of the famous singing Hutchinson family, the most popular singing group in the North. The whole family were abolitionists, sturdy products of the New Hampshire hills. They provided the music for abolitionist conventions, and they had sung for the antislavery political parties in every election since the Free Soil campaign of 1848.[30]

28 *Liberator*, Sept. 28, 1860.
29 C. Carroll Hollis, "R. J. Hinton, Lincoln's Reluctant Biographer," *The Centennial Review of Arts & Science*, v (Winter 1961), 72-75.
30 Carol Brink, *Harps in the Wind, The Story of the Singing Hutchinsons* (New York, 1947), passim.

In the summer of 1860, John Hutchinson published a little book of fifty-one campaign songs, many of them written by members of the Hutchinson family. Most of the songs stayed within the free-soil bounds of the Republican platform, but some of them were out-and-out abolitionist songs. For example, these two stanzas from "Jordan":

> Slavery and Freedom, they both had a fight,
>   And the whole North came up behind 'em,
> Hit Slavery a few knocks, with a free ballot box,
>   Sent it staggering to the other side of Jordan.

> If I was the Legislature of these United States,
>   I'd settle this great question accordin';
> I'd let every slave go free, over land and on sea,
>   Let 'em have a little hope this side of Jordan.
>   Then rouse up, ye freemen, the sword unsheath,
>   Freedom's the best road to travel, I believe.[31]

William H. Burleigh also published a *Republican Campaign Songster* in 1860; he was the brother of Garrisonian abolitionist Charles C. Burleigh and had been a lecturer for the American Anti-Slavery Society in the 1830's. For a time he turned to the quiet life of a poet, but in 1860 he returned to the political fray and edited a little monthly campaign tract, *The Republican Pocket Pistol*, and published his *Songster*. Most of the songs carried a free soil and "Hurrah for Lincoln" message but a few were of a distinctly abolitionist nature, for example, "The Banner of Freedom":

> And the hour hastens on when the Right shall prevail,
> And the banner of Freedom triumphantly wave
> O'er the land of the free and the home of the brave! . . .

> Then a shout for our banner, a shout for our cause,
>   'Tis the noblest on earth, and our watch-word shall be,
> "The whole Constitution, the Union and Laws,
> And freedom to all that by nature are free."[32]

---

[31] John W. Hutchinson, ed., *Hutchinson's Republican Songster, for the Campaign of 1860* (New York, 1860), 25-26.

[32] William H. Burleigh, *Poems by W. H. Burleigh, with a Sketch of his Life*

Another veteran abolitionist, Henry B. Stanton, served the Republican party effectively as a stump speaker in 1860. Stanton had been one of the most forceful lecturers in the American Anti-Slavery Society in the 1830's, but he broke with Garrison in 1840, helped organize the Liberty party, and in 1848 led a majority of Liberty party men into the Free Soil party. In 1860 he stumped New York state for Lincoln. Stanton was as much an abolitionist at heart as ever, but he had lost some of his crusading zeal since the early days when he had been mobbed more than two hundred times, and in 1860 he confined himself to proclaiming the conventional nonextension Republican policy on slavery.[33]

These four and many other Republican abolitionists played active roles in the 1860 campaign. Occasionally they had qualms of conscience about supporting a party whose leaders repeatedly proclaimed that their accession to power would pose no danger to slavery in the states. One abolitionist, Elizur Wright, worked out a careful justification of his support for Lincoln, and his explanation is representative of the feelings of other abolitionists who voted Republican in 1860. Some of Wright's friends charged him with inconsistency in supporting the nonabolitionist Lincoln for president. Replied Wright to one of these critics: "Accepting facts as facts and treating them as facts, I know my vote isn't going to make you or Gerrit Smith or Wm. Goodell president. . . . In the Republican platform . . . are some just and right things. . . . I believe the average sentiment of the party is more anti-slavery than the platform, and the sentiment of the most active & efficient leaders still more so."[34]

Another conscientious Republican abolitionist was John Jay, grandson of the first chief justice of the Supreme Court, and son of William Jay, one of the most faithful of the early abolitionists.

by *Celia Burleigh* (New York, 1871), v-xvii; William H. Burleigh, ed., *The Republican Campaign Songster for 1860* (New York, 1860), 28.

[33] Louis Filler, *The Crusade Against Slavery, 1830-1860* (New York, 1960), 72, 134, 189; Henry B. Stanton, *Random Recollections* (3rd ed., New York, 1887), 50, 213; Henry B. Stanton to Salmon P. Chase, July 10, 1860, Chase Papers, LC; *New York Tribune*, Sept. 12, 1860.

[34] Wright to unknown, Oct. 8, 1860, Wright Papers, LC.

Jay explained the reasons for his support of Lincoln in a long speech to his Westchester County neighbors on the eve of the election. The history of the Republican party showed that "it is the embodiment of the Anti-Slavery sentiment of the country," he said. "I do not intend to intimate that all the Anti-Slavery sentiment of the country is represented in that party, or that all the members of that party sympathize with the Abolitionists." Nevertheless, the inauguration of Lincoln would inaugurate "the beginning of the end of American Slavery." Jay predicted that when the Republicans gained a majority in Congress they would outlaw slavery in the territories, abolish slavery in the District of Columbia, prohibit the foreign and internal slave trade, and so constrict slavery as to put it on the road to imminent extinction. Oliver Johnson printed this speech as a supplement to the *Anti-Slavery Standard*, with an explanation that Jay's views, "in some important respects, differ from ours, but we are glad of the opportunity to lay before our readers a Republican speech so thoroughly imbued with the spirit of abolition that it is not likely to gain admission to any of the leading presses of the party."[35]

Jay, Wright, Stanton, Burleigh, the Hutchinsons, Thomas Wentworth Higginson, George L. Stearns, and the other Republican abolitionists who voted for Lincoln in 1860 did so because they hoped that somehow his election would prove to be the first step toward the eventual abolition of slavery.

✦

Republican indifference and even hostility to equal citizenship for free Negroes was an important reason for the coolness of many abolitionists toward the party. Democratic efforts to pin the Negro equality label on the Republican party usually produced vigorous Republican denials. In his fourth debate with Stephen Douglas in 1858 Lincoln stated with painful clarity:

"I will say then that I am not, nor ever have been in favor of bringing about in any way the social and political equality of the white and black races, (applause)—that I am not nor ever have been in favor of making voters or jurors of negroes, nor of qualifying them to hold office, nor to intermarry with white

[35] *N.A.S. Standard*, Nov. 24, 1860.

people; and I will say in addition to this that there is a physical difference between the white and black races which I believe will for ever forbid the two races living together on terms of social and political equality. And inasmuch as they cannot so live, while they do remain together there must be the position of superior and inferior, and I as much as any other man am in favor of having the superior position assigned to the white race."[36]

"The 'negro question,' as we understand it," wrote an Ohio Republican, "is a *white man's question,* the question of the right of free white laborers to the soil of the territories. It is not to be crushed or retarded by shouting 'Sambo' at us. We have no Sambo in our platform. . . . We object to Sambo. We don't want him about." In the 1860 campaign, Senator Seward explained that "the motive of those who have protested against the extension of slavery" had "always really been concern for the welfare of the white man," and not, as some erroneously assumed, an "unnatural sympathy with the negro."[37]

Republican declarations of white supremacy infuriated many abolitionists. The elevation of free Negroes to civil and political equality was an essential corollary of the abolitionist belief in the right of all men to equal freedom. The Western Anti-Slavery Society denounced the Republican party for its racism, noting that "Ohio, under Republican rule, ostracizes the colored man, refuses his ballot, denies him equal educational rights, and shuts him out of the jury-box, and even out of the county poorhouse." In Massachusetts, the Essex County Anti-Slavery Society resolved that "inasmuch as Abraham Lincoln denies the equality of all men, as taught in the Declaration of American Independence, . . . he is, therefore, unworthy of the votes of all those who love freedom and regard justice." Several other county antislavery societies in New England passed similar resolutions.[38] Gerrit Smith wrote a public letter in October 1860, warning abolitionists not to vote for Lincoln because he "is for a white man's party [and] is opposed to extending equal political rights to the black

---

36 Basler, ed., *Collected Works of Lincoln,* III, 145-46.

37 Ohio Republican quoted in Leon F. Litwack, *North of Slavery* (Chicago, 1961), 270; Seward quoted in the *Twenty-Eighth Annual Report of the American Anti-Slavery Society,* 32.

38 *N.A.S. Standard,* Oct. 13, 1860; *Liberator,* Aug. 31, Sept. 21, Nov. 9, 23, 1860.

man." Among the banners borne by enthusiastic Republicans at a mass meeting in Lincoln's home town of Springfield was one which read: "NO NEGRO EQUALITY IN THE NORTH." The *Anti-Slavery Bugle* commented dryly: "We hope those colored men who are bawling themselves hoarse for Lincoln and Hamlin, will have a good time."[39]

Many northern Negroes did support Lincoln in 1860 for the same reason that many white abolitionists supported him: whatever its shortcomings, the Republican party embodied the anti-slavery sentiment of the North. Several Negro abolitionists, however, sharply criticized the Republican party: H. Ford Douglass, a colored leader from Illinois, declared that Lincoln's nomination held out little hope for the Negro, and noted that Lincoln had once refused to sign a petition requesting repeal of an Illinois law barring Negro testimony in court cases involving whites. If Negroes tried to send their children to public schools in Illinois, charged Douglass, "Abraham Lincoln would kick them out, in the name of Republicanism and anti-slavery! . . . I care nothing about that anti-slavery which wants to make the Territories free, while it is unwilling to extend to me, as a man, in the free States, all the rights of a man."[40]

Frederick Douglass, who early in the campaign had praised Lincoln and his party, was later angered by Republican declarations of white supremacy. In 1860 there was a proposal on the New York state ballot to abolish the $250 property qualification for Negro voters and to admit Negroes to the polls on equal terms with whites. Douglass stumped upstate New York for this proposition, distributing 25 thousand pamphlets published by the New York City and County Suffrage Committee of Colored Citizens. The suffrage amendment had been passed by a Republican legislature and enjoyed the support of a number of Republican newspapers including the powerful *New York Tribune*, but during the campaign most Republican newspapers and stump orators ignored it or manifested only half-hearted support for it. On November 6, Lincoln carried New York by 50 thousand votes, but the Negro suffrage amendment was defeated by nearly a two to one margin.

[39] Gerrit Smith's letter was published in the *Principia*, Oct. 27, 1860; the comment of the *Anti-Slavery Bugle* was quoted in the *Principia*, Sept. 8, 1860.
[40] *Liberator*, July 13, 1860.

25

Scores of thousands of Republicans had voted against the amendment. "The black baby of Negro Suffrage was thought too ugly to exhibit on so grand an occasion," wrote Douglass bitterly. "The negro was stowed away like some people put out of sight their deformed children when company comes."[41]

✦

On the morrow of the election there was general rejoicing among abolitionists—including some who had sharply rebuked the Republicans during the campaign—over the result. There were still some dissenting voices, to be sure. "I do not expect that Lincoln will take high and brave ground against slavery," wrote Gerrit Smith. "I think that their policy will be a very conservative one." George Thompson, noted British abolitionist and close friend of Garrison, warned American abolitionists that Lincoln's victory placed their cause in "a new, a critical and a trying position. . . . You have now to grapple with the new doctrine of Republican *conservatism*. You have now to make genuine converts of those who have as yet only been baptized into the faith of non-extension, and whose zeal in that direction is mere *white-man-ism*."[42]

But the voices of doubt and dissent were few. Joshua Leavitt expressed the feelings of most Republican abolitionists when he exulted that Lincoln's election was the victorious culmination of the battle begun by the Liberty party in 1840. "Thank God! Lincoln is chosen!" wrote Leavitt. "What a growth since 1840. . . . It is a joy to have lived to this day." Whittier rejoiced in Lincoln's victory as "the triumph of our principles—so long delayed." Henry Cheever wrote four days after the election that "since the Republican triumph, even though Lincoln should prove another John Tyler, I think abolitionism will be able to show a bolder hand."[43] Even Frederick Douglass had a good word for

41 Quarles, *Douglass*, 166-67; *Douglass' Monthly*, Aug., Dec. 1860. See also *Principia*, Oct. 13, 1860; *New York Tribune*, Sept. 17, Nov. 3, 1860; *Liberator*, Nov. 2, 1860; and *Twenty-Eighth Annual Report of the American Anti-Slavery Society*, 114-15. The *Anti-Slavery Standard*, Nov. 17, 1860, commented that the defeat of the Negro suffrage amendment was proof that the Republican party could not be trusted.

42 Smith to Charles B. Sedgwick, Nov. 15, 1860, quoted in Ralph Volney Harlow, *Gerrit Smith: Philanthropist and Reformer* (New York, 1939), 428; George Thompson to Garrison, Nov. 23, 1860, published in *Liberator*, Dec. 14, 1860.

43 Leavitt to Salmon P. Chase, Nov. 7, 1860, Whittier to Chase, Nov. 9, 1860, Chase Papers, LC; Henry Cheever to Garrison, Nov. 10, 1860, Garrison Papers, BPL.

the Republican victory. No longer, he said, would the slave power rule the nation: "Lincoln's election has vitiated their authority, and broken their power. . . . More important still, it has demonstrated the possibility of electing, if not an Abolitionist, at least an *anti-slavery reputation* to the Presidency."[44]

Edmund Quincy expressed the views of most Garrisonians in a postelection editorial in the *Anti-Slavery Standard*. "Our readers know that we expect little or no Anti-Slavery help from Mr. Lincoln," wrote Quincy, "but we none the less recognize his election as an Anti-Slavery triumph and the result of long Anti-Slavery labors. It is not the harvest, but it is the green blade that must go before it." Samuel May, Jr. was more enthusiastic. "Is not the result *wonderful?*" he exclaimed. "Not that L. & his administration will be likely to do anything antislavery, but in view of the fact that *the North* has stood fast, and, in face of all the Southern threats & bombast & defiance, chosen the candidate which the South had denounced."[45]

In June, Wendell Phillips had called Abraham Lincoln "The Slave-Hound of Illinois." A brilliant, incisive, intuitive thinker, Phillips believed with Emerson that "a foolish consistency is the hobgoblin of little minds." On the day after the election Phillips stood before a packed auditorium in Boston's Tremont Temple and with prophetic vision told the cheering audience:

"If the telegraph speaks truth, for the first time in our history the *slave* has chosen a President of the United States. (Cheers.) We have passed the Rubicon. . . . It is the moral effect of this victory, not anything which his administration can or will do, that gives value to this success. Not an Abolitionist, hardly an antislavery man, Mr. Lincoln consents to represent an antislavery idea. A pawn on the political chessboard, his value is in his position; with fair effort, we may soon change him for knight, bishop, or queen, and sweep the board. (Applause) . . .The Republican party have undertaken a problem, the solution of which will force them to our position. . . . Not Mr. Seward's 'Union and Liberty,' which he stole and poisoned from Webster's 'Liberty and Union.'

[44] *Douglass' Monthly*, Dec. 1860.
[45] *N.A.S. Standard*, Nov. 24, 1860; Samuel May, Jr. to Samuel J. May, Nov. 11, 1860, Samuel J. May Papers, BPL.

No: their motto will soon be 'Liberty first,' (a long pause) 'Union afterwards.' " (Applause and a solitary hiss)[46]

That solitary hiss perhaps expressed the sentiments of South Carolina, for a member of the Palmetto State's legislature quoted Phillips' speech as one justification for his state's secession from the Union.[47]

[46] Wendell Phillips, *Speeches, Lectures, and Letters,* 1st Series (Boston, 1863), 294, 314.

[47] *Twenty-Eighth Annual Report of the American Anti-Slavery Society,* 44.

II ✦ SECESSION AND THE COMING OF WAR

"WE appear to be on the eve of the oddest Revolution that History has yet seen," wrote Edmund Quincy as the cotton states prepared to leave the Union. "A Revolution for the greater security of Injustice, and the firmer establishment of Tyranny!"[1] The South did indeed launch a revolution in the winter of 1860-1861, but its final outcome was rather different from what the revolutionists hoped.

Even before South Carolina seceded on December 20, 1860, pressure began to build up in the North for concessions and conciliation to save the Union. Dozens of compromise proposals were introduced into Congress. These plans included: repeal of northern personal liberty laws; admission of New Mexico as a slave state; disfranchisement and colonization of free Negroes; and perpetual guaranties of slavery in the states where it already existed, in the District of Columbia, and in all territories lying south of the line 36° 30′. Most antislavery Republicans stood firm against any compromise on the issue of slavery in the territories. In the end the only measures adopted were the repeal or modification of personal liberty laws in three states and congressional passage of a constitutional amendment guaranteeing slavery in the states against federal interference.[2]

For several months during the winter of 1860-1861, however, the various plans to conciliate the South were seriously debated in Congress. Abolitionists did not agree among themselves on the best method of dealing with the secession crisis, but they presented a united front against compromise. The *Anti-Slavery Standard* denounced "Doughface Republicans" who offered "base and humiliating concessions" to the South. William S. Robinson, a member of the Bird Club in Massachusetts, was disgusted with all compromisers. "How many skulking, compromis-

---

[1] *N.A.S. Standard*, Dec. 1, 1860.

[2] The best studies of the North during the secession winter are David M. Potter, *Lincoln and His Party in the Secession Crisis* (New Haven, 1942); and Kenneth M. Stampp, *And the War Came: The North and the Secession Crisis, 1860-61* (Baton Rouge, 1950).

ing creatures there are!" he wrote in his weekly column in the *Springfield Republican*. "For a truce, for a little ease, a chance to live three or four years longer in peace, men are willing to entail on their children a severer struggle than this, or, on their remotest posterity, all the evils of a slaveholding despotism."[3]

The most comprehensive Union-saving measure was popularly known as the "Crittenden Compromise," named for its sponsor, Senator John Crittenden of Kentucky. Crittenden's compromise consisted of a series of constitutional amendments to protect slavery in the states and in the District of Columbia, to exclude slavery north of the line 36° 30′ and guarantee it south of that line in all territories now held "or hereafter acquired," and to provide for the disfranchisement and colonization abroad of free Negroes. These amendments were to be perpetually binding; that is, they could never be repealed.[4] Abolitionists excoriated the Crittenden plan in the strongest language they could command. "This so called Crittenden compromise . . . *nails* Slavery into the Constitution," wrote the Reverend R. C. Waterston, a Massachusetts abolitionist. "To me it seems infamous. This question between Slavery & Freedom may as well be met now, as at any other time. Better now than after the rivets have been made more secure."[5]

Abolitionists were confident that radical Republicans would not betray the antislavery cause by accepting a compromise, but they had less faith in the moderate Republicans and in the northern people generally. "My trust, just now, is in the South rather than the North," wrote Mary Grew in January 1861. "I am not sure the North will not make disgraceful concessions of principles, but I am tolerably confident that the South will not accept them." Lydia Maria Child was bitter toward Republicans who were willing to compromise their principles to prevent secession: "If all this excitement does not settle down into a miserable mush of concession, leaving the country in a worse state than it found it,

---

[3] *N.A.S. Standard*, Dec. 15, 22, 1860; *Springfield Republican*, Jan. 19, 1861.

[4] *Cong. Globe*, 36 Cong., 2 Sess., 112-14, 237, 1093-94, 1259-61, 1368, 1405.

[5] R. C. Waterston to Charles Sumner, Feb. 11, 1861, Sumner Papers, HU. For other examples of abolitionist denunciation of the Crittenden plan, see Samuel May, Jr. to Garrison, Jan. 11, 1861, Garrison Papers, BPL; Milton Sutliff to Salmon P. Chase, Feb. 14, 1861, Chase Papers, LC; and *Liberator*, Feb. 1, Mar. 15, 1861.

we shall owe it less to the steadfastness of Republican leaders, than to the utter impossibility of satisfying the demands of the South, however patiently we may crawl in the dust, or whatsoever quantity of dirt we may consent to eat."[6]

Abolitionists were apprehensive about Lincoln's attitude during the secession crisis. The president-elect maintained a public silence from the time of his election until his departure for Washington in February. Privately, however, he made known his opposition to any concession on the issue of slavery in the territories, and it was due more to his influence than to any other factor that most moderate Republicans voted against compromise when the showdown came.[7] Abolitionists were apprised of Lincoln's position by his law partner, William Herndon. "Mr. Lincoln yet remains firm as a rock," Herndon informed Massachusetts abolitionists in February. "He has told me, not only once, but often & often, that rather than concede to traitors, his soul might go back to God from the wings of the Capitol. . . . Say to the Mass[achusetts] boys 'Stand firm—keep your convictions true to your soul.' " Abolitionists appreciated Lincoln's role in preventing compromise. "It is much to the credit of Mr. Lincoln," wrote Garrison, "that he has maintained his dignity and self-respect intact, and gives no countenance to any of the compromises."[8]

✦

Opposition to compromise was essentially a negative policy. What positive solution of the secession crisis could abolitionists offer? For most Garrisonians the answer was easy: let the South go. For nearly twenty years they had been urging the secession of free states from the slaveholding Union. When secession finally came, it was the South that broke away from the North, but this made little difference to Garrisonians—the end result was the same.

The basic Garrisonian argument for disunion was a simple one.

[6] Mary Grew to Garrison, Jan. 15, 1861, Garrison Papers, BPL; L. M. Child to Sumner, Jan. 28, 1861, Sumner Papers, HU.

[7] Potter, *Secession Crisis*, 133-70, 176-87.

[8] Wm. Herndon to Samuel Sewall, Feb. 1, 1861, Garrison Papers, BPL; *Liberator*, Feb. 15, 1861. Some abolitionists, however, were bitter toward Lincoln because of his approval of the proposed constitutional amendment to guarantee slavery in the states forever against congressional interference. *Principia*, Mar. 9, 16, 23, 1861.

Under the Constitution the national government was pledged to protect slavery. The number of southern slave states had increased from six to fifteen during the existence of the Union. Since the adoption of the Constitution, the slave power had marched on from one victory to another until in 1857 a southern-dominated Supreme Court had declared that Negroes were not citizens of the United States. The national government had failed to suppress the African slave trade. Under the aegis of the Union, Florida and Texas were acquired for slavery. The federal government was pledged to return fugitives into bondage. The national army and the militias of free states could be called upon to crush any slave uprising in the South. "We have a right to call on you to give your blood to maintain the slaves of the South in bondage," taunted Robert Toombs of Georgia in a speech Garrisonians were fond of quoting. "Gentlemen, deceive not yourselves; you cannot deceive others. This is a pro-slavery government. Slavery is stamped on its heart—the Constitution."[9]

Disunion, argued Garrisonians, would relieve the North of responsibility for the sin of slavery. It would remove the powerful protective shield of the United States army from slavery, thus allowing slave insurrections a better chance of success. It would end the North's obligation to enforce the fugitive slave law, and encourage a greater exodus of fugitive slaves from the South. Disunion would isolate the South and hold up its peculiar institution to the moral condemnation of the world. Disunion grew out of American principles. The Declaration of Independence stated that any government which undermined natural and God-given rights should be destroyed and a new one formed. Garrisonians maintained that they were fulfilling the revolutionary tradition of the founding fathers by attacking the proslavery Constitution and Union.[10]

[9] The Toombs statement is quoted in Ralph Korngold, *Two Friends of Man* (Boston, 1950), 164-65.

[10] For an excellent discussion of Garrisonian disunionism see Irving H. Bartlett, *Wendell Phillips: Brahmin Radical* (Boston, 1961), 114-37. Some Negro abolitionists were even more strongly disunionist than Garrison. Philadelphian Robert Purvis denounced the Union as "one of the basest, meanest, most atrocious despotisms that ever saw the face of the sun," and said that any man with decent self-respect would look upon it with *"contempt, loathing, and unutterable abhorrence!"* H. Ford Douglass asserted that "I can hate this Government without being disloyal, because it has stricken down my manhood, and treated me as a saleable commodity." Leon F. Litwack, *North of Slavery* (Chicago, 1961), 265-66.

This was the Garrisonian case for disunion prior to 1860. During the secession winter the argument was refined and amplified in an effort to convince the North to let the slave states depart in peace. At first some Garrisonians feared that the South would not carry out its secession threats. "What a stir at the South!" exclaimed William Fish of New York on November 21, "& what a matter of rejoicing it would be to us, if all the Southern States *would* secede! No such encouraging result, I fear." Even after South Carolina had gone, Marius Robinson of Ohio could not persuade himself that "it is anything more than a magnificent game of bluff, & that she will win thereby such compromises as she wants. The only hope is in her madness & insolence."[11]

Most abolitionists, however, believed in the implacable determination of secessionist leaders to carry their states out of the Union. Edmund Quincy was confident that "the abolition of slavery will be hastened by this Disunion movement, whatever shape it may finally take."[12] Most Garrisonians agreed with Quincy. Samuel May, Jr., rejoiced in the secession movement. "I say, with you, Let the South go—put not a *straw* in her way—interpose not even an objection or a regret; let her go." Bankruptcy and ruin or European dependence awaited her, and the North could form its own Union without slavery. Mattie Griffith, a young Kentucky-born woman who had emancipated her inherited slaves and impoverished herself to help them get a new start in life, and had come North herself to join the Garrisonian crusade, believed that "a calm and peaceable dissolution of the Union would be a splendid point in the history of the country, and surely the most signal blow the 'peculiar institution' has ever received."[13]

At the beginning of the new year Garrison pronounced all Union-saving efforts "simply idiotic." He said, "At last 'the covenant with death' is annulled, and 'the agreement with hell' broken. The people of the North should recognize the fact that THE UNION IS DISSOLVED, and act accordingly." The North would then be free indeed, and the South left with all her dread responsibilities resting on her own head. "In that case, she cannot

[11] Wm. Fish to Samuel May, Jr., Nov. 21, 1860, Garrison Papers, BPL; Marius Robinson to May, Dec. 21, 1860, Samuel May, Jr. Papers, BPL.

[12] *N.A.S. Standard*, Jan. 12, 1861.

[13] May to Samuel J. May, Dec. 9, 1860, Samuel J. May Papers, BPL; Mattie Griffith to S. H. Gay, Dec. 28, 1860, Gay Papers, CU.

long uphold her tottering slave system—speedy emancipation will follow—and the final result will be the formation of a Union stretching from the Atlantic to the Pacific, one in spirit, in purpose, in glorious freedom, the bitter past forgotten, and the future full of richest promise!"[14]

Wendell Phillips fervently welcomed secession. "All my grown-up years," he told a New Haven audience, "have been devoted to creating just such a crisis as that which is now upon us." During the secession winter he lectured widely on behalf of disunion, advocating the South's revolutionary right of secession: "Standing with the principles of '76 behind us, who can deny them the right?"[15] Phillips considered disunion the first step toward emancipation. "What supports slavery?" he asked. "Northern bayonets, calming the masters' fear. . . . Disunion leaves God's natural laws to work their good results. . . . Under God's law, insurrection is the tyrant's check. Let us stand out of the path, and allow the Divine law to have free course." Rather than make concessions to keep the slave states in the Union, Phillips would "build a bridge of gold, and pay their toll over it,—accompany them out with glad noise of trumpets. . . . But let the world distinctly understand why they go,—to save slavery; and why we rejoice in their departure,—because we know their declaration of independence is the jubilee of the Slave."[16]

The Garrisonians' implied endorsement of slave insurrections troubled some observers. The pre-Civil War generation could remember the senseless butchery of Nat Turner's uprising, and all Americans had heard blood-curdling stories about the massacre of Haitian whites by Negroes in 1804. The constitution and "Declaration of Sentiments" of the American Anti-Slavery Society, moreover, explicitly disavowed insurrection as a means of abolishing slavery, and some of the Garrisonians, including Garrison himself, were avowed pacifists. How, then, could they sanction insurrection? Garrison declared in December 1860, that if the patriots of 1776 were justified in their resort to arms against Britain, the slaves were justified a thousand times over in rising

---

[14] *Liberator*, Jan. 4, Feb. 15, Mar. 8, 1861.

[15] *ibid.*, Mar. 22, 1861; George L. Austin, *The Life and Times of Wendell Phillips* (2nd ed., Boston, 1901), 206.

[16] Wendell Phillips, *Speeches, Lectures, and Letters*, 1st Series (Boston, 1863), 350-62.

against their oppressors. "Brand the man as a hypocrite," he wrote, "who, in one breath, exults in the deeds of Washington and Warren, and in the next, denounces Nat Turner as a monster for refusing longer to wear the yoke and be driven under the lash." Garrison personally believed in nonresistance, but most of his countrymen did not, and he measured them by their own standard. "If the doctrine of non-resistance ought to be spurned for oppressed white men, it is equally to be spurned for oppressed black men. . . . I test the nation by its own revolutionary standard, taking Bunker Hill monument for my measuring line."[17]

Phillips was no pacifist, and he had less difficulty than Garrison in justifying his endorsement of insurrection. "The reason why I have advised the slave to be guided by a policy of peace is because he has had, hitherto, no chance," said Phillips in February 1861. In a southern Confederacy, however, his chances for successful insurrection would be much better: "I acknowledge the right of two million and a half of white people in the seven seceding States to organize their government as they choose. Just as freely I acknowledge the right of four million of black people to organize *their* government, and to vindicate that right by arms." The South had never known real peace. "Slavery is a form of perpetual war. . . . I hesitate not to say, that I prefer an insurrection which frees the slave in ten years to slavery for a century. . . . Where is the battle-field, however ghastly, that is not white,— white as an angel's wing,—compared with the blackness of that darkness which has brooded over the Carolinas for two hundred years?"[18]

Garrisonians sincerely believed that disunion would destroy slavery. They overestimated the readiness of slaves to rise in revolt, and they underestimated the potential military strength of the white South, but these were mistakes of judgment committed by most northerners. Indeed, the Garrisonian thesis that disunion meant emancipation found a great deal of support among non-Garrisonians and nonabolitionists. "Phillips' last speech rings gold-like—has the chime of true metal in it," exclaimed William Herndon on February 1, 1861. "I do not agree with Phillips about

[17] *Liberator*, Dec. 7, 1860. See also John L. Thomas, *The Liberator: William Lloyd Garrison* (Boston, 1963), 135-36, 382, 397-98.
[18] Phillips, *Speeches, Lectures, and Letters*, 1st Series, 383-85.

Disunion, though I see that Disunion is liberty to the Slave, and God speed that day." A Republican editor in Indianapolis stated flatly that "the dissolution of the American Union seals the doom of American slavery." A southern Confederacy would be a foreign nation, continued the editor, "No more protection then, no more fugitive slave laws, no more surpressing [sic] of slave insurrections by Federal troops. . . . How long would the abnormal institution of slavery . . . live when brought under the crushing effects of these great influences?" A Des Moines paper declared that "the most effectual way to bring about the enfranchisement of every slave on this continent, is to dissolve this Union." And Samuel Bowles, no sympathizer with abolitionists, affirmed that outside of the Union, slavery "will be pretty certain to come to a violent and bloody death."[19]

When nonabolitionists could argue thus, it is not surprising that William Lloyd Garrison, Jr., could write in February 1861, that "From the standpoint of the Abolitionists never have events looked so propitious for the jubilee of the slave"; or that the *Anti-Slavery Standard* could congratulate abolitionists upon having never "had more abundant reason for satisfaction as to the past and hope as to the future than they have now."[20] Despite this optimism, however, and despite a widespread feeling that secession would spell the doom of slavery, it seems likely that in the short run peaceful disunion would have strengthened rather than weakened slavery, at least in the deep South. If the North had followed the advice of Garrisonians in 1861, the peculiar institution, in all probability, would not have come to an end as soon as it did.

✦

Many non-Garrisonian abolitionists also avowed a willingness to let the South secede peaceably in 1860-1861. Four of the five living members of the "Secret Six"—that group of abolitionists who had helped finance John Brown's exploits in Kansas and

[19] Herndon to Samuel Sewall, Feb. 1, 1861, Garrison Papers, BPL; *Indianapolis Daily Journal*, Dec. 14, 1860; *Des Moines Iowa State Register*, Jan. 23, 1861, quoted in Howard C. Perkins, *Northern Editorials on Secession* (2 vols., New York, 1942), 117-118, 440; *Springfield Republican*, Dec. 22, 1860.

[20] William L. Garrison, Jr., to Samuel Johnson, Feb. 9, 1861, Samuel Johnson Papers, Essex Institute; *N.A.S. Standard*, Mar. 2, 1861.

Virginia—favored disunion rather than concession. Dr. Samuel Gridley Howe opposed any efforts to preserve the Union with the "cancerous excrescences which shoot out from its southern extremities." Thomas Wentworth Higginson said that if the crisis "simply ends in Disunion, even with a state of temporary war, I should be glad—for I think that is a mere question of time & it may as well come now." Frank Sanborn observed in January that "the present condition of National affairs gives me much hope for the Slave. Whatever may be the issue—and I think it will be *real* disunion—Slavery will be greatly weakened."[21] Two days before South Carolina adopted her secession ordinance, Gerrit Smith wrote that it would be "infinitely better" for the Union to be "broken asunder" than to be "recemented by concessions to Slavery." Three months later Smith said: "I insist that the Nation has the right and is therefore bound to abolish Slavery. But if it will not do so, then let there be Disunion & Abolition will follow."[22]

In December 1860, Frederick Douglass declared that "if the Union can only be maintained by new concessions to the slaveholders; if it can only be stuck together and held together by a new drain on the negro's blood . . . then will every rightminded man and woman in the land say, let the Union perish, and perish forever." John Pierpont of Massachusetts, an aged Liberty party veteran, affirmed that secession "would abolish the fugitive slave act and bring the Canada line several degrees of latitude further south."[23] John Jay fervently declared that "if we cannot have liberty & union in any new readjustment, I go for liberty without union." Edward Gilbert reported that "all the Abolitionists I know would hail disunion with delight and hope. We all feel that any further compromise with slavery would render the country unfit for honest men to live in." John G. Whittier summed up the abolitionist position in a poem entitled "A Word for the Hour":

[21] Harold Schwartz, *Samuel Gridley Howe: Social Reformer* (Cambridge, Mass., 1956), 249; Higginson to Louisa Higginson, Nov. 23, 1860, Higginson Papers, HU; Frank Sanborn to Gerrit Smith, Jan. 27, 1861, Smith Papers, SU.

[22] Gerrit Smith to S. P. Chase, Dec. 18, 1860, Smith Papers, SU; Gerrit Smith to Frank Sanborn, Mar. 20, 1861, Sanborn Papers, LC.

[23] *Douglass' Monthly*, Jan. 1861; Pierpont to Charles Sumner, Dec. 10, 1860, Sumner Papers, HU.

They break the links of Union: shall we light
The fires of hell to weld anew the chain
On that red anvil where each blow is pain?
Draw we not even now a freer breath,
As from our shoulders falls a load of death? . . .
Pity, forgive, but urge them back no more
Who, drunk with passion, flaunt disunion's rag
With its vile reptile-blazon. Let us press
The golden cluster on our brave old flag
In closer union, and, if numbering less,
Brighter shall shine the stars which still remain.[24]

✦

Most abolitionists were prepared to acquiesce in peaceable secession. To some, however, this seemed a renunciation of their duty to the slave. Stephen S. Foster, for example, could not see "how the slaves could possibly be benefited by a political separation from the North, where most of their active friends now reside." He was aware that disunion was sometimes "demanded of the North as a matter of consistency, to free herself from the responsibility of slavery." But this would leave the slaves "unprotected in the hands of their plunderers—a deliberate refusal to employ in their behalf the potent agencies on which we depend for the maintenance of our own freedom." Foster thought the federal government had the power under the Constitution to abolish slavery, and during the secession crisis he asserted that by preserv-

---

[24] Jay to Sumner, Feb. 4, 1861, Sumner Papers, HU; Gilbert to George Cheever, Jan. 17, 1861, Cheever Papers, AAS; John G. Whittier, *Songs of Labor and Reform* (vol. III of his *Poetical Works*, Riverside Edition, Boston, 1888), 218-19. Two non-Garrisonian abolitionists wrote lengthy pamphlets supporting peaceable secession in 1861. In the first, James Freeman Clarke asserted that concessions would be far worse than disunion. "The Union is a means to an end," he wrote. "Give up the end in order to preserve the means, and both become worthless. . . . The end of the Union is to secure prosperity, peace, justice, equal rights, and liberty. It is evident, therefore, that these are not to be sacrificed, even to preserve the Union." Clarke, *Secession, Concession, or Self-Possession: Which?* (Boston, 1861), 13. A second disunionist pamphlet, by George Bassett of Illinois, proclaimed that "the tendency of secession will be to terminate . . . American slavery. Separate the slave States from the others, and slavery must stand on its own merits. . . . It is . . . well known that the general government is pledged against any effective measures to bring slavery to a speedy end. In theory and practice, it is the bulwark of chattel slavery." Bassett, *A Northern Plea for the Right of Secession* (Ottawa, Ill., 1861), 22-23.

ing the Union "and enforcing an anti-slavery construction of the constitution, slavery could ere long be wiped out."[25]

William Goodell, who also believed in the right of the government to abolish slavery in the states, could not countenance disunion in any form. The disunionist abolitionist, wrote Goodell, "feels an uncomfortable weight of responsibility for slavery. . . . But he overlooks the still more crushing responsibility of giving over the struggle, and giving up the slaves to the tender mercies of the slaveholders." Abolitionists had "no moral or political right to allow [the slaves] to be kidnapped out of the Union, when it is the religious and constitutional duty of the Union to set them free."[26]

Goodell realized that few persons agreed with his antislavery interpretation of the Constitution, and in January he switched to an argument that was to become familiar to millions in subsequent years: the right of the government to abolish slavery under the war power. Goodell contended that the Republican party was absolved of its pledge of noninterference with slavery in the states by the acts of the seceding states themselves. By seizing United States property, he argued, the South had levied war on the United States and made herself liable to the usages and fortunes of war. "If the . . . rebellion cannot be put down otherwise than by liberating all the slaves of all the slave States, what consideration should hinder its being done?" Meeting in New York City, the Church Anti-Slavery Society adopted Goodell's argument and resolved that the secession crisis gave the government, "by the express provision of the constitution in case of rebellion or insurrection, the right to suppress rebellion and to abolish slavery, the cause of it."[27]

"Instead of looking around for means of reconciling freedom and slavery," declared Frederick Douglass in January 1861, "how immeasurably better would it be if, in our national councils, some Wilberforce or a Buxton could arise, and . . . propose a plan for the complete abolition of slavery." There was no Wilberforce or Buxton in Washington, but here and there in the North a few

[25] *N.A.S. Standard*, Dec. 1, 1860; *Worcester* (Mass.) *Spy*, Feb. 11, 1861. See also Samuel May, Jr., to Garrison, Feb. 17, 1861, Garrison Papers, BPL.

[26] *Principia*, Nov. 24, Dec. 8, 1860.

[27] *ibid.*, Jan. 12, Feb. 2, 1861; *New York Evening Post*, Jan. 24, 1861.

Republican newspapers tentatively suggested plans of compensated emancipation in the border states. In an editorial entitled "The Only Possible Compromise," the *New York Tribune* proposed that the federal government appropriate $240,000,000 over the next fifteen years to purchase and liberate the slaves in Delaware, Maryland, Missouri, Arkansas, Texas, and Louisiana at an average price of $400 per slave.[28] The *Boston Advertiser* suggested an annual appropriation of $50,000,000 or more to compensate slaveholders who wished to participate in a nationwide program of compensated emancipation. This suggestion was advanced as a means of breaking the secession impasse. It would not bring back the Gulf states, but it might hold the border states and inaugurate the abolition of slavery therein at the same time.[29]

Abolitionists had traditionally opposed the idea of compensated emancipation because indemnification implied recognition of the right of property in man. But during the secession winter several abolitionists endorsed the suggestion of compensated emancipation. A convention of Garrisonians in Syracuse, for example, adopted resolutions written by Samuel J. May affirming that "the dissolution of the Union, even, may not relieve us; for if slavery still remains in the land, it will be a perpetual trouble to the inhabitants thereof, whether they be separate or whether they be united." Inasmuch as the North was equally guilty with the South of the sin of slavery, "our wealth, and the wealth of the nation ought to be put in requisition to relieve those who may impoverish themselves by setting their captives free."[30] None of the plans for compensated emancipation got beyond the drawing-board stage, however, and they had little or no effect in stemming the tide of secession.

✦

While abolitionists were thundering against compromise from the platform, pulpit, and press, the compromisers took more direct action against abolitionists, inaugurating a season of mob violence unparalleled since the early years of the antislavery movement. The northern mobs of 1860-1861 were composed of

28 *Douglass' Monthly*, Feb. 1861; *New York Tribune*, Jan. 19, 1861.
29 Elizabeth Peabody to Gerrit Smith, Jan. 25, 1861, Smith Papers, su.
30 Samuel J. May, *Some Recollections of Our Anti-Slavery Conflict* (Boston, 1869), 388-94; *N.A.S. Standard*, Feb. 9, 1861.

two elements: "gentlemen of property and standing" who feared the loss of millions of dollars by secession and blamed the abolitionists for the nation's troubles; and urban workingmen, whose virulent anti-Negro and proslavery prejudices were deeply rooted.

During the secession winter, the Democratic and conservative press was filled with incendiary attacks on abolitionists. "The Anti-Slavery agitation is the true and only cause of all our woes and trouble," proclaimed the *Chicago Times and Herald*. The paper urged concessions to the South, hoping that "this negro question will be again settled, and settled in a manner never again to disturb railroad stocks in this world." The *Cincinnati Daily Enquirer* asserted that the crisis of the Union "was created by crack-brained fanatics, ignorant or careless of their duty to the Government as citizens of the Union. . . . The people of the North must put down this party in their midst, whose only basis is hostility to the institutions of half of the States of this Union." The *Chicago Times* published the following advice to the nation:

"Evil, and nothing but evil, has ever followed in the track of this hideous monster, Abolition. . . . Will you allow the brightest American hopes and prospects to be dashed to earth by this vile struggle . . . to degrade the white man to the negro's level? . . . Let the South have her negroes to her heart's content, and in her own way—and let us go on getting rich and powerful by feeding and clothing them. Let the negroes *alone!*—let them ALONE! . . . Kill the vile cause of disunion, and disunion itself will perish for *lack of food*. ABOLITION IS DISUNION. It is the 'vile cause and most cursed effect.' It is the Alpha and Omega of our National woes. STRANGLE IT!"[31]

With feeling running so high, the desire for compromise with the South was bound sooner or later to manifest itself in mob violence against abolitionists and Negroes. On December 3, a group of Boston abolitionists who believed in John Brown's method of attacking slavery held a meeting in Tremont Temple to discuss the question, "How Can American Slavery be

[31] *Chicago Daily Times and Herald*, Nov. 21, 1860; *Cincinnati Daily Enquirer*, Dec. 6, 1860; *Chicago Times*, Dec. 7, 1860. All these editorials are printed in Perkins, *Northern Editorials on Secession*, 94-97, 140-41, and 429-31.

Abolished?" No sooner had James Redpath called the meeting to order than the hall was invaded by a group of "North end Roughs and Beacon Street Aristocrats" led by lawyers and merchants, "nearly all of whom have uncollected debts [in the South] and many of them mortgages on slaves."[32] They began to shout and stamp their feet, making it impossible for Redpath and his followers to carry on. A few of the "Broadcloth rowdies" marched to the platform, forcibly ejected the astonished Redpath, took over the meeting, and passed resolutions urging concessions to the South "in the interests of commerce, manufactures, and agriculture." The abolitionists organized a counterattack, and a general scuffling broke out. Finally the police, who sympathized with the mob and had refused to protect the abolitionists, dispersed the meeting and ordered everybody home.[33]

The abolitionists decided to continue their meeting in the Negro Baptist church on Joy Street. That night the church was crowded with abolitionists and Negroes, while several hundred "Union men" gathered outside in an ugly mood. Wendell Phillips gave the main speech of the evening, a scorching attack on the Boston authorities for failing to protect free speech. After the meeting the mob assaulted colored people with stones and clubs as they emerged from the church. Phillips was saved from a similar fate by a tight-lipped cordon of friends who escorted him home through the mob. The frustrated rioters retired to the Negro section and expressed their Union-saving sentiments by smashing the windows of several houses.[34]

On four Sundays during the secession winter, Phillips spoke to large crowds in Boston's huge, barn-like Music Hall, and each

[32] This description of the mob is taken from the accounts by William S. Robinson in the *New York Tribune*, Dec. 5, 7, 1860. The leader of this mob was Richard Fay, a wealthy Boston lawyer. Many of his confederates were also prominent lawyers, merchants, or brokers: Rufus Choate, Jr., John Bell, B. F. Russell, Oliver Stevens, Thomas L. Parkins, John C. Boyd, William C. Rogers, T. J. Coolidge, Jr., William Aspinwall, and Amos A. Lawrence. For a discussion of the Boston antiabolitionist mobs of 1860-61, see Edith Ellen Ware, *Political Opinion in Massachusetts during the Civil War and Reconstruction* (New York, 1916), 85-90.

[33] This account of the meeting is drawn from descriptions in the *New York Tribune*, Dec. 7, 1860; *Boston Courier*, Dec. 4, 1860; *Worcester Spy*, Dec. 4, 1860; and *Liberator*, Dec. 7, 14, 1860.

[34] *New York Tribune*, Dec. 7, 1860; *Liberator*, Dec. 7, 14, 21, 1860; *Twenty-Eighth Annual Report of the American Anti-Slavery Society*, 177.

time but the first the hall was surrounded by hundreds of clerks, lawyers, merchants, and common laborers who thought they saw their livelihoods threatened by the breakup of the Union. Their feelings toward Phillips were expressed by one well-dressed young businessman: "Damn him! He has depreciated stocks $3,000,000 by his slang." Alarmed for Phillips' safety, his friends organized a company of about forty men, who stationed themselves in strategic parts of the hall to prevent any attack on Phillips. When Phillips finished speaking his men would form a circle around him and escort him home through the jeering, cursing mobs. Two or three close friends stayed with Phillips several nights, sleeping in the next room with their revolvers near at hand. Phillips himself was a good shot with a revolver, and carried one with him whenever he ventured onto the streets of Boston during the winter.[35]

The convention of the Massachusetts Anti-Slavery Society in Tremont Temple on January 24 erupted into pandemonium. Merchants and shopkeepers gave their employees the day off to attend the meeting, and two or three hundred young clerks and rowdies crowded into the galleries. They heckled and shouted at every speaker, but reserved their greatest fire for Phillips. As he tried to speak they shouted, sang, and threw seat cushions at the platform. "Such yelling, screeching, stamping, and bellowing I never heard," wrote Lydia Maria Child, who was present at the meeting. "It was a full realization of the old phrase, 'All hell broke loose.' " After trying unsuccessfully to make himself heard above the uproar, Phillips suddenly leaned forward and began talking quietly to reporters in the front row. "Abolitionists! Look here!" he said. "These pencils [pointing to the reporters] will do more to create opinion than a hundred thousand mobs. While I speak to these pencils, I speak to a million of men. . . . We have got the press of the country in our hands. Whether they like us or not, they know that our speeches sell their papers. (Applause and laughter) With five newspapers we may defy five hundred boys." The hecklers yelled to Phillips: "Speak louder. We want to hear what you're saying," and having gained their attention Phillips

---

[35] Thomas W. Higginson, *Cheerful Yesterdays* (Boston, 1898), 240-44; George W. Smalley, *Anglo-American Memories,* 1st Series (London, 1911), 91-99; Bartlett, *Phillips,* 225-31; *Liberator,* Dec. 21, 1860, Jan. 25, 1861; Higginson to Louisa Higginson, Jan. 21, 1861, Higginson Papers, HU.

spoke for half an hour without interruption. When he sat down, however, the mob renewed its clamor, drowning out most of the other speakers. Finally the police cleared the galleries, but when the abolitionists returned for their evening meeting they found themselves locked out by order of the mayor, a Democrat.[36] The mob had won this round, and at least one southern newspaper rejoiced. "A John Brown meeting cannot be held in Boston now," wrote a correspondent to an Atlanta newspaper. "We have got a most powerful organization here that will be heard from in due time. . . . Tell the people of Georgia not to be too rash. Tell them to bear with us a little longer and all will be well."[37]

Boston was not the only place where abolitionists were shouted down. In nearly every city where they tried to speak they were greeted by mobs. Susan B. Anthony arranged a series of abolitionist meetings in upstate New York during January and February. In Buffalo a riotous assemblage led by ex-Governor Horatio Seymour hooted down the abolitionists, drove them from the platform, organized the meeting themselves, and adopted Union-saving resolutions denouncing "the wild theories of fanatical abolitionists." At Rochester, Rome, and Auburn abolitionist speakers were howled down. The Utica city council denied them the use of any public hall. In Syracuse the abolitionists were met by a drunken rabble armed with pistols, knives, and rotten eggs. The mob dragged effigies of Susan B. Anthony and Samuel J. May through the streets and burned them in the city square. Only in Albany was free speech vindicated. The Democratic mayor of that city stationed a heavy guard of police around the hall and sat on the platform himself with a revolver in his lap to make sure the meeting was not disturbed.[38]

William H. Furness, abolitionist pastor of a Unitarian Church in Philadelphia, feared mob violence against his church, and members of his congregation came armed to Sunday services from December 1860, until the following April. A gang of young toughs attacked Charles C. Burleigh as he was attempting to lecture in

[36] *Liberator*, Feb. 1, 1861; Lydia Maria Child to Sarah B. Shaw, Jan. ?, 1861, in Harriet W. Sewall, ed., *Letters of Lydia Maria Child* (Boston, 1883), 148; Frank Sanborn to Gerrit Smith, Jan. 27, 1861, Smith Papers, su.

[37] The Atlanta newspaper was quoted in the *Liberator*, Feb. 8, 1861.

[38] *N.A.S. Standard*, Jan. 19, 26, Feb. 2, 9, 16, 1861; *Twenty-Eighth Annual Report of the American Anti-Slavery Society*, 182-88.

the schoolhouse at Westfield, Massachusetts. In the ensuing struggle the rioters knocked over the stove and burned down the building. Some of the most vicious mobs were encountered by Parker Pillsbury, Josephine Griffing, and Giles B. Stebbins in Ohio and Michigan. At Ann Arbor a group of university students and local hangers-on assaulted abolitionists with wooden benches, clubs, and broken glass, injuring several persons and demolishing the inside of the meeting-hall.[39]

Abolitionists believed that the purpose of these mobs was "to conciliate the plotters of treason at the South, to stay the progress of secession, and lure back seceders and armed rebels, by creating an impression that the North is ready to adopt the cowardly policy of concession."[40] Garrison was discouraged by the virulent anti-abolitionist spirit abroad in the land. "I fervently trust this pro-slavery Union is broken beyond the possibility of restoration by Northern compromise," he wrote, "yet, when I see our meetings everywhere mobbed down . . . I am not sure but the whole country is to come under the bloody sway of the Slave Power."[41]

In the final analysis, however, the mobs probably helped the abolitionists by attracting public attention and sympathy to them. "Every sentence that Mr. Phillips utters is read as never before," wrote William Lloyd Garrison, Jr. "The *Tribune* scatters his speeches broadcast thru the North, & the *Herald* prints them likewise to send South."[42] Their enemies could denounce, deride, and mob the abolitionists, but they could not prevent abolitionist words and ideas from being heard and read throughout the land.

✦

To most Americans during the winter of 1860-1861, war was but a dimly glimpsed possibility. The only alternatives seemed to be disunion, concession, or a long period of waiting until south-

[39] Elizabeth M. Geffen, "William Henry Furness, Philadelphia Antislavery Preacher," *Pennsylvania Magazine of History & Biography*, LXXXII (July 1958), 290; Wm. L. Garrison, Jr., to Samuel Johnson, Feb. 9, 1861, Johnson Papers, Essex Institute; Parker Pillsbury to C. K. Whipple, Jan. 30, 1861, Garrison Papers, BPL; *Twenty-Eighth Annual Report of the American Anti-Slavery Society*, 180-81, 188-90.

[40] *ibid.*, 190.

[41] Garrison to Oliver Johnson, Jan. 19, 1861, Garrison Papers, BPL.

[42] Wm. L. Garrison, Jr., to Samuel Johnson, Feb. 9, 1861, Johnson Papers, Essex Institute.

ern Unionists brought their states back into the Union voluntarily. Some abolitionists foresaw war; few desired it.

In spite of their hopes for peace, several abolitionists feared that war would be the outcome of the secession struggle. "I am here at the center of political commotion," wrote Henry B. Stanton from Washington in January, "& I assure you this Union is going to destruction as fast as it can. . . . Civil War is close upon us." A month later Lydia Maria Child observed: "if the Republicans do *not* yield up all they have gained, I suppose the alternative is civil war. It is a horrid alternative. . . . But here lies the alarming fact; we must *always* keep on compromising our principles, or else civil war will be threatened. . . . Freedom must come up manfully to the struggle, or die by a slow but certain poison. Therefore, much as I deprecate civil war, I deliberately say even *that* is better than compromises of principles, at this momentous crisis."[43]

Even as late as the first part of April, however, most abolitionists did not anticipate war. Frederick Douglass believed the North too cowardly and proslavery to fight. "All talk about putting down treason and rebellion by force," he wrote, "are as impotent and worthless as the words of a drunken woman in a ditch. Slavery has touched our government, and the cirute has gone out of its arms." In a speech at New Bedford on April 9, Wendell Phillips alluded to telegraphic reports (false, of course) that Fort Sumter was already under attack. Let South Carolina have the fort, said Phillips—he wanted no war with her. Phillips had as low an estimate of northern courage and patriotism as Douglass: "You cannot go through Massachusetts, and recruit men to bombard Charleston or New Orleans. The Northern mind will not bear it: you can never make such a war popular. . . . Instead of conquering Charleston, you create a Charleston in New England, you stir up sympathy for the South."[44]

Three days after this speech the shore batteries in Charleston opened fire on Fort Sumter in earnest. Contrary to the expectations of abolitionists, the North was galvanized into a frenzy of patriotism by the event. Political differences were temporarily

[43] H. B. Stanton to E. C. Stanton, Jan. 12, 1861, Stanton Papers, LC; L. M. Child to Henrietta Sargent, Feb. 9, 1861, Child Papers, Cornell.

[44] *Douglass' Monthly*, April 1861; George L. Austin, *The Life and Times of Wendell Phillips* (2nd ed., Boston, 1901), 206-09.

forgotten. Every northern hamlet held its war meeting. Abolitionists were astounded by the northern reaction to Sumter. For
thirty years the North had tamely submitted to the demands of the
slave power, but in 1861 the free states decided to submit no more.
Dr. Henry Bowditch, a Boston abolitionist, wrote: "Ye gods,
what a change has come over the spirit of our people since that
occurrence [the firing on Sumter]. We had been lying as in a
state of apparent listlessness. . . . Now . . . the whole North is a
unit. . . . Young and old, men and women, boys and girls, have
caught the sacred enthusiasm. . . . The times are ripening for a
march of a liberating army into the Confederate States. If slavery
is to be the cornerstone of treason, slavery will, must be, undermined."[45]

"You have no idea how the war fever rages here," wrote Oliver
Johnson from New York. "There was never anything like it."
After attending a mass war meeting in Worcester, Higginson
wrote: "Tonight we have more than enthusiasm, we have unanimity. . . . Never before since I lived here (or anywhere else) has
there been [such] absolute unanimity on a single subject." Samuel
May, Jr. rejoiced, "These are very hopeful times indeed. There
is a North at last, and the Southern people are absolutely con-
founded at the sight." Frederick Douglass was compelled by the
mass enthusiasm to change his mind about northern courage and
patriotism. "What a change now greets us!" he wrote two weeks
after Sumter. "The Government is aroused, the dead North is alive,
and its divided people united. . . . The cry now is for war,
vigorous war, war to the bitter end."[46]

Opposed to war before the firing on Sumter, most abolitionists
did an about-face when war finally came, for they saw in the
conflict the imminent destruction of slavery. When he heard the
news of Sumter's bombardment, Samuel Gridley Howe seized a
pen and wrote: "Since they will have it so,—in the name of God,
—Amen! Now let the Governors and Chief men of the people see

[45] Vincent Y. Bowditch, *Life and Correspondence of Henry Ingersoll Bowditch*
(2 vols., Boston, 1902), II, 2-4. The northern reaction to the firing on Sumter is
described in Stampp, *And the War Came*, 288-89.
[46] Oliver Johnson to Samuel May, Jr., Apr. 15, 1861, Johnson Papers, VHS;
Higginson to Louisa Higginson, Apr. 17, 1861, Higginson Papers, HU; Samuel
May, Jr., to C. C. Burleigh, Apr. 25, 1861, Samuel May, Jr., Papers, BPL; *Douglass'
Monthly*, May 1861.

to it that war shall not cease until Emancipation is secure." Henry B. Stanton wrote from Washington a few days after Sumter: "I hear Old John Brown knocking on the lid of his coffin & shouting 'Let me out,' 'let me out!' The doom of slavery is at hand. It is to be wiped out in blood. Amen!"[47]

Some abolitionists voiced tentative doubts about the value of war to the antislavery cause. William Goodell noted sourly that the speakers at a huge Union meeting in New York disavowed any intention to interfere with slavery and proclaimed the sole purpose of the war to be restoration of the Union.[48] Lydia Maria Child thought there was little "of either right principle, or good feeling, at the foundation of this unanimous Union sentiment." She pointed out that within two weeks of the firing on Sumter the federal forces at Fort Pickens had returned thirty fugitive slaves to their masters, and General Benjamin Butler had offered to use his Massachusetts troops to suppress any slave uprising in Maryland. "I want to love and honor the flag of my country," wrote Mrs. Child, "but how can I, when it is used for such purposes?" Her husband David had attended a Union meeting in Wayland, Massachusetts, and was almost mobbed when he said something about the duty of the government to slaves who came within Union lines. He was told in no uncertain terms that the war had "nothing to do with the damned niggers." "In view of these things," lamented Mrs. Child, "the Union-shouts, and hurrahs for the U.S. flag, sound like fiendish mockery in my ears."[49]

Few abolitionists, however, could share this pessimism in the ebullient days after Sumter. They realized perfectly well that the official war aim was Union rather than emancipation, but foresaw that some measure of abolition was inevitable before the war ended. "It matters little, comparatively, that the rallying cry is 'the Union and the Constitution,'" said Oliver Johnson. "We all know that, in spite of every effort to control and qualify it, the war must be, essentially, a war of freedom against slavery." J. Miller McKim boldly declared: "This is to be an abolition war. The South has elected to give it this character. . . . The North has not been

47 Howe to John Andrew, Apr. 13, 1861, Andrew Papers, MHS; H. B. Stanton to E. C. Stanton, Apr. ?, 1861, E. C. Stanton Papers, LC.
48 *Principia*, Apr. 27, 1861.
49 L. M. Child to Lucy Osgood, Apr. 26, May 7, 1861, Child Papers, Cornell.

and is not yet prepared for final action on this question; but she has no alternative." The *Anti-Slavery Standard* said, "This outburst of spirit and enthusiasm at the North may spring chiefly from indignation at the wrongs of the white man, but it will none the less finally right those of the black man."[50]

One of the biggest questions of the day for abolitionists, and for many who were not abolitionists, was the attitude of Wendell Phillips toward the war. "It will be a pity if Wendell Phillips continues to claim for the secessionists that they are only carrying out the doctrine of State Rights," remarked Oliver Johnson. A young abolitionist in New York reported that his friends were asking where Phillips stood. "I replied that I did not know, but if he did not now enlist under the stars & stripes, I was no longer under him."[51]

Phillips passed through an agony of indecision during the first days after Sumter. For twenty years he had urged disunion; could he now renounce his past just because of the loss of one fort? Phillips came into the law office of his young friend George Smalley in Boston one day, looking tired and uneasy. He discussed his problem with Smalley, who told him: "I don't think it matters much what you sacrifice—consistency, principles, or anything. They belong to the past. They have nothing to do with to-day. The war is upon us. You must either support it or oppose it. If you oppose it, you fling away your position and all your influence. You will never be listened to again." As a clinching argument Smalley said: "I will tell you what I once heard a negro say: 'When my massa and somebody else quarrel I'm on the somebody else's side.' Don't you think the negro knows? Do you really doubt that a war between the Slave Power and the North, be the result what it may, must end in Freedom?" Phillips left after a few more words, but when Smalley saw him again that evening Phillips announced his intention to speak in the Music Hall next Sunday, April 21, on the subject of the war.[52]

The word spread rapidly through Boston. Newspapers pre-

---

[50] Oliver Johnson to J. M. McKim, Apr. 18, 1861, McKim Papers, Cornell; *N.A.S. Standard*, Apr. 20, 27, 1861. McKim's statement is from his weekly column in the *N.A.S. Standard*, Apr. 20, 1861.

[51] O. Johnson to J. M. McKim, Apr. 18, 1861, McKim Papers, Cornell; Edward Bunker, Jr., to W. L. Garrison, Jr., Apr. 25, 1861, Garrison Papers, sc.

[52] Smalley, *Anglo-American Memories*, 1st Series, 108-10.

dicted that Phillips would come out for the Union and the war. Four thousand people jammed into the Music Hall on Sunday. The first thing that greeted their eyes was the platform decked with American flags. Phillips came forward and began speaking in his quiet, melodious voice:

"Many times this winter, here and elsewhere, I have counselled peace,—urged, as well as I knew how, the expediency of acknowledging a Southern Confederacy, and the peaceful separation of these thirty-four States. One of the journals announces to you that I come here this morning to retract those opinions. No, not one of them! (Applause) I need them all,—every word I have spoken this winter,—every act of twenty-five years of my life, to make the welcome I give this war hearty and hot. . . . I rejoice . . . that now, for the first tme in my antislavery life, I speak under the stars and stripes, and welcome the tread of Massachusetts men marshalled for war."

At these words the audience sprang to its feet, and four thousand throats made the rafters echo with cheer after cheer. When calm returned, Phillips continued:

"No matter what the past has been or said; to-day the slave asks God for a sight of this banner, and counts it the pledge of his redemption. (Applause) Hitherto it may have meant what you thought, or what I did; to-day it represents sovereignty and justice. (Renewed applause) The only mistake that I have made, was in supposing Massachusetts wholly choked with cotton-dust and cankered with gold. (Loud cheering) The South thought her patience and generous willingness for peace were cowardice; to-day shows the mistake. She has been sleeping on her arms since '83, and the first canon-shot brings her to her feet with the war-cry of the Revolution on her lips." (Loud cheers)

Phillips admitted that Union war aims at this time did not include emancipation, but John Quincy Adams had long ago affirmed the right of the nation in time of war to abolish slavery, and "when the South cannonaded Fort Sumter the bones of Adams stirred in his coffin. (Cheers) And you might have heard him, from that granite grave at Quincy, proclaim to the nation: 'the hour has struck! Seize the thunderbolt God has forged for you, and annihilate the system which has troubled your peace for seventy years!' (Cheers)" Phillips concluded, "I believe in the possibility of justice, in the certainty of union. Years hence, when the smoke of this conflict clears away, the world will see under our banner all tongues, all creeds, all races,—one brotherhood,—and on the banks of the Potomac, the Genius of Liberty, robed in light, four and thirty stars for her diadem, broken chains under her feet, and an olive-branch in her right hand. (Great applause)"[53]

It was the greatest speech of his life. Five years before, when young Richard Hinton was leaving for bleeding Kansas, Phillips had asked what he planned to accomplish there. Hinton replied that he hoped freedom in Kansas would open the road to freedom in South Carolina. Hinton was in the audience on this memorable April 21, 1861, and as the hall rang with cheers at the end of the speech Phillips leaned over and shouted in his ear, "Well, Hinton, we've reached South Carolina at last!"[54]

As Phillips left the hall he met a mob of people milling around outside, but this time the crowd cheered him every step of the way home instead of threatening his life. The *Liberator* published an extra containing Phillips' speech, and newsboys sold sixteen thousand copies on the streets—the largest edition of the *Liberator* ever printed. The *Anti-Slavery Standard* and *Anglo-African* published several thousand copies of the speech and sold them on the streets in New York. Metropolitan papers in several cities printed the address, and more than 200,000 copies were sold in all.[55]

"Wendell's speech is magnificent; I read it with moist cheeks and a throbbing heart," wrote Oliver Johnson from New York. "What a speech!" cried young William Bunker, a friend of the Garrisons, as he rushed off to enlist. The high priest of disunion had taken up the cudgels for Union and liberty, and abolitionists everywhere enthusiastically closed ranks behind him.[56]

[53] The speech was published by many northern newspapers, including the *Boston Advertiser*, Apr. 22, 1861, and the *New York Sunday Times*, Apr. 28, 1861. It is most readily accessible in Phillips, *Speeches, Lectures, and Letters*, 1st Series, 396-414. George Smalley, *Anglo-American Memories*, 1st Series, 110-12, and Charles W. Slack, in Austin, *Phillips*, 217-18, describe the scene at the Music Hall during and after the speech.

[54] C. Carroll Hollis, "R. J. Hinton, Lincoln's Reluctant Biographer," *The Centennial Review of Arts & Sciences*, v (Winter 1961), 75.

[55] *Liberator*, May 10, 1861; O. Johnson to J. M. McKim, Apr. 29, 1861, McKim Papers, Cornell; Austin, *Phillips*, 218.

[56] O. Johnson to McKim, Apr. 25, 1861, McKim Papers, Cornell; Edward Bunker, Jr., to W. L. Garrison, Jr., Apr. 25, 1861, Garrison Papers, sc.

"THIS war plays the deuce with peace principles," declared pacifist William Furness three weeks after the firing on Sumter. Another peace-minded abolitionist, Samuel J. May, confessed at the outbreak of war that "the conduct of the rebels and the impending fate of our country has shaken my confidence in the *extreme* principles of the non-resistants."[1] The coming of a war which they hoped would destroy slavery posed a serious moral dilemma for pacifist abolitionists. Only a small number of abolitionists were actual nonresistants, but nearly all nineteenth-century reformers professed peace sentiments to some degree. The constitutions of most antislavery societies pledged their members to advocate only peaceful means for the overthrow of slavery. When confronted by a choice between a (potentially) antislavery war and a proslavery peace, however, most abolitionists did not hesitate to choose war. Much as they loved peace, they hated slavery more.

After Lincoln's call for troops Garrison announced that "all my sympathies and wishes are with the government, because it is entirely in the right, and acting strictly in self-defence and for self-preservation." The war would be horrible, as all wars were horrible, "but if it shall end in the speedy and total abolition of slavery, the fountain-source of all our national difficulties, it will bring with it inconceivable blessings." Garrison's son and namesake wrote: "As a non-resistant, believing all war to be wicked & unchristian, I can yet delight that this conflict is upon us." Why? The nonresistant favored a peace based on love and compassion for humanity. "But, peace which is the result of cowardice is despicable. Well, the North for the past twenty years has suffered every indignity, submitted to every degradation which the South could inflict." There was cause for rejoicing in the North's awakening from its moral stupor: "Instead of the utter subjection to slavery which we had feared, a regeneration has taken place, & the tyrant now reads in an aroused North, the handwriting on the wall prophecying his destruction. So I hail with acclamation

---

[1] Furness to Moncure Conway, May 7, 1861, Conway Papers, cu; G. B. Emerson, S. May, and T. J. Mumford, *Memoir of Samuel Joseph May* (New York, 1871), 226.

every man who shoulders a musket for the purpose of getting a shot at the slave-power."[2]

The elder Garrison denied that support of the war involved any compromise of his pacifist principles. He would not take up arms himself, but would judge by their own standards "those who, rejecting the doctrine of non-resistance, profess to believe in the right and duty of maintaining their freedom by the sword. The worst thing they can do is to be recreant to their own convictions in such a crisis as this. I thank God when men who believe in the right and duty of wielding carnal weapons, are so far advanced

"Emancipation." Nast in *Harper's Weekly*

that they will take those weapons out of the scale of despotism and throw them into the scale of freedom."[3]

Gerrit Smith, a member of the American Peace Society, rationalized his support for the war on the ground that the government was merely defending itself against "traitors and pirates who are at work to overthrow it. If there are principles of the Society forbidding this, I am not aware of them." Another abolitionist member of the Peace Society said that its meetings had become

[2] Garrison to T. B. Drew, Apr. 25, 1861, Garrison Papers, BPL; W. L. Garrison, Jr., to Edward S. Bunker, Jr., Apr. 28, 1861, Garrison Papers, SC.

[3] *Liberator*, June 14, 1861; John White Chadwick, *Sallie Holley, A Life for Liberty* (New York, 1899), 179-80.

war meetings and that he found himself praying that the sword would not be sheathed until there was no longer a slave in the land.[4] The Peace Society made an official distinction between international wars, which it opposed, and the suppression of domestic rebellion, which it approved.

A few abolitionist-pacifists refused to accept this reasoning. Elihu Burritt, one of the foremost proponents of universal peace, lamented "the insidious drifting that has carried nearly all our peace friends into the wake of this war." Burritt ridiculed the Peace Society's position "that this terrible conflict, in which each party is arraying 500,000 armed men against the other, is not *war* but quelling a mob on the part of the Federal Government. . . . I feel that this sophistry and position have shorn the locks of the Society of all the strength of principle; and I have been saddened to silence."[5]

British pacifists sharply rebuked Garrison for his prowar stand. Garrison's friends replied angrily. "If the editor of the London Herald of Peace does not understand that Slavery is war," cried James Redpath, "and that, therefore, the putting down of Slavery is the true peace policy, . . . Mr. Garrison does, and every other man of good judgment here does." Did Britons think that nonresistant abolitionists should require the government to "sit still, and have the handcuffs applied, the gag forced into their mouth, and consent to be driven out of the seat of government, and allow the slaveholders to walk in & occupy?" asked Samuel May, Jr. "It is plain to me that the non-resistants would have been nothing less than the allies of the slaveholders, to have taken any such ground."[6]

Prowar abolitionists developed the argument that slavery itself was the worst form of war imaginable, and that a civil war, however terrible, was worth the cost if it held out a chance of abolishing slavery. "Tho' a peace man, and a lover of peace, I regard slavery perpetuated as much more deplorable than a . . . bloody war

---

[4] *Gerrit Smith to George C. Becksmith, May 18, 1861* (printed letter, Peterboro, 1861); *Principia*, June 8, 1861.

[5] Elihu Burritt to Henry Richard, May 26, 1861, in Merle Curti, ed., *The Learned Blacksmith: Letters and Journals of Elihu Burritt* (New York, 1937), 138-39. The Peace Society suspended its activities for the duration of the war, and soon disintegrated.

[6] *The Pine and Palm*, Sept. 7, 1861; Samuel May, Jr., to Richard Webb, Dec. 24, 1861, Samuel May, Jr., Papers, BPL.

that may overthrow it," declared an Iowa abolitionist. Moncure Conway, the Virginia-born abolitionist who grew up on a slave plantation, wrote in 1862 that "Slavery is perpetual war. . . . A single day of Slavery and its rule in this country witnessed more wrong, violence, corruption, more actual war, than all that civil war even could bring." Wendell Phillips exclaimed, "In my view, the bloodiest war ever waged is infinitely better than the happiest slavery which ever fattened men into obedience. And yet I love peace. But it is real peace; not peace such as we have had; not peace that meant lynch-law in the Carolinas and mob-law in New York, . . . a gag on the lips of statesmen, and the slave sobbing himself to sleep in curses. No more such peace for me."[7]

✦

At the height of war enthusiasm in the North following the firing on Sumter, Garrison urged abolitionists to " 'stand still, and see the salvation of God' rather than attempt to add anything to the general commotion." This glorious hour was "no time for minute criticism of Lincoln, Republicanism, or even the other parties, now that they are fusing for a death-grapple with the Southern slave-oligarchy."[8]

Similar advice poured into abolitionist headquarters from prominent Garrisonians in Boston, New York, Philadelphia, and elsewhere. The pressure for quiet and conformity became so strong that the executive committees of the American and New England Anti-Slavery Societies took the unprecedented step of canceling the annual conventions of these societies.[9] In an editorial explaining the reason for this cancellation, the *Anti-Slavery Standard* conceded that criticism and agitation had always been the duty of abolitionists, "But, in a crisis like this, criticism may suspend its judgment for awhile and watch the sequence of events." Abolitionists should do nothing to endanger "the storm of Northern in-

[7] Joseph Dugdale to J. Miller McKim, June 27, 1861, McKim Papers, Cornell; Moncure Conway, *The Golden Hour* (Boston, 1862), 12, 33; Wendell Phillips, *Speeches, Lectures, and Letters*, 1st Series (Boston, 1863), 419.

[8] Garrison to Oliver Johnson, Apr. 19, 1861, Garrison Papers, BPL.

[9] J. M. McKim to Garrison, Apr. 20, 1861, O. Johnson to Garrison, Apr. 22, 1861, Garrison to O. Johnson, Apr. 23, 1861, J. S. Gibbons to Garrison, Apr. 25, 1861, Garrison Papers, BPL; John Jay to Charles Sumner, Apr. 18, 1861, Sumner Papers, HU; Edmund Quincy to Sydney Howard Gay, Apr. 19, 1861, Gay Papers, CU; Records of the Board of Managers of the Massachusetts Anti-Slavery Society, p. 118 (in possession of the BPL).

dignation against the South which is now beating against the out-
works of slavery. Should it slacken, or turn its force backward on
its own region, the time of criticism and censure will have come
again."[10]

This action brought protests from some who thought that
abolitionists should remain vigilant and active. After all, they
argued, there were few signs of an antislavery purpose on the part
of the North. In his proclamation of April 15 calling for 75,000
troops to suppress rebellion, Lincoln promised "to avoid any destruction of, or interference with, property," that is, slavery.
General Benjamin Butler offered in April to use his Massachusetts
troops to put down a rumored slave insurrection in Maryland, and
in subsequent months several other northern generals made similar
offers to border-state slaveholders.[11] On April 22 Secretary of
State Seward officially instructed the American minister in Paris
that "the condition of slavery in the several states will remain just
the same whether [the rebellion] shall succeed or shall fail."[12]
The *New York Times,* rapidly becoming the most accurate journalistic spokesman for administration policy, editorially stated
that "it is a great mistake to suppose that the war . . . is a war . . .
against Southern institutions." Even the *New York Tribune* declared a month after the surrender of Sumter that "this War is in
truth a War for the preservation of the Union, not for the destruction of Slavery; and it would alienate many ardent Unionists to
pervert it into a War against Slavery. . . . We believe that Slavery
has nothing to fear from a Union triumph."[13]

Pointing to statements such as these, several abolitionists deplored the cancellation of the annual meetings. Parker Pillsbury
and Aaron M. Powell thought abolitionists should "reserve and
exercise the right of *criticism.*" Susan B. Anthony could not see
"*one good* reason for the abandonment of all our meetings."[14]

10 *N.A.S. Standard,* Apr. 27, 1861.

11 Roy P. Basler, ed., *The Collected Works of Abraham Lincoln* (9 vols., New
Brunswick, N.J., 1955), IV, 332; *The War of the Rebellion: A Compilation of the
Official Records of the Union and Confederate Armies* (128 vols., Washington,
1880-1901), Series 1, vol. II, 593, 47-49, 662, vol. III, 373. (Hereafter cited as *O.R.*)

12 Edward L. Pierce, *Memoir and Letters of Charles Sumner* (4 vols., Boston,
1877-94), IV, 39.

13 *New York Times,* May 10, 1861; *New York Tribune,* May 14, 1861.

14 *N.A.S. Standard,* May 11, 1861; Pillsbury to Wm. Lloyd Garrison, Jr., May
28, 1861, Pillsbury Papers, SC; A. M. Powell to Wm. L. Garrison, May 8, 1861,

From Illinois George Bassett expressed his disgust for the "universal infatuation" of abolitionists who gave unqualified support to the war. "It is not a war for Negro Liberty, but for national despotism. It is a tariff war, an aristocratic war, a *pro-slavery* war." A Garrisonian at Yale College found it "singular" that "Abolitionists and Disunionists of thirty years' standing should now be found lending pen and voice to uphold and urge on a war waged solely and avowedly to preserve and perpetuate the Union." This was no antislavery conflict: "Is any one so blind as to fancy that the capitalists, who last winter were mobbing Mr. Phillips, have now struck hands with him for a crusade against slavery? . . . Point me to a single word or whisper of love or regard for the rights of the slave, in all this disgusting and senseless vaporing about the flag, and the Union, and the dignity of the Government."[15]

Garrison tried to answer these criticisms in a long *Liberator* editorial on May 10. He admitted that the war, at least on the surface, was not an abolitionist war. Garrison considered this, however, "a verbal and technical view of the case." He asserted that "the one great cause of all our national troubles and divisions is SLAVERY: the removal of it, therefore, is essential to our national existence. What can be plainer than this?" It was so plain, he thought, that the North would soon realize it and take steps to remove this pernicious cause of all its troubles. For abolitionists to persist in the old policy of disunion and excoriation of the national government would be a blind and obstinate consistency; abolitionists must be flexible and adjust themselves to the changed situation.

As the weeks passed, however, the war settled into a conservative pattern—a pattern that soon discouraged many abolitionists. Republican newspapers made it painfully clear that, unless unforeseen obstacles arose, it would not be an antislavery war. Said the widely respected *Springfield Republican*: "If there is one point of honor upon which more than another this administration

---

Garrison Papers, BPL; Susan B. Anthony to Martha Wright, May 28, 1861, Anthony Papers, SC.

[15] Bassett to Gerrit Smith, May 9, 1861, Smith Papers, SU; *Liberator*, May 10, 1861. See also George W. Bassett, *A Discourse on the Wickedness and Folly of the Present War, delivered in the Court House, Ottawa, Ill., August 11, 1861* (Ottawa, 1861).

will stick, it is its pledge not to interfere with slavery in the states." Governor Andrew of Massachusetts, seeking advice from Washington on the tone he should take toward national affairs in his message to a special session of the legislature, was bluntly told by Montgomery Blair to "drop the nigger." Even Henry Ward Beecher, a strong antislavery man, trimmed to the conservative breeze of public opinion. "Some people ask if this is to be a crusade of emancipation," noted Beecher in a sermon on June 23. "No, it is not. I hate slavery intensely. . . . Liberty is the birthright of every man, yet ours is not an army of liberation. Why? Because the fifteen States of the South are guaranteed security in their property, and we have no right by force to dispossess them of that property."[16]

Under such circumstances some abolitionists who had interpreted the northern war fever after Sumter as an incipient revolution against slavery began to have second thoughts. "I am beginning to have some fears that this uprising is a sham & that the slave may not be free," wrote Edward M. Davis of Philadelphia on May 30. James Redpath was one of those who had welcomed the outbreak of war as the impending doom of slavery. But six weeks later he was no longer so sure. "The signs of the times have not and do not now indicate to our mind any such hopeful result," he wrote. "On the contrary, the drift of public sentiment appears, day by day, to be steadily setting against even the recognition of the slave in this contest." Especially disheartening were the frequent reports of the return to their masters of fugitive slaves who had sought refuge within Union lines. Lydia Maria Child said that "Every instance of sending back poor fugitive slaves has cut into my heart like the stab of a bowie-knife, and made me dejected for days."[17]

When the Garrisonian abolitionists of New England gathered for their annual Fourth of July picnic at Framingham, Massachusetts, there was a vocal element of opposition to the Garrison-Phillips policy of supporting the Union war effort. Stephen S. Foster brought this discontent to a head by introducing a resolu-

16 *Springfield Republican*, June 8, 1861; Henry G. Pearson, *The Life of John A. Andrew* (2 vols., Boston, 1904), I, 248-49; *New York World*, June 24, 1861.
17 E. M. Davis to S. H. Gay, May 30, 1861, Gay Papers, CU; *Pine and Palm*, June 1, 1861; L. M. Child to Henrietta Sargent, July 26, 1861, in Harriet W. Sewall, ed., *Letters of Lydia Maria Child* (Boston, 1883), 154.

tion which affirmed that until the government proclaimed emancipation, abolitionists could "give it no support or countenance in its effort to maintain its authority over the seceded States." Passage of this resolution would have virtually committed abolitionists to disloyalty, and Garrison, Phillips and others hastened to speak out against it. "I cannot say that I do not sympathize with the Government, as against Jefferson Davis and his piratical associates," declared Garrison, and he continued, "There is not a drop of blood in my veins, both as an abolitionist and a peace man, that does not flow with the Northern tide of sentiment." If the government should try to conclude a peace on the basis of the Union with slavery as secure as ever, "then will be the time for me to open all the guns that I can bring to bear on it. But, blessed be God, that 'covenant with death' has been annulled, and that 'agreement with hell' no longer stands. I joyfully accept the fact, and leave all verbal criticism until a more suitable opportunity."

Phillips thought that despite appearances, "there is a prevailing and unconscious, perhaps, but assured sentiment and purpose at the North, that the Union either does or shall mean liberty in the end." Phillips had been criticized for discarding his disunionism and coming out for the war. He replied to his critics that "no man should flatter himself he can mould the world exactly in his method. . . . I have advocated Disunion for fifteen years, because I thought it a practicable and peaceable method of freeing the North from the guilt of slavery, and of planting at the South the seeds of early and entire emancipation. But it has pleased the Nation to seek that result in a different way." Abolitionists should not renounce the Lincoln administration, said Phillips. They should try to influence public opinion in favor of emancipation, and bring that opinion to bear on the government. Several other speakers supported the position of Garrison and Phillips. When the vote was taken, Foster's antigovernment resolution was defeated by a large margin.[18]

This did not end the matter, however. At the annual celebration of West Indian emancipation on August 1 at Abington, Massachusetts, Parker Pillsbury introduced another resolution denouncing the Lincoln administration. "I have no higher opinion of

[18] *Liberator*, July 12, 1861.

Abraham Lincoln, and his Cabinet . . . than I have of the President and Cabinet . . . of the Confederate States," said Pillsbury in a biting speech. Pillsbury's resolution was also defeated, but in subsequent weeks criticism of the Garrison-Phillips position increased. James McCune Smith, Negro abolitionist and editor of the *Anglo-African* in New York City, wrote a letter to his friend Gerrit Smith rebuking the progovernment stand of Smith and the Garrisonians. "Because the South chose to storm Sumter and rave generally," complained McCune Smith, "you lent the sanction of your great name to the support of an Administration which, with trembling knees and in the face of the enemy endeavored to pacify the South by returning fugitive slaves!"[19] Pillsbury indignantly announced that he was going to the West for a lecture tour "in the hope that all the old Life Guard of Freedom at the West will still be found, as in the past, at their posts. No party, no Administration, no army as yet, has shown itself worthy to be entrusted with the hallowed interests of liberty and humanity."[20]

This kind of criticism was not without effect on progovernment abolitionists. "The situation of persons like ourselves is far from pleasant," Gerrit Smith told Garrison and continued, "While we condemn the Cause of the South, we cannot advocate the Cause of the North. Nevertheless we are filled with the hope that the Cause of the North will become the Cause of Truth." In reply to criticism by British abolitionists, Samuel May, Jr., wrote: "I do not disguise nor apologize for the follies & mistakes of our own Government, but speak of them plainly. But, so far as the Govt. is right, it deserves to be sustained, & we do cheerfully sustain it to that degree."[21]

But by September 1861, the truce that had prevailed between most abolitionists and the Lincoln administration was beginning to wear thin. The fond hopes for a short war and a quick end to slavery had proven illusory; the North had measured the strength of the Confederacy and found that it was in for a long, hard war. Abolitionists began to organize more actively and thoroughly to

[19] *ibid.*, Aug. 16, 1861; James McCune Smith to Gerrit Smith, Aug. 22, 1861, Smith Papers, su.

[20] *N.A.S. Standard*, Aug. 24, 1861.

[21] Smith to Garrison, Sept. 2, 1861, Garrison Papers, bpl; May to Richard Webb, Dec. 24, 1861, Samuel May, Jr., Papers, bpl.

bring pressure on the government to adopt an emancipation policy. There had never actually been a lack of such pressure. From the beginning of the conflict abolitionists had individually and collectively called for emancipation as a war policy. At first they made little impression on public opinion, but as the strife grew hotter, the iron necessities of war began to convince more and more northerners that emancipation was the only road to victory.

One of the first tasks of antislavery propaganda was to persuade a skeptical North that Negro slavery was the fundamental cause and basic issue of the war. Most northerners at first were inclined to agree with Stephen Douglas, who said in an Illinois speech early in the war: "The issue is not the negro; this question is above all the negroes in Christendom; it involves the freedom and independence of the ten millions, soon to be a hundred millions, of free white men in this valley."[22] Elizur Wright retorted that a war merely for Union, "tho' not on a false, is on a superficial issue. The war at its foundation is all about the black man, . . . and before the war is through the black man is almost certain to be fighting for himself on one side or the other." "If the slavery question is ignored," warned John Jay, "& the people are taught to look upon it as a mere sectional struggle for power, it will sink to a mere political question in which they will take but little interest."[23]

Abolitionists pointed out that the Confederates did not consider the Negro question insignificant in this war. In an address at Savannah on March 21 Alexander Stephens, vice president of the Confederacy, criticized Thomas Jefferson and the founding fathers for their erroneous belief that all men were created equal and that slavery was wrong. The statesmen of the Confederacy would not repeat this error. "Our new Government," said Stephens, "is founded upon exactly the opposite ideas; its foundations are laid, its corner stone rests upon the great truth that the negro is not equal to the white man; that slavery, subordination to the superior race, is his natural and normal condition. This, our new Government, is the first in the history of the world, based upon this great physical, philosophical, and moral truth."[24]

[22] *Liberator*, May 3, 1861.

[23] Wright to S. P. Chase, May 4, 1861, Jay to Chase, June 4, 1861, Chase Papers, LC.

[24] *Liberator*, July 5, 1861. Edward McPherson, *The Political History of the United States of America during the Great Rebellion* (Washington, 1865), 103-04, also prints this speech.

This and similar statements by other Confederate leaders caused Thomas Wentworth Higginson to write: "It is impossible to blink the fact that Slavery is the root of the rebellion. . . . Either slavery is essential to a community or it must be fatal to it,—there is no middle ground; and the Secessionists have taken one horn of the dilemma with so delightful a frankness as to leave us no possible escape from taking the other. Never, in modern days, has there been a conflict in which the contending principles were so clearly antagonistic. The most bigoted royal house in Europe never dreamed of throwing down the gauntlet for the actual ownership of man by man." Frederick Douglass declared that "the American people and the Government at Washington may refuse to recognize it for a time; but the 'inexorable logic of events' will force it upon them in the end; that the war now being waged in this land is a war for and against slavery."[25]

Early in the war abolitionists developed the argument that slavery was both a source of strength and weakness to the Confederacy. It was a source of strength because, as Douglass quoted from the *Savannah Republican*, "the labor of the South is not, as elsewhere, the fighting element of the State." The *Montgomery Advertiser* proclaimed that slavery was a "tower of strength to the Confederacy." Ten per cent of the total white population was required to fill the ranks of the army. "In any other country than our own, such a draft could not be met," said the *Advertiser*, "but the Southern States can furnish that number of men and still not leave the material interests of the country in a suffering condition. . . . The institution of slavery in the South alone, enables her to place in the field a force so much larger in proportion to her white population than the North."[26]

Frederick Douglass wholeheartedly agreed that slavery was "a tower of strength" to the Confederacy, and urged the North to convert it into an element of weakness by proclaiming emancipation. "Why? Oh! why, in the name of all that is national, does our Government allow its enemies this powerful advantage?" asked Douglass. "The very stomach of this rebellion is the negro in the

<hr/>

25 T. W. Higginson, "The Ordeal by Battle," *Atlantic Monthly*, VIII (July 1861), 94, 89; *Douglass' Monthly*, May 1861.

26 *Savannah Republican*, quoted in *Douglass' Monthly*, July 1861; *Montgomery Advertiser*, Nov. 6, 1861, quoted in *Principia*, Nov. 16.

condition of a slave. Arrest that hoe in the hands of the negro, and you smite the rebellion in the very seat of its life." There were thousands of slaves doing the heavy physical labor of the southern army—digging trenches, building fortifications, serving as teamsters, drivers, etc.—allowing soldiers to conserve their strength for the actual fighting. Douglass said, "The negro is the key of the situation—the pivot upon which the whole rebellion turns. . . . To fight against slaveholders, without fighting against slavery, is but a half-hearted business, and paralyzes the hands engaged in it."[27] Abolition of slavery, then, became a "military necessity" for victory in the war for the Union. That phrase, "military necessity," became the watchword of abolitionists in subsequent months; and "military necessity" was eventually cited by Lincoln as the main reason for his Emancipation Proclamation.

William Goodell urged abolitionists to keep the following facts before the people: the war was costing a million dollars a day; it could not be terminated without emancipation; every day's delay in proclaiming emancipation would cost the nation another million dollars; liberation of the slaves would transfer more than 500,000 able-bodied men from the Confederate to the Union side; the rebellion was a slaveholder's rebellion, and could not be put down without destroying slavery; and a compromise peace, leaving slavery intact, would fail to remove the cause of the strife and doom the nation to future discord and conflict. The *Anti-Slavery Standard* neatly summed up the abolitionist argument: "Success in the War, without Emancipation, is a Military Impossibility, and a Reunion with Slavery a political one."[28]

Abolitionists argued that emancipation was not only a military necessity, but also a moral necessity if the North hoped to justify the war to itself and to the world. In a popular book, *The Rejected Stone*, which went through three editions in 1861-62, Moncure Conway contended that the war had revealed the nation's fatal weakness. When the founding fathers constructed the edifice of the Union they cast aside one essential foundation stone, and Americans of 1861 were reaping the consequences of this folly. "That stone is, essentially, JUSTICE. The form in which it stands for

[27] *Douglass' Monthly*, July, Aug., Sept. 1861.
[28] *Principia*, Aug. 17, 1861; *N.A.S. Standard*, Dec. 7, 1861. In 1861 the American Anti-Slavery Society issued a pamphlet entitled *The War and Slavery: or Victory only through Emancipation* (Boston, 1861).

us is THE AFRICAN SLAVE." Napoleon once said that God was on the side of the strongest battalions. He found time to ponder his error in the solitude of St. Helena. The northern defeat at Bull Run, asserted Conway, proved that "*God is NOT on the side of the strongest battalions.*" An army fights much better when it has a noble cause for which to fight, and the rebels were "*fighting for their liberty.* True, it was their liberty; the liberty of Wrong, the free course of Anarchy, the untrammelled rule of Passion, the uncurbed privilege of trampling the most sacred rights and hopes of mankind." Nevertheless, they believed they were fighting and dying for a sacred cause. "Now, North-men," asked Conway, "with what do you confront this? Have you any Freedom-frenzy, with its superhuman strength? Do you worship Liberty with a passion?" Until the North acquired such a passion it would not be able to match the South's fighting spirit. When the North began to fight for the liberty of all races, it would learn that God was not on the side of the strongest battalions, but "The strongest battalions are those on the side of God."[29]

Abolitionists argued that England and Europe could have little sympathy for the North so long as it fought merely for political dominion. "Great Britain can see no principle of freedom in the war, as regards the enslaved, no intention of justice or of mercy toward them," wrote George Cheever from England, where he spent the first four months of the war. Zebina Eastman, Illinois abolitionist, served as American consul in Bristol during the war, and continually bombarded Washington with pleas for an emancipation policy. He reported that he was doing his best to foster pro-Union sentiment among the British people, but found it difficult in 1861-1862 because they viewed the war as a mere contest for power, with moral superiority on the side of the South, which was fighting for its own freedom. Once the North proclaimed emancipation, argued Eastman, it would win the powerful hosts of British middle- and lower-class opinion to its side.[30]

Whittier summed up the abolitionist wartime indictment of

[29] Moncure D. Conway, *The Rejected Stone: or Insurrection vs. Resurrection in America* (Boston, 1861), 23-24, 68-73.
[30] George Cheever, Diary, entry of June 12, 1861, in Cheever Papers, AAS; Zebina Eastman to S. P. Chase, Jan. 8, 1862, Chase Papers, LC; Eastman to Seward, Sept. 11, 1862, Seward Papers, RU.

slavery in a widely quoted poem, "Hymn of Liberty," intended to be sung to the tune of Luther's hymn, "A Mighty Fortress Is Our God."

> What gives the wheat-field blades of steel?
> What points the rebel cannon?
> What sets the roaring rabble's heel
>   On the old star-spangled pennon?
>   What breaks the oath
>   Of the men o' the South?
>   What whets the knife
>   For the Union's life?—
> Hark to the answer: Slavery!

> Then waste no blows on lesser foes
>   In strife unworthy freemen.
> God lifts to-day the veil, and shows
>   The features of the demon!
>   O North and South,
>   Its victims both,
>   Can ye not cry,
>   'Let slavery die!'
> And Union find in freedom?[31]

✦

In many ways the Civil War was a revolutionary conflict. The grant of freedom to four million slaves constituted the greatest social and economic revolution in American history. From the beginning of the war, abolitionists hoped for such an outcome and called on their fellow Americans to take up the revolutionary crusade for freedom. In an editorial entitled "The Second American Revolution," written less than three weeks after the fall of Sumter, William Goodell solemnly proclaimed: "It has begun. It is in progress.... The Revolution must go on, to its completion —*a National Abolition of Slavery.* . . . What but the insanity of moral blindness can long delay the proclamation, inviting [the slaves] to a share in *the glorious second American Revolution.*"[32]

The South tried to justify its secession by appealing to the tra-

[31] John G. Whittier, *Anti-Slavery Poems: Songs of Labor and Reform* (vol. III of his *Poetical Works*, Riverside Ed., Boston, 1888), 220.
[32] *Principia*, May 4, 1861.

ditions of '76. Moncure Conway, however, refused to recognize the southern rebellion as a revolution: "Revolution depends for its dignity and heroism purely upon the worth and justice of its cause. Had our American Revolution been for the purpose of forming our Colonies into a band of robbers and pirates" it would not have been a revolution. The South was fighting for slavery, "therefore it is wrongly called Revolution." It was the North that must fight a revolution of freedom. "The revolution is on our side, and as soon as the nation feels that, and acts upon it, the strength of the South is gone. . . . WE ARE THE REVOLUTIONISTS."[33]

It was all very well for abolitionists to urge the North forward on a revolutionary crusade for freedom, but a generation of Americans nurtured in a tradition of veneration for the Constitution could not be moved by such appeals alone. The constitutional inviolability of slavery in the states was held as an article of faith by most Americans. If abolitionists wished to see their dream of universal emancipation come true during the war, they would have to find some constitutional sanction for such a radical measure. They lost no time in doing so. Fortunately for them, there was a ready-made doctrine at hand for just such an emergency—the principle of the war power of the national government over slavery, developed and elaborated by John Quincy Adams twenty years earlier. During the Civil War the "war power" phrase became a companion to "military necessity" as the rallying cries under which wartime emancipationists drove the nation forward to total abolition of slavery.

On the day after the surrender of Fort Sumter, abolitionists began urging Lincoln and Congress to proclaim emancipation under the war power. They circulated petitions, wrote letters, made speeches, or talked personally with their congressmen. "That the President is authorized to liberate the slaves is as clear as that he may, when judging there is military necessity for it, order the destruction of all the rail roads in the Slave States," proclaimed Gerrit Smith on July 12 and continued, "In making war upon us the South has authorized us to cripple her in all the ways we

[33] Conway, *Rejected Stone*, 75-80, 110. For a similar appeal to the North to make the war a revolution for freedom, see [Elizur Wright], *The Programme of Peace, by a Democrat of the Old School* (Boston, 1862), 3-5.

can." The American Anti-Slavery Society published a pamphlet entitled *The Abolition of Slavery the Right of the Government under the War Power*. The pamphlet quoted extensively from John Quincy Adams, and included statements from Joshua Giddings, Orestes Brownson, and several other prominent Americans. It was published anonymously and cleverly edited: none of the articles or statements in it were by abolitionists, yet every one of them asserted the necessity or right of emancipation under the war power. Presumably such arguments would make a deeper impression on conservatives if they were known not to come from "fanatical" abolitionists.[34]

It took more than quotations from Adams and Giddings, however, to convert conservatives. As the emancipation pressure from abolitionists and radical Republicans mounted, the Democratic and conservative press countered with daily assertions that emancipation by the federal government, even under the war power, was manifestly unconstitutional. Clearly the abolitionists would have to wheel forth their heaviest legal artillery to prove the constitutionality of wartime emancipation. Two of the most learned lawyers in the abolitionist camp undertook the task. In the late summer of 1861 the American Anti-Slavery Society published a long pamphlet by David Lee Child entitled *The Rights and Duties of the United States Relative to Slavery under the Laws of War*. Under the United States Constitution slaves were regarded as both persons and property. Whether considered as persons *or* property, asserted Child, the federal government had the right to free them under the laws of war. He wrote: "As 'persons,' slaves stand in the same relation to an enemy conquering and occupying the country of their residence, as their masters do. Here is a principle of the laws of war, perfectly settled and unquestioned: Conquerors have the right, to the extent of their conquests, to establish such government and laws as they see fit. . . . They may dissolve the system of society which they find, and substitute any other which they deem more conducive to the improvement and happiness of the vanquished, and the peace and safety of the conquering na-

[34] *Gerrit Smith to Owen Lovejoy, July 12, 1861* (published letter, Peterboro, 1861), printed in broadside form and in the *New York Tribune*, July 28; *The Abolition of Slavery the Right of the Government under the War Power* (Boston, 1861), passim.

tion." If slaves were considered merely as property, the nation still had every right to emancipate them: "By the laws of war, the victors in a just cause may seize, appropriate to the uses of the war, carry off, confiscate, distribute or destroy every species of property, public or private, belonging to their enemies." As persons *or* property, therefore, slaves could be confiscated "to weaken our enemies, strengthen ourselves, and hasten the achievement of a beneficial and permanent peace."[35]

Another and even more thorough dissertation on the war power was published in the spring of 1862 by William Whiting of Concord, Massachusetts. Whiting was one of the ablest lawyers in New England, and was considered by his colleagues to be the foremost patent lawyer in the country. He was an abolitionist and served as a vice president of the Massachusetts Anti-Slavery Society. His father had been one of Garrison's earliest supporters, and his wife was a leading spirit in the Concord Anti-Slavery Society. The Whitings and the Garrisons were personal friends.[36] In his treatise Whiting pointed out that the Constitution had been adopted to "form a more perfect Union, establish Justice, insure domestic Tranquility, provide for the common defence, promote the general Welfare, and secure the Blessings of Liberty." But what had happened? "A handful of slave-masters have broken up that Union, have overthrown justice, and have destroyed domestic tranquility." Slavery had become irreconcilable with republican institutions, and must be destroyed. In time of war, under martial law, military officers had the undisputed right to seize private property for military purposes. Article I, Section 8 of the Constitution gave Congress the power to provide for the common defense and general welfare of the nation, including the right to abolish slavery should this prove necessary. "This right of seizure and condemnation is harsh," concluded Whiting, "as all the proceedings of war are harsh, in the extreme, but it is nevertheless lawful."[37]

[35] David Lee Child, *Rights and Duties of the United States Relative to Slavery under the Laws of War* (Boston, 1861), 5-6, 11, 24.

[36] Mrs. S. Barker to M. W. Chapman, Jan. 13, 1860, Chapman Papers, BPL; *Liberator*, July 12, 1861; *N.A.S. Standard*, Feb. 1, 1862; Frank Sanborn to unknown, Dec. 28, 1862, Sanborn Papers, Concord Public Library; Garrison to Helen Garrison, June 11, 1864, Mrs. Wm. Whiting to Garrison, Dec. 11, 1864, Garrison Papers, BPL.

[37] William Whiting, *The War Powers of the President, and the Legislative*

Whiting's book enjoyed an amazing popularity. In little more than a year it went through seven editions. In subsequent years chapters on military arrests, reconstruction, military government, and war claims were added, and in 1871 the expanded book of 695 pages was still in such demand as to require the printing of a forty-third edition. On the strength of the original treatise, Whiting was appointed solicitor of the War Department in December 1862, where he gained the friendship of Lincoln and Secretary of War Stanton.[38]

✦

When General Butler put his Massachusetts troops at the disposal of Maryland's Governor Thomas Hicks for the suppression of potential slave insurrections, there was a loud outcry from the Republicans and abolitionists in the Bay State. Governor Andrew curtly informed Butler that "the matter of servile insurrection among the community in arms against the Federal Union is no longer to be regarded by our troops in a political, but solely in a military point of view, and is to be contemplated as one of the inherent weaknesses of the enemy."[39] The chameleon-like Butler quickly discerned the drift of public opinion in Massachusetts. When three fugitive slaves came into his lines at Fortress Monroe in Virginia on May 23, he promptly labeled them contraband of war, refused to return them to their masters, and put them to work

---

Powers of Congress in Relation to Rebellion, Treason, and Slavery (7th ed., Boston, 1863), 3, 26-28, 46-48, 52, 54-55, 58. It should be noted that not all authorities on international and constitutional law were in agreement on the belligerent right of confiscation. The United States Supreme Court, however, later upheld the confiscation measures passed by Congress during the war. For a discussion of this question, see James G. Randall, *Constitutional Problems under Lincoln* (New York, 1926), 294-302, 312-15, 343-51, 373-85.

[38] The 8th edition in 1864 was published under the title *The War Powers of the President, Military Arrests, and Reconstruction of the Union*; the 10th edition in 1864 was published under the title *War Powers under the Constitution of the United States*; the 43rd edition was published in 1871 under the title *War Powers under the Constitution of the United States. Military Arrests, Reconstruction and Military Government.* For Whiting's appointment as War Department solicitor and his friendship with Lincoln, see Frank Sanborn to unknown, Dec. 28, 1862, Sanborn Papers, Concord Public Library; and Basler, ed., *Collected Works of Lincoln*, VIII, 373.

[39] Lewis Tappan to Andrew, Apr. 29, 1861, Andrew to Tappan, Apr. 30, 1861, published letters, clippings in Tappan Papers, LC; Andrew to Butler, Apr. 25, 1861, in Jesse A. Marshall, ed., *Private and Official Correspondence of Gen. Benjamin F. Butler during the Period of the Civil War* (5 vols., Norwood, Mass., 1917), I, 37-38.

constructing a new bake-house. Thenceforth the word "contraband," which technically applied to military goods sold to an enemy nation by a neutral, acquired a new meaning in the United States. By July 30 the number of contrabands behind Butler's lines had reached nine hundred. Their exact status was indefinite and they were by no means yet free, but their presence within Union lines helped partially to offset abolitionist bitterness over the continued return of fugitive slaves to their masters by other Union generals.[40]

Abolitionists were disheartened by Lincoln's renewed pledge in a July 4th message to Congress not to interfere with slavery in the states. They were slightly encouraged a few days later by House passage of Owen Lovejoy's resolution affirming that "it is no part of the duty of the soldiers of the United States to capture and return fugitive slaves." But this resolution was merely an expression of opinion by one branch of Congress and had little effect on army officers who continued to return fugitives. Near-unanimous passage by the House on July 22 and by the Senate three days later of the Crittenden and Johnson resolutions stating that "this war is not waged upon our part . . . for any purpose . . . of overthrowing or interfering with the rights or established institutions of . . . southern States" plunged the abolitionists into deeper gloom.[41]

Little public attention was focused on these resolutions when they were passed because they came immediately after the Union had suffered its setback at Bull Run. While most of the North reacted with despair and dejection, abolitionists took on new hope from the defeat. They foresaw that it would compel the northern people, most of whom had expected a short and easy war, to reassess their war policy and to reflect more seriously on the slavery issue. Many northerners began tentatively to agree with the abolitionists

[40] Edward L. Pierce, "The Contrabands at Fortress Monroe," *Atlantic Monthly*, VIII (Nov. 1861), 627-30. Several Union commanders imitated Butler's example and admitted fugitives to their lines. There was no uniform national policy on this subject in 1861, and each commanding general was allowed to do pretty much as he pleased regarding fugitive slaves.

[41] Basler, *Collected Works of Lincoln*, IV, 439; *Cong. Globe*, 37 Cong., 1 Sess., 32, 222-23, 258-60; Wendell Phillips to Charles Sumner, July 15, 1861, Sumner Papers, HU; *Douglass' Monthly*, Aug., Sept. 1861.

after Bull Run that the Union should convert slavery from a source of Confederate strength to a source of weakness by initiating an emancipation policy.

"The result of the battle was a fearful blow," wrote Moncure Conway two days after Bull Run, but "I think it may prove the means of rousing this stupid country to the extent & difficulty of the work it has to do." Wendell Phillips thought that Bull Run was "just what we wanted, and was perhaps the best thing that could have happened."[42] George L. Stearns considered it "the first step toward emancipation. If we had won a decisive victory, in less than six months the rebellious states would be back in the Union, the government would be out-voted in Congress, and we should have all our work to do over again." David Child believed that "A dozen victories would not have done so much to bring us to the right path as that disgraceful rout. We needed it." The moderate Charles Francis Adams, Jr., feared that "this defeat tends more and more to throw the war into the hands of the radicals, and if it lasts a year, it will be a war of abolition."[43]

In the weeks following Bull Run there was a marked increase of emancipationist feeling among the people of the North. "Public sentiment is changing almost as rapidly since that great disaster as it did after the fall of Fort Sumter," reported veteran Free Soiler Amasa Walker on August 8. "There is less noise made on the subject, but the current is strong and deep." Henry Cheever related the story of a Democrat who told his neighbor: "I went out to Bull's Run battlefield a Breckinridge Democrat, coming home I turned into a fighting Abolitionist."[44] Frederick Douglass thought that the defeat "has much changed the tone of Northern sentiment as to the proper mode of prosecuting the war, in reference to slavery, the cause of the war. . . . A cry has gone forth for the abolition of slavery." The *New York Tribune* began cautiously to hint at an emancipation policy. Even the *New York Times,*

[42] Moncure Conway to Ellen Conway, July 23, 1861, Conway Papers, cu; Phillips' remark is quoted in Sarah Forbes Hughes, ed., *Letters and Recollections of John Murray Forbes* (2 vols., Boston, 1899), i, 227.

[43] Frank P. Stearns, *The Life and Public Services of George Luther Stearns* (Philadelphia, 1907), 254; D. L. Child to Garrison, July 29, 1861, Garrison Papers, BPL; C. F. Adams, Jr., to C. F. Adams, July 23, 1861, in Worthington C. Ford, ed., *A Cycle of Adams Letters, 1861-65* (2 vols., Boston, 1920), i, 23.

[44] *Independent*, Aug. 8, 1861; *N.A.S. Standard*, Aug. 10, 1861.

which had previously tried to stifle any mention of the Negro in connection with the war, proclaimed four days after Bull Run that "there is one thing, and only one, at the bottom of this fight—and that is the *negro*."[45]

Partly in response to the growing public desire for action against slavery, Congress passed on August 6 a confiscation act providing for the seizure of all property used "in aid of the rebellion," including slaves. This bill applied only to slaves who had actually worked on Confederate military fortifications, naval vessels, and so on, and did not specifically *emancipate* such slaves, but it was nevertheless a significant step in the direction of emancipation. Thomas Wentworth Higginson wrote on August 23: "I am satisfied that we are gravitating towards a bolder anti-slavery policy. The desideratum is to approach a policy of emancipation by stages so clear & irresistible as to retain for that end an united public sentiment."[46]

On August 30, General John C. Frémont, commander of the Western Department, electrified the country with a bold and dramatic proclamation instituting martial law in Missouri and freeing the slaves of every rebel in the state. Frémont had taken this step with the advice and consultation of a quartermaster on his staff, Captain Edward M. Davis, a Philadelphia abolitionist and personal friend of the general. Davis telegraphed the first news of the proclamation to his fellow abolitionist, Sydney Howard Gay of the *New York Tribune*, who published Davis' dispatch in the issue of August 31, scoring a tremendous beat for the *Tribune* over its rivals.[47]

Abolitionists applauded Frémont's proclamation. Garrison hailed it as "the beginning of the end"; Gerrit Smith informed Lincoln in a public letter that "this step of General Frémont is the

[45] *Douglass' Monthly*, Aug. 1861; *New York Tribune*, Aug. 6, 12, 1861; *New York Times*, July 25, 1861. See also *New York Times*, July 29. The *Principia*, Sept. 21, 1861, quoted articles and editorials from a large number of northern newspapers in the weeks after Bull Run calling for some degree of emancipation.
[46] McPherson, *Political History of the Great Rebellion*, 195-96; Higginson to Louisa Higginson, Aug. 23, 1861, Higginson Papers, HU.
[47] E. M. Davis to S. H. Gay, May 22, Aug. 27, Sept. 1, 1861, Gay Papers, CU; Allan Nevins, *Frémont: Pathmarker of the West* (New York, 1955), 500, 503. The text of Frémont's proclamation is in *O. R.*, Ser. 1, vol. III, 466-67. See also E. M. Davis to J. M. McKim, Sept. 19, 1861, McKim Papers, Cornell; and Edmund Quincy to Richard Webb, Oct. 25, 1861, Quincy-Webb Correspondence, BPL.

first unqualifiedly and purely right one, in regard to our colored population, which has taken place during the war." Governor Andrew declared that Frémont's order gave "an impetus of the grandest character to the whole cause."[48] From Maine to Missouri the Republican press and a surprising number of conservative and Democratic papers expressed approval of the measure.[49] Lincoln, however, was afraid it would "alarm our Southern Union friends and turn them against us; perhaps ruin our rather fair prospect for Kentucky." On September 11, the president modified the proclamation to make it conform with the Confiscation Act of August 6, which confiscated only those slaves who had directly aided the Confederate military forces.[50]

Many Republicans could scarcely believe the news that Lincoln had revoked Frémont's order. Abolitionists were appalled. Garrison charged Lincoln with a "serious dereliction of duty." His annulment of Frémont's order was "timid, depressing, suicidal." In private Garrison fumed bitterly that even if Lincoln was "six feet four inches high, he is only a dwarf in mind." Edmund Quincy thought that revocation of the order "was one of those blunders which are worse than crimes." Frederick Douglass was disgusted by Lincoln's deference to the wishes of Kentuckians. "What is the friendship of these so-called loyal slaveholders worth?" asked Douglass. "The open hostility of these so-called loyal slaveholders is incomparably to be preferred to their friendship. They are far more easily dealt with and disposed of as enemies than as allies. From the beginning, these Border Slave States have been the mill-stone about the neck of the Government."[51]

From all over the North, abolitionists and antislavery Republicans reported popular opposition to Lincoln's action. "I cannot convey to you the burning sense of wrong which is filling the

---

[48] *Liberator*, Sept. 6, 1861; *Gerrit Smith to President Lincoln, Aug. 31, 1861* (Peterboro, 1861), published as a broadside and in the *New York Tribune*, Sept. 9; Pearson, *Andrew*, I, 249.

[49] *New York Times*, Sept. 2, 1861; *New York Herald*, Sept. 3, 1861; *Worcester Spy*, Sept. 2, 1861; *Springfield Republican*, Sept. 17, 1861. The *Principia*, Nov. 23, 1861, quoted statements from several dozen northern newspapers, including most of the great metropolitan dailies, endorsing Frémont's proclamation.

[50] Basler, *Collected Works of Lincoln*, IV, 506-07, 517-18.

[51] *Liberator*, Sept. 20, 1861; Garrison to Oliver Johnson, Oct. 7, 1861, Garrison Papers, BPL; *N.A.S. Standard*, Sept. 28, 1861; *Douglass' Monthly*, Oct. 1861.

breasts of our people here, as they gradually come to see that there is no President of the United States—only a President of Kentucky," wrote Moncure Conway from Cincinnati. B. Rush Plumly, Philadelphia Quaker abolitionist who was on duty in St. Louis as a special agent of the Treasury Department, wrote to his chief, Salmon P. Chase: "I wish you were here at this hour to see and feel the effect of the 'President's Order' in respect of Genl. Frémont's Proclamation. If the President had emptied the Arsenals of the Government into the Camps of the Rebels, he could not have so effectually strengthened them. . . . Better lose Kentucky, than keep her, at such a price." Plumly came East soon after this, had a talk with Lincoln in Washington, and later vented his wrath privately at the president's "pigheaded stupidity."[52]

Lincoln's revocation of Frémont's proclamation ended the five-months' armistice between abolitionists and the administration. Gone were the fond hopes that the president would quickly perceive the need to strike at slavery in order to win the war. Sharp criticism of Lincoln began to appear more frequently in abolitionist writings; it was not a time for pulling punches or speaking softly. There was a moral and political conflict in the North between conservatives and radicals over the question of human freedom. Abolitionists enlisted wholeheartedly for the duration of this struggle, determined that it should end in nothing less than universal emancipation.

[52] Moncure Conway to Charles Sumner, Sept. 17, 1861, Sumner Papers, HU; B. Rush Plumly to Chase, Sept. 15, Oct. 19, 1861, Chase Papers, LC. See also Henry Wright to Garrison, Sept. 16, 23, 1861, Garrison Papers, BPL; and *Principia*, Nov. 23, 1861.

IV ✦ EMANCIPATION AND PUBLIC

OPINION: 1861-1862

ISSATISFIED with the progress of the antislavery cause, Gerrit Smith and Henry Cheever wanted to hold a national convention of abolitionists in Washington or Philadelphia on September 24 to publicize the demand for emancipation. All branches of the abolitionist movement would be represented at the proposed convention. Cheever consulted Garrison, who threw cold water on the project. "Such a Convention, called by the parties and persons suggested by you, 'pronounced abolitionists,' would be more likely to excite popular prejudice at this crisis, and thus to damage a movement for the abolition of slavery under the war power, than to do good," argued Garrison. As long as the government was fighting a deadly battle with the slave power, "it seems to us the part of wisdom to avoid conspicuity as radical abolitionists in convention assembled, and to merge ourselves, as far as we can without a compromise of principle, in the onward sweeping current of Northern sentiment." Garrison hinted mysteriously at the emergence of a new antislavery organization in Boston, composed of abolitionists and antislavery Republicans alike, whose purpose would be to promote emancipation by means of newspaper articles, lectures, and petitions.[1]

Garrison was referring to a group of prominent Massachusetts abolitionists, including himself, Phillips, Frank Sanborn, George Stearns, William Henry Channing, Edmund Quincy, and Frank Bird, who were invited by Dr. Samuel Gridley Howe to meet at his Boston office on September 5 to discuss ways and means of channeling public opinion toward emancipation. A second meeting took place on September 10.[2] These gatherings became the subject of considerable hush-hush comment among abolitionists. Lydia Maria Child informed Whittier that "the warmest of the Republicans, and the most unprejudiced of the Abolitionists, are laying their

[1] Henry Cheever to Gerrit Smith, Aug. 20, Sept. 13, 1861, Smith Papers, su; Garrison to Henry Cheever, Sept. 9, 1861, Cheever Papers, aas.

[2] Frank B. Sanborn, *Dr. Samuel Gridley Howe: Philanthropist* (New York, 1891), 284; Laura E. Richards, *Letters and Journals of Samuel Gridley Howe: The Servant of Humanity* (Boston, 1909), 499-500; Frank P. Stearns, *The Life and Public Services of George Luther Stearns* (Philadelphia, 1907), 256-57.

heads together, with no more *publicity* than is necessary, to influence popular opinion, through the press, and help on the turning-tide in the right direction." Stearns told J. Miller McKim about the group, warning him to keep the information quiet, for "we do not as yet wish the movement to be made public."[3]

At the second meeting in Howe's office an executive committee was appointed to formulate plans of action. The committee decided that their primary objective should be to educate the public to understand "much better than it now does, the magnitude of the war in which the country is involved, and the bearing of slavery upon its continuance and final issue." They planned to solicit emancipation articles and editorials from prominent abolitionists to be sent out on printed slips to small-town newspapers all over the North. The articles would be anonymous "so that the truths they present may have their due weight, without prejudice." The group tentatively called itself the Boston Emancipation League, and decided to work under cover for the time being because of the prevailing popular prejudice against abolitionists.[4]

The decision of the Emancipation League to inaugurate a propaganda campaign was partly spurred by Lincoln's revocation of Frémont's Missouri proclamation. A large section of the northern press which had welcomed Frémont's order when it appeared now followed Lincoln and condemned Frémont for having gone too far. Emancipationist feeling in the North was fickle and ill-formed at best; a massive program of popular education would be necessary to create a public opinion that would eventually compel the abolition of slavery.[5]

The opening gun in this battle of words was fired by Charles Sumner in his address to the Massachusetts state Republican convention in Worcester on October 1. Sumner was on terms of friendship with most of the founders of the Emancipation League and was well aware of their activities. In his October 1 speech he de-

[3] L. M. Child to Whittier, Sept. 10, 1861, Child-Whittier Correspondence, LC; Stearns to J. M. McKim, Oct. 1, 1861, McKim Papers, Cornell.

[4] Stearns to McKim, Oct. 1, 1861, McKim Papers, Cornell; James M. Stone to Gerrit Smith, Oct. 10, 1861, Smith Papers, SU.

[5] L. M. Child to Whittier, Sept. 22, 1861, Child-Whittier Correspondence, LC; *Principia,* Oct. 26, 1861; *N.A.S. Standard,* Nov. 2, 1861; *Independent,* Nov. 7, 1861; *New York Times,* Dec. 5, 1861.

clared that "Slavery is our Catiline. . . . It is often said that the war will make an end of slavery. This is probable; but it is surer still that the overthrow of slavery will make an end of the war. It is not necessary even . . . to carry the war into Africa; it will be enough if we carry Africa into the war." James Freeman Clarke, a member of the executive committee of the Emancipation League and a delegate to the convention, introduced resolutions from the floor affirming that Massachusetts would "welcome any act under the war power which should declare all slaves within the lines of our armies free . . . compensating all loyal owners." A majority of delegates probably favored such a statement, but fearing that it might be interpreted as a rebuke to Lincoln for his recent modification of Frémont's order, the convention tabled Clarke's resolution.[6]

Sumner's abolitionist friends praised his speech, while Boston conservatives glowered and growled.[7] "Mr. Sumner's speech has created a great sensation," reported a Boston friend of the senator. "The elements of Hunkerism have boiled over. Yet he is hardly in advance of the times more than six months."[8] The *New York Tribune* published the speech in its weekly edition, assuring it a potential reading audience of nearly a million persons. The Emancipation League sent copies of the speech to editors of northern newspapers, to every clergyman and country storekeeper in Massachusetts, and to every member of the Massachusetts legislature.[9]

Abolitionist strategy during October and November 1861, was to remain in the background of the growing emancipation movement, letting others less burdened with the odium of a lifetime of devotion to freedom take the lead. "I have discouraged any distinct antislavery movement by the old abolitionists in New York," reported John Jay in October, "from the belief that such action would rather retard than advance the conversion of the Democratic masses." Lewis Tappan tried to imitate Boston's example and form an Emancipation League in New York, but Jay and other leading Republicans defeated the attempt. "Abolition will

[6] *Boston Advertiser*, Oct. 2, 1861. Sumner's speech is printed in his *Works*, VI, 1-29.

[7] There are about a dozen letters from abolitionists praising Sumner's speech, in the Sumner Papers, HU.

[8] James W. Stone to S. P. Chase, Oct. 5, 1861, Chase Papers, LC.

[9] James M. Stone to Sumner, Dec. 18, 1861, Sumner Papers, HU.

come as a military necessity as our army advances," argued Jay, and "its advocacy at this moment by those who have always opposed [slavery] on moral grounds is calculated rather to divide the North."[10]

Jay was in touch with leading "War Democrats" in New York, trying quietly to persuade them to come out for emancipation as a military necessity. Maria Weston Chapman was also a firm advocate of this approach. "Start the thing by others & then fall in, is our best plan," she wrote. "I have been long in correspondence with leading N.Y. Merchants—Our friend John Jay is doing the same work with the Butler & Dickinson people,—the fire is lighting at every corner." In November this method began to pay off. Daniel S. Dickinson, Colonel John Cochrane, George Bancroft, Benjamin Hallett—all of them prominent Democrats or conservatives before the war—began to deliver emancipation speeches. Cochrane and Secretary of War Simon Cameron made several joint appearances in the Northeast, calling for emancipation and the arming of Negro soldiers as a military necessity. The *New York Tribune* was delighted with these developments. "We now see men like Daniel S. Dickinson and Gerrit Smith," said the *Tribune,* "who have heretofore stood at the antipodes of this controversy, and classes like Hard-Shell Democrats and Garrisonian Abolitionists, who have represented the most antagonistic opinions in regard to it, taking substantially the same view of the part which Slavery ought to play in this sanguinary drama."[11]

On November 27, Sumner spoke for emancipation before a huge audience in New York's Cooper Union. Sitting on the platform next to prominent Republicans were Oliver Johnson, George Cheever, Octavius B. Frothingham, Dexter Fairbanks, William Goodell, Edgar Ketchum, Henry B. Stanton, Theodore Tilton, and Edward Gilbert, all of them veteran abolitionists. Commented Goodell afterwards: "To ourselves and a remnant of our old associates, on the platform and in the meeting, who remembered the scenes of [anti-abolitionist] mob violence in this city, . . . the

---

[10] John Jay to Sumner, Oct. 16, Nov. 8, 1861, Henry Hartt to Sumner, Oct. 18, 1861, Sumner Papers, HU; Lewis Tappan, Journal, entry of Sept. 12, 1861, Tappan Papers, LC; *Principia,* Oct. 26, 1861.

[11] M. W. Chapman to J. M. McKim, Oct. ?, 1861, Garrison Papers, BPL; *New York Times,* Nov. 14, 1861; *New York Tribune,* Nov. 12, 14, 20, 1861. Cochrane was Gerrit Smith's nephew.

contrast was most striking and cheering. To any of our Radical friends in the country who may be surprised at seeing the names of Oliver Johnson, William Goodell, &c. on the list of Vice-Presidents of a meeting invited by a Young Men's *Republican* Association, we may say that our own surprise is equal to theirs. Let them not however infer that we have backslidden from our Radical Abolition faith. The speech and the responses show that our fellow citizens, not ourselves, are changing."[12]

With the growing popularity of emancipation and the consequent increase in the prestige of abolitionists, the founders of the Emancipation League decided to bring their organization into the open. They held a formal inauguration meeting in Boston on December 16, with Samuel Gridley Howe in the chair. George S. Boutwell, onetime Democratic governor of Massachusetts and now a Republican, gave the main address, flanked on the platform by the elite of Massachusetts abolitionism and Republicanism. "The Emancipation League is now in full blast," screamed the hostile *Boston Herald*, "the furnace is heated ten times hotter than ever, and the whole pack of Anti-Slavery, Abolition devils are at work to make Bedlam appear lovely and inviting."[13] The League ignored such outbursts and formally elected its officers on January 27, 1862, choosing Samuel Sewall, one of the original abolitionists, as president. The executive committee was dominated by abolitionists, and George L. Stearns served as treasurer. The League recruited a fairly large dues-paying membership among Massachusetts abolitionists and Republicans, but a large part of the organization's funds were contributed by the wealthy Stearns. During the first year of its existence, the League sponsored nine lectures and six free-discussion sessions, published and circulated nearly 100,000 pamphlets, and supplied scores of northern newspapers with emancipation editorials and articles. During 1862 Stearns kept one clerk busy full time sending out documents, pamphlets, and speeches. In August 1862, a weekly newspaper, the *Boston Commonwealth*, was founded under the auspices of the League.[14]

---

12 *Principia*, Dec. 7, 1861.

13 *Liberator*, Dec. 20, 27, 1861; *Boston Herald*, quoted by *Liberator*, Dec. 27, 1861.

14 Stearns, *Stearns*, 258-59; *Boston Commonwealth*, Jan. 24, May 29, 1863; George Stearns to Frank Sanborn, Apr. 30, 1862, Sanborn Papers, Concord Public Library. The membership book of the Emancipation League is in the Rare Book Department, BPL.

In the winter and spring of 1861-62 the number of emancipation organizations and lecture associations proliferated rapidly. William Goodell and J. Walden, publisher of Goodell's *Principia*, organized a "National Emancipation Association" in New York City on November 6, 1861. The Association served as a clearinghouse for emancipation petitions sent to the president and Congress during the 1861-1862 congressional session. In Boston, Charles W. Slack, chairman of Theodore Parker's old Twenty-Eighth Congregational Society, organized a course of emancipation lectures. Susan B. Anthony arranged a similar lecture series in Rochester, which featured several prominent abolitionist speakers. New York City abolitionists formed an Emancipation League, similar to the Boston organization, in June 1862 and sponsored a course of popular lectures.[15]

One of the most effective emancipation organizations was formed in the national capital. In November 1861, a group of young antislavery officeholders decided to organize a lecture association to bring outstanding antislavery speakers to Washington. One of these young men later told the following story: "About nine o'clock there was a knock at the door and it was opened to admit a venerable man with long flowing white hair and a beard like Raphael's Saint Jerome, a quick, nervous manner, a glowing pink face and vivacious and merry blue eyes. He paused, leaned against the door, and said, 'Gentlemen, I saw an advertisement summoning young men to come here to consult to-night, and here I am!'" The "young" patriarch was John Pierpont, seventy-six years old and a battle-scarred veteran of the abolitionist crusade, who now held a job in the Treasury Department. The younger antislavery clerks were so charmed by Pierpont's enthusiasm that "without much discussion, or even consideration, we elected this 'young man' to be our president, organizing as the Washington Lecture Association."[16]

15 *Principia*, Nov. 9, 30, 1861, June 12, 26, 1862; Stearns, *Stearns*, 260-61; Ida H. Harper, *The Life and Work of Susan B. Anthony* (3 vols., Indianapolis, 1898-1908), I, 217; S. B. Anthony to George Cheever, Mar. 6, 1862, Parker Pillsbury to Cheever, Mar. 11, 1862, Cheever Papers, AAS; S. B. Anthony to Theodore Tilton, Mar. ?, 1862, Apr. 14, 1862, Anthony Papers, NYHS; *New York Tribune*, June 13, 1862.

16 Wm. A. Croffut, *An American Procession, 1855-1914* (Boston, 1930), 56-57. See also Abe C. Ravitz, "John Pierpont: Portrait of a Nineteenth Century Re-

The Association sponsored a course of more than twenty lectures in the hall of the Smithsonian Institution during the winter. Some of the foremost abolitionists and Republicans in the nation were featured in the series. The lectures were an overwhelming success. Lincoln attended several of them, and leading members of Congress were in the audience at every lecture.[17] Pierpont marveled that the series had "been more entirely and triumphantly successful, than the most sanguine of us dared to hope." It did his heart good "to hear the emphatic applause with which the radicalisms of the lectures are received—the more radical the more rapturous —and this in Washington, where nothing of the kind has ever been attempted before."[18] Kentucky's proslavery Senator Garrett Davis was greatly disturbed by the popularity of the lectures. "The utterances they have dared to put forth in this city have desecrated the Smithsonian Institution," he fumed, and continued, "What will you do with these monsters? I will tell you what I would do with them and with the horrible monster Greeley, as they come sneaking around here, like hungry wolves, after the destruction of Slavery. If I had the power, I would take them and the worst Seceshers and hang them in pairs."[19]

✦

William Goodell wrote in December 1861: "Never has there been a time when Abolitionists were as much respected, as at present. Never has there been a time in which their strongest and most radical utterances . . . were as readily received by the people, as at present. . . . Announce the presence of a competent abolition lecturer and the house is crammed."[20]

What had happened in the space of a few short months to change the abolitionists from a set of despised fanatics to a group of reformers whose advice was eagerly sought and listened to? The answer lies, partially at least, in the swelling tide of emanci-

---

former," Ph.D. dissertation, New York University, 1955, 301-02; and W. A. Croffut to George Cheever, Nov. 25, 1861, Cheever Papers, AAS.

[17] Croffut, *American Procession*, 57-74; Ravitz, "Pierpont," 305; T. W. Higginson to Louisa Higginson, Dec. 7, 1861, Higginson Papers, HU; *New York Tribune*, Jan. 15, 1862; *Independent*, Jan. 16, 1862; W. A. Croffut to George Cheever, Mar. 5, 1862, Cheever Papers, AAS.

[18] Pierpont to Wm. Cullen Bryant, Jan. 12, 1862, Pierpont Papers, PML.

[19] *New York Tribune*, Jan. 25, 1862.

[20] *Principia*, Dec. 21, 1861.

pationist opinion in the North. The hard, inescapable necessities of war were pushing the North, slowly and reluctantly, to the extremist position of the abolitionists. Victor Hugo once said that "There is no greater power on earth than an idea whose time has come." By December 1861, the powerful idea of universal freedom was taking deep root in America. As lifelong champions of this idea, abolitionists began to reap the benefits of its growing popularity. For thirty years they had been crying in the wilderness, telling the people that slavery was destroying the moral and political fabric of the nation. The mass of the people paid little attention except to denounce the abolitionists as troublesome fanatics. When the Union broke apart and war erupted, many persons began to regard the abolitionists in a new light. They no longer appeared as zealous crackpots, but as prophets who had tried to save their country before it was too late.[21]

The evidence of the new-found popularity, prestige, and influence of abolitionists in 1861-1862 is overwhelming. In the last two months of 1861, Frederick Douglass and several other abolitionist speakers were welcomed enthusiastically when they spoke in Syracuse, a city that had mobbed them ten months before. A nonpartisan literary journal in New York observed that "one of our most ably edited and uniformly well written journals is the New York Anti-Slavery Standard. Before the great rebellion, the Standard was a tabooed paper, except in exclusively 'abolition' circles; but now the Standard may be read and quoted by anybody without loss of character or business."[22] When Wendell Phillips spoke in New York on December 19, the street in front of Cooper Union was filled with a crowd an hour before the doors opened. The audience packed every corner of the hall and nearly a thousand people were turned away for lack of room. The listeners applauded Phillips' most radical utterances, and afterwards voted unanimously to invite Garrison to speak.[23]

[21] Richard Hofstadter has perceptively analyzed the role of the radical reformer in a time of crisis in his "Wendell Phillips: The Patrician as Agitator," in *The American Political Tradition and the Men Who Made It* (New York, Vintage Books, 1958), 139.

[22] *Douglass' Monthly*, Dec. 1861; *New York Courier*, quoted in *N.A.S. Standard*, Nov. 16, 1861.

[23] *New York Tribune*, Dec. 20, 1861; *N.A.S. Standard*, Dec. 28, 1861; Oliver Johnson to Garrison, Dec. 20, 31, 1861, Theodore Tilton to Garrison, Jan. 1, 1862, Garrison Papers, BPL.

The newborn prominence and prestige of abolitionists was graphically portrayed by a correspondent of the *New York Times* (a paper hostile to abolitionism) who reported the annual meeting of the Massachusetts Anti-Slavery Society in January 1862. The *Times* reporter wrote: "In years heretofore a great deal has been said and much fun has been made of the promiscuous and somewhat peculiar features of these gatherings. The facts that black and white met socially here, and that with equal freedom men and women addressed the conglomerate audience, have furnished themes for humorous reporters and facetious editors; but no such motive has drawn here the representatives of fifteen of the most widely circulated journals of the North." Abolitionist meetings were now notable political events. "Peculiar circumstances have given to this, the oldest Anti-Slavery Society in the country, and to similar organizations elsewhere, an importance which hitherto has not been theirs, and which justifies the most wide circulation of their sayings, doings, prophecies and lamentations."[24]

A small group of Republican congressmen invited George Cheever to preach an antislavery sermon in the House of Representatives on Sunday, January 12. Cheever accepted, and his sermon produced such a powerful effect that forty-three congressmen and senators invited him to preach another one on January 26.[25] These two sermons and Cheever's lecture at the Smithsonian Institution were the talk of Washington for several days. A private in a regiment stationed near the capital heard Cheever's first sermon and wrote to him afterwards: "Previous to this war, I hated the name of an abolitionist. But within the last nine months I have seen enough of the beauties of slavery to turn me right about. And I agree with you that the salvation of the country depends on the adoption by the government of a sweeping emancipation policy." Another Washington observer wrote:

"I have rarely seen an audience more completely magnetized by a speaker than the crowded assembly in the Smithsonian were, last Friday, by Cheever. Almost every sentence elicited applause, and several times the heartiest cheers broke forth irrepressibly. Yester-

[24] *New York Times*, Jan. 25, 1862.

[25] Committee of twelve Republican congressmen to Cheever, Jan. 9, 1862, Committee of forty-three Republican congressmen and senators to Cheever, Jan. 14, 1862, Cheever Papers, AAS.

day, also, he preached to an assembly of two thousand and upwards in the Hall of Representatives, thrilling his auditors with his trumpet calls to action. . . . And when, at the close, the Hutchinsons sang the plaintive Prayer of the Fugitive Slave, and the vast multitude burst out in one tumultuous acclamation, it was startling to think of the utter transformation wrought by one year's tremendous experience."[26]

More than twenty years later a Republican congressman still remembered Cheever's sermons as "the most terrific arraignment of slavery I ever listened to." Invitations to speak showered upon Cheever from all over the Northeast, and he accepted as many of them as he could, including a request to address a joint session of the Pennsylvania legislature.[27]

Other abolitionists who lectured in Washington during the winter made almost as great an impression as Cheever. Gerrit Smith spoke in the capital on March 1, and remarked afterwards: "A great change has taken place in that City. The most radical Abolitionist is now applauded by a Washington audience for his most radical utterances." William Goodell was encouraged by his reception in the capital. "In and out of Congress . . . radical views, in Washington City, . . . are on the advance. To this improved condition of things, the lectures in the Smithsonian Institute, this season, have greatly contributed."[28] Goodell, Moncure Conway, and William Henry Channing had personal interviews with Lincoln while they were in the capital. Conway was impressed by Lincoln, probably because the president complimented his

[26] John B. Geyser to Cheever, Jan. 15, 1862, Cheever Papers, AAS; O. B. Frothingham, *Memoir of William Henry Channing* (Boston, 1886), 323-24. A captain in the Sickles Brigade, stationed in Charles County, Maryland, wrote in a private letter December 15, 1861, that "the more our officers and soldiers see of the institution of slavery the more they detest it. Five months ago, ninety out of every hundred of the Sickles Brigade would have been delighted to mob an abolitionist—now they want to abolish slavery, root and branch." Quoted in the *Anglo-African*, Dec. 28, 1861.

[27] George Julian, *Political Recollections, 1840 to 1872* (Chicago, 1884), 370; Committee of twenty-one members of the Pennsylvania legislature to Cheever, Jan. 17, 1862, Gordon S. Berry (clerk of the Pennsylvania legislature) to Cheever, Jan. 25, 1862, Cheever Papers, AAS.

[28] Gerrit Smith to Richard Webb, Mar. 15, 1862, Smith to Garrison, Mar. 17, 1862, Garrison Papers, BPL; *Principia*, Apr. 10, 17, 1862.

book, *The Rejected Stone*. Lincoln was "astonished to learn that its author was really a native of Virginia."[29]

The greatest triumph for the abolitionists was Wendell Phillips' visit to Washington in March. "A year ago Wendell Phillips would have been sacrificed to the Devil of Slavery anywhere on Pennsylvania Avenue," wrote the Washington correspondent of the *New York Tribune*, but "To-day he was introduced by Mr. Sumner on to the floor of the Senate. The Vice-President left his seat and greeted him with marked respect. The attentions of Senators to the apostle of Abolition were of the most flattering character." Phillips lectured three times to enthusiastic audiences at the Smithsonian Institution; he was guest of honor at a dinner party given by Speaker of the House Galusha Grow; and he had a private interview with Lincoln, from which he emerged with a more favorable impression of the president than he had previously held. The *New York Tribune* drew a significant moral from Phillips' welcome in the capital. It had been little more than a year since he was mobbed in Boston for expressing the same sentiments he now uttered in Washington. "Both then and now he is a representative man," observed the *Tribune* editorially, "and the fierce anger that then sought his death, and the deference and respect now paid to him by men in the highest places of the nation, are tributes to the idea of which he, more than any other one man, is a popular exponent. It is not often that history presents such violent contrasts in such rapid succession."[30]

Phillips had been lecturing in the Northeast most of the winter, and when he left Washington he headed west for a brief tour. In Cincinnati he was greeted by rock- and egg-throwing toughs from Kentucky. It was the first and last occurrence of antiabolitionist mob violence during the war. It helped rather than harmed

[29] Moncure Conway to Ralph Waldo Emerson, Jan. 22, 1862, Conway to Ellen Conway, Mar. 17, 1862, Conway Papers, CU.

[30] *New York Tribune*, Mar. 15, 18, 19, 1862. The Washington correspondent of the *Boston Journal* reported that "the matchless oratory of Wendell Phillips has taken the town by storm." The correspondent of the *Springfield Republican* stated that Phillips had "uttered the most ultra sentiments without the slightest interruption or censure. This is in itself almost a miracle, and will be set down as an 'event' when the history of these times comes to be written. . . . Phillips was a real lion while here. . . . It was the complete triumph of free speech on slave soil." Quoted in the *N.A.S. Standard*, Mar. 29, 1862.

Phillips. Editors throughout the North denounced the Kentucky rioters, and lecture invitations poured in on Phillips at a redoubled rate. He wrote to a Boston friend, "You have no idea how the disturbance has stirred the West. I draw immense houses, and could stay here two months, talking every night." The *New York Tribune* estimated that during the winter and spring of 1861-1862 no less than 5 million people heard or read Phillips' antislavery discourses.[31]

In 1862, Charles A. Dana neared the completion of fifteen years as managing editor of the *New York Tribune*, but he was finding it increasingly difficult to get along with Greeley and in March 1862, Dana resigned. His successor was Sydney Howard Gay, the mild-mannered, intellectual, hard-working Garrisonian abolitionist who had been a member of the *Tribune* staff since 1857. Before that he had edited the *Anti-Slavery Standard* for fourteen years. Greeley had been impressed by the quality of Gay's work on the *Standard* and had personally offered him a position with the *Tribune*. Life on the *Tribune* staff was not always easy for a Garrisonian abolitionist from 1857 to 1861. Greeley was no abolitionist; he was erratic in his devotion to the antislavery cause. Dana, Gay, and other members of the editorial corps worked hard to keep the paper consistently antislavery in spite of Greeley's deviations. When war came in 1861 the *Tribune* did not immediately call for emancipation. Not until after Bull Run did Greeley begin to hint cautiously at abolition, and it was not until the late months of 1861 that the *Tribune* became known as a consistent and thoroughgoing champion of emancipation.[32]

In his five years with the *Tribune*, Gay had proved himself the most valuable member of the editorial staff and he was a natural choice to succeed Dana. Abolitionists were delighted with the news that one of their own had become managing editor of America's most powerful newspaper at a time of America's greatest crisis. Oliver Johnson, a personal friend of both Greeley and Gay, told Garrison that Gay's accession was "a most important change,

---

[31] *Liberator*, Mar. 21, Apr. 11, 25, 1862; *New York Tribune*, Apr. 4, 1862.

[32] Louis M. Starr, *The Bohemian Brigade: Civil War Newsmen in Action* (New York, 1954), 18-19, 98-99; Horace Greeley to S. H. Gay, Aug. 18, 1861, Gay to Wendell Phillips, Oct. 28, 1861, Parker Pillsbury to Gay, Nov. 21, 1861, J. G. Whittier to Gay, Nov. 14, 1861, Gay Papers, cu.

and one that will improve the tone of the paper. This *inter nos*."[33]

As managing editor, Gay soon showed himself a more efficient administrator and harder worker than his predecessor. He was in the office from noon until 3 a.m., six days a week. He wrote editorials, supervised the makeup of the paper, and directed the far-flung corps of *Tribune* war correspondents. As the war progressed, Greeley spent more and more time on his voluminous private correspondence, his lecture tours, and his political activities in Washington and New York. Gay took on a growing amount of responsibility for the paper. Greeley determined the general editorial policy and usually wrote the leading editorial each day when he was in town, but Gay superintended the day-to-day policy of the *Tribune* and gradually acquired a greater power over editorial strategy than even Dana had exercised. Gay soon earned a reputation of excellence among his fellow journalists. Edward Dicey of the *London Spectator*, one of the best foreign correspondents in the United States during the war, considered the *Tribune* under Gay's management "better printed, more thoughtfully written, and more carefully got up than any of its contemporaries." And Charles Congdon, the brilliant, acid-tongued editorial writer for the *Tribune* and a good friend of Dana's, paid Gay a supreme compliment: "You must know that the *Tribune* in my opinion never was a better paper. It is due to you to say this."[34]

A second journalistic event of great importance for abolitionists in 1861-1862 was the change in editorship of the *New York Independent*, the largest and most influential political-religious weekly newspaper in the country. The *Independent* had been founded in 1848 as a Congregational antislavery journal by Henry C. Bowen,

[33] Oliver Johnson to Garrison, Mar. 31, 1862, Garrison Papers, BPL. See also Pillsbury to Gay, Apr. 2, 1862, Gay Papers, CU; and O. Johnson to J. M. McKim, Dec. 29, 1862, McKim Papers, NYPL.

[34] Starr, *Bohemian Brigade*, 98-99, 116-24, 133-34; Elizabeth N. Gay to Sarah M. Gay, Apr. 1, 12, 1862, Gay Papers, CU; S. H. Gay to Garrison, Nov. 1, 1862, Garrison Papers, BPL. The quoted tributes to Gay from Dicey and Congdon are in Starr, *Bohemian Brigade*, 133-34. James R. Gilmore, a friend of Greeley and Gay, wrote in his memoirs that Gay "had more influence with [Greeley] than any other person." Gilmore asserted that "from the resignation of Charles A. Dana, early in 1862, until the close of the war, Mr. Gay controlled the course of the *Tribune*, and in all that time he did what no other man—except Mr. Dana—ever did or could do,—he held Mr. Greeley's great powers to the steady support of the Union." James R. Gilmore, *Personal Recollections of Abraham Lincoln and the Civil War* (Boston, 1898), 81, 94.

New York silk merchant and son-in-law of Lewis Tappan. For thirteen years it was edited by three Congregational clergymen: Leonard Bacon, Joseph Thompson, and Richard S. Storrs. During this period the *Independent* pursued a conservative antislavery course, attacking slaveholders and abolitionists with about the same spirit. In 1861 the three clergymen editors hesitated, vacillated, and refused to declare openly for an emancipation policy. Meanwhile the war had forced Bowen's silk business into bankruptcy, and to save the *Independent* he turned it over temporarily to Tappan in December 1861 without consulting the three editors. The three clergymen resigned, and Tappan persuaded Henry Ward Beecher to become the new editor-in-chief of the *Independent*. [35]

Abolitionists rejoiced at the change. Beecher did not quite measure up to radical antislavery standards, but he was an improvement over his predecessors; abolitionists also knew that Beecher's editorship would be little more than nominal. The real source of the *Independent's* editorial policy after December 1861, was Theodore Tilton, the brilliant young abolitionist who had been on the *Independent* staff since 1856. With his busy schedule, Beecher scarcely had time to write more than one editorial a week. Tilton took over most of the editorial work, and in less than a year his journalistic genius and Beecher's name more than doubled the *Independent's* circulation, bringing it to the amazing total (for a religious journal) of 70 thousand. In the spring of 1863, Beecher resigned and went to England on a lecture tour to win British support for the Union cause. Tilton became editor-in-chief of the *Independent*. Under his editorship it became less a religious journal and more a radical, crusading political weekly. Tilton frequently consulted his friends Garrison and Oliver Johnson about editorial policy, and for all practical purposes the powerful *Independent* became an abolitionist organ. [36]

35 Frank Luther Mott, *A History of American Magazines* (3 vols., New York and Cambridge, 1930-38), II, 367-71; Louis Filler, "Liberalism, Anti-Slavery, and the Founders of the *Independent*," *New England Quarterly*, xxvii (Sept. 1954), 291-306; Edward Gilbert to George Cheever, Nov. 27, 1860, Cheever Papers, AAS; Lewis Tappan, Journal, 1861, entry of Dec. 7, 1861; Tappan, "Resumé of my Life," 1861, Tappan Papers, LC; *Independent*, Dec. 19, 1861. Tappan relinquished the proprietorship of the *Independent* to Bowen after the latter had gotten his business back on its feet in the early months of 1862.

36 Mott, *American Magazines*, II, 371-73; *N.A.S. Standard*, Dec. 21, 1861,

The increasing influence of abolitionists was reflected in the exasperation of their opponents. A writer in the conservative *Boston Courier* denounced Phillips as a treasonable fanatic: "It will not do to represent this torch of incendiarism as a person of no influence or consideration, for the contrary is notoriously the fact. . . . There is not at this moment in Massachusetts a person of more wide influence over the general heart and mind than he is. As a public lecturer, he is by far the most popular man in the State." After Phillips had lectured in Washington, Kentucky's Senator Garrett Davis lamented that the abolitionists "have such skillful and dexterous and able and unscrupulous leaders here that they can cajole the simple, moderate, conservative, constitutional Republicans to their extreme measures." Davis thought Phillips should be "manacled and confined at Fort Warren or Fort Hamilton." Acidulous old James Gordon Bennett of the *New York Herald* demanded that "the Government send these ranters to Fort Lafayette a while, to be seasoned, and then string them up with the rebels, like dried haddock, at the end of the war. Thus the country will be saved, and his Satanic Majesty be enabled to settle his accounts with Phillips very speedily."[37]

Abolitionists themselves never ceased to marvel at their new-found popularity. "It is hard to realize the wondrous change which has befallen us abolitionists," wrote Mary Grew early in 1862. "After thirty years of persecution . . . abolitionists read with wonder, in prominent journals of this city [Philadelphia], . . . respectful tributes to men whose names had hitherto been used as a cry wherewith to rally a mob; and see with joy their own arguments and phraseology adopted by those journals."[38] Another Philadelphian was amazed that she could now make a profit on an

---

Feb. 1, 1862; S. B. Anthony to Tilton, Mar. ?, 1862, Anthony Papers, NYHS; Oliver Johnson to Garrison, May 28, July 25, 1862, Tilton to Garrison, May 27, June 11, 1863, Garrison Papers, BPL; Garrison to Tilton, June 5, 1863, Garrison Papers, NYHS; Frederick Douglass to Tilton, Oct. 21, 1862, Douglass Papers, Misc. MS, NYHS; Tilton to Douglass, Apr. 30, Oct. 22, 1862, Douglass Papers, Anacostia; Amasa Walker to Tilton, July 22, 1864, Tilton Papers, NYHS. On Jan. 1, 1863, the *Independent* claimed twice the circulation of any other weekly religious newspaper in the world.

[37] The statements of the *Courier*, Davis, and Bennett were quoted in the *Liberator*, Feb. 7, May 9, 16, 1862.

[38] Mary Grew to Wendell P. Garrison, Jan. 9, 1862, Garrison Papers, RU; *Twenty-Eighth Annual Report of the Philadelphia Female Anti-Slavery Society* (Phila., 1862), 10.

abolitionist lecture instead of losing money: "To think that the day has come to supply our Treasury instead of emptying it on such an occasion. What next?" Phillips noted that "Lyceums which could not formerly endure an Abolitionist on any topic, now invite them, stipulating that they shall talk on slavery." Henry Ward Beecher thought it "a great day that we have lived to see, when Mr. Garrison is petted, and patted, and invited, and praised by Governors, and judges, and expectants of political preferment. What is the world coming to?"[39]

What indeed? Abolitionists had never known the exhilaration of such power and prestige. Their speakers were in great demand all over the North. Their ranks contained some of the most popular and effective platform lecturers in the country. One of their number was managing editor of the most powerful newspaper in the nation; another was the editor of the largest political-religious weekly journal in the world. Abolitionism was no longer at a discount; abolitionists no longer went begging for listeners. Men who had felt obliged to work under cover to promote emancipation in October 1861, were wined and dined in the nation's capital five months later. Abolitionism had arrived.

✦

There were some abolitionists, however, who wondered whether their newfound popularity had been purchased too dearly. One fact greatly disturbed them: this growing northern zeal for emancipation was not based upon concern for the rights of the Negro as a *person*, but upon the argument of "military necessity" to save the Union. There was no question of Charles Sumner's genuine compassion for the slave, but he refused to express that compassion in his early wartime emancipation arguments. "You will observe that I propose no crusade for abolition, . . . making it a war of abolition instead of a war for preservation of the Union," he wrote on November 3, 1861. He argued instead that the Union could be saved only by striking at slavery. "In short, abolition is not to be the object of the war, but simply one of its agencies." A week later Sumner told John Jay that emancipation "is to be presented strictly as a measure of military necessity, and the argu-

[39] Sarah Pugh to Elizabeth N. Gay, Apr. 6, 1862, Gay Papers, cu; *Liberator*, Jan. 31, Mar. 21, 1862.

ment is to be thus supported rather than on grounds of philanthropy."[40]

Some abolitionists strongly questioned these tactics. "This doctrine of the abolition of slavery at last, as 'a *military necessity*,' is the rock on which we are in more danger of splitting than perhaps any other," cried Parker Pillsbury. "It is, to me, the most God-insulting doctrine ever proclaimed." The pleas of military necessity reminded Pillsbury of the deathbed conversion of a sinner. Emancipation would be worth very little, he thought, unless it proceeded from a conviction of justice and right. Lydia Maria Child was also discouraged by the military necessity argument: "This entire absence of a moral sense on the subject, has disheartened me more than anything else. Even should they be emancipated, merely as a 'war necessity,' everything *must* go wrong, if there is no heart or conscience on the subject. . . . It is evident that a great moral work still needs to be done."[41]

In January 1862, James R. Gilmore and Robert J. Walker launched a new emancipation journal called the *Continental Monthly*. Neither of these men was an abolitionist: Gilmore was a New York businessman and cotton trader; Walker was a former governor of Kansas territory and a friend of Lincoln. Gilmore selected Charles G. Leland as editor of his new journal. In the first two issues of the *Monthly*, Leland and Gilmore frankly stated their indifference to the moral issue of slavery. "This is not now a question of the right to hold slaves, or the wrong of so doing," declared Leland. "All of that old abolition jargon went out and died with the present aspect of the war. So far as nine-tenths of the North ever cared, or do now care, slaves might have hoed away down in Dixie" forever, if their masters had not re-

---

[40] Sumner to R. Schleiden, Nov. 3, 1861, Sumner to John Jay, Nov. 10, 1861, quoted in Edward L. Pierce, *Memoir and Letters of Charles Sumner* (4 vols., Boston, 1877-94), IV, 49. In 1864 Jay told Sumner that "my own view of the most expedient manner of proceeding against slavery in all its phases, has been as you are aware from the commencement of the war, so far at least as the old abolitionists are concerned, in favour of grounding our action on military necessity, & the national safety, & leaving the moral argument which we have used for the last thirty years to be monopolized for the present by the new converts to abolition by whom they can be wielded with the masses with ten-fold effect." Jay to Sumner, Mar. 8, 1864, Sumner Papers, HU.

[41] Pillsbury's statement was quoted by the *N.A.S. Standard*, Nov. 23, 1861; for Mrs. Child, see *Liberator*, Jan. 17, 1862, and L. M. Child to Gerrit Smith, Jan. 7, 1862, Smith Papers, SU.

belled and sought to destroy the Union. Leland continued: "Now let every friend of the Union boldly assume that, so far as the settlement of this question is concerned, he does not care one straw for the Negro. Men have tried for thirty years to appeal to humanity without success, for the Negro, and now let us try some other expedient. Let us regard him not as a man and a brother, but as 'a miserable nigger,' if you please, and a nuisance. But whatever he be, if the effect of owning such creatures is to make the owner an intolerable fellow, seditious and insolent, it becomes pretty clear that such ownership should be put an end to."[42]

Gilmore, Leland, and Walker coined the word "emancipationist" to distinguish themselves from the abolitionists and their disreputable humanitarian motives. Abolitionists were shocked and saddened by the attitude of these "emancipationists." Charles K. Whipple, Garrison's editorial assistant on the *Liberator*, admired the energy of the men who were backing the *Continental Monthly*, but "it is unspeakably saddening to see . . . men so intelligent and sagacious in worldly wisdom . . . deliberately repudiating a higher motive and adopting a lower one." No doubt they would gain more support for emancipation by adopting this course, "for it is a sad fact that most Northerners are afflicted by intense colorphobia." But they could not remain indifferent to human rights with impunity. "It is God's law that injustice shall not prosper," proclaimed Whipple. "Why not have done with oppression? Why not choose justice, and adhere to its dictates?"[43]

A young abolitionist in the army reported to Garrison that many of his fellow soldiers had become "emancipationists" only because they wanted to end the war and go home. They still disliked the Negro as much as ever: "Though these men wish to abolish slavery, it is not from any motive outside of their own selfishness; and is there not a possibility that at some not very distant day, these old rank prejudices, that are now lulled to sleep by selfish motives, may again possess these men and work evil?" Frederick Douglass felt the same fear and expressed it in a speech at Cooper Union: "Much as I value the present apparent

[42] Gilmore, *Personal Recollections*, 39-56, 66-70; *Continental Monthly*, i (Jan. 1862), 97-98, and (Feb. 1862), 113-17.
[43] *Liberator*, Feb. 14, 1862.

hostility to Slavery at the North, I plainly see that it is less the outgrowth of high and intelligent moral conviction against Slavery, as such, than because of the trouble its friends have brought upon the country. I would have Slavery hated for that and more. A man that hates Slavery for what it does to the white man, stands ready to embrace it the moment its injuries are confined to the black man, and he ceases to feel those injuries in his own person."[44]

✦

Nearly every abolitionist shared this fear that the North might discard the Negro as soon as he ceased to be a "military necessity," but in the rush of events and hard work during 1861 and 1862 there was little time to stop and brood about the problem. In the fall and winter abolitionists spent a great deal of time circulating emancipation petitions. Garrison wrote the most widely circulated petition, which urged Congress to decree "the total abolition of slavery throughout the country" under the war power, giving fair compensation to *loyal* masters "as a conciliatory measure, and to facilitate an amicable adjustment of difficulties." Abolitionists had been traditionally hostile to the idea of compensation and there was some opposition to the inclusion of compensation to loyal owners in Garrison's petition, but most abolitionists waived their theoretical objections in this case and signed the petition. For those who refused, William Goodell's National Emancipation Association circulated a petition that did not call for compensation.[45]

Abolitionists worked to obtain signatures to these petitions with a will and energy unknown since the great petition campaigns of 1836 to 1844. They found many people eager to sign. One abolitionist who obtained twenty-five signatures wrote that "not four of these men would have signed this petition previous to the bombardment of Sumpter [sic]."[46] Memorials bearing thousands of signatures began piling up on congressional desks. In January, the Washington correspondent of the *New York Tribune* reported

---

[44] Jacob Allen to Garrison, Oct. 23, 1862, Garrison Papers, BPL; Speech of Frederick Douglass at Cooper Union, Feb. 6, 1863, published in the *New York Tribune*, Feb. 7.

[45] *Liberator*, Sept. 27, 1861; M. W. Chapman to J. M. McKim, Oct. 7, 1861, Garrison Papers, BPL; *Principia*, Nov. 16, Dec. 28, 1861.

[46] *Principia*, Dec. 28, 1861.

(with some exaggeration) that "the petitions for universal emancipation to the present Congress have been more numerous and respectably signed than were those presented to the Parliament which abolished West Indian Slavery, at its opening."[47]

Lincoln's annual message to Congress on December 3, 1861, threw a dash of cold water on abolitionist hopes. His only reference to emancipation was a recommendation that the United States acquire territory in which to colonize slaves freed by the Confiscation Act of August 6. Otherwise he reiterated earlier assurances that he had no intention of interfering with the domestic institutions of the South. We should be "anxious and careful," said the president, that the war did not "degenerate into a violent and remorseless revolutionary struggle."[48]

Abolitionists were appalled. A revolutionary struggle for freedom was precisely what they wanted. Gerrit Smith publicly assailed the message as "twattle and trash" and complained that Lincoln was "bound hand and foot by that Pro-Slavery regard for the Constitution in which he was educated."[49] In the *Liberator* Garrison characterized the message as "feeble and rambling," and complained privately: "What a wishy-washy message from the President! . . . He has evidently not a drop of anti-slavery blood in his veins. . . . If there be not soon an 'irrepressible conflict' in the Republican ranks, in regard to his course of policy, I shall almost despair of the country. A curse on that Southern 'loyalty' which is retained only by allowing it to control the policy of the Administration!" Garrison concluded sorrowfully that Lincoln was "a man of very small calibre, and had better be at his old business of splitting rails than at the head of a government like ours, especially in such a crisis."[50]

47 *New York Tribune*, quoted in *Principia*, Jan. 30, 1862. See also *Principia*, Jan. 23, 1862; *N.A.S. Standard*, Dec. 21, 1861, Jan. 11, 1862; *Liberator*, Feb. 21, May 9, July 4, 1862; S. B. Anthony to Matilda J. Gage, Feb. 27, 1862, Gage Papers, Radcliffe Women's Archives; Samuel May, Jr. to J. M. McKim, Oct. 9, 1861, McKim Papers, Cornell; Samuel May, Jr., Day Book, entries of Mar. 6, 11, 1862, May Papers, BPL.

48 Roy P. Basler, ed., *The Collected Works of Abraham Lincoln* (9 vols., New Brunswick, N.J., 1955), v, 48-49.

49 *Gerrit Smith to Thaddeus Stevens*, Dec. 6, 1861 (published letter, Peterboro, 1861); *Gerrit Smith to George Thompson*, Jan. 25, 1862 (published letter, Peterboro, 1862).

50 *Liberator*, Dec. 6, 1861; Garrison to Oliver Johnson, Dec. 6, 1861, Garrison Papers, BPL.

Some abolitionists found consolation in the belief that Congress and public opinion were in advance of the president. "Foolishly as the President acts," observed Oliver Johnson, "there is much in the aspect of things at Washington and in the state of public opinion to encourage us."[51] Abolitionist confidence in Congress was not misplaced. In an implied repudiation of Lincoln's annual message, the House on December 4 refused to reaffirm the Crittenden resolution. The next day, Senator Trumbull introduced a far-reaching confiscation bill and Thaddeus Stevens offered a resolution urging emancipation under the war power. Owen Lovejoy introduced a bill making it a penal offense "for any officer or private of the Army or Navy to capture or return, or aid in the capture or return, of fugitive slaves." Emancipation petitions continued to pour in on Congress. On one day alone, January 6, 1862, ten such petitions bearing thousands of signatures were presented in the Senate. A week later no less than seven different bills dealing with emancipation and confiscation of rebel property were reported out of congressional committees.[52]

As Congress laboriously debated a variety of emancipation proposals, the mood of abolitionists fluctuated between hope and despair. "Never, since I became an Abolitionist, have I seen such hopeful times as these . . . never a time when the minds & hearts of the people were so receptive of light touching Slavery," wrote Samuel May, Jr., on November 26. Less than two months later, however, Lydia Maria Child confessed that "My courage flags a little, and hope grows faint. The *people* head in the right direction; but we are unfortunate in the men we have placed in power. Lincoln is narrow-minded, short-sighted, and obstinate. . . . Gerrit Smith writes me that his friends Thaddeus Stevens and Gen. Frémont almost despair of the ship of state."[53]

The antislavery cause began to brighten a bit as the spring of 1862 approached. The *New York Tribune* stepped up its demands

[51] Johnson to Garrison, Dec. 5, 1861, Garrison Papers, BPL.

[52] *Cong. Globe*, 37 Cong., 2 Sess., 6, 15-16, 18-19, 33-34, 57-60, 185, 327-32, 334, 497. Republican Congressman George Julian kept the abolitionists well informed on the progress of the antislavery cause in Congress during the 1861-62 session. See the dozens of letters exchanged between Julian and leading abolitionists in the Giddings-Julian Correspondence (LC), Gerrit Smith Papers (SU), Cheever Papers (AAS), and Garrison Papers (BPL).

[53] May to Richard Webb, Nov. 26, 1861, Samuel May, Jr., Papers BPL; L. M. Child to Whittier, Jan. 21, 1862, Child-Whittier Correspondence, LC.

for emancipation. "It is time for us to cease this idle babble about the constitutional guaranties for a vicious system of society which the Constitution nowhere mentions by name," thundered Sydney Gay in the *Tribune* of February 5. He continued, "It is time for us to consider how much longer we can afford to follow the modern device of holding slavery sacred above all other things. . . . As our armies go forward let them find only two classes in the revolted States—Union men and rebels, let their color be what it may."[54] In early March the leading Republicans and abolitionists of New York City organized a huge emancipation rally at Cooper Union —a rally which attracted national attention.[55]

Lincoln could hardly ignore the buildup of emancipation pressure. On March 6, he sent a message to Congress recommending passage of a joint resolution offering federal compensation to any state "which may adopt gradual abolishment of slavery."[56] It was Lincoln's first specific recommendation on the subject of slavery and it touched off a great deal of discussion. Abolitionist reaction to the president's message was generally favorable, with some exceptions. Moncure Conway likened the proposal to "the insertion of a wedge so neatly as to do credit to the President's knowledge of rail-splitting," but he disliked the word "gradual"; emancipation was "one of the Commander-in-Chief's guns; and to make it gradual would be like firing off a gun a little at a time." Maria Weston Chapman was also sorry for the word "gradual" in the message, but supposed it "to be only a make-weight, like the word compensation: a couple of sops thrown to two heads of slaveholders. Meanwhile, events are compelling immediatism." Wendell Phillips welcomed the message as "one more sign of promise. . . . If the President has not entered Canaan, he has turned his face Zionward."[57]

There were some dissenting voices, however. "Multitudes of petitions from all the free states signed by tens of thousands of estimable citizens, are before Congress, asking for the immediate

54 *New York Tribune*, Feb. 5, 1862; J. M. McKim to S. H. Gay, Feb. 8, 1862, Gay Papers, cu.
55 *Liberator*, Mar. 7, 14, 1862.
56 Basler, *Collected Works of Lincoln*, v, 144-46.
57 Moncure Conway to Ellen Conway, Mar. 8, 1862, Conway Papers, cu; Conway, *Golden Hour*, 52; M. W. Chapman to Mary Estlin, Mar. 18, 1862, Estlin Papers, bpl; Phillips' speech published in *Liberator*, Mar. 14, 1862.

abolition of slavery," declared Garrison, and he then asked, "Are these to be satisfied by proposing such a will-of-the-wisp as a substitute?" Privately, Garrison expressed fear that "the President's message will prove 'a decoy duck' or 'a red herring,' so as to postpone that decisive action by Congress which we are desirous of seeing." And George Cheever wrote: "How pitiable the attitude of President Lincoln, beseeching rebel States to do what God, justice, humanity and our Constitution require *him* to do."[58] Congress passed Lincoln's resolution on April 10, but a majority of border-state representatives refused to consider any plan of voluntary emancipation.

Congress enacted several antislavery measures in the spring of 1862. On March 10, the Senate passed (the House had previously acted) a new article of war prohibiting army officers from returning fugitive slaves. On April 16, President Lincoln signed into law a measure for compensated emancipation of all slaves in the District of Columbia. In June, Congress prohibited slavery in all the territories of the United States. Legislation was also enacted providing for the more effectual suppression of the African slave trade and for the education of colored children in the District of Columbia.[59] Abolitionists were pleased by passage of these measures, especially by emancipation in the District of Columbia. "Well, it is something to get slavery abolished in ten miles square, after thirty years of arguing, remonstrating, and petitioning," wrote Lydia Maria Child. "The effect it will produce is of more importance than the act itself. I am inclined to think that 'old Abe' *means* about right, only he has a hide-bound soul." Garrison considered abolition of slavery in the capital "an event of far-reaching importance." Congressman George W. Julian thought Garrison right "in regarding abolition here as a great triumph. We are gaining ground. The current is setting in the right direction." Samuel May, Jr., observed that "Our govt. moves very cautiously, very slowly, and their steps are not strides. But it does seem to me that all these steps are *forward*—none backward."

58 *Liberator*, Mar. 14, 1862; Garrison to Oliver Johnson, Mar. 18, 1862, Garrison Papers, BPL; George Cheever to Charles Sumner, Mar. 22, 1862, Sumner Papers, HU.
59 *Cong. Globe*, 37 Cong., 2 Sess., 1,446-51, 1,526, 1,629-31, 1,640-49, 2,041-64; *U.S. Statutes at Large*, XII, 354, 376-78; Wendell P. Garrison and Francis J. Garrison, *William Lloyd Garrison* (4 vols., Boston, 1885-89), IV, 49-50.

The *Anti-Slavery Standard* regarded emancipation in the District of Columbia as "the Beginning of the End of Slavery."[60]

During the spring of 1862, abolitionists bubbled over with optimism. "I trust I am not dreaming but the events taking place seem like a dream," wrote Frederick Douglass happily. Theodore Tilton joyfully observed that "the cause is striding forward with seven-league boots. If you do not hurry and grow old," he jokingly told Garrison, "you may see Slavery abolished before you have a gray hair on the top of your head!" Mary Grew was delighted by the progress of the antislavery cause, but she knew that politicians had not suddenly become saints: "such things are not expected by sane reformers. It is enough to elicit our deep thanksgiving that, by events over which the govt. has or has not control; from motives pure, selfish, or commingled, the abolition of slavery is at hand." And Wendell Phillips declared on May 6 that slavery was doomed to utter extinction. "Abraham Lincoln may not wish it; he cannot prevent it; the nation may not will it, but the nation can never prevent it," said Phillips, and continued, "I do not care what men want or wish; the negro is the pebble in the cog-wheel, and the machine cannot go on until you get him out. . . . Abraham Lincoln simply rules; John C. Frémont governs."[61]

[60] L. M. Child to Robert Wallcutt, Apr. 20, 1862, Garrison Papers, BPL; Garrison to Julian, Apr. 13, 1862, Giddings-Julian Correspondence, LC; Julian to Garrison, Apr. 16, 1862, Garrison Papers, BPL; Samuel May, Jr., to Samuel J. May, Apr. 14, 1862, S. J. May Papers, BPL; *N.A.S. Standard*, Apr. 26, 1862.

[61] Douglass to Sumner, Apr. 7, 1862, Sumner Papers, HU; Tilton to Garrison, Apr. 3, 1862, Mary Grew to Helen Garrison, June 20, 1862, Garrison Papers, BPL; Phillips' speech published in *Liberator*, May 16, 1862.

V + THE EMANCIPATION PROCLAMA-TION AND THE THIRTEENTH AMENDMENT

A sharp contest still raged within the ranks of the abolitionists between those who supported the government in its war against rebellion and those who refused to support any government that was not thoroughly abolitionist. W. O. Duvall, who belonged to the latter group, criticized Gerrit Smith for his support of the Union. "Of what use, for Heaven's sake, has this government ever been to you or me?" asked Duvall. "It was never anything but a gigantic swindler and robber; and yet you argue that there is no sacrifice too great for its continuance." Duvall also had some harsh words for the Garrisonians: "Edward Everett and Wendell Phillips sitting side by side! The Liberator puffing D. S. Dickinson's blarney!! How has the fine gold become dim! Prophets become partisans! Truly, these are the days of small things." Stephen S. Foster agreed with Duvall and said in January 1862: "There has never been an Administration so thoroughly devoted to slavery as the present. No other ever returned so many fugitive slaves, nor did so much to propitiate the Slave Power. Under these circumstances, is there any sufficient reason for us to . . . give our sanction and support to the Government?"[1]

Phillips and Garrison responded to these criticisms in well-publicized speeches at Cooper Union. In December 1861, Phillips insisted that only emancipation could end the irrepressible conflict and bind the Union together with hooks of steel. He continued: "People may say this is a strange language for me,—a Disunionist. Well, I was a Disunionist, sincerely, for twenty years. I did hate the Union, when the Union meant lies in the pulpit and mobs in the street, when Union meant making white men hypocrites and black men slaves. (Cheers) . . . But now, when I see what the Union must mean in order to last, when I see that you cannot have union without meaning justice, . . . why should I object to it?

---

[1] Duvall to Gerrit Smith, Dec. 15, 1861, Smith Papers, NYPL; Foster's statement quoted in *Liberator*, Jan. 31, 1862.

... Do you suppose I am not Yankee enough to buy union when I can have it at a fair price?" A month later Garrison came before a similar New York audience and reaffirmed all of his abolitionist principles. But he no longer wished to stand apart from the rest of the antislavery North. "What are all your paltry distinctions worth?" he asked. "You are not Abolitionists. Oh, no. You are only anti-slavery." In the eyes of the South, however, there was no real difference. An antislavery man would be hanged in Charleston as soon as an abolitionist: "Why, the President of the United States . . . is an outlaw in nearly every slave State in this Union. . . . I think it is time, under these circumstances, that we should all hang together." Garrison had been charged with inconsistency because he now supported the Union, and he replied, "Well, ladies and gentlemen, when I said I would not sustain the Constitution, because it was a 'covenant with death, and an agreement with hell,' I had no idea that I would live to see death and hell secede. (Prolonged applause and laughter) Hence it is that I am now with the Government to enable it to constitutionally stop the further ravages of death, and to extinguish the flames of hell forever. (Renewed applause)"[2]

Over the objections of Stephen S. Foster, Garrison steered a resolution through the annual convention of the Massachusetts Anti-Slavery Society in January affirming that "this Society regards the Government as wholly in the right, and the Secessionists wholly and atrociously in the wrong, on the issues presented." Two weeks later Garrison submitted the same resolution to the annual meeting of the New York Anti-Slavery Society in Albany. Parker Pillsbury immediately jumped up and offered another set of resolutions denouncing the Lincoln administration's failure to take effective action against slavery. If the war should end in some form of compromise with slavery, said Pillsbury, "the Abolitionists will have more to answer for than any other class of people." The government had no intention "to interfere with

[2] Wendell Phillips, *Speeches, Lectures, and Letters*, 1st Series (Boston, 1863), 440; William Lloyd Garrison, *The Abolitionists, and Their Relation to the War* (*Pulpit and Rostrum*, numbers 26 and 27, New York, 1862), 31, 28, 46. On December 13, 1861, Garrison removed the maxim, "The United States Constitution is a covenant with death and an agreement with Hell" from the head of the first page of the *Liberator* and replaced it with the command, "Proclaim Liberty throughout all the land, to all the inhabitants thereof."

the condition of a single slave in the land. . . . I do not wish this government prolonged another day in its present form." In reply, Garrison pointed to several antislavery acts by the government: the Confiscation Act, Butler's contraband policy, and Union protection of more than 8 thousand fugitive slaves on the South Carolina sea islands. The exchange became heated. Finally Aaron M. Powell stepped in to try to smooth things over, and suggested that both sets of resolutions—Garrison's and Pillsbury's—be adopted. This was done, and the convention adjourned in a spirit of apparent harmony, but beneath the surface the gulf between the Garrison and Pillsbury factions was wider than ever.[3]

The growing division between the two groups was revealed in their private correspondence. Most abolitionists, especially those in Boston, New York, and Philadelphia, supported Garrison's point of view. Pillsbury's following was small, recruited mainly from rural New England and New York, and from some of the western states. Stephen S. Foster was Pillsbury's most faithful ally. In private Foster shook his head sadly over Garrison's course: "How lamentable it is that those who have stood for so many years with their feet firmly planted on the rock of truth should falter in this hour of our nation's greatest peril, & . . . virtually make over our cause & themselves to the government." Pillsbury said privately, "I dare not yet trust the interests of the Anti-Slavery cause in the hands of the present, any more than in any former, Presidential administration. Nor do I see how we can any more change our mottoes, and our glorious old battle cry, 'No Union with Slaveholders,' than we might have done at the election of General Taylor."[4]

Supporters of Garrison considered Pillsbury slightly unbalanced. When slavery was abolished in the District of Columbia, Oliver Johnson asked: "Will not even the croakers now be willing to confess that our cause has made progress? . . . Will not our friend Pillsbury be able to discern a ray of light stealing over the dark picture that seems to be always hanging before his mind's eye?" Pillsbury was evidently not cheered by emancipation in the

---

[3] *Liberator*, Jan. 31, 1862; *N.A.S. Standard*, Feb. 15, 1862. See also S. B. Anthony to E. C. Stanton, Feb. 9, 1862, Stanton Papers, LC.

[4] S. S. Foster to George Thompson, Mar. 16, 1862, Foster Papers, AAS; Pillsbury to Elizabeth B. Chace, Mar. 24, 1862, in Lillie C. Wyman and Arthur C. Wyman, *Elizabeth Buffum Chace* (2 vols., Boston, 1914), I, 229.

nation's capital. "P. P. is . . . not in a quite healthy state of mind," commented Samuel May, Jr. "When he heard of the President's signing the Bill for Abolition in the District of Columbia, he said he dreaded to give way to any rejoicing, for he had noticed that any *good* thing in the Government was quite sure to be followed by some extraordinary baseness!"[5]

Oliver Johnson feared that the abolitionists' intramural squabbles would be revealed to public view at the annual convention of the American Anti-Slavery Society in May. He urged Garrison to prepare careful resolutions for the meeting with a mind to bridging the gap between the two wings of the Society. "You know just how far it will do for us to go in the direction that P. P. would lead us," wrote Johnson, "and if you will put in proper shape the *needed criticism* of the government, not sparing censure where it is deserved, but showing proper discrimination, we shall have no difficulty in carrying with us the common sense of the Society."[6] Garrison prepared and introduced resolutions urging the government to adopt universal emancipation, criticizing Lincoln and Congress for their slowness, but nevertheless supporting the government in its efforts against rebellion. Stephen S. Foster offered another resolution affirming that although the government "from purely selfish motives" had "done many acts favorable to the freedom of the slaves, it has in no instance evinced a genuine regard for their rights as citizens." Foster noted that the administration still enforced the fugitive slave law in the District of Columbia, and in other ways observed the proslavery compromises of the Constitution. Garrison's resolutions were passed and Foster's was laid on the table because of "lack of time" to discuss it.[7]

In the three weeks between the convention of the American Anti-Slavery Society and the meeting of the New England Anti-Slavery Society at the end of May, many other abolitionists began to have doubts about the wisdom of Garrison's course. During these three weeks several events occurred which undermined the confidence and optimism prevailing earlier in the spring: Lincoln

[5] Oliver Johnson to Garrison, Apr. 18, 1862, Garrison Papers, BPL; Samuel May, Jr., to E. B. Chace, Apr. 22, 1862, in Wyman and Wyman, *Chace,* I, 236.
[6] Johnson to Garrison, Apr. 10, 1862, Garrison Papers, BPL.
[7] *Liberator,* May 16, 1862.

revoked General David Hunter's military order proclaiming emancipation in South Carolina, Georgia, and Florida; the administration continued to enforce the fugitive slave law in the District of Columbia; and the House narrowly defeated a confiscation bill emancipating all the slaves of rebels. At the New England meeting there was a great deal of oratory denouncing these actions, and Foster introduced resolutions affirming that abolitionists could give no more support to the Union than to the Confederate government. "Abraham Lincoln is as truly a slaveholder as Jefferson Davis," said Foster. "He cannot even contemplate emancipation without colonization." Many of the speakers supported Foster's side of the argument, but Wendell Phillips, who had earlier in the meeting denounced Lincoln in the strongest terms, nevertheless could not agree that Lincoln was as bad as Jefferson Davis. Foster and Pillsbury were trying to create the impression that the Society had abandoned its principles by supporting the government, said Phillips. "No such body has proposed to support the Government *as it is*. It *advises*, not supports the Government." Phillips declared that he had "supported it by trying to force it on to a better position." This expressed the will of a majority of the delegates, and Foster's resolutions were defeated by a vote of nearly two to one.[8]

The meeting left a bitter taste in the mouths of many abolitionists. "There was . . . some unpleasant feeling caused, by Pillsbury's pretty openly charging, & Powell's (& others) *insinuating* . . . that the Anti-Slavery Societies & their Committees had lowered their moral standard," reported Samuel May, Jr., to a friend. May agreed completely with Garrison's position: "We hold the Government, the parties, the churches,—as ever,—to their highest duty. But we hope not to part with our common sense." This was precisely what May thought Pillsbury had done in suggesting that "the present administration is the worst one we have ever had" and that "Jeff. Davis would be preferable as a President to Abraham Lincoln." "These and kindred positions," concluded May, "seem to us to be really and truly characterized by fanaticism."[9] The truth was that Pillsbury and Foster were

[8] *Liberator,* June 6, 1862.

[9] Samuel May, Jr., to Richard Webb, June 30, 1862, Samuel May, Jr. Papers, BPL.

temperamentally incapable of supporting any government. They had been oppositionists and "come-outers" so long that their hostility to authority was ingrained, no matter what the authority stood for. Their inflexible opposition to the Union cause during the first year of the war brought into the open the growing schism in the American Anti-Slavery Society.

Even as the Society seemed to be splitting into two factions, however, there was on another plane a trend toward reconciliation of those abolitionists who had been bitterly opposed to each other since the schism of 1840. The war rendered academic all the old constitutional and methodological disputes among the various schools of abolitionism. James Redpath recognized this in November 1861, when he proclaimed that "the policies both of the Gerrit Smith and the Garrisonian school of abolitionists have been practically suspended. Events have so changed the position of affairs that their old-time policies are no longer applicable." An old abolitionist who had broken with the Garrisonians in 1840 and had gone into the Liberty party, wrote to Garrison in February, 1862: "There never was any but an imaginary chasm between us, and the providential events of the last few months have bridged it all over."[10] Early in 1862 Garrison invited Gerrit Smith to attend the Garrisonian antislavery meetings of that year. Smith could not come, but he responded handsomely with praise of the Garrisonians and their work, an acknowledgment that there was no longer any reason for differences among abolitionists, and a check for $50 for the American Anti-Slavery Society.[11]

An article by Frederick Douglass in his *Monthly* of March 1862, strikingly illustrated the progress of reconciliation among old abolitionist enemies. For years there had been bitterness between Douglass and Garrison, dating from the early 1850's when Douglass had repudiated Garrisonian disunionism. But in 1862 Douglass was ready to bury their differences. "Every man who is ready to work for the overthrow of slavery, whether a voter or non-voter, a Garrisonian or a Gerrit Smith man, black or white, is both clansman and kinsman of ours," he wrote. "Whatever polit-

10 *The Pine and Palm*, Nov. 23, 1861; Charles W. Denison to Garrison, Feb. 24, 1862, Garrison Papers, BPL.

11 Gerrit Smith to Wendell P. Garrison, Jan. 16, 1862, Garrison Papers, RU; Gerrit Smith to Wm. Lloyd Garrison, Apr. 16, 1862, Garrison Papers, BPL; *Liberator*, May 9, 1862.

Contrabands Coming into Camp in Consequence of the Emancipation
Proclamation. A. R. Waud in *Harper's Weekly*

ical or personal differences, which have in other days divided and distracted us, a common object and a common emergency makes us for the time at least, forget those differences." Douglass praised the work of Garrisonians during the war. "No class of men are doing more according to their numbers, to conduct this great war to the Emancipation of the slaves than Mr. Garrison and the American Anti-Slavery Society."[12] Garrisonians responded heartily to Douglass' magnificent gesture, and Douglass once again became a featured speaker at Garrisonian antislavery meetings.

There were many other examples of wartime cooperation among old abolitionist rivals. The American Anti-Slavery Society used George Cheever's Church of the Puritans in New York for its business meetings, and a bond of friendship grew up between Garrisonians and members of Cheever's Church Anti-Slavery Society. Garrisonians and John Brown men worked together in the Boston Emancipation League. It was Garrison who arranged Theodore Weld's return to the antislavery lecture platform during the war, and brought Weld once again to meetings of the American Anti-Slavery Society.[13]

Some breaches, of course, were too wide and too personal to be healed even by the wartime emergency. The gulf between Garrison on the one hand, and Lewis Tappan and Joshua Leavitt on the other, had been too wide to be easily bridged. But on the whole, while a rift was developing within the American Anti-Slavery Society during the war, Garrisonians as a group were closing ranks with the rest of the abolitionist movement to fight a common battle against slavery and rebellion.

✦

Most abolitionists were riding the crest of a wave of optimism in the early spring of 1862, but far back in their minds was a nagging doubt about the basis for this confident outlook. What if the rebellion should suddenly collapse? Would not the old devil of compromise enter into the peace settlement, leaving slavery essentially intact?

12 *Douglass' Monthly*, Mar. 1862.

13 Oliver Johnson to Samuel May, Jr., July 31, 1861, Johnson Papers, vhs; Frank Preston Stearns, *The Life and Public Services of George Luther Stearns* (Philadelphia, 1907), 274; Oliver Johnson and Theodore Tilton to Garrison, Sept. 25, 1862, Weld to Garrison, Oct. 8, 31, 1862, Johnson to Garrison, Apr. 9, 1863, Garrison Papers, bpl; Garrison to Weld, Apr. 6, 1863, Weld Papers, lc.

In February 1862, Union arms won a series of victories climaxed by the capture of Fort Donelson. The North was exultant; editors assured their readers that "the rebellion is crumbling" and "the end is approaching."[14] Higginson noted in his diary that "there is such a glare of victory that we only count the months or perhaps weeks until Richmond and New Orleans shall have submitted." But he discerned danger in this development. "The less success on our part, the more likelihood of an emancipatory policy —& so the other way." Charles Sumner stated privately that "these victories have a good side and a bad side. They will set us up in Europe, but I fear they will put back our ideas at home." George Cheever was not happy with the turn of events, "for our victories, if continued, will just result in bringing back those States as slaveholding States again in the Union."[15]

In April 1862, abolitionists put these fears out of mind while they rejoiced over the abolition of slavery in the District of Columbia, but three events in the second half of May brought back all their doubts and apprehensions stronger than ever. On April 25, General David Hunter, commander of the Union forces occupying the islands and coastline of South Carolina, Georgia, and Florida, had proclaimed martial law in the "Department of the South," comprising all of these three states. On May 9, he issued a second order stating that "Slavery and martial law in a free country are altogether incompatible" and declaring all slaves in the three states "forever free." The edict was published in northern newspapers on May 16. It was immediately acclaimed by abolitionists, who assumed that Lincoln had authorized it. "Has not the President used a very sharp knife, in Genl. Hunter's hands, to cut the knot?" exclaimed Francis George Shaw joyfully.[16]

But Lincoln had not authorized Hunter's action; he did not even know of the order until he read it in the newspapers. The conservative and Democratic press demanded that Lincoln re-

[14] For examples of northern editorial assurances that the rebellion was crumbling, see the *Springfield Republican*, Feb. 2, 8, 27, 1862, and the *New York Tribune*, Feb. 5, 1862.

[15] Higginson, Diary, entry of Feb. ?, 1862, Higginson to Louisa Higginson, Feb. 21, 1862, Higginson Papers, HU; Charles Sumner to S. H. Gay, Feb. 18, 1862, Gay Papers, CU; George Cheever to Elizabeth C. Washburn, Apr. 4, 1862, Cheever Papers, AAS.

[16] Shaw to Garrison, May 16, 1862, Garrison Papers, BPL.

scind the order. Secretaries Chase and Stanton, on the other hand, assured President Lincoln that nine-tenths of the Republicans approved of Hunter's proclamation, and urged him to let it stand. The president deferred to the wishes of conservatives and border state Unionists, however, and revoked Hunter's order on May 19. Lincoln renewed his plea to the border states to take advantage of his offer of compensated emancipation, and hinted ominously that should they not do so he might find it necessary eventually to proclaim military emancipation.[17]

Abolitionists were deeply disappointed by Lincoln's action. William Goodell wrote, "He has grieved and weakened his best friends. He has gladdened and strengthened his worst enemies— the worst enemies of the country." "Shame and confusion to the President for his halting, shuffling, backward policy!" cried Garrison.[18] Anna Dickinson, a rising young abolitionist orator, denounced the president as "not so far from . . . a slave-catcher after all," and privately wrote that Lincoln was "an Ass . . . for the Slave Power to ride."[19]

Some abolitionists, however, found grounds for hope in Lincoln's reiteration of the offer of compensated emancipation and his implied warning of possible future military emancipation. Samuel May, Jr., observed that the president had "again sadly disappointed the Anti-Slavery portion of the country & the army,— which now has grown to be a very large portion," by annulling Hunter's proclamation. But May thought Lincoln sincere in his wish to abolish slavery through a program of voluntary, compensated emancipation: "Slow, timid, altogether too patient with & too trustful of the Slaveholders, as he is, I do think his appeal a very solemn one to those States."[20]

In the last week of May, the northern press was full of the shocking story that open season on fugitive slaves had been declared in Washington. Slave catchers from neighboring states were invading the District, seizing Negroes on the streets and claiming

[17] T. Harry Williams, *Lincoln and the Radicals* (Madison, Wisc., 1941), 137-38; Roy P. Basler, ed., *The Collected Works of Abraham Lincoln* (9 vols., New Brunswick, N.J., 1955), v, 222-23.

[18] *Principia*, May 22, 1862; *Liberator*, May 23, 1862.

[19] *Liberator*, June 6, 1862; Anna Dickinson to Susan Dickinson, May 27, 1862, Dickinson Papers, LC.

[20] May to Richard Webb, May 27, 1862, Samuel May, Jr., Papers, BPL; see also *Independent*, May 22, 1862.

them as fugitives. One report told of a fugitive who ran up the steps of the Capitol with heavy chains on his legs in a frantic effort to escape his pursuers. "Is it possible that such a deed can be perpetrated by the Government and not be branded by the nation as a disgrace?" asked Theodore Tilton in the *Independent*. The New England Anti-Slavery Society angrily condemned the Lincoln administration for allowing the national capital to be turned into a slave pen.[21]

On May 26, the House of Representatives defeated by four votes a bill for the confiscation and emancipation of all slaves belonging to rebel masters. Five congressmen from Massachusetts voted against the bill, providing the narrow margin of defeat. The New England Anti-Slavery Society denounced the House for its "astounding infatuation" and "utter moral cowardice." The Society passed a resolution urging Massachusetts voters to send the five recusant congressmen into a "dishonored retirement at the next election." George Cheever was profoundly depressed by the defeat of this bill. "The first time, the very first time in all our history that the possibility of emancipation has been distinctly presented . . . it is decided in the negative—by the votes from Massachusetts!" he lamented. "Which *now* is the most guilty, the North or the South? And what reason has England to sympathize with the North rather than the South?"[22]

The events of May plunged abolitionists from the pinnacle of confidence to the depths of despair. For more than two months following his interview with Lincoln in March, Wendell Phillips had praised the president's virtues and predicted an early end to slavery. By June, however, Phillips' patience was wearing dangerously thin. He began to doubt his policy of supporting the administration. "This cabinet *fears opposition* more than it *values support*," he told Charles Sumner. "Let them feel that *we* can *criticize* & *demand* as well as the Border States & Conservative Side." Phillips urged congressional Republicans to get tough and threaten to withhold supplies unless the administration adopted a more radical policy. "Lincoln is doing twice as much to-day to break this Union as Davis is," he charged. "We are paying thou-

[21] *Independent*, May 29, 1862; *Liberator*, June 6, 1862.

[22] *Cong. Globe*, 37 Cong., 2 Sess., 2,363; *Liberator*, June 6, 1862; Cheever to Elizabeth C. Washburn, June 3, 1862, Cheever Papers, AAS.

sands of lives & millions of dollars as penalty for having a *timid* & *ignorant* President, all the more injurious because *honest*."[23]

As the summer progressed and McClellan's army mired itself in the mud flats of the Chickahominy, the pressure for emancipation mounted ever higher. On June 20, a delegation from the Society of Progressive Friends, a small liberal Quaker association dominated by Garrisonian abolitionists, presented to Lincoln a memorial urging emancipation under the war power. The memorial had been written by Garrison and was read to the president by Oliver Johnson. Lincoln replied politely to the delegation, agreeing with them that slavery was wrong, but questioning whether a proclamation of emancipation would have any effect in the South when he could not even enforce the Constitution there. Johnson replied briefly, conceding that "the Constitution cannot now be enforced at the South, but you do not on that account intermit the effort to enforce it, and the memorialists are solemnly convinced that the abolition of Slavery is indispensable to your success." Lincoln made no promises, but intimated that he would take action against slavery when he thought, under God's guidance, that such action would be helpful and effective.[24]

In July, John Jay organized an emancipation meeting of prominent conservative New Yorkers at Cooper Union. "Our old Conservative solid men are ready for the most radical measures," Jay informed Sumner, "& we can speak in their names in such a way as to give voice to the whole country and demand not for the blacks but for ourselves & for the Union as our only hope an emancipation policy."[25] In the same month the *Independent* began publishing a series of widely quoted editorials by Beecher and Tilton militantly calling for the abolition of slavery.[26] Susan B. Anthony started on a whirlwind speaking tour through the smaller towns of upstate New York. In New Jersey, Angelina Grimké Weld published a petition entitled "A Declaration of War on Slavery" and circulated it herself in the Perth Amboy neighborhood, obtaining hundreds of signatures even in that Democratic

---

[23] Phillips to Sumner, June 7, 29, 1862, Sumner Papers, HU.

[24] Garrison to Helen Garrison, June 9, 1862, Garrison Papers, BPL; *New York Tribune*, June 21, 1862; Basler, ed., *Collected Works of Lincoln*, v, 278-79.

[25] Jay to Sumner, July 4, 16, 1862, Sumner Papers, HU; Jay to S. P. Chase, July 3, 1862, Chase Papers, LC.

[26] *Independent*, July 10, 24, 31, Aug. 14, 1862.

stronghold.[27] Throughout the North abolitionists and Republicans were engaging in similar activities, while the Republican press became increasingly bold in calling for emancipation.

"The great phenomenon of the year," observed the conservative Republican *Boston Advertiser* in August 1862, "is the terrible intensity which this [emancipation] resolution has acquired. A year ago men might have faltered at the thought of proceeding to this extremity in any event. The majority do not now seek it, but, we say advisedly, they are in great measure prepared for it." Senator John Sherman wrote from Ohio to his brother, General Sherman: "You can form no conception of the change of opinion here as to the Negro Question. . . . I am prepared for one to meet the broad issue of universal emancipation." Oliver Johnson thought "the slowness and the stupidity of the President are very trying, but the constantly improving state of the public mind gives me hope, or at least keeps me from despair."[28]

Lincoln felt the pressure. On July 12 he summoned the congressmen and senators from the border slave states to the White House and pleaded with them to accept his offer of compensated emancipation. If they delayed much longer "the institution in your states will be extinguished by mere friction and abrasion." When he repudiated General Hunter's proclamation, Lincoln continued, "I gave dissatisfaction, if not offence, to many whose support the country can not afford to lose. And this is not the end of it. The pressure, in this direction is still upon me, and is increasing. By conceding what I now ask, you can relieve me." The border state representatives thought it over for two days, and on July 14 a majority of them sent a reply rejecting Lincoln's appeal. Eight days later the president submitted the first draft of an emancipation proclamation to his cabinet, but was persuaded by Seward to withhold it until Union arms won a victory.[29]

Congress felt the pressure too, and on July 17 it passed the

[27] Alma Lutz, *Susan B. Anthony, Rebel, Crusader, Humanitarian* (Boston, 1959), 95-96; Catherine H. Birney, *The Grimké Sisters: Sarah and Angelina Grimké, The First American Women Advocates of Abolition and Women's Rights* (Boston and New York, 1885), 285.

[28] *Boston Advertiser*, Aug. 20, 1862; John Sherman to William T. Sherman, Aug. 24, 1862, in Rachel S. Thorndike, ed., *The Sherman Letters, Correspondence between General and Senator Sherman from 1837 to 1891* (London, 1894), 156-57; Oliver Johnson to Samuel May, Jr., July 25, 1862, Garrison Papers, BPL.

[29] Basler, ed., *Collected Works of Lincoln*, v, 317-19, 336-37.

second Confiscation Act, declaring all slaves of rebel masters "forever free" as soon as they came within Union lines. But abolitionists no longer considered a confiscation act sufficient. In the first place the emancipation clause of the act was buried in the middle of several paragraphs of dry legal language. Secondly, the law freed only one, a dozen, or a hundred slaves at a time, as they came within Union lines. Abolitionists desired a bold and sweeping edict declaring all slaves immediately free and proclaiming to the world that the North was fighting for universal freedom. Finally, abolitionists realized that lengthy litigation would be necessary to determine whether each individual slave-owner had been engaged in rebellion under the terms of the law, and whether, therefore, his slaves were actually freed by the act. Maria Weston Chapman expressed the opinion of most abolitionists when she called the Confiscation Act "an Emancipation bill with clogs on."[30]

Moreover, to the public eye it appeared that Lincoln had no intention of enforcing the act. Abolitionists pointed out that the law would remain a dead letter unless antislavery generals were appointed to important commands. Lincoln appointed few anti-slavery generals to important commands; instead on July 11 he named General Henry Halleck, who had tried to exclude fugitive slaves from his lines while in command of the Department of the West, as general in chief of the United States Army. After passage of the Confiscation Act, abolitionists hoped for a ringing proclamation from the president ordering his generals to put the law into effect.[31] But nothing of the kind was forthcoming. The administration "is blind as a bat to its true line of policy," cried Garrison in despair. "Stumbling, halting, prevaricating, irresolute, weak, besotted," were the only words he could find to describe Lincoln's course.[32]

In a speech at Abington, Massachusetts, on August 1 Wendell Phillips released his pent-up frustration in a savage attack on the

[30] *U.S. Statutes at Large*, XII, 589-92; M. W. Chapman to Anne G. Chapman, July 20, 1862, Weston Papers, BPL. For a discussion of the meaning of the Second Confiscation Act as it applied to slavery, see James G. Randall, *Constitutional Problems under Lincoln* (New York, 1926), 358-63.

[31] Williams, *Lincoln and the Radicals*, 148-49; *New York Tribune*, Aug. 6, 13, 1862; *N.A.S. Standard*, July 26, 1862.

[32] *Liberator*, July 25, 1862.

administration. "I do not believe in the government," he said.
"I do not believe this government has got either vigor or a purpose.
It drifts with events." Phillips dismissed Lincoln as "a first-rate
second-rate man. . . . He has not uttered a word which gives even
a twilight glimpse of any antislavery purpose. He may be honest,
—nobody cares whether the tortoise is honest or not; he has neither
insight, nor prevision, nor decision." McClellan and his proslavery
ideas were ruining the country. "I do not say that McClellan is
a traitor," declared Phillips, "but I say this, that if he had been
a traitor from the crown of his head to the sole of his foot, he could
not have served the South better than he has done since he was
commander-in-chief (applause) ; . . . and almost the same thing
may be said of Mr. Lincoln."[33]

The speech was denounced by the northern press. "WENDELL
PHILLIPS SPOUTING FOUL TREASON," screamed the *New
York Herald*. One editor claimed that imprisonment of Phillips
would be worth 100,000 men to the Union cause. The *Philadelphia
Press* proclaimed that "Wendell Phillips is a traitor in his soul.
He differs from Jefferson Davis in this only, that Davis has drawn
the sword, while Phillips is effective without it."[34] George Livermore, Massachusetts Republican, wrote to Sumner on August 10:
"Cannot you have influence with some of Wendell Phillips' friends
and have him sent to a madhouse before he is arrested as a traitor?
. . . If he is sane, the prison is too good for him; if crazy, have
him gently treated but not suffered to go at large." Most abolitionists sprang to Phillips' defense. But some of them regretted
the severity of the speech. "I disapprove & regret [the course]
of W. Phillips," wrote John Jay. "The President is to be sustained
by us as far as possible, & we are not to throw away our influence
over him & give him up to our opponents."[35]

Phillips came to his own defense in a letter to the *New York
Tribune*. He denied that he was disloyal or that he was still a dis-
unionist at heart. He fervently believed in the Union *with freedom*.
"But government and the Union are one thing. This *administra-*

[33] Excerpts of the speech were published in many northern newspapers. It is
published in full in Phillips, *Speeches, Lectures, and Letters*, 1st Series, 448-63.
[34] Press reaction to the speech was quoted in the *Liberator*, Aug. 15, 22, 1862;
Philadelphia Press, Aug. 11, 1862.
[35] Livermore to Sumner, Aug. 10, 1862, Jay to Sumner, Aug. 7, 1862, Sumner
Papers, HU.

tion is quite another. Whether the administration will ever pilot us through our troubles, I have serious doubts: that it never will, unless it changes its present policy, I am quite certain." Phillips believed that he must "educate, arouse, and mature a public opinion . . . by frankly and candidly criticizing [the administration's] present policy. . . . Such criticism is always every thinking man's duty. War excuses no man from this duty: least of all now, when a change of public sentiment to lead the administration to and support it in a new policy, is our only hope of saving the Union." If he were in the Senate, said Phillips, he would refuse to vote the administration a dollar until it proclaimed emancipation. "My criticism is not, like that of *The Boston Courier* and its kindred, meant to paralyze the Administration, but to goad it to more activity and vigor."[36] Phillips' letter seemed to achieve its desired effect. At any rate the Republican press ceased to assail him and resumed its demand for an emancipation policy—the same demand Phillips was making.

Sydney Gay was not having an easy time as managing editor of the *Tribune* in the summer of 1862. His boss, Greeley, was prone to sudden whims and was becoming increasingly impatient with Lincoln and talking of issuing some kind of public ultimatum for emancipation. Gay desired emancipation as much or more than Greeley, but wanted to keep the *Tribune* an administration paper and avoid extreme anti-Lincoln criticism. Letters from impatient Republicans denouncing Lincoln were coming into the *Tribune* every day, and on July 30 Gay sent a private note to the president, enclosing a typical letter. These letters evinced "a deep-seated anxiety on the part of the people," Gay told Lincoln. "I do not publish them because I know they would exercise a most serious influence on the public mind. I cannot, however, justify it to myself that . . . [you should be] left in ignorance of that which so many thousands of people desire [you to] hear. Taking a middle course, therefore, I send you one letter as a specimen of all the rest." The letter was from George Rathbun, a prominent Republican and former congressman from upstate New York, who charged that "the President . . . hangs back, hesitates, & leaves the country to drift. . . . The people are uneasy, anxious, and

[36] Phillips to the editor of the *New York Tribune*, Aug. 16, 1862, in the *Tribune*, Aug. 20.

suspicious. They begin to fear . . . that we are trifled with, that there is not & never has been any serious determination to put down the rebels."[37]

Upon reading these letters Lincoln immediately telegraphed Gay an invitation to the White House, asking that he bring Rathbun with him. Gay replied that a death in the family would prevent him from coming at once, but promised to come as soon as possible. When he had heard nothing from Gay for eight days, Lincoln telegraphed him again, asking imploringly "When will you come?"[38] Gay turned up in Washington the next day, without Rathbun, who had declined to come. Gay had a long and pleasant conversation with the president, and presented the argument for emancipation calmly and firmly. Lincoln regaled the editor with apt anecdotes, but made no promises. Gay left the interview with a favorable impression of the president; Lincoln later told a friend that he considered Gay "a truly good man & a wise man."[39]

Lincoln hoped the interview would mollify the *Tribune* and silence Greeley's criticisms—he once said that having Greeley "firmly behind me will be as helpful to me as an army of one hundred thousand men"—but from this standpoint his meeting with Gay was a failure. Greeley was not in a mood to be mollified. On August 7 he wrote to Sumner: "Do you remember that old theological book containing this: 'Chapter One—Hell; Chapter Two—Hell Continued.' Well, that gives a hint of the way Old Abe *ought to be* talked to in this crisis."[40] Gay tried unsuccessfully to calm his irate colleague. James R. Gilmore, a friend of both Lincoln and Greeley, reported the editor's intractability to the president, who reluctantly authorized Gilmore to inform Greeley of the draft emancipation proclamation reposing in a White House desk drawer. Gilmore rushed back to New York, but arrived just hours

[37] Gay to Lincoln, July 30, 1862, Lincoln Papers, LC, copy also in Gay Papers, CU; George Rathbun to the editor of the *New York Tribune*, July 28, 1862, Gay Papers, CU.

[38] Lincoln to Gay, Aug. 1, 9, in Basler, ed., *Collected Works of Lincoln*, v, 353, 364; Gay to Lincoln, Aug. 1, 1862, Lincoln Papers, LC.

[39] Louis M. Starr, *Bohemian Brigade: Civil War Newsmen in Action* (New York, 1954), 126-27; Lincoln's statement quoted in H. L. Stevens to Gay, Sept. 7, 1862, Gay Papers, CU.

[40] William H. Hale, *Horace Greeley, Voice of the People* (Collier Books edition; New York, 1961), 268-69.

too late; Greeley's famous "Prayer of Twenty Millions," demanding of the government an emancipation policy, had already gone to press.[41]

Wendell Phillips thought Greeley's Prayer "superb, terrific. If I could rouse myself to envy anybody I could almost envy G. for the power to do it. . . . Just the man. Just the act."[42] Many abolitionists agreed with Phillips, although some, like Gay, probably regretted the timing of the "Prayer." Lincoln took the unusual step of replying publicly to Greeley's manifesto. "My paramount object in this struggle *is* to save the Union, and is *not* either to save or to destroy slavery," wrote the president. "If I could save the Union without freeing *any* slave I would do it, and if I could save it by freeing *all* the slaves I would do it; and if I could save it by freeing some and leaving others alone I would also do that."[43]

Abolitionist reaction to Lincoln's reply was mixed. Edmund Quincy wrote that the president's position was "what we had always believed that it must be." Abolitionists had never expected Lincoln to interfere with slavery in the states except as a military necessity to preserve the Union. "A President of the United States, under an oath to support the Constitution, is not to be expected to act upon motives of mere morality and humanity," wrote Quincy with perhaps a trace of irony. Abolitionists, however, believed that Lincoln had been too slow to recognize the military necessity that now urgently demanded an emancipation policy. "The President has tried 'to save the Union without freeing any slave,' and has failed; is it not time to see what effect 'freeing some,' if not 'all,' would have?"[44]

Most abolitionists probably agreed with Quincy. Gay told Lincoln that "your letter to Mr. Greeley has infused new hope among us. . . . I think the general impression is that . . . you mean presently to announce that the destruction of Slavery is the price of our salvation. The loyal North longs to hear that word from you." Phillips, however, did not agree. Lincoln "won't be flattered," thought Phillips; "he can only be frightened and bullied

41 Starr, *Bohemian Brigade*, 127-28; James R. Gilmore, *Personal Recollections of Abraham Lincoln and the Civil War* (Boston, 1898), 76-84.
42 Phillips to Gay, Sept. 2, 1862, Gay Papers, cu.
43 Lincoln to Greeley, Aug. 22, 1862, published in *New York Tribune*, Aug. 25.
44 *N.A.S. Standard*, Aug. 30, 1862.

into the right policy." Admitting that most Boston abolitionists concurred with Gay, Phillips nevertheless considered Lincoln's reply to Greeley "the most disgraceful document that ever came from the head of a free people." A Vermont abolitionist thought the reply proved that Lincoln regarded the slavery question as "one of mere policy." "Was ever a more heartless policy announced? . . . With the President public policy is *everything*, humanity and justice nothing."[45] But the very nature of the presidency compelled Lincoln to proceed more cautiously than radicals desired. The multitude of conflicting pressures on the president and the crushing responsibilities of the war forced him to base his actions primarily on "public policy."

In the early days of September a sense of despondency settled heavily upon the northern people. General Pope's loss of the second Battle of Bull Run was a fearful blow. "The war is upon us like a dead weight," wrote Robert Collyer, a Unitarian minister and abolitionist from Chicago. "Surely we cannot go much longer as we are—God help us." Lincoln seemed to be further away from emancipation than ever. On September 13 he told a delegation of Chicago clergymen that an emancipation proclamation would do no more good than "the Pope's bull against the comet."[46] "I am growing more and more skeptical as to the 'honesty' of Lincoln," wrote Garrison. "He is nothing better than a wet rag." Frederick Douglass expressed his "ineffable disgust" with the president's conduct. Gerrit Smith could only lament: "Our poor, guilty, wretched, wicked nation! Very faint is my hope that it will be restored."[47]

From depths of despondency the abolitionist mood was suddenly catapulted to heights of joy by Lincoln's unexpected issuance of a preliminary Emancipation Proclamation on September 22. On September 17 McClellan had turned back Lee's invasion of Maryland at Sharpsburg, and seizing upon this as the victory

[45] Gay to Lincoln, undated, but probably about Aug. 26, 1862, Lincoln Papers, LC; Phillips to Gay, Sept. 2, 1862, Gay Papers, CU; "J. S." to Garrison, Sept. 1, 1862, in *Liberator*, Sept. 5.
[46] John H. Holmes, *The Life and Letters of Robert Collyer* (2 vols., New York, 1917), I, 288; Basler, ed., *Collected Works of Lincoln*, V, 420.
[47] Garrison to Oliver Johnson, Sept. 9, 1862, Garrison Papers, BPL; Frederick Douglass to Gerrit Smith, Sept. 8, 1862, Smith Papers, SU; Smith to Garrison, Sept. 20, 1862, Garrison Papers, BPL.

for which he had waited, the president issued his Proclamation five days later. On January 1, 1863, all slaves in rebellious states would be declared "forever free"; loyal slave states and any rebellious states which returned to the Union before that time would be exempt from the terms of the edict. Lincoln also promised to present to Congress in December a plan for the gradual, compensated abolition of slavery in loyal states.[48]

"I have been in a bewilderment of joy ever since yesterday morning," Theodore Tilton informed Garrison on the day after publication of the Proclamation. "I am half crazy with enthusiasm! I would like to have seen whether *you* laughed or cried on reading it: *I* did both." Frederick Douglass happily declared, "We shout for joy that we live to record this righteous decree. Border State influence, and the influence of half-loyal men, have been exerted and have done their worst. The end of these two influences is implied in this proclamation." Both Gerrit Smith and Moncure Conway cried, "God Bless Abraham Lincoln!" And Wendell Phillips echoed dryly, "How decent Abe grows."[49]

A few abolitionists were disappointed by the conservative, conditional nature of the Proclamation. "How cold the President's Proclamation is!" shivered Sallie Holley of Rochester. George Cheever denounced it as "nothing but a bribe to win back the slaveholding states to loyalty by giving and confirming to them the privilege of tyrannizing over millions of their fellow creatures in perpetual slavery." Garrison's first reaction upon reading the Proclamation was one of disappointment. He had hoped that an emancipation edict, when forthcoming, would be immediate and complete; instead Lincoln had confined it to rebellious states, given them one hundred days of grace, and coupled it with his favorite scheme of gradual, compensated emancipation. "The President can do nothing for *freedom* in a direct manner, but only by circumlocution and delay," complained Garrison. "How prompt was his action against Frémont and Hunter!"[50]

---

[48] Basler, ed., *Collected Works of Lincoln,* v, 433-36.

[49] Tilton to Garrison, Sept. 24, 1862, Garrison Papers, BPL; *Douglass' Monthly,* Oct. 1862; Gerrit Smith to Lincoln, Oct. 9, 1862, Lincoln Papers, LC; Conway in *Commonwealth,* Sept. 27, 1862; Phillips to Elizabeth Gay, Sept. 23, 1862, Gay Papers, CU.

[50] Sallie Holley to A. K. Foster, Sept. 30, 1862, Foster Papers, Worcester Historical Society; George Cheever to Elizabeth C. Washburn, Sept. 29, 1862,

Nevertheless Garrison publicly rejoiced in the Proclamation as "an important step in the right direction, and an act of immense historic consequence." Governor John Andrew declared, "It is a poor *document*, but a mighty *act*." Samuel May, Jr., would not "stop to criticize now, & say this freedom ought (as indeed it ought) to have been made immediate, that it ought to have been proclaimed (as it ought) seventeen months ago. . . . I cannot stop to dwell on these. Joy, gratitude, thanksgiving, renewed hope and courage fill my soul."[51]

The principal worry of abolitionists between September and January was whether Lincoln could withstand the strong conservative pressure for modification or revocation of the Proclamation. The Democratic press unleashed a savage attack on the edict, calling it unconstitutional, dictatorial, and ruinous. Democrats made opposition to emancipation one of their main issues in the 1862 congressional elections, appealing to northern race prejudice and to the white workingman's fear of low-wage competition from free Negroes.[52]

Abolitionists were distressed by Democratic electoral victories in several key states, but were encouraged by Lincoln's removal of the conservative McClellan from command of the Army of the Potomac on November 7. "The removal of McClellan lights up the whole horizon," wrote Oliver Johnson. "From all that I can learn, the President is not contemplating any change of policy, so far as emancipation is concerned, in consequence of the result of the recent election. The removal of McClellan tends to show that . . . he is satisfied, at last, that all attempts to conciliate the pro-slavery Democracy are vain."[53]

But Lincoln's annual message to Congress on December 1 dealt a sharp blow to abolitionist confidence. The president urged adoption of a constitutional amendment granting compensation to

---

Cheever Papers, AAS; Garrison to Fanny Garrison, Sept. 25, 1862, Garrison Papers, BPL.

[51] *Liberator*, Sept. 26, 1862; John Andrew to Albert G. Browne, Sept. 23, 1862, in Henry G. Pearson, *The Life of John A. Andrew* (2 vols., Boston, 1904), II, 51; May to Richard Webb, Sept. 23, 1862, Samuel May, Jr., Papers, BPL.

[52] William G. Cochrane, "Freedom without Equality: A Study of Northern Opinion and the Negro Issue, 1861-1870," Ph.D. dissertation, University of Minnesota, 1957, 46-49. See also *New York World*, Sept. 24, 1862; and John Jay to S. P. Chase, Sept. 27, 1862, Chase Papers, LC.

[53] Johnson to Garrison, Nov. 10, 1862, Garrison Papers, BPL.

any state that undertook to abolish slavery by 1900. Slaves freed "by the chances of the war" would remain "forever free"; but all others would remain slaves until they were gradually emancipated by the respective states or individual owners.[54]

Abolitionists were astounded by this proposal. "We cannot refrain from expressing our astonishment at the folly and infatuation evinced in his plan for buying up Southern treason 'in lots to suit purchasers,' " declared Garrison in the *Liberator*. Did this message mean that Lincoln had decided against issuing his emancipation proclamation on January 1 after all? The *New York World* and *Herald* gleefully said that it meant just that, and many abolitionists feared they were right. "If the President means to carry out his edict of freedom on the New Year," asked Moncure Conway, editor of the newly established *Boston Commonwealth*, "what is all this stuff about gradual emancipation?"[55]

As the decisive New Year's Day drew near, abolitionists grew tense and anxious. They asked each other apprehensively whether Lincoln would remain true to his promise. They wrote to friends in Washington for information on the president's intentions.[56] Oliver Johnson did not doubt that Lincoln would "fulfill the promise of Sept. 22, but I presume he will do it in such a cold, formal, uninspiring way, that we shall feel ourselves under a wet blanket. . . . 'Old Abe' seems utterly incapable of a really grand action." Garrison observed on December 26 that "it seems to be the general conviction" that Lincoln would stand by his Proclamation, "though we shall not be greatly surprised if he substitute some other project for it. A man so manifestly without moral vision . . . cannot be safely relied upon in any emergency." After a talk with Lincoln, Charles Sumner assured his abolitionist friends that "the Presdt. is firm. He says that he would not stop the Procltn. if he could, & he could not if he would."[57]

On New Year's Day 1863, Boston's Negro and white abolitionists crowded into Tremont Temple to celebrate the expected proc-

54 Basler, ed., *Collected Works of Lincoln*, v, 529-37.

55 *Liberator*, Dec. 5, 1862; *Commonwealth*, Dec. 6, 1862.

56 Gerrit Smith to Garrison, Dec. 13, 1862, Garrison Papers, BPL; William Goodell to Sumner, Dec. 24, 1862, S. E. Sewall to Sumner, Dec. 28, 1862, Sumner Papers, HU; *N.A.S. Standard*, Dec. 27, 1862; *Principia*, Jan. 1, 1863.

57 Johnson to Garrison, Dec. 27, 1862, Garrison Papers, BPL; *Liberator*, Dec. 26, 1862; Charles Sumner to S. G. Howe, Dec. 28, 1862, Sumner-Howe Correspondence, HU.

lamation of freedom. The festivities began gaily enough, but as speech followed speech and no news of the Proclamation came over the telegraph wires, doubt began to gnaw at the hearts of the assembled crusaders. Perhaps Sumner had been misinformed; perhaps Lincoln would not issue the great edict of freedom after all! In the evening several speakers, climaxed by Frederick Douglass, tried to entertain and distract the audience while they waited for the Proclamation. But a general restlessness, a mood almost of despair, began to pervade the hall. Just as Douglass himself was about to succumb to despondency a messenger ran through the door shouting "It is coming! It is on the wires." "A thrill shot through the crowd; the enthusiasm was intense," wrote an eyewitness the next day. When the complete Proclamation was received, Charles Wesley Slack (a young white abolitionist who had led the fight in the Massachusetts legislature to abolish segregated schools) read it aloud to the crowd. As he finished, the cheers, applause, and yells erupted into pandemonium for several minutes. "The people seemed almost wild with delight," wrote the eyewitness. "It is the dawning of a New Day!"[58]

All over the North, and in Union-occupied portions of the South, similar jubilee meetings took place. It was a day of joy and thanksgiving, the climax of the first phase of the abolitionist movement. In the first flush of enthusiasm, abolitionists lavished lofty praise on Lincoln and his Proclamation. "This is a great Era! A sublime period in History! The Proclamation is grand. The President has done nobly," exclaimed the Reverend R. C. Waterston, a Massachusetts abolitionist and official of the Church Anti-Slavery Society. "Hurrah! Hosanna! Hallelujah! Laudamus! Nunc dimittis! Jubilate! Amen!" cried the usually restrained Maria Weston Chapman. Garrison hailed the Proclamation as "a great historic event, sublime in its magnitude, momentous and beneficent in its far-reaching consequences."[59]

As they studied the Proclamation more closely, however, abolitionists found one important shortcoming: it applied only to the

[58] *Liberator*, Jan. 9, 16, 1863; *N.A.S. Standard*, Jan. 10, 1863; eyewitness account quoted from R. C. Waterston to Charles Sumner, Jan. 2, 1863, Sumner Papers, HU.

[59] Waterston to Sumner, Jan. 2, 1863, Sumner Papers, HU; M. W. Chapman to A. H. Gibbons, Jan. 5, 1863, in Sarah H. Emerson, *Life of Abby Hopper Gibbons* (2 vols., New York, 1896-97), I, 384; *Liberator*, Jan. 2, 1863.

Confederate states, and of these Tennessee and parts of Louisiana and Virginia were exempted "for the present." The executive committee of the American Anti-Slavery Society accused Lincoln of being "derelict in his duty in exempting any part of the slave states, or any portion of the slave population." Most abolitionists, however, were inclined to be lenient on this point; they noted that Lincoln had exempted certain portions of the Confederacy only "for the present," and that slavery was doomed in the border states anyway. "I regret, of course, that the Act was not universal," wrote Tilton. "But Providence means to supplement it *de facto,* by adding the omitted states in good time."[60]

Some nonabolitionist critics laughed at the Proclamation as a *brutum fulmen,* a harmless threat. They pointed out that it "emancipated" only those slaves beyond the power of the federal government, and exempted those within Union lines. This was true, replied abolitionists, but the Proclamation constituted a promise of freedom to all slaves in nonexempt rebel states as soon as the Confederacy was conquered. Edmund Quincy admitted that actual physical emancipation could only be accomplished by the Union army as it advanced southward; but news of the Proclamation would "not only spread with immense rapidity over every portion of the South, but [would] . . . exercise everywhere a moral influence mightily efficacious for the freedmen, and against the slaveholder." William Robinson observed dryly: "That old Declaration of July 4, 1776, remained a ridiculous *brutum fulmen* for seven years. No doubt many a mad wag among the Tories of that day had his jeer at it, comparing it to the Pope's bull against the comet."[61]

✦

January 1, 1863, was the climax of the drive for emancipation. But the events of the next two years constituted an important anticlimax. There were still many obstacles to be overcome before the decision to abolish slavery was secure beyond recall. Thomas Wentworth Higginson, colonel of the first regiment of freed slaves enlisted in the Civil War, feared a reaction from the onsweeping

[60] *Liberator,* Jan. 16, 1863; Tilton to Garrison, Jan. 9, 1863, Garrison Papers, BPL. See also *Principia,* Jan. 8, 1863; J. F. Clarke to N. A. Staples, Jan. 1, 1863, Clarke Papers, HU; Lewis Tappan to Sumner, Jan. 9, 1863, Sumner Papers, HU; and *N.A.S. Standard,* Jan. 10, 1863.

[61] Quincy in *N.A.S. Standard,* Jan. 10, 1863; Robinson in *Springfield Republican,* Jan. 3, 1863.

revolution of emancipation. "Sometimes I feel anxious about the ultimate fate of these poor [Negro] people," he confided to his journal a week after Lincoln had issued the Emancipation Proclamation. "After Hungary, one sees that the right may not triumph, & revolutions may go backward, & the habit of inhumanity in regard to them seems so deeply impressed upon our people, that it is hard to believe in the possibility of anything better. I dare not yet hope that the promise of the President's proclamation will be kept."[62]

Higginson had good reason for his fears. Since the summer of 1862 the antiemancipation "Copperhead" movement had grown alarmingly. Capitalizing on northern war-weariness, "Copperheadism" reached a peak of strength in the winter and spring of 1863 when the Army of the Potomac, decisively defeated at Fredericksburg and Chancellorsville, seemed mired in the incompetency of its generals. In order to counter the Copperhead movement, Republicans organized Union Leagues throughout the North in 1863. These societies were virtual adjuncts of the Republican party, and were formed to promote loyalty to the Republican war policy of emancipation and total victory over the South. Many abolitionists belonged to the Union Leagues, and John Jay helped organize Leagues in New York and other cities; he later served as president of the New York League. New York and Boston Republicans established the Loyal Publication Society and the New England Loyal Publication Society to print and distribute thousands of pamphlets, speeches, and editorials calling for loyalty, emancipation, and a vigorous war policy. Several abolitionist speeches were published by these societies.[63]

The Union capture of Vicksburg and the victory at Gettysburg in July 1863, caused great rejoicing in the North and put a temporary damper on the Copperhead movement. But for abolitionists there was a somber side to Yankee success. Once again northern editors told their readers that the rebellion was on the verge of collapse. There was talk of a peace overture to the Confederacy,

[62] Higginson, Journal, entry of Jan. 8, 1863, Higginson Papers, HU.

[63] John Jay to Charles Sumner, Mar. 18, 1863, Sumner Papers, HU; Jay to S. P. Chase, Sept. 13, Oct. 6, 1863, Chase Papers, LC; Frank Freidel, "The Loyal Publication Society: A Pro-Union Propaganda Agency," *Mississippi Valley Historical Review*, XXVI (1939), 191-210; George W. Smith, "Broadsides for Freedom; Civil War Propaganda in New England," *New England Quarterly*, XXI (Sept. 1948), 291-312.

and abolitionists feared that the price of peace at this time would be compromise on the issue of slavery. "We are too victorious; I fear more from our victories than our defeats," wrote Charles Sumner. "If the rebellion should suddenly collapse, Democrats, copperheads, and Seward would insist upon amnesty and the Union, and 'no question asked about slavery.' God save us from any such calamity!"[64]

Radicals and abolitionists asked each other apprehensively whether Lincoln would bow to conservative pressure and modify his Proclamation. The president relieved their anxiety in a public letter of August 26 to James Conkling of Springfield, Illinois. Echoing the war-power arguments of William Whiting, Lincoln affirmed that he possessed full constitutional power to declare military emancipation. He had done so, and he would not retract his action. He had promised freedom to the slaves, "and the promise being made, must be kept."[65]

Abolitionists praised the letter. "We thank the President for that declaration," wrote William Goodell in the *Principia*. "We thank God, and take courage."[66] Republican victories in the 1863 elections gave proponents of emancipation another injection of hope. Lincoln provided abolitionists with further cause for rejoicing in his annual message to Congress on December 8, 1863, when he firmly declared that "while I remain in my present position I shall not attempt to retract or modify the emancipation proclamation; nor shall I return to slavery any person who is free by the terms of that proclamation, or by any of the acts of Congress." Henry Wright wrote fervently, "God bless thee, Abraham Lincoln! With all my heart I bless thee, in the name of God & Humanity."[67] Lincoln's declaration was an important victory for abolition. The president had refused to succumb to the counter-emancipation pressures exerted during 1863, and had placed himself firmly and irrevocably on the side of freedom.

[64] Sumner to John Bright, July 21, 1863, in E. L. Pierce, *Memoir and Letters of Charles Sumner* (4 vols., Boston, 1877-94), IV, 143. See also Sumner to E. L. Pierce, July 29, 1863, *ibid.*, 142; George Cheever to Elizabeth C. Washburn, July 7, Aug. 5, 1863, Cheever Papers, AAS; Cheever to S. P. Chase, Aug. 7, 1863, Chase Papers, LC.

[65] Basler, ed., *Works of Lincoln*, VI, 406-10.

[66] *Principia*, Sept. 10, 1863.

[67] Basler, ed., *Works of Lincoln*, VII, 51; Henry Wright to Lincoln, Dec. 16, 1863, Lincoln Papers, LC.

In the spring of 1863 Elizabeth Cady Stanton and Susan B. Anthony had organized the Women's Loyal National League to promote loyalty and propagandize for emancipation. Abolitionists had been calling for a congressional emancipation act to reinforce Lincoln's Proclamation, and the Women's League decided that their main function would be to circulate petitions urging passage of such an act.[68]

The women hoped to obtain one million signatures to their petition by the end of the 1863-1864 congressional session. This was a lofty goal, far exceeding the number of signatures ever before secured for a single objective in America, but Mrs. Stanton and Miss Anthony went to work with great energy and optimism. Women abolitionists all over the North rallied to the cause. Senator Sumner cooperated gallantly with the ladies, sending out blank petitions under his frank. The League employed lecturing agents to travel through key areas giving speeches, circulating petitions, and establishing auxiliary societies. By the fall of 1863 the petition campaign was in full swing, but the women were plagued by a shortage of funds. Susan B. Anthony persuaded the executive committee of the American Anti-Slavery Society to lend its resources to the petition campaign. The Society decided to send out an expanded corps of lecturers during the winter of 1863-1864 to supplement the work of the Women's Loyal National League. One of the Society's new lecturers was William Andrew Jackson, Jefferson Davis's former slave and coachman.[69]

Late in 1863 there was a growing conviction that the confiscation acts and the Emancipation Proclamation, although legitimate wartime measures, might become legally inoperative once peace was concluded. To be permanent, therefore, emancipation must be

[68] *N.A.S. Standard*, May 23, 30, June 6, 1863; Elizabeth Cady Stanton, et al., *History of Woman Suffrage* (6 vols., New York, 1881-1922), II, 50-78.

[69] Eleanor Flexner, *Century of Struggle: The Woman's Rights Movement in the United States* (Cambridge, Mass., 1959), 109-10; Lillie B. C. Wyman and Arthur Wyman, *Elizabeth Buffum Chace* (2 vols., Boston, 1914), I, 223-24; Ida Harper, *The Life and Work of Susan B. Anthony* (3 vols., Indianapolis, 1898-1908), I, 232-34; E. C. Stanton to Fanny Garrison, May 25, 1863, Garrison Papers, BPL; Mattie Griffith to Mary Estlin, July 27, 1863, copy in Weston Papers, BPL; S. B. Anthony to E. C. Stanton, Oct. 10, 1863, Gerrit Smith to E. C. Stanton, Oct. 23, 1863, Stanton Papers, LC; Giles Stebbins to Gerrit Smith, Oct. 6, 1863, Mar. 22, 1864, Smith Papers, SU; *Commonwealth*, Oct. 2, 30, 1863; *Liberator*, Oct. 2, 16, Nov. 13, Dec. 11, 25, 1863, Jan. 1, 8, Mar. 4, June 3, 1864; *N.A.S. Standard*, Oct. 31, Nov. 21, Dec. 5, 1863, Apr. 9, 1864.

written into the Constitution. Realizing the force of this argument, abolitionists in December 1863, decided to press for a constitutional amendment to abolish and prohibit forever the institution of slavery in the United States. The request for a constitutional amendment was included in all petitions circulated by the antislavery societies after December 1863, and in all petitions circulated by the Women's Loyal National League after February 1864.[70]

By early 1864 2,000 men, women, and children were at work circulating petitions. In February Miss Anthony and Mrs. Stanton sent the first installment of petitions bearing 100 thousand signatures to Senator Sumner.[71] On February 9 two tall Negroes, symbolizing the struggle for freedom, carried the huge bundles of petitions into the Senate and placed them on Sumner's desk. The senator rose to speak. "This petition is signed by one hundred thousand men and women, who unite in this unparalleled manner to support its prayer," he told the Senate. "They are from all parts of the country and every condition of life. . . . Here they are, a mighty army, one hundred thousand strong, without arms or banners, the advanced guard of a yet larger army."[72]

It was clear that the women would come nowhere near their goal of one million signatures. Such a goal was unrealistically high for the resources and womanpower of the League. By the time Congress adjourned in July 1864, the League had sent in petitions bearing nearly 400 thousand signatures. Even though they had not reached their goal of one million, this was an impressive achievement. No other petition for a single objective had ever received so many signatures. Senators Sumner and Henry Wilson assured the League that their petition campaign had been of great assistance in the struggle to secure congressional passage of the Thirteenth Amendment.[73]

The Senate adopted the Thirteenth Amendment on April 8, 1864, but it failed to obtain the necessary two-thirds majority

[70] Samuel May, Jr., to Garrison, Dec. 28, 1863, Garrison Papers, BPL; *Liberator*, Jan. 15, 1864; S. B. Anthony to Charles Sumner, Mar. 1, 1864, Sumner Papers, HU.
[71] Stanton et al., *History of Woman Suffrage*, II, 78-87; S. B. Anthony and E. C. Stanton to Sumner, Feb. 4, 1864, Sumner Papers, HU.
[72] *Cong. Globe*, 38 Cong., 1 Sess., 536.
[73] *Liberator*, Mar. 11, 1864; *Independent*, Apr. 7, 1864; *New York Tribune*, May 17, 1864; *N.A.S. Standard*, May 28, June 4, 1864; Harper, *Anthony*, I, 238.

in the House, which the Republicans controlled by only a bare majority. Most Democrats voted against the Amendment, still hoping to preserve the framework of slavery. Lincoln's victory in the election of 1864, however, convinced many Democrats that public opinion desired emancipation. Emancipationists had gained control of most of the border slave states and were rapidly extinguishing slavery therein. Enough Democrats changed their votes or abstained from voting in the lame duck session of Congress to enable the House to pass the Thirteenth Amendment on January 31, 1865.[74] Ratification by the necessary three-fourths of the states was completed before the end of the year.

✦

Abolitionist influence and prestige continued to climb in the last two years of the war. In January 1863, a friend of General Butler returned from a Wendell Phillips speech and wrote to the general that Phillips had praised Butler's work in New Orleans. This was an important endorsement, for "Phillips, in these winter months, manufactures a vast amount of popular opinion. No man will speak oftener or to larger audiences in America for the next few months. . . . These masses in New England and New York and Ohio are reached by men like Phillips who have the public ear in Lyceum Halls." A Philadelphia abolitionist reported that the antislavery office in that city "has become the resort of a class of men who have hitherto kept from Abolitionists, as dangerous & fanatical, and who now seem surprised to find that the abolitionists have but spoken the words of truth & soberness." Officials of the Pennsylvania Freedmen's Relief Association, including some of the city's leading businessmen, frequently consulted with J. Miller McKim on freedmen's affairs. They "almost sit at his feet and are eager for the information and experience which only an old Abolitionist can give."[75]

In the summer of 1863 James Redpath published a book of Phillips' lectures and speeches. The first printing sold out in four days. The book went through four printings in six months.[76]

---

[74] *Cong. Globe*, 38 Cong., 1 Sess., 1,490, 2,995, 2 Sess., 531.

[75] J. O. A. Griffin to Butler, Jan. 18, 1863, in Jesse A. Marshall, ed., *Private and Official Correspondence of Gen. Benjamin F. Butler during the Period of the Civil War* (5 vols., Norwood, Mass., 1917), II, 580; Abby Kimber to R. D. Webb, Feb. 22, 1863, Garrison Papers, BPL.

[76] *Liberator*, July 24, 1863; Frank Sanborn to Moncure Conway, Sept. 16,

When the United States acquired Alaska in 1867 the only English-language book in the territory's only public library was a copy of Phillips' speeches.[77] In a review of the book the conservative *Newburyport Herald* (Massachusetts) tried to analyze the reasons for Phillips' wartime popularity. "He was the foreteller of this day which we have lived to see," stated the *Herald*. "Few heard him once; but now many will read him, for his ideas are the popular ones of the day, and he holds the ear of the nation, and his audience embraces continents. Garrison and Phillips have been among the most successful reformers the world has ever known."[78]

One of the more remarkable events of abolitionist history was the rise of young Anna Dickinson from obscurity to fame as an abolitionist orator second in demand only to Wendell Phillips. Anna Dickinson was born in 1842, eleven years after Garrison had launched the *Liberator*. She followed in the footsteps of her father, a zealous Quaker abolitionist of Philadelphia. In 1856, at the age of fourteen, Miss Dickinson penned her first contribution to the *Liberator*. In 1860 she pleasantly surprised the abolitionists by delivering an eloquent speech at a Philadelphia antislavery meeting.[79] In the spring of 1862 Garrison signed her on as a lecturer for the Massachusetts Anti-Slavery Society. She made a speaking tour of Rhode Island, and immediately created a sensation. Her rapid-fire manner of delivery, her simple, direct style, her withering sarcasm, and the novelty of a teen-ager attacking political leaders nearly three times her age left audiences gasping and cheering. "We are at a loss to conceive whence sprung this new champion in petticoats of an antislavery war," wrote a correspondent of the *Providence Press* in April 1862, "but in sending her

---

1863, Conway Papers, cu. In 1863 the enterprising James Redpath formed a publishing company and printed several antislavery books to help promote the cause of emancipation. Books published by him included Phillips' lectures; William Wells Brown's *The Black Man*; a biography of Toussaint L'Ouverture; Augustin Cochin's *Results of Emancipation* and *Results of Slavery*; and Louisa May Alcott's first book, *Hospital Sketches*. See Madeleine B. Sterne, *Imprints on History: Book Publishers and American Frontiers* (Bloomington, Ind., 1956), 76-83.

[77] *N.A.S. Standard*, Feb. 8, 1868.

[78] *Newburyport Herald*, quoted in *Liberator*, Dec. 4, 1863.

[79] Giraud Chester, *Embattled Maiden: The Life of Anna Dickinson* (New York, 1951), 10-25; *Philadelphia Press*, Oct. 27, 1860; *N.A.S. Standard*, Nov. 2, 1860; J. Miller McKim to Samuel May, Jr., Nov. 22, 1860, Garrison to Helen Garrison, Oct. 29, 1861, Garrison Papers, bpl.

forth, her coadjutors have made a wise selection—for, with the tongue of *a dozen women*, she combines the boldness of forty men." On April 20 she climaxed her whirlwind tour with a speech before 4,000 eager listeners in Boston's Music Hall. It was a triumphant success. Afterwards Wendell Phillips told her that he had never been so "gratified and deeply moved by a speech." Anna Dickinson soon acquired a reputation as the Joan of Arc of the abolitionist crusade. At the age of nineteen she suddenly blossomed forth as one of the most sensational public speakers of the day.[80]

In March and April 1863, important state elections were scheduled in New Hampshire and Connecticut. Democrats had hopes of recapturing these states and continuing the reaction against the Republicans begun in the 1862 fall elections. In New Hampshire the Democrats nominated a gubernatorial candidate who favored a compromise peace and opposed emancipation. The eyes of the nation were turned toward the Granite State, for a Republican defeat there would be interpreted as a popular rebuke of Lincoln's emancipation policy. Both parties spent vast amounts of money in the campaign and brought in their best speakers.

The young secretary of the New Hampshire Republican state committee, Benjamin Prescott, had heard Anna Dickinson speak at an antislavery meeting the previous year, and in February 1863, he invited her to speak for the Republicans in the campaign. She accepted, and spoke about twenty times in towns throughout the state. At first the seasoned politicians ridiculed the idea of paying good cash to a twenty-year-old girl stump speaker. But her phenomenal success in the first towns where she spoke soon changed their minds. "We must have Miss Dickinson in our town if possible, for it may be the means of saving us," wrote one local Republican leader late in the campaign. "A few of our Copperheads heard her at Moultonboro and they are completely shelled out. . . . Our people say they must have her, or we are 'stuck in the mud.' " The Republicans triumphed narrowly in the election, and many of the state's Republican newspapers gave Anna chief

80 Chester, *Embattled Maiden*, 32-38; Anna Dickinson to Garrison, Mar. 16, 1862, Garrison Papers, BPL; Garrison to Anna Dickinson, Mar. 22, 27, 30, Apr. 3, 1862, Charles W. Slack to Anna Dickinson, May 14, 1862, Dickinson Papers, LC; the statement by the *Providence Press* was quoted in the *Liberator*, Apr. 18, 1862; other press comment quoted in the same issue; Wendell Phillips' remark is quoted in Anna Dickinson to Susan Dickinson, Apr. 28, 1862, Dickinson Papers, LC.

credit for the victory. If she had spoken in every town in the state, said one journal, the Republican margin would have been greater. The governor-elect praised her efforts. Though it is probable that federal patronage and the furloughing home of soldiers to vote had at least as much to do with the outcome as Anna Dickinson, her personal triumph and soaring fame were nevertheless very gratifying to abolitionists.[81]

The Connecticut election in April was equally important. The Democrats nominated an antiemancipation peace man for governor and prepared for an all-out effort to elect him. Anna Dickinson entered the campaign on March 25, with only two weeks to go before the election. The Democratic tide was running strongly when she began speaking. After her first speech in Hartford the Connecticut Republican state chairman joyfully wired Prescott: "MISS DICKINSON SPOKE TO A CROWDED HOUSE LAST NIGHT. SHE HAS NO EQUAL IN CONNECTICUT. PEOPLE WILD WITH ENTHUSIASM."[82] She spoke all over the state in the next two weeks, creating a sensation. She was so successful that the Republican committee selected her as the speaker for an election eve rally in Hartford, the most important speech of the campaign. The hall was packed three hours before she spoke. Nearly every sentence she uttered was cheered to the echo. One enthusiastic listener remarked the next day: "I am excited. I admit it, I am; it seems as if I was on fire, and everyone else that heard her are about as bad off. . . . [I] never heard anything that would begin to equal it."[83] The Republican candidate won by 3,000 votes, and both parties gave Anna credit for turning the tide and leading the Republicans to victory. The Republican press was ecstatic in its praise. The state committee paid her $100 for every speech she made, plus $400 for the last speech at Hartford.[84]

Fresh from her triumphs in New Hampshire and Connecticut, Anna Dickinson took New York by storm in early May. Five

[81] Chester, *Embattled Maiden*, 45-49; Prescott to Anna Dickinson, Jan. 2, 28, 29, Feb. 1, 10, 11, 12, 15, 25, 26, 27, 1863, Dickinson Papers, LC. Clippings of press comment in the Dickinson Papers, LC. The statement by the local Republican leader was quoted in Chester, *Embattled Maiden*, 48.

[82] Chester, *Embattled Maiden*, 52.

[83] *ibid.*, 58.

[84] *ibid.*, 49-59, is an excellent account of Miss Dickinson's part in the Connecticut campaign. See also the press clippings in the Dickinson Papers, LC.

thousand people crowded into Cooper Union to hear her speak, and she gratified them with a rousing abolitionist address. "The audience at Cooper Union went crazy," wrote a correspondent of a Connecticut newspaper. "Applause came often and in long-continued storms, hats were swung and handkerchiefs waved and at times the whole house was like a moving, tumultuous sea, flecked with white caps. Never have I seen in New York any speaker achieve such a triumph."[85]

In December 1863, a group of more than one hundred Republican congressmen and senators invited Anna Dickinson to deliver an address in the House Chamber. She accepted, and came before an elite assemblage of Washington dignitaries on the evening of January 16, 1864.[86] President and Mrs. Lincoln were present and joined in a standing ovation accorded the speaker when she had finished. "We have heard wonderful stories of her power to win over seemingly the most confirmed old Hunkers," reported the correspondent of the *Boston Journal* after listening to Anna Dickinson's Washington address, "and can now realize their truth." The *Washington Chronicle* declared, "Joan of Arc never was grander, and could not have been better, in her mail of battle, than was this Philadelphia maid in her statesmanlike demand that this war do not cease till slavery lies dead and buried."[87]

Abolitionists marveled at Anna Dickinson's phenomenal success. She was not an original thinker; her speeches were little more than a hodgepodge of other people's ideas. Wendell Phillips and Frederick Douglass owed their preeminence as orators partly to their original, creative minds; Anna Dickinson owed her success to a staccato-like delivery, a sarcastic wit, a youthful exuberance, the inevitable comparison with Joan of Arc, and the emotional fervor generated by the war itself. Yet her success was not transitory; she remained one of the most popular lecturers in the nation for a decade after the war. She was a valuable asset to the abolitionist movement for many years.

[85] Chester, *Embattled Maiden*, 60-63; *Liberator*, May 8, 1863; *N.A.S. Standard*, May 9, 16, 1863. The statement by the Connecticut newspaper correspondent is quoted in Chester, *Embattled Maiden*, 61.

[86] Susan Dickinson to Anna Dickinson, Dec. 23, 1863, Whitelaw Reid to Anna Dickinson, Dec. 16, 1863, Dickinson to Reid, Jan. 7, 1864, Dickinson Papers, LC.

[87] *Boston Journal*, quoted in *Liberator*, Feb. 19, 1864; *Washington Chronicle*, Jan. 18, 1864.

Abolitionist lecturers were drawing larger crowds than any other speakers in the winter of 1863-1864. In January the *Independent* noted that most lectures had been financial failures in New York during the season, but that the appearances of Phillips, Douglass, and Dickinson had drawn huge crowds and made large profits. Douglass reported in February that "I am, this winter, doing more with my voice than with my pen. I am heard with more than usual attention." The Democratic *Hartford Times* remarked sourly after the annual meeting of the Massachusetts Anti-Slavery Society that "it is deemed a sufficiently important matter, now, to telegraph all over the country the sayings and doings of these chronic fanatics and sworn enemies of the Union, though they and their treasonable opinions were held, four years ago, in silent abhorrence by the very men who now strive to be foremost in the race to do them reverence."[88]

In February 1864, the *New York Times*, spokesman of middle-of-the-road Republicanism, paid an unwitting compliment to the abolitionists. "It is extraordinary how completely the idea of gradual emancipation has been dissipated from the public mind everywhere, by the progress of events," commented the *Times*. "Before the rebellion, it was accounted the very extreme of Anti-Slavery fanaticism to believe in the possibility of immediate emancipation without social ruin. . . . Even when it had become a generally accepted fact that Slavery must come to an end, the idea still adhered that the emancipation must be gradual in order to be safe." But the pressures of war changed all that, and "all these gradual methods are now hardly more thought of than if they had been obsolete a century." The "very extreme of Anti-Slavery fanaticism" had become the accepted policy of the American nation, and as prophets of this policy abolitionists found themselves respected and influential for the first time in their lives. "All true reformers have been ridiculed & despised in their own day," observed Lewis Tappan. "We are coming out of the slanderous valley sooner than most reformers have done, for we have lived to hear old opponents say 'I was wrong.' "[89]

✦

[88] *Independent*, Jan. 21, 1864; Douglass to anonymous, Feb. 17, 1864, in Philip Foner, *The Life and Writings of Frederick Douglass* (4 vols., New York, 1950-55), III, 40; *Hartford Times*, quoted in *Liberator*, Feb. 26, 1864.

[89] *New York Times*, Feb. 25, 1864; Lewis Tappan to Gerrit Smith, Oct. 3, 1864, Smith Papers, su.

Most abolitionists reacted with qualified jubilation to the Emancipation Proclamation and the subsequent events culminating in the Thirteenth Amendment. Emancipation was only the penultimate climax of their crusade for freedom and equality. Freedom had been achieved; but only an incomplete "paper" freedom. Emancipation had proceeded not from an overwhelming conviction on the part of the American people of its justice and humanity, but from "military necessity." The massive job of aiding the transition of 4 million bondsmen to a new life of freedom, and of persuading white America to accept the Negro as an equal, still lay in the future. Abolitionists could not yet retire from the conflict; it was still too early to celebrate the final victory.

VI ✦ THE NEGRO: INNATELY
INFERIOR OR EQUAL?

O NE of the most formidable obstacles to the abolition of slavery and the extension of equal rights to free Negroes was the widespread popular and scientific belief, North as well as South, in the innate inferiority of the Negro race. Most white Americans took it for granted that Negroes were by nature shiftless, slovenly, childlike, savage, and incapable of assimilation as equals into white society. Since the beginning of the antislavery movement abolitionists had been confronted by arguments that Negroes belonged to a separate and inferior species of mankind; that they would work only under compulsion; that they could not take care of themselves in freedom and would revert to barbarism; and that emancipation would bring economic and social ruin to the South and the nation.[1]

For thirty years abolitionists had worked tirelessly but without much success to combat these arguments. When war came in 1861 and emancipation became an imminent possibility, the debate about the Negro's racial character reached new heights of intensity and bitterness. Conservatives urged their thesis of Negro inferiority and unfitness for freedom with desperate energy; abolitionists argued from the pulpit, platform, and press that a hostile environment, not innate inferiority, had created the servile, comic creature that was the American concept of the Negro in 1860. The abolitionists affirmed that if this environment were transformed by the abolition of slavery and of racial discrimination, the Negro would prove himself a constructive, capable, and creative member of society.

[1] The following studies treat this subject in considerable detail: William S. Jenkins, *Pro-Slavery Thought in the Old South* (Chapel Hill, 1935), 242-84; Guion G. Johnson, "A History of Racial Ideologies in the United States with Reference to the Negro," MS in the Schomburg Collection, NYPL; William R. Stanton, *The Leopard's Spots: Scientific Attitudes Toward Race in America, 1815-59* (Chicago, 1960). For a good example of the many pamphlets and books arguing the innate inferiority of the Negro, see J. H. Van Evrie, *Negroes and Negro "Slavery"; The First an Inferior Race—the Latter its Normal Condition* (New York, 1853).

Abolitionists were well aware that the common belief in the Negro's racial inferiority constituted one of the main justifications for slavery. In the final analysis, wrote Sydney Howard Gay in 1860, slavery was based "upon the assumed fact that the negroes are an inferior race, over whom the whites possess not merely an artificial superiority dependent upon the existing circumstances of their mutual position, but a natural superiority, which exists and ever must exist." Frederick Douglass said, "In truth, this question is at the bottom of the whole [slavery] controversy." Until the doctrine of the diversity and inequality of races was discredited, abolitionists reasoned, the theory and practice of slavery would remain strongly entrenched in America. "We cannot expect," said Gilbert Haven, the militant, red-headed Methodist clergyman, "the complete removal of this curse from our land until we stand boldly and heartily upon the divine foundation—the perfect unity of the human race."[2]

With the coming of war in 1861 and the impending prospect of emancipation, proslavery advocates roused themselves to even greater efforts to show that bondage was the normal and only possible condition of the Negro. When the emancipationist drive was gathering momentum at the end of 1861, the *New York Journal of Commerce* published a concise summary of the conservative argument against abolition. "A year ago, no thoroughly sane man in America would have consented to a decree of absolute emancipation," declared the *Journal*, and the war was no reason why the nation should suddenly go insane. "Let no man say this is a base and sordid view of a question of personal freedom." It was a matter of racial common sense. The Negro simply could not take care of himself in freedom. "Unless the reformer can, with his emancipation scheme, introduce new and superhuman industry, economy, thrift and perseverance into the negro, it will result that he will not earn a support for himself alone, much less for his family." The attempt "to make use of the war for the purposes of emancipation," concluded the *Journal*, "is virtually a proposition to plunge the South into the depths of poverty."[3] The northern proslavery press echoed these sentiments throughout the war.

[2] *New York Tribune*, Dec. 1, 1860; Philip S. Foner, *The Life and Writings of Frederick Douglass* (4 vols., New York, 1950-55), II, 294; Gilbert Haven, *National Sermons, Speeches, and Letters on Slavery and Its War* (Boston, 1869), 150.

[3] *New York Journal of Commerce*, quoted in *Liberator*, Jan. 3, 1862.

135

The abolitionist attack on the concept of racial inequality centered on two fronts: one, an attempt to demonstrate, from the Bible, from science, from history, and from observed facts, the essential unity and equality of races; and two, an attempt to show that the unfavorable environmental conditions of slavery and segregation, rather than natural inferiority, had caused the vices and disabilities of the American Negro.

The antebellum generation was fond of quoting the Bible as a weapon in the slavery controversy, and abolitionists could point to several passages of scripture which "proved" the unity of the human race. The book of Genesis told the story of the creation of *man* (not men) in God's own image. In his famous sermon on Mars Hill, St. Paul told the people of Athens that God "hath made of one blood all nations of men for to dwell on the face of the earth." Gilbert Haven contended that the Bible sanctioned the complete equality and fraternity of the races. Solomon treated the Queen of Sheba, an Ethiopian, "with the utmost respect and cordiality." Moses married an Ethiopian; a Negro was called by God to be one of the prophets and teachers of the Church at Antioch. "More than this," declared Haven, "the Bible constantly proclaims the absolute oneness of the race of man, in Adam, Noah, and Christ."[4]

By 1860, however, the Bible argument was pretty well played out. Thirty years of controversy had only shown that the Bible could be quoted effectively on both sides of the slavery issue. Science, especially ethnology and anthropology, commanded a large and growing influence in the mid-nineteenth century. Ethnology in the hands of Josiah Nott, Louis Agassiz, Samuel G. Morton, and George Gliddon (a group that came to be known as the "American School" of anthropology), who taught that the various races of mankind constituted separate species with the Negro at the bottom of the scale, had become a major weapon in the defense of slavery. Abolitionists realized that to combat these teachings they must themselves use the weapons of ethnology. Few abolitionists had any formal anthropological training, but as a group they were well educated and highly literate; and given the rather crude state of nineteenth-century ethnological knowledge, the industrious

[4] Haven, *National Sermons*, 137.

layman could become almost as well informed as the professional scientist.

Several abolitionists made intensive studies of the question of race. To refute the "American School" of anthropology, abolitionists quoted prominent European naturalists who argued for the unity and equality of races. In 1861, for example, the *Anti-Slavery Standard* published a review of *L'Unité de l'Espèce Humaine*, by M. de Quatrefarges, professor of natural history and ethnology at the Museum of Natural History in Paris. Using the classifications of Linnaeus and Lamarck, M. de Quatrefarges defined mankind as a single species; racial differences were the result of varieties within the species developed by conditions of environment and transmitted by heredity. M. de Quatrefarges used his vast knowledge to deny the existence of any fundamental and immutable differences in the mental capacities of various races.[5]

Abolitionists cited several other outstanding European scientists who maintained the unity and equality of races: Dr. R. G. Latham, the British ethnologist; Dumont d'Urville, the French geographer and navigator; George Louis Leclerc Buffon, the brilliant naturalist; and finally, most important of all, the renowned Alexander von Humboldt, who wrote: "Whilst we maintain the unity of the human species, we at the same time repel the depressing assumption of superior and inferior races of men." Through Humboldt, said Charles Sumner, "Science is enlisted for the Equal Rights of All."[6]

Sumner may have overstated his case, since American science, at least, spoke overwhelmingly for inequality. But the ethnologists of the world spoke with a discordant and divided voice on the subject of race in 1860. Abolitionists argued forcefully and accurately that science had failed to *prove* the racial inferiority of the Negro. "You may read Prichard, and Pinkerton, and Morton, and Pickering, and Latham, and all the rest—the whole library of Ethnology," said Theodore Tilton in 1863, "and in the confusion of knowledge you will find one thing clear—and that is, science has not yet proved, in advance, that the negro race is not to be

[5] *N.A.S. Standard,* Nov. 9, 1861.

[6] Charles Sumner, *Works of Charles Sumner* (15 vols., Boston, 1870-73), XIII, 155-57. Curiously enough, none of the disputants in the racial controversy referred to Darwin before 1866, although *The Origin of Species* was known in America soon after its publication in 1859.

a high-cultured, dominant race—rulers of their own continent, and perhaps dictators to the world."[7]

The endless refinements of the scientific racial arguments probably passed over the heads of the general public. The average man was more interested in concrete examples; and the advocates of Negro inferiority thought they had one incontrovertible example to show him: the supposed barbarous and uncivilized condition of Africa. What contribution to civilization and progress had Africa ever made, asked proslavery writers derisively?

This was a potentially damaging argument, and abolitionists advanced boldly to meet it. Negro abolitionists were in the forefront of the struggle to vindicate Africa. The central theme of their argument was that the inhabitants of ancient Egypt, fountainhead of western civilization, were a Negroid or partially Negroid race. "The ancient Egyptians were not white people," declared Frederick Douglass, "but were, undoubtedly, just about as dark in complexion as many in this country who are considered Negroes." Their hair "was far from being of that graceful lankness which adorns the fair Anglo-Saxon head." William Wells Brown, a prominent Negro abolitionist, lecturer, and author, said in 1862, "I claim that the blacks are the legitimate descendants of the Egyptians." While the ancestors of the proud Anglo-Saxons were roaming the forests of northern Europe as savages, declared Brown, Africa had created the foundations of western civilization and passed on this precious heritage to the Jews, Greeks, Romans, and ultimately to western Europe.[8] Martin Delany, another Negro abolitionist, cited the historians Herodotus and Diodorus Siculus in support of his contention that the world was indebted to ancient Egypt and Ethiopia "for the propagation of that glorious light of progressive civilization—religion, philosophy, arts, science and literature in general, which now illuminate the world." In reply to a derisive reference to Negroes by Senator William L. Yancey of Alabama, William Wells Brown told a group of Boston abolitionists in 1860: "When Mr. Yancey's ancestors were bending their backs to the yoke of William the Conqueror, the ancestors of his

[7] Theodore Tilton, *The Negro* (New York, 1863), 5. This was a speech delivered by Tilton at the annual meeting of the American Anti-Slavery Society in 1863. Several thousand copies were published and distributed by the Society.

[8] Foner, *Douglass*, II, 296; *Liberator*, June 6, 1862, quoting speech by William Wells Brown.

slaves were revelling in the halls of science and learning. If the Hon. Senator from Alabama wants antecedents, he shall have them; and upon such, I claim a superiority for the negro. (Loud applause)"[9]

These arguments were most vigorously advanced by Brown in a book entitled *The Black Man, His Antecedents, His Genius, and His Achievements,* published in 1863. Brown wrote the book for the express purpose of dispelling popular notions about the Negro in order to help mobilize popular support for Lincoln's newly adopted emancipation policy. The book was an immediate success; the first edition was sold out soon after publication, and in the next three years ten printings came off the presses. "Such a rapid sale of a book devoted entirely to an exhibition of the genius, the talent and the heroism of the hated Negro," said the *Anti-Slavery Standard,* "shows that a great change has come over the minds of the American people, and that justice to a long injured race is not far off." Lewis Tappan exclaimed, "This is just the book for the hour. It will do more for the colored man's elevation than any work yet published."[10]

But the glories of ancient Ethiopia were not sufficient to convince many skeptics of the inherent equality of Negroes. Modern Africa stood in the way. Most nineteenth century Americans considered Africa a backward, barbaric continent, devoid of any trace of civilization or culture. Most world travelers who visited the dark continent concurred with Bayard Taylor's opinion that the Negro was "the lowest type of humanity on the face of the earth." Not being world travelers themselves, abolitionists perforce obtained much of their information on Africa from such unflattering sources. Consequently they admitted that contemporary Africa stood low in the scale of civilization, but they advanced a kind of cyclical theory of history, by which nations rose and fell, and would rise again. At one time Africa was the center of learning and culture, said Gerrit Smith, but in the course of events she declined in importance. Africa's "inherent, inborn faculties," however, "are

[9] Martin Delany, *Principia of Ethnology: The Origin of Races and Color* (Philadelphia, 1879), 42-48; Brown was quoted in *Liberator,* Oct. 26, 1860.

[10] *N.A.S. Standard,* Aug. 1, 1863; Tappan was quoted in William Wells Brown, *The Rising Son* (Boston, 1874), introduction by Alonzo D. Moore, 24. See also *Commonwealth,* Oct. 30, 1863; and Samuel May, Jr., to Richard Webb, Sept. 19, 1865, Samuel May, Jr., Papers, BPL.

neither multiplied nor diminished because developed in one age, and undeveloped in another. . . . Changes of circumstances, along with other causes, alternately lift up and depress a people." Theodore Tilton asked in 1863:

"Do you call the negro race inferior? No man can yet pronounce that judgment safely. How will you compare races, to give each its due rank? . . . You must compare them in their fulfillments, not in their beginnings. . . . How will you estimate the rank of the Roman people? By its beginnings? By its decline? By neither. You rank it at the height of its civilization. . . . The Germans, to-day, give philosophy to Europe—but you can count the years backward when the Germans, now philosophers, were barbarians. . . . No man can now predict the destiny of the negro race. That race is yet so undeveloped—that destiny is yet so unfulfilled—that no man can say, and no wise man pretends to say, what the negro race shall finally become."[11]

Some abolitionists, moreover, did not entirely accept the dark portrait of modern Africa drawn by most travelers. Several months after the outbreak of the Civil War a remarkable little book, written anonymously and entitled *Record of an Obscure Man,* was published in Boston. It purported to be the memoir of a man who had visited a friend in the South in 1842 and had talked with him about the capabilities of the Negro race. In reality it was a fictional essay by Mrs. Mary Putnam, elder sister of James Russell Lowell and an abolitionist sympathizer. Mary Putnam asserted that most travelers who visited Africa penetrated no farther than the coastal areas, whose inhabitants had been subjected to debasing contact with rapacious slave traders, "to which their degradation is to be attributed, rather than to inherent depravity or stupidity." Travelers who had ventured into the interior of Africa found people of finer appearance, gentler manners, greater industry and honesty. "When Central Africa has been fully laid open to the world," she argued, "we shall be called upon to revise many of our opinions."[12]

Displaying great learning, Mrs. Putnam quoted from world-famous travelers and explorers who had ventured into Central

[11] Gerrit Smith to Montgomery Blair, Apr. 2, 1862, in *Liberator*, Apr. 18; Tilton, *The Negro*, 4-5.

[12] [Mary Putnam], *Record of an Obscure Man* (Boston, 1861), 91-92.

Africa: Hugh Clapperton, Mungo Park, and Dixon Denham. "Read what Denham says of the inhabitants of the interior," she urged; "of their industry, their skill in weaving and dyeing, of their love of music and poetry." Denham described the natives as "hospitable, kind-hearted, honest, and liberal." Anticipating the findings of modern scholars, Mrs. Putnam decried the notion that Negroes had been civilized and uplifted by slavery and Christianity. Slavery, she said, had only suppressed their native virtues and intelligence.[13]

In one of the best expressions of "cultural relativism" to come out of the nineteenth century, Mary Putnam warned against accepting at face value the somber descriptions of Africa by certain westerners. "All men are prone to judge the manners of other countries by the standard of their own," she wrote, "and the civilized world views from its own stand-point that which it calls savage. We find the Africans barbarians, wherever customs differ from ours; but they are on the road to civilization, when their nonsense suits our nonsense."[14]

Abolitionists praised Mary Putnam's little book. "Such a studied tribute to the negro, in this way, we have never had the fortune to see," said Garrison in his review of *Record of an Obscure Man*. "The African is contemplated as a man apart from his accidents, and heavy must be the load of prejudice against color that is not lightened by the spirit and the truthfulness with which his claims are urged."[15] Abolitionists adopted many of Mrs. Putnam's arguments in their crusade for emancipation and equal rights.

The advocates of racial equality did not have to confine their researches to Africa to find persuasive examples of the manhood, ability, and achievements of the Negro race. There were plenty of authentic black heroes in the western hemisphere. By all odds, the greatest of these was Toussaint L'Ouverture, the Haitian

---

[13] *ibid.*, 92-96.

[14] *ibid.*, 123.

[15] *Liberator*, Nov. 29, 1861. The *Anglo-African*, a weekly newspaper published by Negroes in New York City, pronounced *Record of an Obscure Man* "the fullest and most satisfactory record it has been our fortune to meet with, after reading all we could find in print on the subject. . . . She recognizes in the negro an original, inherent germ force of his own, solemn, grand, endowed with energy and vitality enough to develop civil, social, and intellectual greatness out of his own resources." *Anglo-African*, Feb. 15, 1862.

liberator who led his people out of slavery and defeated the armies of Napoleon when the French tried to reenslave the Caribbean island. One of Wendell Phillips' most powerful and compelling lectures was a biography of Haiti's warrior statesman. In 1862-63 Phillips gave this lecture to dozens of audiences throughout the Northeast as a means of dramatizing the Negro's fitness for freedom. "The negro race, instead of being that object of pity and contempt which we usually consider it, is entitled, judged by the facts of history, to a place close by the side of the Saxon," said Phillips. Did anyone doubt the Negro's courage? "Go to 50,000 graves of the best soldiers France ever had, and ask them what they think of the negro's sword." Could the Negro take care of himself in freedom? "Hayti, from the ruins of her colonial dependence, is become a civilized state, the seventh nation in the catalogue of commerce with this country, inferior in morals and education to none of the West Indian isles. Toussaint made her what she is. Courage, purpose, endurance—they are the tests." The *Semi-Weekly New York Tribune* printed a special edition containing Phillips' speech on March 13, 1863, for circulation among the troops in the Union army.[16]

The Negro had proved his physical courage in Haiti, in the American Revolution and War of 1812, and would soon prove it again in the Civil War; but what about mental ability and intellectual achievement? It was while asking himself this question that Moncure Conway stumbled across the remarkable story of Benjamin Banneker. Conway did some research on Banneker's life and published an article on him in the *Atlantic Monthly* at the end of 1862. A free-born, self-taught Maryland Negro, Banneker had devoted all his spare time to scientific research. He corrected some of the errors of the greatest astronomers of his age; in 1790 he compiled an accurate almanac based on his studies, and continued to publish annual almanacs until shortly before his death in 1804. His work was praised by Jefferson and internationally acclaimed by scientists. "History must record," concluded Conway,

[16] *New York Tribune* (Daily), Mar. 12, 14, 1863; *Semi-Weekly Tribune*, Mar. 13, 1863. In 1863 James Redpath edited and published an old biography of Toussaint by John R. Beard as a part of the effort to win public respect for the courage and resourcefulness of the Negro race. James Redpath, ed., *Toussaint L'Ouverture: a Biography and Autobiography* (Boston, 1863).

"that the most original scientific intellect which the South has yet produced was that of the pure African, Benjamin Banneker."[17]

Abolitionists industriously gathered statistics on the intellectual, professional, and business achievements of free Negroes. The American Anti-Slavery Society's *Annual Report* for 1859 pointed to the Negro actor Ira Aldridge, who was delighting European audiences with his portrayal of Othello; to three young Haitian students who had won highest honors at the concourse of all French colleges in Paris; to the New York Negro, Ditz, who had submitted a plan for a Broadway railroad; and the Philadelphia Negro, Aaron Roberts, who had developed a new and improved fire-extinguishing apparatus. These and many other accomplishments by Negroes demonstrated "the black man's capacity for mental culture and improvement . . . wherever a fair chance to test it has been given." In the business world Negroes boasted George T. Downing of Rhode Island and Stephen Smith of Philadelphia, both of them wealthy men by any standards. Some Negro lawyers of mark were John Mercer Langston of Ohio, and Robert Morris and John Rock of Boston. Frederick Douglass was one of the foremost orators in America, and in the pulpit the Reverend Henry Highland Garnet of New York and the Reverend J. Sella Martin of Boston ranked high. In sum, wrote William Wells Brown, the Negroes of the North, though "shut out, by a cruel prejudice, from nearly all the mechanical branches, and all the professions," had "learned trades, become artists, gone into the professions. . . . If this is not an exhibition of capacity, I don't understand the meaning of the term."[18]

✦

Many abolitionists, while arguing vigorously for the inherent equality of the Negro race, nevertheless believed in racial *differences*. "It is a mistake to speak of the African as an inferior race to the Caucasian," said James Freeman Clarke. "It is doubtless *different* from this, just as this is also different from the Malay, the Indian, the Mongolian. There are many varieties in the human

[17] Moncure D. Conway, "Benjamin Banneker, the Negro Astronomer," *Atlantic Monthly*, xi (Jan. 1863), 79-84.

[18] *Annual Report of the American Anti-Slavery Society for the Year Ending May 1, 1859* (New York, 1860), 77-78; Brown, *Black Man*, 49. This book contains short biographies of 57 eminent Negroes.

family." This was an accurate statement by today's ethnological standards, but Clarke parlayed it into a more questionable thesis: that the Negro was innately inferior to the Caucasian in some respects and superior in others. He stated:

"The colored man has not so much invention as the white, but more imitation. He has not so much of the reflective, but more of the perceptive powers. The black child will learn to read and write as fast or faster than the white child, having equal advantages. The blacks have not the indomitable perseverance and will, which make the Caucasian, at least the Saxon portion of it, *masters* wherever they go—but they have a native courtesy, a civility like that from which the word "gentleman" has its etymological meaning, and a capacity for the highest refinement of character. More than all, they have almost universally, a strong religious tendency, and that strength of attachment which is capable of any kind of self-denial, and self-sacrifice. Is this an inferior race—so inferior as to be only fit for chains?"[19]

Several other abolitionists subscribed to the notion of the Negro's superiority in the realm of manners, religion, and the arts, and inferiority in certain aspects of the hard-headed, practical business world. In an effort to convince readers of the Negro's ability to make positive contributions to American culture, Moncure Conway penned an article for the *Boston Commonwealth* in 1862, signing himself "A Native of the South." Negroes were a graceful people, he said, full of exuberance and picturesque charm. It was the Negro who gave to the South its warmth and radiance. The colored people had fertile, poetic imaginations. They had contributed much to southern culture, and would contribute more in freedom. "In our practical, anxious, unimaginative country, we need an infusion of this fervid African element, so child-like, exuberant, and hopeful," wrote Conway. "We ought to prize it, as we do rare woods and glowing gems imported from the gorgeous tropics." One year later, writing for an English audience, Conway stated that Negroes "seem to me to be weaker in the direction of the understanding, strictly speaking, but to have strength and elegance of imagination and expression. Negro

[19] James Freeman Clarke, *Slavery in the United States: A Sermon Delivered on Thanksgiving Day, 1842* (Boston, 1843), 24.

sermons, fables, and descriptions are in the highest degree pictorial, abounding in mystic interpretations which would delight a German transcendentalist. My belief is, that there is a vast deal of high art yet to come out of that people in America. Their songs and hymns are the only original melodies we have."[20]

In his widely publicized speech on "The Negro," Theodore Tilton proclaimed the Negro "the most religious man among men. Is not the religious nature the highest part of human nature? Strike out the negro then, and you destroy the highest development of the highest part of human nature." It was a mistake, thought Tilton,

"to rank men only by a superiority of intellectual faculties. God has given to man a higher dignity than the reason. It is the moral nature. . . . In all those intellectual activities which take their strange quickening from the moral faculties—processes which we call instincts, or intuitions—the negro is superior to the white man—equal to the white woman. The negro race is the feminine race of the world. . . .

"We have need of the negro for his . . . aesthetic faculties. . . . We have need of the negro for his music. . . . But let us stop questioning whether the negro is a man. In many respects he is a superior man. In a few respects, he is the greatest of men. I think he is certainly greater than those men who clamor against giving him a chance in the world, as if they feared something from the competition."[21]

Among American natural scientists of the mid-nineteenth century, Louis Agassiz was foremost in prestige and authority. His adherence to the "American School" of anthropology gave it an influence it could not otherwise have commanded. As a Harvard Professor, Agassiz had many acquaintances in Boston's intellectual circles; several of these acquaintances were abolitionists, and Agassiz's racial ideas could not help but have some effect on their thinking. Samuel Gridley Howe was one such friend. In 1863-1864 Howe served as a member of the American Freedmen's In-

---

[20] *Commonwealth*, Oct. 18, 1862; Conway, *Testimonies Concerning Slavery*, 71. Conway had gone to England in 1863 as a sort of ambassador of good will from the American abolitionists. He liked London so well that he settled down and lived there for the next 20 years.

[21] Tilton, *The Negro*, 11-13.

quiry Commission (see Chapter VIII). In connection with his research for the Commission, Howe asked Agassiz for his views on the effect of race on the problems of emancipation and reconstruction. Agassiz replied that he welcomed the prospect of emancipation, but warned against granting equal political and social rights to freedmen. He reviewed the history of the Negro in Africa and the western hemisphere, and concluded that Negroes were "indolent, playful, sensual, imitative, subservient, good-natured, versatile, unsteady in their purpose, devoted and affectionate." The Negro had never shown himself qualified for self-government. "I cannot," concluded Agassiz, "think it just or safe to grant at once to the negro all the privileges which we ourselves have acquired by long struggles. . . . Let us beware of granting too much to the negro race in the beginning, lest it become necessary hereafter to deprive them of some of the privileges which they may use to their own and our detriment."[22]

Howe was torn between his respect for Agassiz's learning and his own equalitarian principles. "I would not only advocate entire freedom, equal rights and privileges," he told Agassiz, but "open competition for social distinction." Howe was nevertheless influenced by some of Agassiz's notions regarding the mental inferiority of Negroes. In a book on Canadian Negroes published in 1864, Howe lamented that the younger generation, who had never known slavery and who enjoyed equal civil and political rights in Canada, had failed to produce as many outstanding individuals, in proportion to their numbers, as the white community. Howe took into account the prejudice, discrimination, and lack of opportunity that might account for this failure, but concluded that even with these disabilities the Negro community should have produced more superior men. Teachers to whom he talked testified that Negroes learned just as fast as whites in the lower grades, but fell behind at the higher levels "when they come to studies which tax the higher mental powers, or the reasoning and combining faculties." Colored people, thought Howe, were "quick of perception; very imitative; and they rapidly become intelligent. But they are rather knowing, than thinking people. They occupy

[22] Howe to Agassiz, Aug. 3, 1863; Agassiz to Howe, Aug. 9, 10, 1863, in Elizabeth C. Agassiz, *Louis Agassiz: His Life and Correspondence* (2 vols., Boston, 1885), II, 591-608.

useful stations in life; but such as require quick perceptions, rather than strong sense."[23]

To the modern reader familiar with the view of contemporary anthropology that there is no proof of significant differences in the mental capacities of various races, the opinions of Howe and other abolitionists who thought like him appear to border on racism. Even the belief of Tilton, Conway, and others in the inherent superiority of the Negro in the "feminine" virtues—religion and the arts—imply an assumption of Negro *inferiority* in the "masculine" virtues of reason and enterprise. Thus a case of modified racism could be made out against certain of the abolitionists, but only by ignoring the fact that in the contemporary spectrum of opinion on race, the abolitionists were far in the liberal vanguard. The remarkable fact about the abolitionists was not that as champions of the Negro *some* of them believed in racial differences, but that in a nation where popular belief *and* scientific learning overwhelmingly proclaimed the Negro's absolute inferiority, there were men and women who dared to affirm their faith in the innate equality of all men, regardless of race.

✦

Then as now, one of the most explosive aspects of the race question was the issue of intermarriage. "Would you like your daughter to marry a nigger?" was the derisive question hurled at abolitionists hundreds of times through the years. It is not recorded whether any daughter of a white abolitionist did marry a Negro, but it is known that the abolitionists did not shrink from discussing the issue. In the face of popular odium and violence, abolitionists struggled to remove laws barring intermarriage from the statute books of Massachusetts and other states. Marriage "is a personal and private matter, with which neither Congress nor any other law-makers have aught to do," said Gerrit Smith. "When a man and woman want to be married it is *their* business, not mine, nor anybody's else," declared Theodore Tilton. "But to read what some newspapers say of the 'monstrous doctrine of amalgamation,' one would think it consisted in stationing a provost-marshal at street corners, to seize first a white man and then a black woman,

[23] Howe to Agassiz, Aug. 18, 1863, *ibid.*, 614; Samuel G. Howe, *The Refugees from Slavery in Canada West* (Boston, 1864), 81-82.

147

and to marry them on the spot, against their will, for a testimony to human equality." Tilton pointed out the obvious fact, usually ignored by proslavery partisans, that amalgamation occurred under slavery, not freedom, at the bidding of the white man, not the Negro. Tilton declared that "a slave-woman's master, who makes himself the father of her children, is in honor bound to make himself her husband. So far from denouncing the marriage of blacks and whites, I would be glad if the banns of a hundred thousand such marriages could be published next Sunday."[24]

Abolitionists Louisa May Alcott, Lydia Maria Child, and Anna Dickinson defended intermarriage in short stories and novels. Gilbert Haven frequently vindicated amalgamation from his pulpit.[25] Moncure Conway proclaimed boldly that "I, for one, am firmly persuaded that the mixture of the blacks and whites is good; that the person so produced is, under ordinarily favourable circumstances, healthy, handsome, and intelligent. Under the best circumstances, I believe that such a combination would evolve a more complete character than the unmitigated Anglo-Saxon," because it would combine the best traits of both races. "Amalgamation!" exclaimed Wendell Phillips dramatically. "Remember this, the youngest of you; that, on the 4th of July, 1863, you heard a man say, that in the light of all history, in virtue of every page he ever read, he was an amalgamationist to the utmost extent. (Applause)" Phillips had no hope for the future "but in that sublime mingling of races which is God's own method of civilizing and elevating the world. (Loud applause) Not the amalgamation of licentiousness, born of slavery, . . . but that gradual and harmonizing union, in honorable marriage, which has mingled all other races, and from which springs the present phase of European and Northern civilization."[26]

✦

Most modern sociologists and psychologists agree that discrimination, segregation, and "cultural deprivation" rather than

[24] Gerrit Smith to the Hon. John Gurley, Dec. 16, 1861, in *Liberator*, Jan. 3, 1862; Tilton, *The Negro*, 10.

[25] Louisa May Alcott, "M. L.," a short story published serially in the *Commonwealth*, Jan. 24, 31, Feb. 7, 14, 21, 1863; Lydia M. Child, *A Romance of the Republic* (Boston, 1867); Anna Dickinson, *What Answer?* (Boston, 1868); Haven, *National Sermons*, 146.

[26] Conway, *Testimonies Concerning Slavery*, 76; Phillips' speech quoted in *Commonwealth*, July 17, 1863.

innate inferiority are responsible for the inferior status which the Negro occupies in American society. Abolitionists advanced this argument more than a century ago. Like modern sociologists, they maintained that environment, not racial deficiency, was the cause of the Negro's inferiority.

"I well remember what amazement was excited when Mr. Garrison and his partner first took a black boy as an apprentice in the office of 'The Liberator,' " wrote Oliver Johnson in his memoirs. "It was declared on every side that no 'nigger' could learn the art of printing, and it was held to be evidence of arrant folly to try the experiment. If the negroes, under such circumstances, sometimes seemed dull and even stupid, who can wonder? What race or class of men is strong enough to keep its feet under such a load of prejudice and contumely?" Theodore Tilton agreed that discrimination was responsible for the Negro's disabilities. "We put a stigma upon the black man's color, and then plead that prejudice against the commonest fair dealing," he stated. "We shut him out of schools, and then bitterly inveigh against the ignorance of his kind. We shut up all learned professions from his reach, and withhold the motives for ordinary enterprise, and then declare that he is an inferior being, fitted only for menial services."[27]

Prejudice and discrimination against the free Negro were debilitating enough, but the effects of slavery were worse still. "Take any race you please, French, English, Irish, or Scotch," said Frederick Douglass; "subject them to slavery for ages—regard and treat them every where, every way, as property. . . . Let them be loaded with chains, scarred with the whip, branded with hot irons, sold in the market, kept in ignorance . . . and I venture to say that the same doubt would spring up concerning either of them, which now confronts the negro." It was little wonder that "the colored people in America appear stupid, helpless and degraded. The wonder is that they evince so much spirit and manhood as they do." Theodore Tilton conceded that "slavery has reduced the blacks to the lowest point of ignorance and humiliation of which humanity . . . is capable." The "peculiar institution" had produced some singular effects on the Negro, making him childlike and dependent, lacking in initiative and

[27] Oliver Johnson, *William Lloyd Garrison and His Times* (2nd ed., Boston, 1885), 101-02; *Independent*, May 29, 1862.

self-respect. "Man is, to a certain extent, the creature of circum-stances," argued Tilton, "and two centuries of slavery must needs have molded the character of the slave. . . . The faults of the slave . . . come of training, rather than of natural endowment."[28]

In the *New York Tribune* of February 5, 1863, Sydney Gay presented a cogent and eloquent summary of the environmentalist argument. "We have never supposed that the liberation of so many human beings, heretofore irresponsible, would be without some embarrassments," he wrote in reply to proslavery arguments that slaves were not fit for freedom. "It is Freedom that fits men for Freedom. . . . The crime of Slavery has been that it has found the incapacity of its victims an argument for the continuation of its emasculating influences, and has continually pointed to the ruin it has wrought as an apology for postponing reparation." Nobody in his right senses, continued Gay,

"has expected to find the Freedman . . . a miracle of virtue, a wonder of wit, a paragon of prudence, and a marvel of industry. In him who was yesterday a Slave, we should expect to find the vices of the Slave—the traces of that falsehood which heretofore had been his sole protection against cruelty—of that thievishness which may have saved him from the pangs of hunger, or guarded him from the inclemency of the elements—of that insubordination of the animal passions which his superiors in society have encour-aged for their own profit and by their own example. . . . Eman-cipation will not remove the scars which Slavery has inflicted. There is many a brow from which the brand can never be erased. . . . So much the sooner should we, with all the courage of a genuine repentance, dock this entail of human misery, and at least turn the faces of future generations toward kindlier opportunities and less discouraging vicissitudes!"[29]

The effects of slavery and racial discrimination on the Negro's character, according to abolitionists, were felt primarily in three areas: intelligence, industry, and morals. The Negro's defects of intelligence, remarked Douglass, could be found among the peas-ants, laborers, and lower classes of all races. "A man is worked upon

---

[28] Speech by Douglass in Cooper Union, Feb. 12, 1862, published in *New York Tribune*, Feb. 13; article by Tilton in *Independent*, Aug. 20, 1863.

[29] *New York Tribune*, Feb. 5, 1863. See also J. M. McKim to Gay, Jan. 28, 1863, Gay Papers, cu.

by what *he* works on. He may carve out his circumstances, but his circumstances will carve him out as well." Douglass recalled his trip to Ireland in the 1840's, where he found the population of the poorer districts much like plantation slaves in every respect save color. "The open, uneducated mouth—the long, gaunt arm—the badly formed foot and ankle—the shuffling gait—the retreating forehead and vacant expression—and, their petty quarrels and fights—all reminded me of the plantation, and my own cruelly abused people."[30]

Moncure Conway, born and raised on a Virginia plantation, recounted the story of a companion of his youth, a slave boy who was popular with the white boys of the neighborhood and excelled in telling stories, playing games, and so on. The boy had a great native intelligence. He accompanied young Moncure to school every day, but of course was not allowed in the schoolroom. He wanted to know what happened in there, and when he found out he too wanted to learn to read. He could not understand why he was denied this privilege, and soon grew bewildered, then saddened, and finally rebellious, forcing Moncure's father to sell him South. Conway never forgot the boy. "I have dwelt upon this case," he wrote in his *Testimonies Concerning Slavery*, "because it is that which represents, in my own experience, one of the most tragical forms in which Slavery outrages human nature." On the basis of his experience, Conway also denied the theory that because of some natural disability, Negroes learned quickly until the age of ten or twelve, and then fell behind. "It has been my lot to have much to do with the poor whites of the South, and I have observed precisely the same arrest of development, both physical and mental, in those poor whites. . . . They learn well at first, even with a kind of voracity; but, at about the same age with the Negro child, they become dull." This was the result, not of inherent inferiority, but of the child's sudden realization of the cramped circumstances, limited opportunities, and unhappy future that faced the poor whites, as well as Negroes, of the South.[31]

The lazy, shiftless Negro who would work only under compulsion was a byword among those who defended slavery and ridiculed the idea of emancipation. Of course slaves were lazy, wrote Lydia

[30] Foner, *Douglass*, II, 304-05.
[31] Conway, *Testimonies Concerning Slavery*, 4-7, 65-66.

Maria Child in her study of emancipation in the West Indies. Slavery "takes away the motive power from the laborers, who naturally desire to shirk as much as possible of the work, which brings them no pay. . . . It makes them indifferent to the destruction of property on estates, in whose prosperity they have no interest. . . . It kills their ingenuity and enterprise." She cited the testimony of planters and missionaries in the West Indies, who said that emancipation had "almost wholly put an end to sulking, or pretending to be sick. . . . Planters treat their laborers more like fellow-men, and that leads them to be respectful, in their turn. They have now a growing regard for character; a feeling unknown to them in the days of slavery."[32]

The alleged immorality, dishonesty and untruthfulness of the Negro were cited by proslavery propagandists as additional proofs of his inferiority. Of course the slave was immoral, replied abolitionists. Under slavery promiscuity was encouraged, marriage had no legal validity, and the father had no personal responsibility for his children, who belonged, not to their parents, but to their master. "Being regarded as animals, and treated like live-stock, [slaves] unavoidably lived like animals," wrote Mrs. Child. "Modesty and self-respect were impossible to their brutalized condition." In the West Indies, she contended, there was much less immorality a generation after emancipation than there had been under slavery.[33]

"To tell us that Slavery fosters in the enslaved habits of deception, is not to communicate to us any startling novelty," wrote Sydney Gay in 1862. Gay and Conway admitted that Negroes were prone to petty thievery, "but it should be remembered that the rights of property involve some very refined problems," said Conway. "If the Negro is inclined to sympathize with the views of Rousseau on such questions more than the English schools would approve, it must be admitted that the systematic disregard of his own right to his earnings is scarcely the best method of giving him better views. I have never heard yet of a slave who had managed to filch back so much as had been filched from him." Samuel Gridley Howe declared that "the offences against property, with which by

---

[32] Lydia Maria Child, *The Right Way the Safe Way* (2d ed., New York, 1862), 5-6, 15-16.

[33] Charles K. Whipple, *The Family Relation, as Affected by Slavery* (Cincinnati, 1858), passim; Child, *Right Way Safe Way*, 6.

public voice the [Negroes] are charged, . . . grow directly out of slavery. . . . The owner, in his daily practice, violates the most sacred right of property, by taking the slave's labor without pay; and the slave imitates him by violating the less sacred right of property, in stealing what he can lay his hands on." Upon the basis of his observations of free Negroes in Canada, Howe concluded that "with freedom and the ownership of property, the instinct of family will be developed, marriages will increase, and promiscuous intercourse decrease. . . . [Canadian Negroes] are, upon the whole, sober, industrious, and thrifty, and have proved themselves to be capable of self-guidance and self-support."[34]

"The difference between the Black and White," thought Sydney Gay, "is no other than the difference between the White and the White—differences occasioned by the accidents of location, and susceptible of removal by the opportunities of culture." Abolitionists realized, however, that these differences would not be wiped out in a year or two. "Men going from slavery to freedom cannot change their habits as they change their garments," wrote Howe. "The effects of Slavery will last more than one generation or even two," predicted Wendell Phillips. "It were a very slight evil if they could be done away sooner." The Negro was potentially the equal of the white man, but he had a long, hard road to travel before he reached that potentiality.[35]

In the final analysis, argued abolitionists, the question was not one of race, but of human rights. "I think races are of secondary importance," said Wendell Phillips in 1863. "I despise an empire resting its claims on the blood of a single race. My pride in the future is in the banner that welcomes every race and every blood, and under whose shelter all races stand up equal. (Applause)" Theodore Tilton proclaimed, "Looked at through the centuries, the question of races sinks into insignificance. The only generalization that will stand is, not that there are five races of men, or seven, or twelve, but only one—the universal human race in which all men are brothers, and God is father over all!"[36]

[34] *New York Tribune*, Jan. 13, 1862; Conway, *Testimonies Concerning Slavery*, 70; Howe, *Refugees in Canada West*, 86-87, 103, 101.

[35] *New York Tribune*, Sept. 17, 1863; Howe, *Refugees in Canada West*, 86; speech by Wendell Phillips in Boston Music Hall, Dec. 16, 1860, in *New York Tribune*, Dec. 18.

[36] *Liberator*, May 29, 1863; Tilton, *The Negro*, 8.

VII ✦ FREEDMEN'S EDUCATION,

1861-1865

IN an optimistic mood, Wendell Phillips told an assemblage of abolitionists on the Fourth of July 1861, that "these days of anti-slavery gatherings for the purpose of emancipation, I believe, will be soon over." Emancipation was sure to come as a result of the war, and the duty of abolitionists would then be "to watch for the welfare of this victim race, guard it during its pupilage, shelter it by patronage, by protection, by privilege, by recognizing its claim to an equal manhood." A year later William Goodell asserted that "as soon as slavery shall be abolished, there will be an opportunity for Christian philanthropists to commence the arduous work of educating, enlightening, and guiding the emancipated colored people." In 1863 Whittier thanked God for the virtual abolition of slavery by the war, but warned his fellow abolitionists that "we must not for a moment forget that, from this hour, new and mighty responsibilities devolve upon us to aid, direct and educate these millions, left free, indeed, but bewildered, ignorant, naked and foodless in the wild chaos of civil war. We have to undo the accumulated wrongs of two centuries; to remake the manhood that slavery has well-nigh unmade."[1]

During the early war years, northern conservatives conjured up terrifying visions of servile insurrection and barbarism as consequences of emancipation. Abolition would mean social and economic anarchy in the South, with horrible scenes of bloodshed and carnage the result of inevitable race war. "The Negro will not work except under compulsion," they cried. "The two races cannot live side by side in freedom." Slavery was an absolute necessity to the South's social and economic system. "What will you *do* with the freed slaves?" they asked the abolitionists. Conservatives cited the alleged failure of emancipation in the West Indies as an example of the baneful consequences of letting black men go free. Abolitionists replied with an outpouring of scholarly and popular studies, based on official British and French sources, designed to

[1] Phillips was quoted in *Liberator*, July 12, 1861; Goodell in *Principia*, Oct. 23, 1862; and Whittier in *Proceedings of the American Anti-Slavery Society at its Third Decade Anniversary* (New York, 1864), 7.

demonstrate the economic and social *success* of emancipation in the West Indies.[2]

Many conservatives, however, remained unconvinced that large numbers of freed slaves could remain in the United States without causing social upheaval. In 1861-1862 there was widespread support among conservative Republicans and Democrats for the colonization abroad of Negroes emancipated by the war. Abolitionists and northern Negroes, of course, were overwhelmingly opposed to the idea of colonization as a solution of the Negro question. James Redpath promoted the emigration of northern Negroes to Haiti in an effort to help build that island republic into a strong nation and make it a showcase of Negro abilities. But Redpath as well as other abolitionists denounced all wartime colonization plans having the general purpose of getting Negroes out of the United States. Most colored men had little desire to leave their homeland. "Sir," said Robert Purvis to an advocate of Negro colonization, "this is our country as much as it is yours, and we will not leave it."[3]

Nevertheless Lincoln lent his support to several unwise colonization schemes during the war. In 1862 the president actually signed a contract with one Bernard Kock, a fly-by-night promoter, for the colonization of more than 450 freed slaves on the Ile A'Vache, a small island off the southern coast of Haiti. This venture proved a tragic failure. Kock confiscated the American dollars of the colonists and failed to provide them with adequate housing. Smallpox and actual starvation decimated the ranks of the emigrants. Lincoln finally admitted failure and sent a ship to bring the surviving Negroes back to the United States in February 1864. Abolitionists hoped that the government had

[2] The most important wartime writings by abolitionists on emancipation in the West Indies were: Lydia Maria Child, *The Right Way the Safe Way* (1st ed., New York, 1860; 2nd ed., 1862); Lewis Tappan, *Immediate Emancipation: The Only Wise and Safe Mode* (New York, 1861); a series of articles by Richard J. Hinton in *The Pine and Palm*, June 15, 22, 29, July 6, 13, Aug. 10, Sept. 14, 1861; a series of articles by Frank Sanborn in the *Springfield Republican*, Nov. 13, 16, 23, Dec. 7, 1861, Jan. 18, 25, Feb. 1, 8, 1862; Frank Sanborn, *Emancipation in the West Indies*, a pamphlet published by the Emancipation League in Boston in March 1862; a series of articles by Sanborn in the *Commonwealth*, Oct. 25, Nov. 8, 22, Dec. 13, 20, 1862, Jan. 10, 1863; and Mary Louise Booth, translation of Augustin Cochin's *Results of Emancipation* and of the same author's *Results of Slavery* (both books published in Boston, 1863).

[3] Purvis to Samuel C. Pomeroy, Aug. 28, 1862, published in the *New York Tribune*, Sept. 20, 1862.

learned something from the failure of its colonization schemes. Edmund Quincy asserted that the collapse of emigration projects showed colonization to be a "wild, delusive and impractical scheme," while emancipation without expatriation, for which abolitionists had always contended, had been successful. "Thus does the boasted wisdom of 'Conservatism' turn out to be folly, while the 'fanaticism' of the 'crazy Radicals' is proved by experience to be the highest wisdom."[4]

The failure of colonization confronted America with the problem of absorbing 4 million freed slaves into the social structure. Abolitionists were ready for this challenge. Opportunities for abolitionists to demonstrate the Negro's fitness for liberty and to help the freedmen in their difficult transition from slavery to freedom came early in the war. As contrabands began pouring into Union lines at Fortress Monroe near Hampton, Virginia, in the summer of 1861, General Butler assigned Private Edward L. Pierce to the job of ministering to their needs and superintending their labor on Union fortifications. Pierce was picked for this task because of his antislavery background, his administrative ability, and his eagerness to prove the Negro's capacity for freedom. He had studied law in the office of Salmon P. Chase, was a friend of Charles Sumner and Wendell Phillips, and had served as a member of Phillips' bodyguard during the antiabolitionist riots of the secession winter.[5]

Pierce worked with the contrabands only a short time before he was mustered out and returned to private life (he had enlisted for three months). But during that brief period he laid down certain basic principles that governed future contraband policy at Monroe. The contrabands were to work the same number of hours per day as white laborers, and receive the same rations as soldiers. They were to be paid for their labor. Part of their wages was to be deducted for support of sick and aged contrabands.

---

[4] *N.A.S. Standard*, Mar. 19, 1864. There are several studies of wartime colonization projects. The best of these are: Warren A. Beck, "Lincoln and Negro Colonization in Central America," *Abraham Lincoln Quarterly*, VI (Sept. 1950), 162-83; Willis D. Boyd, "Negro Colonization in the National Crisis, 1860-1870," Ph.D. dissertation, UCLA, 1953; Paul J. Scheips, "Lincoln and the Chiriqui Colonization Project," *Journal of Negro History*, XXXVI (1952), 418-53.

[5] Edward L. Pierce, *Enfranchisement and Citizenship, Addresses and Papers*, ed. by A. W. Stevens (Boston, 1896), 4-5, 19; Edward L. Pierce, "The Contrabands at Fortress Monroe," *Atlantic Monthly*, VIII (Nov. 1861), 632-36.

Pierce published an article on "The Contrabands at Fortress Monroe" in the *Atlantic Monthly*. He stated that the Negroes had worked hard in the July heat and had shown little of the indolence of which they were usually accused. Many officers had sneered at Pierce's idea of getting Negroes to work by kind treatment and wage incentives, but Pierce asserted that the result proved him right: the contrabands worked better when treated well than when they were whipped and driven like cattle. Pierce had held long conversations with several contrabands, and when he mentioned that most whites considered their race lazy and shiftless, they replied scornfully: "Who but the darkies cleared all the land round here?" Pierce concluded that there were lazy

Letterhead of the National Freedmen's Relief Association.

Negroes, but that there were a great many lazy white men as well. With good wages, promptly paid, the Negro would prove as industrious as the southern white, perhaps more so.[6]

Less than two weeks after the firing on Fort Sumter, *The American Missionary*, organ of the American Missionary Association (A.M.A.) proclaimed that the war would create in the South "one of the grandest fields of missionary labor the world ever furnished." By June 1861, the abolitionist-dominated A.M.A. was making plans to send teachers and books to educate the 700 Negroes within Union lines in Virginia. The Reverend L. C. Lockwood went to Fortress Monroe in early September and opened a Sunday school on September 15. Two days later a day school for freedmen was established near the site where the first shipload of slaves landed in America in 1619. The school was a success, and several more schools and churches were started under A.M.A. auspices in subsequent months. The Association also helped the government provide for the physical needs of the freedmen. The Boston auxiliary alone sent more than one hundred barrels of clothing to the contrabands during the winter of 1861-62.[7]

On the morning of November 7, 1861, a Union fleet steamed into Port Royal Sound with guns ablaze, and by nightfall Port Royal Island and the adjacent South Carolina sea islands 50 miles southwest of Charleston were in Union hands. Most of the islands' white population escaped to the mainland, leaving behind scores of fertile cotton plantations and more than 8,000 confused slaves. Here indeed was a challenge to abolitionists. Because of their physical and cultural isolation, these slaves were among the most ignorant and backward of the entire South. If *they* proved themselves capable of a productive and peaceful life in freedom, antiemancipation arguments based on the alleged barbarism and shiftlessness of the Negro race would crumble to pieces. Abolitionists were quick to grasp the significance of this opportunity. Two weeks after the capture of Port Royal, the *Anti-Slavery Standard*

[6] Pierce, "Contrabands at Fortress Monroe," *op.cit.*, 635-40.

[7] Augustus F. Beard, *A Crusade of Brotherhood, A History of the American Missionary Association* (Boston, 1909), 117-18; Richard B. Drake, "The American Missionary Association and the Southern Negro, 1861-1888," Ph.D. dissertation, Emory University, 1957, 1-31; S. S. Jocelyn to Gerrit Smith, June 17, 1861, Smith Papers, su; Lewis Tappan to Charles Sumner, Jan. 16, 1862, Sumner Papers, hu; L. C. Lockwood to George Cheever, Jan. 29, 1862, Cheever Papers, aas; Gerrit Smith to Lewis Tappan, Nov. 23, 1862, Tappan Papers, lc.

urged the government to grant freedom to the slaves and hire them to harvest the cotton crop. "Here, within the protection of the arms of the United States, might a new experiment of tropical culture by free labor be tried," declared the *Standard*. "Succeeding there, as succeed it must and would, how simple the process by which it might be extended wherever the arms of the nation may be predominant!"[8]

In December the Treasury Department sent special agents to the islands to collect and sell the 1861 cotton crop. The agents were to supervise the labor of contrabands and keep records of their work for future payment of wages. Secretary of the Treasury Chase realized, however, that such an arrangement was not satisfactory on a long-term basis since the cotton agents had no interest in the welfare of the Negroes and would do little or nothing to further the great social experiment of freedom on the islands. On December 20 Chase sent a telegram to Edward L. Pierce asking him to accept a commission to investigate the condition and needs of the freedmen at Port Royal. Pierce accepted, and departed for the sea islands on January 13, 1862.[9] After two weeks of intensive observation Pierce drew up a report to Chase on February 3. He thought that "when properly organized, and with proper motives set before them," the contrabands "will as freemen be as industrious as any race of men are likely to be in this climate." Because of their past dependence the Negroes were not yet self-reliant, but "in spite of their condition, reputed to be worse here than in many other parts of the rebellious region, there are such features in their life and character that the opportunity is now offered to us to make of them, partially in this generation and fully in the next, a happy, industrious, law-abiding, free, and Christian people." Pierce recommended that the government appoint labor superintendents for each plantation or group of smaller plantations, "selected with reference to peculiar qualifications, and as carefully as one would choose a guardian for his children." The contrabands, said Pierce, should be treated "with sole reference" to their preparation for the rights and duties of freedom and citizenship.[10]

[8] *N.A.S. Standard*, Nov. 23, 1861.

[9] Willie L. Rose, "Rehearsal for Reconstruction: The Port Royal Experiment," Ph.D. dissertation, Johns Hopkins University, 1962, 19-32.

[10] Pierce, *Enfranchisement and Citizenship*, 77, 82-85.

Pierce talked with President Lincoln on February 15. Afterwards Lincoln gave Chase *carte blanche* to go ahead with the sea island experiment on the basis of Pierce's recommendations. Chase appointed Pierce a special agent of the Treasury Department with full powers to select superintendents and teachers for the contrabands. The government would supply the superintendents with rations, housing, and transportation, but their salaries would have to be paid by private philanthropic societies.[11]

Shortly after arriving on the sea islands Pierce had written to Jacob Manning, abolitionist pastor of the Old South Church in Boston, describing the "strange and chaotic condition" of the contrabands. They were confused, destitute, and in danger of demoralization by their contact with Union soldiers. "If this critical moment be not availed of and some means not taken to make them industrious, orderly and sober, they will become hopelessly demoralized," Pierce informed Manning. "You must see that the heathen to whom we owe a special duty . . . are nearer to us than the Ganges."[12]

Manning published this letter in the *Boston Transcript*, and called a meeting at his home for the formation of a society to send supplies, teachers, and labor superintendents to the contrabands. At a second meeting on February 7 the "Boston Educational Commission" was organized. Its purpose was "the industrial, social, intellectual, moral and religious elevation of persons released from Slavery in the course of the War for the Union." Governor John Andrew was chosen president of the Commission, whose membership included every shade of antislavery conviction from radical abolitionist to moderate Republican. In New York City the Reverend Mansfield French, an abolitionist and a friend of Chase, took the lead in organizing the National Freedmen's Relief Association. In Philadelphia, abolitionist J. Miller McKim took steps to form a similar society. At a public meeting on March 5 the Philadelphia Port Royal Relief Committee was organized, with McKim as executive secretary.[13]

The inception of the freedmen's aid movement touched off a debate within abolitionist ranks over the purpose and strategy

[11] *ibid.*, 90-91.
[12] *Boston Transcript*, Jan. 27, 1862.
[13] Pierce, *Enfranchisement and Citizenship*, 67-68; Rose, "Rehearsal for Reconstruction," 36-45; *Liberator*, Mar. 7, 1862.

of antislavery societies. Early in 1862 McKim submitted his resignation as corresponding secretary of the Pennsylvania Anti-Slavery Society. Slavery was crumbling under the weight of war, argued McKim, and there was no longer any need for agents, lecturers, and other traditional appurtenances of the abolitionist movement. "In my judgment, the old anti-slavery routine is not what the cause now demands," he wrote. "Iconoclasm has had its day. For the battering-ram we must substitute the hod and trowel. . . . We have passed through the *pulling-down* stage of our movement; the building-up—the constructive part—remains to be accomplished." McKim proposed that abolitionists dissolve their old societies or convert them into freedmen's aid associations.[14]

Most abolitionists disagreed with McKim. The officers of the Pennsylvania Anti-Slavery Society refused to accept his resignation, and McKim consented to stay on as corresponding secretary until a replacement could be found. Pillsbury, Powell, and other abolitionist lecturers maintained that lectures, meetings, and so on, were more important to the antislavery cause than ever. "If emancipation comes as a mere 'necessity of war,'" declared the *Anti-Slavery Standard,* "it will come unsanctioned by any considerations of justice or humanity toward the victims of our oppression, and the strenuous exertion of moral influence in their behalf will still be greatly needed." The end of slavery may be near, wrote Giles Stebbins of Michigan, but there was still grave danger of compromise. "Surely the Abolitionists, with tongue and pen, can help to the right answer. Never were their words so earnestly and widely heard as now. . . . Why seal our lips when, more than ever, the people hear and ponder our words?"[15]

McKim hastened to deny the implication that he favored abandonment of the antislavery crusade. He merely wanted to channel it in a new direction. "This *freedmen* business is an immensely 'big job,'" he explained. "It is abolition already begun. It is all important that the first instalment should be well managed. The experiment of freedom should be initiated with as much care as possible." Abolitionists could not do the whole work, of course, but they should take the lead. "We are to continue to be

---

14 *N.A.S. Standard,* May 3, 1862.

15 *N.A.S. Standard,* Feb. 15, 1862; Stebbins to Garrison, May 20, 1862, in *Liberator,* May 30. See also *N.A.S. Standard,* May 3, 1862, and *Liberator,* May 16, 1862.

what we have always been, a wheel within a wheel; an original motive power. . . . Our presence & influence should be seen and felt in this & all other important movements."[16]

Meanwhile the freedmen's aid societies selected 41 men and 12 women as the first group of plantation superintendents and teachers for the sea island freedmen. This contingent sailed from New York early in March 1862. Among these "Gideonites," as they soon called themselves, were many abolitionists. Miss Laura Towne, a Philadelphia abolitionist who was destined to become one of the outstanding personalities on the islands, declared when she arrived there in 1862 that "we have come to do antislavery work, and we think it noble work and mean to do it earnestly." Another antislavery veteran observed in August 1862, that some of the foremost young abolitionists in Philadelphia had left comfortable homes to go to Port Royal and teach the freedmen.[17] Charlotte Forten, a highly cultured young Negro from Salem, Massachusetts, complained on the other hand that some of the plantation superintendents were prejudiced against the Negroes and spoke of them in contemptuous terms. Reuben Tomlinson, another Philadelphia abolitionist who became a prominent figure on the islands, deplored the shortcomings of several of the superintendents. "There is also a lukewarmness among them on the subject of anti-Slavery," he wrote, "which I think interferes very materially with their usefulness." The northern societies were forced to dismiss several of the superintendents who had treated the Negroes badly. The great majority of Gideonites were genuinely concerned for the freedmen's welfare, however, and most of those who were not, were quickly weeded out of the enterprise.[18]

[16] McKim to Samuel May, Jr., May 20, 1862, McKim Papers, Cornell.

[17] Rupert S. Holland, ed., *Letters and Diary of Laura M. Towne, Written from the Sea Islands of South Carolina, 1862-84* (Cambridge, Mass., 1912), 8; Sarah Pugh to Mary Edmundson, Aug. 5, 1862, Garrison Papers, BPL.

[18] Ray Allen Billington, ed., *The Journal of Charlotte Forten* (Collier Books, New York, 1961), 165; Tomlinson to J. M. McKim, Sept. 20, Oct. 17, 1862, Jan. 16, 1863, McKim Papers, Cornell. See also Rose, "Rehearsal for Reconstruction," 54-66; William H. Pease, "Three Years Among the Freedmen: William C. Gannett and the Port Royal Experiment," *Journal of Negro History*, XLII (April 1957), 98-117; Sarah Pugh to Elizabeth Gay, Apr. 6, 1862, Gay Papers, CU; Frank Sanborn to Gerrit Smith, Apr. 13, 1862, Smith Papers, SU; Maria W. Chapman to Anne G. Chapman, July 6, 1862, Weston Papers, BPL; T. W. Higginson to Louisa Higginson, Oct. 24, 1863, Higginson Papers, HU.

The Gideonites encountered many trials and difficulties in their first months on the islands. The sea island Negroes spoke a dialect almost unintelligible to northern ears. Harriet Ware, a Massachusetts abolitionist stationed on St. Helena Island, reported in April 1862, that it required a "great deal of tact and ability" to gain the friendship and confidence of the contrabands. "We are not used to these people—it is even very difficult to understand what they say." After her first day in Beaufort, Laura Towne wrote that "it certainly takes great nerve to walk here among the soldiers and negroes and not be disgusted or shocked or pained so much as to give it all up." Charlotte Forten considered the first Negroes she encountered upon her arrival "certainly the most dismal specimens I ever saw."[19] The teachers faced a herculean task in trying to teach Negro children of all ages to read and write in overcrowded schoolrooms. Laura Towne described one of her early classroom experiences: the pupils "had no idea of sitting still, of giving attention or ceasing to talk aloud. They lay down and went to sleep, they scuffled and struck each other. They got up by the dozen, made their curtsies, and walked off to the neighboring field for blackberries, coming back to their seats with a curtsy when they were ready. They evidently did not understand me, and I could not understand them, and after two hours and a half of effort I was thoroughly exhausted."[20]

In the face of such discouragements a few Gideonites gave up and returned home. Most of them stuck it out, however, and soon sang a happier tune. Laura Towne forgot her early disheartenment, and in June 1862, she wrote to a friend:

"I wish you were as free from every fret as I am, and as happy. We found the people here naked, . . . afraid and discontented about being made to work as slaves, and without assurance of freedom or pay, of clothes or food,—and now they are jolly and happy and decently fed and dressed, and so full of affection and gratitude to the people who are relieving them that it is rather too flattering to be enjoyed. It will not last, I dare say, but it is genuine now and they are working like Trojans. . . . It is such

[19] Harriet Ware to ?, Apr. 21, 1862, in Elizabeth Pearson, ed., *Letters from Port Royal* (Boston, 1906), 20-21; Holland, *Letters and Diary of Laura Towne*, 7; Billington, *Journal of Charlotte Forten*, 142.
[20] Holland, *Letters and Diary of Laura Towne*, xiv-xv.

163

a satisfaction to an abolitionist to see that they are proving conclusively that they can and will and even *like* to work enough at least to support themselves and give something extra to Government."[21]

After they learned to keep order and communicate with the pupils, teachers found to their delight that the children learned to read rapidly. All of the freedmen showed great eagerness to learn to read and write. Most of the teachers agreed that Negro children were fully equal to whites on the lower levels of learning. At the higher levels, such as mathematics, original composition, grammar, and so on, they did not do as well, but most of the teachers attributed this to lack of background, motivation, and opportunity rather than to any innate inferiority. On the whole, most teachers were satisfied with the progress made by their students during the first year. Pierce wrote after observing the contrabands for several weeks that "I was never so impressed as at this hour with the conviction that the lifting of these people from bondage to freedom . . . is a very easy thing, involving only common humanity, and reasonable patience and faith. If white men only did as well under such adverse circumstances, they would be regarded as prodigies."[22]

The Port Royal experiment received a great deal of national publicity in both the proslavery and antislavery press. Much was at stake on the South Carolina islands. If the contrabands there showed themselves capable of an industrious and productive life in freedom, the main argument against emancipation would dissolve into nothingness. For this reason the Democratic and conservative press in the North tried to discredit the whole enterprise. The attempt by Pierce and his "band of Abolition socialists, free lovers, and disorganizers of society generally" to "put in practice the theory of Abolition at Port Royal, will be the beginning of the downfall of the now rampant and powerful Abolition party in the North," declared the *New York Express*. The *Express* charged that the contrabands had become paupers living on the United States Treasury, revelling in idleness at the expense of the

[21] *ibid.*, 68.
[22] Rose, "Rehearsal for Reconstruction," 300-03; Pease, "Three Years Among the Freedmen," *op.cit.*, 100-01; Pearson, *Letters from Port Royal*, 11, 18, 60, 75; Pierce to Sumner, Mar. 20, 1862, Sumner Papers, HU.

northern taxpayer. "The question now arises, if this is the result of letting loose a few thousand negroes in South Carolina, what will it be when the contrabands shall be counted by hundreds of thousands?" The *New York Journal of Commerce* intoned that "the nonsensical, wild and fanatical plans of irresponsible men and women which are having their trial at Port Royal are a subject of sorrow and disgust to the intelligent world." And the *Louisville Democrat* commented that "the abolitionists propose to elevate the black races. Nothing but hemp could do the same thing properly for them."[23]

The abolitionist and antislavery press countered these aspersions with facts, figures, and opinions based on actual observation and study of the situation on the sea islands. On June 2, 1862, Pierce submitted his final report as special agent of the Treasury Department. Under the supervision of Gideonites the Negroes had planted nearly 15,000 acres of cotton, corn, potatoes, and grain. Despite their initial disinclination to plant cotton (they considered it a badge of slavery), and the six weeks' late start on the growing season, the crops were coming along well. The contrabands worked industriously under the stimulus of wages even though they were frequently not paid on time. Their behavior, said Pierce, gave the lie to the old proslavery assertion that Negroes would work only under compulsion. "It is not pretended that many of these laborers could not have done more than they have done, or that in persistent application they are the equals of races living in colder and more bracing latitudes," he wrote. But they worked hard enough to make themselves self-supporting, and with the additional incentives of complete freedom they would work even harder. Nearly 2,500 children were taught in the day schools during the first two months of the experiment, and almost the whole adult population attended Sunday schools. "The success of the movement, now upon its third month, has exceeded my most sanguine expectations," concluded Pierce. "Industrial results have been reached which put at rest the often reiterated assumption that this territory and its products can be cultivated only by slaves.

---

[23] *New York Express*, quoted in *N.A.S. Standard*, Apr. 5, 1862; *New York Journal of Commerce*, quoted in *Liberator*, May 9, 1862; *Louisville Democrat*, quoted in the *Columbus Crisis*, Dec. 31, 1862.

A social problem which has vexed the wisest approaches a solution."[24]

In the summer of 1862 J. Miller McKim visited the sea islands as the official representative of the Philadelphia Port Royal Relief Committee. McKim was shocked by what he saw of the lingering effects of slavery. Even in his most radical moments as an abolitionist he had never suspected the depths of the soul-corroding and personality-warping effects of human bondage. Nevertheless, after a two weeks' tour of the islands McKim expressed optimism about the future of the Negroes as free men. Most of the anti-Negro stories circulating in the North, he said, came from reporters of the *New York Herald* and *New York World* stationed on the islands, who moved among "the ribald and unprincipled, picking up their items in bar-rooms, . . . and thus it is that at least half of what they write is absolutely false."[25]

McKim returned to Philadelphia and on July 9 gave a public lecture summarizing his observations on the islands. The lecture was widely published by the antislavery press and printed in pamphlet form for distribution throughout the North. Many people were asking: "Has the negro the spirit—the *pluck*, to do his part in maintaining the status now, or hereafter to be, assigned him?" McKim tried to answer this all-important question as fairly as he could. "Servitude is not a condition favorable to the growth of courage," he said. "Slavery in fact as well as law, unmans its victims." But given the incentives and responsibilities of freedom, the Negroes would develop pluck enough. McKim quoted the testimony of one of the plantation superintendents: The freedmen "have their vices. Deception and petty thieving prevail. They are careless, indolent and improvident. They have a miserable habit of scolding and using authoritative language to one another." But "all these vices are clearly the result of *slave education*, and will gradually disappear under improved conditions." McKim stated his firm conviction that the free-labor experiment at Port Royal had thus far been "entirely successful."[26]

24 Pierce, *Enfranchisement and Citizenship*, 97-102. Pierce's report was widely publicized by the antislavery press.

25 McKim to Sarah McKim, June 19, 1862, McKim Papers, NYPL. See also Oliver Johnson to Garrison, June 27, 1862, McKim to Garrison, July 13, 1862, Garrison Papers, BPL.

26 J. M. McKim, *The Freedmen of South Carolina: an Address Delivered in Sansom Hall, July 9, 1862* (Philadelphia, 1862), 18, 30, and passim.

Many other abolitionists and Gideonites contributed their testimony to the positive results of the first months of the Port Royal experiment. Charles P. Ware, a plantation superintendent from Massachusetts, observed in October 1862 that the enterprise had operated under many handicaps during the preceding summer. "The sudden reaction consequent upon the change from slavery to what they hardly knew as freedom; the confusion incident upon military occupation . . . the lateness of the cotton crop, the poorness of the seed . . . and lastly, the shameful delay in the payments" of wages—with all these hindrances it would not have been surprising if the experiment had failed entirely. But it had not failed. Under such adverse circumstances "it is wonderful how much they have done and in what an excellent state they are." E. S. Philbrick wrote after a year on the islands: "If our Northern croakers could only be made to realize as we do here the ease with which we have reduced a comparative degree of order out of the chaos we found, and see how ready this degraded and half-civilized race are to become an industrious and useful laboring class, there would not be so much gabble about the danger of immediate emancipation."[27]

Evidence of the success of the Port Royal experiment and similar efforts elsewhere did not rest upon the testimony of abolitionists alone. John Murray Forbes, a businessman who visited the sea islands in the spring of 1862, wrote in June of that year: "I used to think emancipation only another name for murder, fire and rape, but mature reflection and considerable personal observation have since convinced me that emancipation may, at any time, be declared without disorder."[28] Many others like Forbes were becoming convinced in 1862 by the pressures of war, the reports of teachers of the freedmen, the statements of impartial observers, and personal observation that immediate emancipation was both safe and practicable.

While the freedmen's aid societies were winning converts among conservatives, a few abolitionists warned against the dangers of paternalism inherent in the very concept of freedmen's aid.

[27] Ware and Philbrick quoted in Pearson, *Letters from Port Royal*, 98-99, 180.
[28] Forbes to Charles Sumner, June 21, 1862, in Sarah Forbes Hughes, ed., *Letters and Recollections of John Murray Forbes* (2 vols., Boston, 1899), I, 317-18.

Lydia Maria Child complained about the practice at Fortress Monroe of withholding a portion of the freedmen's wages for support of the sick and aged. "I wish white people could get rid of the idea that they must manage *for* them," she said. "*White* laborers would not work with much heart under such circumstances. They ought to pay them *wages* in proportion to their *work*, and let *them* form Relief Societies among themselves, so that they might feel that *they* did the benevolent work themselves." Wendell Phillips also believed in a greater degree of laissez-faire for the freedmen. "I ask nothing more for the negro than I ask for the Irishman or the German who comes to our shores," said Phillips in May 1862. "I thank the benevolent men who are laboring at Port Royal—all right!—but the blacks at the South do not need them. They are not objects of charity. They only ask this nation—'Take your yoke off our necks.' "[29]

In one sense this criticism was unfair. There was a very real danger of excessive paternalism, to be sure, but the abolitionist teachers and superintendents in the field were no more in favor of paternalism as a permanent policy than Phillips. They were confronted by a set of circumstances, however, which made a certain amount of paternalism necessary at first. The contrabands were just emerging from slavery, an institution that had deeply implanted in their character the habits of dependence and servility. It would take months and years of patient labor, education, and experience before this attitude of dependence on the one side, and the corresponding necessity of a certain amount of paternalism on the other, ceased to exist. The function of the limited paternalism practiced by Gideonites was to help the Negroes take the first steps to freedom, to set them on the path that led to eventual self-reliance, when paternalism would no longer be necessary.[30]

Most of the Gideonites fully recognized the dangers of falling into an attitude of benevolent condescension toward the contrabands. They were annoyed at first by the servile attitude of the Negroes. "These people show their subserviency in the way they put Marm or Sir into their sentences every other word, . . . and in always agreeing to everything you say," wrote Harriet Ware

[29] L. M. Child to Francis G. Shaw, Jan. 28, 1862, Shaw Correspondence, NYPL; Phillips' statement quoted in *Liberator*, May 16, 1862.
[30] Rose, "Rehearsal for Reconstruction," 205-06.

from St. Helena Island in April 1862. "In school it is rather annoying to have them say, 'Yes Marm,' 'zackly Marm,' before it is possible for an idea to have been reached their brains."[31] In many ways the adult freedmen were like children. They had been treated like children, in a sense, all their lives, and for a time they continued to act toward the northern missionaries as they had acted toward their old masters. "The great mass of these people are to all intents and purposes children," observed Reuben Tomlinson early in 1863, "except that they are children with fixed habits, the growth of years, & are therefore even more difficult to manage than children." In view of this childlike behavior, it is not surprising that some of the Gideonites were unconsciously flattered and wheedled into an overindulgent attitude toward their "people." Tomlinson warned against such overindulgence, declaring that it was the worst way to prepare the Negroes for the responsibilities and duties of freedom.[32]

When the Gideonites first came South the contrabands were destitute, in desperate need of food, clothing, and benevolent assistance. The government distributed rations, and the freedmen's aid societies sent thousands of dollars worth of clothing to the islands. This natural impulse to treat the poverty-stricken freedmen as objects of charity was soon overcome, however. The societies set up stores on the islands where the freedmen could buy clothing and supplies at cost, and in November 1862, the government discontinued the issuance of rations to able-bodied freedmen and their families. Most of the Gideonites made conscious efforts to avoid an excess of paternal benevolence, and as time passed the freedmen themselves began to act more like free men.[33]

✦

Port Royal and Fortress Monroe were not the only places where northern teachers and missionaries worked with the freedmen. As the war progressed the A.M.A. established schools and churches in just about every part of the Confederacy penetrated by Union armies. The Boston and Philadelphia Educational and Relief Societies, organized in February and March 1862, later

[31] Pearson, *Letters from Port Royal*, 25.
[32] Tomlinson to J. M. McKim, Feb. 19, Mar. 16, 1863, McKim Papers, Cornell.
[33] Pearson, *Letters from Port Royal*, 33-34; Francis George Shaw to S. P. Chase, Jan. 13, 1864, Chase Papers, LC.

changed their names to the New England Freedmen's Aid Society and the Pennsylvania Freedmen's Relief Association. These two societies plus the National Freedmen's Relief Association of New York expanded the scope of their activities during 1862-1863, established auxiliary societies, and sent an ever-increasing quota of supplies and teachers to the South.[34]

Abolitionists were prominent in the organization and leadership of freedmen's aid societies. A substantial percentage of the officers of the New England, New York, and Pennsylvania societies were old-line abolitionists. The A.M.A. was dominated by abolitionists.[35] In March 1862, George E. Baker, an old abolitionist, helped to organize the National Freedmen's Relief Association in Washington, which distributed supplies, conducted schools, and provided hospital and medical care for freedmen in the District of Columbia and northern Virginia. Joseph Parker, an abolitionist Baptist minister from Boston, became corresponding secretary of the New England Educational Commission for the Freedmen, an organization which directed the freedmen's aid efforts of New England Baptists during the war. In February 1862, Richard J. Hinton founded the Kansas Emancipation League to provide relief, establish schools, and find jobs for the 4,000 contrabands who escaped into Kansas during the first year of the war.[36] In Syracuse Samuel J. May organized an auxiliary freedmen's relief association and spent much of his time and energy directing the work of the association during the rest of the war. The Rochester Ladies Anti-Slavery Society supported a school in Alexandria, Virginia. As the Union armies in the West advanced southward into Tennessee and Mississippi in 1862, thousands of contrabands crowded into filthy camps set up for them behind Union lines. Levi Coffin, famous Cincinnati abolitionist and legendary "President" of the underground railroad, visited a contraband camp at Cairo, Illinois,

[34] Beard, *Crusade of Brotherhood,* passim; Julius H. Parmelee, "Freedmen's Aid Societies, 1861-1871," in *Negro Education: A Study of the Private and Higher Schools for Colored People in the United States; U.S. Dept. of Interior: Bureau of Education Bulletin,* 1916, no. 38 (Washington, 1917), 269-80.

[35] Henry Lee Swint, *The Northern Teacher in the South, 1862-1870* (Nashville, 1941), 26-28.

[36] George E. Baker to Gerrit Smith, July 25, 1864, Smith Papers, su; Joseph W. Parker, "Memoirs," typescript of MS written by Parker in 1880, supplied to the author by Parker's granddaughter, Mrs. Perce J. Bentley, pp. 105-28; Richard J. Hinton to Charles Sumner, Feb. 27, 1862, enclosing circular of the Kansas Emancipation League, Sumner Papers, hu.

late in 1862 and helped start a school there. He returned to Cincinnati and in January 1863, organized the Western Freedmen's Aid Commission. Coffin served as general agent of the Commission, and spent the rest of the war organizing auxiliary societies, raising money, and overseeing the activities of his organization.[37]

Abolitionists also predominated among the teachers and missionaries who went South to instruct and assist the freedmen in their transition to freedom. Few of the old-line abolitionists actually went into the field to teach: that work was usually left to younger and more adventurous persons of antislavery backgrounds, while the older people remained in the North to serve in administrative capacities. A few of the veteran crusaders, however, went South and served on the firing line of freedom. Frances Dana Gage arrived at Port Royal in 1862. Josephine S. Griffing went to work among the freedmen in Washington in 1863 and stayed there until her death in 1872, devoting herself entirely to the work of caring for sick and aged freedmen and finding jobs for the able-bodied.[38] At the outbreak of the war the sixty-year-old Quaker abolitionist, Abigail Hopper Gibbons, offered her services to the government as a nurse. The government accepted, and assigned her to army camps in northern Virginia in the first year of the war. In 1862 she was put in charge of the army hospital at Point Lookout in southern Maryland. A contraband camp was established next to the army hospital. Mrs. Gibbons took charge of the distribution of supplies from freedmen's aid societies, and found jobs in the North for several of the freedmen. She was disliked by the local white populace, most of whom were Confederate sympathizers. She received several threatening letters from irate Marylanders. The following was a typical example of these missives: "Old Lady you are not needed at this place and you had better leave double quick or else the soldiers [Maryland Unionist soldiers] will give you an introduction to the bay you never came here for any good to soldiers as they have found it out you old nigger lover yea worse an old hypocrit the devil has his

[37] Samuel J. May to Garrison, Sept. 9, 24, 1862, Garrison Papers, BPL; *Thirteenth Annual Report of the Rochester Ladies' Anti-Slavery Society* (Rochester, 1864); Levi Coffin, *Reminiscences* (Cincinnati, 1880), 619-50.

[38] F. D. Gage to S. P. Chase, Mar. 4, 1863, Chase Papers, LC; F. D. Gage to Matilda Joslyn Gage, Nov. 20, 1863, Gage Papers, Radcliffe Women's Archives; Elizabeth Cady Stanton et al., *History of Woman Suffrage* (6 vols., New York, 1881-1922), II, 26-39.

house full of better people than ever you were you old Hell hound you must know that you cant rule this whole point now hum yourself away pretty soon."[39]

At the end of the war the various secular and religious freedmen's aid societies had more than 900 teachers in the South. In August 1865, General O. O. Howard, newly appointed head of the Freedmen's Bureau, said that more than 200,000 freedmen had received instruction during the past four years.[40] In the early postwar years there was a great expansion of freedmen's aid activity, especially among the church-connected societies (see Chapter XVII).

+

Abolitionists made use of every opportunity to proclaim the success of the Port Royal experiment and other free labor enterprises. Edward Pierce and Charlotte Forten published their observations in the *Atlantic Monthly*. Mansfield French and Frances Gage wrote articles about the sea islands for the *New York Tribune*. Mrs. Gage went on an extensive lecture tour in the winter of 1863-64, giving more than 75 lectures about the Port Royal freedmen.[41]

An ever-increasing number of northern conservatives were becoming convinced by the success of the scattered free labor experiments that immediate emancipation was safe and practicable. But the glowingly optimistic reports written for publication by teachers, labor superintendents, and other freedmen's aid workers contained only part of the truth. For many years abolitionists had argued that the dehumanizing institution of slavery destroyed nearly every vestige of manhood, morality, and intelligence in its victims. When the Gideonites first came South and saw for themselves the abject, servile character of many contrabands, their

[39] Sarah Hopper Emerson, *Life of Abby Hopper Gibbons* (2 vols., New York, 1896-97), I, 248, 296-395, II, 1-42, 70-101, 108-32. The letter to Mrs. Gibbons is quoted from *ibid.*, II, 39.

[40] Parmelee, "Freedmen's Aid Societies," *op. cit.*, 273, 277, 284; *Nineteenth Annual Report of the American Missionary Association* (New York, 1865), 18-29; *Philadelphia Ledger*, Aug. 10, 1865.

[41] Edward L. Pierce, "The Freedmen at Port Royal," *Atlantic Monthly*, XII (Sept. 1863), 302-15; Charlotte Forten, "Life in the Sea Islands," *Atlantic Monthly*, XIII (May 1864), 587-96, and (June 1864), 666-76; Mansfield French to S. H. Gay, Oct. 14, 21, 23, 1862, Gay Papers, CU; Frances D. Gage to Matilda Joslyn Gage, Nov. 20, 1863, Gage Papers, Radcliffe Women's Archives; *N.A.S. Standard*, Dec. 12, 1863, Mar. 26, 1864.

theories about slavery were quickly confirmed. But to report the objective truth about the freedmen would only confirm the stereotype of the servile, shiftless, barbarous Negro. Hence in most of their *published* reports and letters they played down the ignoble qualities of the freedmen and emphasized their rapid progress and remarkable achievements under freedom. The countless trials, heartbreaks, and disillusionments faced by the Gideonites were rarely mentioned in public accounts of their work.

Typical of some of the teachers' published reports was this statement by Linda Slaughter, an Ohio abolitionist and teacher for the A.M.A.: "Already has the Freedman been quickened intellectually. . . . What has not freedom done for him? The brutish mind, the servile demeanor, and the clouded soul have given place to noble impulses. . . . A nation has been born in a day. . . . Steadily are they rising; steadfastly are they progressing. . . . The Freedmen are destined shortly to become the ruling race in the South. Labor and education . . . soon will elevate them above the aristocratic level of their former masters."[42]

Such rosy accounts may have been necessary to convince the North of the success of emancipation, but many abolitionists recognized the dangers inherent in these enthusiastic statements. In the first place they did not accurately reflect the facts of the freedmen's character, the difficulty of the transition to freedom, and the many disappointments experienced by the freedmen's aid workers. Secondly, if the Negro found the transition to freedom as easy as Linda Slaughter and others represented it, slavery could not have been such a bad institution after all—but most abolitionists who went South agreed privately that slavery was even worse than they had suspected. Thirdly, these optimistic and exaggerated reports of progress could only build up such high expectations that disillusionment would be inevitable when the real facts of the freedmen's character, abilities, and status became known.

Many teachers of the freedmen warned against rosy distortion of the condition of affairs in the South. A Massachusetts abolitionist teaching in an A.M.A. school at Norfolk wrote in 1863 that on the whole the Negroes were behaving well in freedom. But "some injudicious letter-writers from the South would make them

[42] Linda Slaughter, *The Freedmen of the South* (Cincinnati, 1869), 177, 179.

out *better* than other men and women, almost angelic. . . . This is as unjust and foolish as to go to the other extreme, like the New York *Herald*. They are human, and then, from their births, outraged and wronged, their ideas of morals are very vague and few. How could they be otherwise? . . . Some are honest, some are not. Some are stupid and dull, some brilliant and learn quick. . . . Well, I think it was just so, up in the Old Bay State . . . and, I presume, it is so still, and ever will be with 'white folks' children."

Another A.M.A. teacher at Norfolk wrote in July 1863: "I have sometimes feared, when reading letters from friends of the negro, south, who naturally enough want to look upon the bright side of the slave's character, that false impressions would be made regarding the capabilities of the negroes. . . . We must stand face to face with stern and revolting facts. The contrabands *are* low and degraded, but is it *their* reproach? They *are* unfit for freedom, but are they any more fit for oppression, or will longer servitude ever better prepare them to receive the glorious heritage of liberty? They are what the accursed system of slavery has made them."[43]

An abolitionist friend of Garrison, serving as a Union army chaplain at New Bern, North Carolina, wrote a letter to the *Liberator* asserting that the condition of some of the freedmen was appalling, their morals low, their minds ignorant. "But when we think of the circumstances under which they have been raised, we cannot wonder at their condition. Herded and worked like cattle, . . . kept in total ignorance, governed through their fears, bought and sold, beaten and bruised at will,—no wonder that they are unloving, suspicious, treacherous, impure, passionate, degraded." Abolitionists and all friends of the freedmen should confront these realities with a clear eye. "There must be nothing sentimental or romantic. They, the freedmen, are not angels, they are not even civilized men. . . . We must begin at the root. We must deal with them as children in intellect, but men in instincts and passions. . . . It is useless, it is folly to disguise the difficulties, or to throw a false halo of romance about the negro. It is the highest proof of a genuine sympathy and interest, to admit all

[43] The two letters were published in the *Principia*, June 25 and July 23, 1863.

the disagreeable features of the work, to realize all the difficulties, and *still to go on*."[44]

William Channing Gannett was one of the most thoughtful and objective participants in the Port Royal experiment. Not yet twenty-two years old when he arrived on the sea islands in the spring of 1862, Gannett was the son of one of New England's foremost Unitarian ministers. While attending Harvard he had become an abolitionist and an admirer of Wendell Phillips. He graduated Phi Beta Kappa from Harvard in 1860, and joined the first shipload of Gideonites to Port Royal in March 1862. Gannett stayed on the islands until 1865. After the war he became a prominent Unitarian clergyman and a leader in the Social Gospel movement.[45]

Gannett was a penetrating and lucid thinker. During the war he commented frequently on the progress of the Port Royal experiment. Taken together, his observations constitute a remarkably objective and valuable analysis of the experiment by a participant in it. Gannett considered the experiment a success. "I feel no doubt," he wrote in 1863, "that under conditions of peace, three years would find these people, with but very few exceptions, a self-respecting, self-supporting population." Their behavior had suggested the capacity and power of development. "Their principal vices—dishonesty, indolence, unchastity, their dislike of responsibility, and unmanly willingness to be dependent on others for what their own effort might bring,—their want of forethought and inability to organize and combine operations for mutual benefit . . . can be traced naturally and directly to slavery."[46]

In 1865 Gannett concluded his tour of duty among the freedmen. He published an important article on the freedmen in the *North American Review* of July 1865; and in the fall of the year he visited England, lecturing frequently to eager British audiences on his experiences at Port Royal. In his article and lectures Gannett constantly reiterated that "the real wrong in slavery did not affect the body, but it was a curse to the soul and mind of the

[44] *Liberator*, Apr. 3, 1863.
[45] William H. Pease, "William Channing Gannett, A Social Biography," Ph.D. dissertation, U. of Rochester, 1955, passim.
[46] Pearson, *Letters from Port Royal*, 177-79.

slave. The aim of the master was to keep down every principle of manhood and growth."[47] As a result the slave became childlike and dependent. "In slavery, not only are natural rights denied, but, what is quite as injurious, necessary wants are supplied; everything contributes to the repression of faculty. The slaveholder's institution is a nursery for perpetuating infancy."[48]

In mental ability, said Gannett, the Negroes showed surprising quickness in the faculties of perception and intuition, but were slow in constructive reasoning. This was a defect of training, not of innate capacity. "They have capacity, but lack ability,—the term properly applicable to the mind which by discipline has control of its powers. That the faculty exists dormantly and awaits its training is indicated by the fact that in many individuals it is already partially developed."[49]

Slavery had also dulled the Negro's sense of conjugal fidelity. Sexual promiscuity was encouraged by the example and regulations of the master race. "On the Sea Islands the plantation is a rare exception on which the white family has not contributed to populate the negro houses." There were no proper marriages among slaves; husbands or wives could be sold away from each other, or from their children. "Thus all the props which society usually affords to chastity are changed under slavery into stumblingblocks."[50] In reply to the charge of dishonesty and mendacity commonly leveled against the Negro race, Gannett pointed out that the slave had virtually no protection under law, so he lied to protect himself from abuse and punishment. A piece of property himself, he could have little appreciation of the sanctity of the rest of his master's property. "Laziness, dishonesty, and licentiousness," wrote Gannett, "are the very habits which it is impossible, even in conception, to dissociate from slavery."[51]

Gannett presented a cautiously optimistic view of the future. "If a people were really unfit for freedom," he declared, "it seems likely that emancipation would render them not only paupers, but a race of beggars." Nothing of the kind had occurred at

---

[47] Clipping from *Bristol Post* (England), Oct. 23, 1865, in the Gannett Papers, RU.

[48] [William C. Gannett], "The Freedmen at Port Royal," *North American Review*, CI (July 1865), 1.

[49] *ibid.*, 2-3.

[50] *ibid.*, 13.

[51] *ibid.*, 11-13.

Port Royal. But the road to freedom would not be smooth. "Not only do their old habits cling to the freedmen as they rise, but their ignorance will betray them into new and perilous mistakes. We look for slow progress and much disappointment. . . . For a time discouragement and failure await the eager restorer." But Gannett concluded that these disappointments and setbacks should never dissuade America from her goal of equal rights and opportunities, under law, for all men.[52]

[52] *ibid.*, 25-28.

VIII ✦ THE CREATION OF THE FREED-
MEN'S BUREAU

T HE abolitionists began urging the government to adopt a uniform administrative policy toward the freedmen as soon as it became clear that some degree of emancipation would result from the Civil War. The administrative situation during most of the war was chaotic. One system of caring for the contrabands and utilizing their labor prevailed in Virginia, another at Port Royal, another in Louisiana, and still another in the Mississippi Valley north of Louisiana. There were frequent conflicts of authority regarding freedmen's affairs between the Army and the Treasury Department. Military officers in command of occupation forces believed that the disposition of the contrabands should be under their authority, while the Treasury Department, which had charge of abandoned lands and estates, tried to control the Negro labor that cultivated these lands. Military commanders often placed the Negroes in unsanitary, overcrowded contraband camps where disease and death were common. Lessees of abandoned estates frequently treated their contraband laborers as if they were still slaves.[1]

Foreseeing this unsatisfactory situation, abolitionists in the early months of the war recommended the creation of a federal bureau of emancipation to coordinate and administer the treatment of freedmen. In a sermon at New Bedford, Massachusetts in July 1861, abolitionist William J. Potter stated that "with an act of emancipation, let there be a new Executive Bureau established . . . to care for and protect, and educate these four millions of new born freemen." In January 1862, John Jay urged upon Senator Sumner the necessity of a bureau "to take charge of the blacks wherever our army lands in the Southern States, under rules & regulations to be prepared by the War Department."[2]

In 1862 the Emancipation League initiated a campaign to

---

[1] George R. Bentley, *A History of the Freedmen's Bureau* (Philadelphia, 1955), 16-29; Bell I. Wiley, *Southern Negroes, 1861-1865* (New Haven, 1938), 175-259.

[2] *N.A.S. Standard*, July 27, 1861; Jay to Sumner, Jan. 4, 1862, Sumner Papers, HU.

persuade the government to create an emancipation bureau.[3] In September, Samuel Gridley Howe visited Washington, talked with Chase and other officials, and reported that he found them friendly to the idea of a bureau.[4] The League sent a memorial to the United States Senate, signed by leading abolitionists and Republicans in Massachusetts, requesting creation of an emancipation bureau. "The exigencies of the hour demand more than aught else a Bureau at Washington which shall be devoted to the emancipation of slaves, and their employment," declared the *Commonwealth* in an editorial supporting the memorial. The cruelty and outrages inflicted upon the freedmen by the Army and by Treasury agents, argued the *Commonwealth*, were the result of administrative anarchy in dealing with the freedmen. Freedmen's aid societies could not help the Negroes unless they were assisted by a sympathetic and powerful government agency. An emancipation bureau was needed "to see that Justice, that the right of fair trial, that a field for his labor, are secured to the Negro."[5]

Garrisonian abolitionists seconded the demand for an emancipation bureau. "Without fitting measures, [the Emancipation Proclamation] is worth little to our generation," said Wendell Phillips in January 1863. "Long before this, there should have been created a 'Bureau of Freedmen,' to guard and aid the advent of these millions into the condition of freedmen." Edmund Quincy wanted an agency "to make provision for the first necessities of the freedmen, to allot them lands out of those forfeited by the rebels, [and] to organize and protect their labor." The Massachusetts and New York Anti-Slavery Societies passed resolutions urging creation of a bureau "for the special purpose of guarding the rights and interests of the liberated bondsmen, providing them with land and labor, and giving them a fair chance to develop their faculties and powers through the necessary educational instrumentalities."[6]

[3] Frank Bird to John Andrew, Nov. 15, 1862, Andrew Papers, MHS; S. G. Howe to S. P. Chase, Nov. 19, 1862, Chase Papers, LC; Frank Bird to Benjamin Butler, Dec. 11, 1862, Butler Papers, LC; Frank Sanborn to S. P. Chase, Dec. 8, 1862, Sanborn to Charles Sumner, Dec. 9, 1862, James Redpath to Sumner, Feb. 7, 1863, Sumner Papers, HU; Sanborn to ?, Dec. 28, 1862, Sanborn Papers, Concord Public Library; *Commonwealth*, Dec. 13, 1862.

[4] S. G. Howe to Frank Bird, Sept. 17, 1862, in Laura E. Richards, *Letters and Journals of Samuel Gridley Howe* (Boston, 1909), 502.

[5] "Memorial of the Emancipation League," *Senate Misc. Docs.*, 37 Cong., 3 Sess., no. 10; *Commonwealth*, Jan. 17, 1863.

[6] Phillips' statement quoted in *Liberator*, Jan. 9, 1863; Quincy's statement

Abolitionists realized that they would have a better case for a freedmen's bureau if they could present reliable facts about the condition of the freedmen. "We must be able to present," wrote Samuel Gridley Howe, "as early as possible, a general and reliable coup d'oeil of the actual condition of those who are actually out of the house of bondage; their wants and their capacities. We must collect facts and use them as ammunition." In pursuance of Howe's suggestion the Emancipation League in December 1862 sent a questionnaire to superintendents and supervisors of freedmen's affairs. They received prompt replies from eight supervisors, which were published by the League in the *Commonwealth* and in pamphlet form.[7]

The questionnaire sought information on the industriousness of the freedmen, their scale of wages, whether white men were paid more than freedmen for the same work, and whether freedmen's wages were promptly paid; the habits of the freedmen with regard to intemperance, chastity, honesty, and religion; and the capacity and desire of the freedmen for education. The purpose of the questionnaire was to bring facts "to bear upon the problem as to what is to be the *status* of the negro after the Rebellion is suppressed." On the basis of this information the League hoped to persuade Congress to establish a freedmen's bureau.

The replies came from the District of Columbia, Virginia, South Carolina, Arkansas, and Missouri. Most of them agreed that with proper incentives the freedmen worked well. Average wages paid by the government varied from $7 to $10 per month, plus rations and clothing. White laborers were usually paid more for the same work. Several of the replies stated that freedmen's wages were usually paid late, sometimes not at all, causing distrust and a tendency to shirk. Most of the replies agreed that the freedmen's sexual morals could stand a great deal of improvement. Some of

---

published in *N.A.S. Standard*, Jan. 24, 1863; resolutions of Massachusetts and New York Anti-Slavery Societies published in *Liberator*, Feb. 6, 1863, and *N.A.S. Standard*, Mar. 7, 1863. The Massachusetts Society sent a copy of its resolution to President Lincoln, Lincoln Papers, LC.

7 S. G. Howe to F. W. Bird, Sept. 17, 1862, in Richards, *Letters and Journals of S. G. Howe*, 502; *Commonwealth*, Jan. 24, 1863; *Facts Concerning the Freedmen, Their Capacity and Their Destiny, Collected by and Published by the Emancipation League* (Boston, 1863). See also *New York Tribune*, Dec. 26, 1862; and *N.A.S. Standard*, Jan. 17, 1863.

the reports declared that slavery had fostered in the Negroes the vices of lying and stealing, but others emphasized that the freedmen were remarkably honest in view of their past training. All replies agreed that the freedmen showed a strong desire for education and were capable of learning as fast and as well as comparable classes of whites. Most replies stated that the Negroes were a religious people but that their piety seemed to have little relation to morality. Several reports complained of ill treatment and contemptuous conduct toward the freedmen by Union officers and soldiers.

The final series of questions asked by the Emancipation League was: "Are the freedmen in your department fit to take their place in society . . . with a fair prospect of self-support and progress? or do they need any preparatory training and guardianship? . . . And would they need any different training and guardianship from what other men, equally ignorant, would need?" Most of the replies stated that a temporary system of government protection would be necessary during the difficult transition period and until some degree of recovery was achieved in the war-torn South. Once peace and order were restored, however, "equal laws *faithfully* administered" would be better than any program of guardianship or apprenticeship. Most of the replies compared the Negroes favorably with southern "poor whites" and asserted that the freedmen, with education and a minimum of guidance, could become capable members of society. Some of the replies emphasized that settlement of the freedmen on land of their own would greatly facilitate the transition from slavery to a prosperous freedom. The Emancipation League presented the questionnaire and replies to the government in the hope that Congress could use them as a guide in framing a freedmen's bureau bill.

After his visit to Port Royal in June 1862, J. Miller McKim began to advocate the creation of a government commission to investigate the condition and needs of the freedmen and make a formal report. McKim visited Washington in December 1862, and urged his idea of a freedmen's inquiry commission upon Senator Sumner, Congressmen Thaddeus Stevens and John Bingham, and Secretary of War Stanton. All of these men seemed to favor the project, although Stanton advised caution. McKim thought that a congressional commission would be best, and Stevens agreed with him. Stanton and Sumner, however, favored an executive commission that could be appointed quietly and go to work without the possibly harmful fanfare of a congressional debate. McKim was convinced by their reasoning. Sumner, McKim, and Stanton discussed possible appointees to the commission. Someone suggested McKim himself as a member but he declined, arguing that no old-line Garrisonian should be included on the commission because his presence might prejudice conservatives against its findings. Several names of possible members were mentioned, but McKim left Washington without anything final having been decided. He returned to the capital in January for another discussion, but still nothing was decided. McKim expressed a desire to be secretary of the proposed commission, and he evidently left for Philadelphia with the understanding that he would be appointed secretary.[8]

In March 1863, the War Department announced the formation of the "American Freedmen's Inquiry Commission" (A.F.I.C.) to investigate the condition and needs of the freedmen within Union lines. The Commission consisted of three members: Robert Dale Owen, Samuel Gridley Howe, and James McKaye. All were wartime emancipationists, and Howe was a prewar abolitionist. Instead of a secretary, a stenographer would accompany the commissioners to the South and take down verbatim testimony of military commanders, labor superintendents, teachers, and the freedmen themselves. McKim and his Garrisonian friends were chagrined that McKim was not appointed secretary, but they swallowed their disappointment and praised the membership of the Commission. McKim furnished Owen with memoranda of his visit to the sea islands and copies of the reports of British and French commissions on the results of emancipation in the West Indies. Owen could use these reports as models for the report of the A.F.I.C., of which he was chairman.[9]

8 McKim to Frank Bird, Dec. 23, 1862, McKim Papers, NYPL; McKim to Sumner, Dec. 24, 1862, Jan. 2, 20, 1863, Sumner Papers, HU; Gerrit Smith to McKim, Dec. 27, 1862, S. H. Gay to McKim, Jan. 15, 1863, Sumner to McKim, Jan. 13, 30, 1863, Thaddeus Stevens to McKim, Nov. 27, 1862, McKim Papers, Cornell; Oliver Johnson to McKim, Dec. 29, 1862, Sumner to McKim, Jan. 18, 1863, McKim Papers, NYPL; McKim to S. H. Gay, Jan. 3, 1863, Gay Papers, CU.

9 O.R., Ser. 3, vol. III, 73-74; N.A.S. Standard, Mar. 28, 1863; Liberator, Apr. 17, 1863; Commonwealth, Mar. 27, 1863; Sumner to Howe, Mar. 14, 1863, Sumner-

The three commissioners set up headquarters in New York and began to plan their method of procedure. They decided to visit personally as many parts of the Union-occupied South as possible and send questionnaires to areas they were unable to visit. All three commissioners inspected freedmen's camps in Virginia in the spring of 1863, and McKaye went to Port Royal in June. On June 30, 1863, the Commission submitted a brief preliminary report of their activities and conclusions up to that point, written primarily by Owen. Owen had not been a prewar abolitionist, although he was active in other reform movements. He came to Washington at the beginning of the war and soon became an articulate wartime emancipationist. He met and formed friendships with several abolitionists and worked closely with them during the war. Owen had a receptive rather than original mind. His biographer states that he absorbed many abolitionist ideas during the war. This is probably true, because both the preliminary and final reports of the A.F.I.C. contained numerous abolitionist ideas and recommendations.[10]

The preliminary report asserted that freedmen worked well for wages if they were promptly paid. Their vices "are such as appertain to their former social condition." Thievery and lying were common among them, but "men who are allowed no property do not learn to respect the rights of property. Men who are subjected to despotic rule acquire the habit of shielding themselves from arbitrary punishment by subterfuges." The report recommended the establishment of a freedmen's bureau to bring order out of the chaos of freedmen's affairs. The bureau should function at least until the end of the war, should supervise the employment and wage contracts of freedmen, and should establish courts to adjudicate disputes relating to freedmen. The preliminary report

---

Howe Correspondence, HU; Sumner to Frank Bird, Mar. 19, 1863, Bird Papers, HU; McKim to Sumner, Mar. 21, 23, 1863, W. H. Furness to Sumner, Mar. 30, 1863, Sumner Papers, HU; Oliver Johnson to McKim, Mar. 25, 1863, McKim Papers, Cornell; McKim to W. H. Furness, Mar. 28, Apr. 3, 6, 1863, McKim to Caroline Weston, Sept. 14, 1863, McKim to R. D. Owen, Mar. 30, 1863, McKim Papers, NYPL. The stenographer who accompanied the commissioners on their investigations was J. M. W. Yerrington, a Boston abolitionist who usually reported the speeches of Wendell Phillips and the proceedings of antislavery conventions.

[10] Richard W. Leopold, *Robert Dale Owen: A Biography* (Cambridge, Mass., 1940), vii, 350-51.

The Contraband Camp at City Point—an Evening Prayer Meeting.
Joseph Becker in *Leslie's Illustrated Newspaper*

emphasized the need for teaching the Negroes self-reliance. Charity was acceptable as a means of temporary relief, but freedmen should be put to work as soon as possible on abandoned or confiscated plantations. They should be paid regular and adequate wages and should be given the opportunity to purchase or otherwise acquire confiscated land. The report conceded that the transition to freedom would be difficult, but advised against any system of permanent or semipermanent guardianship of the freedmen. The Negroes were hungry for education, and a school system, staffed by teachers of the freedmen's aid societies, should be established under the auspices of the proposed freedmen's bureau.[11]

[11] The preliminary report is most conveniently accessible in *O.R.*, Ser. 3, vol. III, 430-54.

During the summer Howe went to Ontario to investigate conditions among Negroes there, most of whom had escaped from American slavery. Owen remained in New York and spent the summer doing research on Negro history and preparing a questionnaire which was sent in August to officials all over the country who had anything to do with freedmen. It was modeled on the questionnaire sent out by the Emancipation League the previous December, and the replies were similar. At the end of 1863 Owen and Howe made a tour of contraband camps in Kentucky, Tennessee and Missouri. The following February, McKaye went to New Orleans. The main burden of writing the Commission's final report fell to Owen. He completed it and submitted it to the War Department in May 1864. Its conclusions reflected the thinking of all three commissioners.[12] In the final analysis the report embodied the results of thirty years of abolitionist research and reflection. "Extensive experience in the West Indies has proved that emancipation, when it takes place, should be unconditional and absolute," stated the report. "The experiment of a few years' apprenticeship, plausible in theory, proved, in practice, a failure." This was taken directly from abolitionist writings on emancipation in the West Indies.[13] The report repeated its earlier recommenda-

[12] Harold Schwartz, *Samuel Gridley Howe: Social Reformer* (Cambridge, Mass., 1956), 261-66; Leopold, *Owen*, 360-63.

[13] In their studies of emancipation in the British West Indies, abolitionists emphasized the failure of the gradualist approach. In 1833 the British Parliament had enacted a law emancipating the 668,000 slaves in its West Indian colonies on August 1, 1834. Instead of becoming immediately free, however, the slaves were to remain bound to their masters as apprentices until 1840. Anticipating difficulties under the apprenticeship system, the planters on Antigua granted their slaves immediate and unconditional freedom in 1834. The apprenticeship policy was designed to "prepare" the slaves for freedom, but it proved burdensome, expensive, and unsatisfactory to planter and slave alike. Several planters on the other islands followed Antigua's example and freed their slaves unconditionally, and in 1838 all of the colonial assemblies officially recognized the failure of apprenticeship by decreeing the unconditional emancipation of all slaves on August 1 of that year. Abolitionists were fond of emphasizing the contrast between Antigua and Jamaica. Whereas in Antigua emancipation was immediate, in Jamaica the planters vigorously attempted to keep the Negroes in a state of quasi-slavery by means of the apprenticeship system. As a result the transition to freedom in Antigua was quick and relatively painless; in Jamaica it was slow and painful. Antigua became the most prosperous of the islands, with a high percentage of land ownership and a relatively low illiteracy rate. Jamaica became the least prosperous of the islands. The moral? Immediate emancipation was far superior to gradual emancipation. "If the experience of Antigua and Jamaica teaches anything," concluded Frank Sanborn, "it teaches that simultaneous and entire emancipation is the safest, the cheapest, and the wisest course." Frank Sanborn, *Emancipation in the West*

tion of a freedmen's bureau. "For a time we need a freedmen's bureau, but not because these people are negroes, only because they are men who have been, for generations, despoiled of their rights." Such federal guardianship should be replaced as soon as possible by equal laws equally administered. The same civil and political rights enjoyed by whites should be granted to freedmen. "The essential thing is that we secure to them the means of making their own way; that we give them, to use the familiar phrase, 'a fair chance.' If, like whites, they are to be self-supporting, then, like whites, they ought to have those rights, civil and political, without which they are but laboring as a man labors with hands bound."[14]

A recent historian has called the Commission's report a "Blueprint for Radical Reconstruction." Certain it is that the work of Owen, Howe, and McKaye laid the foundations for the Freedmen's Bureau. One of the first results in Congress of the Commission's activities was the creation of a Senate Committee on Emancipation (later renamed the Committee on Slavery and Freedmen), with Sumner as chairman. Immediately after submission of the Commission's final report, Sumner introduced a resolution calling for copies of the two official reports for his Senate Committee. Several days later he offered a motion to publish 3,000 extra copies of the final report, calling it "one of the most able contributions to this question that has ever appeared in this country or any other country." Republicans carried the motion over Democratic opposition. Congressmen debating the Freedmen's Bureau bill had copies of the report on hand at all times.[15]

Owen published separately in book form a slightly modified version of the final report.[16] Howe also published a book setting forth the results of his investigation of Canadian Negroes. He strongly endorsed the equalitarian laissez-faire approach to eman-

Indies (Boston, 1862), 15. See also Lydia M. Child, *The Right Way the Safe Way* (2nd ed., New York, 1862), 18, 30-31, 33, 58-60, 67; and an article in the *Pine and Palm*, June 21, 1861, by Richard Hinton.

14 "Final Report of the American Freedmen's Inquiry Commission," *O.R.*, Ser. 3, vol. IV, 289-382. Quoted passages from 381-82.

15 John G. Sproat, "Blueprint for Radical Reconstruction," *Journal of Southern History*, XXIII (February 1957), 25-44; *Senate Journal*, 37 Cong., 1 Sess., 649-50; *Cong. Globe*, 38 Cong., 1 Sess., 3,285-87; *Senate Exec. Docs.*, 38 Cong., 1 Sess., no. 53 (ser. no. 1,176).

16 Robert D. Owen, *The Wrong of Slavery, the Right of Emancipation, and the Future of the African Race in the United States* (New York, 1864).

cipation and the transition to freedom emphasized by the A.F.I.C. reports. "The negro does best when let alone," argued Howe, and "we must beware of all attempts to prolong his servitude, even under pretext of taking care of him. The white man has tried taking care of the negro, by slavery, by apprenticeship, by colonization, and has failed disastrously in all; now let the negro try to take care of himself."[17] At the beginning of 1864, Howe wrote a public letter to Congressman Thomas D. Eliot of Massachusetts, chairman of the House Committee considering a freedmen's bureau bill. Howe warned Eliot that "whatever plan is adopted, should be founded on the principle that the negro, once emancipated, is as free as a white man; free to go or to come; free to accept or reject employment; free to work or to starve." A system of guardianship or apprenticeship would be nothing less than "a prolongation of slavery or servitude disguised under the name of *protection*." What was needed, said Howe, was not guardianship but "some general system for putting the negroes upon their own legs, and defending them against those who will strive to push them down, and keep them down."[18]

Most abolitionists favored this equalitarian laissez-faire approach. Frederick Douglass was one of the strongest proponents of such a policy. In reply to the oft-repeated question, "What shall we do with the Negroes?", Douglass said:

"Our answer is, do nothing with them; mind your business, and let them mind theirs. Your *doing* with them is their greatest misfortune. They have been undone by your doings, and all they now ask and really have need of at your hands, is just to let them alone. ... If you see [a Negro] on his way to school, with spelling book, geography and arithmetic in his hands—let him alone. Don't shut the door in his face. ... We would not for one moment check the outgrowth of any benevolent concern for the future welfare of the colored race in America or elsewhere; but in the name of reason and religion, we earnestly plead for justice before all else. Benevolence with justice is harmonious and beautiful; but benevolence without justice is a mockery. Let the American people, who have thus far only kept the colored race staggering between partial

[17] Samuel G. Howe, *The Refugees from Slavery in Canada West* (Boston, 1864), 104.
[18] *Commonwealth*, Jan. 8, 1864.

philanthropy and cruel force, be induced to try what virtue there is in justice."[19]

While the A.F.I.C. was doing its work, abolitionists kept up the pressure for a freedmen's bureau. In 1863 abolitionist Josephine S. Griffing came to Washington as an agent of the Western Freedmen's Aid Commission. She was appalled by the destitution and misery of the thousands of freedmen who had flocked to the city. She served also as an agent of the National Freedmen's Relief Association in Washington, and was put in charge of doling out governmental and philanthropic aid to the Negroes. She established sewing schools for the women, some of whom became proficient enough to support themselves by making clothes. She found jobs and homes in the North for hundreds of freedmen and their families. But Mrs. Griffing soon discovered that the task was too big for haphazard government relief and private philanthropy. She began to urge the creation of a freedmen's bureau to dispense emergency relief, foster education, and help settle the freedmen in remunerative occupations. Her winning personality and obvious sincerity made a favorable impression on Lincoln, Stanton, Sumner, and other government officials with whom she discussed the subject of a freedmen's bureau.[20]

On November 9, 1863, officials of the freedmen's aid societies of Boston, New York, and Philadelphia held a rally at Cooper Union to bring pressure on the government in behalf of a freedmen's bureau. These three societies plus the Cincinnati organization sent a delegation to Lincoln. The president expressed

[19] *Douglass' Monthly*, Jan. 1862; speech of Douglass at the annual meeting of the Massachusetts Anti-Slavery Society, Jan. 25, 1865, in *Liberator*, Feb. 10, 1865. The idea of some sort of temporary apprenticeship or guardianship for a people emerging from slavery and woefully ignorant of the responsibilities of freedom has a certain attractiveness, even for the liberal. A wisely administered paternal guardianship might have moderated some of the excesses of Reconstruction and paved the way for ultimately better race relations in the South. But in the context of the 1860's and 1870's a wise paternal guidance was probably impossible. After all, apprenticeship had failed in the British West Indies under better conditions than those which existed in the postwar South. Abolitionist fears that temporary guardianship would become a device for perpetual subordination of the Negro were well founded, for this was pretty much what happened in the South after 1877.

[20] Mrs. Griffing's activities are discussed in Elizabeth Cady Stanton et al., *History of Woman Suffrage* (6 vols., New York, 1881-1922), II, 26-30. See also Mrs. Griffing to Garrison, Aug. 19, 1864, published in *Liberator*, Aug. 26, 1864.

his sympathy with their objective and suggested that they draw up a memorial which he would submit to Congress. A committee drafted the memorial and sent it to Lincoln on December 1, 1863. It urged the president to "interpose" with Congress and recommend "the immediate creation of a bureau of emancipation." The care of the freedmen had become a matter beyond the resources of private benevolent societies. The problem required "the best ability the country offers" and a "regularly constituted government bureau, with all the machinery and civil powers of the government behind it." Congressman Thomas Eliot of Massachusetts had introduced a freedmen's bureau bill at the previous session of Congress, but his measure had died quietly in committee. He reintroduced the bill in the 1863-64 session, and shortly afterwards Lincoln sent the memorial of the freedmen's aid societies to Congress as part of a special message endorsing the idea of a freedmen's bureau. J. Miller McKim, Francis George Shaw, Levi Coffin, and other officials of the freedmen's societies spent several weeks in Washington during the winter lobbying for the bill.[21]

Eliot's bill provided for the establishment of a bureau within the War Department to dispense relief, supervise the labor of freed Negroes, provide them with educational facilities, make rules and regulations for their treatment, establish freedmen's courts, and settle the Negroes on abandoned or confiscated lands. Democrats charged that the bill was unconstitutional and would centralize too much power in the federal government. But it passed the House on March 1, 1864. In the Senate, however, it ran into a roadblock set up by its friends. Sumner reported the bill out of committee with an amendment placing the Bureau under the Treasury instead of the War Department. He believed that the most important part of the bill was the provision for settling freedmen on confiscated land. Such land was under the control of the Treasury Department, and Sumner wanted the Bureau to be in the same Department. Military men, however, argued that the Bureau logically belonged in the War Depart-

[21] *Commonwealth*, Dec. 11, 1863; *Senate Exec. Docs.*, 38 Cong., 1 Sess., no. 1 (serial no. 1,176); *New York Tribune*, Dec. 28, 1863; Elizabeth Gay to Sarah Pugh, Feb. 21, 1864, Gay Papers, cu; Levi Coffin, *Reminiscences* (Cincinnati, 1880), 647-48.

ment since the army controlled the occupied South. Abolitionists warned Sumner against pressing his version of the bill: the House had passed the act by such a narrow margin that any Senate changes might jeopardize final passage. Sumner persisted, however, and the Senate passed his version on June 28, 1864.[22]

Consequently no bill at all was enacted in 1864, and the matter carried over to the next session. When Congress met in December it was confronted by several more petitions from freedmen's aid societies and other groups urging creation of a bureau. Abolitionists continued to press Sumner to accept a bureau as an autonomous agency within the War Department. Sumner finally agreed to this proposal provided that control of confiscated lands was also placed in the War Department. This was done and the bill finally passed both Houses and was signed by Lincoln on March 3, 1865.[23]

Some abolitionists hoped that Lincoln would appoint a prominent antislavery man as head of the new Bureau.[24] But the president and his military commanders wanted to keep it under army control. Most of the commissioners and assistant commissioners of the Bureau were generals, and a majority of the subordinate posts were filled by lower-grade army officers. Several abolitionists, however, were appointed to important positions in the Bureau. Josephine Griffing served as sub-assistant commissioner in the District of Columbia. John W. Alvord, one of the earliest abolitionists, was appointed superintendent of schools of the Freedmen's Bureau. Reuben Tomlinson served as superintendent of schools for the Bureau in South Carolina. Several other abolitionists who came South with the freedmen's aid societies held positions in the Bureau. In addition, General O. O. Howard, head of the Bureau, was sympathetic with the antislavery cause. Several

---

[22] Bentley, *Freedmen's Bureau*, 36-43; *Cong. Globe*, 38 Cong., 1 Sess., 566-73, 760-63, 893-95, 908, 2,457, 2,798-2,801, 2,931-35, 3,350, 3,527; *Commonwealth*, Apr. 22, 1864.

[23] *Liberator*, Dec. 9, 1864; *Independent*, Feb. 9, 1865; Bentley, *Freedmen's Bureau*, 46-49; *Cong. Globe*, 38 Cong., 2 Sess., 563-66, 766-68, 983-90, 1,348, 1,402; *U.S. Statutes at Large*, xiii, 507-09.

[24] Martin Conway to Garrison, Jan. 1, 1864, J. S. Griffing to Garrison, Mar. 24, 1864, Garrison Papers, BPL; James Birney to S. P. Chase, Jan. 25, 1864, Chase Papers, LC; John Andrew to S. H. Gay, Feb. 16, 1864, Gay Papers, CU; *Liberator*, Jan. 29, 1864; *N.A.S. Standard*, Mar. 11, 1865; *Commonwealth*, Mar. 18, 1865.

assistant commissioners had been antislavery sympathizers before the war. General Rufus Saxton, assistant commissioner for South Carolina, had been raised by an abolitionist father and had associated with abolitionists during much of his life.[25]

Abolitionists played a major role in the formation of the Freedmen's Bureau. It is probable that some kind of a bureau would have been established without abolitionist urging, but much of the credit for the liberal features of the Freedmen's Bureau bill must go to the abolitionists. They were the first to call for establishment of a bureau. The Emancipation League exerted great pressure on Congress and laid some of the groundwork for a bureau with its questionnaire of 1862. The abolitionist-dominated freedmen's aid societies paved the way for inclusion of education as one of the main objectives of the Bureau. J. Miller McKim fathered the establishment of the Freedmen's Inquiry Commission which in turn formulated the basic principles of the Freedmen's Bureau bill. Abolitionist Samuel Gridley Howe served on that Commission. The opposition of the Commission and of abolitionists to any sort of apprenticeship or guardianship for the freedmen helped prepare the way for the Bureau's treatment of freedmen as free men. Abolitionists could be justly proud of their part in the creation of the Freedmen's Bureau.

[25] Stanton et al., *History of Woman Suffrage*, II, 33-39; Henry Lee Swint, *The Northern Teacher in the South, 1862-1870* (Nashville, 1941), 6, 143; Reuben Tomlinson to J. M. McKim, May 14, 1869, McKim Papers, Cornell; T. W. Higginson to Louisa Higginson, June 22, 1863, Rufus Saxton to Higginson, Dec. 13, 1905, Higginson Papers, HU.

IX ✦ MEN OF COLOR, TO ARMS!

THE enlistment of Negro troops in the Union Army beginning in late 1862 was one of the most revolutionary features of the Civil War. Colored men had fought in the American Army during the Revolution, and New Orleans Negroes had helped Andrew Jackson defend the city against the British in 1815, but since 1792 Negroes had been barred by federal law from the state militias and there were no Negroes in the regular United States Army. In 1859 the Massachusetts legislature passed a bill repealing the ban on Negro militia service. But Governor Nathaniel Banks vetoed the measure because it conflicted with the federal law of 1792. Public opinion in 1860, except perhaps in a few of the New England states, was overwhelmingly opposed to allowing Negroes in the militia or the army.[1]

With the outbreak of war in 1861 many Negroes and abolitionists believed the national emergency would compel the North to waive its prejudices and accept regiments of Negro volunteers. Frederick Douglass and other abolitionists urged Negroes in northern cities to form militia companies. Within 36 hours of Lincoln's first call for troops, Boston Negroes met and resolved to organize militia units. Philadelphia Negroes began to recruit two regiments. Colored men in New York began drilling in a privately hired hall. In many parts of the North free Negroes were prepared to join the army if the government would accept them.[2] The Negro knew that if he demonstrated his patriotism, manhood, and courage on the battlefields of the Union, the nation would be morally obligated to grant him citizenship and equal rights. As Frederick Douglass put it: "Once let the black man get upon his person the brass letters, *U.S.*; let him get an eagle on his button, and a musket on his shoulder and bullets in his pocket, and there is no power on earth which can deny that he has earned the right to citizenship in the United States."[3]

[1] Francis W. Bird, *Review of Gov. Banks' Veto of the Revised Code, on Account of its Authorizing the Enrollment of Colored Citizens in the Militia* (Boston, 1860).

[2] Benjjamin Quarles, *The Negro in the Civil War* (Boston, 1953), 24-29; Dudley Taylor Cornish, *The Sable Arm: Negro Troops in the Union Army, 1861-65* (New York, 1956), 2-3, 6-7; *Liberator*, May 3, 10, 17, 1861.

[3] *Douglass' Monthly*, Aug. 1863.

But the North was not ready in 1861 to let Negroes help save the nation. "We don't want to fight side and side with the nigger," wrote Corporal Felix Brannigan of the New York 74th. "We think we are a too superior race for that." In April Secretary of War Cameron informed a Negro who had offered 300 colored volunteers to help defend the capital that "this Department has no intention at present to call into the service of the Government any colored soldiers."[4]

Abolitionists reacted with predictable wrath to the government's refusal to employ Negro troops. "What upon earth is the matter with the American Government and people?" asked Frederick Douglass in an angry editorial entitled "Fighting Rebels with only One Hand." The government screamed "Men, men! send us men," but refused to accept the services of Negroes. "Why does the Government reject the negro? Is he not a man? Can he not wield a sword, fire a gun, march and countermarch, and obey orders like any other? . . . This is no time to fight only with your white hand, and allow your black hand to remain tied."[5] Abolitionists extolled the courage of the black man in the war for independence and the War of 1812. They quoted Andrew Jackson's praise of the New Orleans Negroes who had helped defeat the British in 1815.[6] "Colored men were good enough to fight under Washington, but they are not good enough to fight under McClellan," said Douglass sarcastically. "They were good enough to help win American independence, but they are not good enough to help preserve that independence against treason and rebellion."[7]

After the northern defeat at Bull Run many Republicans began to reconsider their belief that white men alone could quickly crush the rebellion. Republican congressmen privately urged the arm-

---

[4] Brannigan quoted in Quarles, *Negro in the Civil War*, 31; the exchange of letters between the Negro volunteer and Cameron is in *O.R.*, Ser. 3, vol. I, 107, 133.

[5] *Douglass' Monthly*, Sept. 1861.

[6] In the fall of 1861 the American Anti-Slavery Society published a pamphlet entitled *Loyalty and Devotion of Colored Americans* (Boston, 1861), detailing the services of Negro soldiers in the Revolution and the War of 1812 and urging the government once again to call black men to the colors to help preserve freedom and Union. For other examples of abolitionist efforts in behalf of the enrollment of Negro soldiers, see John Jay to Sumner, June 19, July 25, 28, 1861, Sumner Papers, HU; *New York Tribune*, July 7, Aug. 8, 1861; *N.A.S. Standard*, May 25, 1861; *Liberator*, Aug. 9, Oct. 18, Nov. 22, Dec. 13, 20, 1861.

[7] Speech by Douglass in New York, Feb. 12, 1862, in *New York Tribune*, Feb. 13.

ing of freed slaves. Republican newspapers began cautiously to broach the proposition in the fall of 1861.[8] At the outbreak of the war Elizur Wright had written several editorials urging the employment of Negro soldiers and had sent them to the *New York Tribune*. They were not printed. But at the end of 1861 when the *Tribune* committed itself to a policy of Negro troops, Wright's editorials, altered slightly to bring them up to date, began appearing in its columns.[9]

More and more northerners were becoming receptive to the idea of Negro soldiers. In a November speech to Colonel John Cochrane's regiment near Washington, Secretary of War Cameron openly advocated the arming of freed slaves as a military necessity. Colonel Cochrane, a nephew of Gerrit Smith and a War Democrat, made a series of speeches in late 1861 urging the use of Negro troops. Conservatives threw up their hands in horror at these suggestions. "Putting arms into the slaves' hands!" exclaimed the *New York Express*. "If this be attempted to any extent, the whole world will cry out against our inhumanity, our savagery, and the sympathies of all mankind will be turned against us." The *New York Journal of Commerce* charged that Cameron and Cochrane had taken "a desperate plunge into the embrace of the Garrison and Phillips party."[10]

Cameron was not disturbed by these cries of alarm. In his annual report to Congress in December he recommended the freeing and arming of slaves of rebels coming into the Union lines. He released the report to the press before Lincoln had read it. The angry president ordered him to recall the report and delete the offending section, but the press and public had already seen the original report. Abolitionists welcomed Cameron's recommendation as the "straightforward and common sense view of the subject." The government would be foolish not to use every resource at its command to win the war. But Lincoln, ever-solicitous of conservative border-state and northern opinion, refused to take this view of the subject.[11]

[8] T. Harry Williams, *Lincoln and the Radicals* (Madison, Wis., 1941), 33; *New York Evening Post*, quoted by *Liberator*, Nov. 8, 1861; *New York Tribune*, Dec. 4, 13, 1861, Jan. 30, 1862.

[9] Wright to Whitelaw Reid, Jan. 30, 1873, Reid Papers, LC.

[10] Cornish, *Sable Arm*, 22; *New York Express* and *New York Journal of Commerce*, quoted by *N.A.S. Standard*, Nov. 30, 1861.

[11] Williams, *Lincoln and the Radicals*, 59; *Liberator*, Dec. 13, 1861.

General Thomas W. Sherman, commander of the Union forces occupying the South Carolina sea islands, had been authorized by Cameron to arm the slaves there "if special circumstances seem to require it." Sherman was opposed to the idea of Negro soldiers, however, and did nothing in the direction of arming slaves. His successor, General David Hunter, was an antislavery sympathizer and decided in May 1862, to organize a Negro regiment on the islands. Most of the Gideonites on the islands were less convinced than their northern abolitionist brethren of the courage and martial ardor of freed slaves. William Gannett wrote in May 1862, that "Negroes—plantation negroes, at least—will never make soldiers in one generation. Five white men could put a regiment to flight."[12] Events seemed to bear out the Gideonites' skepticism, for few freedmen volunteered and Hunter was compelled to order a draft to fill up his regiment. This was a serious mistake. Squads of white soldiers marched into the cotton fields and dragged freedmen off to headquarters, often without explanation. The Negroes began to fear that their old masters' tales about Yankee plans to sell them to Cuba were true after all. They hid in swamps and woods to escape the draft, but were rounded up and driven to General Hunter's headquarters at bayonet point. Teachers and labor superintendents were appalled by Hunter's brutal and ill-advised tactics. The draft was destroying much of the freedmen's confidence in Yankees which had been laboriously built up by the Gideonites. Edward L. Pierce sent strong protests against the draft to Hunter and Chase. Hunter finally filled up his regiment, the first slave regiment to be recruited in the Civil War, but at the cost of sowing no little distrust among the freedmen.[13]

Hunter faced other difficulties as well. Democrats and conservatives in Congress attacked his efforts to arm the freedmen. The Lincoln administration refused to sustain him. The general's repeated requests for uniforms, pay for the soldiers, and authorization for his regiment went unanswered. The government was not yet prepared to commit itself to the arming of Negroes.

[12] Elizabeth Pearson, ed., *Letters from Port Royal* (Boston, 1906), 43.

[13] Cornish, *Sable Arm*, 33-40; Willie Rose, "Rehearsal for Reconstruction: The Port Royal Experiment," Ph.D. dissertation, Johns Hopkins University, 1962, 186-92; Rupert S. Holland, ed., *Letters and Diary of Laura M. Towne, Written from the Sea Islands of South Carolina, 1862-84* (Cambridge, Mass., 1912), 41-54.

Hunter gave up in August 1862, and disbanded all but one company of his regiment. The first attempt to arm the freedmen was an utter failure.[14]

Antislavery Union generals in Kansas and Louisiana also made limited efforts in 1862 to enroll Negro soldiers, but they were not sustained by the administration. In the summer of 1862, however, McClellan's soldiers were bogged down before Richmond and finally driven back by Lee after severe fighting. The defeat was a sharp blow to northern morale. Early in July Lincoln issued a call for 300,000 volunteers, but war-weariness was beginning to creep over the North and few men came forward to join the colors. Public opinion was becoming more favorable to the use of Negro troops to supplement declining white manpower. On July 17, 1862, Congress passed two acts authorizing the president to enlist Negroes as soldiers. The first was the Confiscation Act, which empowered Lincoln to "employ as many persons of African descent as he may deem necessary and proper for the suppression of this rebellion." The second was a militia act repealing the provisions of the 1792 law barring Negroes, and providing for the employment of free Negroes and freedmen as soldiers. Abolitionists applauded these acts and urged President Lincoln to begin immediately to recruit a Negro army from every section of the nation.[15]

But Lincoln was not yet prepared to arm the black man. On August 4 an Indiana delegation offered the government two regiments of colored men from their state, but the president declined the offer. The nation "could not afford to lose Kentucky at this crisis," said Lincoln. "To arm the negroes would turn 50,000 bayonets from the loyal Border States against us that were for us." In vain did abolitionists point out that arming the Negroes would bring many times 50,000 bayonets to the aid of the Union. Lincoln was still solicitous of conservative opinion, and conservatives applauded his speech to the Indiana delegation.[16]

[14] Cornish, *Sable Arm*, 40-53.

[15] Edward L. Pierce, *Memoir and Letters of Charles Sumner* (4 vols., Boston, 1877-94), IV, 112; *U.S. Statutes at Large*, XII, 589-92; *Liberator*, Aug. 8, Sept. 5, 12, 1862.

[16] Roy P. Basler, ed., *The Collected Works of Abraham Lincoln* (9 vols., New Brunswick, N. J., 1955), V, 356-57; *New York Times*, quoted by *New York Tribune*, Aug. 16, 1862.

Yet in the next three weeks the president's opinion on the issue of Negro troops evidently underwent a change, for on August 25 Secretary of War Stanton authorized General Rufus Saxton, military governor of the South Carolina sea islands, to raise five regiments of black soldiers on the islands. Pressure from Republicans and abolitionists, declining white manpower, continuing lack of success of Union arms, and increasing sentiment in the army itself favoring the use of Negro troops were important factors in Lincoln's change of mind. On the sea islands most of the Gideonites had overcome their earlier skepticism about the possibility of making soldiers out of freedmen. Instead of instituting the hated draft, General Saxton relied on volunteers, using the one remaining company of General Hunter's abortive regiment as a nucleus. The Gideonites cooperated enthusiastically, urging the freedmen to enlist to fight for their own freedom and to prove the manhood of their race. Volunteers came forward slowly at first, but by November 7 the regiment was filling up rapidly and was mustered in as the First South Carolina Volunteers. It was the first Negro regiment of the Civil War officially authorized by Washington.[17]

Saxton began looking for the right man to command the regiment. He knew that the eyes of the nation would be focused on this experiment, and he wanted nothing to go wrong. The colonel of the regiment must be fully sympathetic with the experiment, intelligent and flexible but at the same time a strict disciplinarian. J. H. Fowler, a Massachusetts abolitionist serving as chaplain on the sea islands, recommended Thomas Wentworth Higginson as the best man for the job. Several other Gideonites seconded the recommendation. Saxton knew Higginson by reputation, and on November 5 he sent him an official invitation to become colonel of the First South Carolina Volunteers.[18]

Higginson was a true nineteenth century intellectual, a scholar and author imbued with romantic zeal. A leading contributor to the *Atlantic Monthly*, he was also one of New England's most militant abolitionists. He was excited by the prospect of com-

[17] Cornish, *Sable Arm*, 53-55, 80-84, 92-93; O.R., Ser. 1, vol. xiv, 377-78; Rose, "Rehearsal for Reconstruction," 247-51; Holland, *Letters and Diary of Laura Towne*, 86, 93.

[18] Saxton to Higginson, Nov. 5, 1862, Fowler to Higginson, Nov. 10, 1862, Higginson Papers, HU.

manding the first regiment of black men officially mustered into the Union Army. He told the publisher of the *Atlantic Monthly* that he would rather command such a regiment "than anything else in the world."[19] A trip to the sea islands convinced him that the government intended to carry through the enterprise in good faith, and he accepted the colonelcy of the regiment on the spot. "Will not Uncle Wentworth be in bliss!" exclaimed his young niece. "A thousand men, every one as black as coal."[20]

Higginson fully realized the importance of his undertaking. "The first man who organizes and commands a successful black regiment will perform the most important service in the history of the war," he wrote in his journal the day before he assumed his new duties. Chaplain Fowler had observed that "the success or failure of this reg[iment] is to be a most important fact in the solution of this whole Negro question." In May 1863, after his soldiers had proved themselves in several minor battles, Higginson wrote that "there is no doubt that for many months the fate of the whole movement for colored soldiers rested on the behavior of this one regiment. A mutiny, an extensive desertion, an act of severe discipline, a Bull Run panic, a simple defeat, might have blasted the whole movement for arming the blacks." Higginson reported that he had been informed by Secretary Chase that "the Cabinet at Washington kept their whole action in regard to enlisting colored troops waiting to hear from us in Florida, and when the capture of Jacksonville was known [two Negro regiments under Higginson captured Jacksonville in March 1863], the whole question was regarded as settled, the policy avowed."[21]

The performance of Higginson's men was not quite so crucial to the whole policy of Negro soldiers as he pictured it, but it was nevertheless important. After two months of intensive drilling Higginson took his troops on several minor raids into the interior to capture supplies and lumber and to run off slaves. Whenever his men encountered Confederate soldiers they fought

[19] Higginson to James T. Fields, Nov. 17, 1862, A. W. Anthony autograph MS Collection, NYPL.

[20] Higginson to Louisa Higginson, Nov. 16, 1862, Higginson Papers, HU; Higginson's niece quoted in Mary Higginson, *Thomas Wentworth Higginson* (Boston, 1914), 215.

[21] Higginson, Journal, entry of Nov. 23, 1862, J. H. Fowler to Higginson, Nov. 10, 1862, Higginson to Louisa Higginson, May 18, 1863, Higginson Papers, HU.

well, holding their own or besting the rebels. Higginson sent an enthusiastic report of his first expedition to the secretary of war, which found its way into the newspapers. "Nobody knows anything about these men who has not seen them in battle," wrote Higginson. "There is fiery energy beyond anything of which I have read, unless it be the French Zouaves. . . . It would have been madness to attempt with the bravest white troops what I have accomplished with the black ones. . . . No officer in this regiment now doubts that the key to the successful prosecution of the war lies in the unlimited employment of black troops."[22]

The *New York Tribune* prominently featured this report and commented editorially: "It will not need many such reports as this—and there have been several before it—to shake our inveterate Saxon prejudice against the capacity and courage of negro troops." A *New York Times* reporter on the sea islands was even more exuberant. "Our colored troops are more than a match for any equal number of white rebels which can be brought against them," he wrote to his paper, and the *Times*, which had once opposed the use of Negro troops, printed his dispatch happily.[23]

Higginson insisted that the white officers of his regiment treat the Negro soldiers as men. He prohibited the officers from inflicting "degrading punishments" on the troops and from calling them "insulting epithets." He banned the use of the word "nigger" and threatened severe punishment of any officer who uttered it. He inspired respect in his officers and confidence and self-respect in his men.[24] At first most white soldiers sneered or grumbled at the prospect of freed slaves serving in the same army as they. But by the spring of 1863 Higginson's soldiers had won a grudging if not always generous respect from the white troops. Higginson reported that while reviewing a dress parade of his regiment he overheard a white soldier behind him say: "By——, to think of my living to see a nigger regiment drill better than the 104th Pennsylvania." After Higginson's regiment had relieved the 55th Pennsylvania on picket duty one day, Edward L. Pierce asked a private of the 55th: "Isn't this rather new, to be relieved by a negro regiment?" "All right," answered the white soldier.

[22] *O.R.*, Ser. 1, vol. xiv, 194-98.
[23] *New York Tribune*, Feb. 11, 1863; *New York Times*, Feb. 10, 1863.
[24] Cornish, *Sable Arm*, 88-89; Mary Higginson, *Higginson*, 216-18.

"They've as much right to fight for themselves as I have to fight for them."[25]

While serving as colonel of the First South Carolina Volunteers, Higginson kept a journal in which he recorded his observations and experiences. This journal formed the basis of a subsequent series of articles published from 1864 to 1867 in the *Atlantic Monthly*. These articles in turn formed the basis of a book published in 1869 under the title *Army Life in a Black Regiment*, surely one of the true classics of Civil War literature, and according to Howard Mumford Jones "one of the few classics of military life in the national letters."[26]

Higginson's comments in his journal and in his published writings on the character of the freedmen and their adaptability to military life are especially interesting. He found the freedmen equal in courage and superior in enthusiasm to white troops. They took more readily to drill than whites because their plantation background had made them amenable to discipline. They made better over-all soldiers than whites, thought Higginson, because of their "Indian-like knowledge of the country and its ways" and their grim comprehension that they were fighting for the freedom of themselves and their race.[27]

Higginson described the freedmen on the islands as "a simple and loveable people, whose graces seem to come by nature and whose vices by training." He conceded that "they are not truthful, honest, or chaste," but asked, in view of their past training, "why should they be?"[28] His observations dispelled one stereotype of the Negro. Several of the white officers had their wives in camp, and the white women were never molested or annoyed in any way by the black troops. These women, wrote Higginson, "declared that they would not have moved about with anything like the same freedom in any white camp they had ever entered and it

[25] Higginson to Louisa Higginson, June 20, 1863, Higginson Papers, HU; Edward L. Pierce, "The Freedmen at Port Royal," *Atlantic Monthly*, XII (Sept. 1863), 313.

[26] T. W. Higginson, *Army Life in a Black Regiment*, with an introduction by Howard Mumford Jones (Lansing, Mich., 1960 [1869]), xi.

[27] Higginson, Journal, entries of Nov. 27, Dec. 1, 3, 1862, Jan. 12, 13, 1863, Higginson to Louisa Higginson, Dec. 10, 22, 1862, Feb. 24, June 20, 1863, Higginson Papers, HU; Higginson, *Army Life*, 42, 190-94.

[28] Higginson, Journal, entries of Nov. 27, Dec. 1, 3, 1862, Higginson Papers, HU.

The Battle at Milliken's Bend. T. R. Davis in *Harper's Weekly*

always aroused their indignation to hear the negro race called brutal or depraved."[29]

Higginson tended to fall into the same attitude of benevolent paternalism toward the freedmen which overtook several of the Gideonites. "They seem the world's perpetual children, docile & gay & loveable, in the midst of this war for freedom upon which they have intelligently entered," he wrote. "I think it is partly from my own notorious love of children that I like these people so well."[30] But Higginson realized the dangers inherent in excessive paternalism and consciously strove to avoid them. "It saves a great deal of trouble, while it lasts, this childlike confidence," he wrote of his troops; "nevertheless, it is our business to educate them to manhood, and I see as yet no obstacle." Even so, Higginson viewed the transition of the freedmen from childhood to manhood with mixed emotions. "In every way I see the gradual change in them, sometimes with a sigh as parents watch their children growing up and miss the droll speeches and the confiding ignorance of children," he wrote near the end of his tour of duty on the islands. "Sometimes it comes over me with a pang that they are growing more like white men, less naive and less grotesque."[31]

✦

More than any other northern governor, John Andrew of Massachusetts favored the employment of Negro troops. In January 1863, Andrew finally obtained authorization from Stanton to recruit a Negro regiment in his state. Stanton said, however, that all commissioned officers must be white men. Andrew wanted to grant a few lieutenancies to qualified Negroes and give them opportunities for promotion, but Stanton and Lincoln feared the reaction of the northern people if black men became officers. The enlistment of Negro privates was a great leap forward, they said, and public opinion must be allowed to digest this advance before making a further one. Andrew reluctantly agreed, but obtained a promise from Stanton that in all matters relating to pay, status, and treatment his Negro regiment would be equal to other Union regiments.[32]

[29] Higginson, *Army Life*, 197.
[30] Higginson, Journal, Dec. 16, 26, 1862, Higginson Papers, HU.
[31] Higginson, Journal, entries of Dec. 21, 1862, Feb. 11, 1864, Higginson Papers, HU.
[32] Henry G. Pearson, *The Life of John A. Andrew* (2 vols., Boston, 1904), II, 71-74.

Andrew wanted the new regiment to be the grandest achievement of his governorship, and he took great care in selecting its officers. "I am desirous to have for its officers, particularly its field officers, young men of military experience, of firm anti-Slavery principles," wrote Andrew to his friend, abolitionist Francis G. Shaw of New York. "I shall look for [such officers] in those circles of educated Anti-Slavery Society, which next to the colored race itself have the greatest interest in the success of this experiment."[33] Andrew invited Shaw's son Robert to become colonel of the 54th Massachusetts Volunteers. After some initial hesitation, Robert Gould Shaw accepted. A Harvard graduate, young Shaw was then a captain in the Second Massachusetts Infantry with considerable combat experience. For lieutenant colonel, Andrew selected Norwood P. Hallowell, member of a well-known abolitionist family. Most of the rest of the officers were abolitionists, some of them having been frequent visitors at the Garrison home in prewar days.[34]

The next problem was recruitment of men for the regiment. Negroes were much less eager to flock to the colors now than they had been at the outbreak of the war when the North did not want them. There were several reasons for this. In the first place, the booming war economy had created full employment and prosperity for Negroes in many parts of the North. A white Bostonian wrote in February 1863, that "the blacks here are too comfortable to do anything more than talk about freedom."[35] In the second place, despite Stanton's promises to Andrew there were disturbing rumors that Negro volunteers would receive less pay than white soldiers. Thirdly, and perhaps most important, intelligent and educated northern Negroes deeply resented the ineligibility of black men to become officers in the new regiments.

Abolitionists and radical Republicans sympathized with the complaints of northern Negroes. If the experiment of arming Negroes was to be "hedged about by every restriction or annoy-

[33] Andrew to Francis G. Shaw, Jan. 30, 1863, in Pearson, *Andrew*, II, 74-76.
[34] Lawrence Lader, *The Bold Brahmins: New England's War Against Slavery, 1831-1863* (New York, 1961), 279-83; Wendell P. Garrison and Francis J. Garrison, *William Lloyd Garrison* (4 vols., Boston, 1885-89), IV, 79.
[35] Charles Russell Lowell to his mother, Feb. 4, 1863, in Edward W. Emerson, *Life and Letters of Charles Russell Lowell* (Boston, 1907), 233-34.

ance," wrote Sydney Gay in the *New York Tribune*, "if they are
to have inferior pay, privileges and consideration, to other soldiers
—if they are forewarned that they can never win promotion or
commendation, . . . we presume all they will do is of small account.
Spartans would not volunteer to fight in defiance of such in-
dignities."[36] Garrisonian abolitionists passed resolutions protesting the exclusion of Negroes from officer's rank, "believing that
it serves to retard enlistment, to perpetuate an unnatural caste,
and to stifle high and honorable aspiration in the mind of the
common soldier." The Church Anti-Slavery Society urged the
government to give Negro troops "an open field and a fair chance,
and let the colored soldier fight on equal terms with the white
soldier."[37]

While striving to remove injustices in the treatment of Negro
troops, abolitionists nevertheless urged colored men to join the
army no matter what the terms. If they fought well they would
win equal rights and promotion for themselves; if they refused
to enlist, they would only confirm the stereotype of the cowardly,
incompetent Negro. "Every race has fought for Liberty and
its own progress," Governor Andrew told Massachusetts Negroes.
"If Southern slavery should fall by the crushing of the Rebellion,
and colored men should have no hand and play no conspicuous
part in the task, the result would leave the colored man a mere
helot." Speaking to a group of New York City Negroes, George
Stearns said, "This is the time God has given your race to conquer its freedom from Northern prejudice and Southern pride
and avarice." "You must fight or be slaves," Stearns told the
Negroes. "You must fight . . . to obtain a right to fight on terms
of equality. . . . It is the duty as well as the privilege of the black
man to fight without standing on terms. . . . If he refuses to fight
or turns his back on the enemy his doom is sealed for this generation." In March 1863, Frederick Douglass published a stirring
broadside entitled *Men of Color, To Arms!* "Liberty won by
white men would lack half its lustre. Who would be free themselves
must strike the blow," proclaimed Douglass. "The chance is now

36 *New York Tribune*, Mar. 4, 1863.

37 *N.A.S. Standard*, Mar. 7, 1863; *Liberator*, June 5, 1863; copy of resolutions
adopted by the Church Anti-Slavery Society on May 25, 1863, in the Cheever
Papers, AAS.

given you to end in a day the bondage of centuries, and to rise in one bound from social degradation to the plane of common equality with all other varieties of men. . . . Action! action! not criticism, is the plain duty of this hour."[38]

Recruiting proceeded slowly at first. Massachusetts' small Negro population filled less than two companies. Governor Andrew called on abolitionist George L. Stearns, a wealthy lead-pipe manufacturer and a leading advocate of Negro troops, to form a committee of "prominent citizens" to recruit soldiers for the Massachusetts 54th from all over the North. The legislature appropriated funds for bounties and transportation of recruits to Massachusetts. Stearns went to Buffalo to organize a central recruiting office. He hired prominent Negro abolitionists such as Douglass, William Wells Brown, Charles L. Remond, John Mercer Langston, Henry Highland Garnet, and Martin Delany as recruiting agents. Whenever the funds subscribed by the committee and the legislature ran short, Stearns dipped into his own pocket. His agents crisscrossed the North, making speeches and urging Negroes to join up. Frederick Douglass was extremely active, and his own sons were the first recruits from New York. By the end of April recruits were coming in at the rate of 30 to 40 per day, and Andrew soon had enough men to form a second Negro regiment, the 55th Massachusetts.[39]

There had been much sneering among conservative Bostonians at the idea of a Negro regiment. But as the men of the 54th began drilling at Readville, near Boston, curiosity gradually overcame prejudice and thousands of Bostonians went out to the camp to watch. Many of them came away with changed opinions after witnessing this fine-looking set of colored men march, drill, and shoot with a skill and élan equal to that of most white regi-

[38] Pearson, *Andrew*, II, 69-70; Stearns quoted in *Commonwealth*, May 22, 1863; Frederick Douglass, *Men of Color, To Arms!*

[39] Frank P. Stearns, *The Life and Public Services of George Luther Stearns* (Philadelphia, 1907), 286-92; Pearson, *Andrew*, II, 81-84; Benjamin Quarles, *Frederick Douglass* (Washington, 1948), 204-08; George Stearns to Gerrit Smith, Feb. 15, Mar. 13, 1863, Smith Papers, SU; John Andrew to Gerrit Smith, Feb. 17, 1863, Smith Papers, NYPL; Gerrit Smith to Frederick Douglass, Mar. 10, 1863, Stearns to Douglass, Mar. 24, 1863, Douglass Papers, Anacostia. Garrison's oldest son, George, joined the 55th as a lieutenant, abandoning his father's non-resistance teachings to take an active part in the war. Garrison reluctantly acquiesced in his son's decision. William L. Garrison, Jr., to Ellen Wright, May 26, 1863, Garrison Papers, SC.

ments. Abolitionists visited the camp nearly every day. The New England Freedmen's Aid Society sent tobacco, stoves, and other items to the men and dispatched a corps of teachers to instruct those soldiers who were illiterate. In May Governor Andrew presented the colors to Colonel Shaw in an impressive ceremony at Readville. "I know not, Mr. Commander, when, in all human history, to any given thousand men in arms there has been committed a work at once so proud, so precious, so full of hope and glory as the work committed to you," Andrew told Shaw. "I stand or fall, as a man and a magistrate, with the rise or fall in history of the Fifty-Fourth Massachusetts Regiment."[40]

At the end of May the regiment marched in review through Boston on its way to embark for South Carolina. Twenty thousand eager spectators lined the streets to watch a Negro regiment march along the same route taken by Anthony Burns in his return to bondage nine years earlier. Thousands cheered as the regimental band played the John Brown song and the troops swung smartly through Boston Common. No other Massachusetts regiment had received such a send-off. Abolitionist leaders gathered in Wendell Phillips' house on Essex Street to view the parade. As the troops passed the house Garrison stood on the balcony, his hand resting on a marble bust of John Brown. Colonel Shaw paused briefly as he passed the veteran abolitionist, and several officers lifted their hats as the troops marched by. It was a symbolic and memorable day in the history of the Negro's struggle for freedom, and those abolitionists who watched the parade of the 54th through Boston never forgot the scene.[41]

✦

Andrew's success in raising two regiments of colored troops encouraged other northern governors to take similar steps to help fill their state troop quotas. In 1862 John Mercer Langston, Ohio Negro abolitionist, had suggested to Governor David Tod a project to raise colored volunteers to be credited against Ohio's quota. Langston was coolly shown out of the governor's office with the words, "Do you not know, Mr. Langston, that this is a *white man's* government; that white men are able to defend and

---

[40] Garrison and Garrison, *Garrison*, IV, 79; Ednah Bow Cheney, *Reminiscences* (Boston, 1902), 83-84; Pearson, *Andrew*, II, 87-89.
[41] *Liberator*, June 5, 12, 1863.

protect it? . . . When we want you colored men we will notify you."
By June 1863, Tod had changed his mind. He notified Langston
and gave him authority to enlist Negro soldiers. Using his experience gained as a recruiting agent under Stearns, Langston
completed the enlistment of a regiment of Ohio Negroes by
November. Professor G. W. Shurtliff of Oberlin, an abolitionist,
was selected as colonel of the regiment.[42]

Martin Delany helped recruit colored soldiers for Rhode
Island, Connecticut, and Ohio. In Philadelphia, J. Miller McKim,
a member of the Union League, started a movement within the
League to enlist Negro regiments in Pennsylvania. The committee
formed to raise these troops, according to McKim, was composed
of "the antislavery elite" of the Union League. McKim organized
a huge rally at Philadelphia's National Hall on July 6 to kick off
the drive for enlistment of Pennsylvania colored regiments. Frederick Douglass and Anna Dickinson were featured speakers at
the rally. Their eloquence helped swell the ranks of Pennsylvania's
Negro regiments. Within ten months ten regiments of Negro
troops from Pennsylvania and neighboring states were recruited
and organized.[43]

In New York City a group of abolitionists in George Cheever's
Church of the Puritans asked Lincoln for permission to recruit
10,000 Negro soldiers to march South under General Frémont
as a "Grand Army of Liberation." Many prominent New York
Republicans endorsed their request, and a delegation headed by
Cheever talked with Lincoln at the end of May 1863. The presi-
dent expressed interest in the project and promised to appoint
Frémont to a command if the 10,000 troops could be raised.
Frémont, however, was not interested in such a command.[44] The
New Yorkers went ahead anyway in their efforts to raise the
troops, applying to John Jay and the Union League for as-

[42] John M. Langston, *From the Virginia Plantation to the National Capital*
(Hartford, Conn., 1894), 205-17.

[43] Frank A. Rollin, *Life and Public Services of Martin R. Delany* (Boston,
1883), 145-53; McKim to Charles Gibbons, Feb. 12, 1863, McKim Papers, NYPL;
Charles Follen McKim to Frank Garrison, Sept. 11, 18, 1863, Charles Follen
McKim Papers, NYPL; J. M. McKim to Garrison, July 10, 1863, Sarah Pugh
to R. D. Webb, Aug. 11, 1863, Garrison Papers, BPL; *Commonwealth*, July 31,
1863; *Liberator*, July 31, 1863; *N.A.S. Standard*, June 11, 1864.

[44] *New York Tribune*, June 1, 1863; *Principia*, June 18, 1863; Basler, *Collected
Works of Lincoln*, VI, 239; Frémont to Charles Sumner, June 9, 1863, Sumner
Papers, HU.

sistance. They sought authorization from Governor Horatio Seymour to begin recruiting, but the Democratic Seymour was strongly opposed to Negro soldiers and refused to grant the desired permission. Jay and his Union League committee finally obtained permission from Stanton to recruit New York Negroes directly under national authority. The first regiment marched proudly down Broadway in March 1864, and two more followed soon afterward.[45]

In May 1863, General Banks began to organize Negro regiments in Louisiana into a *Corps d'Afrique*. B. Rush Plumly, a Philadelphia abolitionist serving as general appraiser of the Treasury Department in New Orleans, was put in charge of recruitment in the city. He resigned his position in the Treasury Department and was commissioned a major in the army. Plumly reported great success in gaining the confidence of New Orleans' colored people. "I have helped 'get up' their concerts; attended their meetings; churches, balls, parties, funerals, &c. &c. besides visiting constantly in their houses," he wrote. "A man must go among them; personally, he must *like* them. They must *believe* in him. Their instinct is as subtle as any reasoning. They want to know that their leader is fighting for the principle of Freedom, by which they are to benefit. They don't want him to fight for 'niggers.' " Plumly's son commanded one of the Negro regiments. By the end of August, Plumly had raised five regiments in New Orleans, and in the whole of Union-occupied Louisiana Banks had enrolled 12,000 black soldiers.[46]

Perhaps George Stearns' greatest contribution to the Civil

---

[45] John Jay to Sumner, Mar. 8, 1864, Sumner Papers, HU; John Jay, "The Union League Club of New York, Its Memories of the Past," speech delivered to the Union League Club on Mar. 13, 1868, in John Jay, *Slavery and the War* (New York, 1868), #21.

[46] Cornish, *Sable Arm*, 126-29; Plumly to S. P. Chase, July 4, 10, Aug. 1, 28, 1863, Chase Papers, LC; quotation from letter of July 4. In March 1863, Secretary Stanton had sent Adjutant-General Lorenzo Thomas to the Union-occupied portions of the lower Mississippi Valley to arm and equip as many freedmen as he could. A graduate of West Point and a career army officer, but no abolitionist, Thomas went about his work with an unexpected heartiness and efficiency. By the end of the war he had raised 76,000 black troops, more than 40 per cent of the entire number of Negroes who served in the Union Army. Although Thomas sometimes resorted to impressment to fill up his regiments, abolitionists were happy with the over-all effect of his work, for the large number of troops he raised helped convince the nation of the value and contribution of black soldiers. Cornish, *Sable Arm*, 110-26.

War was his work in recruiting the 54th Massachusetts, the most celebrated Negro regiment in American history. But he did not retire from the recruiting field after organizing the 54th and 55th. In May 1863, Secretary Stanton formed the Bureau of Colored Troops to facilitate the enlistment of black soldiers. At the beginning of June, Stearns went to Washington and offered to put his efficient and far-flung recruiting service at the disposal of the government. "I have heard of your recruiting bureau," Stanton told Stearns, "and I think you would be the best man to run the machine you have constructed. I will make you an Assistant Adjutant-General with the rank of Major, and I will give you authority to recruit colored regiments all over the country." Stearns accepted the job. He could draw upon the secret service funds of the War Department to finance his activities. In addition he raised $50,000 by private subscription in the North.[47]

Stearns went first to Philadelphia to help organize the enlistment of Pennsylvania Negroes. The camp where the troops were trained, located on land donated by abolitionist Edward M. Davis, was named by Stearns "Camp William Penn." "The Quakers wince," Stearns told his wife, "but I tell them it is established on peace principles; that is, to conquer a lasting peace."[48] From Philadelphia Stearns proceeded to Maryland to help General William Birney, son of the renowned abolitionist James G. Birney, recruit colored soldiers in that state. In August Stearns was ordered to Nashville, where a large body of freedmen had congregated in the rear of General William Rosecrans' army. When Stearns arrived he found the brutal practice of impressment in force, producing chaos, confusion, and distrust on the part of the freedmen. Union officers and agents of Military Governor Andrew Johnson were indiscriminately drafting Negroes for heavy labor, placing them in filthy compounds, and neglecting to pay them wages. Stearns was appalled by the situation and immediately sent a protest to Stanton.[49]

Secretary Stanton did not give much support to Stearns' efforts

---

[47] Stearns, *Stearns*, 295-96; O.R., Ser. 3, vol. III, 374, 676, 682-85.

[48] Stearns, *Stearns*, 301-302; quotation from p. 302. See also Sarah Pugh to R. D. Webb, Aug. 11, 1863, Garrison Papers, BPL.

[49] Stearns, *Stearns*, 307-308; N.A.S. Standard, Sept. 5, 1863; O.R., Ser. 3, vol. III, 676-77, 840.

to put an end to such practices. But with his personal tact, charm, good sense, and exceptional administrative talents Stearns set about to bring order out of chaos. His first task was to win suspicious Tennesseans to support a policy of humane treatment, prompt payment, education, and enlistment rather than impressment of the freedmen. Two of his agents spent their full time holding public meetings, explaining Stearns' policy and appealing to loyal Tennesseans for support. These methods were eminently successful. Within a few weeks Major Stearns had won the confidence of important Tennessee Unionists, including Governor Johnson. Stearns put an end to impressment. He sent his recruiting agents among the freedmen to hold meetings in churches, cabins, and camps. Stearns established clean and well-run contraband camps for the wives and children of recruited soldiers. He organized schools among the colored troops and their families, and through his contacts with northern freedmen's aid societies he obtained teachers and supplies for these schools.[50]

Stearns' tenure as recruiting agent in middle Tennessee produced a great change in public opinion there toward slavery and Negro soldiers. His successor wrote in October 1864, that Stearns' wise and firm actions had been primarily responsible for "causing the great revolution in public opinion, patent in the last year. Whereas some then opposed, I know of no prominent loyal Tennessean who does not now believe in, advocate, and encourage the raising of colored troops."[51] Stearns enlisted approximately seven regiments, and his successor, Captain R. D. Massey, who followed Stearns' methods, raised another thirteen. But Stearns' most important contribution was not the number of regiments he enlisted. His activities in Tennessee, according to J. Miller McKim, "augmented the power and helped to lick into shape the antislavery sentiment in that part of the country. His dozen recruiting agencies, scattered through middle Tennessee and extending into Alabama, have been a dozen anti-slavery agencies; a dozen education agencies; a dozen Freedmen's agencies; a dozen agencies for promoting Northern ideas."[52]

✦

[50] *O.R.*, Ser. 3, vol. III, 793, 816, 819-20, 823, vol. IV, 762-63, 770-74, vol. V, 120; Stearns to the Boston Committee for Recruiting Colored Soldiers, Oct. 10, 13, 1863, copies in Charles Sumner Papers, HU. See also Cornish, *Sable Arm*, 236-38.
[51] *O.R.*, Ser. 3, vol. IV, 772.
[52] *N.A.S. Standard*, Mar. 26, 1864.

On May 1, 1863, the *New York Tribune* observed that most northerners now acquiesced in the policy of arming Negroes, but that there was still considerable doubt whether they would make good soldiers. "Loyal whites have generally become willing that they should fight," declared the *Tribune*, "but the great majority have no faith that they will really do so. Many hope they will prove cowards and sneaks—others greatly fear it."[53] Abolitionists confidently predicted that Negroes would prove themselves courageous fighting men, but they nevertheless awaited the first important battle fought by Negroes with some anxiety.

Higginson's soldiers had performed well in skirmishes, but as yet no Negro troops had engaged in a major battle. In the early summer in 1863, however, Negro regiments fought courageously in two major engagements at Port Hudson and Milliken's Bend in the Mississippi Valley. The performance of colored soldiers in these battles converted many skeptics into ardent supporters of the policy of arming Negroes. Even more important was the assault of the 54th Massachusetts regiment on Fort Wagner, a Confederate outpost guarding the entrance to Charleston harbor, in July 1863. The attack was repulsed with heavy loss to the regiment, including the death of Colonel Shaw, but the heroic conduct of the 54th during the battle has become enshrined in the history of the Negro race.[54] Colonel Shaw and the men who fell with him were virtually canonized by the abolitionists and by a large segment of northern public opinion. Fort Wagner was "a holy sepulchre" to the Negro race, declared the *Anti-Slavery Standard*. The battle "made Fort Wagner such a name to the colored race as Bunker Hill had been for ninety years to the white Yankees," observed the *New York Tribune*. "Through the cannon smoke of that black night," said the *Atlantic Monthly*, "the manhood of the colored race shines before many eyes that would not see."[55] Angelina Weld asked Gerrit Smith, "Do you not rejoice & exult in all the praise that is lavished upon our brave colored troops even by Pro-slavery papers? I have no tears to shed over their graves, because I see that their heroism is working a great change in public opinion, forcing all men to see the

[53] *New York Tribune*, May 1, 1863.
[54] Cornish, *Sable Arm*, 142-45, 151-56.
[55] *N.A.S. Standard*, Aug. 8, 1863; *New York Tribune*, Sept. 8, 1865; *Atlantic Monthly* quoted in Lader, *Bold Brahmins*, 290.

sin & shame of enslaving such men." Mary Grew wrote, "Who asks now in doubt and derision, 'Will the negro fight?' The answer is spoken from the cannon's mouth; it is written in sunlight on flashing steel; it comes to us from . . . those graves beneath Fort Wagner's walls, which the American people will surely never forget."[56]

Perhaps the greatest tribute to the courage of black soldiers came from President Lincoln in a public letter of August 26, 1863, in which he rebuked the opponents of emancipation. "Some of the commanders of our armies in the field who have given us our most important successes, believe the emancipation policy, and the use of colored troops, constitute the heaviest blow yet dealt to the rebellion," wrote Lincoln. "You say you will not fight to free negroes. Some of them seem willing to fight for you." When the war was won "there will be some black men who can remember that, with silent tongue, and clenched teeth, and steady eye, and well-poised bayonet, they have helped mankind on to this great consummation; while, I fear, there will be some white ones, unable to forget that, with malignant heart, and deceitful speech, they have strove to hinder it."[57]

✦

Words of praise were very pleasant to the ears of Negro soldiers, but many of them would have been happier if the Union had shown its appreciation by paying them the same wages as white troops. Higginson's regiment and the 54th and 55th Massachusetts regiments had enlisted under a specific War Department promise of equal pay. But Stanton in fact had no legal authority to make such a promise. The only law applying specifically to colored soldiers was the militia act of July 17, 1862, which stated that Negroes would be paid $10 per month, $3 of which could be deducted for clothing. White privates received $13 per month *plus* a clothing allowance of $3.50. At the time the law was passed it was envisaged that Negroes in the army would serve primarily as laborers rather than soldiers. When Stanton formed the Bureau

[56] Angelina Weld to Gerrit Smith, July 28, 1863, Smith Papers, su; [Mary Grew], *Thirteenth Annual Report of the Philadelphia Female Anti-Slavery Society* (Phila., 1864), 17.

[57] Lincoln to James Conkling, Aug. 26, 1863, in Basler, ed., *Collected Works of Lincoln*, vi, 408-10.

of Colored Troops in May 1863, he asked the legal adviser of the War Department for a ruling on the pay of Negro soldiers. He was informed that under the law their pay would have to be $10 per month. Beginning in June 1863, all Negro soldiers were paid at this rate.[58]

Abolitionists were outraged by this inequality in pay. The Negro soldier fought the same battles, faced the same and even greater dangers than his white comrade-in-arms, but was paid only three-fifths as much as the white soldier. To abolitionists this looked like another three-fifths compromise. On August 1, 1863, Frederick Douglass addressed a public letter to George Stearns declaring his intention to resign from Stearns' recruiting agency. He had been enlisting black soldiers for five months, Douglass explained, but the government had not kept good faith with its Negro troops. "When I plead for recruits," he said, "I want to do it with all my heart, without qualification. I cannot do that now. The impression settles upon me that colored men have much overrated the enlightenment, justice and generosity of our rulers at Washington."[59]

Stearns agreed with Douglass and privately urged him to seek an interview with Lincoln to lay the colored man's grievances before the president. Douglass did so, and was shown into Lincoln's office on August 10, 1863. The president listened quietly and sympathetically to Douglass' protests against the inequality in pay and the lack of opportunity for Negroes to become commissioned officers. Lincoln replied that he appreciated the justice of Douglass' complaints, but that there was still a great deal of popular opposition in the North to the use of Negro soldiers and that discrimination in pay and promotion took the edge off some of this opposition—it was "a necessary concession to smooth the way to their employment at all as soldiers." Ultimately, Lincoln promised, Negro soldiers would receive the same pay and treatment as white troops.[60]

[58] Cornish, *Sable Arm*, 184-87; Quarles, *Negro in the Civil War*, 200; *O.R.*, Ser. 3, vol. III, 252; *U.S. Statutes at Large*, XII, 269, 599; Fred A. Shannon, *The Organization and Administration of the Union Army, 1861-1865* (2 vols., New York, 1928), I, 71-72.

[59] Douglass to Stearns, Aug. 1, 1863, in *Douglass' Monthly*, Aug. 1863.

[60] Stearns to Douglass, Aug. 8, 1863, Douglass Papers, Anacostia; Frederick Douglass, *Life and Times of Frederick Douglass* (Hartford, Conn., 1884), 301-04.

In South Carolina the men of the 54th and 55th Massachusetts regiments were angered by the news that their pay was to be only $10 per month. Deciding to meet the challenge head-on, the two regiments refused on principle to accept any pay at all until they were treated as equals. Governor Andrew sympathized with their stand and hurried to Washington to find out why Stanton's promise to his troops had been broken. He saw Lincoln, Stanton, and several other officials. All agreed that the 54th and 55th had been promised equal pay, but pointed lamely to the law of July 17, 1862, as an excuse for discrimination. Andrew was partially mollified by an administration promise to support legislation to equalize pay at the next session of Congress. He returned to Boston and called a special session of the state legislature to appropriate funds to pay the 54th and 55th the difference between their promised and actual wages. The legislature quickly passed the law, but the regiments refused again to accept any pay until Washington abolished the degrading distinction between white and colored troops. They would prefer, they stated, to serve out their enlistments without pay than to be insulted by the federal government. As Theodore Tilton expressed it, they were unwilling "that the Federal Government should throw mud upon them, even though Massachusetts stands ready to wipe it off."[61]

In his annual report of December 1863, Stanton asked Congress to enact legislation equalizing the pay of white and colored soldiers. Thaddeus Stevens immediately introduced a bill to accomplish this objective. Abolitionists expected quick congressional approval of the bill. But a considerable segment of northern opinion still opposed this elementary measure of justice. Democrats and even some Republicans reasoned that to pay Negro troopers the same wages as white soldiers would degrade the white man. The *New York World* declared that "to claim that the indolent, servile negro is the equal in courage, enterprise and fire of the foremost race in all the world is a libel upon the name of an American citizen. . . . It is unjust in every way to the white soldier to put him on a level with the black."[62]

In the face of this kind of pressure from conservatives, Con-

---

[61] Pearson, *Andrew*, II, 99-104; Quarles, *Negro in the Civil War*, 201.
[62] *House Exec. Docs.*, no. 1, 38 Cong., 1 Sess., p. 8; *Commonwealth*, Dec. 18, 1863; *New York World*, Dec. 13, 1863.

gress dawdled and hesitated. Abolitionists and Republicans organized counterpressure to convince lawmakers of the need for speedy action. The Middlesex County (Massachusetts) Anti-Slavery Society sent Lincoln a resolution denouncing the government's policy of using Negroes "to fight its battles, die miserably in its ditches, without a dollar of bounty, on only part pay, and always under white officers, and against all hope of preferment or promotion." Antislavery meetings all over the North adopted similar resolutions demanding equal pay.[63]

Congress seemed disposed to act favorably on a bill to equalize the *future* pay of white and colored troops. "The public seems to suppose that all required justice will be done by the passage of a bill equalizing the pay of all soldiers for the future," wrote Higginson in a letter published by Gay in the *Tribune*. But this was only half the question. Several Negro regiments, including Higginson's, had enlisted with the promise of equal pay from the date of enlistment. His men had been nearly sixteen months in the service and for them the issue was not only a question of future pay but of arrears for deficiencies in past wages. Higginson declared that there was "nothing mean or mercenary" about his soldiers. If they were convinced that the government needed the money they "would serve it barefooted and on half-rations, and without a dollar—for a time." But they saw white troops all around them receiving higher pay and huge bounties for re-enlisting, and they questioned the good faith of the government. Washington's delay in rectifying its injustice, said Higginson, "has already inflicted untold suffering, has impaired discipline, has relaxed loyalty, and has begun to implant a feeling of sullen distrust in the very regiments whose early career solved the problem of the nation, created a new army, and made peaceful emancipation possible."[64]

Higginson wrote privately to prominent senators urging them to act promptly or sacrifice the good will of Negro soldiers. At Higginson's behest Sydney Gay lashed out in the *Tribune* against conservative Republican senators who were blocking passage of a

[63] Resolution adopted by the Middlesex County Anti-Slavery Society, Dec. 27, 1863, copy in Lincoln Papers, lc; *Liberator*, Jan. 29, Feb. 5, 1864.

[64] Higginson, *Army Life*, 218-21. This letter was printed in broadside form and sent to every member of Congress and to many northern newspapers.

bill to make equal pay retroactive to the date of enlistment.[65] Senator William Pitt Fessenden of Maine was a leading opponent of retroactive equal pay because he had calculated that it would cost the government an extra million and a half dollars. "Has he 'calculated' how much it will cost the country not to pass it?" asked the *Boston Commonwealth* angrily. "Has he calculated the price in infamy to the Government of this country, and to every man who votes against this bill, of denying to these colored soldiers what nobody pretends to say is not justly their due? . . . Would he dare to treat a single squad of Maine white men in this way?"[66]

Massachusetts' Senators Sumner and Wilson were leading the fight in the Senate for equal pay. Realizing that a majority of the Senate was opposed to the retroactive clause of the bill, Wilson introduced an amendment to make equal pay for all Negro regiments retroactive only to January 1, 1864. Boston abolitionists seethed with anger at Wilson's apparent concession to the forces of evil.[67] Wilson sent an indignant letter to Garrison explaining the reasons for his action. "It is not pleasant to be sharply censured by friends when one does the best he can," wrote Wilson. He stated that three-fourths of the Senate was opposed to full retroactive equal pay, and he had moved to make such pay retroactive to January 1 in order to salvage at least part of the retroactive feature. "I had caucussed the Senate and secured a majority and we all felt here that the friends of the colored soldiers had won a great victory," Wilson told Garrison. "Judge then of my amazement when I learned that our friends at home were censuring me." Abolitionists accepted Wilson's explanation and the *Commonwealth* publicly retracted its criticism of the senator. Abolitionists turned their wrath instead on Fessenden and other conservatives who had forced the compromise. "Our Senators [Wilson and Sumner] managed the case of the wronged soldiers with great ability and tact," declared the *Commonwealth*, "but

[65] Higginson to William P. Fessenden, Feb. 13, 1864, Higginson Papers, NYHS; Higginson to S. H. Gay, Feb. 13, 1864, Gay Papers, CU; *New York Tribune*, Jan. 14, 20, Feb. 5, 11, 1864. See also Higginson to the *New York Times*, Feb. 14, 1864, in the *Times*, Feb. 21, 1864.

[66] *Commonwealth*, Feb. 12, 1864.

[67] *ibid.*, Feb. 19, 1864.

were overborne by bigotry, jealousy and copperheadism. And so, this simple act of justice is postponed."[68]

Discontent and even mutiny were mounting among Negro troops who were becoming impatient with Congress's failure to grant them equal pay. Sergeant William Walker of the Third South Carolina Volunteers marched his company to his captain's tent and ordered them to stack arms and resign from an army that broke its contract with them. Walker was court-martialed and shot for mutiny. Edward N. Hallowell, who had succeeded Robert Shaw as colonel of the 54th Massachusetts, reported a desperate situation in his regiment. "I do not wish to continue to keep the men in a condition worse than slavery," wrote Hallowell angrily. His regiment was in a state of near rebellion because they refused to accept unequal pay and hence had received no pay at all for nearly a year. "I believe them to be entirely right, morally, and yet military necessity has compelled me to shoot two of them," declared Hallowell. "We are willing to give our lives to the country, but it is too much to sacrifice our honor & self respect."[69]

On June 15, 1864, Congress finally enacted legislation granting equal pay to Negro soldiers. The law was made retroactive to January 1, 1864, for all Negro soldiers, and retroactive to the time of enlistment for those Negroes who had been free men on April 19, 1861.[70] Justice had been meted out to colored soldiers—but belated and partial justice. Frank Sanborn denounced the discrimination in retroactive pay between free Negroes and freedmen as a travesty on justice, an admission of the legality of property in man. It "divides the colored soldiers into two grades" and "does honor to injustice with a vengeance." It conceded to the Confederacy much of what it was fighting for. "The Government says to the rebels—'Some of these men are free; some of them were once *your slaves. We* discriminate between the two grades; what do you intend to do about it?' Let Fort Pil-

---

68 Wilson to Garrison, Feb. 22, 1864, Garrison Papers, BPL; *Commonwealth*, Feb. 26, 1864.

69 Higginson, *Army Life*, 218; E. N. Hallowell to Sumner, June 30, 1864, Henry I. Bowditch to Sumner, July 1, 1864, Sumner Papers, HU.

70 *U.S. Statutes at Large*, XIII, 129-30.

low tell of the effect of these bloody instructions of pro-slavery prejudice and meanness."[71]

On August 18, 1864, the adjutant general's office issued an order directing commanders of Negro regiments to determine which of their men had been free on April 19, 1861. These men would be given full pay from the date of their enlistment; all others from January 1, 1864. This posed a serious problem for many regiments. Most northern regiments had both free Negroes and freedmen in their ranks; even the 54th and 55th Massachusetts regiments contained a few men who had escaped from slavery after April 19, 1861. Morale in such regiments might be impaired if some of the men received more back pay than others. Colonel E. N. Hallowell of the 54th worked out an ingenious method to avoid this problem. The fact of freedom before April 19, 1861, was established by the soldier's oath. Hallowell devised the following oath: "You do solemnly swear that you owed no man unrequited labor on or before the 19th day of April, 1861. So help you God." This became known as the "Quaker Oath," and even those men of the 54th who had been slaves took the oath in good conscience "by God's higher law, if not by their country's." Several other northern Negro regiments imitated Hallowell's oath.[72]

This did not solve the problem for regiments recruited solely in the South. Such an oath for them would be too patently transparent and would probably invite rebuke from Washington. Higginson urged Sumner to keep up the fight for full justice to freedmen soldiers. Failure to secure full retroactive pay for them "will be the greatest blow ever struck at successful emancipation in the Department of the South," he wrote, "for it will destroy all confidence in the honesty of the government."[73] Higginson fired off more letters to northern newspapers, conceding that under the new law the Massachusetts regiments "will get their

[71] *Commonwealth*, June 24, 1864. See also *Liberator*, Aug. 19, 1864, and *Commonwealth*, Aug. 12, 1864. On April 12, 1864, Confederate troops under General Nathan Bedford Forrest allegedly slaughtered several score Negro soldiers in cold blood after surrender of the Union garrison at Fort Pillow, Tennessee.

[72] *O.R.*, Ser. 3, vol. IV, 565; Pearson, *Andrew*, II, 120; Luis F. Emilio, *History of the Fifty-Fourth Regiment of Massachusetts Volunteer Infantry, 1863-65* (Boston, 1891), 220-21.

[73] Higginson to Sumner, June 20, 1864, Sumner Papers, HU.

pay at last, and be able to take their wives and children out of the almshouse, to which, as Gov. Andrew informs us, the gracious charity of the nation has consigned so many." But the refusal of full back pay to the First South Carolina Regiment was "a deliberate repudiation of the debt deliberately incurred by the Secretary of War." Higginson concluded in disgust, "If a year's discussion . . . has at length secured the arrears of pay for the Northern colored regiments, possibly two years may secure it for the Southern."[74]

Higginson intended to carry on the fight for the next two years or for the rest of his life, if necessary. When the next session of Congress met he wrote more letters to northern newspapers and sent a memorial to Congress, which was presented to the Senate by Henry Wilson on December 12, 1864. Higginson's persistence finally paid off. Wilson guided to passage on March 3, 1865, a law granting full retroactive equal pay to all Negro regiments that had been promised equal pay when they were enrolled.[75]

In spite of all the delays, vacillations, and injustices, the employment of Negro troops by the North was one of the most revolutionary features of the war. More than any other single factor the performance of Negro soldiers earned their race the respect of the North, made emancipation secure, and helped pave the way for the gains made by the Negro during Reconstruction. Abolitionists played an important part in the conception and execution of the policy of arming Negroes. George L. Stearns, John Andrew, J. Miller McKim, John Jay, Frederick Douglass, John

[74] Letters from Higginson in the *New York Times*, July 3, 1864; *New York Evening Post*, July 10, 1864; and *New York Tribune*, Aug. 12, 1864.

[75] Higginson, *Army Life*, 227-28; *N.A.S. Standard*, Dec. 17, 1864; *U.S. Statutes at Large*, xiii, 488; Henry Wilson to Higginson, March 26, 1865, Higginson Papers, HU. One of the most constant complaints of abolitionists and Negroes regarding the government's policy toward its Negro soldiers, aside from the matter of unequal pay, was the denial of officers' commissions to Negroes. Public prejudice and the inexperience of most Negro soldiers were the main reasons for this policy. As prejudice toward the Negro lessened in the last months of the war, the army promoted several Negroes to the rank of lieutenant. Eight Negro physicians were given major's commissions as surgeons during the war, and in the last weeks of the war Martin Delany was commissioned a major of infantry. Several other colored men were given complimentary commissions before being mustered out of the service in 1865. Of course several thousand colored men served as noncommissioned officers, but fewer than 100 Negroes were actually commissioned during the war. Cornish, *Sable Arm*, 214-17; Quarles, *Negro in the Civil War*, 208.

Mercer Langston, Martin Delany, William Birney, and others recruited dozens of Negro regiments. Colonels Shaw, Higginson, Edward and Norwood Hallowell, and many other abolitionist officers of Negro troops contributed to the success of the policy. Finally, abolitionists played a leading role in the efforts to rectify the discrimination in pay between white and Negro soldiers. The success of Negro soldiers was in part a triumph of abolitionism.

X ✦ THE QUEST FOR EQUAL RIGHTS IN THE NORTH

B Y 1863 the Civil War had become a revolution of freedom for 4 million slaves. The antislavery crusade, however, envisaged not only a negative freedom—the absence of chattelism—but a positive guaranty of equal protection of the laws to all men. Once freedom was won, most abolitionists were ready to proceed with the next step in the revolution—equality.

"This is a war not of geographical sections, nor of political factions, but of principles and systems," declared Theodore Tilton in 1863. "Our war against this rebellion is . . . a war for social equality, for rights, for justice, for freedom." In 1863 Moncure Conway wrote that "the war raging in America must be referred to a higher plane than that of Liberty. It is a war for Equality. It is to decide whether the Liberty which each race claims for itself, and knows to be good, shall be given impartially to all, of whatever colour or degree."[1]

These statements were summaries of an idea expressed many times by abolitionists during the war. The most eloquent and persistent spokesman for this revolution of racial equality was Wendell Phillips. His program of reconstruction, said Phillips early in 1862, was the creation of a nation in which there was "no Yankee, no Buckeye, no Hoosier, no Sucker, no native, no foreigner, no black, no white, no German, no Saxon; . . . only American citizens, with one law impartial over all." Phillips wanted to destroy the aristocratic society of the Old South and replace it with a new social order based on equal rights, universal education, and the dignity of labor. He declared: "I hold that the South is to be annihilated. I do not mean the geographical South. . . . [I] mean the intellectual, social, aristocratic South—the thing that represented itself by slavery and the bowie-knife, by bullying and lynch law, by ignorance and idleness. . . . I mean a

[1] *Independent*, June 25, 1863; Moncure D. Conway, *Testimonies Concerning Slavery* (2nd ed., London, 1865), 131-32. For a brilliant discussion of the evolution of equal rights as a northern war aim, see C. Vann Woodward, "Equality: the Deferred Commitment," in *The Burden of Southern History* (Vintage Books, New York, 1961), 69-87.

society which holds for its cardinal principle of faith, that one-third of the race is born booted and spurred, and the other two-thirds saddled for the first to ride. . . . That South is to be annihilated. (Loud applause)" This social revolution must be accomplished primarily by the freedmen. "I want the blacks as the very basis of the effort to regenerate the South," said Phillips. "We want the four millions of blacks—a people instinctively on our side, ready and skilled to work; the only element the South has that belongs to the nineteenth century."[2]

Most abolitionists realized that free Negroes were treated little better in the North than in the South. The revolution of equality, they knew, must embrace North as well as South. "No Abolitionist condemns our Northern oppression of negroes one whit less than he does Southern Slavery," declared Sydney Gay in 1862. "North as well as South, this outraged people encounter DENIAL everywhere," asserted Gerrit Smith in a ringing denunciation of racial discrimination in the North. "Even the noblest black is denied that which is free to the vilest white. The omnibus, the car, the ballot-box, the jury box, the halls of legislation, the army, the public lands, the school, the church, the lecture-room, the social circle, the table, are all either absolutely or virtually denied to him."[3]

Abolitionists could not hope to revolutionize the southern social order without first improving the status of northern Negroes. Gilbert Haven stated the problem succinctly. When southerners observed "no recognition of the unity of man" in the North, he said, "when they see these, our brethren, set apart in churches and schools, or, if allowed to enter our churches, driven into the lowest seats; when they behold every avenue of honorable effort shut against them,—that no clerk of this complexion is endured in our stores, no apprentice in our workshops, no teacher in our schools, no physician at our sick-beds, no minister in our pulpits, —how can we reproach them for their sins, or urge them to repentance?"[4]

---

[2] Speeches by Phillips published in *Liberator*, Apr. 25, May 23, Nov. 28, 1862.

[3] *New York Tribune*, Mar. 21, 1862; Gerrit Smith to the editor of the *New York Tribune*, July 1, 1861, published in the *Tribune*, July 7.

[4] Gilbert Haven, *National Sermons, Speeches, and Letters on Slavery and Its War* (Boston, 1869), 139.

When the militant phase of abolitionism began in 1831 the status of northern Negroes was deplorable. Shut out from white schools and churches, forced to live in city slums and ghettos, denied equal civil and political rights, subject to Jim Crow legislation and degrading "black laws" in many states, confined to menial occupations, almost universally despised as members of an inferior race, the northern Negroes' lot in 1830 was a harsh one. In some respects their status actually deteriorated in the next thirty years. The huge influx of immigrants in the 1840's and 1850's drove colored people out of many of their former occupations and subjected them to the mob fury of socially and economically insecure immigrants. Some of the western states made their black laws more severe between 1830 and 1860.

At the same time, however, northern Negroes made significant gains in other areas, especially in New England, the center of abolitionist influence. By a combination of moral suasion and political pressure, abolitionists and free Negroes helped to bring about the desegregation of most public schools in New England and the abolition of Jim Crow on New England stage coaches, horse cars, and railroads. Abolitionist efforts were partly responsible for the defeat of the Rhode Island constitution of 1842, which had established *white* manhood suffrage, and the substitution of a new constitution which granted Negro suffrage. Abolitionists registered their protests against "Negro pews" by withdrawing from churches that practiced this form of segregation and by joining or founding congregations which admitted Negroes on an equal basis. Abolitionist and antislavery lecturers almost singlehandedly ended segregated seating in many lecture halls by refusing to speak before segregated audiences. The Hutchinson family refused to sing before segregated groups. In many ways abolitionists tried to bear witness against the system of racial discrimination which prevailed in the antebellum North.

In 1860 Negroes enjoyed equal political rights in all the New England states except Connecticut. In New York, Negroes possessing property worth $250 could vote. In all other northern states colored men were denied suffrage.[5] All but a handful of

---

[5] In Ohio, men with a greater visible admixture of Caucasian than Negro genes could vote. In some respects, of course, this was a greater insult to the Negro than the denial of suffrage to all colored men.

public schools in New England were open to both races. Public transportation in most of the North was nonsegregated. But Jim Crow still prevailed on the New York, Philadelphia, Cincinnati, and San Francisco streetcars. Public schools in most of the North outside of New England were segregated, and in some areas no public schools at all were open to Negroes. In several western states Negroes were subjected to severe legal discrimination and denied equal rights in the courts. In many parts of the North, including New England, Negroes were discriminated against in housing, employment, restaurants, hotels, and places of recreation.[6]

NEGRO SUFFRAGE.

"Negro Suffrage." From the *Boston Commonwealth*

[6] For the best discussion of the status of northern Negroes before the Civil War and of the efforts of abolitionists to improve that status, see Leon F. Litwack, *North of Slavery* (Chicago, 1961). Most histories of the abolitionist movement and biographies of abolitionist leaders contain references to the attempts of abolitionists to secure equal civil and political rights for Negroes in the antebellum North. For additional descriptions of the condition of northern Negroes on the eve of the Civil War, see *Anglo-African*, Jan. 7, 1860; and *Liberator*, Oct. 5, 26, Nov. 2, Dec. 7, 1860, Jan. 4, Mar. 15, 1861.

With the outbreak of war, some abolitionists feared that the campaign for equal rights in the North might be buried by the confusion and excitement of armed conflict. "The laws respecting the colored man, in Iowa, Illinois, and other Western States, notwithstanding the predominance of Republican majorities, are disgraceful and proscriptive," wrote a western abolitionist. "It seems to me that the work of the Anti-Slavery Society ought to be carried on unrelaxingly. Legislation of a just character needs to be inaugurated. It will not answer to trust these reforms to this war." The Essex County (Massachusetts) Anti-Slavery Society resolved at the end of 1861 that "we still deem the mission of the Abolitionists *unaccomplished* so long as a . . . nominally free colored man is subjected to any proscription, political, educational, or ecclesiastical."[7] Stephen S. Foster declared in January 1862, that the object of the American Anti-Slavery Society was "not merely to destroy the *form* of slavery, but to destroy the *spirit of oppression*, which shows itself at the South, in the form of slavery, and at the North, in the bitter and relentless prejudice against color." Later in the year a Boston Negro reminded abolitionists that there was still much work for them to do right in Boston, where Negroes suffered discrimination in housing, employment, and some restaurants.[8]

In 1861 Susan B. Anthony pronounced a severe indictment of racial discrimination in the North. The northern people were horrified by tales of southern cruelty to slaves, she said, "and yet, what better do we? While the cruel slave-driver lacerates the black man's mortal body, we, of the North, flay the spirit." Even when the northern Negro obtained an education, he found the doors to many vocations shut in his face. Miss Anthony declared that reconstruction of the nation on the basis of equality for all men must begin in the North. She concluded: "Let us open to the colored man all our schools, from the common District to the College. Let us admit him into all our mechanic shops, stores, offices, and lucrative business avocations, to work side by side with his white brother; let him rent such pew in the church, and occupy such seat in the theatre, and public lecture room, as he pleases; let him be admitted to all our entertainments, both public &

[7] *N.A.S. Standard*, June 22, 1861; *Liberator*, Dec. 27, 1861.
[8] *Liberator*, Jan. 31, 1862, Aug. 15, 1862.

private; let him share all the accommodations of our hotels, stages, railroads and steamboats. . . . Extend to him all the rights of Citizenship. Let him vote and be voted for; let him sit upon the judge's bench, and in the juror's box. . . . Let the North thus prove to the South, by her acts, that she fully recognizes the humanity of the black man."[9]

Individually and in small groups, by private persuasion, precept, or example, abolitionists did what they could during the war to lessen prejudice and mitigate discrimination in the North. A Michigan abolitionist who owned a large farm told Garrison that he employed several Negro farmhands, paying them the same wages, serving them at the same table, and sleeping them in the same bunkhouse as his white laborers. Henry Cheever organized a "Freedom Club" in Worcester, containing men of both races, whose object was to break down the barriers between white and colored workingmen.[10] William H. Channing, abolitionist chaplain of the U.S. House of Representatives, invited Negro minister Henry Highland Garnet to occupy his pulpit in the House chamber one Sunday morning in February, 1865. Channing considered this event an important step in the campaign against discrimination in the nation's capital. At about the same time Charles Sumner presented Boston Negro lawyer John Rock as a candidate to argue cases before the Supreme Court. Chief Justice Chase accepted Rock and swore him in, making him the first Negro ever to be accredited as a Supreme Court lawyer. This affair was regarded by abolitionists as a symbol of the revolution in the Negro's status since 1857, when Chief Justice Taney had denied the citizenship of black men.[11]

Abolitionists tried also to cleanse northern churches of segregation. It was not always an easy task. In 1863 the Reverend Horace Hovey, abolitionist pastor of the Congregational church in Florence, Massachusetts, preached that "the negro has the same right that we have . . . to obtain a first-rate education and to rise in social position according as he rises in worth; the same right to

[9] MS of speech, marked "1861," in S. B. Anthony Papers, LC.

[10] H. Willis to Garrison, June 20, 1861, Garrison Papers, BPL; Henry Cheever to Gerrit Smith, July 20, 1864, Smith Papers, SU.

[11] Octavius B. Frothingham, Memoir of William Henry Channing (Boston, 1886), 316; Channing to L. M. Child, Mar. 8, 1865, published in Commonwealth, Mar. 25, 1865; New York Tribune, Feb. 9, 1865.

vote and to sit in legislative and congressional halls." Fifteen or twenty of his parishioners took offense at these words and walked out of the church. But there were some encouraging signs of progress. Maria Weston Chapman rejoiced in 1863 that the Park Street Church in Boston had reversed its long-standing policy of refusing to rent pews to Negroes.[12] Gilbert Haven succeeded in desegregating many New England Methodist churches, in expunging the word "colored" from the minutes of the New England Methodist Conference, and in securing admission of a Negro minister to the Conference as pastor of an integrated church.[13]

Education was another area in which abolitionists worked to promote desegregation wherever they were in a position to do so. Segregation had been abolished in Boston's public schools in 1855 largely through the efforts of abolitionists and antislavery Republicans. During the war abolitionists extended their school desegregation efforts to New York. In 1863 Andrew D. White, antislavery Republican and future president of Cornell University, was elected to the New York legislature to represent the Syracuse district. Because of his teaching experience, White was appointed chairman of the Education Committee and given the task of codifying New York's education laws. A statute of 1841 had authorized the establishment of segregated schools in any district that wished to maintain them. White wanted to repeal this statute and abolish school segregation in the state. One of his closest friends in Syracuse was Samuel J. May, the veteran abolitionist crusader. White asked May for information and arguments against segregation. May supplied him with abolitionist writings on the inherent equality of the Negro, reports of the success of integration in New England schools, and a long letter outlining the main arguments for desegregation. Separate schools for Negroes, wrote May, were "a perpetual imputation of fault, unworthiness or inferiority, which must tend to discourage and keep them depressed" even if the facilities were equal to those of

[12] Horace C. Hovey to M. W. Chapman, July 15, 1864, Weston Papers, BPL; M. W. Chapman to Mary Estlin, Dec. 29, 1863, Estlin Papers, BPL.

[13] William Haven Daniels, *Memorials of Gilbert Haven* (Boston, 1880), 151, 182; William G. Cochrane, "Freedom without Equality: A Study of Northern Opinion and the Negro Issue, 1861-1870," Ph.D. dissertation, University of Minnesota, 1957, 294-96.

white schools. Colored children should enjoy "not only equal educational privileges, but the same, as the white people enjoy." The common schools were the nursery of the Republic, argued May, and the fostering of caste distinctions in the schools would create class and racial divisions in the nation which could prove fatal to democracy. The mission of America was "to show the world that *all* men, not white men alone, but all, of every complexion, language and lineage have equal rights to life, liberty and the pursuit of happiness. . . . Let then our common schools, from the lowest to the highest grade, be equally open to the children of all the people." The efforts of May and White were unavailing, however, and New York did not prohibit segregation in its public schools until nearly forty years later.[14]

In 1861 there were still five New England cities that maintained segregated public schools: Hartford and New Haven, Connecticut, and Providence, Newport, and Bristol, Rhode Island. Abolitionists and Negroes in Rhode Island kept up a steady antisegregation pressure on school officials, city councilmen, and state legislators. They petitioned these bodies repeatedly, arguing that segregation placed a stigma of inferiority on Negro children and that the colored schools were provided with inferior funds and equipment. In May 1864, abolitionists won a preliminary victory when the General Assembly's committee on education recommended abolition of separate schools in Rhode Island. In 1865 the lower House passed a bill embodying this recommendation. But the Senate defeated the measure by a narrow margin, largely because of the determined opposition of Newport senators. Thomas Wentworth Higginson had moved to Newport after his dis-

---

[14] James M. Smith, "The 'Separate But Equal' Doctrine: An Abolitionist Discusses Racial Segregation and Educational Policy during the Civil War," *Journal of Negro History,* XLI (April 1956), 138-47. This article publishes the letter from May to White, Mar. 11, 1864, which can be found in the Collection of Regional History, Cornell University. The public schools of Syracuse, a center of antislavery activity in upstate New York, had been desegregated for more than twenty years. In his report on the condition of Canadian Negroes, Samuel Gridley Howe observed that "the colored children in the mixed schools do not differ in their general appearance and behavior from their white comrades. They are usually clean and decently clad. They look quite as bright as the whites. . . . The association is manifestly beneficial to the colored children. . . . The appearance, and the acquirements of colored children in the separate schools, are less satisfactory." Howe made a strong plea for school desegregation in the United States. Howe, *The Refugees from Slavery in Canada West* (Boston, 1864), 78-79.

charge from the army in 1864 and was elected to the School Board in 1865. As a result of Higginson's efforts, Newport abolished its separate schools in September 1865. With the opposition of Newport legislators thus removed, the Rhode Island legislature in 1866 outlawed school segregation in the entire state. Abolitionists rejoiced in the removal of "this last relic of slavery" from Rhode Island. The Connecticut legislature followed the example of its neighbor and abolished segregated public education in the Nutmeg State in 1868.[15]

Normal schools in New England were open to both races, but many of the private academies and preparatory schools were not. Abolitionists played an important role in desegrating two prominent New England private schools in 1865. John G. Whittier and Theodore Weld were instrumental in securing the admission of colored girls to Dr. Dio Lewis' girls' school in Lexington, Massachusetts, where Weld and his wife Angelina taught from 1864 to 1867.[16] The energetic Rhode Island Quaker abolitionist, Elizabeth Buffum Chace, decided in 1865 that the refusal of the Friends' school in Providence to admit colored applicants was a disgrace that could no longer be tolerated. Through her friend Dr. Samuel Tobey, a wealthy New England Quaker who was one of the main financial supporters of the school, Mrs. Chace obtained a promise from the trustees to admit henceforth all qualified applicants, regardless of race. The action of these two private schools paved the way for the lowering of the color bar at several other New England academies.[17]

More widely publicized than these school desegregation measures were the efforts to remove discrimination in the courts, trans-

[15] *Liberator*, Sept. 6, 1861, Mar. 11, 18, 1864, Sept. 29, 1865; *Commonwealth*, Mar. 4, 18, 1865; *N.A.S. Standard*, Oct. 7, 1865, May 26, 1866; Higginson to Anna and Louisa Higginson, Apr. 19, 1874, Higginson Papers, HU; Irving H. Bartlett, *From Slave to Citizen: The Story of the Negro in Rhode Island* (Providence, 1954), 52-59; *Special Report of the Commissioner of Education on the Condition and Improvement of Public Schools in the District of Columbia . . .* (Washington, 1871), 328, 334-35.

[16] Dio H. Lewis to Whittier, Sept. 11, 1865, Whittier Papers, Essex Institute; Benjamin Thomas, *Theodore Weld: Crusader for Freedom* (New Brunswick, N.J., 1950), 253-57.

[17] Albert K. Smiley to J. B. Smith, Sept. 5, 1865, E. B. Chace to Samuel Tobey, Sept. 15, 1865, Tobey to Mrs. Chace, Sept. 18, 1865, Smiley to J. B. Smith, Sept. 18, 1865, in Lillie B. C. Wyman and Arthur C. Wyman, *Elizabeth Buffum Chace* (2 vols., Boston, 1914), I, 276-78.

portation, and other areas. Charles Sumner was a leader of anti-discrimination activity at the national level. In 1862 he guided to Senate passage a bill to repeal an 1825 law barring colored persons from carrying the mail. Democrats and conservative Republicans defeated the measure in the House, but it finally passed both Houses and became law on March 3, 1865. In 1862 Massachusetts abolitionists called on Congress to enact legislation granting Negroes equal rights in federal courts. Sumner introduced a bill providing that in all proceedings of District of Columbia courts there would be no exclusion of witnesses because of race. The measure passed both Houses. In 1864 Sumner finally secured enactment of a law prohibiting the exclusion of witnesses from federal courts on grounds of race or color. During the war, Congress admitted Negroes to its visitors' galleries for the first time. Many white persons in Washington complained that it was an insult to every white man in the land to admit "niggers" to the congressional galleries, and called down direful maledictions upon the heads of "Sumner and the nasty abolitionists" for perpetrating this vulgar act, but their complaints were of no avail.[18]

In 1863 Sumner and the abolitionists opened an attack on segregation and exclusion of Negroes from the horsecars and railroads of the District of Columbia. Supported by a series of militant editorials in the *New York Tribune* (probably written by Gay), Sumner introduced amendments to the charter renewal grants of several Washington companies prohibiting them from excluding or segregating passengers on account of race. Finally in 1865 Sumner obtained passage of a bill prohibiting segregation on every streetcar line in the District.[19] Desiring to test the effectiveness of this statute, the venerable Sojourner Truth, ageless Negro abolitionist who was working among the freedmen at Arlington, rode on the horsecars of several Washington lines. One conductor tried to make her ride on the outside platform. She threatened to sue him if he persisted, and he gave in. Another

[18] McPherson, *History of the Rebellion*, 239-40, 242-43, 593; *U.S. Statutes at Large*, XII, 351, 407, XIII, 515; *New York Tribune*, Apr. 12, 1862, June 30, 1864; *Liberator*, June 27, 1862; *Commonwealth*, Sept. 27, 1862; *Boston Advertiser*, quoted in *Liberator*, Jan. 6, 1865; *Anglo-African*, Jan. 4, 1862.

[19] McPherson, *History of the Rebellion*, 241-42, 593-94; *U.S. Statutes at Large*, XII, 805, XIII, 537; *New York Tribune*, Feb. 4, 11, 17, Mar. 1, 18, 1864; *Liberator*, Mar. 20, 1863; *Commonwealth*, Mar. 11, 1864.

conductor pushed her roughly against the door in an effort to eject her from the car, causing a painful injury to her shoulder. She had him arrested and caused him to lose his job. Soon after this a conductor was seen to stop his car unasked and beckon kindly to some colored women standing timidly in the street. The right of Washington Negroes to ride in the horsecars was henceforth unquestioned.[20]

Nowhere in the North were Negroes and abolitionists more hated than in New York City. Irish laborers feared economic and social competition from the black man and had little use for a war fought to free the slave. Sparked by the enforcement of the draft, New York's immigrant and lower-class population rioted during four days of bloody mob violence in July 1863. The mob lynched Negroes in the streets and burned the Colored Orphan Asylum to the ground. The rioters attacked the offices of the *New York Tribune* and ransacked the homes of abolitionists and Republicans. New York police and federal troops finally brought the mobs under control.[21]

Abolitionists went immediately to work to get New York's stricken Negro population back on its feet after the riots. The American Missionary Association disbursed temporary relief and assistance. Gerrit Smith contributed $1,000 to help the work. Abolitionists were unexpectedly aided in their efforts by New York City merchants, who organized a relief society and raised thousands of dollars for assistance and for the rebuilding of the orphan asylum. In fact, despite the murders and suffering, the riots in the long run helped to improve the status of New York Negroes. Angelina Weld reported two weeks after the uprising that a reaction against the Irish and in favor of colored people was setting in among the city's middle and upper classes. Wealthy families discharged Irish servants and hired Negroes. The average

---

[20] Lillie B. C. Wyman, *American Chivalry* (Boston, 1913), 110-12.

[21] Albon P. Man, Jr., "Labor Competition and the New York Draft Riots of 1863," *Journal of Negro History*, xxxvi (1951), 375-405; *New York Tribune*, July 13-20, 1863; Angelina Weld to Gerrit Smith, July 28, 1863, Smith Papers, su; Oliver Johnson to Garrison, July 16, 1863, Garrison to Johnson, July 25, 1863, Sarah Pugh to R. D. Webb, Aug. 11, 1863, Garrison Papers, bpl. In 1862 and 1863 there were anti-Negro riots in many northern cities, caused by real and labor competition between white and Negro workingmen. Williston Lofton, "Northern Labor and the Negro during the Civil War," *Journal of Negro History*, xxxiv (July 1949), 251-73.

middle-class New Yorker began to realize that he had been partly responsible for the murderous outrages against Negroes. All classes of white citizens had held Negroes in contempt, spoken disrespectfully of them, and refused to admit them to streetcars, schools, restaurants and hotels. Little wonder then that the lower classes mobbed and lynched them. A more kindly spirit toward colored people began to manifest itself in New York in the weeks and months after the draft riots.[22]

Taking advantage of this shift in public opinion, the three abolitionist newspapers in New York City (*Independent, Anti-Slavery Standard,* and *Principia*) plus the *Tribune* and the *Evening Post* inaugurated a campaign to abolish Jim Crow on all of the city's street railroads. Most streetcar companies allowed Negroes to ride in their cars, but the Fourth Avenue and Eighth Avenue roads permitted their conductors to exclude colored people, and the Sixth Avenue company segregated them in special cars. Abolitionists contended that the railroads were common carriers and were required by law to provide transportation equally to everyone. They threatened to take the matter to court. The Fourth Avenue road finally began admitting Negroes to its cars in February 1864, but the other two companies still refused to change their policy. In June 1864, the controversy came to a head when the conductor of an Eighth Avenue car, aided by an Irish policeman, forcibly ejected the widow of a Negro sergeant who had been recently killed in battle. The *Tribune* exploded in anger: "It is quite time to settle the question whether the wives and children of the men who are laying down their lives for their country . . . are to be treated like dogs." Public opinion was hostile to the railroad. The policeman who had helped eject the woman was reprimanded by his superiors. The city police commissioner prohibited his men from helping conductors eject Negroes from the cars. The Eighth Avenue road capitulated to the surge of public opinion and ended its exclusion of Negroes. A few days later the Sixth

22 Mattie Griffith to Elizabeth Gay, Aug. 6, 1863, Gay Papers, cu; S. S. Jocelyn to Gerrit Smith, July 22, 1863, Gerrit Smith Papers, su; Jocelyn to Lewis Tappan, July 30, 1863, Tappan Papers, lc; W. E. Whiting to Gerrit Smith, July 20, 1863, Angelina Weld to Smith, July 28, 1863, Smith Papers, su; L. M. Child to Frank Shaw, July 27, 1863, Child Papers, Wayland Historical Society; *Principia,* Jan. 7, 1864.

Avenue road likewise surrendered. All of New York City's public transportation was thenceforth integrated.[23]

Philadelphia in 1860 had a larger Negro population than any other northern city. Several Philadelphia Negroes had amassed considerable wealth and resided in comfortable, even luxurious homes. Most colored residents of the City of Brotherly Love, however, lived in squalor and poverty in unsanitary slums. Philadelphia was a rigidly segregated city. Negro children attended separate schools when they attended any schools at all. Some of the city's nineteen streetcar and suburban railroad companies refused to admit Negroes to their cars; those that did admit colored people forced them to ride on the front platform. Negroes seeking transportation in the city were often compelled to walk or hire an expensive carriage.[24]

This extreme Jim Crowism in transportation came under powerful attack by Philadelphia abolitionists. Garrisonian abolitionism was stronger in Philadelphia than anywhere outside New England. A large number of the city's colored people were Garrisonians. Philadelphia's Negroes also supported thriving organizations of their own, particularly the Social, Civil, and Statistical Association of Colored People, which sponsored lectures, provided legal assistance to Negroes, and served as a pressure group in behalf of the interests of all colored people. William Still, a prominent Philadelphia Negro, was leader of this Association and was also an official in the Pennsylvania Anti-Slavery Society.[25]

[23] George Cheever to Elizabeth Washburn, Aug. 5, 1863, Cheever Papers, AAS; *New York Tribune*, Aug. 4, 5, 7, 1863, June 21, 24, 30, 1864; *Principia*, Aug. 13, 1863; *Independent*, Jan. 21, 1864; *Liberator*, Mar. 4, 1864; *Boston Commonwealth*, June 24, 1864; *N.A.S Standard*, July 2, 9, 16, 1864. Quotation is from *New York Tribune*, June 21, 1864. Segregation on San Francisco's street railroads was abolished by a district court ruling in October 1864. *Liberator*, Nov. 18, 1864, quoting *San Francisco Bulletin*, Oct. 3, 1864. In Cincinnati, however, Jim Crow in public transportation was not ended until after the war.

[24] Ira V. Brown, "Pennsylvania and the Rights of the Negro, 1865-1887," *Pennsylvania History*, xxviii (Jan. 1961), 45-46; *Liberator*, Sept. 21, 1860; *Twenty-Seventh Annual Report of the Philadelphia Female Anti-Slavery Society* (Phila., 1861), 17.

[25] Brown, "Pennsylvania and the Rights of the Negro," *op.cit.*, 49-50; Alberta S. Norwood, "Negro Welfare Work in Philadelphia, Especially as Illustrated by the Career of William Still, 1775-1930," M.A. thesis, U. of Pennsylvania, 1931, 18-24; Larry Gara, "William Still and the Underground Railroad," *Pennsylvania History*, xxviii (Jan. 1961), 33-39.

The Colored People's Association, the Pennsylvania Anti-Slavery Society, and the Philadelphia Female Anti-Slavery Society all maintained standing committees to work for the abolition of discrimination in Philadelphia's transportation system. William Still inaugurated the militant phase of the antisegregation campaign in 1859 with a long letter to the press detailing the insults and hardships suffered by Negroes on Philadelphia's street railroads. The letter was widely reprinted and focused national attention on the subject. In 1862 Still obtained the signatures of 360 prominent white Philadelphians, including all of the city's leading abolitionists, to a petition requesting the Board of Presidents of the City Railways to end segregation on their lines. The board took no action on the petition, but from this time forward the anti-Jim Crow campaign grew in scope and intensity. The three abolitionist committees kept up the pressure by means of petitions, speeches, letters to the press, and private interviews with railroad presidents. In 1863 Still wrote an eloquent letter to the city's leading newspapers, the *Philadelphia Press*, describing in detail the humiliation suffered by a Negro who tried to obtain transportation in the City of Brotherly Love. The letter was widely published. It appeared in the *London Times*, and was reported by Moncure Conway to have done more harm to the Union cause in England than a military defeat.[26]

The emergence of a national policy of arming Negroes to fight for the Union gave an important fillip to the antisegregation efforts. The antislavery press began to publish stories of wounded colored soldiers who had been ejected from Philadelphia horsecars. Sensing a change in public opinion, abolitionists and Negroes, now supported by the whole Republican press of Philadelphia, stepped up their struggle against segregation. In October 1864, a National Colored Men's Convention met in Syracuse and urged the formation of state Equal Rights Leagues throughout the North to work for desegregation and Negro suffrage. The first (and strongest) such League was formed in Philadelphia, and its initial target was streetcar segregation. It joined in the growing

[26] Norwood, "William Still and Negro Welfare Work," 52-60; William Still, *A Brief Narrative of the Struggle for the Rights of the Colored People of Philadelphia in the City Railroad Cars* (Phila., 1867), 3-10; *Twenty-Seventh Annual Report of the Philadelphia Female Anti-Slavery Society*, 17; *Thirtieth Annual Report of the Philadelphia Female Anti-Slavery Society* (1864), 23-24.

outcry for an end to discrimination in Philadelphia transportation.[27]

William Still suggested to J. Miller McKim the idea of holding a mass meeting at Philadelphia's Concert Hall to demand the abolition of Jim Crow. McKim used his contacts with leading Philadelphia Republicans and businessmen to arrange a meeting for January 13, 1865, sponsored by prominent white Philadelphians. The meeting adopted resolutions calling on the railroads to end their Jim Crow policy, and appointed a committee to negotiate with the railroad presidents. McKim and James Mott, secretary and president respectively of the Pennsylvania Anti-Slavery Society, were two of the leading members of this committee. Their efforts obtained some immediate results. The Philadelphia and Darby Railroad, a suburban line, put an end to segregation on its trains. A few days later a streetcar company also abolished segregation, and another line began admitting Negroes to *some* of its cars. After a month the first company reported that because of integration it had lost white passengers and its revenue had declined; therefore it would henceforth allow Negroes only in special "Colored" cars. The Board of Railway Presidents took a public "poll" in the streetcars and announced that a majority of white Philadelphians still opposed integration. But McKim's committee did not give up. They made a direct appeal to the mayor, a Democrat, who rebuffed them with the statement that he did not wish "the ladies of his family to ride in the cars with colored people."[28]

Defeated at the city level, advocates of equal rights turned hopefully to the state legislature. There they found a staunch ally, Senator Morrow B. Lowry from northwestern Pennsylvania, who for six years had been urging passage of a state law to prohibit segregation in public transportation. Described by Garrison as "a most radical abolitionist, and reminding me alike of Gerrit

[27] *New York Tribune*, Nov. 19, 1864; *N.A.S. Standard*, Oct. 15, Nov. 19, 1864, Jan. 14, 21, 1865; *Liberator*, Dec. 23, 1864, Jan. 6, 27, Mar. 24, 1865; *Thirty-First Annual Report of the Philadelphia Female Anti-Slavery Society* (1865), 17-18.

[28] Still, *Brief Narrative*, 11-13; [Benjamin C. Bacon], *Why Colored People in Philadelphia Are Excluded from the Street-Cars* (Phila., 1866), 3-4; *Thirty-Third Annual Report of the Philadelphia Female Anti-Slavery Society* (1867), 26-27; *Liberator*, Jan. 27, 1865; *Boston Commonwealth*, Jan. 28, 1865; *N.A.S. Standard*, Jan. 28, Feb. 25, 1865; *New York Tribune*, Feb. 10, May 3, 1865; William Still to J. Miller McKim, Nov. 10, 1871, McKim Papers, NYPL.

Smith and Charles Sumner," Lowry was a genuine crusader for equal rights.[29] The State Senate passed Lowry's bill by a close vote, but it was shelved in the House. Lowry persisted, and in March 1867, his bill finally passed both Houses and became law. It prohibited discrimination in every form of public transportation in the entire state of Pennsylvania. It was an impressive victory for equal rights, and to abolitionists and Negroes must go the main credit for the triumph. It was they who initiated the struggle and kept up the pressure; and it was an abolitionist who piloted the bill through the state legislature.[30]

Not content with the policy of arming Negroes in separate regiments, a few enthusiastic integrationists among the abolitionists called for the abolition of colored regiments and the complete integration of the army. "I want to sink the differences of race," wrote Samuel Gridley Howe. "I do not believe in black colonies, or black regiments." Gilbert Haven said, "We must abolish colored regiments. . . . A citizen, if he volunteers, should join what regiment he chooses; if he is drafted, those that most need his musket."[31] Such a policy, however, was too radical for the 1860's. The enlistment of Negroes on any basis was a revolutionary step forward; full-scale integration of the armed forces would not come until nearly a century later.

In addition to the antidiscrimination measures described above, northern Negroes made other advances in civil rights during and immediately after the war. California abolished its laws excluding Negro testimony against whites in the courts in 1863. Illinois did the same in 1865, and repealed all the rest of her infamous "black laws" except the exclusion of Negroes from the polls. Chicago's public schools were desegregated in 1865. In 1866 the Indiana Supreme Court declared unconstitutional the worst of that state's black laws. In 1865 Massachusetts enacted the first comprehensive public accommodations law in American history, forbidding the

29 Garrison to Helen Garrison, Nov. 5, 1865, Garrison Papers, BPL.

30 Brown, "Pennsylvania and the Rights of the Negro," op.cit., 48-49; Lewis Tappan to Morrow B. Lowry, Jan. 18, 1865, Tappan letterbook, Tappan Papers, LC; *Liberator*, Feb. 3, Mar. 3, 1865; *N.A.S. Standard*, Apr. 1, June 3, 1865, Dec. 1, 1866, Feb. 23, Mar. 30, 1867; *Report of the Committee Appointed for the Purpose of Securing to Colored People in Philadelphia the Right to the Street-Cars* (Phila., 1867).

31 Howe to John Andrew, n.d., but sometime in spring of 1863, Andrew Papers, MHS; Haven, *National Sermons*, 405, 510. The United States Navy had always been integrated.

exclusion of any person because of race or color from restaurants, inns, theaters, and places of amusement. The *New York Tribune* and *Anti-Slavery Standard* called for passage of a federal law to prohibit discrimination in public transportation. Such a law, said Sydney Gay, would be "a fit corollary to the Amendment which abolishes slavery." Senator Henry Wilson introduced a bill in February 1865, providing for a fine of $500 against any railroad or steamship in the United States which discriminated against Negroes.[32]

The time was not yet ripe for such a sweeping national law, and Wilson's bill was buried in committee. But the very fact that such a bill could be introduced in 1865 was an indication of the revolution in the status of colored men since 1861. Under the pressure of military necessity the Negro had been freed and given an opportunity to fight for the Union. He fought courageously and well, winning the grudging respect of millions of northern whites. The Negro's contribution as a soldier combined with the patient, effective work of civil rights advocates won large gains for the northern Negro during the war. Black laws and discrimination in civil rights were slowly crumbling away and Jim Crow was gradually disappearing from many parts of the North. Race prejudice, however, remained powerful and discrimination continued to prevail in many walks of life. Negroes in 1865 could vote on equal terms with whites in only five states, and these states contained only 7 per cent of the *northern* Negro population. Negro suffrage would soon become the main issue of southern reconstruction, and so long as most northern states refused the ballot to black men, the North was in a false and stultifying moral position. Abolitionists appreciated this fact and kept up their agitation for equal suffrage in the North. Despite the pre-eminence of the southern problem during Reconstruction, the status of the northern Negroes continued to occupy much of the attention of abolitionists.

[32] *Commonwealth*, Apr. 17, 1863, Nov. 10, 1866; Benjamin Quarles, *The Negro in the Civil War* (Boston, 1953), 313; *New York Tribune*, Feb. 6, 10, 1865; *Special Report of the Commissioner of Education* . . . (Washington, 1871), 343; Milton R. Konvitz, *A Century of Civil Rights, with a Study of State Law Against Discrimination*, by Theodore Leskes (New York, 1961), 155; *Independent*, Aug 3, 1865; *N.A.S. Standard*, Feb. 11, 1865. Gay's statement from *New York Tribune*, Feb. 5, 1865.

XI ✦ THE BALLOT AND LAND FOR THE

FREEDMEN: 1861-1865

RECONSTRUCTION emerged as a burning issue even before the war began. At first the word "reconstruction" was used by Democrats and conservatives to designate a restoration of the Union on the basis of compromise with the Confederacy. In this form radicals and abolitionists shunned the term. By the second year of the war, however, "reconstruction" was beginning to acquire its later meaning of a genuine *reconstruction* of southern society and politics. In January 1862, George Cheever published an article in the *Independent* outlining a theory of reconstruction very similar to the later "conquered provinces," "state suicide," and "forfeited rights" theories of Thaddeus Stevens, Charles Sumner, and Samuel Shellabarger. Cheever argued that by virtue of their rebellion the Confederate states had forfeited all rights and protection under the United States Constitution. They were out of the Union *de facto*. When finally conquered they should be administered as territories until they could return to statehood under conditions imposed by Congress.[1]

This was the essence of reconstruction as conceived by abolitionists and radical Republicans throughout the war. The theories of Stevens, Sumner, and Shellabarger varied slightly in details, but at their core was the idea that conquered Confederate states had no rights under the Constitution. Their social and political systems lay prostrate and malleable. It was the job of Congress to remodel southern institutions into a form that would guarantee liberty and equal rights to all men.[2] In February 1862, Sumner introduced a series of Senate resolutions embodying these ideas in his "state suicide" theory of reconstruction. Several abolitionists expressed support for Sumner's resolutions. John Jay succinctly summed up the radical theory of reconstruction as it emerged in 1862: "The Southern states have ceased to be states of the Union—their soil has become National territory."[3]

[1] *Independent*, Jan. 16, 1862.
[2] Eric L. McKitrick, *Andrew Johnson and Reconstruction* (Chicago, 1960), 99-101, 110-19; *Liberator*, Mar. 28, July 11, 1862; *Independent*, May 22, 1862; *Principia*, Nov. 28, 1862.
[3] *Cong. Globe*, 37 Cong., 1 Sess., 736-37; Elizur Wright to Sumner, Feb. 16,

This theory was certain to come into collision with the presidential plan of reconstruction as developed tentatively and experimentally by Lincoln and hardened into doctrinal rigidity by Andrew Johnson. The presidential theory denied that the Confederate states, *as states*, had ever really left the Union. It was a rebellion of individuals, not states. Therefore the function of reconstruction was to appoint loyal state officials to breathe the spark of loyalty and life back into the states. When certain minimum requirements were met these states would again take their place in the Union, their institutions unimpaired and their rights unchanged except for slavery, which was a casualty of the war.[4] In line with these ideas Lincoln appointed a military governor for Tennessee early in 1862 and for several other Confederate states as they came under partial Union control in subsequent months. Some abolitionists expressed opposition to this policy of establishing provisional governments in rebel states. George Cheever protested that such a procedure usurped Congress's powers of reconstruction and defeated the very purpose of Sumner's "state suicide" resolutions, which had envisaged the administration of conquered states as territories under congressional control. In this argument can be found the germ of the later clash between Congress and the executive over the terms of reconstruction.[5]

From the start of the war abolitionists pondered the conditions of reconstruction that would best secure the permanent freedom of emancipated slaves. As early as 1862 many abolitionists came to the conclusion that there could be no security for freedmen without Negro suffrage. But suffrage for the newly emancipated slaves seemed to be an impractical idea in 1862-1863, and several abolitionists hesitated to demand it as a condition of reconstruction. Samuel Sewall declared that he would be satisfied with a policy that granted equal civil rights and left the question of suffrage in abeyance. Not so Wendell Phillips and Frederick Douglass, who were in the vanguard of the movement to require Negro suffrage as a condition of reconstruction.

1862, Thomas Garrett to Sumner, Feb. 24, 1862, George Cheever to Sumner, Feb. 27, 1862, John Jay to Sumner, Feb. 12, 1862, Sumner Papers, HU.

[4] McKitrick, *Andrew Johnson and Reconstruction*, 101-10.

[5] Cheever to Sumner, Feb. 27, 1862, Sumner Papers, HU; *Principia*, June 19, 1862.

Phillips drew a parallel between the Irish immigrant and the emancipated Negro. When the number of Irishmen in the United States was small and politically insignificant, they were the butt of jokes and derision by politicians. But as soon as they became numerous and acquired political power, the attitude of politicians underwent a miraculous change. Phillips asked: "Do you know a politician who dares to make a speech to-day, without a compliment to green Erin? The moment a man becomes valuable or terrible to the politician, his rights will be respected. Give the negro a vote in his hand, and there is not a politician, from Abraham Lincoln down to the laziest loafer in the lowest ward in this city [New York] who would not do him honor. . . . From the possession of political rights, a man gets means to clutch equal opportunities of education, and a fair space of work. Give a man his vote, and you give him tools to work and arms to protect himself." In May 1863, Douglass stated boldly that he would demand for the emancipated Negro "the most perfect civil and political equality." Negro suffrage was "the *only solid*, and *final solution* of the problem before us."[6]

After the Union victories at Gettysburg and Vicksburg in July 1863, there was a great increase in public discussion of reconstruction. The North believed that these victories heralded the collapse of the Confederacy, and the upsurge in reconstruction debate resulted from the assumption that peace was just around the corner. Northern opinion on the issue of reconstruction ranged from the Democratic demand that emancipation not be made a condition of peace to the call of radical abolitionists for Negro suffrage. The whole country looked to Lincoln for a statement on reconstruction. As a supplement to his annual message on December 8, 1863, the president announced his long-awaited policy of restoration. He offered a full pardon to all Confederates (except a small class of prominent military and civilian leaders) who would take an oath of *future* loyalty to the Constitution and swear to uphold all acts of the executive and Congress relative to slavery. Furthermore, whenever a number of white voters equal to one-tenth of those who had voted in 1860 took the oath, they could proceed to reestablish a state government that

---

[6] Samuel Sewall to Sumner, Jan. 4, 1863, Sumner Papers, HU; speech of Wendell Phillips at Cooper Union on May 12, 1863, published in *Liberator*, May 29, 1863; *Douglass' Monthly*, June 1863.

would be recognized by the president. Lincoln declared that any provision adopted by reconstructed states with respect to the freedmen, "which shall recognize and declare their permanent freedom, provide for their education, and which may yet be consistent, as a temporary arrangement, with their present condition as a laboring, landless, and homeless class" would be acceptable to him.[7] In other words, southern whites were to be allowed to handle the race problem in their own way, even if they adopted a temporary apprenticeship system and excluded Negroes from equal civil and political rights.

Recognizing that the president's plan was designed more as a measure to weaken the rebellion than as a permanent policy of reconstruction, the *New York Tribune* and several abolitionists approved the message. Even Theodore Tilton, who disliked parts of Lincoln's program, wrote that "the Message is only a suggestion, not a final plan—only a hint for the hour. It will create a good deal of wholesome discussion; and while this discussion goes on, the public sentiment marches steadily forward, & makes the politicians ready for a better plan."[8]

But many abolitionists feared the consequences of Lincoln's conservative policy. Wendell Garrison, son of the pioneer abolitionist, denounced the president's exclusion of freedmen from the suffrage. "To free the slave, and then to abandon him in an anomalous position betwixt bondage and manhood, is not this as cruel as slavery?" asked young Garrison. He called for a total reorganization of southern society and politics. "There is no safety short of absolute justice. The reconstruction of Southern society must be thorough, and affect constitutions, statutes, and customs." The *Anti-Slavery Standard* thought that "the proposition to commit the care and education of the freedmen to those revived States is too much like giving the lambs to the nurture and admonition of wolves. That is a duty which belongs, by eminence, to the Nation, and should be entrusted to none but trustworthy hands."[9]

---

[7] Roy P. Basler, ed., *The Collected Works of Abraham Lincoln* (9 vols., New Brunswick, N.J., 1955), VII, 53-56.

[8] Tilton to W. P. Garrison, Dec. 16, 1863, Garrison Papers, BU. See also *New York Tribune*, Dec. 10, 11, 1863; John Jay to Sumner, Dec. 10, 1863, Sumner Papers, HU; *Commonwealth*, Dec. 11, 18, 1863; *Independent*, Dec. 17, 1863.

[9] Wendell Garrison, writing under the pen-name, "M. du Pays," in the *Liberator*, Dec. 18, 1863; *N.A.S. Standard*, Dec. 19, 1863.

The *Boston Commonwealth* published a blistering editorial denouncing the concept of states' rights which allowed the individual states to determine and regulate the rights of citizenship. "Are [we] going to slink any longer behind the sham, the miserable evasion, that the protection of personal rights and liberty for every citizen of the United States within the limits of any State belongs entirely to the State and in no case to the United States?" asked the *Commonwealth*. "This deplorable nonsense cost us the war, and the nation's life within an inch." Taking Tennessee as an example, the *Commonwealth* produced figures which showed that under Lincoln's 10 per cent plan, 14,000 voters could establish the government of a state that contained more than one million inhabitants. These figures illustrated "the thoroughly anti-republican, undemocratic character of the President's proposition," asserted the *Commonwealth*. "This insignificant fraction determines who shall govern the State hereafter. They have the power to prevent every colored man from voting, and, in the present state of public opinion in all the slave States, *they will prevent it*. . . . Besides being such a burlesque upon popular sovereignty, the thing is impossible."[10]

During the winter of 1863-1864 more and more abolitionists began to condemn Lincoln's reconstruction policy. In January the *Principia* warned that "there is danger that some scheme of apprenticeship—such as that adopted but repudiated in Jamaica —may defeat, delay, or greatly impede and embarrass the progress of the country toward peace, unity, and freedom." The *Principia* joined the growing list of radicals calling for Negro suffrage to avert this danger.[11] Theodore Weld and Anna Dickinson lectured frequently during the winter, raising their eloquent voices in impassioned pleas for equal justice to the freedmen.[12] The Massachusetts Anti-Slavery Society adopted a resolution written by Wendell Phillips demanding for the Negro "an equal share with the white race in the management of the political institutions for which he is required to fight and bleed, and to

10 *Commonwealth*, Dec. 25, 1863, Jan. 1, 1864.

11 *Principia*, Jan. 14, 1864.

12 *Independent*, Feb. 18, 25, 1864; Theodore Weld to Samuel Johnson, Jan. 23, Feb. 4, 1864, Johnson Papers, Essex Institute.

which he is clearly entitled by every consideration of justice and democratic equality."[13]

Phillips was the most persistent, eloquent, and biting critic of the administration's reconstruction program. He traveled up and down the East Coast in the winter of 1863-1864 giving his lecture on reconstruction to scores of audiences in crowded halls. Phillips called for a constitutional amendment to prohibit every state from passing laws "which make a distinction among her citizens on account of race. (Cheers)" Reconstruction was impossible on any other basis. Phillips declared: "Never will this nation be a unit until every class God has made, from the lakes to the Gulf, has its ballot to protect itself. (Applause) . . . The negro has earned land, education, rights. Before we leave him, we ought to leave him on his own soil, in his own house, with the right to the ballot and the school-house within reach. (Loud applause) Unless we have done it, the North has let the cunning of politics filch the fruits of this war."[14]

Radical censure of Lincoln's reconstruction policy focused on Louisiana in early 1864. The president had ordered General N. P. Banks, commander of the Department of the Gulf, to proceed with the reconstruction of Louisiana under the amnesty and reconstruction proclamation of December 8, 1863. The nucleus of a Unionist political force existed in New Orleans in the form of a Free State General Committee, controlled by native radicals. Many members of the Committee supported a moderate degree of suffrage for the free Negroes of the city. The Committee favored the calling of a convention to write a new constitution prior to the election of state officers. With the approval of Lincoln, however, Banks scheduled elections for state officials on February 22, 1864, *under the old Louisiana Constitution.* White men who took the oath of allegiance would be eligible to vote. New Orleans radicals and Negroes were outraged by what they considered Banks' high-handed proceedings. By scheduling state elections *before* the convening of a constitutional convention, Banks had cut the ground from under the radicals. New Orleans' free Negroes sent a delegation to Washington armed with a petition requesting

[13] *Liberator,* Feb. 5, 1864.

[14] *New York Tribune,* Feb. 16, 17, 1864; *Liberator,* Feb. 5, Mar. 25, Apr. 8, May 20, 1864.

the ballot. Abolitionists in the North loosed a barrage of attacks on Banks for restricting the suffrage to whites.[15]

Three parties in Louisiana nominated candidates for governor in the February 22 election: conservative, moderate, and radical. Both the moderate and radical parties were pledged to end slavery, but the moderate candidate, Michael Hahn, attacked the radicals for their support of Negro equality. Banks threw his support to Hahn, and with the backing of the United States Army, Hahn won an easy victory.[16] Abolitionists denounced the whole affair. The exclusion of Negroes from the polls, protested the *Commonwealth*, "has no parallel for meanness." Tilton asserted: "Prejudice, even with Gen. Banks to back it, and President Lincoln to confirm it, is a weak foundation for an enduring State. Official injustice is the very worst disturber of the public peace. . . . Let us establish no skin-deep discrimination among our citizens."[17]

The representatives of New Orleans' free Negroes arrived in Washington in March 1864, bearing their petition for suffrage. They cited the high rate of literacy and the large amount of property owned by free colored men in Louisiana. Their request, added to other radical pressures, prompted Lincoln to write a private letter to Governor Hahn, who was preparing for the Louisiana constitutional convention scheduled for early April. "I barely suggest for your private consideration," wrote the president, "whether some of the colored people may not be let in [to the suffrage]—as, for instance, the very intelligent, and especially those who have fought gallantly in our ranks."[18] This idea of a qualified Negro suffrage was gaining considerable support in the North. But most abolitionists wanted no qualifications which were not applied equally to both races. To give the ballot to only a limited number of Negroes would elevate them "into a caste which is dangerous to its members, humiliating to those of inferior grade, an anomaly in free republican society," argued Til-

15 Fred H. Harrington, *Fighting Politician: Major General N. P. Banks* (Philadelphia, 1948), 140-44; *New York Tribune*, Jan. 18, 1864; *Independent*, Jan. 28, Feb. 18, 1864; *Commonwealth*, Mar. 4, 1864; *N.A.S. Standard*, Jan. 28, 1865.

16 Harrington, *Banks*, 144-46.

17 *Commonwealth*, Mar. 18, 1864; *Independent*, Mar. 10, 1864.

18 *New York Tribune*, Mar. 16, 18, 1864; *Liberator*, Mar. 11, 1864; *N.A.S. Standard*, Mar. 19, 1864; Lincoln to Hahn, Mar. 13, 1864, in Basler, *Collected Works of Lincoln*, VII, 243.

ton. "One rule must be applied to all classes, or no rule must be made."[19]

In Louisiana most of the radicals boycotted the constitutional convention that opened in April, declaring angrily that the whole thing was a farce and that Banks had packed the convention with moderates. Banks responded to northern radical pressure to the extent of forcing the convention to empower the legislature to enfranchise Negroes. The provision was permissive, not mandatory, and the legislature elected under the new constitution did nothing whatever in the direction of Negro suffrage. Tennessee and Arkansas, the other states reconstructed under Lincoln's plan in 1864-1865, also refused to enfranchise colored men. Frustrated radicals and abolitionists turned increasingly to Congress in their efforts to obtain equal civil and political rights for freedmen as a condition of reconstruction.[20]

Congress was in a mood to listen to radical demands. Under the leadership of Henry Winter Davis and Benjamin Wade, congressional Republicans had been slowly maturing their reconstruction policy. On March 22 Davis finally got his bill before the House for its third reading. By implication the Wade-Davis bill endorsed the "state suicide" theory of reconstruction. It asserted that restoration of the Union was a congressional rather than executive function. Whereas Lincoln's policy envisaged the reestablishment of state governments by 10 per cent of those voters who took an oath of future loyalty, the Davis bill stipulated that not until 50 per cent of the white men of voting age took such an oath could a civil government be reestablished. Moreover, no one who had voluntarily participated in or supported the rebellion could vote for delegates to the constitutional convention, and no rebel officeholder could vote or hold office under the new state constitution.[21]

Abolitionists approved many features of this bill, but sharply disapproved of its limitation of the franchise to whites. "And this is called 'guaranteeing to the States a Republican form of Government,' is it?" asked William Goodell sarcastically. "What

---

[19] *Independent*, Mar. 10, 1864. See also *Commonwealth*, Mar. 18, Apr. 29, 1864.

[20] Harrington, *Banks*, 146-49; J. M. Ashley to Garrison, Mar. 22, 1864, Garrison Papers, BPL; *Liberator*, Apr. 8, 1864; *Independent*, Apr. 14, 1864.

[21] Charles H. McCarthy, *Lincoln's Plan of Reconstruction* (New York, 1901), 224-85; *Cong. Globe*, 38 Cong., 1 Sess., Appendix, 82-85.

shall be said of the folly of excluding the votes of that part of the community that is most decidedly and unquestionably loyal [that is, the freedmen]?"[22] Josiah Grinnell in the House and Charles Sumner in the Senate tried to amend the bill to include Negro suffrage, but their amendments were voted down by large majorities in both Houses. Wade explained that he favored the Negro suffrage amendment in principle, but "I would rather it should not be adopted, because, in my judgment, it will sacrifice the bill."[23] Many proponents of the Wade-Davis bill probably considered it a stopgap measure to mark time until northern public opinion could be educated up to the point of accepting Negro suffrage as a basis of reconstruction.

The Wade-Davis bill was finally passed by Congress on July 2, but Lincoln slapped a pocket veto on the radicals' handiwork. Incensed by the president's action, Davis and Wade issued a blistering manifesto denouncing Lincoln's usurpation of Congress's rightful function of controlling reconstruction.[24] Wendell Garrison sympathized with their anger, but declared that he was just as glad to see the bill vetoed because it had left the Negro entirely out of the reconstruction process. The *Commonwealth* had "no tears to shed over the loss of this bill, which though in the main a good one, was . . . disfigured by a requisition that none but 'white' persons should take part in the work of reconstruction. Until Congress has sense enough and decency enough to pass bills without the color qualification, we care not how quickly they are killed."[25]

✦

Education and the ballot for the Negro were two of the most important abolitionist requirements for a sound reconstruction of the South. But many abolitionists realized that political equality and education would mean little to the freed slave without a solid foundation of economic independence. The freedmen must "be made proprietors of the soil in fee simple, as speedily as pos-

[22] *Principia*, May 12, 1864.

[23] *New York Tribune*, May 5, 1864; *Liberator*, May 13, 1864; Wade quoted in *Cong. Globe*, 38 Cong., 1 Sess., 3,449.

[24] Basler, *Collected Works of Lincoln*, VII, 433-34; Wade-Davis Manifesto published in *New York Tribune*, Aug. 5, 1864.

[25] Wendell Garrison quoted in *Liberator*, Aug. 19, 1864; *Commonwealth*, July 15, 1864.

sible," wrote a correspondent of the *Liberator* in 1864. Otherwise the white planter would keep the Negro in a state of semi-serfdom by paying him low wages and making him economically dependent on the old master class. "It is going to make a mighty difference to the 'landless and homeless,' whether they are to get only the poor pittance of twenty-five or thirty cents per day, and be thus kept dependent, or whether they shall receive four or five times this amount by planting on their own land," asserted the *Liberator* correspondent. "The conflict between capital and labor is as old as the world; but in this case the contest could never be more unequal."[26]

This was not a new idea to abolitionists. From the outset of the war many of them had desired the breakup of large southern plantations and their redistribution among landless farmers, black and white. Such action would accomplish two important objectives: it would promote democracy in the South by destroying the economic basis of the "landed aristocracy"; and it would promote the economic independence of the freedmen. Less than a month after the firing on Fort Sumter, William Goodell called for the confiscation of land belonging to rebels and its redistribution among freed slaves.[27] In subsequent months many other abolitionists repeated and endorsed this proposal. When Congress opened its special session in July 1861, several drastic confiscation bills were introduced. But the bill that finally passed was a very mild measure confiscating only property (including slaves) used in direct support of the Confederate military effort.[28]

Abolitionists continued to press for full-scale expropriation. "By all the laws and usages of civilized nations," declared Charles K. Whipple in the *Liberator* in June 1862, "rebels against a government forfeit their property, as well as their other rights and privileges, under it." He urged the administration to confiscate rebel lands and allot a portion of them to the landless laborers who had worked them under compulsion for generations and had thus earned a clear title to the land. This act of simple

---

[26] *Liberator*, Feb. 5, 1864.

[27] *Principia*, May 4, 1861.

[28] *N.A.S. Standard*, July 13, 1861; *Liberator*, Oct. 18, 1861; *Anglo-African*, Nov. 23, 1861; *Principia*, Dec. 1, 1861; article by Lewis Tappan in the *New York Evening Post*, Jan. 30, 1862; John Jay to Sumner, Nov. 19, 1861, Sumner Papers, HU; *Cong. Globe*, 37 Cong., 1 Sess., 11, 23, 120, 142, 218-20, 415, 430-31, 434, 454.

justice to the freedmen would build the new South on a foundation of small landowners thoroughly loyal to the government. It would expiate the sin incurred by the nation in allowing men to be kept in slavery for so many generations.[29]

The Confiscation Act of July 1862, as originally passed by Congress, met many of the abolitionists' demands. It provided for the permanent confiscation of all property belonging to traitors. Lincoln objected, however, that this provision violated the constitutional ban on bills of attainder that worked forfeiture of property beyond the life of offenders. Under presidential pressure Congress passed a joint resolution declaring that nothing in the act should be construed to work a forfeiture of real estate beyond the life of the offender. Abolitionists were dismayed. If such an interpretation of the Constitution were sustained, the possibility of confiscation and redistribution of southern lands would disappear. In the third edition of his *War Powers of the President*, William Whiting argued learnedly that the constitutional prohibition of bills of attainder did not debar Congress from confiscating property permanently by separate legislative act as a punishment for treason.[30]

Whiting's legal erudition was widely respected, and his arguments were later utilized by Republican congressmen in their efforts to repeal the joint resolution of 1862. Meanwhile, some abolitionist spokesmen explored other means of accomplishing a revolution in southern land ownership. Even before passage of the 1862 Confiscation Act, Elizur Wright had published anonymously a pamphlet suggesting confiscatory taxation as a method of abolishing the southern landed aristocracy. Wright proposed that a tax of $15 per acre be levied on all Confederates who owned more than 300 acres or who had owned slaves before the war. In nearly all cases this tax would not be paid and the government could seize the land and sell part of it to help defray the cost of war. The remainder could be sold or granted to the freedmen. "If the Federal Government, under its war power, has a right to charge batteries with projectiles that sweep down the active and

29 *Liberator*, June 13, 1862.
30 Williams, *Lincoln and the Radicals*, 164-66; Basler, *Collected Works of Lincoln*, v, 328-31; William Whiting, *The War Powers of the President, and the Legislative Powers of Congress in Relation to Rebellion, Treason, and Slavery* (Boston, 1862), 95-128.

[passive] rebels alike," declared Wright, "can it not charge a battery with an agrarian law which will only annihilate without killing the real rebels?" In a later article for the *Commonwealth* Wright asserted that "a free Republic is utterly impossible . . . where the soil chiefly belongs to a limited small number of princes, patroons, nabobs or ex-slave-holders." He realized that northern conservatives would throw up their hands in horror and conjure up visions of the Jacobin's excesses in the French Revolution. "But an agrarian law for the South is just the next inevitable question," Wright stated. "Let the programme be, not only liberty to the loyal, but the SOIL TO THE TILLER."[31]

When emancipation became an official northern war aim in 1863, abolitionist demands for agrarian reform in the South became more insistent. In an oft-repeated address entitled "Amen to the Proclamation," Wendell Phillips declared that "the whole social system of the Gulf States is to be taken to pieces; every bit of it." All vestiges of slavery and the old aristocracy must be wiped out, said Phillips, and this could be done only by granting land to the freedman, for to him land was the symbol and substance of freedom.[32] Senator Sumner introduced in February 1863, a bill to grant 10 acres of land to every Negro soldier. The bill did not pass, but it was a sign of the increasing congressional concern over the land question in the South. Early in 1863 Indiana Congressman George Julian, a veteran antislavery crusader and foe of land monopoly, urged Congress to adopt "an equitable homestead policy, parcelling out the plantations of rebels in small farms for . . . the freedmen . . . instead of selling it in large tracts to speculators, and thus laying the foundation for a system of land monopoly in the South scarcely less to be deplored than slavery itself."[33]

Julian's remarks probably referred in part to the land sales about to take place on the South Carolina sea islands. In August 1861, Congress had levied a direct tax on every state to raise revenue for carrying on the war. Of course this tax could not be collected in most parts of the Confederacy, and the 1861 law

---

31 [Elizur Wright], *The Programme of Peace. By a Democrat of the Old School* (Boston, 1862), 15-22; *Commonwealth*, Nov. 15, 1862.

32 *New York Tribune*, Jan. 23, 1863.

33 E. Wright to Sumner, Feb. 1, 1863, Sumner Papers, HU; *New York Tribune*, Feb. 12, 1863; Julian's speech quoted in *Cong. Globe*, 37 Cong., 3 Sess., 1,069.

made no provision for collection in the Union-occupied portions of rebel states. This was rectified by an act of June 7, 1862, authorizing the president to appoint tax commissioners to assess the proportion of taxes owed by occupied areas of the Confederacy and to offer the land of delinquent taxpayers for sale at public auction. In effect this was a confiscation act similar to Elizur Wright's proposal.[34]

The tax commissioners arrived at Port Royal in October 1862. They scheduled a public auction of lands for February 11, 1863. Many of the Gideonites became alarmed, fearing that northern speculators would descend upon the islands and buy up most of the desirable land, leaving the Negro with little or nothing. Led by Mansfield French, some of the Gideonites began putting pressure on their friends in Washington to reserve part of the land for the freedmen. "I am greatly troubled in view of the land sales," wrote French to Secretary Chase. "The sharp-sighted speculators are on hand & with larger purses than those of the friends of humanity. If the plantations fall into their hands, *most* of the colored people will suffer greatly." French proposed that General Rufus Saxton, military governor of the islands, be allowed to purchase some of the land with the proceeds of the cotton fund and resell it in small lots to the freedmen.[35] At the beginning of February 1863, Laura Towne suggested to Saxton that he should request a postponement of the sales on grounds of "military necessity." Saxton, who sympathized entirely with the Gideonites, thought this a good idea and persuaded General Hunter to order a postponement of the auction until the whole question was clarified. News soon reached the Gideonites that their efforts in Washington had paid off. On February 6 Congress amended the tax law to allow the tax commissioners to reserve a certain amount of land for educational and charitable purposes. There was "general jubilation" on the islands. The land sales were rescheduled for March 9 and the tax commission reserved most of the saleable property for the future benefit of the freedmen.[36]

34 Willie Rose, "Rehearsal for Reconstruction: The Port Royal Experiment," Ph.D. dissertation, Johns Hopkins University, 1962, 260-61; *U.S. Statutes at Large*, XII, 294ff., 422-23.

35 French to Chase, Jan. 2, 1863, Chase Papers, LC; French to Chase, Jan. 6, 1863, Lincoln Papers LC.

36 Rupert S. Holland, ed., *Letters and Diary of Laura M. Towne, Written from*

Many of the Gideonites believed with Mansfield French that the freedmen had earned a grant of land by long years of suffering and toil. Another group of northern plantation superintendents, led by Edward S. Philbrick of Boston, disagreed with them. Philbrick was a hard-headed practical businessman with years of experience as a successful civil engineer and entrepreneur. He was inclined at times to regard the philanthropic wing of the Gideonites as naïve do-gooders. Philbrick was alert to the danger of speculators grabbing all the good land. But instead of a direct grant of land to the freedmen or the sale of property to them on special terms, he wanted an opportunity for sympathetic northern capitalists to purchase plantations and continue the free-labor experiment on a private-enterprise basis.[37] William Gannett agreed with Philbrick. He thought the freedmen would learn self-reliance best by being thrust into the labor market just like other men. Special grants of land would only reinforce their lack of initiative and self-reliance bequeathed by slavery. "To receive has been their natural condition," argued Gannett. "Give them land, and a house,—and the ease of gaining as good a livelihood as they have been accustomed to would keep many contented with the smallest exertion."[38]

At the land sales of 1863 on the sea islands, 16,479 acres were put up for general sale (the rest of the land was reserved by the government). About 2,000 acres were purchased by freedmen who had pooled their savings. Most of the rest—nearly 8,000 acres—was bought by Edward Philbrick, representing a group of Boston capitalists, at an average price of less than $1 per acre. Philbrick hired several of the government's plantation superintendents, including Gannett and Charles Ware, to run his plantations in 1863 on the basis of private enterprise. The freedmen raised a large cotton crop on these plantations in 1863, and Philbrick cleared a huge profit. He publicized his successful crop and profits in the northern press as an unanswerable argument for emancipa-

---

the *Sea Islands of South Carolina, 1862-84* (Cambridge, Mass., 1912), 100-03; Elizabeth Pearson, ed., *Letters from Port Royal* (Boston, 1906), 154, 159-60; Rose, "Rehearsal for Reconstruction," 262-65, 276-77; *U.S. Statutes at Large*, XII, 640.

[37] Rose, "Rehearsal for Reconstruction," 277-80; Pearson, *Letters from Port Royal*, 117-18, 147-48, 165-67.

[38] William Pease, "Three Years Among the Freedmen: William C. Gannett and the Port Royal Experiment," *Journal of Negro History*, XLII (Apr. 1957), 106.

tion and free labor. Many of the Gideonites, however, remained unconvinced that Philbrick's motives were entirely unselfish. During 1863 there was an undercurrent of belief among the more philanthropic-minded abolitionists that Philbrick's protestations of concern for the freedmen's welfare were mostly a cover for his own desire to make money.[39]

Most northern abolitionists who gave serious thought to the land question agreed with the "do-gooder" wing of the Gideonites. "The confiscated lands of the Southern Rebels ought to be given in suitable portions to the colored people, who so long have tilled them without wages," wrote Samuel J. May in April 1863. A month later the annual meeting of the American Anti-Slavery Society adopted a sweeping resolution calling for permanent confiscation of property owned by Confederates and the allotment of homesteads from these lands to freedmen, loyal southern whites, and Union soldiers.[40] Wendell P. Garrison attacked Lincoln's pardon and amnesty proclamation because it provided for the restoration of confiscated property to southerners who took a loyalty oath. Wendell Phillips was angry because the president's reconstruction plan "leaves the large landed proprietors of the South still to domineer over its politics, and makes the negro's freedom a mere sham. Until a large share of those estates are divided, the aristocracy is not destroyed, neither is any *fair* chance given for the development of a system of free labor."[41]

During the winter of 1863-1864 the abolitionist-controlled *Boston Commonwealth* published a series of powerful editorials urging agrarian reform as a condition of reconstruction. "What do we gain in point of peace, union, republicanism, or genuine

[39] Rose, "Rehearsal for Reconstruction," 280-85; Pearson, *Letters from Port Royal*, 170-72. Despite his good year, Philbrick's cotton crop was not as large as the better crops raised under slavery, and his profits were due mainly to the war-inflated price of cotton.

[40] S. J. May to Garrison, Apr. 16, 1863, Garrison Papers, BPL; *Liberator*, May 29, 1863.

[41] W. P. Garrison, in *Liberator*, Dec. 18, 1863; Phillips to Benjamin Butler, Dec. 13, 1863, Butler Papers, LC. In his lectures on reconstruction during the winter of 1863-64, Phillips called repeatedly for a confiscation policy. See, for example, reports of his speeches in the *New York Tribune*, Dec. 23, 1863, and Feb. 17, 1864. The *New York Herald* predicted that the Republicans would eventually adopt Phillips' radical confiscation proposals. "Emancipation, abolition, confiscation, southern lands for landless negroes! This is the programme," declared the *Herald*. "The *Tribune* will, as usual, wait six months, and then follow Wendell Phillips' lead, face foremost. The *Times* will wait about ten months, and then follow, as usual, back foremost." *New York Herald*, Dec. 23, 1863.

democracy by converting Jeff Davis and his patriarchs into Lord Palmerston and a fox-hunting, rent-roll gentry?" asked the *Commonwealth*. A landless peasant class in the South would be a constant source of social unrest. "To be safe, peaceable and permanent," reconstruction "must be primarily economical and industrial; it must commence by planting a loyal population in the soil of the South, not only as its cultivators but its rightful and actual owners." The *Commonwealth* denounced Lincoln's pardon and amnesty program. "If the President can restore to these traitors all their rights to the land," wrote the editor, "then the Confiscation Act is a farce, and the war will have been a gigantic crime and failure."[42]

In February 1864, a committee of prominent abolitionists and antislavery Republicans representing the secular freedmen's aid societies petitioned Congress "to give to the slaves made free by the power of the government, a legal and quiet possession of adequate land for their residence and support."[43] On the South Carolina sea islands, plans were being carried out for precisely that purpose. In September 1863, Lincoln had ordered the tax commissioners to put up for public sale at auction most of the lands reserved by the government at the previous auction in March 1863. The president specified that certain tracts of this land were to be sold to freedmen in 20-acre lots at the special price of $1.25 per acre. Gideonites and freedmen on the islands were overjoyed by Lincoln's order. General Saxton and the Reverend Mansfield French went even further than the order allowed in their zeal to obtain land for the freedmen. They encouraged the Negroes to preempt not only their allotted 20 acres each, but to build cabins on adjoining lots in the hope that bidders would respect their squatters' rights on these adjoining properties. Saxton and French defended their action on the ground that Lincoln's order reserved only 16,000 of 60,000 government-held acres for the freedmen. This, they argued, was hardly enough to support the 15,000 freedmen on the islands. Preemption would enable the Negroes to acquire much more property at the special price of $1.25 per acre than specified in Lincoln's orders.[44]

[42] *Commonwealth*, Dec. 25, 1863, Jan. 1, 8, 15, 22, Mar. 4, 1864.
[43] *Liberator*, Feb. 12, 1864.
[44] Rose, "Rehearsal for Reconstruction," 355-59; Basler, *Collected Works of Lincoln*, VI, 453-59.

Saxton actually issued instructions of his own on November 3 telling the freedmen to stake their claims wherever they wished. He was supported by most of the Gideonites, by Colonel Higginson, and by the *Free South,* a small Port Royal newspaper edited by Philadelphia abolitionist James Thompson. The tax commissioners, supported by Philbrick, were strongly opposed to the scheme, and put pressure on Washington to stop the activities of Saxton and French. But French went personally to Washington in December 1863, to obtain a new set of instructions to ratify General Saxton's preemption orders. French returned triumphantly to Port Royal in January, bearing a new order dated December 31, 1863, allowing Negro heads of families to preempt any government-owned property on the islands up to 40 acres apiece.[45]

The Gideonites were elated. They immediately informed the freedmen of their rights. The tax commissioners' office was soon swamped with preemption claims. But the commissioners were adamantly opposed to preemption. They carried out passive resistance to the new instructions, ignoring some of the preemption claims, attacking the legality of the instructions, and complaining to Washington. Philbrick was outspoken in his opposition to special privileges for the freedmen. They had not earned the land, he argued, and special consideration would break down their moral fiber and vitiate their self-reliance. The Gideonites counterattacked. French and others denounced Philbrick as a selfish capitalist seeking to build a fortune on the sweat and toil of an "agricultural peasantry." In a milder tone Higginson remarked that few of the men in his regiment agreed with Philbrick's arguments. "Sergeant Rivers . . . summed it up in conversation the other day," Higginson reported. "Every colored man will be a slave, & feel himself a slave until he can raise him own *bale of cotton* & put him own mark upon it & say *dis is mine!*" Philbrick lost some of his allies; Gannett, for example, was converted to the proposition that the freedmen must have land and deserved special opportunities to acquire it because of their lifetime of unrequited toil. Nevertheless the tax commissioners persuaded Washington to reverse its policy and cancel the preemption privileges.[46]

[45] Rose, "Rehearsal for Reconstruction," 359-73; *Commonwealth,* Jan. 15, 1864; Higginson to Louisa Higginson, Jan. 14, 1864, Higginson, Journal, entry of Jan. 20, 1864, Higginson Papers, HU.

[46] Rose, "Rehearsal for Reconstruction," 373-80; Pearson, *Letters from Port*

French was dismayed, but he was not through fighting. He asked Chase to allow those claims to stand that had been filed before the preemption instructions were rescinded. Since more than a thousand claims had been filed, this would have accomplished nearly everything French desired. Meanwhile in a series of incendiary speeches he urged the freedmen to take the land they needed and defend it with their hoes if necessary. French received no word from Chase, however, and when the sales took place on February 18 there was the utmost confusion over preemption rights, property claims, and so on. In most cases the tax commissioners ruled against the preemptors and sold large slices of preempted land to the highest bidders at an average price of $11 per acre. The freedmen purchased only 2,276 acres at the special rate of $1.25 per acre. In addition several groups of freedmen pooled their resources and purchased 470 acres at an average price of just over $7.00 per acre in the competitive bidding. The whole affair left a sour taste in everybody's mouth. French and the "do-gooder" Gideonites were furious with Philbrick, the tax commissioners, and the government for what they considered deliberate treachery to the freedmen. Philbrick was irritated by abolitionist attacks on him in the press. The freedmen themselves were angry, resentful, and distrustful toward the Yankees who first promised them land and then withdrew the promise.[47]

Meanwhile there was increasing support in Congress for some degree of confiscation. Early in 1864 George Julian introduced a bill to extend the Homestead Act of 1862 to cover the abandoned and confiscated estates of the South. Under Julian's bill these estates would be carved into 40 and 80 acre tracts and made available to Union soldiers, southern freedmen, and loyal southern whites on the homestead principle of full ownership after five years' residence and cultivation. Lydia Maria Child congratulated Julian for his speech in support of the bill, and proclaimed her opinion that land monopoly was "only another phase of Slavery; another form of the absorption of Labor by Capital,

---

Royal, 247-49, 251, 254-55, 257, 265-66, 276-77; quotation is from Higginson, Journal, entry of Nov. 21, 1863, Higginson Papers, HU.

[47] Rose, "Rehearsal for Reconstruction," 382-88; Holland, *Letters and Diary of Laura Towne*, 129-30; Pearson, *Letters from Port Royal*, 251, 254-55, 257, 265-66, 277-78; Higginson to S. H. Gay, Feb. 13, 1864, Gay Papers, CU; *Independent*, Apr. 21, May 5, 1864, Jan. 26, 1865.

which has tormented and degraded the world from the beginning." The House passed Julian's bill on May 12, 1864, by a vote of 75-64; it was reported from Senate committee, but did not come up for discussion before the end of the session in July.[48]

Julian realized that his confiscation-homestead measure would be of little value unless Congress repealed the joint resolution of 1862 (tacked on to the second Confiscation Act) limiting forfeiture of property to the life of the offender. In February 1864, the House voted to amend the joint resolution to read no forfeiture "contrary to the Constitution," hoping that the Supreme Court would uphold permanent confiscation of rebel property. Julian confidently expected an endorsement of repeal by the Republican National Convention. The National Union League convention meeting the day before the Republican conclave approved repeal, but conservatives on the resolutions committee squelched a similar endorsement by the Republican convention. On June 28, however, the Senate passed an amendment to the Freedmen's Bureau bill repealing the 1862 joint resolution outright. Encouraged, Julian went to see Lincoln on July 2, hoping to convince the president of the constitutionality of permanent confiscation. Lincoln admitted that when he had forced Congress to adopt the joint resolution in 1862 he had not examined the question thoroughly. William Whiting's written and spoken arguments, the president said, had since convinced him of his error, and he was now ready to sign a bill repealing the joint resolution of 1862. The 1864 session of Congress ended, however, without House and Senate agreement on the precise form such a repeal should take. On February 24, 1865, the House repealed the joint resolution outright by the margin of one vote. But in the final conference committee report on the Freedmen's Bureau bill the repeal amendment was dropped in order to win conservative support for the Bureau. Thus, although Congress had voted on three separate occasions to repeal the 1862 joint resolution, failure of both houses to get together on the exact form of repeal had defeated the measure. Nor was Julian's confiscation-homestead

[48] Patrick W. Riddleberger, "George W. Julian: Abolitionist Land Reformer," *Agricultural History*, v (July, 1955), 109-10; L. M. Child to Julian, Mar. 27, 1864, Giddings-Julian Correspondence, lc. For additional expressions of abolitionist support for Julian's bill, see Gerrit Smith to Julian, Mar. 25, 1864, and Lewis Tappan to Julian, Mar. 28, 1864, *ibid*.

measure passed during the 1864-65 session.[49] Abolitionists and radical Republicans were disappointed, but they looked hopefully to the next session of Congress for favorable action on the land question.

One provision of the Freedmen's Bureau bill encouraged this hope. William Whiting had used his influence with members of Congress to get a land proviso inserted in the bill. As finally passed on March 3, 1865, the act contained a section stating that to every male refugee or freedman "shall be assigned not more than forty acres" of abandoned or confiscated land at rental for three years and an option to purchase at the end of that time with "such title thereto as the United States can convey." This was rather vague and indefinite, but it was the best Congress could do at the time. Friends of the freedmen hoped that subsequent legislation would provide the freedmen with clear and definite titles to land of their own in the reconstructed South.[50]

As Sherman marched through Georgia in the last month of 1864, thousands of ragged and destitute freedmen straggled along behind his troops. When the army reached Savannah the problem of providing for the refugees became acute. General Sherman and Secretary of War Stanton, who was visiting Savannah, held a conference on January 12 with twenty Negro leaders of the city. Four days later Sherman issued Special Field Order no. 15, designating the coastline and riverbanks 30 miles inland from Charleston to Jacksonville as an area for exclusive Negro settlement. Freedmen settling in this area could take up not more than 40 acres of land per family, to which they would be given "possessory titles" until Congress "shall regulate the title." No white persons except authorized military personnel were to be allowed in the area. Sherman's order gave General Saxton full power over freedmen's affairs from Charleston to Key West.[51]

Abolitionist reaction to the order was mixed. Sydney Gay commended the provision granting land to the freedmen, but he dis-

[49] LaWanda Cox, "The Promise of Land for the Freedmen," *Mississippi Valley Historical Review*, XLV (Dec. 1958), 432-34; George Julian, *Political Recollections, 1840 to 1872* (Chicago, 1884), 242, 245-46; *Cong. Globe*, 38 Cong., 1 Sess., 519, 3,327, 38 Cong., 2 Sess., 1,026, 1,125.

[50] Cox, "Promise of Land for the Freedmen," *op.cit.*, 414-18, 426, 432; *U.S. Statutes at Large*, XIII, 507-09.

[51] *O.R.*, Ser. 1, vol. XLVII, part ii, 60-62.

liked the feature setting the Negroes apart from the white race. This smacked too much of colonization. Sherman was known as a conservative on the Negro question, and Gay distrusted his motives. The *Commonwealth* also criticized the order and asserted that "all this effort at segregating the negroes will fail. If they were good enough to live in the presence of white men as slaves, they are good enough to dwell in their presence as freemen."[52]

On the other hand, Tilton wholeheartedly approved of the measure, considering it a long-overdue effort to settle a large number of freedmen on land of their own. He discounted the colonization fears of other abolitionists, and expressed the belief that white teachers and officials of freedmen's aid societies would be allowed in the area. Secretary Stanton sent a private letter to Garrison seeking to allay the suspicions of abolitionists, pointing out that the Negro leaders themselves had expressed a desire to be set apart from whites. Stanton enclosed the minutes of the conference with Savannah Negroes, which Garrison published in the *Liberator* along with a defense of Sherman's order.[53] Abolitionists received private assurances from General Saxton that white teachers and missionaries would be allowed in the area. In fact, said Saxton, the segregation aspect of the order had been designed to keep out speculators, slick traders, and other whites who might take advantage of the freedmen. Saxton had full power over admission or exclusion of whites, and any who had legitimate business in the area would be admitted.[54]

These assurances mollified suspicious abolitionists and converted them to supporters of Sherman's order. Saxton, however, had been by no means as confident at first of the advantages of the plan as he appeared later in his assurances to abolitionists. He was reluctant to accept the duties of administering the order, fearing that it was just one more promise of land to the freedmen destined to be broken. Stanton, however, assured him that all would be well, and Saxton went vigorously to work to place

---

[52] *New York Tribune*, Jan. 30, 1865; *Commonwealth*, Feb. 4, 1865. See also W. L. Garrison, Jr. to Ellen Garrison, Feb. 5, 1865, Garrison Papers, sc; and S. B. Anthony to E. C. Stanton, Feb. 14, 1865, Stanton Papers, lc.

[53] *Independent*, Feb. 2, 1865; Edwin M. Stanton to Garrison, Feb. 12, 1865, Garrison Papers, bpl; *Liberator*, Feb. 17, 24, 1865.

[54] T. W. Higginson to Anne and Louisa Higginson, Mar. 6, 1865, Saxton to Higginson, Apr. 4, 1865, Higginson Papers, hu.

thousands of Georgia and South Carolina freedmen on the land. He appointed Reuben Tomlinson inspector general of Freedmen's Affairs. French and Gannett also assisted Saxton in the massive project. By the end of June 1865, they had settled more than 40,000 freedmen on the coastal lands. Many of the Negroes were growing good crops on their new land. The experiment seemed to be a success.[55]

By 1865 abolitionists had achieved partial success in their drive to obtain land for the freedmen. Powerful congressional leaders such as Julian, Sumner, and Thaddeus Stevens were committed to the principle. Congress had gone on record in favor of repealing the joint resolution of 1862 forbidding permanent confiscation. The promise of land for the freedmen was embodied in legislation creating the Freedmen's Bureau. Freedmen on the South Carolina sea islands had purchased several thousand acres of land at tax sales. Freedmen from all over the southeastern United States were being settled with "possessory titles" on thousands of acres in South Carolina, Georgia, and Florida. Abolitionists looked ahead hopefully to action by future Congresses guaranteeing these titles and setting aside more land for the freedmen. During the war abolitionist spokesmen had called for a three-cornered policy to insure the safety and permanence of reconstruction: education, land, and the ballot for the freedmen. At the war's end there were encouraging signs in favor of the realization of all three objectives.

[55] Rose, "Rehearsal for Reconstruction," 428-30; Holland, *Letters and Diary of Laura Towne,* 151, 153; *The Freedmen's Record,* i (August 1865), 128.

XII + THE REELECTION OF LINCOLN

THE announcement of Lincoln's reconstruction policy in December 1863, crystallized radical opposition to the president. The resulting Republican intraparty struggle over the 1864 presidential nomination produced a schism in abolitionist ranks. Ever since the issuance of the Emancipation Proclamation, Wendell Phillips had been growing impatient with Lincoln's apparent failure to recognize that the revolutionary character of the war required more than mere freedom for the Negro. Garrison, on the other hand, while critical of many presidential policies, was inclined to approve the growth of Lincoln's antislavery sentiments since 1861 and to trust to the future for further advances. During 1864 Phillips became the leader of an anti-Lincoln faction of abolitionists while Garrison championed the president's renomination and reelection.

An epic debate between Phillips and Garrison at the annual meeting of the Massachusetts Anti-Slavery Society in January 1864, brought their disagreements into sharp focus. Phillips offered a resolution affirming that "the Government, in its haste, is ready to sacrifice the interest and honor of the North to secure a sham peace . . . leaving the freedmen and the Southern States under the control of the late slaveholders." In a speech supporting his resolution Phillips conceded that Lincoln had done a great work in freeing the slaves. "All honor to Abraham Lincoln for so much!" But mere negative freedom would leave the Negro in a condition little better than slavery. "There stands the black man naked, homeless; he does not own a handful of dust; he has no education; he has no roof to shelter him." President Lincoln had "no desire, no purpose, no thought, to lift the freed negro to a higher status, social or political, than that of a mere labourer, superintended by others." This was not the man, said Phillips, to undertake the difficult job of reconstruction.

Garrison moved to amend Phillips' resolution by striking out the words "is ready to sacrifice" and inserting "is in danger of sacrificing." Phillips' wording, argued Garrison, implied an impeachment of the president's motives. Garrison was prepared to criticize certain aspects of Lincoln's policy, but he believed in the president's honesty and good will. "There was a time when I had little confidence in Abraham Lincoln, and very little respect for him," confessed Garrison. His revocation of Frémont's and Hunter's emancipation edicts had drawn Garrison's sharp censure. But then came the Emancipation Proclamation and the enrollment of Negro soldiers. "I have changed my opinion of Abraham Lincoln," said Garrison. "True, he is open to criticism for his slowness, and needs spurring on to yet more decisive action; but I am not willing to believe that he is 'ready to sacrifice the interest and honor of the North to secure a sham peace.' " Lincoln was pledged never to revoke his emancipation policy. He had shown great capacity for moral growth while in office. "In my judgment," concluded Garrison, "the re-election of Abraham Lincoln to the Presidency of the United States would be the safest and wisest course."

Phillips replied that he could not accept Garrison's amendment, for he believed that "the Government was knowingly preparing for a peace in disregard of the negro." The unequal treatment of Negro soldiers "is proof that the Government is *ready* for terms which ignore the rights of the negro." The Emancipation Proclamation, moreover, did not "bestow those rights which this [Anti-Slavery] Society was established to secure. The technical liberty which the black man gets is no better than apprenticeship. Equality is our claim, but it is not within the intention of the Government to grant it to the freedmen. I cannot trust the Government, therefore." Garrison replied briefly, arguing that the president had moved ahead as fast as public opinion would allow. When the vote was taken, Garrison's amendment lost by a narrow margin and Phillips' original resolution was adopted. The Massachusetts Anti-Slavery Society had by implication committed itself against Lincoln's renomination.[1]

The outcome of the Massachusetts meeting caused widespread speculation about an impending schism between Garrison and Phillips. The Associated Press telegraphed an account of their debate to newspapers all over the North. The conservative press chortled gleefully over the prospect of a division in radical ranks, but abolitionists hastened to deny that any such division existed. The disagreement between Phillips and Garrison was a mere dif-

[1] *Liberator*, Feb. 5, 1864.

ference of opinion about men and measures, they said, and did not represent a fundamental break between the two men. Garrison published an editorial defending Phillips' right to express any opinion he wished from the antislavery platform. The *Anti-Slavery Standard* stated flatly that "no schism exists in, or impends over, the Anti-Slavery body."[2] But the clash between Garrison and Phillips was more serious than abolitionists were ready to admit publicly. One young abolitionist who was present at the meeting thought "there was something terrible in . . . Phillips' and Garrison's quarrel."[3] Garrison received several letters from abolitionists supporting his position and criticizing Phillips sharply. Oliver Johnson warned privately that nothing but grief could come of abolitionists injecting themselves into partisan politics.[4]

But his warning went unheeded. It was inevitable that abolitionists should become politically involved in 1864. In 1860 the politicians had shied away from them, but by 1864 the situation was reversed, and some abolitionists had become respected spokesmen of the radical wing of the Republican party. Their advice and support was sought by politicians. Two presidential aspirants had been making use of covert abolitionist support for more than a year in their bids to wrest the Republican nomination from Lincoln in 1864.

Secretary of the Treasury Chase was the abolitionists' strongest ally in the cabinet. Chase was a man of inordinate ambition. He wanted very much to become president. Since early 1862 he had been building an organization of loyal supporters in the patronage-rich Treasury Department. Several abolitionists participated in this activity. B. Rush Plumly, special agent of the Treasury Department in Missouri and New Orleans, was quietly preparing for the 1864 nomination as early as April 1862. "*I am* for you," Plumly told Chase. "I do not avow it, but I prepare for it thro' a thousand channels. While I scrupulously discharge every duty of my Office, I *do* use it, here and all over the country—

---

[2] *Liberator*, Feb. 26, 1864; *N.A.S. Standard*, Feb. 13, 1864. See also *Independent*, Feb. 4, 1864; *Commonwealth*, Feb. 12, 1864; and *Principia*, Feb. 18, 1864.

[3] Lillie B. Chace to Lucy Lovell, Feb. 7, 1864, in Lillie B. C. Wyman and Arthur C. Wyman, *Elizabeth Buffum Chace* (2 vols., Boston, 1914), I, 258-59.

[4] Henry C. Badger to Garrison, Feb. 3, 1864, J. M. McKim to Garrison, Feb. 9, 1864, Samuel J. May to Garrison, Feb. 10, 1864, Oliver Johnson to Garrison, Feb. 18, 1864, Garrison Papers, BPL.

quietly but effectively, for the *future*!"[5] With the knowledge of Governor Andrew and other members of the Bird Club in Massachusetts, a strong Chase organization was formed in the Boston Custom House. Tilton and Joshua Leavitt of the *Independent* were sympathetic to the Chase movement, and stood ready to give it their support. James Redpath offered to publish a book of Chase's writings and speeches to publicize the secretary's fitness for the presidency.[6]

Many radical Republican leaders, dissatisfied with Lincoln's moderate war and reconstruction policies and resentful of the influence of William H. Seward and Montgomery Blair in the cabinet, supported the Chase movement. Greeley and Gay were sympathetic and were prepared to swing the *Tribune* to Chase's support at the proper time.[7] On the day after Lincoln announced his reconstruction policy in December 1863, Chase's supporters held a strategy conference in Washington. Activity continued behind the scenes until February 18, when Tilton published an editorial in the *Independent* calling for the nomination of a man committed to equalitarianism and justice in the solution of the reconstruction problem. Without mentioning any names, Tilton made it clear that Chase fulfilled these requirements and Lincoln did not. Two days later came publication of the famous Pomeroy Circular, a statement issued by the manager of the Chase forces, Senator S. C. Pomeroy, declaring that the interests of the country required a change of administration and that Chase was the man to crush the rebellion and reconstruct the nation in accordance with the principles of justice. Taking the Circular as a cue, the *New York Tribune* came out cautiously for Chase.[8]

The Pomeroy Circular backfired and destroyed Chase's candi-

---

[5] Plumly to Chase, Apr. 21, 1862, Chase Papers, LC. See also Plumly to Chase, Jan. 2, June 20, Aug. 20, Oct. 3, Dec. 1, 1863, Feb. 26, 1864, *ibid.*

[6] James W. Stone to Chase, Jan. 15, May 5, July 2, 1862, May 29, 1863, Joshua Leavitt to Chase, Sept. 30, Nov. 12, 1863, Feb. 12, 1864, James Redpath to Chase, Jan. 15, 1864, Chase Papers, LC; Joshua Leavitt to Charles Sumner, Nov. 18, 1863, Sumner Papers, HU. See also John Jay to Chase, Sept. 25, 1862, Chase Papers, LC.

[7] Whitelaw Reid to Horace Greeley, Jan. 19, 1864, Gay Papers, CU.

[8] William F. Zornow, *Lincoln and the Party Divided* (Norman, Okla., 1954), 32-36, 41-49; Charles R. Wilson, "The Original Chase Organization Meeting and *The Next Presidential Election*," *Mississippi Valley Historical Review*, XXIII (June 1936), 61-63; *Independent*, Feb. 18, 1864; *New York Tribune*, Feb. 23, 24, 1864. The *Boston Commonwealth* also endorsed the Chase movement. *Commonwealth*, Mar. 4, 1864.

dacy. Angry protests arose from local Republican leaders all over the North. The Republican National Committee endorsed Lincoln for renomination by a margin of four to one. State legislatures voted approval of Lincoln. The legislature of Ohio, Chase's home state, came out for "old Abe." In the light of this overwhelming popular support for Lincoln, the Chase boom collapsed. Chase's friend, James Freeman Clarke, advised him to issue a statement declining to be a presidential candidate. Such a statement, said Clarke, would increase the respect of the country for Chase and preserve his influence in the cabinet. Chase received similar advice from Greeley and James Garfield, and on March 5 he announced that he was not a candidate for the presidency. His statement did not preclude a possible draft if Lincoln's support should suddenly falter, and some of Chase's friends continued to hope for a miracle to catapult the secretary back into the presidential race.[9]

Like Chase, John C. Frémont had a strong desire to be president. Frémont had been a special hero of the abolitionists since his issuance of an emancipation edict in Missouri in 1861. A year later, in August 1862, Moncure Conway attacked Lincoln's conservatism on the slavery issue and nominated Frémont as the next president. Later in the month Frémont spoke to a huge crowd in the Boston Music Hall, flanked on the platform by several abolitionist leaders who were beginning to speak more openly of him as a possible presidential candidate in 1864.[10] In 1863 Frémont bought a summer home in Nahant, Massachusetts, and began to consult frequently with abolitionist leaders in the Old Bay State. His wife, Jessie Benton Frémont, exercised her well-known charm on abolitionists in an effort to secure their support for her husband's candidacy. Frémont himself gained the ear and the friendship of Wendell Phillips, who encouraged his presidential aspirations.[11]

Frémont was popular with German-Americans, who were gen-

9 Zornow, *Lincoln and the Party Divided*, 49-57; James Freeman Clarke to Chase, Feb. 26, 1864, Chase Papers, LC; *New York Tribune*, Mar. 11, 1864; *Independent*, Mar. 17, 1864.

10 *Liberator*, Aug. 8, Sept. 5, 12, 1862; W. L. Garrison, Jr., to Fanny Garrison, Aug. 30, 1862, Garrison Papers, SC; B. Rush Plumly to S. H. Gay, Nov. 28, 1862, Gay Papers, CU.

11 M. W. Chapman to "Lizzy and Anne," May 15, 1863, Weston Papers, BPL; Phillips to Charles Sumner, Nov. 27, 1863, Sumner Papers, HU.

erally radical on the slavery question. Karl Heinzen, a militant abolitionist, was the leader of the German-American community in Boston. In May 1863, Heinzen announced his support for Frémont as the next president and set about to rally German-American support for the "Pathfinder." Early in July the "German National Central Committee" issued an appeal for the organization of German-American voters into political clubs. Such clubs were formed in most of the North's major cities. Heinzen organized the Boston club, which adopted a radical platform and endorsed Frémont for president. Delegates from several German clubs came together in Cleveland on October 20, 1863, for a national convention. Heinzen played a major role at this meeting, which adopted a platform calling for revision of the Constitution to bring it into line with the Declaration of Independence; treatment of the southern states as "territories for the purpose of reconstruction"; and the confiscation and redistribution among freedmen of the estates of slaveholders.[12]

The Frémont movement began to gather momentum. Radical German-Americans in Missouri and Illinois endorsed the "Pathfinder" in March 1864. Frémont and his friends began to woo abolitionist support openly. A few young radicals in New York City formed a "Freedom and Frémont Club" in the office of the Women's Loyal National League. On March 18 a Frémont Club was formally organized in the city. Several abolitionists, including Parker Pillsbury, David Plumb, and George Cheever, took part in the meeting; resolutions were passed denouncing Lincoln's reconstruction policy and calling for the equality of all men before the law. A week later the *Principia* placed the Frémont banner at the head of its editorial columns. All over the North radical Germans and the Phillips wing of the abolitionists organized Frémont clubs.[13]

While remaining hostile toward Lincoln, however, many abolitionists refused to follow Phillips into the Frémont movement.

[12] Carl Wittke, *Against the Current, The Life of Karl Heinzen* (Chicago, 1945), 189-91; Ruhl Jacob Bartlett, *John C. Frémont and the Republican Party* (Columbus, Ohio, 1930), 88-97.

[13] *Ibid.*, 96-100; George Thompson to Garrison, Feb. 29, Mar. 2, 1864, Oliver Johnson to Garrison, Mar. 1, 2, 1864, Frémont to Garrison, Mar. 5, 1864, Garrison Papers, BPL; Susan B. Anthony to Charles Sumner, Mar. 6, 1864, John Jay to Sumner, Mar. 7, 8, 1864, Sumner Papers, HU; *Principia*, Mar. 3, 17, 24, Apr. 14, 21, 1864; *Liberator*, Mar. 25, 1864.

Some of Chase's supporters had not given up hope of overturning the Lincoln bandwagon. Tilton, Greeley, and other Chase men urged postponement of the Republican convention (scheduled for June 7) until the beginning of September, hoping that the tide of war or politics would turn in their favor in the interval. The *Boston Commonwealth* endorsed this suggestion and continued to hammer away at the president in strong language. But Lincoln's popularity with rank and file Republicans was too great for the postponement ruse to succeed. The pro-Lincoln Republican National Committee ignored the pressure for postponement. Chase's abolitionist supporters were left temporarily dangling in mid-air.[14]

While Phillips, Cheever, and Goodell threw themselves into the Frémont movement, and while Tilton, Anna Dickinson, and the *Boston Commonwealth* refused to support either Lincoln or Frémont, several other abolitionists publicly committed themselves to Lincoln's renomination. On February 27 Garrison wrote privately to McKim that Lincoln's renomination was in the best interests of the antislavery cause. "I am not his partisan, nor a member of the Republican party, nor a politician," said Garrison, "but I believe it will be the game of the rebels on the one hand, and of the Copperheads on the other, to urge rival Republican candidates to take the field, and thus to 'divide and conquer.'" McKim sent a copy of this letter to the powerful *Philadelphia Press*, which published it to counteract the widespread belief that Phillips spoke for most abolitionists in opposing Lincoln. "Whatever William Lloyd Garrison says has weight," commented the *Press* editorially. "He is still, as he has been for more than thirty years, the leader of the American Abolitionists. . . . Mr. Garrison, in sustaining Mr. Lincoln, proves conclusively that the President is not the candidate of the weak, semi-pro-slavery conservative faction." The managing editor of the *Press* told McKim privately that "the publication of Mr. Garrison's opinion must do great good. Everything that identifies the Government with Abolitionism is a benefit. . . . If the anti-

---

14 Zornow, *Lincoln and the Party Divided*, 57-62; Frank Sanborn to Moncure Conway, Mar. 31, 1864, Conway Papers, cu; Ralph Ray Fahrney, *Horace Greeley and the* Tribune *in the Civil War* (Cedar Rapids, Iowa, 1936), 175, 184-85; *Independent*, Apr. 7, 1864; *Commonwealth*, Apr. 22, 1864.

slavery radicals cease to give the government support it must of necessity fall into the hands of the conservatives."[15]

Garrison repeated his warning against Republican factionalism in an important editorial in the March 18th *Liberator*. Lincoln was not perfect, said Garrison, but there was nevertheless "much to rejoice over and to be thankful for; and a thousand incidental errors and blunders are easily to be borne with on the part of him who, at one blow, severed the chains of three millions three hundred thousand slaves." Pro-Frémont abolitionists sharply criticized Garrison's editorial, which was widely reprinted or cited in the Republican press. Noting the influence of the editorial among wavering antislavery men, Phillips remarked sadly that "a million dollars would have been a cheap purchase for the Administration of the *Liberator's* article on the Presidency."[16] But Garrison received many approving letters from fellow abolitionists and Republicans.[17] Some of the veteran crusaders who remembered the days when they had received nothing but abuse from politicians were amused by the Republican lionization of Garrison. "It is vastly entertaining to see how Forney's 'Press' . . . quotes from the Liberator, & extols Mr. Garrison as a man of the soundest judgment, . . . and repeats again & again, that *he* is in favor of Lincoln," wrote Mary Grew. "Verily, the abolitionists have wakened up to find themselves famous."[18]

Meanwhile the preparations for Frémont's nomination went forward. On May 6 a group of German-American radicals and several abolitionists, including Stephen S. Foster, Karl Heinzen, and James Redpath issued a call for a nominating convention to be held in Cleveland on May 31. A few days later the Central Frémont Club of New York City issued a similar call, urging as a platform the principles of Negro suffrage and southern land redistribution. Several abolitionists, including Phillips, Goodell,

[15] Garrison to McKim, Feb. 27, 1864, published with editorial comment in *Philadelphia Press*, Mar. 17, 1864; John S. Stockton to McKim, Mar. 16, 1864, enclosed with letter from McKim to Garrison, Mar. 18, 1864, in Garrison Papers, BPL.

[16] *Philadelphia Press*, Mar. 23, 1864; *N.A.S. Standard*, Mar. 26, 1864; E. M. Davis to Garrison, Mar. 17, 1864, E. C. Stanton to Garrison, Apr. 22, 1864, Garrison Papers, BPL; Phillips' statement quoted in *Liberator*, May 20, 1864.

[17] Alfred Love to Garrison, Mar. 10, 1864, J. S. Griffing to Garrison, Mar. 24, 1864, Isaac W. Arnold to Garrison, Apr. 2, 1864, George W. Curtis to Garrison, May 7, 1864, Garrison Papers, BPL.

[18] Mary Grew to Samuel May, Jr., Mar. 31, 1864, Garrison Papers, BPL.

George and Henry Cheever, Elizabeth Cady Stanton, Susan B. Anthony, and Frederick Douglass signed this call or endorsed the convention.[19]

The atmosphere was electric with tension as abolitionists gathered in New York on May 10 and 11 for the annual meeting of the American Anti-Slavery Society. Everyone expected a sharp debate between the partisans of Lincoln and Frémont. They were not disappointed. At the beginning of the meeting Phillips offered a resolution affirming that abolitionists saw "no evidence of [an administration] purpose to put the freedom of the negro on such a basis as will secure it against every peril." Phillips charged that Lincoln's whole philosophy during the war had been to touch slavery as lightly as possible, and then only to save the Union. His philosophy of reconstruction was similar. "What McClellan was on the battle-field—'Do as little hurt as possible!'— Lincoln is in civil affairs—'Make as little change as possible!' " Phillips would consider Lincoln's election "the end of Union in my day, or its reconstruction on terms worse than Disunion." Phillips was booed and hissed by the nonabolitionist spectators in the galleries at Cooper Union. Garrison's pro-Lincoln speeches were applauded by the same spectators. But the hard-core abolitionists were with Phillips by a small majority and the Society adopted his resolution by a margin of three votes.[20]

With an impressive show of unanimity the Church Anti-Slavery Society on May 25 denounced Lincoln's reconstruction policy and came out against his reelection.[21] But the real fireworks were reserved for the meeting of the New England Anti-Slavery Society at the end of May. The prospect of a lively debate drew the largest crowd in the Society's history. They were treated to a pyrotechnic display of oratory. The best speakers were on the anti-Lincoln side and included Phillips, Pillsbury, and Foster. Garrison, Samuel May, Jr., and Henry Wright led the array of speakers supporting Lincoln. Both sides repeated the same arguments they

[19] *Principia*, May 12, 26, June 2, 1864; *New York Tribune*, May 18, 1864; *Commonwealth*, May 13, 1864.

[20] *Liberator*, May 20, 27, 1864. See also Garrison to Helen Garrison, May 13, 1864, Garrison Papers, BPL; and Parker Pillsbury to Sumner, May 8, 24, 1864, Sumner Papers, HU.

[21] Resolutions of the Church Anti-Slavery Society adopted in annual meeting, May 25, 1864, copy in Cheever Papers, AAS.

had been using for several months. Pillsbury introduced resolutions condemning the Lincoln administration for its reconstruction policy, its refusal to support Negro suffrage, and its slowness to grant equal treatment to Negro soldiers. Garrison offered a series of counterresolutions praising the administration for its antislavery achievements and "respectfully but earnestly" urging Lincoln "to use his utmost constitutional power to secure equal rights for all under the national flag." As the debate became acrimonious Andrew T. Foss, veteran abolitionist lecturer, appealed for compromise and good will between the two sides. "I accept Wendell Phillips' criticism" of the administration, said Foss. "On the other hand, I accept the favorable view taken by Mr. Garrison of the reelection of Abraham Lincoln. I will rather accept him for four years more than run the risk of McClellan, or any Copperhead of that sort." When the vote finally came, Garrison's resolutions lost by a slim margin and Pillsbury's were adopted. Then in a gesture of belated magnanimity, Garrison's resolutions, with slight modifications, were also passed.[22] This effort to smooth over differences went for naught. Witnesses reported privately that the discussion had been even more bitter than appeared from the published accounts. The *Anti-Slavery Standard* admitted editorially that the debates had been "marked . . . by the passionate partisanship of the caucus."[23]

Numerous abolitionists were among the 400 delegates who gathered in Cleveland on May 31 to nominate General Frémont as the presidential candidate of the "Radical Democratic Party." The other two groups represented at the convention were radical German-Americans and dissatisfied War Democrats. Wendell Phillips was unable to attend the convention, but his personality nevertheless dominated the proceedings. A letter from Phillips was read to the cheering delegates. "Mr. Lincoln's model of reconstruction is the experiment in Louisiana, which puts all power into the hands of the unchanged white race," proclaimed the letter. "Such reconstruction makes the freedom of the negro a sham, and perpetuates Slavery under a softer

[22] *Liberator*, June 3, 10, 1864.

[23] S. B. Anthony to E. C. Stanton, May 30, 1864, Gerrit Smith Papers, su; Pillsbury to Sumner, May 29, 1864, Sumner Papers, hu; Lillie B. C. Wyman, "Reminiscences of Wendell Phillips," *New England Magazine*, xxvii (Feb. 1903), 725-26; *N.A.S. Standard*, June 4, 1864.

name." Phillips urged the convention to "demand a reconstruction of States as speedily as possible, on the basis of every loyal man, white or black, sharing the land and the ballot."

Several abolitionists served on the convention's resolutions committee, which presented a radical platform to the meeting. This platform called for a constitutional amendment to prohibit slavery and "secure to all men absolute equality before the law"; for control of reconstruction by Congress; and for the distribution of confiscated rebel lands "among the soldiers and settlers." Parker Pillsbury had tried to write into the platform a specific endorsement of Negro suffrage and land for *freedmen*, but the phrases about equality before the law and land for *settlers* were the best he could do. Both points were left deliberately vague because of the presence of War Democrats at the convention. This disturbed some of the abolitionists, and the adoption of another plank denouncing Lincoln's suspension of habeas corpus disturbed them even more, for this was the main objection of "Copperheads" to the Lincoln administration. Coupled with the nomination of Colonel John Cochrane (who had voted for Pierce, Buchanan, and Breckinridge before the war) for vice president, the habeas corpus plank created suspicion that the War Democratic wing of the Frémont movement was bidding for an alliance with the Copperhead Democracy.[24]

Pro-Frémont abolitionists were not entirely satisfied with the outcome of the convention, but publicly they praised its work and stepped up their attacks on Lincoln.[25] Phillips at this time believed that Frémont had a good chance to win the election. If the regular Republican convention in Baltimore nominated Lincoln he thought the radicals should stay with Frémont until the end. Phillips had some illusory hopes that the Republicans would drop Lincoln at the last moment and nominate a more radical candidate—Chase, Butler, Frémont, or Grant—in which case the

[24] The proceedings of the convention were reported in the *New York Tribune*, June 1, 1864; *Liberator*, June 3, 1864; *N.A.S. Standard*, June 4, 1864, and many other newspapers. See also *Commonwealth*, June 10, July 8, 1864; S. B. Anthony to E. C. Stanton, June 12, 1864, Stanton Papers, LC; and William F. Zornow, "The Cleveland Convention, 1864, and the Radical Democrats," *Mid-America*, XXXVI (Jan. 1954), 39-53.

[25] *Principia*, June 9, 1864; Henry Cheever to George Cheever, June 8, 1864, Cheever Papers, AAS; Parker Pillsbury to Sumner, June 18, 1864, Sumner Papers, HU.

Frémont party could dissolve itself and endorse the Republican candidate. In any event Phillips was sure the Frémont movement would scare the Baltimore convention into adopting a more radical platform than they would otherwise have done. Phillips got himself elected as a delegate to the Massachusetts Republican convention and tried there to secure an unpledged delegation to Baltimore. He also used his influence in an effort to elect an anti-Lincoln or unpledged delegation from Vermont. Both efforts failed. Phillips' views of politics at this time were curiously unrealistic. His hopes of defeating Lincoln's renomination had no basis in fact. The Baltimore convention unanimously renominated the president on June 7.[26]

Garrison attended the Baltimore convention in company with Theodore Tilton. Strong emotions overcame the veteran crusader as he sat in the galleries and watched the convention adopt a resolution pledging the Republican party to the extinction of slavery by constitutional amendment. He reported to his *Liberator* readers that when this resolution was read "the whole body of delegates sprang to their feet as by one impulse, giving vent to their feelings in prolonged cheering. . . . Was not a spectacle like that rich compensation for more than thirty years of universal personal opprobrium?" Garrison wrote privately that "even my friend Phillips would have been highly gratified with the tone and spirit of the Convention. In the speeches made, every allusion made to slavery as a curse to be extirpated . . . has been most enthusiastically responded to."[27]

From Baltimore Garrison and Tilton proceeded to Washington for Garrison's first visit to the capital. He was cordially welcomed everywhere. He visited the Senate Chamber and sent in his card to Wilson and Sumner, who immediately came out and escorted him to one of the Senate desks on the floor. There he sat for a time while several Republican senators came over to shake his hand and talk with him. He also visited Secretary of War Stanton. The brusque secretary, who usually dispatched callers with haste, took time for a long private interview with Garrison. The next

[26] Phillips to Moncure Conway, Mar. 16, 1864, Conway Papers, cu; *Liberator*, May 27, 1864; *Commonwealth*, May 27, 1864; Wendell P. Garrison and Francis J. Garrison, *William Lloyd Garrison* (4 vols., Boston, 1885-89), iv, 110.

[27] *Liberator*, June 24, 1864; Garrison to Helen Garrison, June 8, 1864, Garrison Papers, bpl.

day Garrison and Tilton visited Lincoln and talked with him for more than an hour. The president thanked Garrison for his support, and confided that the antislavery plank in the Republican platform had been inserted at presidential request. Garrison found his interview with Lincoln "very satisfactory." "There is no mistake about it in regard to Mr. Lincoln's desire to do all that he can . . . to uproot slavery, and give fair-play to the emancipated. I was much pleased with his spirit."[28]

Many Republican papers printed Garrison's praises of Lincoln after the nomination. "Our papers are publishing all of Garrison's eulogies on Lincoln and calling the attention of all abolitionists and radical republicans to them," noted Susan B. Anthony, a Frémont supporter, with disgust. "In their eyes, Mr. Garrison is now a sound philosopher and wise statesman."[29] Several abolitionists who had previously opposed Lincoln's renomination now came out in his favor, arguing that anything which split the Republican party created a danger of Democratic victory.[30]

The *Liberator* and the Republican press began to excoriate the Frémont movement. Frémont's supporters struck back hard. General G. P. Cluseret, French-born radical and former officer on Frémont's staff, had established a Frémont organ in New York City called the *New Nation*. After Lincoln's nomination Cluseret published a bitter criticism of Garrison, calling him "a lost leader . . . drunk with the wine of political expediency." Garrison the reformer had descended to the level of a conservative politician. "Mr. Garrison is in his dotage," charged the *New Nation*. "The old man is no longer the prophet whom we revered. . . . Either Garrison has been wrong for a quarter of a century; or he is wrong now."[31] Several pro-Frémont abolitionists canceled their subscriptions to the *Liberator*. The Hovey trust fund committee, dominated by anti-Lincoln abolitionists, cut off its subsidy to the *Liberator*. For a time it appeared that Garrison might have to suspend publication of the paper. But abolitionist friends who agreed with his political views came to the rescue. Gerrit

28 Garrison to Helen Garrison, June 9, 11, 1864, Garrison Papers, BPL.

29 S. B. Anthony to E. C. Stanton, June 12, 1864, Stanton Papers, LC.

30 C. A. Stackpole to Garrison, June 6, 1864, M. W. Chapman to Elizabeth Pease Nichols, July 18, 1864, Francis George Shaw to Garrison, Aug. 12, 1864, Garrison Papers, BPL; Wm. Channing to W. L. Garrison, Jr., Aug. 20, 1864, Garrison Papers, SC.

31 Reprinted in *Liberator*, June 24, 1864.

Smith sent a check for $200. E. D. Draper and Samuel Sewall raised enough money to replace the Hovey fund subsidy. Scores of abolitionists all over the North sent small contributions, and the *Liberator* was saved.[32]

In June, Oliver Johnson published in the *Anti-Slavery Standard* a sharp editorial attack on the Frémont movement. This editorial set the tone for pro-Lincoln abolitionists during the rest of the campaign. Johnson asserted that the habeas corpus plank in the Cleveland platform and the acceptance letters of Frémont and Cochrane, both of which passed lightly over the slavery question and dwelt on points calculated to appeal to Democrats, proved that Frémont's political managers were bidding for an alliance with the Copperhead Democracy. Johnson called Cochrane an "unscrupulous and slippery politician" who had been proslavery before the war and now posed as an antislavery radical. "And this man, without a drop of anti-slavery blood in his veins, and whose life has been one long chapter of intrigue, is led in triumph to the chair of a Political Anti-Slavery Convention by a non-voting Abolitionist [Pillsbury] who can find no ground for confidence in President Lincoln, the emancipator of 3,000,000 slaves!" Johnson believed that there was Copperhead money behind the *New Nation*. The Frémont party was "an ally of Jeff Davis," he told George Cheever. "Frémont I believe is a scoundrel, in alliance with the corrupt leaders of the Copperhead Democracy to divide the loyal voters of the country in the Presidential election. The Anti-Slavery of the Cleveland platform is Homeopathic, its Copperheadism conspicuous and emphatic; and so . . . [are] the letters of its candidates."[33]

And indeed there appeared to be much truth in Johnson's statements. The editorial policy of the *New Nation* seemed to be "anything to beat Lincoln." Cluseret actively sought an alliance with the Democrats. "There is so little difference between this party and the Democratic party," said the *New Nation*, "that it would be easy to adopt a common ticket, which would sweep every thing before it." The *New York World* and other Demo-

---

[32] Gerrit Smith to Garrison, Aug. 1, 1864, Tilton to Garrison, Sept. 6, 1864, Garrison Papers, BPL; *Liberator*, July 8, 15, 22, 29, Aug. 19, 26, Sept. 2, 16, Oct. 7, 14, Dec. 30, 1864.

[33] *N.A.S. Standard*, June 18, 1864; Oliver Johnson to George Cheever, June 16, 1864, Cheever Papers, AAS.

cratic papers praised the Frémont movement and publicly chortled over the prospect of facing a divided Republican party at the polls.[34] In the light of these facts many abolitionists who opposed Lincoln were forced to repudiate Frémont also. "Applying the same rule of judgment to that political movement that we habitually apply to all others," wrote Aaron M. Powell, "I cannot see how Mr. Phillips, or any other truly conscientious Abolitionist can give it support." Yet Powell could not bring himself to support Lincoln either, and thought that abolitionists should remain completely independent of politics in this campaign as they had done in the past. Lydia Maria Child had disliked the Frémont movement from the beginning, and after the developments of June 1864, she liked it even less. "I am exceedingly sorry for the course Wendell Phillips is pursuing," she wrote. "Since Frémont has written a letter so obviously courting the Copperheads, I don't see how he *can* stand by him."[35]

Even Frank Sanborn, who had little use for Lincoln, turned against the Frémont movement. If there was a prospect of the success of any other Republican, said Sanborn, "we would denounce Lincoln tomorrow. But bad as Lincoln is, he is better than Wood and Vallandigham. . . . Of all evils we wish to avoid throwing power into the hands of the peace Democrats." Frémont had destroyed himself by his behavior since his nomination. "His *New Nation* has been wretchedly edited and his strength since the Cleveland letter has fallen off two thirds. So much for dallying with Copperheads. . . . Except Phillips, who is not very confidently for Frémont, there is not a leading man in N[ew] E[ngland] who favors him. . . . It is a great pity—for Frémont had good stuff in him."[36]

But Frémont's abolitionist backers were not yet ready to give up on the general. On July 11 George Cheever delivered a power-

---

[34] Statements by the *New Nation* and Democratic papers quoted in *N.A.S. Standard*, June 18, July 2, 1864; and *Liberator*, June 24, July 1, 1864.

[35] Powell to Samuel May, Jr., June 25, 1864, Samuel May, Jr., Papers, BPL; L. M. Child to Whittier, June 19, 1864, in John Albree, ed., *Whittier Correspondence from Oakknoll* (Salem, Mass., 1911), 147-48. See also Sarah Shaw to Elizabeth Gay, June 25, 1864, Gay Papers, CU; and H. C. Neall to Whittier, June 20, 1864, Whittier Papers, Essex Institute.

[36] Sanborn to Moncure Conway, July 10, 1864, Conway Papers, CU. See also *Commonwealth*, July 8, 22, 1864. Fernando Wood and Clement Vallandigham were prominent Copperheads.

ful attack on Lincoln which was later published in pamphlet form. He reviewed Lincoln's slowness to act against slavery, his revocation of emancipation edicts issued by his generals, his efforts to delay emancipation thirty-seven years and colonize the Negroes abroad, his unequal treatment of Negro troops, and his reconstruction policy which would restore the slaveholding element to power and leave the freedman little more than a serf on the soil of his former master. Contrast this man, said Cheever, with John C. Frémont, who throughout the war had been in the forefront of the revolution of freedom and equality. How could any abolitionist hesitate to choose between these two men?[37] William Goodell, Parker Pillsbury, Phillips, and several other abolitionists continued their active support of Frémont.

In June, however, Theodore Tilton came out flatly against the Frémont movement. The Republican platform, he said, was better than the platform of the "Radical Democratic Party" despite the radicalism of the latter, because the *real* purpose of the Frémont movement was an alliance with the Democratic forces. "Our chief regret in view of the Cleveland Convention is, that it has unhappily led a number of excellent friends of the Good Cause into a snare," wrote Tilton. "Those well-known Abolitionists identified with the Cleveland movement—and whose sincerity and uprightness we do not for a moment question—have unwittingly placed themselves in a false position, where their influence is working against the best interests of the country, and is bringing a lamentable discredit upon themselves." Tilton admired Phillips and agreed with most of his criticisms of Lincoln, but he could see no reason to support a party which, in the end, would turn out far worse than the Lincoln party.[38]

Phillips replied in the next issue of the *Independent*. He denounced the conservatism of the Republican party and stated that he preferred the whole loaf of the Cleveland platform to the half-loaf of Baltimore. The Cleveland platform called for a constitutional amendment not only to abolish slavery, but to guarantee to all men equality before the law. "To me this is the chief gem of its crown," said Phillips. "There can be no possible

[37] George B. Cheever, *A Change of Administration, for the Security of the Government, a Christian Duty and a National Necessity* (New York, 1864).
[38] *Independent*, June 23, 1864.

salvation for the Union, and no safety for the negro in his freedom, except on the basis of every man of every race equal in privilege, right, and franchise before the law. This idea, again, owes its birth to the Cleveland Movement, and is, as yet, the high-water mark of American politics." Phillips would welcome an alliance between Frémont and the Democrats if it came on the basis of the Cleveland platform. Even if unsuccessful at the ballot box, the Frémont movement would have served its purpose if it forced the Republican party to adopt a more radical policy.

Tilton answered Phillips' arguments in the same issue of the *Independent*. Preserving a tone of respect and admiration for the great orator, Tilton nevertheless accused him of political naiveté for believing that any alliance could be forged between the Frémont party and the Peace Democracy on terms favorable to the former. Tilton recounted his experience at the Frémont ratification meeting in New York on June 27. Nearly all the speakers were Peace Democrats! The loudest cheers were for McClellan! The chief speaker, Colonel Cochrane, alluded to Frémont and McClellan as "twin cherries on one stalk!" It should have been obvious, said Tilton, that the Democrats were using the Frémont movement as a weapon to wound the Republican party. The "equality before the law" plank of the Cleveland platform, he declared, was a sham. "Now, we would be glad if a great political party could go before the country on the high issue of giving every black man a vote," wrote Tilton. "But the country is not ready for such an issue. . . . If the next election were to turn upon the question of giving every black man a vote, the Copperheads would achieve the next administration. If the country were ready for such an issue, the Baltimore Convention would have made it. . . . Any man who knows the meaning of the Cleveland movement laughs at the idea that Frémont and Cochrane are fighting a battle for the sake of the negro's right to vote. Neither of these men, in their letters of acceptance, said a word about the rights of the negro." Tilton was not happy with the Republican nomination either. "If the great Union party represented at Baltimore had chosen some other candidate, we would have had no regrets. If, before November, some strange change in events should put another name at the head of this great party, we would cheerfully acquiesce. But we shall not join the Copperheads in a coalition to make bad worse."[39]

Phillips restated his position in the next issue of the *Independent*, chiding Tilton for his declaration that the country was not ready for Negro suffrage. That may be true, said Phillips, but since when did radicals wait until the country was ready for a reform before advocating it? Phillips avowed himself an agitator, not a politician. He had taken an advanced position in the Frémont movement not for political reasons, but for purposes of reform. He criticized Tilton for rejecting his abolitionist training and supporting Lincoln on grounds of expediency. In a brief reply, Tilton repeated his earlier arguments and asserted that he was as much in favor of Negro equality as Phillips. But before that measure became acceptable to public opinion there would have to be a great deal more discussion and agitation of the issue than there had been. "We are in for the agitation, heart and soul —as zealously as Mr. Phillips. But it is simply unwise to push a great question to an untimely defeat at the ballot-box." Phillips was foolish if he really believed that the Cleveland movement was genuinely in favor of Negro suffrage. "Let Mr. Phillips go to a Frémont ratification meeting, and speak on the 'absolute equality' of negroes and Irishmen, and he will be rioted out of the house," wrote Tilton. "We are willing to join Mr. Phillips in any new and needful labors to make the country ready for the negroes' fullest rights; but the Frémont meetings are just the places where such ideas are not welcome."[40]

This exchange between two of the foremost radicals in the country was widely reprinted and commented on by the northern press. Tilton conceded privately that his set-to with Phillips had been the most unpleasant experience of his editorial career. He was worried that his friend Phillips would take it personally. That worry was erased when Phillips sent him a cordial note

[39] *ibid.*, June 30, 1864. Tilton informed a friend privately that "the Frémont meeting at Cooper Institute was the most complete and disastrous Copperhead display that could possibly have happened. The genuine antislavery men who have joined this company are in great sorrow and confusion." Tilton to Hugh Bond, June 30, 1864, Tilton Papers, NYHS.

[40] *Independent*, July 7, 1864.

declaring that their difference of opinion in no way impaired their friendship.[41]

But if the exchange between Phillips and Tilton was conducted in a spirit of cordiality, the same could not be said of the dispute within the American Anti-Slavery Society itself. Phillips was incensed by the *Anti-Slavery Standard's* criticisms of the Frémont movement. He accused Oliver Johnson of making the *Standard* a partisan Lincoln sheet. Phillips maintained that the anti-Lincoln resolutions adopted in 1864 by the Massachusetts, American, and New England Anti-Slavery Societies bound the *Standard*, as official organ of the American Society, to pursue an anti-Lincoln course. He called a meeting of the Society's executive committee and demanded suspension of the *Standard* unless it changed its policy.[42] Oliver Johnson was just as adamant. "If I am required either to set the Standard in opposition to Lincoln's election," he told the executive committee, "or to suppress my honest convictions in regard to the Frémont movement, its candidates and platform, I shall resign the editorial chair."[43] Despite Phillips' fulminations, a majority of the executive committee, led by Garrison, supported Johnson and passed a vote of confidence in his editorial policy. The committee told Johnson only to avoid "undue partiality" toward Lincoln. The *Standard* subsequently followed a course of "non-partisan" support of the president. Its position was the same as in 1860, explained Johnson, when the *Standard* was not a partisan proponent of Lincoln but nevertheless hoped for his victory.[44] This did not satisfy Phillips and his adherents, who denounced the *Standard* as "a disgrace to the Society & a fraud upon it," and withdrew their financial support from the paper. The schism in the Society grew so bitter that the executive committee canceled the usual Fourth of July and August First (anniversary of West Indian emancipa-

[41] Tilton to Garrison, June 30, 1864, Garrison Papers, BPL; Tilton to Anna Dickinson, July 13, 1864, Dickinson Papers, LC.

[42] Garrison to Samuel May, Jr., June 17, 1864, Garrison to Oliver Johnson, June 17, 20, 1864, George Thompson to Garrison, June 18, 1864, Garrison Papers, BPL.

[43] Johnson to Garrison, June 20, 1864, Garrison Papers, BPL.

[44] Samuel May, Jr., to S. J. May, June 22, 1864, S. J. May Papers, BPL; Oliver Johnson to Samuel May, Jr., June 23, 30, 1864, Samuel May, Jr., Papers, BPL; Johnson to Garrison, June 23, 1864, Johnson to Phillips, June 22, 1864, Garrison Papers, BPL; *N.A.S. Standard*, Aug. 6, 1864.

tion) celebrations in order to prevent additional public quarrels.[45]

The *Standard, Liberator,* and *Independent* continued to hammer away at the theme that pro-Frémont abolitionists were playing into the hands of Copperheads. Some radical Republicans who disliked Lincoln warned the Frémont abolitionists that their activities endangered the Republican party.[46] Late in July, Phillips and Karl Heinzen, sensitive to Republican criticism of their course and of Frémont's alleged dalliance with Copperheads, had a long talk with the "Pathfinder" and published the results. Frémont reaffirmed his support of the radical planks in the Cleveland platform. "The negroes ought to have all the rights of whites," he said. "The word white must disappear from the laws and Constitutions." Frémont indignantly denied the rumors that he would throw over the radical planks in the Cleveland platform in return for the regular Democratic nomination. He would like to make an alliance with the War Democrats to beat Lincoln, Frémont said, but he would accept such an alliance on none but his own terms. Phillips, Heinzen, and other abolitionist backers of Frémont were satisfied with the interview. If the Democratic convention in Chicago at the end of August nominated McClellan and repudiated the antislavery portion of the Cleveland platform, said Goodell, the Frémont ticket would go its own way and have nothing to do with the Democrats. If, on the other hand, the Democratic party split apart at Chicago, the Frémont party would be glad to absorb the War Democrats on the basis of the Cleveland platform.[47]

The Boston Emancipation League and its organ, the *Commonwealth,* represented those abolitionists who were opposed to Lincoln but who were suspicious of the Frémont movement. George Stearns, chief backer of the *Commonwealth,* invited a group of abolitionists to meet with Frémont at Stearns' home on August 9 to discuss the political situation. Present at the meeting besides Stearns and Frémont were Phillips, Frank Bird, Elizur Wright, Bronson Alcott, and two lesser-known officials of the Emancipa-

---

[45] Oliver Johnson to Samuel May, Jr., Oct. 15, 1864, Garrison Papers, BPL; Johnson to Samuel May, Jr., Sept. 22, 1864, Samuel May, Jr., Papers, BPL; W. L. Garrison, Jr., to Martha Wright, Oct. 6, 1864, Garrison Papers, SC; *Liberator,* June 24, July 22, 1864.

[46] *N.A.S. Standard,* July 16, 1864; *Liberator,* July 29, 1864; *Principia,* July 21, 1864; Henry Wilson to George Cheever, July 27, 1864, Cheever Papers, AAS.

[47] *Principia,* Aug. 4, 1864; *Commonwealth,* Aug. 5, 1864.

tion League. They questioned Frémont closely. The general stated that he expected a contest between the War Democrats and the Copperheads at the Chicago convention. The former would prevail, he believed, and nominate him on a radical platform. Frémont thought that with the support of the War Democrats and radical Republicans he had a good chance of beating Lincoln. Stearns and some of the others were skeptical, but Phillips came away from the meeting with renewed enthusiasm for the Frémont cause. He wanted to call an immediate convention of New England radical Republicans to endorse Frémont.[48]

But two weeks later Phillips' optimism had vanished and he told Elizabeth Cady Stanton that McClellan would be nominated at Chicago on a peace platform.[49] What had happened to dull Phillips' hopefulness? Northern morale dropped to its lowest point in August 1864. Grant was stalemated in Virginia and casualty lists were mounting. Sherman was stymied before Atlanta. Frustration, despair, and defeatism overcame the northern people in July and August. Early in August Sydney Gay reported that things were "never so gloomy." "The people would vote today for any compromise that would bring peace without sacrifice of the Union," and there was "a growing party for peace at any price, even disunion." Lincoln's "chances of reelection grow daily less & less, & the chances of any Copperhead traitor better and better." Many other abolitionists echoed Gay's somber observations. Henry Raymond, chairman of the Republican National Committee, received letters from dozens of Republican politicians reporting defeatism and an alarming growth of anti-Lincoln sentiment around the country. On August 23 Lincoln wrote his famous memorandum stating that he would probably not be reelected and that it would be his duty to cooperate with the president-elect to save the Union before the next inauguration.[50]

The North's defeatism, plus the growing exasperation of radical Republicans with the president after his pocket veto of the

[48] George Stearns to Bronson Alcott, Aug. 8, 1864, Alcott Papers, Concord Public Library; Alcott, Diary, entries of August 9 and 10, *ibid.*

[49] Phillips to E. C. Stanton, Aug. 22, 1864, in Theodore Stanton and Harriot Stanton Blatch, *Elizabeth Cady Stanton* (2 vols., New York, 1922), II, 98.

[50] Gay to Elizabeth Gay, Aug. 6, 1864, Gay Papers, CU; Francis Brown, *Raymond of the* Times (New York, 1951), 259-60; Roy P. Basler, ed., *The Collected Works of Abraham Lincoln* (9 vols., New Brunswick, 1955), VII, 514.

Wade-Davis bill, combined to produce a movement to replace Lincoln on the Republican ticket with someone more likely to unite the party and win the election—such as Chase, Butler, or Grant. Several abolitionists were active in this movement. On July 21 Henry Winter Davis, one of the radical congressional leaders, got in touch with George Cheever and suggested the possibility of persuading both Lincoln and Frémont to withdraw in favor of a new candidate. Cheever wrote to several abolitionist friends to ask them what they thought of this idea. He received favorable replies from Tilton and from the leaders of the Emancipation League. At the end of July Cheever drew up a list of men to consult about the project. Davis approved the list and on August 14 and 18 a group of abolitionists and radicals, including Cheever, Tilton, Greeley, and Parke Godwin (managing editor of the *New York Evening Post*) met at the homes of David Dudley Field and George Opdyke in New York to formulate plans. Senators Chandler, Wade, and Sumner, ex-Secretary Chase, and Governor Andrew gave cautious and qualified support to the project.[51]

The radicals tentatively scheduled a new Republican convention for September 28 in Cincinnati.[52] Meanwhile on August 21 a group of Boston abolitionists headed by Stearns apprised Frémont in a public letter of the movement for a new convention and "emphatically advise[d]" both Frémont and Lincoln to withdraw their candidacies. They asked Frémont to state definitely whether he would withdraw if Lincoln agreed to do so. Frémont replied four days later that he would pull out of the race if Lincoln did the same and if the new convention nominated a candidate pledged to total victory over the Confederacy and a complete abolition of slavery.[53]

The radical leaders of this movement met again in New York

[51] Zornow, *Lincoln and the Party Divided*, 108-16; Henry Winter Davis to George Cheever, July 21, 31, 1864, Smith Regnas to George Cheever, July 25, 1864, Cheever Papers, AAS; George Cheever to Tilton, July ?, 1864, Amasa Walker to Tilton, July 22, 1864, Tilton Papers, NYHS; Elizur Wright to Gerrit Smith, Aug. 13, 19, 1864, Smith Papers, SU; Sumner to Whittier, Sept. 1, 1864, Whittier Papers, Essex Institute; Henry G. Pearson, *The Life of John Andrew* (2 vols., Boston, 1904), II, 156-63; Fahrney, *Greeley and the* Tribune *in the Civil War*, 198-200.

[52] John A. Stevens to Henry Cheever, Aug. 25, 1864, Amasa Walker to Henry Cheever, Aug. 26, 31, 1864, Cheever Papers, AAS.

[53] *Commonwealth*, Aug. 26, 1864; *Liberator*, Sept. 9, 16, 1864.

at the end of August and decided to sound out northern Republican governors on the plan to replace Lincoln. On September 2, letters written by Tilton and signed by Tilton, Greeley, and Godwin went out to all Republican governors asking them three questions: Can Lincoln be elected? Can he carry your state? Should another candidate be substituted for him? Before these letters were sent, the Democrats had nominated McClellan for president on a virtual peace-at-any-price platform. This was expected, but somehow its actual accomplishment tended to unite Republicans behind Lincoln as the only alternative to McClellan and disaster. Suddenly on September 3 the news flashed across the country that Sherman had taken Atlanta. The North went wild with joy. The long summer of discontent was over. The long-awaited victory was here at last. In this new mood of exhilaration and enthusiasm northern war-weariness and defeatism dissolved like a fog at sunrise. Republican governors received Tilton's inquiry at just the time when this mood was manifesting itself. Consequently the replies were overwhelmingly opposed to the replacement of Lincoln by another candidate. Before the capture of Atlanta a majority of Republican governors might have favored a new convention. But military victory transformed the situation overnight. Lincoln was no longer the discredited leader of a lost cause; he was the mighty captain of a victorious nation, confident of vindication at the polls in November. The plans for a Cincinnati convention were quietly abandoned.[54]

Even before he received the replies of northern governors, Tilton had concluded that unqualified support of Lincoln's candidacy was the only sensible course. "I was opposed to Mr. Lincoln's nomination; but now it becomes the duty of all Unionists to present a united front," he wrote to Anna Dickinson on September 3. "The Baltimore platform is the best in American history—we can pardon something to a second-rate candidate." In an *Independent* editorial Tilton wholeheartedly endorsed the

[54] The replies of the governors to Tilton's letters are in the Tilton Papers, NYHS. See also Sydney Gay to Elizabeth Gay, Sept. 3, 1864, Gay Papers, CU; *New York Tribune*, Sept. 3, 1864; *Liberator*, Sept. 9, 1864; Fahrney, *Greeley and the Tribune in the Civil War*, 202; John Nicolay to Tilton, Sept. 6, 1864, and Tilton to Nicolay, Sept. 6, 1864, Lincoln Papers, LC; George Cheever to Elizabeth Washburn, Sept. 10, 1864, and John Austin Stevens to Henry Cheever, Sept. 14, 1864, Cheever Papers, AAS.

Republican party and repeated his lukewarm endorsement of Lincoln. He privately advised Miss Dickinson to come out in favor of Lincoln. She did so in a letter to the *Independent* which attracted wide attention. "This is no personal contest," she declared; "I shall not work for Abraham Lincoln; I shall work for the salvation of my country's life, . . . for the defeat of this disloyal peace party, that will bring ruin and death if it comes into power." In the weeks after the capture of Atlanta many other abolitionists who had previously withheld support from Lincoln followed Tilton's and Dickinson's lead.[55]

On September 6 the *New York Tribune* unequivocally endorsed Lincoln's reelection in an editorial universally attributed to Greeley, but actually written by Sydney Gay.[56] Despite its faults the Lincoln administration, said Gay, was ten thousand times better than the Copperhead Democracy. "Henceforth we fly the banner of ABRAHAM LINCOLN for the next Presidency, choosing that far rather than the Disunion and a quarter of century of wars, or the Union and political servitude which our opponents would give us." Gay agreed with much of the radicals' criticism of Lincoln, but the president "has done seven-eighths of the work after his fashion; there must be vigor and virtue enough left in him to do the other fraction. . . . We MUST re-elect him, and, God helping us, we WILL."

McClellan partly repudiated the Democratic peace platform, but his letter of acceptance stated that peace should be concluded solely on the basis of Union and the southern states readmitted with all their rights unimpaired. This seemed to mean that if elected, McClellan would seek to preserve slavery in a restored Union. Since all abolitionists and most Republicans by this time linked Union with emancipation as inseparable war aims, McClellan's position was as abhorrent to them as Vallandigham's.[57]

Several abolitionists took the stump for Lincoln. Anna Dickinson made numerous well-publicized speeches. Tilton threw himself into the campaign with such abandon that he fainted from ex-

[55] Tilton to Anna Dickinson, Sept. 3, 5, 1864, Dickinson Papers, LC; Tilton's and Miss Dickinson's public endorsements of the Republican party published in *Independent*, Sept. 8, 1864. In a letter to the *Liberator* of Sept. 23, 1864, Frederick Douglass retracted his earlier opposition to Lincoln and declared that every friend of the slave should now rally to the president's support.

[56] S. H. Gay to Elizabeth Gay, Sept. 9, 1864, Gay Papers, CU.

[57] *Liberator*, Sept. 16, 1864.

haustion on the speaker's platform at a rally three days before the election. Henry Wright stumped for Lincoln in Illinois and Michigan. William Burleigh spoke frequently in and around New York City. Andrew T. Foss gave forty speeches for Lincoln during the campaign. Gerrit Smith spoke nearly every day for five weeks in upstate New York. Worthy of note is the fact that many of these speeches, especially those by Anna Dickinson, consisted mainly of attacks on McClellan and contained little praise of Lincoln or his administration.[58]

After the capture of Atlanta, Republicans generally were confident of victory. But Frémont was still in the race, and there was a danger that he would take away enough votes from Lincoln to put McClellan in the White House. Republican Senator Zachariah Chandler journeyed to New York in an effort to persuade Frémont to withdraw from the race. Chandler may have been authorized by Lincoln to promise that in return for Frémont's withdrawal, Montgomery Blair, the *bête noire* of the radicals, would be dropped from the cabinet.[59] Meanwhile a number of Boston abolitionists, headed by George Stearns, put pressure on Frémont to pull out of the race. Frémont consulted several abolitionist friends. Whittier advised him to withdraw for the good of the country. Wendell Phillips, implacable to the end, urged Frémont to stay in the race as a symbol of radical ideas. But Phillips was the only prominent figure to give Frémont this advice, and on September 17 the "Pathfinder" decided to withdraw. In a letter on that day to Stearns and his associates, Frémont grudgingly urged his backers to support Lincoln for reelection. The letter was published on September 22, and the next day Lincoln accepted Montgomery Blair's resignation. Frémont's

58 Tilton to Anna Dickinson, Sept. 14, Oct. 4, 1864, Dickinson Papers, LC; Tilton to John Nicolay, Nov. 12, 1864, Lincoln Papers, LC; *Liberator*, Sept. 16, Oct. 7, 28, Nov. 4, 1864, Feb. 3, 17, 1865; William H. Burleigh, *Poems by W. H. Burleigh, With a Sketch of His Life by Celia Burleigh* (New York, 1871), xxv-xxvi; Gerrit Smith to Garrison, Oct. 10, 1864, Garrison Papers, BPL; *Commonwealth*, Sept. 16, 1864; *N.A.S. Standard*, Sept. 24, 1864.

59 For a discussion of the Chandler mission, see Winfred A. Harbison, "Zachariah Chandler's Part in the Re-election of Abraham Lincoln," *Mississippi Valley Historical Review*, XXII (Sept. 1936), 267-76; and Charles R. Wilson, "New Light on the Lincoln-Blair-Frémont 'Bargain' of 1864," *American Historical Review*, XLII (Oct. 1936), 71-78.

withdrawal united the Republican party once more. Republicans now looked forward confidently to victory in November.[60]

Some of Frémont's supporters were angered by his withdrawal. Elizabeth Cady Stanton, Susan B. Anthony, and George Cheever refused to follow the general into the Lincoln camp.[61] There were rumors that Phillips would take the stump for Lincoln, but Phillips himself squelched these with the statement that he would "cut off both hands before doing anything to aid Abraham Lincoln's election."[62] Phillips tried to make his position clear in speeches to hostile Boston and New York audiences in October. He avowed himself a reformer, not a politician. He judged Lincoln by the reform standards of equality and justice for the freedmen. The president had fallen short of these standards, said Phillips, and hence he could not support him for reelection. Most of Phillips' fellow abolitionists regretted these speeches, for by giving them Phillips had sacrificed some of the influence and prestige he had gained since the outbreak of the war.[63] Phillips' stand in 1864 revealed a lack of political realism. If all antislavery sympathizers had followed his advice and refused to support Lincoln, the abolitionist cause would have suffered a disastrous defeat. Fortunately for the cause and for the nation, all but a handful of antislavery men followed Garrison rather than Phillips in 1864.

All abolitionists, even Phillips, hailed the Republican triumph in November as a great victory for freedom. "The people pronounced for the prosecution of the war in the first place, and in the next for the abolition of slavery," said the *Commonwealth*.

---

[60] George Stearns to Bronson Alcott, Sept. 11, 1864, Alcott Papers, Concord Public Library; George Stearns, S. R. Urbino, James Stone, Frank Bird, Samuel G. Howe, and Elizur Wright to Frémont, Sept. 9, 1864, and Frémont to Stearns et al., Sept. 17, 1864, published in the Boston papers, Sept. 22, 1864, and the rest of the northern press, Sept. 23, 1864. Jessie Benton Frémont later recalled that Whittier's advice had been decisive in her husband's decision to withdraw. Allan Nevins, *Frémont: Pathmarker of the West* (2nd ed., New York, 1955), 582. See also *ibid.*, 579-82; and *Commonwealth*, Oct. 8, 1864.

[61] Stanton and Blatch, *Elizabeth Cady Stanton*, II, 100-01; George Cheever to Elizabeth Washburn, Nov. 1, 1864, Cheever Papers, AAS; Oliver Johnson to Gerrit Smith, Nov. 23, 1864, Smith Papers, SU.

[62] Stanton and Blatch, *Elizabeth Cady Stanton*, II, 100-01n.

[63] *Liberator*, Oct. 28, 1864; *Commonwealth*, Oct. 29, 1864; W. L. Garrison, Jr., to Martha Wright, Oct. 23, Nov. 13, 1864, Samuel J. May to W. L. Garrison, Jr., Oct. 26, 1864, Garrison Papers, SC; W. P. Garrison to W. L. Garrison, Oct. 27, 1864, W. P. Garrison Papers, HU.

"With a logic which never fails them, they linked together these two things and made them one and inseparable." Phillips urged all abolitionists to forget past differences and work together for the common cause. "Now our common duty is to throw all personal matters behind us and rally together to claim of the Republican party the performance of their pledge [the Thirteenth Amendment]," he told Elizabeth Cady Stanton. "On that issue the canvass was conducted, and now we have a right to demand the 'bond,' and they a right to demand that we shall help them attain the capability of granting it." Universal freedom for the Negro was assured by Lincoln's reelection; abolitionists must work to persuade the people and their government to take the next step forward—universal equality.[64]

[64] *Commonwealth*, Nov. 19, 1864; Wendell Phillips to E. C. Stanton, Nov. 20, 1864, Stanton Papers, LC. See also *Liberator*, Nov. 18, 1864; and a speech by Phillips published in the *Philadelphia Press*, Dec. 19, 1864.

XIII ✦ SCHISM IN THE RANKS:

1864-1865

In 1865 there occurred a schism in the Garrisonian abolitionist movement comparable in importance to the division of 1840. One of the main causes of the schism of 1865 was the sharp clash between the followers of Garrison and Phillips over the presidential election of 1864, but there were other causes, dating back many years. The controversy between Pillsbury and Foster, on the one hand, and Garrison on the other regarding the attitude of abolitionists toward the Republican party was long-standing and foreshadowed the conflict of 1864. During the early war years Wendell Phillips exercised a mediating influence between the two factions, but as the war progressed his increasingly revolutionary concept of reconstruction drove him closer to the Pillsbury-Foster camp.

Disputes among Garrisonians over the future of their antislavery societies broke out in the first year of the war. McKim's attempt to resign from the Pennsylvania Anti-Slavery Society and devote himself full-time to freedmen's aid work sparked the controversy. After Lincoln made emancipation an official war aim, the discussion of the fate of organized abolitionism became more heated. At the annual meeting of the Massachusetts Anti-Slavery Society in 1863, Garrison hinted that before another year went by abolitionists might be able to proclaim the jubilee and disband their societies. Stephen S. Foster and Charles Remond, a fiery New England Negro abolitionist, were angered by this kind of talk. After all, they argued, malignant prejudice and discrimination against the Negro would still exist after slavery was gone. One of the declared purposes of the antislavery societies was to end this discrimination. The societies could not consider their work done when slavery was abolished. Garrison agreed that abolitionists were pledged to remove racial discrimination, but maintained that "as Abolitionists, distinctively, our special work is . . . the utter annihilation of slavery." The work of educating, uplifting, and securing equal rights for the freedmen should be done through other organizations or through the established social and political institutions of the nation. The historic mission of antislavery societies, he asserted, would be fulfilled when slavery disappeared from the nation.[1]

Many abolitionists could not see it this way. America's hostility to emancipation had compelled them to organize separately, and they anticipated as much opposition to their drive for equality as they had encountered in the struggle for liberty. Pillsbury and Phillips registered their protest against what they considered Garrison's conservatism by staying away from the Third Decade Anniversary Celebration of the founding of the American Anti-Slavery Society at Philadelphia in December 1863. This meeting was planned partly as a joyous jubilee anticipating the end of the antislavery crusade. Pillsbury and Phillips, ever-mindful of the dangers of a conservative reconstruction, could see little to be thankful for and hence stayed away.[2] Aware of the reasons for their absence, Garrison tried to assuage the apprehensions of the Pillsbury-Phillips faction in his opening speech to the Philadelphia meeting. "We may now confidently hope that our labors are drawing near to an end, so far as the abolition of slavery is concerned," he said. "But our labors in the field of a common humanity, and in the cause of reform, are never to terminate here, except with our mortal lives." Emancipation would confront the nation with the task of lifting generations of enforced ignorance from the minds of the freedmen. "This is a work of mercy and benevolence, in the doing of which we believe the great mass of the people of all denominations, and parties, and sects will flow together."[3]

Frederick Douglass was not entirely satisfied with Garrison's statement. "A mightier work than the abolition of slavery now looms up before the Abolitionist," he told the veteran crusaders at Philadelphia. "The work of the American Anti-Slavery Society will not have been completed until the black men of the South, and the black men of the North, shall have been admitted, fully and completely, into the body politic of America." A month later

---

[1] *Liberator*, Feb. 6, 1863.

[2] W. L. Garrison, Jr., to Ellen Wright, Dec. 11, 1863, Garrison Papers, sc.

[3] *Proceedings of the American Anti-Slavery Society at its Third Decade Anniversary* (New York, 1864), 5.

Douglass warned a New York audience of the reaction that usually followed revolutions. When the Confederacy was conquered and slavery abolished, there would be danger of a reaction that could rob the black man of his rights. "There never was a time when Anti-Slavery work was more needed than right now. The day that shall see the Rebels at our feet, their weapons flung away, will be the day of trial."[4]

The controversy over presidential politics in 1864 intensified abolitionist differences, but other issues were also driving a wedge between the two wings of the Garrisonian movement. One of these issues was General N. P. Banks' freedmen's labor system in Louisiana. Many Louisiana planters within Banks' department had taken the oath of allegiance and were allowed to continue working their plantations with Negro labor. The Negroes were now free, but Banks had established a system of regulations to govern their conduct that, according to some abolitionists, left the planter-laborer relationship very little different from what it had been under slavery.

When he arrived in New Orleans in December 1862, Banks had found the contrabands in a pitiable condition, crowded into filthy camps and huts, living on half-rations handed out by the army. In an effort to get them back to work on the plantations, Banks issued a general order establishing rules and regulations for a system of labor on January 29, 1863, supplemented by an additional order of February 3, 1864. These orders were designed to put every able-bodied male Negro to work. All freedmen not assigned to plantations were required to labor on public works without wages. The Negro could choose his own employer, but once having chosen he must remain with him for one year. Banks' officers encouraged the Negroes to go to work for their old masters. The order regulated the wage scale by ability up to $10 a month, and stipulated that payment of half the wages would be reserved until the end of the year. Workers were promised "just treatment, healthy rations, comfortable clothing, quarters, fuel, medical attendance, and instruction for children." But plantation hands would not be allowed to leave the plantation without a pass, and provost marshals were ordered to enforce the "continuous and

[4] *ibid.*, 111; *New York Tribune*, Jan. 14, 1864.

faithful service, respectful deportment, correct discipline and perfect subordination" of the freedmen.[5]

Abolitionists denounced Banks' order of 1863 as an "execrable proclamation" and called Banks a "born slave-driver." A Massachusetts abolitionist stationed with the army in Louisiana declared that the Banks system was tantamount to a "reestablishment of slavery." Some of Banks' officers, he declared, were Negrophobes and treated the freedmen with cruelty and contempt.[6] Charles K. Whipple asserted that Banks' system "substitutes serfdom for slavery, and seems merely a modification of that intermediate state which Great Britain found to work so ill." A British abolitionist agreed that Banks' policy was similar to the West Indian apprenticeship system which had worked so badly "that it was obliged to be thrown to the dogs."[7]

"It is not easy," wrote Theodore Tilton, "to conceive all the injustice, the oppression, the wrong to inalienable rights, the insult to men keenly capable of feeling it, the misery inflicted on those without redress or opportunity to appeal, [and] the general degradation of a race struggling up toward freedom" produced by Banks' system. Sydney Gay asserted in a *New York Tribune* editorial that Banks' labor system was little better than serfdom. "The negro bound to the soil for a year, compelled to work for wages two-thirds less than he could command in open market, not permitted . . . to have a voice in the contract by which he becomes bound, exposed to the tyrannous caprices of lifelong slaveholders. . . . Such is the serfage which predominates on the soil of Louisiana," wrote Gay angrily.[8]

Abolitionist attacks on Banks found a sympathetic hearing among radical Republicans, but Lincoln supported the general's policy, and it was not substantially changed until after the end of the war. Banks defended himself publicly against radical attacks, and even persuaded some abolitionists, including Garri-

[5] Fred. H. Harrington, *Fighting Politician: Major General N. P. Banks* (Philadelphia, 1948), 104-05; Banks' orders were published in *O.R.*, Ser. 1, vol. xv, 666-67, vol. xxxiv, pt. ii, 227-31.

[6] *Commonwealth*, Feb. 14, 1863; Daniel Mann to S. H. Gay, Feb. 11, 1864, Gay Papers, cu.

[7] *Liberator*, Mar. 11, 1864; J. Perronet Thompson to George Cheever, Mar. 22, 1864, Cheever Papers, aas.

[8] *Independent*, May 5, 1864; *New York Tribune*, July 16, 1864. See also *Independent*, Apr. 7, 1864; and *N.A.S. Standard*, Apr. 23, 1864.

son, that his policy was humanely conceived and wisely carried out for the good of the freedmen. Garrison had never criticized Banks very sharply, and during 1864 he began to reexamine the Banks system more sympathetically. A major reason for this reexamination, of course, was Garrison's support of Lincoln. The president had authorized Banks' policy, and Garrison soon began to defend Banks as part of his effort to vindicate Lincoln. This angered the Phillips wing of the American Anti-Slavery Society and confirmed their belief that Garrison had unaccountably become conservative.

Garrison had several friends stationed with the Union forces in Louisiana who assured him of the essential benevolence of the Banks system. Two men in particular played an important role in shaping Garrison's thinking on this question: Major B. Rush Plumly and the Reverend Edwin Wheelock. Both were veteran abolitionists. Plumly served as special treasury agent in New Orleans and later as a major in the *Corps d'Afrique*. Wheelock had come South as chaplain of a New Hampshire regiment and on February 20, 1863, was appointed deputy superintendent of labor in Louisiana.[9]

Plumly stated that he had been consulted by Banks before issuance of the labor orders, which were drafted primarily with an eye to the best interests of the freedmen. Before Banks came, said Wheelock, the freedmen had been huddled together in filthy camps, and some policy such as that initiated by Banks was absolutely necessary to save them from disease or starvation. Under the Banks system the planter had to provide his laborers with food, clothing, housing, and medical care plus a small plot of land on which the Negroes could grow some of their own food. As a deputy superintendent of labor, Wheelock was assigned to inspect conditions on the plantations. At first there was much disorder. The planters were wedded to their old ways and did not comprehend the revolution going on around them. They did their best to obstruct Banks' policy and make it fail. Wheelock reported planter abuses and obstructionism to Banks, who took

9 Charles Kassel, "Edwin Miller Wheelock," *Open Court*, xxxiv (Sept. 1920), 564-69, "A Knight-Errant in the Department of the Gulf: Episode in the Life of Edwin Miller Wheelock," *Open Court*, xxxix (Sept. 1925), 563-76, "The Labor System of General Banks—A Lost Episode of Civil War History," *Open Court*, xliii (Jan. 1929), 35-50.

prompt corrective action. Undesirable overseers and provost marshals were removed; some planters were fined or deprived of their plantations. Order gradually emerged from chaos, and by the end of 1863, Wheelock reported, the system had proved a success.[10]

One abolitionist criticism of Banks' labor policy was its fixed rate of low wages. But Garrison pointed out that the provision of food, clothing, housing, and medical care must be added to the wage rate to form a true picture. When this was done, he said, the Louisiana freedmen's standard of living compared favorably with other parts of the South. In the fall of 1864 General Banks spoke in vindication of his policy to a crowded audience in Boston's Tremont Temple. Garrison published the entire speech in the *Liberator* and editorially praised Banks for his successful efforts "to deliver the oppressed from the yoke of bondage, give vitality and success to paralyzed industry, . . . reconcile employers and the employed, . . . [and] establish and multiply schools for those hitherto forbidden to learn the alphabet." Louisiana Negroes were guaranteed equal rights in the courts under the new state constitution, a provision which, said Garrison, some northern states would do well to emulate. Several other abolitionists joined Garrison in approving Banks' policy.[11]

These champions of the Banks system were especially impressed by its provision for education of the freedmen. Banks' labor order of 1863 envisioned creation of a public school system for freedmen financed by property taxes. Under the leadership of Major Plumly a few schools were opened in October 1863. In March 1864, Banks issued a general order creating a "Board of Education for the Department of the Gulf" with power to levy and collect the school tax, establish common schools, employ teachers, and erect schoolhouses. Plumly served as chairman and Wheelock as secretary of the Board. These veteran abolitionists virtually ran the public school system of Louisiana for more

[10] Plumly to Garrison, Sept. 6, Oct. 20, 1864, in *Liberator*, Sept. 23, Nov. 11, 1864; Wheelock to Garrison, Feb. 8, 1865, in *Liberator*, Mar. 3. See also *Liberator*, Apr. 8, July 29, Nov. 11, 1864; and George Hepworth to Garrison, July ?, 1864, Garrison Papers, BPL.

[11] *Liberator*, July 29, Nov. 11, 1864; *N.A.S. Standard*, Nov. 19, 1864; Oliver Johnson to Garrison, July 16, 1864, Garrison Papers, BPL; Gerrit Smith to Gen. Banks, Nov. 21, 1864, in *Liberator*, Dec. 16. Statement by Garrison quoted from *Liberator*, Nov. 11, 1864.

than a year. By May 1864, they had established 49 schools with an average daily attendance of 5,200 pupils. By the end of July 1865, Plumly and Wheelock had organized 126 schools for the freedmen with 230 teachers giving instruction to 15,000 children in day classes and 5,000 adult freedmen in night and Sunday schools. Garrison pointed to these accomplishments as evidence of the benevolent operation of General Banks' policy.[12]

In spite of these educational achievements, most abolitionists were, in the words of Elizabeth Cady Stanton, astonished that "Garrison should defend the proposed apprenticeship system for the emancipated negroes [in Louisiana]. We say now, as ever, Give us immediately unconditional emancipation, and let there be no reconstruction except on the broadest basis of justice and equality." James McCune Smith, a Negro abolitionist in New York City, was profoundly sorry that his friend Gerrit Smith had expressed approval of the Banks system. "If I had a century of life secured to me," said McCune Smith, "I would not hope to live to see the day of Negro Emancipation, while serfdom of Banks' kind is endorsed by progressive friends of freedom to-day." The *Boston Commonwealth* lamented that Garrison's endorsement of Banks had convinced many Republicans of the safety of reconstruction on the basis of the Banks-Lincoln policy. The *Commonwealth* asserted: "No middle course between acknowledgement and denial of the negro's manhood is possible. If abolition is to be held to mean simply that the negro shall no longer be sold at the auction-block; no longer separated from his wife and children; no longer denied the alphabet; but that he may be put under guardianship; bound out to long terms of service; compelled to work for inadequate wages; made subject to all the old policy regulations . . . of chattelhood; . . . if this is the definition which the administration and the people prefer, we have got to go through a longer and severer struggle than ever."[13]

12 Charles Kassel, "Educating the Slave—A Forgotten Chapter of Civil War History," *Open Court*, XLI (Apr. 1927), 239-56; "Education of the Freedmen," *North American Review*, CI (Oct. 1865), 531; *Liberator*, Apr. 15, Sept. 30, 1864, Feb. 24, 1865.

13 E. C. Stanton to S. B. Anthony, Dec. 29, 1864, in Theodore Stanton and Harriot Stanton Blatch, *Elizabeth Cady Stanton* (2 vols., New York, 1922), II, 104; James McCune Smith to Gerrit Smith, Feb. 17, 1865, Smith Papers, SU; *Commonwealth*, Nov. 19, 1864.

Another issue dividing abolitionists in 1864 was the question of Negro suffrage as a condition of reconstruction. Theoretically all abolitionists were pledged to secure equal civil and political rights for Negroes. Under the leadership of Wendell Phillips a majority of abolitionists had committed themselves to impartial or universal manhood suffrage in the South as a practical condition of reconstruction. But some abolitionists maintained that the American Anti-Slavery Society *as an organization* had nothing to do with the suffrage issue. "I am in favor of universal suffrage, without regard to color," said J. Miller McKim, "but as a member of the American Anti-Slavery Society my work will be accomplished when the slave shall be emancipated." Garrison asserted that the antislavery societies were "not organized specifically to determine" the question of Negro suffrage. "It is a new issue, and one to be settled upon a new basis, as much as the voting of women."[14]

Thus far the abolitionist discussion of Negro suffrage had been confined to procedural problems. But in July 1864, Garrison injected a substantive flavor to the debate in a public letter to Professor Francis W. Newman, an English abolitionist who had criticized Lincoln's failure to include Negro suffrage as part of his reconstruction policy. "The elective franchise is a conventional, not a natural right," said Garrison. Lincoln should not be censured for his refusal to require Negro suffrage, for in the United States the right of suffrage was granted by the states rather than the federal government. Moreover, asked Garrison, "when was it ever known that liberation from bondage was accompanied by a recognition of political equality? Chattels personal may be instantly translated from the auction block into freemen; but when were they ever taken at the same time to the ballot-box, and invested with all political rights and immunities?" Garrison believed that even if Lincoln had the power to enfranchise the freedmen, such action might backfire. "Submitted to as a necessity at the outset, as soon as the [reconstructed] State was organized and left to manage its own affairs, the white population, with their superior intelligence, wealth and power, would unquestionably alter the franchise in accordance with their prejudices." Universal

[14] McKim to Garrison, Mar. 17, 1864, Garrison to Oliver Johnson, May 5, 1864, Garrison Papers, BPL.

suffrage in the South, said Garrison, would come slowly only "by a struggle on the part of the disfranchised, and a growing conviction of its justice."[15]

Garrison's statement shocked many of his fellow abolitionists. "Often during the last thirty years, Anti-Slavery men have denounced the black laws of some of the States which disfranchise citizens on account of color, as part and parcel of Slavery, the work of doughface politicians," declared the *Commonwealth*. "When before now did Mr. Garrison aid and comfort these doughfaces, by saying that 'the elective franchise is a conventional not a natural right?' When did he petrify his zealous friends by telling them majestically that 'according to the laws of development and progress it is not practicable' to extend the right of suffrage to colored men?" Liberty included the right of self-government, said the *Commonwealth*, and without the ballot the Negro's freedom would be a mere sham. "O Garrison, this is not abolitionism," proclaimed the *Commonwealth*. "Black men may well enough rejoice that they have got, out of our military necessity, a certain instalment of liberty. . . . But for a prophet to say they may well be contented with this . . . is of the madness which goes before ruin."[16]

The *Commonwealth's* strictures probably represented the opinion of most abolitionists. But no matter how much they might publicly deprecate Garrison's course, several abolitionists privately conceded some of his points. After all, they had been arguing for thirty years that slavery deadened the intellect and dulled the moral sense of the Negro. How then could they ask immediate suffrage for this creature degraded by generations of slavery? This question posed a serious dilemma for many abolitionists. "Suffrage to me, is a difficult problem of solution," said Parker Pillsbury. "I cannot believe it should be enjoyed by those who cannot both write and read their ballots."[17] Some abolitionists thought the solution lay in a literacy test applied impartially to both races. Others admitted the injustice of the North trying to impose Negro suffrage on a reconstructed South while most northern states barred black men from the polls.

15 *Liberator*, July 22, 1864.
16 *Commonwealth*, Aug. 5, 1864. See also *ibid.*, Sept. 9, 1864; and Lillie B. Chace to Anna Dickinson, Aug. 21, 1864, Dickinson Papers, LC.
17 Pillsbury to Sumner, July 3, 1864, Sumner Papers, HU.

For most abolitionists, however, these considerations gave way to their belief in the overwhelming practical necessity of Negro suffrage in the postwar South. Professor Newman stated the case succinctly: "In all history I know not where to find so sense-less an infatuation as that of putting power into the hands of your disloyal conquered enemies, and casting your loyal friends under their feet." Thomas Wentworth Higginson declared that "if under any other circumstances we might excuse ourselves for de-laying the recognition of the freedmen's right to suffrage, yet it would be utterly disastrous to do so now, when two-thirds of the white population will remain disloyal, even when conquered." Charles K. Whipple affirmed that Negro suffrage was necessary for two reasons: to give the freedmen the means to protect their freedom; and to "secure an immediate loyal population to trans-act political affairs and uphold the United States government in the Southern States." Whipple was not much impressed by the argument that the southern Negro was too ignorant to vote. Since the nation had "refused to make ignorance a bar in the case of Irish immigrants, it would not be fair to set up the plea of similar ignorance against these other new comers. Let us stick by the principle stated in the Declaration of Inde-pendence, that the right of the governing power depends on the consent of the governed."[18]

Wendell Phillips proclaimed that universal suffrage was a vital requisite of genuine democracy. "I do not believe in an English free-dom," said Phillips, "that trusts the welfare of the dependent class to the good will and moral sense of the upper class. This is aristoc-racy. . . . Our philosophy of government, since the 4th day of July, 1776, is that no class is safe, no freedom is real, . . . which does not place in the hands of the man himself the power to protect his own rights." Benevolent enterprises to educate the freedmen were not sufficient. "Gen. Banks says that he has set up schools for the blacks. . . . I have no doubt there are some hundreds of scholars in those schools; but I undertake to say that Gen. Banks cannot educate a mass of men by any system of benev-olence." Only when the state feared the power of the ballot in

18 Newman quoted in *Liberator*, July 1, 1864; Higginson quoted in *Atlantic Monthly*, xiv (Oct. 1864), 517-18; Whipple's statements published in *N.A.S. Standard*, June 11, Dec. 17, 1864.

the hands of ignorant men did it take steps to provide universal education in order to insure social stability. Universal suffrage, therefore, was a prerequisite to universal education in the South.[19]

Negro suffrage was rapidly becoming the central issue of reconstruction, and Garrison came under increasing pressure to make his position on this issue clear. In January 1865, he published an editorial reaffirming his belief in equal rights for all men. But the national government, said Garrison, had no more right to require Negro suffrage in Louisiana than in Connecticut. Moreover, so long as most northern states denied the ballot to Negroes the North had no *moral* right to impose equal suffrage on the South. Abolitionists should rejoice in the great revolution of opinion that had made emancipation possible instead of grumbling that liberty was worthless without the ballot. Garrison believed that emancipation "would open the way for ultimate social, civil and political equality; but this through industrial and educational development, and not by any arbitrary mandate."[20]

Most abolitionists were far from satisfied with this explanation of Garrison's position. Even his allies in the contest with the Phillips-Pillsbury wing of the antislavery society urged him to make his endorsement of equal suffrage more emphatic. "As abolitionists, we are the friends and *advocates* of Negro suffrage," McKim told Garrison. "For there is not, and in the nature of things cannot be, any difference of opinion among abolitionists on any essential point connected with this subject." McKim urged Garrison "to say, in terms not to be mistaken—'The right to vote for the negro on the same terms that it is given to the white man.' " The *Anti-Slavery Standard* stated flatly that "the black men must have their political rights asserted and maintained, or they cannot long retain their personal rights. . . . These are questions which naturally grow out of such a revolution as we are now enacting, and now is the time to settle them in the right way forever." Oliver Johnson, editor of the *Standard*, urged Garrison to take a clear stand in favor of impartial suffrage at the forthcoming meeting of the Massachusetts Anti-Slavery Society. "Don't let Phillips & Co. drive you too far by their attempts to put you in a

[19] *Liberator*, Feb. 10, 1865. See also speeches of Phillips published by *Liberator*, Dec. 16, 1864, and *Commonwealth*, Dec. 31, 1864.
[20] *Liberator*, Jan. 13, 1865.

false position," wrote Johnson. "Obliged as we are to defend the Administration from their unjust assaults, we must still stand firmly for the equal rights of the colored race."[21]

At the Massachusetts meeting Phillips introduced a series of resolutions affirming that "no emancipation can be effectual and no freedom real, unless the negro has the ballot." Garrison offered a counterresolution asserting that "if, as reconstructed, Louisiana ought not to be admitted to the Union because she excludes her colored population from the polls, then Connecticut, New Jersey, Pennsylvania, and all the Western States ought not to be in the Union for the same reason." Garrison agreed with Phillips that racial discrimination would be intolerable in the reconstructed Union, and he therefore proposed that "Congress should lose no time in submitting to the people an amendment of the Constitution, making the electoral law uniform in all the States, without regard to complexional distinctions." The suggestion of a constitutional amendment prohibiting racial discrimination was not new, for Phillips had broached the idea nearly a year before. But it was an important statement coming from Garrison, since it represented his first firm declaration in favor of equal suffrage as a condition of reconstruction. But the Phillips wing of the Society now regarded the method of constitutional amendment inadequate. If the southern states were once readmitted without Negro suffrage they could form a bloc large enough to defeat ratification of such an amendment. Negro suffrage must be secured by congressional act *prior* to the readmission of southern states as a *fundamental condition* of readmission. The time to strike for equal rights was *now*, while the national government wielded absolute power over the rebel states. After reconstruction was completed on the basis of Negro suffrage, said Phillips, the principle of equal suffrage could be nailed down permanently by a constitutional amendment.[22]

[21] McKim to Garrison, Jan. 17, 1865, in *Liberator*, Jan. 27, 1865; *N.A.S. Standard*, Jan. 21, 1865; Oliver Johnson to Garrison, Jan. 24, 1865, Garrison Papers, BPL.

[22] A year later Garrison had come around to Phillips' point of view on the suffrage question. In February 1866, Garrison wrote that "the ballot must be insisted on at least as strenuously for the loyal blacks as for the pseudo-loyal whites, and as a *sine qua non* to the recognition of State independence." Garrison to George Julian, Feb. 11, 1866, Giddings-Julian Correspondence, LC.

There was a great deal of acrimonious discussion of this and other issues at the Massachusetts meeting. Stephen S. Foster denounced Garrison's support of Banks and accused Garrison of making "a compromise with the devil." Garrison's partisans rushed to his defense and excoriated Foster in harsh language. The meeting threatened to erupt into an orgy of name-calling. Cooler heads finally prevailed and the vote was taken on Phillips' and Garrison's resolutions. The former were adopted overwhelmingly and the latter laid on the table. The Massachusetts Anti-Slavery Society had rejected Garrison's leadership and raised the standard of Phillips.[23]

Ironically, at the same time that Garrison's influence was declining among his fellow abolitionists, it was rising among the people at large. Because of his support of Lincoln in 1864 and his defense of the administration against the attacks of other abolitionists, Garrison had acquired great prestige among moderate Republicans.[24] He reciprocated their praise by trusting them with the future of the Negro. So many of his old enemies had come to believe in his doctrine of immediate emancipation, Garrison reasoned, that there was no reason to doubt the eventual triumph of equality as well. It was a time to sing praises and thanksgiving. Garrison seemed to have reached the pinnacle of success in 1865, and the protests of Phillips, Foster, and others that the success was not yet complete rankled his nerves. He considered the Thirteenth Amendment the crowning victory of the antislavery crusade. He was not indifferent to the problem of the freedmen's future; far from it. But he wanted nothing to mar his sense of triumph in the Thirteenth Amendment.[25]

23 *Liberator*, Feb. 3, 10, 17, 1865. See also Samuel May, Jr., to Richard Webb, Feb. 14, 1865, S. May, Jr., Papers, BPL; and Oliver Johnson to Samuel May, Jr., Feb. 9, 1865, Johnson Papers, VHS.

24 Charles Eliot Norton, editor of the *North American Review*, told Garrison in January 1865: "You are teaching the nation a most important lesson by your present course, in showing them that it is possible to unite common sense & moderation . . . with the most uncompromising fidelity to principles,—and by convincing them that the leader of the Abolition movement is not, as he has been esteemed, a fanatic but a calm and wise man." Norton to Garrison, Jan. 14, 1865, Garrison Papers, BPL.

25 For evidence of Garrison's new popularity among Republicans and moderates generally, see George Putnam to Garrison, Nov. 24, 1864, John Murray Forbes to Garrison, Jan. 18, 1865, Garrison to Forbes, Jan. 21, 1865, Garrison to Helen Garrison, July 23, 1865, Edwin M. Stanton to Garrison, Sept. 18, 1865, Garrison Papers, BPL; Edmund Quincy to Richard Webb, Oct. 16, 1865,

One of the high points of Garrison's career was an invitation from the United States government to attend as a guest of honor the ceremonial raising of the flag over Fort Sumter on April 14, 1865, exactly four years after the surrender of the fort to the Confederacy. Along with George Thompson (the noted British abolitionist) and Henry Ward Beecher, who was to deliver the main address at the celebration, Garrison traveled to Charleston in a government steamship. Several New York abolitionists and members of Beecher's church chartered another ship and came South to help liven the festivities. Left behind to edit the *Liberator*, Samuel May, Jr., commented that the honor done to Garrison and Thompson was a just recognition of their great services to the cause of freedom. "Mr. Garrison is no longer a proscribed, but an honored man—in the land of his birth. . . . He bears a name and has acquired a reputation,—to be enjoyed while yet he lives— which the most greedy of fame might covet."[26]

While in Charleston Garrison experienced some of the most gratifying moments of his life. He was lionized by a throng of 3,000 freedmen, several of whom lifted him to their shoulders and bore him triumphantly to the speakers' stand in Citadel Square. He visited Calhoun's tomb in the cemetery of St. Phillip's Church and solemnly intoned, "Down in a deeper grave than this slavery has gone, and for it there is no resurrection." He visited the offices of the *Charleston Courier*, now in Yankee hands, and set in type a paragraph of Beecher's oration. Everywhere he went in Charleston, Garrison was the center of attention. A week after his return to Boston one of Garrison's sons reported that "father has [not] quite 'come to himself' yet, his trip was so crowded with delightful wonders. It was like dreamland."[27] The prophet scorned and ridiculed for thirty years had lived to receive a king's homage in the city of his bitterest enemies. Little wonder that Garrison was elated by the strong wine of success. Little wonder

Quincy-Webb Correspondence, BPL; *Commonwealth*, Feb. 11, 1865; *Boston Traveller*, quoted in *Liberator*, Mar. 24, 1865; *Boston Transcript*, quoted in *N.A.S. Standard*, Apr. 8, 1865.

[26] Wendell P. Garrison and Francis J. Garrison, *William Lloyd Garrison* (4 vols., Boston, 1885-89), IV, 136-39; May's statement published in *Liberator*, Apr. 14, 1865.

[27] Garrison and Garrison, *Garrison*, IV, 139-52; W. L. Garrison, Jr., to Martha Wright, Apr. 25, 1865, Garrison Papers, SC.

that for a time he considered his crusade gloriously consummated and could not comprehend the jeremiads of men like Phillips.

During the interval between the meeting of the Massachusetts Anti-Slavery Society in January and the annual convention of the American Anti-Slavery Society in May, the infighting among abolitionists intensified. Roughly speaking, there were two main factions among Garrisonians regarding the future of their societies. One group, led by Garrison and Edmund Quincy, favored a formal dissolution of the American Anti-Slavery Society in May 1865. Phillips, Pillsbury, and Foster led the other faction that believed the Society should continue the battle until equal civil and political rights were granted to all Negroes.[28] By making it clear that he would resign as president of the Society whether it disbanded or not, Garrison rallied a majority of the executive committee to his side. On March 16 the committee voted to recommend disbandment of the Society at the annual meeting.[29] Oliver Johnson warned that on the issue of immediate dissolution Phillips would probably defeat Garrison, and urged that the whole question be postponed until after ratification of the Thirteenth Amendment. Garrison remained firm in his intention to retire, however, and Johnson reluctantly decided to vote for dissolution at the May meeting.[30]

In *Anti-Slavery Standard* editorials, Johnson and Edmund Quincy urged abolitionists to devote themselves to the work of the freedmen's aid societies as a logical continuation of their anti-slavery crusade. "The work of the *Anti-Slavery* Societies will obviously be done when slavery is abolished," said Johnson, "but the work of the friends of Liberty and Equality will not be done so long as any form of injustice or oppression exists in the world." Johnson also expressed approval of the idea of forming a new society to agitate the question of Negro suffrage. "There is not

[28] Samuel May, Jr., to Richard Webb, Feb. 14, 1865, Oliver Johnson to May, Mar. 2, 13, 1865, Mary Grew to May, Mar. 7, 1865, Samuel J. May to May, Mar. 10, 1865, S. H. Gay to May, Mar. 12, 27, 1865, Samuel May, Jr., Papers, BPL; Samuel May, Jr., to S. J. May, Mar. 5, 1865, S. J. May Papers, BPL.

[29] Henry Wright to Garrison, Mar. 13, 15, 1865, Garrison Papers, BPL; Oliver Johnson to Samuel May, Jr., Mar. 17, 31, Apr. 6, 24, 1865, Johnson Papers, VHS; Samuel May, Jr., to S. H. Gay, Mar. 22, 1865, Elizabeth Gay to Sarah Pugh, Apr. 3, 1865, Gay Papers, CU.

[30] Oliver Johnson to Samuel May, Jr., Mar. 17, 31, Apr. 6, 1865, Johnson Papers, VHS.

an Abolitionist in all the land," he declared, who would not "heartily cooperate" with such an organization. "But to keep an *Anti-Slavery* Society alive after slavery is abolished would seem, in our judgment, to be folly."[31]

Phillips protested against this reasoning. In a letter to the *Standard* he pointedly quoted the clauses of the American Anti-Slavery Society's constitution relating to the attainment of equal rights for free Negroes. A man was still a slave, argued Phillips, until he enjoyed all the rights of free men, including the ballot. Therefore it was entirely appropriate for an *antislavery* society to continue its work after the technical abolition of chattelism. Phillips depreciated the value of freedmen's aid associations. "Alms giving to the Negro is very well, highly honorable to the newly-converted givers, very useful to the Negro, and may be necessary for a little while," he said. "But I protest against its continuance for any length of time. I am still an Abolitionist, still a believer in the 'Negro's ability to take care of himself,' and do not intend to insult him by holding him up before the country as a chronic pauper. Let us . . . stand claiming for the Negro JUSTICE, not privileges; RIGHTS, not alms." In a reply to Phillips, Johnson asserted that the freedmen's aid societies went far beyond mere alms-giving. They were as resolute in their determination to secure equal suffrage for the Negro as Phillips himself. "But in order that there may be Negro Suffrage, there must be Negroes, and self-supporting and intelligent ones," wrote Johnson. "That there may be Negroes, they must be fed during the transition stage; . . . they must be furnished with . . . protection against extortion and oppression; that they may be intelligent, they must have school teachers."[32]

In February Phillips had feared that Garrison might carry the Society with him for dissolution at the May convention.[33] But as the meeting drew near, Phillips acquired important allies. His friends Elizabeth Cady Stanton and Susan B. Anthony rallied many of the women abolitionists to his side. Robert Purvis and Charles Remond assured him of the support of Philadelphia and Boston Negroes. On May 1 a group of New York Negroes passed

[31] *N.A.S. Standard*, Feb. 11, Mar. 18, Apr. 8, 1865.
[32] *N.A.S. Standard*, Apr. 22, 1865.
[33] Frank Sanborn to Moncure Conway, Feb. 17, 1865, Conway Papers, cu.

a resolution affirming that the American Anti-Slavery Society "cannot, in good faith, without violation of assumed honorable trust, at present dissolve." The executive committees of the Pennsylvania and the Philadelphia Female Anti-Slavery Societies voted to oppose dissolution. The *Boston Commonwealth* published an editorial urging the Society to keep itself intact for the upcoming struggle for equal rights. George Stearns and other backers of the *Commonwealth* made plans to go to New York City and help Phillips defeat Garrison's bid to dissolve the Society.[34]

An unusually large crowd filled the hall of Cooper Union for the public meetings of the Society, anticipating a sharp debate. They were not disappointed. Before the convention met, Johnson had urged Garrison to prepare careful resolutions explaining his motives for wishing to dissolve the Society. "Set the question of Negro Suffrage in such a light as to destroy the advantage which Phillips seeks to gain over us by his vehement partizan talk on that subject," Johnson advised Garrison. "Make it clear that in dissolving we do not withdraw ourselves from any work that needs to be done for the protection of the rights of the colored people. The strength of our opponents lies in cunningly making a false issue at this point." Garrison accepted the advice. In his opening speech to the convention he stated flatly that "there is no difference among Abolitionists . . . in regard to this matter of giving the ballot to those who have been so long disfranchised. We are one in this measure, and we must endeavor to see that it is carried without delay."[35]

34 S. B. Anthony to E. C. Stanton, Apr. 19, 1865, Stanton Papers, LC; S. B. Anthony, Diary, entry of Apr. 27, 1865, Anthony Papers, LC; Oliver Johnson to Garrison, May 1, 3, 1865, Garrison Papers, BPL; Mary Grew to Samuel May, Jr., Apr. 28, 1865, Garrison Papers, SC; Oliver Johnson to M. W. Chapman, May 4, 1865, Weston Papers, BPL; *Commonwealth*, Apr. 29, 1865; Frank P. Stearns, *The Life and Public Services of George Luther Stearns* (Phila., 1907), 352-53. Resolution passed by New York Negroes published in *New York Times*, May 3, 1865. The interest of New York Negroes, the *Boston Commonwealth*, George Stearns, and other non-Garrisonian abolitionists in the fate of the Garrisonian societies may seem strange until it is recalled that the war had put an end to most of the old constitutional and methodological disputes among abolitionists. The distinctions between Garrisonians and non-Garrisonians were now little more than academic, and many former non-Garrisonians, such as Gerrit Smith, Frederick Douglass, Theodore Weld, and George Stearns, had begun to take part in the activities of the American Anti-Slavery Society. (See Chapter V of this study.)

35 Johnson to Garrison, Apr. 24, May 3, 1865, Garrison Papers, BPL; *Liberator,*

Garrison introduced a resolution affirming that slavery was virtually abolished and that the American Anti-Slavery Society could therefore dissolve itself amid a chorus of thanksgiving and hallelujahs. "We organized expressly for the abolition of slavery," he said. "We called our Society an *Anti-Slavery* Society." It would be "an anomaly, a solecism, an absurdity to maintain an anti-slavery society after slavery is dead." Garrison repudiated the intimation that he meant to abandon the cause of the Negro. "Of course, we are not to cease laboring in regard to whatever remains to be done; but let us work with the millions, and not exclusively as the American Anti-Slavery Society." Edmund Quincy, Samuel May, Jr., and a few other speakers supported Garrison's resolution. May thought that abolitionists could do more good now for the Negro outside the antislavery societies than in them. "Take the leaven of this Society," he said, "and infuse it into every Freedmen's Aid Society in the land, and every other society, and my word for it, that leaven will leaven the entire mass, and its power will be multiplied a thousandfold."[36]

Phillips introduced a counterresolution calling for the continuation of the Society until "the liberty of the negro" was placed "beyond peril." "Now, friends," said Phillips, "my abolitionism, when I pledged my faith to that Declaration of Sentiments and Constitution of the American Anti-Slavery Society, was, 'Absolute equality before the law; absolute civil equality'; (Loud applause) and I shall never leave the negro until, so far as God gives me the power, I achieve it." A whole array of eloquent speakers supported Phillips' resolution. Anna Dickinson spoke for continuation of the Society. Senator Henry Wilson expressed the hope of radical Republicans that the Society would remain in existence. Negro abolitionists especially insisted on the need for keeping up the antislavery organizations. Charles L. Remond asserted that despite the great wartime revolution in the Negro's status, there

---

May 19, 1865. Garrison's statement represented a departure from his earlier opposition to immediate enfranchisement of the freedmen (see discussion earlier in this chapter). What had caused his change of mind? There is no definite evidence on this point, but abolitionist criticism of his earlier position probably had something to do with it.

[36] *Liberator*, May 26, 1865.

was still a crushing load of prejudice bearing down the colored man in America. Frederick Douglass recalled the earlier struggles against Jim Crow in the North and the victories for equal rights in New England. "That was good anti-slavery work twenty years ago; I do not see why it is not good anti-slavery work now," said Douglass. "Slavery is not abolished until the black man has the ballot. While the Legislatures of the South retain the right to pass laws making any discrimination between black and white, slavery still lives there. (Applause)"[37]

After two days of debate the vote was finally taken on Garrison's dissolution resolution. It was rejected by a vote of 118-48. As a gesture of harmony the Society then reelected Garrison as its president for the ensuing year. But the pioneer abolitionist had already announced his intention to withdraw from the Society, and he refused the presidency. Phillips was thereupon elected as the new president. Samuel May, Jr., Edmund Quincy, Anne Warren Weston, and several other allies of Garrison also resigned from the Society. Oliver Johnson and Edmund Quincy resigned as editors of the *Anti-Slavery Standard*. Though the over-all strength of the Society was undoubtedly weakened by these resignations, there was an infusion of new abolitionists—men who had stood aloof from the Garrisonians before the war—that helped offset the absence of those who withdrew. Gerrit Smith, George Cheever, and John G. Whittier were elected vice presidents of the reorganized Society; George L. Stearns was appointed to the executive committee; Parker Pillsbury took over as editor of the *Standard*, assisted by Phillips' son-in-law, George W. Smalley. Phillips henceforth wrote many of the *Standard*'s lead editorials.[38]

The schism in the Garrisonian antislavery societies left a legacy of bitterness. Phillips and Garrison remained friends, but relations between them were strained. Phillips was alienated from his old friends Quincy and Johnson. The hostility that had been building for years between Pillsbury and Foster on the one hand, and Garrison, McKim, and Johnson on the other erupted into an open

---

[37] *ibid.*, May 26, June 2, 1865.
[38] *ibid.*, June 2, 1865; *N.A.S. Standard*, May 27, 1865. After resigning as editor of the *Anti-Slavery Standard*, Oliver Johnson became managing editor of the *Independent*, a post he held for five years. Garrison published the final issue of the *Liberator* on December 29, 1865, eleven days after the Thirteenth Amendment was declared ratified.

break after the events of 1865. Both sides blamed the other for the schism. Garrison and his friends ascribed motives of "personal pique and an ulterior purpose" to Pillsbury and Foster.[39] Johnson considered Phillips' course "disgraceful." "What a shame that he should put himself at the head of this clique that has so long waged an insidious and venomous war upon you!" Johnson told Garrison. Samuel May, Jr., thought Phillips *"mainly* to blame— because the sympathy & countenance he has given this set [Pillsbury and Foster] has magnified their self-importance & encouraged their petty plots."[40]

Those who advocated continuation of the antislavery societies, on the other hand, disclaimed personal motives for their action. They emphasized the need to continue active work on behalf of equal rights and intimated that Garrison and his allies had abandoned the cause. Pillsbury was sorry that he had alienated Garrison and others, "but it was Mr. Garrison who taught me to be true to myself." In Pillsbury's opinion "suffrage for the negro is now what immediate emancipation was thirty years ago. If we emancipate from slavery and leave the European doctrine of serfdom extant, even in the mildest form, then the colored race, or we, or perhaps both, have another war in store." One of the younger followers of Phillips sadly accused Garrison of "deserting the true banner."[41]

The truth, as usual, probably lay somewhere between the claims of either side. The schism of 1865 resulted partly from an honest difference of opinion over substantive and procedural issues. It was also caused partly by a power struggle between the Pillsbury and Garrison factions that had been going on for at least ten years. So long as Phillips took no sides or stood with Garrison, the Pillsbury faction was an insignificant minority. But when Phillips sided with the Pillsbury-Foster group because of his distrust of Lincoln and his concern for the freedmen's future, he took a majority of the American Anti-Slavery Society with him and displaced Garrison as leader of the abolitionist move-

[39] Garrison to Helen Garrison, May 10, 1865, Garrison Papers, BPL.

[40] Johnson to Garrison, May 18, 1865, Garrison Papers, BPL; Samuel May, Jr., to Richard Webb, May 29, 1865, S. May, Jr., Papers, BPL.

[41] Pillsbury to S. B. Anthony, May ?, 1865, in Ida Harper, *The Life and Work of Susan B. Anthony* (3 vols., Indianapolis, 1898-1908), I, 246; Lillie B. Chace to Anna Dickinson, May 22, 1865, Dickinson Papers, LC.

ment. Garrison's assertion that his opponents were actuated only by spite and personal enmity was unfair, although there was a germ of truth in the accusation. Pillsbury's charge that Garrison had forsaken the Negro was equally unfair. Garrison and his allies were subsequently active in the freedmen's aid movement and availed themselves of every opportunity to speak out for civil rights and Negro suffrage. Yet there *was* an element of ideological conflict between some of the participants in the 1865 schism. Garrison, Quincy, Johnson, McKim, and May were essentially moderates in their social and political ideas. They had joined the antislavery movement because they saw in slavery an enormous injustice demanding cauterization. Phillips, Pillsbury, and Foster were motivated by the same belief in the injustice of slavery, but in addition they were genuine, thoroughgoing radicals in their social philosophy. It was no mere coincidence that Phillips, Pillsbury, and Foster were active in the labor reform movements of the 1870's while Garrison opposed militant labor agitation. These ideological and temperamental differences played a significant part in the schism of 1865.

XIV + ANDREW JOHNSON AND RECON-
STRUCTION: 1865

THE problem of reconstruction occupied the mind of every politician and reformer in the winter of 1864-1865. Abolitionists applauded an intimation by Lincoln in his annual message of a willingness to compromise with congressional radicals on the issue.[1] The thorny problem of the readmission of Louisiana under the Banks-Hahn Constitution of 1864 was dumped into the House Committee on Rebellious States in December. The chairman of this committee was James Ashley of Ohio, a radical antislavery man and a friend of several leading abolitionists. Ashley and Thomas Eliot, a radical Republican from Massachusetts, evidently negotiated a compromise with Lincoln whereby Ashley promised to accept the admission of Louisiana, Tennessee, and Arkansas under Lincoln's 10 per cent plan in return for the administration's acceptance of the right of Congress to prescribe the terms of reconstruction in the other Confederate states. Charles Sumner participated in the negotiation of this compromise and reluctantly approved its terms.[2]

Phillips and most other abolitionists denounced the compromise. Phillips argued that no matter what conditions Congress laid down for other states, the readmission of Louisiana would create a dangerous precedent for presidential reconstruction of the rest of rebeldom.[3] "If Congress allows the President to determine the conditions on which Louisiana shall return to the Union," asked the *Commonwealth*, "what resistance can it make when he brings Florida and Alabama along?"[4] Phillips and George Stearns hurried to Washington for consultation with radical leaders. Henry Winter Davis and William D. Kelley told Phillips that most radicals favored Negro suffrage but that they were powerless in the

---

[1] Roy P. Basler, ed., *The Collected Works of Abraham Lincoln* (9 vols., New Brunswick, N.J., 1955), VIII, 152; *Independent*, Dec. 8, 1864; *Liberator*, Dec. 9, 1864; *Commonwealth*, Dec. 10, 1864.

[2] Charles H. McCarthy, *Lincoln's Plan of Reconstruction* (New York, 1901), 286-91; *N.A.S. Standard*, Dec. 24, 31, 1864; Edward L. Pierce, *Memoir and Letters of Charles Sumner* (4 vols., Boston, 1877-94), IV, 221.

[3] Phillips to Moncure Conway, Jan. 8, 1865, McKim-Maloney-Garrison Papers, NYPL.

[4] *Commonwealth*, Dec. 24, 1864.

face of Lincoln's control of a majority of the party. The only hope was in an aroused public opinion that would convince the president that the North wanted equal suffrage as a condition of reconstruction. They urged Phillips and the abolitionists to keep up the demand for Negro suffrage. Meanwhile the radical leaders promised to do all they could to defeat the admission of Louisiana.[5]

Ashley drafted a proposal for equal suffrage in the eight nonreconstructed Confederate states, but a coalition of Democrats and moderate Republicans voted down his plan in committee. Instead, Ashley was forced to report to the House a bill to admit Louisiana, Arkansas, and Tennessee under Lincoln's reconstruction plan and to admit the rest under conditions similar to those of the Wade-Davis bill vetoed by Lincoln the previous summer. By prior arrangement with Ashley, Congressman William D. Kelley introduced an amendment on the House floor enacting impartial suffrage. Kelley was a prominent radical from Pennsylvania, allied to Philadelphia's abolitionist circles by friendship and marriage. He pleaded for his amendment in a speech that became a classic in the struggle for equal suffrage. The House was impervious to his eloquence, however, and refused to pass the amendment.[6]

Ashley was criticized by abolitionists who were not aware of his backstage maneuvers in the House and thus did not understand why he had reported out his reconstruction bill without Negro suffrage. He explained in a House speech of February 22 that he had no choice; an adverse committee majority had compelled him to report the emasculated bill. He frankly expressed the hope that the House would pass no reconstruction measure at all this session. He wanted the question to go over to the next Congress in which the radicals would be stronger. Ashley also sent a private note to Tilton and to Charles Slack, editor of the *Commonwealth,* explaining the complex maneuvers in Congress. The *Independent*

[5] Phillips to Moncure Conway, n.d., but sometime in January or February, 1865, Conway Papers, cu.

[6] McCarthy, *Lincoln's Plan of Reconstruction,* 291-313; Ira V. Brown, "William D. Kelley and Radical Reconstruction," *The Pennsylvania Magazine of History and Biography,* lxxxv (July 1961), 317, 321; *Commonwealth,* Jan. 28, 1865; *Independent,* Mar. 16, 1865.

and *Commonwealth* published these letters in order to vindicate Ashley's fidelity to the cause.[7]

As Ashley had hoped, the House laid all reconstruction proposals on the table. The real battle, however, was shaping up in the Senate where moderate Republicans were trying to force passage of a resolution recognizing Louisiana as a legitimate state "entitled to the guaranties and all other rights of a State government." Abolitionists feared that adoption of this resolution would establish a precedent against the requirement of equal suffrage as a condition of reconstruction. Garrison was silent on the issue, but Phillips and the *Commonwealth* frantically urged antislavery Republicans to defeat "this suicidal act."[8] Sumner and a small band of radical associates were equal to the occasion. They introduced dilatory motions and filibustered against the resolution, preventing it from coming to a vote before Congress adjourned on March 4.[9] Sumner received the fervent thanks of abolitionists for his decisive role in defeating the admission of "the sham state of Louisiana." The Bird Club in Boston unanimously approved Sumner's course and praised him as the savior of Negro suffrage.[10]

The defeat of Louisiana's bid for readmission buoyed up the spirits of abolitionists. During the winter they professed to discern a favorable movement of northern public opinion toward Negro suffrage. Phillips reported that his audiences cheered his most radical utterances. Henry Ward Beecher came out strongly for Negro suffrage, and several northern Protestant denominations followed suit. Prominent public figures such as Salmon P. Chase and important Republican newspapers such as the *New York Tribune* and the *Boston Journal* endorsed the principle of equal suffrage.[11] Charles Slack informed Sumner at the end of February

[7] *Cong. Globe*, 38 Cong., 2 Sess., 968-69, 1,002; Ashley to editor of the *Commonwealth*, Feb. 27, 1865, published in *Commonwealth*, Mar. 4; Ashley to Tilton, Feb. 27, 1865, Garrison Papers, BPL; *Independent*, Mar. 2, 1865.

[8] *Commonwealth*, Feb. 25, Mar. 4, 1865.

[9] *Cong. Globe*, 38 Cong., 2 Sess., 903, 1,011-12, 1,091-99, 1,101-11; Edward McPherson, *The Political History of the United States of America during the Great Rebellion* (Washington, 1865), 579-81.

[10] Sumner received nearly a dozen letters from abolitionists thanking him for his stand against the admission of Louisiana. The quotation is from Elizur Wright to Sumner, Mar. 6, 1865; the information on the action of the Bird Club is from E. L. Pierce to Sumner, Mar. 4, 1865, Sumner Papers, HU.

[11] O. B. Frothingham to Moncure Conway, Jan. 2, 1865, Conway Papers, CU;

that "the idea of negro suffrage in the disloyal states grows daily in favor and advocacy among [Boston] business men." Lydia Maria Child believed that many northerners had been converted to equal suffrage by the performance of Negro troops in the war. In early April Frank Sanborn observed that "the question of Reconstruction on the basis of negro suffrage is coming up for discussion everywhere, and the converts to Phillips' view are increasing fast."[12]

But a new danger to abolitionist hopes appeared as the war drew to a close. With victory assured there was a noticeable softening of the northern attitude toward rebels. Lincoln's inaugural plea for malice toward none and charity for all appealed to a growing number of Yankees. The fall of Richmond and Lee's surrender sent the North into paroxysms of joy. The war was virtually over, and many Americans stood ready to forgive their enemies. Abolitionists feared that this mood boded ill for the freedmen. A soft attitude toward southern whites might be translated into a reconstruction policy that failed to secure the rights of Negroes. Abolitionists warned against sentimentality in dealing with the South. "I am astonished at the gammon still prevailing at the North about our Southern brethren, and their softened feelings and longings to come back, etc., etc.," wrote Laura Towne from the South Carolina sea islands. "They are hungry, and long for loaves and fishes, but . . . they are bitter and spiteful and 'cantankerous' as ever, and show extreme contempt for Northerners while they are accepting their benefactions." Sanborn rejoiced in Lee's surrender at Appomattox but lamented that "the danger of neglecting the colored men in our plans of Reconstruction is still great."[13]

M. W. Chapman to Mary Estlin, Feb. 5, 1865, Estlin Papers, BPL; Phillips to E. C. Stanton, Feb. 8, 1865, Stanton Papers, LC; *Liberator*, Feb. 10, Mar. 3, 1865; *N.A.S. Standard*, Feb. 4, 18, 1865; *New York Tribune*, Feb. 22, 1865; *Commonwealth*, Mar. 4, 11, 18, 1865.

12 Slack to Sumner, Feb. 28, 1865, Sumner Papers, HU; L. M. Child to George W. Julian, Apr. 1, 1865, Giddings-Julian Correspondence, LC; Frank Sanborn to Moncure Conway, Apr. 6, 1865, Conway Papers, CU.

13 Rupert S. Holland, ed., *Letters and Diary of Laura M. Towne, Written from the Sea Islands of South Carolina, 1862-84* (Cambridge, Mass., 1912), 155-56; Sanborn to Gerrit Smith, Apr. 10, 1865, Smith Papers, SU. See also Sumner to Garrison, Mar. 29, 1865, Garrison Papers, BPL; Amasa Walker to Sumner, Apr. 5, 1865, Sumner Papers, HU.

"PARDON. Columbia—'Shall I Trust These Men'?" Nast
in *Harper's Weekly*

"FRANCHISE. 'And Not This Man'?" Nast in *Harper's Weekly*

In a speech to a group of happy White House serenaders on the evening of April 11, Lincoln appealed for public acceptance of the reconstructed government of Louisiana. He wished that suffrage could have been extended to black soldiers and literate Negroes, but he felt that colored men would get the ballot sooner by working through the established Louisiana government than by tearing it down and starting anew. Lincoln regarded his reconstruction policy as a promise to Louisiana to be broken only if it proved a bad promise.[14]

Some abolitionists were discouraged by the president's renewed commitment to the Louisiana policy, but others found grounds for hope in Lincoln's willingness to break a "bad promise." It would be the task of radicals to convince the president that reconstruction, Louisiana-style, was a "bad promise." Many abolitionists, remembering Lincoln's step-by-step progress from a war policy of noninterference with slavery to one of universal emancipation, looked forward hopefully to his conversion to Negro suffrage.

Less than four days after his speech of April 11, the president was dead. Abolitionist reaction to his assassination was mixed. All, of course, were shocked and appalled by the enormity of the crime. Nonetheless some abolitionists interpreted Lincoln's murder as a warning against leniency in the reconstruction of the South. It was widely believed that Andrew Johnson held more radical ideas on reconstruction than Lincoln. Johnson seemingly confirmed this belief by his thundering denunciations of traitors during the week after the assassination. "Mr. Lincoln's too great kindness of heart led him to a mistaken leniency," wrote William Lloyd Garrison, Jr., "but Andy Johnson has fought the beasts of Ephesus on their own soil and has learned by bitter experience their implacable nature. 'Thorough' will be the word now. . . . The nation sails into new waters now and it may be providential that a new hand grasps the rudder." But here and there arose a dissent. William Robinson recorded in his diary that the Bird Club had great confidence in Johnson, but that he personally thought Lincoln's death "an unmixed evil." Lincoln had possessed the confidence of the country as had no other man since Washington, but Johnson was a relatively unknown quantity. "Lincoln had no adequate idea of what ought to be done," wrote Robinson, "but

[14] Basler, *Collected Works of Lincoln*, VIII, 399-405.

I fear Johnson has still less. Lincoln was, at least, master of himself, and master of the situation: Johnson *may* be the tool of anybody and everybody. Lincoln we have summered and wintered for four years, and knew exactly what he was: Johnson is wholly untried."[15]

Abolitionists welcomed the hardening of northern opinion toward the South produced by Lincoln's assassination. In the weeks before that tragic event, wrote Higginson, the North seemed to be "swiftly sliding back" into "a mush of concession." But Booth's bullet "restored us to our senses" and united the North as it had not been united since the firing on Fort Sumter. The chances for a reconstruction based on justice, he thought, were far better now than before the assassination.[16]

One manifestation of the post-assassination reaction of the North, however, was unwelcome to abolitionists. A cry for bloody vengeance against traitors rent the air. A few abolitionists echoed this demand for blood, but most of them were opposed to execution as a punishment for rebellion. They feared that the cries for vengeance would distract attention from the real issues of reconstruction. "We [don't] want a reign of blood and terror," wrote William Robinson; "we should have, instead, a settled and firm policy of reconstruction on the basis of *justice to the negro*." Tilton argued that *slavery*, not individual rebels, was the real criminal. The rebellion should be punished not by hanging traitors but by exterminating slavery and by putting the Negro's freedom on an indestructible foundation. Phillips declared that executions would only create martyrs. Confiscation of rebel lands and the grant of suffrage to freedmen, not mass hangings, were the proper punishments for rebellion. "What, cover the continent with gibbets!" exclaimed Phillips. "We cannot sicken the nineteenth century with such a sight. . . . [This country] needs for its safety

15 W. L. Garrison, Jr., to Martha Wright, Apr. 16, 1865, Garrison Papers, sc; Wm. S. Robinson, Diary, entry of Apr. 16, 1865, in Mrs. Wm. S. Robinson, ed., *"Warrington" Pen-Portraits: A Collection of Personal and Political Reminiscences from 1848 to 1876, from the Writings of William S. Robinson* (Boston, 1877), 304-05. See also S. B. Anthony to E. C. Stanton, Apr. 19, 1865, Stanton Papers, LC; *Liberator*, Apr. 21, 1865; and *N.A.S. Standard*, Apr. 22, 1865.

16 *Commonwealth*, Apr. 29, 1865. See also Caroline Weston to Mary Estlin, Apr. 18, 1865, Estlin Papers, BPL; *Independent*, Apr. 20, 27, 1865; and Vincent Y. Bowditch, *Life and Correspondence of Henry Ingersoll Bowditch* (2 vols., Boston, 1902), II, 48-52.

no such policy of vengeance; its serene strength needs to use only so much severity as will fully guarantee security for the future."[17]

Abolitionists had another reason for opposing the popular clamor for bloody revenge. Many of them were opposed to capital punishment and were active in the movement to outlaw it. Gerrit Smith, John G. Whittier, and the *New York Tribune* took the lead in calling for clemency to traitors. Smith sent personal letters to President Johnson pleading for leniency, and published two broadsides, a speech, and a sermon urging clemency. Whittier publicly deplored the cries for vengeance. Almost alone among leading Republican newspapers, the *New York Tribune* pleaded for sanity and mercy toward rebel leaders. In a pointed editorial the *Tribune* noted that more than any other single group in the North the abolitionists desired clemency for rebels. They had the good sense, said the *Tribune*, to see that the real enemy was not Jefferson Davis but the spirit of slavery and aristocracy which had spawned the rebellion.[18]

The desire for wholesale executions soon passed away, but the problem of reconstruction remained. Despite William Robinson's prescient fears, most abolitionists had great confidence in Andrew Johnson in April 1865. This confidence was based partly on Johnson's stern denunciations of rebels and partly on his record as wartime military governor of Tennessee. Abolitionists had been impressed by Johnson's vigorous efforts to make Tennessee a free state in 1864-1865 and especially by his famous "Moses" speech to the Negroes of Nashville in October 1864, in which he promised to be their Moses and lead them out of bondage. George L. Stearns had known Johnson during his tenure as recruiting agent of Negro troops in Tennessee. Stearns had been sufficiently convinced of Johnson's radicalism to invite him to join a Negro suffrage association that Stearns was organizing in the fall of 1864.[19]

---

[17] Robinson, *"Warrington" Pen-Portraits*, 305; *Independent*, Apr. 20, 27, 1865; Wendell Phillips, *Speeches, Lectures and Letters*, 2nd Series (Boston, 1900), 449-50.

[18] Gerrit Smith to Andrew Johnson, Apr. 19, 24, 1865, Johnson Papers, LC; *Gerrit Smith to President Johnson*, April 24, 1865, published letter (Peterboro, 1865); Gerrit Smith, *No Treason in Civil War* (New York, 1865); O. B. Frothingham, *Gerrit Smith* (New York, 1879), 294-95; Whittier to the editor of the Amesbury (Mass.) *Villager*, reprinted in *Liberator*, May 26, 1865; *New York Tribune*, Apr. 20, May 5, 8, 1865.

[19] Stearns to Johnson, Sept. 26, 1864, Johnson Papers, LC. See also L. M. Child to Whittier, Nov. 8, 1864, Child-Whittier Correspondence, LC; W. L. Gar-

Abolitionists did not realize that Johnson's opposition to slavery, like that of Hinton Rowan Helper, sprang not from sympathy for the Negro but from the yeoman farmer's traditional hatred of large slaveowners. Johnson had despised abolitionists before the war. He identified himself with the white yeoman class which disliked both the Negroes and the large planters. His private secretary once wrote in his diary that Johnson "exhibited a morbid distress and feeling against the negroes." During the war a friend in Tennessee reminded Johnson that the abolitionists hoped to make free citizens out of the slaves. "Damn the negroes," replied Johnson. "I am fighting these traitorous aristocrats, their masters."[20]

In the weeks after Lincoln's assassination abolitionists were unaware of the new president's feelings toward Negroes. Stearns assured friends that Johnson would do the right things in reconstructing the South. John M. Langston led a delegation of Negroes to see the president, who told them that he was a firm friend of their race. Wendell Phillips declared that Johnson's whole life was pledged to the extirpation of caste and aristocracy in the South. "I believe in him," said Phillips, "I believe he means suffrage." Abolitionists applauded every reference to Johnson at the annual meeting of the American Anti-Slavery Society on May 9-10.[21]

There was one report from Washington, however, that disturbed some radicals. Johnson told a visiting Indiana delegation that he agreed with Lincoln's theory of the legal indestructibility of the states. Radicals were startled, for logically pursued this theory denied the right of Congress to establish suffrage require-

---

rison, Jr., to Martha Wright, Nov. 13, 1864, Garrison Papers, sc; John Pierpont to L. M. Child, Nov. 20, 1864, Pierpont Papers, pml; and *N.A.S. Standard*, May 6, 1865.

20 Benjamin Thomas and Harold Hyman, *Stanton: The Life and Times of Lincoln's Secretary of War* (New York, 1962), 440; Clifton Hall, *Andrew Johnson, Military Governor of Tennessee* (Princeton, 1916), 221.

21 George Stearns to Gerrit Smith, Apr. 21, 1865, Smith Papers, su; Stearns to Sumner, Apr. 30, 1865, Sumner Papers, hu; *Commonwealth*, Apr. 22, 1865; *N.A.S. Standard*, Apr. 29, May 6, 13, 1865; *Liberator*, Apr. 28, May 12, June 2, 1865. Phillips' statement quoted from *ibid.*, June 2, 1865. Lewis Tappan wrote in his journal on April 23, 1865, "we have the encouragement to believe that [Johnson] will prove an able & faithful magistrate." A year later, however, Tappan made a note in the margin next to this entry: "This prophecy falsified by his *treachery!*" Tappan Papers, lc.

ments as a condition of readmission because the states were already *in* the Union and hence possessed the right to regulate their own suffrage qualifications. There were also rumors from Washington that Montgomery Blair was cultivating a close relationship with the new president. Worried Boston abolitionists urged Sumner to establish contact with Johnson and make sure that he was influenced in the right direction. "Save him from the Blairs," Frank Bird told Sumner.[22] The Massachusetts senator needed little urging. Along with Senators Wade and Chandler and Chief Justice Chase, Sumner paid several visits to the White House in the last two weeks of April "with the view of conversing on negro suffrage." The senators seemed to be satisfied with Johnson's views on this question. "He is as radical as I am and as fully up to the work," Chandler wrote to his wife. Sumner informed friends that Johnson was "well-disposed, & sees the right and necessities of the case. . . . Our new President accepts the principle and application" of Negro suffrage. Phillips thanked Sumner for his assurances of Johnson's fidelity to equal rights. "I am glad & *strengthened* by the knowledge," said Phillips.[23]

In letters to George Stearns, however, Sumner expressed less confidence. The president had declared himself in favor of a broadened franchise, said Sumner, but Johnson thought that Negro suffrage should be granted by the states *after* reconstruction rather than imposed by Congress on the states as a condition of restoration. Sumner was worried, because he believed that once readmitted to the Union, southern states would never voluntarily adopt Negro suffrage. He therefore hoped that a decision on reconstruction could be postponed until the next session of Congress. Meanwhile radicals should try to educate public opinion up to the level of demanding Negro suffrage as a condition of readmission. If public opinion supported such a policy, Sumner was sure that Johnson, like Lincoln, would acquiesce in the will of the majority. Stearns agreed, and promised to do everything possible to help mature a correct public opinion.[24]

[22] *Commonwealth*, Apr. 29, 1865; Frank Bird to Sumner, Apr. 15, 1865, Sumner Papers, HU.

[23] Sumner to Bird, Apr. 25, 1865, Bird Papers, HU; Chandler quoted in Joseph B. James, *The Framing of the Fourteenth Amendment* (Urbana, Ill., 1956), 5-6; Sumner to R. Schleiden, May 1, 1865, in Pierce, *Sumner*, IV, 242; Wendell Phillips to Sumner, May 5, 1865, Sumner Papers, HU.

[24] Sumner to Stearns, May 4, 11, and May ?, 1865, quoted in Frank P. Stearns,

Radicals began their intensified campaign for equal suffrage in May 1865. The *Commonwealth* published trumpet blasts warning the nation of the injustice and danger of reconstruction without Negro suffrage. "Refuse this, and the Southern States will make such laws as will allow the freedmen only to be 'hewers of wood and drawers of water,' and, uniting with Northern copperheads, will control the legislation of the country." Phillips promised that the slogan of the American Anti-Slavery Society under his leadership would be "No Reconstruction without Negro Suffrage." "No matter what else we yield, here our demand is to be inexorable," said Phillips. "Abolitionists are to be educated to see that, without this, freedom, so called, is a sham."[25] George L. Stearns published at his own expense in April 1865, a pamphlet entitled *The Equality of All Men before the Law*, containing speeches in behalf of Negro suffrage by Phillips, Douglass, and William D. Kelley. Stearns printed 50,000 copies for distribution throughout the North in April; he prepared another edition of 40,000 in May, and told Sumner that he had enough money on hand or pledged by interested parties to finance the eventual printing of 500,000 copies.[26]

During his trip to South Carolina for the flag-raising ceremonies at Fort Sumter, Theodore Tilton had come to the conclusion that "if the whip-using gentry who formerly held sway in those regions are to return to their former crown and kingdom, the North will have won only half a victory over the rebellion." In a series of militant editorials Tilton argued that the Negro must be granted land and the ballot as inexorable conditions of reconstruction. He admitted that many well-intentioned men had doubts about the constitutional right of the federal government to impose such conditions. But "he is the statesman of a great occasion who is not hampered by mere usage, bigotry, or narrow technicality. It is criminal to let a nation die while hunting after a precedent by which to save it." Whether the rebel states were

---

The Life and Public Services of George Luther Stearns (Phila., 1907), 343-44; Stearns to Sumner, May 8, 1865, Sumner Papers, HU.

[25] *Commonwealth*, May 6, 1865; *N.A.S. Standard*, May 27, June 3, 1865.

[26] Stearns to William Still, Apr. 29, 30, 1865, quoted in Alberta S. Norwood, "Negro Welfare Work in Philadelphia, Especially as Illustrated by the Career of William Still," M.A. thesis, U. of Pennsylvania, 1931, 136-37; Stearns to Sumner, Apr. 30, 1865, Sumner Papers, HU.

theoretically in or out of the Union was a moot question, said Tilton, but no one could deny that legitimate governments did not exist in those states. There was no prescription in the Constitution for the problem of reconstruction. Whatever action was taken by the federal government on this question would be extraconstitutional, not unconstitutional. "The people of the rebel states, having been conquered in war, are at the mercy of the conqueror, and have no other recourse but in his clemency," declared Tilton. "The restoration of the states to their rank in the Union, is an act of pure clemency; of course the entire details as to the manner and form rest in the discretion and judgment of the conquering power."[27]

The radicals were alarmed by continuing rumors that Johnson would soon announce a reconstruction policy without Negro suffrage. On May 17 Stearns sent a personal entreaty to the president recalling their friendship in wartime Nashville and appealing to Johnson's well-known hatred of aristocracy. The rebellion was more than a slaveholder's war against Union and liberty, said Stearns. "It was the deadly strife of the Aristocratic Principle against the Democratic, of the Capital of the country against its Labor." Negroes constituted a majority of the southern laboring class, and without guaranties for their future security and equal rights, aristocracy would continue to rule the South. Would Andrew Johnson "be true to the Democratic principle of Government," asked Stearns, "or will he like all his predecessors ally himself with Capital and continue the war against labor?" Frank Sanborn reported on May 26 that Phillips and Stearns were afraid Johnson would go wrong on the suffrage question unless pressure was brought to bear upon him. An imposing array of radicals gathered in Boston on May 29 for the annual meeting of the Emancipation League. Hoping to impress Johnson with the strength of radicalism in New England, several abolitionists and Republican speakers made eloquent appeals for Negro suffrage.[28]

But it was too late. On that very day the president issued an amnesty proclamation and a reconstruction proclamation for

[27] *Independent*, May 4, 11, 25, 1865.
[28] Stearns to Johnson, May 17, 1865, Johnson Papers, LC; Sanborn to Moncure Conway, May 26, 1865, Conway Papers, CU; *Commonwealth*, June 3, 1865.

North Carolina. The latter named William Holden as provisional governor and stipulated that when a majority of the state's qualified white voters had taken an oath of future loyalty they could form a new constitution and bring the state back into the Union.[29] The reaction of abolitionists was swift and angry. Meeting in Boston on May 31, the New England Anti-Slavery Society unanimously passed a resolution condemning the North Carolina proclamation. "The reconstruction of rebel states without Negro suffrage is a practical surrender to the Confederacy," said Phillips. "Better, far better, would it have been for Grant to have surrendered to Lee than for Johnson to have surrendered to North Carolina." Phillips feared that reconstruction on the basis of white suffrage would doom the freedmen to "a century of serfdom." He pointed to the black code already passed by one house of the Tennessee legislature and predicted that all the reconstructed states would enact such codes unless the black man was enfranchised. Charles C. Burleigh charged Johnson with inconsistency in his reconstruction theory. If the rebel states were actually in the Union, as Johnson claimed, the president had no right to create the extraconstitutional office of provisional governor. But if he *did* have the right to create such an office, he had the same right to require Negro suffrage.[30]

On June 13 the president issued a reconstruction proclamation for Mississippi identical to the North Carolina edict. Even moderate abolitionists who wanted to believe in Johnson's good intentions were depressed by this sign that the president had drawn up the North Carolina proclamation as a pattern for the rest of the South. "If reconstruction is to go on as in North Carolina and Mississippi the slave is not yet free nor is the Union secure," wrote Edgar Ketchum. "People inquire with amazement, believing fully in the patriotism and integrity of President Johnson, whether he can persevere in the exclusion of the freedmen from the suffrage in view of what is now going on in the South. It is a great mystery." Just one small glimmer of light penetrated Phillips' gloomy appraisal of Johnson's actions. "We can only hope the North Carolina policy is adopted

[29] James D. Richardson, ed., *The Messages and Papers of the Presidents* (20 vols., Washington, 1897-1913), viii, 3508-12.

[30] *N.A.S. Standard*, June 3, 10, 1865. See also *Independent*, June 8, 1865; *Commonwealth*, June 3, 1865; and *New York Tribune*, May 31, June 1, 1865.

as an experiment, not as a finality," said Phillips. "The government, let us trust, is only feeling its way, and has no purpose to plunge headlong into such a vortex as reconstruction on the present theory would set whirling."[31]

Only an experiment! This was the straw of hope grasped by many abolitionists and Republicans in the summer of 1865. Alarmed by the efforts of Democrats and conservative Republicans to drive a wedge between the president and radicals, the *Commonwealth* hastily reaffirmed its support of Johnson as head of the Republican party. "We expect him to see, before long if he does not now see, that the spirit of the Rebellion, and the spirit which denies the loyal black man the suffrage, are one and the same," declared the *Commonwealth*. Despite the unfortunate North Carolina reconstruction proclamation, "it is not yet too late to modify or wholly change that plan of reorganization." Samuel May, Jr., expressed willingness to accept Johnson's policy as an experiment. If the southern states demonstrated their good faith by granting equal rights to the freedmen, abolitionists would applaud Johnson's policy as a success. But if the new constitutions of former rebel states showed a continuing devotion to the spirit of slavery and oppression, "let such States remain under Provisional or Military Governorship, until the true light dawns upon them." "I cannot doubt," concluded May, "that such essentially will be the reply of Congress to any State presenting a Constitution excluding the freed people from citizenship and suffrage."[32]

In the summer of 1865 George L. Stearns, chief executive of the abolitionist campaign for Negro suffrage, had three separate but interrelated projects on hand. The first of these was an organization to distribute throughout the nation pamphlets, speeches, and newspapers favoring Negro suffrage. In the fall of 1864 Stearns had decided to organize a league of antislavery men to finance the dissemination of radical material. He collected a list of 2,000 sympathizers who could be called upon for contribu-

[31] Ketchum to Sumner, June 17, 1865, Sumner Papers, HU; *N.A.S. Standard*, June 3, 1865. See also *Liberator*, June 9, 1865; *Principia*, June 29, July 6, 1865; *N.A.S. Standard*, June 24, July 1, 1865; and George Cheever to Elizabeth Washburn, June 14, 1865, Cheever Papers, AAS.

[32] *Commonwealth*, June 10, 17, 1865; May's statement published in *Liberator*, June 23, 1865.

tions and for service as local agents to distribute pamphlets. Using mainly his own money, Stearns had printed nearly 90,000 pamphlets by June 1, 1865. The initiation of Johnson's reconstruction policy and the consequent need for stepped-up radical activity brought the Emancipation League and interested Massachusetts Republicans into Stearns' network. In June he sent out a circular proposing the formation of a "Universal and Equal Suffrage Association." The response was favorable, and within three months Stearns had compiled a list of 20,000 "members" of this association. By July 1 he was employing between six and ten clerks to send out 10,000 newspapers and 3,000 pamphlets per week. The pamphlets contained speeches by Phillips, Douglass, William D. Kelley, Sumner, Henry Ward Beecher, Benjamin Butler, Richard Henry Dana, and other prominent figures. At the end of July Stearns began mailing 12,000 copies of the *Commonwealth* each week to selected subscribers, trebling the circulation of that radical journal. By September he was sending out 20,000 newspapers and 5,000 pamphlets per week, and looking forward to a weekly total of 100,000 newspapers and 50,000 pamphlets if he could raise enough money. He had already distributed a total of 230,000 newspapers and 3 million pages of pamphlets.[33]

Stearns' second project was the founding of a weekly newspaper to represent the interests of the freedmen. J. Miller McKim and the freedmen's aid societies were also laying plans for a weekly. Each group had raised several thousand dollars by the spring of 1865, when they decided to pool their resources and put the proposed paper on a sound financial basis. Wendell P. Garrison, soon to marry McKim's daughter, was appointed associate editor of the new paper. Stearns and McKim cast about for an experienced journalist to serve as editor-in-chief. After George William Curtis and Whitelaw Reid had turned them down, they approached Edwin L. Godkin, a young British-born journalist who had been recommended to Stearns by friends in Boston.

[33] Stearns, *Stearns*, 351-52; Stearns to Gerrit Smith, Sept. 20, 1864, Smith Papers, su; Stearns to Benjamin Butler, June 10, Sept. 16, 1865, enclosing circulars of the "Universal and Equal Suffrage Association," Butler Papers, lc; Stearns to Sumner, Apr. 30, Oct. 4, 1865, Sumner Papers, hu; *N.A.S. Standard*, June 10, Aug. 19, 1865; *Commonwealth*, June 10, July 29, Aug. 5, Sept. 30, 1865.

Stearns and Wendell Phillips interviewed Godkin for four hours, discussing the questions of reconstruction, Negro suffrage, the freedmen, and so on. Godkin gave them the impression that he agreed with their views on all important aspects of reconstruction. They approved of him as editor with the understanding that he was to have complete independence in editorial matters but that the paper was to represent primarily the interests of the freedmen.[34] The stockholders sent out circulars to announce the publication of the first issue of the *Nation* in July 1865. All abolitionist papers gave generous publicity to the new enterprise, and Garrison gave his blessing to the *Nation* as the logical successor of the *Liberator*. Several abolitionists were listed among the contributors to the *Nation*.[35]

With a capitalization of $100,000 and the backing of prominent abolitionists and Republicans, the *Nation* appeared headed for top rank among radical journals. But difficulties plagued the undertaking from the outset. In the first place the *Nation* was caught in the middle of the schism in the American Anti-Slavery Society. McKim had supported Garrison's effort to dissolve the Society and was bitter toward the Phillips faction that now controlled the organization. Stearns, on the other hand, had sustained Phillips in his successful effort to preserve the Society. Godkin disliked the radical crusading fervor of the Phillips wing, and sided with McKim. The early issues of the *Nation* contained oblique disparagements of Phillips and Stearns. Godkin also made a derisive remark about Stearns in a private letter, a report of which came to Stearns' ears. Stearns and Phillips were outraged by these insults. Stearns had contributed and raised more money for the *Nation* than any other person, and he felt that at the very least he deserved respect from its editor. Secondly, Godkin hoped to make the *Nation* into an outstanding

[34] Stearns, *Stearns*, 332-35; Rollo Ogden, ed., *Life and Letters of Edwin Lawrence Godkin* (2 vols., New York, 1907), I, 223-41; W. P. Garrison to W. L. Garrison, Dec. 11, 1864, Apr. 3, May 5, 1865, W. P. Garrison Papers, HU; Lucretia Mott to Martha Wright, Apr. 17, 1865, Mott Papers, SC; Stearns to Sumner, Apr. 30, 1865, Sumner Papers, HU; McKim to Gerrit Smith, May 18, 1865, Smith Papers, SU; Frank Sanborn to Moncure Conway, May 26, 1865, Conway Papers, CU; McKim to M. W. Chapman, June 6, 1865, Weston Papers, BPL.

[35] *N.A.S. Standard*, May 6, 1865; *Commonwealth*, May 13, June 17, 1865; *Liberator*, June 30, 1865.

political and literary review, modeled on English weekly reviews. Its abolitionist backers had conceived of it primarily as a radical freedmen's paper. Thirdly, Phillips and Stearns desired a hard-hitting, no-holds-barred radical journal that would sound the trumpet call of equality in stentorian tones. Instead the *Nation* offered long and scholarly editorials designed to appeal to the intellectual elite rather than to the masses. The editorials of the early months of the *Nation* favored Negro suffrage and equal justice to the freedmen, but they were characterized by a conservative restraint and impartial flavor which rendered them totally inadequate in the eyes of many radicals.[36]

Even Garrison and McKim were slightly unhappy with the first issues of the *Nation*, and Godkin adopted some of their friendly suggestions for improvement. But Phillips, Stearns, and other Boston radicals were entirely dissatisfied. They tried to force Godkin to change the style and spirit of the paper, and failing that, to force him out of the editor's chair. Charging bad faith on the part of Godkin, Stearns and most of the Boston stockholders withdrew their capital from the *Nation* in May 1866. Godkin reorganized the paper and became its proprietor as well as editor. Thenceforth the *Nation* turned gradually more conservative on the reconstruction question. What Stearns had originally conceived of as a large-circulation radical journal crusading for social reform and racial equality became under Godkin a genteel political-literary review of limited circulation but of considerable influence among the patrician class of intellectuals and businessmen in America.[37]

[36] Stearns, *Stearns*, 336-37, 351n.; Ogden, *Godkin*, I, 241-48; *Nation*, I (July 6, 1865), 1, 4-5 (July 13, 1865), 40 (July 20, 1865), 69, 73-74 (Sept. 21, 1865), 357, 359; *Liberator*, July 7, 1865; *Commonwealth*, July 15, 1865; *Independent*, July 13, 1865; McKim to E. L. Pierce, July 10, 1865, Godkin to McKim, July 10, 1865, Pierce to Benjamin Butler, July 11, 1865, in Jesse Marshall, ed., *Private and Official Correspondence of Gen. Benjamin F. Butler during the Period of the Civil War* (5 vols., Norwood, Mass., 1917), V, 491; Mary Stearns to A. Bronson Alcott, July 25, 1865, Alcott Papers, Concord Public Library.

[37] Stearns, *Stearns*, 337-38, 366; Ogden, *Godkin*, I, 242, 246-48; Alan P. Grimes, *The Political Liberalism of the New York Nation, 1865-1932* (Chapel Hill, 1953), 5-12; McKim to Samuel May, Jr., July 19, 1865, Quincy to May, Aug. 16, 1865, McKim to Richard Webb, Aug. 31, 1865, Garrison Papers, BPL; McKim to M. W. Chapman, Aug. 26, 1865, Weston Papers, BPL; Quincy to Webb, Oct. 21, 1865, Quincy-Webb Correspondence, BPL; Samuel May, Jr., to Webb, Sept. 19, 1865, Samuel May, Jr., Papers, BPL; *Nation*, I (Oct. 26, 1865), 520-21; *Liberator*, Sept. 22, Dec. 8, 1865; *Commonwealth*, Feb. 17, 1866, May 30, Nov. 14, 1868;

Made wiser by his experience with the *Nation*, Stearns kept control in his own hands of the next newspaper he founded (see discussion near the end of this chapter). Before the collapse of his hopes for the *Nation*, however, he set on foot his third major project to win public support for Negro suffrage: a mass meeting of the leading men of New England in Boston's Faneuil Hall on June 21, 1865. In an effort to portray this convention as an assemblage of moderates, Stearns engineered the selection of his friend Theophilus Parsons, Harvard law professor and nationally known jurist, as chairman and keynote speaker of the occasion. Richard Henry Dana, a respected lawyer and conservative anti-slavery veteran gave the main address. Although Stearns organized the convention and several abolitionists served as vice presidents and secretaries, radicals generally remained in the background and allowed the solid, substantial men of New England to take the lead. Parsons and Dana both emphasized the need of Negro suffrage to insure the success of reconstruction. Dana frankly admitted that "to introduce to the voting franchise four millions of slaves is a revolution. If we do not secure that now in the time of revolution, it can never be secured except by a new revolution. (Loud applause)"[38]

Stearns considered the Faneuil Hall meeting a great success. It attracted nationwide attention and inspired similar meetings in other cities. All over the North the subject of reconstruction and Negro suffrage was a vital topic of political discussion in the summer of 1865. Abolitionists held several meetings to promote the cause of equal suffrage. Northern Negroes organized rallies and demanded the franchise for themselves and their southern brethren. Radical Republican leaders spoke out for Negro suffrage. Southern freedmen held meetings and asked for the ballot to guarantee their freedom and security. Abolitionists spared no effort to bear witness for equal rights. "I have again and again, in sermon, speech and conversation urged the necessity of universal suffrage and emphatically of black suffrage—on grounds of humanity, justice, equity, reason and safety," re-

---

McKim to William Still, May 26, 1866, quoted in Norwood, "Negro Welfare Work in Philadelphia," 145; Sarah Pugh to McKim, Dec. 20, 1866, McKim Papers, NYPL. Garrison later became critical of the *Nation*'s conservative course.

[38] Stearns, *Stearns*, 346-50; *Commonwealth*, June 24, 1865.

ported O. B. Frothingham in August 1865. "And I shall continue to do so as long as I have breath."[39]

The Democratic and conservative Republican press was annoyed by the outburst of Negro suffrage propaganda in the summer of 1865. The *Chicago Times* lamented: "This is an afflicted nation. To-day the negro is the one thing in every man's mouth from the Gulf to the St. Lawrence. The entire press of the country is wrangling over the negro; Boston philanthropists are holding secret meetings and arranging plans with reference to the negro. . . . Orators are shouting about the negro; preachers are advocating higher law for the benefit of the negro; and, in short, the whole country is . . . 'going it' exclusively on account of the negro." The *New York Times* was tired of the Negro question but was resigned to a continuation of the agitation. "It is evident," said the *Times*, "that this whole negro question can only be got rid of by getting rid of the negroes; and as this is impossible, we must rest content with our lot."[40]

In the discussion of Negro suffrage several phrases were bandied about, often indiscriminately. The four phrases most frequently used were "Negro suffrage," "impartial suffrage," "equal suffrage," and "universal suffrage." There were real differences in the meanings of these phrases, but as time went on the differences tended to disappear. "Impartial suffrage" and "equal suffrage" meant that whether the franchise was unrestricted or qualified it would be open equally to both races. Any qualifications, such as a literacy test or property ownership, must be applied impartially to both races. "Universal suffrage" meant universal manhood suffrage for both races, unrestricted except for age and residence requirements. "Negro suffrage," the phrase most often used, could mean either universal or impartial suffrage. Sometimes it was also used (but seldom by abolitionists) to mean a limited grant of suffrage to Negroes who met special requirements not applicable to whites.

At first several abolitionists, including Theodore Tilton, Gerrit Smith, and Lydia Maria Child, were willing to accept impartial

---

[39] O. B. Frothingham to Charles Sumner, Aug. 3, 1865, Sumner Papers, HU. Antislavery newspapers were filled with details of speeches, meetings, etc. on behalf of Negro suffrage in the summer of 1865.

[40] *Chicago Times*, July 7, 1865; *New York Times*, quoted by *N.A.S. Standard*, July 1, 1865.

suffrage. Conceding the argument that the freedmen were ignorant and lacked political experience, they endorsed a literacy qualification applied equally to both races. They hoped that the rapid spread of education in the South would soon enable most of the freedmen to qualify for the franchise.[41]

Most abolitionists, however, called for universal rather than impartial suffrage. It was unfair, they argued, to impose a literacy qualification on the franchise when the southern Negro for generations had been denied educational opportunities.[42] As time passed the distinction between impartial and universal suffrage became less important. By the end of 1865 nearly all those who advocated Negro suffrage meant, in effect, universal suffrage. There were two reasons for this. In the first place the creation of impartial literacy and/or property qualifications would have disfranchised many white men who already enjoyed suffrage. The principle of universal (white) manhood suffrage was deeply rooted in America, and it was a rare politician who would vote to disfranchise any man except for treason. Secondly, abolitionists and Republicans soon realized that impartial suffrage would give the freedmen negligible political power at first. There would not be a literate colored electorate large enough to counterbalance the white voters or to build the foundations of a strong Republican party in the South. "All my first impressions were for the writing and reading qualification; but on reflection it seemed to me impracticable," wrote Charles Sumner in August 1865. "You cannot get votes of Congress to disfranchise, which you must do in imposing this qualification. . . . Besides, there are very intelligent persons, especially among the freedmen, who cannot read or write. But we need the votes of all, and cannot afford to wait."[43]

✦

41 Tilton to Garrison, Jan. 11, 1865, Garrison Papers, BPL; Lydia M. Child to Tilton, Mar. 7, 1865, in *Independent,* Mar. 16; *Independent,* July 20, Nov. 9, 1865; *Liberator,* Apr. 21, June 16, 1865; *N.A.S. Standard,* Apr. 8, 1865; Gerrit Smith, *Thoughts for the People,* broadside published April 14, 1865 (Peterboro, 1865).

42 See, for example, *Commonwealth,* Mar. 11, June 3, 17, 24, Oct. 14, 1865; Wendell Phillips, *Lectures, Speeches, and Letters* (2nd Series; Boston, 1900), 451-52; *Liberator,* May 19, 1865; *N.A.S. Standard,* Sept. 30, 1865, Feb. 17, 1866; Parker Pillsbury to Charles Sumner, Sept. 16, 1865, Sumner Papers, HU.

43 Sumner to Francis Lieber, Aug. 14, 1865, in Pierce, *Sumner,* IV, 256.

Despite the criticisms of radical abolitionists, most Republican leaders reserved judgment on President Johnson's reconstruction policy in 1865. The desire to regard that policy as an "experiment" which Johnson would abandon if it proved a failure was all-powerful. Moderate Republicans were unwilling to risk a party split over Negro suffrage.[44] Disgusted with the pusillanimity of politicians, Wendell Phillips decided to launch a full-scale attack on Johnson in a deliberate attempt to alienate him from the Republican party and to force the party to repudiate his policy. Phillips was the first prominent figure to come out squarely against the president, blazing a trail followed by thousands of abolitionists and Republicans in the next twelve months.

In powerful editorials in the *Anti-Slavery Standard* of June 24 and July 1, Phillips declared that Johnson's reconstruction program could no longer be considered an experiment. His extension of it to all Confederate states indicated a settled purpose. "We must make up our minds that we have to deal henceforth with a President implacably hostile to the only method of reorganization which is safe, peaceful, and permanent," wrote Phillips. Johnson had surrounded himself with conservative advisers and had rejected the counsels of true Republicans. Like President Tyler before him, he was in the process of abandoning the party that had elected him. Phillips was not deaf to the pleas of Republicans to avoid splitting the party. But Johnson had already gone over to the enemy, and "in these circumstances, he is manifestly a force to be resisted, not one to be counted on our side; a power to be subdued, not one to be waited on and conciliated." Most of the speakers at the abolitionist Fourth of July picnic in Framingham, Massachusetts, echoed Phillips' sentiments. The picnickers resolved unanimously that any reconstruction policy that failed to recognize "the absolute equality of every man before the Law" would be "a practical surrender of the North to the South" and "the essential triumph of the Slave Power."[45]

Theodore Tilton was also apprehensive about Johnson's course, but in midsummer of 1865 he was not yet prepared to declare a

[44] Eric McKitrick, *Andrew Johnson and Reconstruction* (Chicago, 1960), 42-84.

[45] *Liberator*, July 14, 1865. See also Parker Pillsbury to Samuel Johnson, Aug. 3, 1865, Johnson Papers, Essex Institute.

total break with the president. Instead he implored Johnson to reject the counsels of Democrats and remember that he had been elected by a party that meant to safeguard the Negro's freedom won at so dear a cost in war. Charles Slack, editor of the *Commonwealth* and spokesman for the old John Brown wing of Massachusetts abolitionists, expressed confidence that Johnson would soon recognize the failure of his "experiment" and move closer to the radical idea of reconstruction. "Andrew Johnson still stands before the tribunal," wrote Slack on July 22. "Press and people as yet only cry, 'He is going wrong, but he is honest and will come right.' So be it then. We will wait. But . . . if he wants the outspoken, unflinching support . . . of just men everywhere, he must bid for it soon."[46]

"I feel anxious at Pres. Johnson's course & think he mistakes it lamentably by his method of reconstruction, but am not ready to join in the hasty impeachment of him which is getting so popular," wrote William Lloyd Garrison, Jr., on July 9. "I prefer to believe in his good intentions & integrity till otherwise convinced." His father shared these sentiments. The elder Garrison censured Phillips and other abolitionists who had openly declared war on the president. There was "no ground for discouragement or alarm," said Garrison. "There is positive growth and constant progress." Garrison's continued faith in Johnson was echoed by many abolitionists in the summer of 1865. William H. Channing asserted that the president had not "a shade of a purpose to betray the cause of freedom. Let us stand by him and uphold his hand & so at once impel & guide him onward." An abolitionist friend of Frederick Douglass urged the Negro leader to be more charitable in his judgment of the president. "Did you not once have as little faith in Pres. Lincoln when you said he was 'wrong from choice, & right from necessity,' as you have now in Johnson?" she asked. "Does the past justify the present?"[47]

Wendell Phillips did more than denounce Johnson in the summer of 1865. In a July 4th speech he made a positive suggestion

---

[46] *Independent*, July 6, 13, 1865; *Commonwealth*, July 8, 22, 1865.

[47] W. L. Garrison, Jr., to Martha Wright, July 9, 1865, Garrison Papers, sc; *Liberator*, July 14, 1865; Wm. H. Channing to R. H. Dana, July 13, 1865, quoted by McKitrick, *Andrew Johnson and Reconstruction*, 63n.; Martha Greene to Douglass, Aug. 2, 1865, Douglass Papers, Anacostia. Charles Sumner was disturbed by Garrison's endorsement of Johnson. "Has not the time come for

that became the keystone of Republican strategy at the next session of Congress. If Clerk of the House Edward McPherson called the names of southern congressmen elected under Johnson's plan when Congress convened in December, warned Phillips, the game would be up, for the southerners would vote with the Democrats, organize Congress, and enact a reconstruction policy of their own. In a letter to the *Anti-Slavery Standard* of July 8 Phillips amplified his discussion of this question. Under House rules the clerk called the role before organization of the House or choice of a speaker. If the clerk called the names of southern representatives these former rebels would be in a position to control legislation. Phillips urged Clerk McPherson and the Republicans to make sure that this did not happen.[48] Phillips' speech and letter were the first public references to this problem, and they were widely reprinted and discussed in both the northern and southern press. Democrats denounced Phillips' proposal for the omission of southern names from the clerk's roll as "revolutionary" and "fanatical." But many Republicans were jarred into an awareness of the danger by Phillips' warning. McPherson privately assured Phillips in September that he would not call the names of southerners, and a month later the clerk publicly announced his position. When Congress met in December the members from former rebel states were automatically excluded by McPherson's omission of them from the roll, allowing the Republicans to proceed freely with their discussion of the proper method of reconstruction.[49]

In an effort to gather information on southern conditions for use as a weapon against Johnson's policy, Boston abolitionists and radicals helped finance Carl Schurz's southern tour in the summer of 1865 and arranged for publication of Schurz's letters in the *Boston Advertiser*. J. M. W. Yerrington, the abolitionist stenographer, accompanied Schurz and took down the testimony

---

your voice?" Sumner asked the veteran abolitionist on July 22. "This unwise and evil experiment of the Prest. must be exposed. I would not break with him, but let him know frankly the opportunity he has lost, & the mischief he has caused." Sumner to Garrison, July 22, 1865, Garrison Papers, BPL.

48 *Liberator*, July 14, 1865; *N.A.S. Standard*, July 8, 1865.

49 *N.A.S. Standard*, July 15, Aug. 26, Sept. 2, 1865; *New York Times*, July 9, 1865; *New York Herald*, July 15, 1865; *Richmond Commercial Bulletin*, July 19, 1865; LaWanda Cox and John H. Cox, *Politics, Principle, and Prejudice, 1865-1866* (New York, 1963), 140-41.

of all classes of southerners.[50] But radicals did not have to await Schurz's report for evidence of southern oppression of the freedmen. The lower house of the Tennessee legislature had already passed a black code barring Negroes from juries, inflicting more severe punishments on Negroes than whites for the same crime, subjecting Negroes to sale into temporary bondage for vagrancy, and giving the courts power to bind out colored children to white men as apprentices. Reports by military personnel, newspaper correspondents, and teachers in the South of whippings, shootings, and lynchings began to make their way into the northern press. Antislavery and Republican papers ran daily and weekly columns filled with stories of southern outrages against Negroes. The chaotic condition of affairs in the South had its bright side for abolitionists, because it convinced many northerners of the dangers of Johnson's program. Tilton recalled that Lincoln had advanced from a proslavery to an antislavery policy under the pressure of events and of public opinion, "So we believe will President Johnson yet [advance] if the press and the people persist in their just demands."[51]

In Mississippi, Provisional Governor William Sharkey began reorganizing the state militia in August 1865, using Confederate veterans as a nucleus. Union General Henry W. Slocum issued an order prohibiting the formation of militia units, but upon appeal from Sharkey the president overruled his general and allowed the organization of state troops to proceed. More than almost anything Johnson had done thus far, this action aroused the suspicion and distrust of the North.[52] Abolitionists who had not already done so began to turn against the president. "What can be hatched from such an egg but another rebellion?" asked the *Commonwealth*. "If rebels in Mississippi are to be thus armed, then also will they be in every rebel State. Can there be but one end to such a beginning?" Still protesting that he was not a member of the Phillips-Pillsbury party of "doubt, distrust, and denunciation," Samuel May, Jr., nevertheless feared that "if the coming Congress does not present itself, like an immovable wall

[50] F. W. Bird to Garrison, July 5, 1865, Garrison Papers, BPL; Howard K. Beale, *The Critical Year: A Study of Andrew Johnson and Reconstruction* (2nd ed., New York, 1958), 70-71.

[51] *Independent*, Aug. 10, 1865.

[52] McKitrick, *Andrew Johnson and Reconstruction*, 163-64, 193-94.

of adamant, to the encroachments of the Southern managers & their friends, . . . we shall be left in a most singular position, and the culmination of our terrible struggle . . . will be a most absurd, a most lamentable, & at the same time a most farcical one." Even Garrison, who had managed to preserve his jaunty optimism all through the summer, confessed at the beginning of October that "the aspect of things at the South is somewhat portentous. I begin to feel more uneasy about the President."[53]

Radicals realized that to impose Negro suffrage on the South while ignoring the same issue at home would leave them open to charges of hypocrisy. Only five northern states allowed Negroes to vote on equal terms with whites in 1865. Since "we of the North have a great battle to fight in order to secure suffrage to the negro at the South," wrote Sydney Gay in May 1865, "it behooves us to clear our own skirts from stain as rapidly as possible."[54] Republican legislatures in Connecticut, Wisconsin, and Minnesota put Negro suffrage constitutional amendments on their ballots for the fall elections. As the elections approached, however, abolitionists detected a tendency among Republican politicians to hedge on the question of Negro suffrage in their own states. The Minnesota Republican convention endorsed equal suffrage, but the conventions of Wisconsin, New York, Pennsylvania, Ohio, and New Jersey evaded the issue. Connecticut Republicans issued a broadside urging voters to approve the amendment, but the state committee showed a notable lack of enthusiasm for the measure. In truth, Negro suffrage *in the North* was by no means popular among northern voters, and Republican politicians knew it.[55]

---

[53] *Commonwealth*, Sept. 30, 1865; Samuel May, Jr., to S. J. May, Sept. 17, 1865, S. J. May Papers, BPL; Garrison to Henry Wright, Oct. 2, 1865, Garrison Papers, BPL. Lydia Maria Child commented in October that "I feel more uneasy about public affairs than I care to say. . . . I have called to mind my impatience with Lincoln, and I have tried to think the best of Andy Johnson, and to hope for the best; but I confess faith and hope are dying out." L. M. Child to Elisa Scudder, Oct. 22, 1865, Child Papers, Cornell.

[54] *New York Tribune*, May 27, 1865.

[55] *ibid.*, Sept. 12, 26, 1865; *N.A.S. Standard*, Aug. 19, Sept. 30, 1865; *Independent*, Aug. 24, Sept. 28, 1865; G. W. Curtis to S. H. Gay, Aug. 23, 1865, Gay Papers, CU; Henry Stanton to Gerrit Smith, Sept. 22, 1865, Smith Papers, SU; Leslie H. Fishel, Jr., "Northern Prejudice and Negro Suffrage, 1865-1870," *Journal of Negro History*, XXXIX (Jan. 1954), 12-15.

A great deal was at stake in the Connecticut election early in October. A victory for Negro suffrage in the pivotal Nutmeg State would imply a repudiation of Johnson's reconstruction policy and an endorsement of the radicals. A defeat, on the other hand, would be interpreted as a victory for Johnson. The administration and the Democrats did their best to defeat the amendment, using appeals to race prejudice as their main weapon. Republicans failed to make similar efforts on the other side, and the amendment lost by 6,000 votes. A month later Minnesota and Wisconsin voters also turned down Negro suffrage. Abolitionists and radicals were inconsolable. The Connecticut vote was "the most disastrous event since the death of Mr. Lincoln and the inauguration of the present policy of his successor," wrote Wendell P. Garrison in the *Liberator*. "We feel humiliated and a-shamed of this ingratitude and shortsightedness," declared the *Boston Commonwealth* a few days after the Connecticut vote. "It was an unworthy, unmanly and discreditable act, and will cover the New England name with shame the world over." The *Commonwealth* frankly conceded that the defeat of Negro suffrage in Connecticut "jeopardizes—at least, delays—the permanent settlement of the questions in dispute in the rebellious States." Tilton was disenchanted with moderate Republican leadership after the Connecticut election, and abandoned all efforts to promote reconciliation between moderates and radicals. "The Republican party must stand either *for* or *against* Equal Suffrage," announced Tilton. "If this party refuses to fulfill its moral mission, it will go to pieces. . . . We shall be glad to stand with the great body of the Republican party in so far as that body shall stand inflexibly for Freedom and Justice; but we have no intention of abandoning moral principles for the sake of keeping company with political friends."[56]

Abolitionists were discouraged by the entire course of events in the autumn of 1865. A reaction in favor of Johnson and of reconstruction without Negro suffrage seemed to have set in. Southern constitutional conventions were refusing to grant even equal *civil* rights to the freedmen. Unless something intervened

[56] *Liberator*, Oct. 13, 1865; *Commonwealth*, Oct. 7, 1865; *Independent*, Oct. 12, 1865. See also George Cheever to Elizabeth C. Washburn, Oct. 3, 1865, Cheever Papers, AAS; *New York Tribune*, Oct. 3, 7, 1865; and *N.A.S. Standard*, Oct. 14, 1865.

it appeared that these states would be readmitted to the Union with constitutions and "Black Codes" relegating the Negroes to a permanent subordinate status. Hoping against hope, abolitionists looked forward to the meeting of Congress to remedy the situation. Meanwhile they did not sit back and wring their hands in despair. Anna Dickinson, Tilton, Phillips, Douglass, and several lesser abolitionists embarked on lecture tours that would take them before hundreds of audiences during the winter. Reconstruction was virtually the sole topic of their lectures. Nearly every abolitionist speaker kept up a relentless fire against President Johnson's policy throughout the winter.[57]

The title of Phillips' most oft-repeated lecture was "The South Victorious." This jarring title brought thousands who had thought the North victorious to hear Phillips in Boston and New York in October. Judging by the present hour, Phillips told skeptical listeners, the South was indeed victorious. Beaten on the field of battle, she had a good prospect of winning the political game of reconstruction. Phillips reminded his audiences of the revolution of 1848 in France, when the people deposed a king only to install an emperor in his place. "Now, we stand exactly as France stood," said Phillips. The North had overthrown slavery but was in danger of installing a new version of the aristocratic slave power in its place. Under Johnson's plan, said Phillips, the South would return to the Union "with the same theories, with the same men to work them, and the same element to work them with. . . . It must be evident to any reasoning man that the single advantage the North has gained in changing the political and social condition of the Southern States was the elimination, possibly, of this single element of chattelhood." Phillips denounced the Republican party for its timid failure to take a stand against Johnson's policy. "There is really no political force in existence worthy the name of the Republican party," he declared. "We

[57] For examples of abolitionist discouragement, see *Commonwealth*, Oct. 14, 21, 1865; Wendell Phillips to Benjamin Butler, Oct. 24, 1865, Butler Papers, LC; Tilton to Sumner, Nov. 11, 1865, Sumner Papers, HU; *N.A.S. Standard*, Sept. 16, 23, Oct. 21, 1865. Phillips wrote privately in October 1865, that "we have no hope but in such utterly abominable conduct on the part of [Johnson's] protégés at the South as will cause the North & Congress to checkmate his plan." Phillips to Moncure Conway, Oct. ?, 1865, Conway Papers, CU.

can trust neither Congress, nor Andrew Johnson, nor the Republican party. The only hope remaining is in the People."[58]

Charles Sumner had remained in Washington during the summer of 1865 in a futile effort to hold Johnson to the radical line. He returned to Boston at the end of August and confessed his failure to Phillips, Howe, and Stearns. Sumner was prepared to follow Phillips into open opposition to the president. Stearns, however, was not yet ready to give up. He had known Johnson well in Tennessee, and he believed that he could accomplish more in a single conversation with the plebeian president than the scholarly, polished Sumner had achieved all summer. Stearns journeyed to Washington early in October and spent a pleasant hour chatting with Johnson. The president denied that he was going over to the Democrats. On the burning question of Negro suffrage Johnson restated his belief that the federal government had no more right to prescribe suffrage conditions for Alabama than for Pennsylvania. If he were back in Tennessee, said Johnson, he would favor a gradual extension of suffrage to Negroes who had served in the army or could meet a property or literacy qualification. He was opposed to an immediate grant of universal suffrage, fearing that it would cause a war of races in the South.[59]

Stearns returned to his hotel and immediately wrote down the substance of the president's remarks. He requested Johnson's permission to publish the interview, believing that "it will go far to promote a good understanding between you and our leading men."[60] Johnson acquiesced, and Stearns returned to Boston for consultation with his colleagues before publishing the interview. Sumner and Boston's leading abolitionists attended a meeting to discuss the question. Stearns argued that publication would cut the ground from under Democrats who were claiming Johnson as one of themselves, repair the widening breach in the Republican party, and insert an opening wedge for Negro suffrage. The interview put Johnson on record as favoring qualified suffrage, said Stearns, and after six months an improved public opinion would make it possible to get a stronger presidential endorsement of Negro suffrage. Johnson would move, like Lincoln, with the

[58] *N.A.S. Standard*, Oct. 21, Nov. 4, 1865.
[59] Stearns, *Stearns*, 358-60; *New York Tribune*, Oct. 23, 1865.
[60] Stearns to Johnson, Oct. 8, 1865, Johnson Papers, LC.

advancing tide of public opinion. "All my former intercourse with the President taught me to respect his honesty, sincerity and ability," said Stearns, "and I shall trust him until he for the *first time* deceives me." Sumner, Phillips, and others were opposed to publication of the interview. They believed Johnson to be an implacable foe of radical reconstruction, and did not favor anything that would increase the president's stature in the eyes of the Republican party. They considered Johnson less dangerous as an avowed enemy than as a false friend. Stearns nevertheless published the interview in the Boston and New York papers on October 23, and it was reprinted or summarized by nearly every newspaper in the North.[61]

Most of the Republican press reacted precisely as Stearns desired, hailing the interview as evidence that Johnson was still a loyal Republican and a friend of the Negro.[62] But most abolitionists failed to find any reason for encouragement in the interview. Johnson's assertion that universal suffrage would breed a war of races reminded Tilton of the old conservative argument that *emancipation* would spark a race war. The *Anti-Slavery Standard* ridiculed Johnson's statement that he could no more interfere with suffrage requirements in Alabama than in Pennsylvania. Had he appointed a provisional governor for Pennsylvania? Had he ordered Pennsylvania to repudiate her state debt? He had taken such steps in the former rebel states, proving by his own actions that the government possessed the power of a conqueror over the southern states and could mold their institutions into any shape it desired. The *Standard* was opposed to any efforts to reconcile Johnson and the radicals, for it believed Johnson irrevocably hostile to nearly everything the radicals stood for. "We assure Mr. Stearns that the Radicals mean to *smash* the reconstruction policy of the President," declared the *Standard*, "and believe they can do it if their friends and the true friends of the Negro will stand by them."[63]

By the end of October 1865, many abolitionists had come to agree with Higginson that "what most men mean to-day by the

[61] Stearns, *Stearns*, 360-61; quotation from Stearns to Moncure Conway, Oct. 23, 1865, Conway Papers, cu.

[62] *New York Tribune*, Oct. 23, 1865; *Right Way*, Nov. 18, 1865; Stearns to Andrew Johnson, Nov. 13, 1865, Johnson Papers, lc; Stearns, *Stearns*, 361-62.

[63] *Independent*, Oct. 26, Nov. 9, 1865; *N.A.S. Standard*, Oct. 28, 1865.

'President's plan of reconstruction' is the pardon of every rebel for the crime of rebellion, and the utter refusal to pardon a single black loyalist for the crime of being black. . . . The truth is that we are causing quite as much suffering as a conqueror usually does. It is simply that we are forgiving our enemies and torturing only our friends." The Garrison family was finally becoming convinced of Johnson's bad faith. "Notwithstanding Stearns' interview which amounts to nothing," wrote William Lloyd Garrison, Jr., "it will take a different course of action on the President's part to inspire much trust in his administration."[64]

But there were some abolitionists not yet ready to give up on Johnson. J. Miller McKim told a fellow abolitionist that "I share your fears in regard to President Johnson, and yet my hopes exceed my fears."[65] George Stearns still had faith in the president. In November 1865, Stearns began publishing a weekly radical newspaper called the *Right Way*. The purpose of this journal was to win public support for Negro suffrage as the right way to accomplish a successful reconstruction. Stearns employed Alpheus Crosby, an abolitionist and the leading American authority on ancient Greece, as editor of the *Right Way*. William W. Thayer, a John Brown abolitionist, served as business manager of the paper and wrote many of its shorter editorials. The *Right Way* was published in the *Liberator* office, and every week 60,000 copies were sent to members of Stearns' Universal and Equal Suffrage Association. Negroes in the South formed clubs to distribute the *Right Way* among the freedmen. In its early issues the paper advocated Stearns' policy of reconciliation between the radicals and President Johnson. It praised Johnson as a "patriotic President" who needed the support of all "faithful men" in the difficult task of reconstruction. The *Right Way* was convinced that Negro suffrage was necessary for reconstruction and equally convinced that Johnson would soon realize this fact.[66]

As the important 1865-66 session of Congress approached, abolitionists' spirits revived somewhat from the doldrums of

[64] Higginson's statement published in *Independent*, Oct. 26, 1865; W. L. Garrison, Jr., to Martha Wright, Nov. 5, 1865, Garrison Papers, sc.

[65] McKim to S. J. May, Nov. 7, 1865, McKim letterbook, I, 55, McKim Papers, Cornell.

[66] Stearns, *Stearns*, 357; W. W. Thayer, ms. autobiography, fragment in the MS Division, lc; *Right Way*, Nov. 18, 25, Dec. 9, 23, 1865.

October. Leading Republicans were giving signs of opposition to Johnson's policy. Phillips and some of the other ultraradical abolitionists believed congressional Republicans to be almost as culpable as Johnson because of their indecisive stand on Negro suffrage. But most abolitionists expressed confidence in Congress. In November Garrison embarked on a lecture tour that took him as far west as Springfield, Illinois. The veteran abolitionist was heartily welcomed and loudly cheered wherever he appeared. His lectures urged the exclusion of southern representatives from Congress until the freedmen were granted equal rights.[67] Garrison returned to the East on the same train with several Republican congressmen on their way to Washington. Most of them agreed, reported Garrison, that the South should not be readmitted without further examination of the problem and greater safeguards for the freedmen.[68] As the senators and representatives gathered in Washington, John G. Whittier published an Ode to the Thirty-Ninth Congress:

> Make all men peers before the law,
> Take hands from off the negro's throat,
> Give black and white an equal vote.[69]

At the end of 1865, abolitionists were divided roughly into four groups in their opinion of President Johnson. Some abolitionists, including Stearns and McKim, still believed that Johnson would prove faithful to his trust. Others such as Garrison, Lydia Maria Child, and Samuel May, Jr., were disappointed with the president but still possessed a glimmer of hope that he would change his policy under the pressure of congressional action and public opinion. A third group of abolitionists, including Tilton, Higginson, and Charles Slack, had preserved a precarious trust in the president until October, when it became obvious to them that Johnson considered his policy a finality rather than an experiment. They had turned against him and now reposed their confidence solely in Congress, still hoping against hope, however, that the president could somehow be persuaded to abandon his disastrous policy. Finally, the abolitionists led by

---

[67] *Liberator*, Nov. 10, Dec. 8, 15, 1865; *Cleveland Leader*, Nov. 9, 1865; *Chicago Tribune*, Nov. 17, 1865.

[68] Garrison to Helen Garrison, Nov. 27, 29, 1865, Garrison Papers, BPL.

[69] The *Nation*, I (Dec. 7, 1865), 714.

Phillips had long since relegated Johnson to the status of an enemy who must be overcome before the Negro could obtain equal justice. As the representatives of the people gathered in Washington for their weighty deliberations, Phillips and his followers openly challenged President Johnson and dared him to do his worst.

XV ✦ THE FOURTEENTH AMENDMENT
AND THE ELECTION OF 1866

IN his first annual message to Congress on December 2, 1865, President Johnson restated his belief that he had no right to prescribe suffrage qualifications in the southern states and declared that the reconstructed state governments provided ample protection and security for all citizens. Radical abolitionists derided the message. They noted again the president's inconsistency in appointing provisional governors and prescribing certain conditions for reconstruction but denying the right to fix suffrage requirements. As for the protection and security of citizens, one needed only to read the black codes or scan the daily reports of atrocities against freedmen to perceive the falsity of Johnson's assertion.[1] A good example of the southern attitude, said abolitionists, was a box received by Charles Sumner in the mail containing the severed finger of a Negro and a note: "You old son of a bitch, I send you a piece of one of your friends, and if that bill of yours passes I will have a piece of you."[2]

Abolitionists were gratified when Congress, in effect, repudiated Johnson's annual message by refusing to admit southern congressmen and by creating the Joint Committee of Fifteen to formulate a reconstruction policy.[3] A few days later the American Freedmen's Aid Commission, a union of the secular freedmen's aid societies, memorialized Congress for a continuation and enlargement of the Freedmen's Bureau. In an address written by McKim, the societies noted that freedmen could not get justice in the civil courts of the South, where they were excluded as jurors and sometimes as witnesses. McKim urged Congress to create military courts for the Negroes under the auspices of the Freedmen's Bureau.[4] Soon after this Senator Lyman Trumbull introduced two bills intended to clarify and protect the status of

[1] James D. Richardson, ed., *Messages and Papers of the Presidents* (20 vols., Washington, 1897-1913), VIII, 3551-60; *N.A.S. Standard*, Dec. 9, 30, 1865, Jan. 6, 27, 1866; *Commonwealth*, Dec. 9, 23, 30, 1865, Jan. 20, 1866; *Liberator*, Dec. 15, 1865; *Independent*, Jan. 4, Feb. 8, 1866.
[2] *Right Way*, Jan. 27, 1866.
[3] Tilton to Thaddeus Stevens, Dec. 6, 1865, Stevens Papers, LC.
[4] *Liberator*, Dec. 22, 1865.

southern freedmen. One bill enlarged the scope of the Freedmen's Bureau; the second defined the civil rights of freedmen and empowered federal district courts to enforce these rights.[5]

While Congress debated these measures, abolitionists continued to urge Negro suffrage as a minimum condition of restoration. The first test of the suffrage question came on a bill to grant the ballot to colored men in the District of Columbia. Petitions for enactment of this bill poured in from abolitionists and Negroes all over the North. The House passed the bill on January 18, 1866, to the thundering applause of 300 Negroes in the galleries. Abolitionists hailed the event as the greatest victory for the Negro since the Thirteenth Amendment.[6]

While the District of Columbia suffrage bill rested in Senate committee, the full Senate took up an enabling act to admit Colorado as the newest state of the Union. Republicans backed the Colorado bill in order to gain two additional Republican senators to help override Johnson's vetoes. But Sumner and the abolitionists opposed admission because Colorado's constitution limited the franchise to white men. They appreciated the partisan advantages of two more Republican senators, but they were trying to make Negro suffrage the main issue of reconstruction, and admission of a new northern state without equal suffrage would stultify their efforts and create a disastrous precedent. Senator Henry Wilson took the lead in urging Colorado's admission, and abolitionists denounced him unmercifully for his action. Despite the efforts of Sumner and the abolitionists, Congress passed the enabling act. But Johnson vetoed it on the ground that Colorado's population was insufficient for statehood, and Congress could not muster enough votes to override the veto. It was the only Johnson veto of which abolitionists ever approved.[7]

Meanwhile the tension between President Johnson and the Republican congressional majority was mounting. At the be-

[5] Eric McKitrick, *Andrew Johnson and Reconstruction* (Chicago, 1960), 277-79.

[6] *Liberator*, Dec. 15, 1865; *N.A.S. Standard*, Dec. 16, 30, 1865, Jan. 27, Feb. 3, 1866; *Commonwealth*, Jan. 20, 1866; *Right Way*, Dec. 23, 1865, Jan. 20, 27, 1866; *Independent*, Jan. 25, 1866.

[7] Edward McPherson, *Political History of the United States of America during the Period of Reconstruction* (Washington, 1871), 81-83; Edward L. Pierce, *Memoir and Letters of Charles Sumner* (4 vols., Boston, 1877-94), IV, 284-86; *Independent*, Feb. 8, Mar. 15, May 3, 1866; *N.A.S. Standard*, May 12, 19, 1866; *Right Way*, Apr. 28, 1866; *Commonwealth*, Jan. 27, Apr. 21, 28, May 5, 19, 1866.

ginning of the session Horace Greeley, George Stearns, and John Andrew made several attempts to preserve harmony between the president and Congress. Greeley journeyed to Washington in an effort to prevent a breach between Johnson and Republican leaders. Stearns made a personal appeal to his old friend Johnson for reconstruction on the basis of equal rights. In his valedictory address to the Massachusetts legislature on January 5, 1866, Andrew pleaded for the good will and cooperation of all classes, North and South, in solving the complex problem of reconstruction.[8]

Many abolitionists disapproved of these efforts to reconcile President Johnson and the Congress. Phillips thought that Republicans had carried conciliation far enough and that it was time for them to strike boldly against Johnson's policy. In reply to the moderate Republican argument that precipitate action would drive the president into the Democratic party, Phillips said: "If he is capable of being there, he ought to be. If he means to betray his party, the sooner the better." In January Senator Fessenden, chairman of the Joint Committee of Fifteen, publicly stated that there was no breach between the president and the Republican congressional majority. A special meeting of the American Anti-Slavery Society in Boston on January 24, denounced Fessenden's attempt to harmonize Johnson and Congress. "Those who bestow general approval of the President take off the edge of public vigilance," said Phillips. If Fessenden and his associates really thought there was no major difference of opinion between themselves and Johnson, "the leaders of the Republican party are to be watched, not trusted. . . . We need outside pressure and remorseless criticism upon Congress and the President."[9]

During the congressional session a delegation of Negro abolitionists, headed by George Downing, came to Washington to lobby for Negro suffrage. On February 7 Downing, Frederick Douglass, and three other Negroes held an important interview

8 Glyndon G. Van Deusen, *Horace Greeley, Nineteenth Century Crusader* (Phila., 1953), 342-43; *Right Way*, Dec. 16, 1865; Stearns to Johnson, Dec. 14, 1865, Johnson Papers, lc; Henry G. Pearson, *The Life of John A. Andrew* (2 vols., Boston, 1904), ii, 276-87.

9 *N.A.S. Standard*, Jan. 20, Feb. 3, 1866. See also Phillips to Sumner, Dec. 25, 1865, Sumner Papers, hu; *Principia*, Jan. 11, 1866; and *Commonwealth*, Jan. 27, 1866.

"Andrew Johnson's Reconstruction and How It Works."
Nast in *Harper's Weekly*

with President Johnson. In short introductory speeches Downing and Douglass assured the president that they came in a spirit of respect and friendship. They urged Johnson to enfranchise the Negro as a measure of justice and necessity. In his reply the president declared that he had always been a friend of the colored race. "If I know myself, and the feelings of my own heart, they have been for the colored man. I have owned slaves and bought slaves, but I never sold one." Warming to his subject, Johnson declared that Negro suffrage in the South would cause a war of races. If enfranchised the freedmen would become mere political pawns of the planter class, who would use them to grind down further the small white farmers. The president could see no solution of the race problem except emigration of the Negroes from the South. Stunned by Johnson's remarks, Douglass tried to reply, but was cut off by the president before he could utter more than a few sentences. The delegation was ushered out of Johnson's office.[10]

After consultation with radical congressional leaders, Douglass penned a reply to the president's statement and published it in the *Washington Chronicle*. Douglass denied that Negro suffrage would create a race war or that the Negro voter would become the pawn of the planter class. Enmity between Negro and poor white grew out of slavery. In freedom the Negroes and the small white farmers would have similar interests and would vote accordingly. Even if hostility between poor white and Negro did continue in freedom, said Douglass, how was the freedman to protect himself without equal rights? Experience proved that "Men are whipped oftenest who are whipped easiest." To keep the Negro politically powerless would only invite abuse and oppression of the defenseless freedmen. "Peace between races is not to be secured by degrading one race and exalting another," concluded Douglass, "but by maintaining a state of equal justice between all classes."[11]

[10] *Washington Chronicle*, Feb. 8, 1866. One of Johnson's private secretaries reported to a friend that after the "darkey delegation" had left his office, the president "uttered the following terse Saxon: 'Those d----d sons of b----s thought they had me in a trap! I know that d----d Douglass; he's just like any nigger, and he would sooner cut a white man's throat than not.'" P. Ripley to Manton Marble, Feb. 8, 1866, quoted by LaWanda Cox and John H. Cox, *Politics, Principle, and Prejudice, 1865-1866: Dilemma of Reconstruction America* (New York, 1963), 163.

[11] *Washington Chronicle*, Feb. 8, 1866. An account of the interview and a copy

The interview and Douglass' reply attracted widespread attention. The Republican press was almost unanimously critical of Johnson's behavior toward the Negroes. Abolitionists exploded in anger at this new evidence of Johnson's race prejudice. In an editorial entitled "Our Poor White President" the *Anti-Slavery Standard* assailed Johnson's address to the colored delegation as "one of the most brutal and insolent speeches anywhere on record." Elizabeth Cady Stanton commented that the interview showed "how much better Douglass understands the philosophy of social life and republican institutions than the President." The Worcester Freedom Club resolved that the interview had revealed the real attitude of the president toward the Negro: there was no longer any doubt that Johnson's policy was based on the belief that the country belonged to white men alone.[12]

Most abolitionists had given up hope of securing Johnson's cooperation for a just reconstruction program, but there were still many Republicans seeking a basis of accommodation with the president. In mid-February their hopes centered on Trumbull's Freedmen's Bureau bill, recently passed by large majorities in both houses of Congress. Senators Trumbull and Fessenden fully expected Johnson to approve the act. Speaker of the House Schuyler Colfax wagered a box of Havana cigars that the president would sign. J. Miller McKim scouted Democratic rumors that the president would veto the bill. "I can hardly think he will be so unwise as to do so," wrote McKim. "That bill . . . is a growth of the loyal and virtuous public sentiment of the land. To veto it . . . would be to fly in the face of the whole people."[13]

But on February 19 Johnson shocked Republicans by vetoing the act. The *Anti-Slavery Standard* was not surprised. Phillips tossed an "I told you so" editorial at Republicans who had labored to reconcile President Johnson and the Congress. Two days after the veto Theodore Tilton told his friend Greeley that "it is a crime henceforth to deceive the Nation by the pretence

---

of Douglass' reply are in McPherson, *History of Reconstruction*, 52-56. See also *New York Tribune*, Feb. 12, 1866.

[12] *N.A.S. Standard*, Feb. 17, 1866. See also *ibid.*, Feb. 24, 1866; *Commonwealth*, Feb. 17, 1866; *Independent*, Feb. 15, Mar. 1, 1866; *Right Way*, Feb. 24, Mar. 3, 1866.

[13] McKitrick, *Andrew Johnson and Reconstruction*, 284; *New York Tribune*, Feb. 14, 15, 1864; *N.A.S. Standard*, Feb. 24, 1866; McKim to Joseph Simpson, Feb. 16, 1866, McKim letterbook, I, 273, McKim Papers, Cornell.

that Andrew Johnson is the head of the Republican Party. . . .
All disguise is now taken off. The way to victory is no longer
by going *with* him but *against* him." Greeley was stunned by
the veto and expressed his grief in a series of *Tribune* editorials.
He did not yet take Tilton's advice to break completely with
the president, but his editorials were henceforth much more critical of the administration.[14]

Among abolitionists there was hardly one who ever again said
a good word for Johnson. Stearns, Oliver Johnson, McKim,
Garrison, and others who had been hoping against hope that the
president could be dissuaded from his wrongheaded course were
completely disillusioned by the veto. "What is to be done with
Andrew Johnson?" asked Samuel May, Jr., dejectedly. "It looks
to me now that he has *betrayed his friends,* when he might have
easily prevented any rupture if he chose." General Howard,
head of the Freedmen's Bureau, told McKim that the veto had
emboldened white southerners to increase their attacks on the
Bureau and had made freedmen's aid efforts in the South more
difficult. "I have talked hopefully of the President," reported
McKim from Washington. "We have kept our fears to ourselves.
But it is no use. Loyal and virtuous men here, who are well informed, as a general thing have no confidence in & no sanguine
hope of much good from President Johnson."[15]

Johnson followed his veto with one of the most remarkable
public speeches ever uttered by an American president. On
February 22 a group of Democrats held a Washington's birthday celebration at Grover's Theatre in the capital. They adopted
resolutions endorsing Johnson's reconstruction policy and affirming that "the grand old declaration that 'all men are created equal'
was never intended by its authors . . . [to place] the African race
in this country on a civil, social, or political level with the Caucasian."[16] In a festive mood the revelers trooped to the White

[14] *N.A.S. Standard,* Feb. 24, 1866; Tilton to Greeley, Feb. 21, 1866, Tilton
Papers, Misc. Mss, NYPL; *New York Tribune,* Feb. 20, 21, 23, 1866.

[15] Samuel May, Jr., to McKim, Feb. 20, 1866, McKim Papers, NYPL; McKim to
Joseph Simpson, Feb. 28, 1866, McKim letterbook, I, 398-400, McKim Papers,
Cornell. See also *Right Way,* Mar. 3, 1866; Oliver Johnson to Garrison, Feb. 20,
1866, Garrison Papers, BPL; George Thompson to Oliver Johnson, Feb. 22, 1866,
Dickinson Papers, LC.

[16] Garrison to W. P. Garrison, Feb. 22, 1866, Garrison Papers, BPL; *Independent,* Mar. 1, 1866.

House to serenade President Johnson, who responded with a long speech full of diatribes against radical leaders. Johnson compared himself to Christ; he denounced the radicals as traitors and disunionists, and when asked to name his tormentors, he called out the names of Thaddeus Stevens, Charles Sumner, and Wendell Phillips. These plotters were planning to assassinate him, charged Johnson. "If my blood is to be shed because I vindicate the Union and the preservation of this government in its original purity and character," he proclaimed, "let it be shed; let an altar to the Union be erected, and then, if it is necessary, take me and lay me upon it, and the blood that now warms and animates my existence shall be poured out as a fit libation to the Union of these States."[17]

The nation was mortified by the president's speech. Some of his best friends were appalled. Even abolitionists who believed Johnson capable of any villainy were taken aback. "Has the [presidential] office *ever* been so degraded before?" asked Samuel May, Jr. J. Miller McKim, usually restrained of speech, was moved by Johnson's behavior to call the president "an obstinate, pigheaded, ill-conditioned, border-state, 'poor white,' and locofoco Democrat." Garrison delivered a few well-publicized speeches and wrote several articles for the *Independent* denouncing Johnson and calling for his impeachment.[18]

Radical abolitionists who had long urged an unremitting war against the president were delighted by the public reaction to his Freedmen's Bureau veto and his February 22 speech. Many moderate Republicans turned against the president. Eight state legislatures passed resolutions rebuking Johnson.[19] The disillusionment with the president raised the stock of abolitionists who had been declaiming against him for months. Republican newspapers that had previously criticized the abolitionists for inciting ill will between President Johnson and the Congress now printed their speeches with editorial endorsement. Abolitionists

---

17 The speech is reprinted in McPherson, *History of Reconstruction*, 58-63.

18 Samuel May, Jr., to McKim, Mar. 5, 1866, McKim Papers, NYPL; McKim to Arthur Albright, Mar. 23, 1866, McKim Papers, BPL; *New York Tribune*, Feb. 28, 1866; *N.A.S. Standard*, Mar. 10, 1866; *Independent*, Mar. 29, April 26, 1866. See also McKitrick, *Andrew Johnson and Reconstruction*, 295.

19 *Commonwealth*, Feb. 24, 1866; *New York Tribune*, Mar. 5, 1866; *N.A.S. Standard*, Mar. 3, 10, 24, 1866; *Philadelphia Press*, Feb. 27, 1866; *Right Way*, Mar. 17, 1866.

spoke to cheering crowds on the lecture circuit. Radical congressional leaders encouraged their work of agitation. "Every school district in the country should be canvassed in the cause of justice and equality," Congressman William D. Kelley told Phillips. In March 1866, Sumner urged Phillips to hold the antislavery societies together. "You and they are doing indispensable work; in this I express the conviction of every Senator and every Representative on our side of the pending questions."[20]

One of the pending questions was Trumbull's Civil Rights bill. This measure was passed by Congress in March. Again there was much speculation about whether Johnson would veto or sign it. Recovered somewhat from the debacle of February, moderate Republicans were negotiating for a reconciliation with Johnson on the basis of the Civil Rights bill. But again the president spurned their overtures and vetoed the bill. For most Republicans this was the last straw. From that time forward there was a virtually irreparable breach between the president and the party that had elected him. On April 9 Congress passed the Civil Rights bill over Johnson's veto. Abolitionists were overjoyed. At last the Republicans had shown a bold and united front against the perfidious president. "Things begin to look a little brighter," commented young Frank Garrison, "and if we can only keep the two-thirds majority obtained for the bill, we can snap our fingers at the wretched occupant of the White House." Abolitionist David Plumb praised Congress for its defiance of the executive. "Now for the *Main Question*—the Suffrage of the Negro," wrote Plumb. "I do not expect great things from the 'Civil Rights Bill,' unless backed by Negro Suffrage. . . . Since half-measures cannot win the President, now, why not go for a whole one?"[21]

Plumb expressed the sentiments of many abolitionists. Despite their happiness with the passage of the Civil Rights bill, they were far from satisfied. The Civil Rights bill, said Tilton, was

[20] Kelley quoted in *N.A.S. Standard*, May 12, 1866; Sumner to Phillips, Mar. 17, 1866, quoted by Carlos Martyn, *Wendell Phillips: The Agitator* (New York, 1890), 353. See also *N.A.S Standard*, Mar. 10, 17, 1866.

[21] McKitrick, *Andrew Johnson and Reconstruction*, 298-324; *Independent*, Mar. 22, 29, Apr. 5, 12, 1866; *New York Tribune*, Mar. 28, Apr. 9, 10, 1866; Francis Jackson Garrison to Fanny Garrison Villard, Apr. 8, 1866, F. G. Villard Papers, HU; David Plumb to Sumner, Apr. 12, 1866, Sumner Papers, HU.

all right as far as it went, but "the negro will never be thoroughly protected, even in person and property, until he has the ballot." Gerrit Smith wrote an open letter to Senator Henry Wilson declaring that "the Civil Rights Bill cannot serve the black man in place of the ballot." "What is suffrage, if it be not a civil right?" asked the *Anti-Slavery Standard*. "What are civil rights worth that do not include suffrage?" The *Standard* welcomed Congress's display of backbone in passing the bill over Johnson's veto, but nevertheless considered the measure only "half the loaf. And if this be, as many fear, *the substitute for suffrage*, it may prove far worse than no bread."[22]

Abolitionists looked hopefully but not confidently to the Joint Committee of Fifteen for favorable action on the suffrage question. Since the beginning of January the Committee had been deliberating the problem of reconstruction. One of the first questions to come before it was the increase in southern representation occasioned by the abolition of slavery. Before emancipation the slave had counted as three-fifths of a man in determining congressional representation; the freed Negro now counted as a whole man. Without a constitutional amendment the South could return to the Union stronger than ever in Congress, her Negro population disfranchised but counted for representation purposes. In January the Joint Committee sent to Congress a constitutional amendment which would reduce the size of a state's congressional delegation if that state denied or abridged the franchise on account of race or color. Believing that northern public opinion would not sanction a direct grant of Negro suffrage, moderate Republicans rallied behind the apportionment amendment as the best attainable substitute.[23]

Abolitionists denounced the amendment. In a public letter Gerrit Smith asserted that if the South were readmitted under such a plan she would gladly accept reduced representation in order to keep her Negro population disfranchised. Tilton assailed the proposed amendment because it "puts the Negro into the hands of the Rebel. . . . It proves that a Republic is ungrateful." The

22 *Independent*, Feb. 8, 1866; *Gerrit Smith's Reply to Henry Wilson*, Mar. 26, 1866, broadside (Peterboro, 1866); *N.A.S. Standard*, Apr. 7, 14, 1866.

23 Joseph James, *The Framing of the Fourteenth Amendment* (Urbana, Ill., 1956), 55-56; McKitrick, *Andrew Johnson and Reconstruction*, 336-37.

American Anti-Slavery Society resolved that the amendment was "only fitted to protect the North and the white race, while it leaves the Negro to his fate. . . . In times of revolution the decisions, the mistakes, of a single hour may settle the opinions of a nation and its forms of civil life for centuries." Therefore it would be better to defeat this half measure than to accept it and run the risk of it becoming the final basis of settlement.[24]

Sumner was in complete accord with abolitionists on this question. The amendment was passed by the House at the end of January, but in the Senate it ran into the opposition of the powerful senator from Massachusetts. In a marathon Senate speech occupying two days (February 5 and 6), Sumner uttered an exhaustive excoriation of the Amendment and pleaded for congressional enactment of Negro suffrage. Abolitionists and northern Negroes praised Sumner's speech as the greatest effort of his life. They moved quickly to back up his efforts with petitions and memorials against the proposed Amendment.[25] Democrats as well as radical Republicans opposed the Amendment, and by the middle of February Sumner claimed to have enough Senate votes to defeat it. When the vote was taken on March 9 it fell short of the two-thirds majority necessary for passage. Abolitionists rejoiced in its failure and heaped renewed praise on Sumner.[26]

Victory in the battle of the ballot, however, still seemed remote. Convinced that northern public opinion opposed Negro suffrage, moderate Republican leaders continued to seek a less radical solution to the reconstruction puzzle. Abolitionists denounced these Republicans for their willingness to sacrifice the Negro on the altar of political expediency. "They have sought only to tinker, not to *change* 'the President's plans'; to merely prune,

[24] *Gerrit Smith to Senator Sumner*, Feb. 5, 1866, published letter (Peterboro, 1866); Tilton to Sumner, Feb. 2, 1866, Sumner Papers, HU; *N.A.S. Standard*, Feb. 3, 1866. See also *Commonwealth*, Jan. 27, 1866; *Principia*, Feb. 8, 1866; *Independent*, Feb. 1, 8, 15, 1866.

[25] Pierce, *Sumner*, IV, 277-81; "Memorial of a Delegation Representing the Colored People," *House Misc. Docs.*, #109, 39 Cong., 1 Sess.; *Commonwealth*, Feb. 10, 17, 1866; *N.A.S. Standard*, Feb. 17, Mar. 24, Apr. 21, 1866. There are nearly a dozen letters from abolitionists to Sumner praising his speech against the proposed Fourteenth Amendment in the Sumner Papers, HU.

[26] *Cong. Globe*, 39 Cong., 1 Sess., 1,224-35, 1,275-89; *Commonwealth*, Mar. 17, 1866; *N.A.S. Standard*, Mar. 17, 1866.

not to uproot and destroy," charged the *Anti-Slavery Standard* in April. "Were the Democrats in power, they could not possibly be worse."[27] In an effort to improve the climate of public opinion and exert pressure on Congress, the Boston Emancipation League reorganized in March 1866, as the Impartial Suffrage Association. The Association sponsored lectures and aided George Stearns in the circulation of newspapers and pamphlets throughout the nation.[28]

Disturbed by Congress's failure to propose an effective reconstruction program, Robert Dale Owen came to Washington at the end of March and laid before Thaddeus Stevens a comprehensive plan. Owen proposed a constitutional amendment that would prohibit discrimination in civil rights, enact impartial suffrage in every state after July 4, 1876, and provide for proportional reduction of the representation of any states that denied Negro suffrage before that date. Stevens professed enthusiasm for the plan, but Sumner and the abolitionists disliked the postponement of equal suffrage until 1876. Even this modest Negro suffrage proposal, however, was too strong for the Joint Committee. With the congressional elections of 1866 looming on the horizon, they were extremely sensitive to political considerations. The Committee rewrote Owen's amendment. On April 30 Fessenden and Stevens reported to Congress a constitutional amendment that prohibited states from abridging the civil rights of citizens or denying any person the equal protection of the laws; provided for the proportional reduction of the congressional representation of any state that abridged or denied suffrage to any of its male citizens; disfranchised until 1870 all persons who had voluntarily supported the rebellion; and forbade payment of the Confederate debt. Congress struck out the section disfranchising all rebels and substituted a provision to disqualify from political office certain classes of leading Confederates. Otherwise the proposal submitted on April 30 was substantially the same as the measure eventually adopted as the Fourteenth Amendment.[29]

27 *N.A.S. Standard,* Apr. 14, 1866. See also *ibid.,* Apr. 21, June 23, 1866; *Independent,* Apr. 19, 1866.

28 Loring Moody to Gerrit Smith, Mar. 20, 1866, Smith Papers, su; *Right Way,* Mar. 17, 31, Apr. 14, May 5, 1866.

29 James, *Framing of Fourteenth Amendment,* 100-02, 109-16; McKitrick, *Andrew Johnson and Reconstruction,* 343-49.

The *Anti-Slavery Standard* denounced the Joint Committee's proposed Amendment as a "fraud." On the central issue of Negro suffrage it was no better than the Amendment defeated in March. "It is a substitute for suffrage and citizenship," said the *Standard.* "It is the blighted harvest of the bloodiest sowing the fields of the world ever saw." Phillips told Thaddeus Stevens that the report of the Joint Committee was "a fatal & total surrender. The South carries off enough of the victory to enable her to control the Nation, mould its policy & shape its legislation for a dozen years to come." Tilton vigorously criticized the Amendment in the columns of the *Independent.*[30]

Not all abolitionists reacted so sharply to the action of the Joint Committee. George Stearns expressed unwillingness "to accept as a finality any thing less than Impartial Suffrage," but thought that Congress should pass the Amendment "rather than have 'no policy.' " Adoption of the Amendment would not preclude radicals "from asking all we need at a future time. . . . Our support of Congress would be more efficient and direct, if, without denouncing this scheme we claim all we ought to have." The *Boston Commonwealth* regretted that Negro suffrage had not been incorporated into the proposed Fourteenth Amendment. But with an eye to the 1866 elections, the editor commended the Amendment as the best that could be obtained at this time. The *Right Way* considered it "criminal and idiotic" to enfranchise rebels and withhold the ballot from black loyalists. Nevertheless adoption of the Fourteenth Amendment would be "of great value for national security and national justice." Meanwhile, declared the *Right Way*, abolitionists should urge the inclusion of Negro suffrage in the enabling acts admitting southern states and the adoption of a Fifteenth Amendment incorporating equal manhood suffrage into the Constitution.[31]

Abolitionists therefore were divided into two camps in their attitudes toward the proposed Fourteenth Amendment. Neither group approved the measure as the final condition of reconstruction. One faction, led by Phillips, condemned the Amendment un-

[30] *N.A.S. Standard*, May 5, 1866; Phillips to Stevens, Apr. 30, 1866, Stevens Papers, LC; *Independent*, May 3, June 14, 1866.

[31] Stearns to Sumner, May 1, 1866, Sumner Papers, HU; *Commonwealth*, May 5, 19, 26, June 2, 1866; *Right Way*, May 12, June 9, 1866.

equivocally and hoped for its defeat, fearing that adoption would lead to the admission of southern states when they had ratified the Amendment. The other faction, led by George Stearns, approved the Amendment as far as it went, urged its passage, and hoped by an enabling act or a Fifteenth Amendment to secure Negro suffrage.

The House passed the Fourteenth Amendment in its original form on May 10. While the Senate deliberated, Phillips and his followers stepped up their attacks. In *Anti-Slavery Standard* editorials Phillips charged that by failing to enact Negro suffrage Congress had, in effect, surrendered to President Johnson and the South. The vaunted "practical statesmanship" of Fessenden, Trumbull, and other Republican leaders who had formulated the Fourteenth Amendment was nothing but "hypocrisy, fear, and a compromise." In a series of powerful sermons and discourses, several of which were published in pamphlet form, George Cheever excoriated the Amendment as a fraud, a sham, a political trick, and a "robbery of the colored race." Frederick Douglass considered the measure a personal insult to every Negro. "For to tell me that I am an equal American citizen, and, in the same breath, tell me that my right to vote may be constitutionally taken from me by some other equal citizen or citizens, is to tell me that my citizenship is but an empty name," declared Douglass. "To say that I am a citizen to pay taxes . . . obey the laws, support the government, and fight the battles of the country, but, in all that respects voting and representation, I am but as so much inert matter, is to insult my manhood."[32] The New England Anti-Slavery Society resolved that admission of rebel states under the proposed Fourteenth Amendment would be "total surrender" and "an unworthy trick to mislead the nation." In a speech at the Society's annual convention Phillips expressed hope for defeat of the Republican party if it fought the 1866 elections on the basis of the Fourteenth Amendment. "The Re-

[32] *N.A.S. Standard*, May 27, June 2, June 30, 1866; George B. Cheever, *Impartial Suffrage a Right; and the Infamy of the Revolution Against It in the Proposed Amendment of the Constitution* (New York, 1866), *Protest Against the Robbery of the Colored Race by the Proposed Amendment of the Constitution* (New York, 1866), *The Republic or the Oligarchy? Which? An Appeal Against the Proposed Transfer of the Right to Vote from the People to the State* (New York, 1866); Douglass' statement quoted in *N.A.S. Standard*, July 7, 1866.

publicans are occupied chiefly in keeping up their own organization," charged Phillips. "Let that party be broken that sacrifices principle to preserve its own existence."[33]

Garrison, Oliver Johnson, and McKim condemned Phillips' anti-Republican speeches and called for support of Congress and the Fourteenth Amendment. They professed to be no less ardent in their desire for Negro suffrage than Phillips, but declared that this objective would sooner be reached by cooperating with the Republican majority than by defying it. Stearns organized a mass meeting at Faneuil Hall on May 31 under the auspices of the Impartial Suffrage Association. The meeting adopted resolutions endorsing the Fourteenth Amendment and urging Congress to pass enabling acts requiring southern states to enact impartial suffrage before returning to the Union.[34]

Meanwhile a Senate Republican caucus bound all Republicans to vote for the Fourteenth Amendment on the Senate floor. Sumner and a few other radicals were opposed to the Amendment. But they were bound by the caucus decision and voted for the measure when it passed the Senate on June 8. The battle line for radicals now became the enabling act setting forth the conditions under which former Confederate states would be readmitted. Sumner introduced a bill drafted by abolitionist lawyer Samuel Sewall requiring equal suffrage as a condition of readmission. Congressional radicals rallied behind this measure, and Tilton gave it the support of the powerful *Independent*. But moderate Republicans considered Negro suffrage in an enabling act just as much a political liability as in a constitutional amendment. A majority of Republicans were reluctant to commit themselves to any final conditions of readmission. They preferred to go to the country on the basis of the Fourteenth Amendment as it stood, leaving the final terms of reconstruction to the next session of Congress after the 1866 elections. Congress adjourned in July without passing any enabling legislation.[35]

[33] *N.A.S. Standard*, June 9, 1866.

[34] Oliver Johnson to Garrison, June 16, 1866, Garrison Papers, BPL; McKim to John Bingham, July 20, 1866, McKim letterbook, II, 144, McKim Papers, Cornell; *N.A.S. Standard*, June 23, 1866; *Commonwealth*, June 2, 1866; *Right Way*, June 9, 1866.

[35] James, *Framing of Fourteenth Amendment*, 142-52, 169-70; S. E. Sewall to Sumner, June 1, 1866, Sumner Papers, HU; Sumner to Tilton, June 27, 1866, Tilton Papers, NYHS; *Independent*, June 7, 21, 1866; *Commonwealth*, June 16,

Most abolitionists were not reluctant to see this issue postponed until the next session, hoping that time, circumstances, and an improved state of public opinion would make Congress more radical in December. But in the last weeks of the 1865-66 session Tennessee, having ratified the Fourteenth Amendment, knocked on the congressional door for readmission. Moderate Republicans seized upon Tennessee's application as an opportunity to display the good faith of Congress and the success of its reconstruction policy by admitting the state with no other conditions than those contained in the Fourteenth Amendment. Sumner in the Senate and Boutwell in the House tried to incorporate an equal suffrage provision in the act of admission, but their motions were defeated. Tennessee was restored to the Union by joint resolution on July 23. Sumner was deeply discouraged and many abolitionists were sullen. Tilton feared that Tennessee's restoration would create a precedent for the admission of other southern states without Negro suffrage. "Tennessee is permitted to deny to her blacks a voice in the state, while she herself is permitted to resume her voice in the nation," he wrote in the *Independent*. "The spectacle is a national humiliation."[36]

Meanwhile Phillips had been thinking over his statement of May 31 that a Republican defeat in the 1866 elections would be better than a victory on the platform of the Fourteenth Amendment. Phillips' radical friends warned him that expression of such opinions could destroy his influence in the Republican party. At a Fourth of July celebration in Framingham, Massachusetts, Phillips renewed his attacks on the Fourteenth Amendment. But this time instead of calling for the defeat of the Republican party, he proclaimed his belief that the Amendment would not be ratified. He predicted that the South would reject it. Phillips announced that his radical Republican friends did not want the Amendment

July 14, 1866. In line with the decision of the Republican majority to play down the suffrage issue, the Senate quietly shelved the House bill granting the ballot to colored men in the District of Columbia. The *Anti-Slavery Standard* could hardly find words to express its disgust with Republicans for this new act of cowardice. *N.A.S. Standard*, June 23, July 28, 1866.

36 James, *Framing of Fourteenth Amendment*, 171-72; Pierce, *Sumner*, IV, 286-87; Sumner to Moncure Conway, July 30, 1866, Conway Papers, CU; *Right Way*, July 28, 1866; *N.A.S. Standard*, July 28, Aug. 11, 1866; *Commonwealth*, July 28, 1866; *Independent*, July 26, 1866.

ratified; they considered it nothing more than a platform for the fall elections, and hoped to enact a more thorough reconstruction program at the next session of Congress. Phillips therefore hoped the Republican party would succeed. "I know no other channel, this summer, in which to work. I cannot tell you to desert the Republican party; I know nowhere else for you to go."

This advice was not entirely welcome to some abolitionists. Gerrit Smith said that he could never support a party that campaigned on the basis of the infamous Fourteenth Amendment. Stephen S. Foster introduced a resolution declaring that abolitionists would support no party that did not recognize the absolute equality of all men before the law. Phillips hastily replied that he had not meant that abolitionists should give unqualified support to the party. They should condemn Republican shortcomings, as they had always done, but "let us support any one in that organization who does maintain, and promises to support, the true ideas of freedom." In the end Foster's resolution was adopted unanimously, with the understanding that it did not preclude abolitionist support of individual radical Republicans who were true to the idea of equality.[37]

As election day approached, abolitionists toned down their criticism of Republicans and concentrated their fire on President Johnson and his supporters, who were making a determined bid for electoral endorsement of Johnson's reconstruction policy. In June, conservatives issued a call for a National Union convention on August 14 in Philadelphia to rally all of Johnson's supporters in a new party. Republicans and abolitionists directed their main attacks on this new conservative threat. The *Anti-Slavery Standard* described the National Union movement as a bid for power by those who "agree that this is a white man's government. . . . It is virtually a movement for the re-establishment of slavery."[38]

One of the major issues of the 1866 campaign was the increasing oppression of freedmen in the South. In May a mob of white men in Memphis, aided by part of the police force, went on

[37] *N.A.S. Standard*, July 14, 1866. See also *New York Tribune*, July 6, 1866; *Commonwealth*, July 7, 14, 1866; and *N.A.S. Standard*, July 28, Aug. 4, 11, 18, 1866.

[38] *New York Tribune*, July 6, 1866; *Independent*, July 12, 19, 1866; *Commonwealth*, July 7, 1866; *N.A.S. Standard*, July 7, 1866.

a drunken, murderous rampage against the city's Negro population, burning, raping, and pillaging in the colored section of town and killing 46 Negroes. Northerners were appalled. Republicans charged that the riot was the inevitable result of Johnson's reconstruction policy. With Memphis as an example, observed the *New York Tribune* sarcastically, "who doubts that the Freedmen's Bureau ought to be abolished forthwith, and the blacks remitted to the paternal care of their old masters, who 'understand the nigger, you know, a great deal better than the Yankees can?' "[39] The Republican and abolitionist press continued to publish reports of outrages against freedmen all through the summer. Despite conservative charges that the Republican press exaggerated these reports for political purposes, the atrocity stories had some basis in fact. In September 1866, the assistant commissioner of the Freedmen's Bureau in Arkansas reported officially that crimes against freedmen had increased sharply since March. He stated that southern whites felt that "any effort to secure justice for the Freedmen is simply the work of 'abolitionists' . . . and [was] in direct opposition to the wishes of the President of the United States."[40]

The most spectacular anti-Negro violence occurred in New Orleans on July 30. A convention of radical whites and Negroes which had been called to consider a Negro suffrage amendment to Louisiana's Constitution was attacked by a mob of New Orleans whites containing many policemen and former Confederate soldiers. Scores of Negroes and their white allies were killed or wounded by the cold-blooded assault. In the North the affair redounded with great discredit to President Johnson and his policy. Republicans were quick to depict the riot as the inevitable consequence of Johnson's reconstruction program. Some abolitionists went even further and blamed the affray partly on the conservative policy of Congress. Gerrit Smith hoped that the New Orleans murders had "opened the eyes of Congress to its folly in restoring Tennessee, & to the folly of restoring any other Rebel State whilst such State was continuing to oppress the negro." Most radicals joined Elizur Wright in hoping that the

[39] *Independent*, May 17, 1866; *New York Tribune*, May 22, 1866.
[40] Quoted in George R. Bentley, *A History of the Freedmen's Bureau* (Phila., 1955), 158.

riots would prove a blessing in disguise by rousing the people to the necessity of a thorough reconstruction.[41]

Abolitionists unleashed a volley of ridicule and denunciation of the National Union convention when it met in Philadelphia on August 14. The convention adopted a resolution stating that "there is no section of the country where the Constitution and the laws of the United States find more prompt and entire obedience than in [the former Confederate] States." Gerrit Smith was appalled by the mendacious effrontery of this resolution. "This is said of that half of our country in every part of which it is unsafe to be a black man or the friend of a black man," wrote Smith. "Can the people respect the men who so trifle with truth?" Another radical described the Philadelphia convention as "a meeting of marvelous odds and ends, the reconstructed shreds and patches of rebellion; cunning men from down East, . . . gangs of rough and ready men from New York, freebooters in politics; several solemn old men from Pennsylvania, who will stand by the Constitution as it ought to have been two thousand years ago; . . . old pro-Slavery fossils from North Carolina; South Carolina implacables, with the whip-hand itching; . . . Mississippi gentlemen, who are determined to reconstruct by burying the negro." These men had come together "to stand by the Union, and the Constitution, and Andrew Johnson, to defend the New-Orleans massacre, and indorse the policy which gave us the murders at Memphis."[42]

To counter the National Union movement, a convention of Southern Loyalists met in Philadelphia in early September. Hundreds of northern Republicans attended as observers and as "honorary" delegates. The issues of Negro suffrage and the Republican party's relation to the Negro nearly broke up the convention. Trouble began when Rochester Republicans elected Frederick Douglass as a delegate. Many Republicans feared that Douglass' attendance would hurt the party in parts of the North where "social equality" was anathema. One Republican

41 Gerrit Smith to Garrison, Aug. 5, 1866, Garrison Papers, BPL; article by Wright in *Independent*, Aug. 16, 1866. McKitrick, *Andrew Johnson and Reconstruction*, 422-27, is the best brief discussion of the New Orleans riot and its political consequences.

42 Article by Gerrit Smith in *N.A.S. Standard*, Sept. 1, 1866; *New York Tribune*, Aug. 14, 1866. See also *Independent*, Aug. 23, 30, 1866.

urged Thaddeus Stevens to use his influence to keep Douglass away from Philadelphia. "If he goes it will certainly injure our cause and we may lose some Congressmen in doubtful districts."[43]

Douglass was not deterred by the fears of white Republicans. He told Governor Oliver Morton of Indiana that if he was prevented from attending the convention the Republican party would gain a reputation for "hypocrisy and cowardice." Failing to persuade Douglass to stay away from Philadelphia, Republican leaders decided to ignore him as much as possible at the convention. When the delegates assembled at Independence Hall for a grand procession to National Hall where the convention was to be held, all Republicans but General Butler shied away from Douglass. The delegates were supposed to march two abreast, but it appeared that Douglass would have to walk alone until Theodore Tilton came up, locked arms with Douglass, and marched proudly with him down streets lined with cheering onlookers.[44] Despite the cheers, many Republicans were alarmed by the incident. "A good many people here are disturbed by the practical exhibition of racial equality in the arm-in-arm performance of Douglass and Tilton," wrote Thaddeus Stevens to Congressman William D. Kelley. "It does not become radicals like us particularly to object, but it was certainly unfortunate at this time. The old prejudice, now revived, will lose us some votes."[45]

At the convention itself there was some reluctance to seat Douglass as a delegate, and a motion to invite him to sit on the platform was ignored. But Douglass and a Negro delegate from Louisiana were finally seated. The significance of their presence, however, was soon overshadowed by the mighty struggle over Negro suffrage. Without Negro votes, Republicans from the deep South would be politically powerless. Most of the delegates from former Confederate states, therefore, wanted a declaration by the convention in favor of Negro suffrage. They were encouraged in this direction by a number of abolitionists at the convention. Under the leadership of Tilton the New York delega-

[43] Samuel Shock to Thaddeus Stevens, Aug. 27, 1866, Stevens Papers, LC.

[44] Philip S. Foner, *The Life and Writings of Frederick Douglass* (4 vols., New York, 1950-55), IV, 25-26; Benjamin Quarles, *Frederick Douglass* (Washington, 1948), 229-31.

[45] Stevens to Kelley, Sept. 6, 1866, Stevens Papers, LC.

tion passed a Negro suffrage resolution. But the "practical politicians" of the Republican party exerted all their influence to prevent any statement on the suffrage question. A caucus of northern Republican governors resolved that the question of Negro suffrage must be kept out of the campaign. Governor Samuel Cony of Maine said that he favored equal suffrage as much as any man in the country, "but I don't believe in making negro suffrage an issue now. Our great object now is to secure the next Congress. If we don't get that, then all is lost; if we do get it, then all is safe."[46]

In this temper the convention spent three days attacking Andrew Johnson and the Democrats. But on the fourth day the Committee on Unreconstructed States submitted a report that included an endorsement of Negro suffrage. Border-state delegates tried to force an adjournment, and failing that, most of them withdrew, leaving an unorganized and confused mass of delegates from former Confederate states. Seizing the opportunity, Theodore Tilton, Frederick Douglass, and Anna Dickinson marched to the platform and proposed a reorganization of the convention into a popular mass meeting. The enthusiastic southerners agreed, and selected Tilton as chairman. Douglass, Dickinson, and Tilton made rousing speeches that evoked thunderous cheers from the crowd. The southerners, most of whom had never before heard a woman speak in public, were absolutely entranced by Anna Dickinson. After several hours of oratory the meeting broke up in high spirits. The next morning the Southern Loyalists met again formally and the Committee on Unreconstructed States again submitted its Negro suffrage resolutions. At the climax of the debate which followed, reported Tilton, Dr. Randolph, the Negro delegate from New Orleans, "leaped to the stage, and made an electric speech, picturing the wrongs of his race, demanding redress, claiming the ballot, and, suddenly turning to a colossal portrait of Mr. Lincoln behind the platform, exclaimed, 'We are coming, Father Abraham, three hundred thousand more!' The effect was irresistible. The house sprang to its feet, and gave cheer after cheer." The Negro

46 *New York Herald*, Sept. 5, 6, 1866; *Independent*, Sept. 13, 1866; Foner, *Douglass*, IV, 26-27; Howard K. Beale, *The Critical Year: A Study of Andrew Johnson and Reconstruction* (2nd ed., New York, 1958), 185-86.

suffrage resolution was adopted by an overwhelming majority. Moderate northern Republicans were chagrined, but abolitionists were jubilant. The endorsement of Negro suffrage by southern Republicans was an important victory for the radical cause. Many observers agreed that had it not been for the prompt action and persuasive eloquence of Tilton, Douglass, and Dickinson the Southern Loyalists would have adjourned in confusion without declaring for Negro suffrage.[47]

In a campaign speech at Cleveland on September 3, President Johnson repeated his familiar argument that northern radicals who opposed restoration of the Union under his reconstruction policy were traitors. "He who is opposed to the restoration of this Government and the reunion of the States is as great a traitor as Jeff Davis or Wendell Phillips," shouted Johnson. "I would ask you, Why not hang Thad Stevens and Wendell Phillips?"[48] Phillips laughed off the president's bloodthirsty question. But Johnson's designation of Phillips and Stevens as his greatest enemies pointed up an important fact: despite his strictures of the Republican party, Phillips was an influential leader of the party's radical wing. It was an era highly charged with excitement; Phillips was a bold, exciting, uncompromising spokesman for radicalism, and every word he uttered attracted attention. He might have been elected to Congress in 1866. He was nominated for Congress by a workingmen's party in Boston, and a word from Phillips probably would have given him the Republican nomination also. But the great orator declined, believing that he could be more influential as an independent, unfettered spokesman of radicalism than as a member of Congress where he would be hampered by party responsibilities and the exigencies of party politics.[49]

[47] *Independent*, Sept. 13, 1866. See also *New York Herald*, Sept. 7, 8, 1866; *N.A.S. Standard*, Sept. 15, 22, 1866; *Commonwealth*, Sept. 15, 1866; Frederick Douglass to E. C. Stanton, Feb. 6, 1882, Douglass Papers, Anacostia; Douglass to Anna Dickinson, Sept. 10, 1866, Ben Butler to Anna Dickinson, Sept. 8, 1866, Whitelaw Reid to Anna Dickinson, Nov. 11, 1866, Dickinson Papers, LC. Miss Dickinson received many letters of praise and thanks from Southern Loyalists for her part in the convention.

[48] McPherson, *History of Reconstruction*, 135.

[49] *Commonwealth*, Aug. 18, 1866; *Independent*, Sept. 13, Oct. 4, 1866; *New York Times*, Aug. 28, 1866; *N.A.S. Standard*, Sept. 15, 29, Oct. 6, 1866; *New York Herald*, quoted in *N.A.S. Standard*, Oct. 6, 1866.

Phillips was not the only abolitionist held in high regard by radical Republicans. The party recruited an army of abolitionist speakers for the 1866 campaign, headed by Anna Dickinson. But despite the participation of abolitionists in the campaign, Republican strategy in most parts of the North was to avoid the Negro question and concentrate on excoriating Johnson and extolling the Fourteenth Amendment. The Amendment was praised not so much as a benefit to the Negro but as a defense of the North from the renewed ascendancy of the South in national politics. The *Anti-Slavery Standard* complained in September that "most Republicans on the stump, and most Republicans in the press, are alike in this: they denounce the President unsparingly, praise the Congress and its proposed Amendment unmeasuredly, and threaten the rebels unfearingly. But *the negro* is, with them, nowhere remembered: 'The South Carolina rebel shall not have two votes to the New York loyalist's one;' but whether the loyalist of South Carolina shall have one or not, our halting Republican friends do not say. Northern Unionists —being all white—are to be protected; Southern Unionists— being nineteen-twentieths black—are to be left to rebel discretion."[50]

The question whether the Fourteenth Amendment constituted Congress's final terms of reconstruction emerged as a major campaign issue. Moderate Republicans insisted in stump speeches and newspaper editorials that Congress would readmit southern states when they had ratified the Amendment. They pointed to Tennessee as an example. "There can be no question that the amendment was proposed with the distinct intention of submitting it as the final condition of restoration," declared the influential *Boston Advertiser*. The *Nation* stated that enough Republican candidates had committed themselves on the issue to insure southern readmission in return for ratification. Even the *New*

---

[50] *N.A.S. Standard*, Sept. 8, 1866. Republican speakers tailored their remarks to the temper of the area in which they were speaking. In the middle states and the Old Northwest they carefully avoided any mention of Negro suffrage. In New England and parts of upstate New York, northern Ohio, etc., where antislavery sentiment had always been strong, Republican orators frequently advocated equal suffrage. As one Ohio correspondent of Chief Justice Chase explained: "In the Reserve counties, some of our speakers have openly advocated impartial suffrage, while in other places it was thought necessary, not only to repudiate it but to oppose it." B. R. Cowan to Chase, Oct. 12, 1866, Chase Papers, LC.

York Tribune, while continuing to plead for impartial suffrage and universal amnesty, conceded that readmission on the basis of the Fourteenth Amendment was favored by a majority of the party. In September the Republican National Committee issued an official address which proclaimed the Amendment to be "a just and safe plan of reconstruction" upon acceptance of which the southern states would be readmitted.[51]

Abolitionists and radical Republicans were alarmed by this renewed evidence of Republican perfidy to the Negro. They hastened to denounce the moderates and to deny that the Fourteenth Amendment constituted the final terms of reconstruction. Congress had made no formal commitment, argued the *Right Way,* and the admission of Tennessee was in no way a binding precedent. "We know personally every prominent member of Congress, and we know that the leaders do not mean to admit the unadmitted States on the mere adoption of the amendment," asserted Theodore Tilton emphatically. "In the name of the radical party, whose heart we know, and whose voice we speak, we repudiate the Committee's pledge to the rebels as wholly unauthorized, invalid, and void. . . . The radical party . . . can assent to no reconstruction short of Impartial Suffrage."[52]

In a rousing New York speech on October 25, Phillips unleashed another broadside against the Fourteenth Amendment. "The Constitutional amendment, so far as the negro is concerned, is a swindle," he said. "The absent, the unheard, the disfranchised race is sacrificed between the upper and nether millstones of Rebeldom, while the Republican party knowingly, systematically and persistently sacrifice it to preserve their political supremacy."[53] But despite their anger with the Republicans, abolitionists were gratified by the overwhelming Republican victory in the 1866 congressional elections. "The House of Representatives can send a dozen members off to a picnic," exulted Tilton, "and yet leave a majority large enough to pass a radical measure over the

[51] *Boston Advertiser,* Sept. 29, 1866; *Nation,* III (Oct. 4, 1866), 270; *New York Tribune,* Sept. 26, 1866; address of the Republican National Committee reprinted in *Right Way,* Sept. 29, 1866. For a discussion of the part this issue played in the 1866 election, see James, *Framing of Fourteenth Amendment,* 169-73.

[52] *Right Way,* Sept. 29, 1866; *Independent,* Sept. 27, 1866. See also *Commonwealth,* Sept. 29, Oct. 6, 13, 1866; *N.A.S. Standard,* Sept. 22, Oct. 6, 13, 1866.

[53] *New York Tribune,* Oct. 26, 1866.

President's veto." Both Tilton and Phillips interpreted the election results as a thumping repudiation of Johnson but not necessarily a popular endorsement of the Fourteenth Amendment as the final condition of reconstruction. "The Radical men of the North are neither to be conquered by the Democratic, nor trifled with by the Republican, party," wrote Tilton. Phillips declared that Congress, "which abdicated leadership and postponed action till they were 'certain sure' what the elections would be, can now resume their places. Let them go back and, throwing this chaff of Reconstruction out of one window and swindling amendments out of the other," enact a thorough reconstruction program granting the ballot to the freedmen.[54]

The *New York Daily News* affirmed that "where Mr. Phillips stood a few months ago the Radicals stand to-day; where he stands to-day they will doubtless be a few months hence." But despite this comment, most of the evidence in November 1866, indicated that if southern states ratified the Amendment, the moderate Republican majority would admit them to the Union with few if any additional conditions. If this happened the future of Negro suffrage would be dark. Abolitionists and radicals looked hopefully to the South for negative action on the Fourteenth Amendment and girded themselves for a sharp struggle in Congress.[55]

[54] *Independent*, Nov. 15, 1866; *N.A.S. Standard*, Nov. 17, 1866.
[55] *New York Daily News,* quoted in *N.A.S. Standard*, Nov. 24, 1866; James, *Framing of Fourteenth Amendment*, 174-77; McKitrick, *Andrew Johnson and Reconstruction*, 449-54.

XVI ✦ MILITARY RECONSTRUCTION AND IMPEACHMENT

THE prestige and influence of the abolitionists climbed to new heights after the 1866 elections. The mood of the North reached a postwar peak of radicalism in the winter of 1866-1867, and as the chief exponents of this mood the abolitionists saw their popularity increase correspondingly. Abolitionist lecturers reaped a rich harvest. Phillips, Anna Dickinson, Tilton, and Frederick Douglass embarked on ambitious tours of the Middle West, delivering an average of nearly one hundred political lectures apiece during the season. Everywhere they went these orators enriched the treasuries of local lecture bureaus. During the winter of 1866-67 the small town of Mount Pleasant in southeastern Iowa enjoyed a rare treat. No less than five prominent abolitionist lecturers spoke there: Anna Dickinson, C. C. Burleigh, Tilton, Douglass, and Phillips. Joseph Dugdale, a local abolitionist, reported that the words of these speakers had made such an impression in the small Iowa town that the people abandoned their policy of school segregation and allowed the community's Negro children to attend the new school on the same basis as whites.[1]

Phillips was by far the most popular and influential abolitionist lecturer. By 1867 he had become practically a national institution. On his tour of the Middle West he lectured in many towns where he had never before appeared, and delighted the audiences with his quiet but penetrating voice, his magnetic personality, his sharp thrusts at prominent politicians, and his bold ideas. Thousands of St. Louis' leading citizens came to hear him speak in that city, where he put on one of his best performances. Afterwards even the hostile *St. Louis Dispatch* remarked that Phillips was "a man who, as a private citizen, has exercised a greater influence upon the destinies of this country than any public man or men of his age." After listening to a Phillips lecture the editor of the *Keokuk* (Iowa) *Gate City* wrote: "It is

---

[1] *Independent*, Mar. 14, May 2, 1867; *New York Tribune*, Feb. 22, 1867; *N.A.S. Standard*, Dec. 29, 1866, Mar. 30, June 15, 1867. The Mt. Pleasant incident was recounted in *ibid.*, Mar. 30, 1867.

easy to understand why Wendell Phillips had so large a share in abolitionizing New England. His arguments grow upon you. . . . Impracticable? Fanatical? Why, he is one of the most entirely plain, common-sense, practical and practicable men we ever heard. . . . He gives you clear-impressed, new-minted, intellectual coin. . . . The difference between Wendell Phillips and other men, on the score of character, is his boldness. He speaks what other men think."[2]

Phillips' weekly editorials in the *Anti-Slavery Standard* also reached a wide audience. His terse, trenchant prose, so different from the ornate style of many editorial writers of the day, made Phillips' written words almost as popular as his lectures. The *New York Times*, the *New York Herald*, and dozens of smaller papers frequently reprinted Phillips' editorials. Senator Sumner testified to the good effect of the *Standard* among radical congressmen, to whom it was sent gratis every week. The moderate *Times* commented in May 1867, that "the political history of the past two years has been little more than a record of the triumphs of what was originally the abolition party, and which has since become the ultra absolutist element in the Republican party." Thus "it becomes a matter of considerable importance to watch carefully all indications as to what this restless, insatiate and potent element of the dominant party proposes to do next. What they *propose* today may be *law* tomorrow." The Democratic *New York World* observed ruefully that radicalism was like a marching army: "Mr. Weed lags in the rear; Mr. Raymond is only six months behind Mr. Greeley, and Mr. Greeley is only six weeks behind Thad Stevens, and Thad Stevens is only six days behind Wendell Phillips, and Wendell Phillips is not more than six inches from the tail and the shining pitchfork of the master of them all."[3]

Phillips was not the only abolitionist who commanded respect among the politicians. Early in the 1866-67 session of Congress, Speaker of the House Schuyler Colfax wrote to John G. Whittier:

[2] *St. Louis Dispatch* and *Keokuk Gate City*, quoted in *N.A.S. Standard*, Apr. 27, 1867; see also the issues of Mar. 2, Apr. 6, May 18, June 15, 1867.

[3] *N.A.S. Standard*, Dec. 8, 1866; *New York Times*, quoted in *N.A.S. Standard*, May 11, 1867; *New York World*, quoted in *N.A.S. Standard*, May 25, 1867. See also Phillips to Gerrit Smith, Jan. 19, 1867, Smith Papers, su. The circulation of the *Standard* was less than 3,000, but its influence reached far beyond its circulation.

"I respect your good opinion so highly that I take the liberty of enclosing you the last speech made by me on political questions, to be certain that it shall fall under your eye." Phillips modestly told the Pennsylvania Anti-Slavery Society that his wide influence was not due so much to personal qualities as to the fact that he was a spokesman for organized abolitionism. "What do you suppose ever entitled me to the distinction of having the President wish I were hung?" asked Phillips. "I was not a Senator, like Charles Sumner. . . . I did not have the Republican party behind me. I had nothing but the Anti-Slavery Society behind me; but as long as I had that, the President knew it weighed as heavy as the Commonwealth of Pennsylvania, because the people had learned to look at it and give it respect, and heed its teachings."[4]

✦

By the fall of 1866 several abolitionists were calling for the impeachment of President Johnson. In a speech at Cooper Union on October 25, Phillips declared that it was necessary to go one step beyond the defeat of the president's policy: the author of that policy must be removed from office. A thorough reconstruction program enacted by Congress would be worth little if its enforcement was left in the hands of an executive wholly unsympathetic to it. "The very first task I would set before the reassembled Congress," said Phillips, "is to impeach the Rebel at the White House. (Loud Cheers) . . .What is the advantage? Then *we* run the machine. (Laughter)" Phillips branded as irrelevant the argument that President Johnson had committed no specific impeachable act. An ordinary citizen could be indicted only for a specific crime, he said, "but an officer may be impeached for any grave misuse of his powers, or any mischievous nonuse of them —for any conduct which harms the public or perils its welfare."[5]

Most abolitionists fell into line with Phillips' demand for impeachment. The Pennsylvania Anti-Slavery Society unanimously adopted an impeachment resolution. The *Commonwealth* began urging Congress to depose Johnson. The *Right Way* deprecated the impeachment agitation at first, fearing that it might weaken

---

4 Colfax to Whittier, Dec. 13, 1866, Whittier Papers, Essex Institute; *N.A.S. Standard*, Dec. 8, 1866.

5 *New York Tribune*, Oct. 27, 1866. There is a copy of Phillips' Cooper Union address in the Andrew Johnson Papers, LC.

the Republicans by making a martyr of Johnson, but in January 1867, that journal also committed itself to impeachment. Garrison came out strongly for the deposition of Johnson, declaring that while the president remained in office "neither Union men nor negroes will possess any rights on Southern soil that rebels will be bound to respect."[6] There was a certain amount of popular support for the removal of Johnson. Phillips' audiences cheered his references to impeachment. But the *New York Tribune* and other Republican journals approached the question with caution. The House of Representatives directed the Judiciary Committee to investigate Johnson's conduct and determine whether he had done anything impeachable. The Committee undertook its task, but nothing came of the matter at the 1866-67 session of Congress.[7]

Phillips' suggestions to Congress went far beyond impeachment. In 1865 he had thought that when Negro suffrage was enacted, the southern states could be safely readmitted. But by November 1866, he had modified his ideas on this point. Even with Negro suffrage, he said, "you cannot govern the South against its educated classes. . . . Four millions of uneducated negroes, with none of that character which results from position, with none of that weight that comes from one or two generations of recognized manhood, cannot outweigh that element at the South." Through no fault of their own the freedmen were illiterate, landless, penniless. It would be criminal of the North, Phillips now thought, to turn them over to their former masters with nothing more than the ballot to protect them. "This is primarily a social revolution," he said. "You must plant at the South the elements which make a different society. You cannot enact four millions of slaves, ignorant, down-trodden, and despised, into personal equals of the old leaders of the South." The nation must hold the former Confederate states as national territory for several years. During that time the federal government should enact measures to provide the freedmen with education, land, and economic independence. "We do not mean to leave the negro at

[6] *N.A.S. Standard*, Dec. 1, 1866; *Commonwealth*, Nov. 10, 1866; *Right Way*, Oct. 27, Nov. 24, 1866, Jan. 12, 19, 1867; Garrison's statement published in *Independent*, Jan. 10, 1867.

[7] *New York Tribune*, Jan. 8, 1867; Eric McKitrick, *Andrew Johnson and Reconstruction* (Chicago, 1960), 491-93.

The First Vote. A. R. Waud in *Harper's Weekly*

the bottom of the ladder," proclaimed Phillips. "We mean to make a thoroughly developed reconstruction. We mean that Northern brains and ideas and capital shall go down there, and help him . . . until he actually gets education and wealth; until he actually stands on his feet in comparative equality with the white race. We mean to hold [those states] in some shape, until that is done."[8]

Phillips' speeches and editorials on this subject attracted widespread attention and condemnation. His policy of indefinite territorialization of the South was too radical for most antislavery men. But a few abolitionists endorsed portions of Phillips' program. The *Boston Commonwealth*, for example, urged legislation "to secure *education and land*" as well as the ballot "to the poor and ignorant masses at the South. For without education and land even suffrage would be found, for the immediate future, a somewhat illusory boon. . . . We have no doubt of the power of Congress to do whatever is best for the welfare of the South and the country—to cut up and divide among the poor and loyal the great plantations of the rebels . . . to enforce, if need be, universal education under loyal auspices . . . in short, to do everything to civilize and assimilate the South."[9]

At the end of 1866, however, the Fourteenth Amendment was still at the center of the reconstruction controversy. Moderate Republicans urged southern legislatures to ratify the Amendment. "There is no one thing so much dreaded to-day by Wendell Phillips, Sumner, Boutwell, Stevens, and the rest of that school," declared the *New York Times*, "as the acceptance of the Constitutional Amendment by the Southern States—followed, as they know it would be, in spite of their opposition, by the admission of the Southern members into Congress."[10] When Congress convened in December, three southern states had already rejected the Amendment. Prospects appeared bright for the radical cause. But moderate Republican leaders were still committed to the Amendment as the final condition of readmission. Senator Sherman, Congressman Bingham, and many other moderates reaffirmed their belief that Congress would admit southern states if

[8] *N.A.S. Standard*, Nov. 17, 24, Dec. 1, 8, 1866.
[9] *Commonwealth*, Dec. 15, 1866.
[10] *New York Times*, quoted in *N.A.S. Standard*, Nov. 10, 1866.

and when they ratified the Amendment. *Harper's Weekly* anticipated no other conditions of reconstruction than adoption of the Amendment. The *Nation* stated flatly that most of the party considered the Fourteenth Amendment the final condition of restoration. This opinion was not confined to moderates, for on December 14, in reply to a direct question by Sumner, Senator Benjamin Wade stated his intention to vote for readmission when the South accepted the Amendment.[11]

Abolitionists and radical leaders were alarmed by these developments. They feared that the moderate Republican assurances might induce southern states to reconsider their actions, ratify the Amendment, and apply successfully for readmission to Congress. Phillips warned of dire consequences for the Negro if this should happen, and urged Congress "to give the negroes land, ballot and education and to hold the arm of the Federal government over the whole Southern Territory until these seeds have begun to bear fruit beyond any possibility of blighting."[12]

Abolitionists took direct action to counter the apparent Republican willingness to reconstruct on the basis of the Fourteenth Amendment. Henry Cheever in Massachusetts and George Cheever in New York circulated petitions to their respective state legislatures urging them not to ratify the Amendment. The Equal Rights Association led by Elizabeth Cady Stanton and Susan B. Anthony memorialized the New York legislature to reject the Amendment on the grounds that it would permit the continued disfranchisement of both Negroes and women. On January 24 Wendell Phillips appeared before a Massachusetts legislative committee and uttered an eloquent protest against ratification of the Amendment by the Old Bay State. Behind the scenes, Massachusetts radicals and abolitionists were struggling successfully to postpone the state's ratification.[13] By this

11 *Cong. Globe*, 39 Cong., 2 Sess., 124-28, 500, 1,104; *Harper's Weekly*, x (Nov. 17, 1866), 722; *Nation*, iii (Dec. 20, 1866), 485. For a discussion of this issue, see Joseph James, *The Framing of the Fourteenth Amendment* (Urbana, Ill., 1956), 164-77, and McKitrick, *Andrew Johnson and Reconstruction*, 450-55.

12 *N.A.S. Standard*, Jan. 5, 1867. See also Phillips to Sumner, Dec. 27, 1866, Sumner Papers, HU; *Commonwealth*, Dec. 22, 1866; *Right Way*, Dec. 22, 29, 1866; *Independent*, Jan. 17, 1867.

13 Henry Cheever to Gerrit Smith, Dec. 22, 1866, Smith Papers, SU; James L. Child to Henry Cheever, Dec. 26, 1866, Henry Cheever to Elizabeth C. Washburn, Dec. 27, 1866, Cheever Papers, AAS; S. B. Anthony to Frederick Douglass,

time, however, the question had become academic. With the exception of Massachusetts, every northern state had ratified the Amendment by February 7, 1867, and every former Confederate state (except Tennessee) had refused to ratify it. With the encouragement of President Johnson the South had rejected the Amendment. They had cut the ground from under congressional moderates and had given radicals and abolitionists a new lease on life.[14]

As it became clear that southern states were unconditionally rejecting the Fourteenth Amendment, Congress settled down to formulate a comprehensive reconstruction policy.[15] After a bewildering series of amendments and counteramendments, the House on February 13 finally passed a bill sponsored by George Julian and Thaddeus Stevens providing for the simple territorialization and indefinite military administration of the unreconstructed South. The measure contained no provision for the readmission of southern states to the Union. Phillips was delighted with the bill. It was similar to the program he had been advocating since November. "We consider Stevens's bill the best thing yet offered," he wrote on February 16.[16]

Several abolitionists and radicals agreed with Phillips, but political exigencies dictated some provision for the readmssion of southern states when they had fulfilled certain requirements. Moderate Republicans in the Senate passed on February 17 the Sherman substitute for the Julian-Stevens bill. The Sherman substitute would have readmitted southern states when they had

---

Dec. 15, 1866, Douglass Papers, Anacostia; Alma Lutz, *Susan B. Anthony, Rebel, Crusader, Humanitarian* (Boston, 1959), 125; *N.A.S. Standard*, Feb. 2, 1867; Sumner to Frank Bird, Jan. 10, 1867, Bird Papers, HU; Phillips to Sumner, Feb. 1, 1867, Frank Bird to Sumner, Mar. 7, 8, 1867, Sumner Papers, HU; *Boston Commonwealth*, Mar. 9, 16, 1867. Massachusetts finally ratified the Fourteenth Amendment after the Reconstruction Act of March 2 had made Negro suffrage the basis of reconstruction.

14 McKitrick, *Andrew Johnson and Reconstruction*, 469-72.

15 During the session Congress passed over Johnson's veto two bills enacting Negro suffrage in the District of Columbia and admitting Nebraska as a state with a provision for equal suffrage. President Johnson allowed another bill forbidding the denial of suffrage on grounds of race or color in all the territories to become law without his signature. Edward McPherson, *The Political History of the United States of America during the Period of Reconstruction* (Washington, 1871), 154-66, 184.

16 McKitrick, *Andrew Johnson and Reconstruction*, 474-81; *N.A.S. Standard*, Feb. 16, 1867.

ratified the Fourteenth Amendment and adopted new constitutions guaranteeing Negro suffrage. Radicals and abolitionists were opposed to the Sherman bill for two reasons: it did not disfranchise any former rebel leaders, who would take the lead in the reconstruction process and perhaps nullify the effects of Negro suffrage unless they were disfranchised; and it made the reorganization of civil government permissive instead of mandatory, thus allowing the Johnson governments in southern states to continue in power indefinitely if they so wished. Under Stevens' leadership the House refused to concur in the Senate bill. The deadlock was finally broken on February 20 by passage in both Houses of the Wilson and Shellabarger amendments disfranchising all persons disqualified from officeholding under the Fourteenth Amendment and declaring the existing southern state governments "provisional only, and in all respects subject to the paramount authority of the United States." Johnson vetoed this Reconstruction Act on March 2, but it was immediately passed over his veto. The reconstruction process was still permissive, and to remedy this defect the Fortieth Congress on March 23 passed over Johnson's veto an act making civil reorganization mandatory and authorizing military commanders to register voters and set the machinery in motion for the convening of constitutional conventions.[17]

There was some abolitionist dissatisfaction with the Reconstruction Acts as finally passed. Phillips would have been happier with the Julian-Stevens bill. Several abolitionists pointed out that once those southern states with white majorities were readmitted to the Union, there would be nothing to stop them from disfranchising their Negroes. Others urged Congress to enact legislation to guarantee universal public education in the South and to help the freedmen obtain land of their own. Numerous abolitionists denounced Congress for failing to impeach Johnson. They affirmed that the Reconstruction Acts would be little more than a dead letter with an unsympathetic president to administer them. These com-

[17] McKitrick, *Andrew Johnson and Reconstruction*, 481-85; George Julian, *Political Recollections* (Chicago, 1884), 306-08. See also Lewis Tappan to Julian, Feb. 19, 1867, Giddings-Julian Correspondence, LC; Whittier to Sumner, Feb. 27, 1867, Sumner Papers, HU; *Commonwealth*, Feb. 9, 23, Mar. 2, 16, 23, 1867; *Right Way*, Feb. 16, 1867; *New York Tribune*, Feb. 18, 21, 25, 1867; *Independent*, Feb. 21, 28, Mar. 14, 1867; *N.A.S. Standard*, Feb. 23, Mar. 2, 9, 1867.

plaints were outweighed, however, by abolitionist jubilation over the adoption of Negro suffrage and the belief that additional measures necessary to safeguard the Negro's freedom would be enacted in the future. It was reported on good authority from Washington that Johnson would faithfully administer the Reconstruction Acts as the law of the land, and radicals temporarily dropped their cry of impeachment and settled back to await events. There was a general mood of confidence among abolitionists in the spring of 1867. At the annual meeting of the American Anti-Slavery Society in May, Phillips addressed his auditors in an unwonted tone of optimism. "We seem to be on the very eve," he said, "of the accomplishment of all that the friends of freedom have ever asked of the nation; . . . that is, the absolute civil and political equality of the colored man under our institutions of government."[18]

But abolitionists did not rest on their oars. The greatest single shortcoming of the Reconstruction Acts, in their eyes, was the fact that the question of Negro suffrage still rested with the individual states. Abolitionists renewed their demand for a Fifteenth Amendment. "The friends of the negro will never rest satisfied with any scheme that does not place that right [suffrage] beyond contingency," proclaimed the *Independent*. "They demand that it be incorporated into the Federal Constitution." The Philadelphia Female Anti-Slavery Society affirmed that it would accept "no schemes of reconstruction which will leave [the Negro's] highest right of citizenship at the mercy of State legislation or action, after the Southern States shall be restored to sovereignty."[19]

[18] *Independent*, Feb. 28, Mar. 7, 14, Apr. 4, 1867; *Commonwealth*, Mar. 9, 16, 23, 1867; Samuel May, Jr., to Richard Webb, Apr. 2, 1867, Samuel May, Jr., Papers, BPL; E. L. Pierce to McKim, Apr. 20, 1867, McKim Papers, Cornell; *N.A.S. Standard*, Mar. 2, 9, 23, 30, 1867. Statement by Phillips published in *ibid.*, May 18, 1867. The *Right Way*, founded as a spokesman for equal suffrage, ceased publication after passage of the Reconstruction Acts. A shortage of funds was the main reason for the paper's demise, but the achievement of Negro suffrage in the South was also an important factor in the decision to cease publication. *Right Way*, Mar. 2, 1867; Frank P. Stearns, *The Life and Public Services of George Luther Stearns* (Phila., 1907), 377-78. George Stearns, main financial backer of the *Right Way* and one of the most respected abolitionists during the early years of Reconstruction, died suddenly of pneumonia in April 1867.

[19] *Independent*, Feb. 21, 1867; *Thirty-Third Annual Report of the Philadelphia*

Before a Fifteenth Amendment could be passed, however, the majority of northern people who opposed Negro suffrage in their own states must be persuaded to overcome their prejudices. "The states that now need reconstruction are the Northern," declared Tilton in an *Independent* editorial entitled "A Beam to be Plucked from Our Own Eyes." The *Commonwealth* denounced northern Republicans who had voted for Negro suffrage in the South but refused to support it in their own states as "hypocrites and cowards."[20] Abolitionists launched a drive to convince northern voters of the moral and political necessity of equal suffrage in *every* state. New York held a state constitutional convention in the summer of 1867, and abolitionists mobilized their resources to put equal suffrage into the new constitution. They had a staunch ally in Horace Greeley, who served as chairman of the convention's suffrage committee. Although Greeley refused to heed the pleas of Elizabeth Cady Stanton and Susan B. Anthony for woman suffrage, he persuaded the committee to report in favor of universal manhood suffrage (at this time New York Negroes had to meet a $250 property qualification in order to vote). The full convention accepted the committee's report, but over Greeley's protest the convention voted to submit the suffrage article to the voters separately from the rest of the constitution, thereby virtually assuring its defeat.[21]

The question of the Negro's status in the North was important for the future of reconstruction, but in 1867 it was overshadowed by events in the South. In the wake of the Reconstruction Acts, conservative southern leaders, following the example of Wade Hampton, began urging the enfranchised freedmen to vote in harmony with their old masters. Hampton told South Carolina Negroes that the planter class was in the best position to help them achieve stability and prosperity in freedom. Northern Republicans viewed this development with ill-concealed alarm. Some abolitionists declared that the Negro's right to vote was the

Female Anti-Slavery Society (Phila., 1867), 22. See also *N.A.S. Standard*, Mar. 9, 16, 23, Apr. 6, 27, May 11, 1867.

[20] *Independent*, Apr. 18, 1867; *Commonwealth*, Mar. 2, 1867.

[21] Van Deusen, *Greeley*, 361-64. See also *Independent*, Apr. 11, Aug. 1, 1867; *N.A.S. Standard*, May 25, July 6, Sept. 28, 1867; *New York Tribune*, Apr. 3, 4, June 20, 26, 28, July 10, 13, 17, 19, 26, 31, Aug. 6, 9, Sept. 27, Oct. 12, 1867.

important thing, and professed unconcern whether he voted Republican or not. But one of the political reasons for the enactment of Negro suffrage had been the hope of extending Republican power into the South. Abolitionist Reuben Tomlinson, serving as superintendent of education for the Freedmen's Bureau in South Carolina, wrote that "I am a universal suffrage man, but I do not care a cent for it unless we can keep Northern influence here along with it." A Democratic victory in the Connecticut state election in April 1867, startled Republicans out of their lethargy and convinced them of the need to organize and control the southern Negro vote.[22]

Radical leaders Henry Wilson and William D. Kelley immediately started on a southern speaking tour to explain the virtues of Republicanism to the freedmen. Republican officials urged Phillips, Tilton, and Anna Dickinson to speak in the South also. Despite considerable Republican pressure, they refused. They valued their position as radical spokesmen independent of partisan politics. Tilton stated privately that the massive Republican effort in the South was nothing more than "a crusade of politicians—a stumping tour of the old stagers" looking toward the 1868 presidential election. This was important work, but it was not the work of reformers.[23]

Many other abolitionists, however, did not recognize the fine line between reform and politics drawn by Tilton, and proceeded to make their influence felt in southern affairs. Frederick Douglass and Frances E. W. Harper (a Negro abolitionist and poet) undertook speaking tours of the South in the summer of 1867, urging the freedmen to vote for the party that had emancipated and enfranchised them. In April 1867, John Mercer Langston, prominent Negro abolitionist from Ohio, was appointed inspector of schools of the Freedmen's Bureau. For more

---

[22] Francis Butler Simkins and Robert H. Woody, *South Carolina during Reconstruction* (Chapel Hill, 1932), 85-86; Reuben Tomlinson to J. M. McKim, Dec. 4, 1866, McKim Papers, Cornell. See also *New York Tribune*, Mar. 27, 29, Apr. 3, 4, 12, 22, 1867; *Independent*, Mar. 14, 1867; *New York World*, Apr. 19, 1867; *Commonwealth*, Apr. 13, 1867; *N.A.S. Standard*, Apr. 20, May 11, 1867; Henry Wilson to Angelina G. Weld, Apr. 12, 1867, Weld Papers, LC.

[23] *New York Tribune*, Apr. 22, 1867; L. Edwin Dudley, secretary of the Union Republican Congressional Executive Committee, to Anna Dickinson, May 7, June 15, 26, 1867, S. B. Anthony to Anna Dickinson, May 15, 1867, Dickinson Papers, LC; the quotation is from Tilton to Anna Dickinson, May 16, 1867.

than two years he traveled through the South inspecting the facilities of the Bureau and helping to organize the freedmen into the Republican party and the Republican-sponsored Union Leagues. In the spring of 1867 Loring Moody of Boston, a one-time Garrisonian who later became a political abolitionist, was appointed general agent of the National Union League. He was put in charge of organizing Union Leagues throughout the South to marshal votes for the Republican party. In the summer of 1867 a delegation of northern Republicans, including abolitionists John Jay and Charles W. Slack, intervened to quell a factional struggle in the Virginia Republican party.[24]

Uncounted dozens of abolitionists residing in the South were also active in politics. Nearly every official and teacher of the freedmen's aid societies was to some degree a Republican organizer. Edwin M. Wheelock, one of the creators of the Louisiana public school system (see Chapter XIII), moved to Texas after the war where he served successively as the state superintendent of education, reporter of the state supreme court, and superintendent of the state Institute for the Blind. Reuben Tomlinson was elected state auditor of South Carolina in 1868 and was politically prominent in the state until the end of Reconstruction. Gilbert Pillsbury, the abolitionist brother of Parker Pillsbury, came to South Carolina in 1863. In 1867 he was one of the architects of the new South Carolina Constitution, and was later elected mayor of Charleston. Henry Purvis, son of the wealthy Philadelphia Negro abolitionist Robert Purvis, was a member of the South Carolina legislature during Reconstruction. These are only a few examples of the activities of the many abolitionists who became permanent or semipermanent residents of the South after the war.[25]

24 Rosetta Douglass Sprague to Frederick Douglass, Apr. 24, 1867, Douglass Papers, Anacostia; Douglass to Anna Dickinson, May 21, 1867, Dickinson Papers, LC; John M. Langston, *From the Virginia Plantation to the National Capital* (Hartford, Conn., 1894), 258-95; George Bentley, *A History of the Freedmen's Bureau* (Phila., 1955), 187-89; information on the activities of Loring Moody obtained from the Loring Moody Papers, BPL, which include several dozen letters relating to his activities as an organizer for the National Union League in 1867; Union League Club of New York, *Report of the Proceedings of the Conference at Richmond, June 11 and 12, 1867* (New York, 1867), in John Jay, *Slavery and the War*, #18.

25 Charles Kassel, "Edwin Miller Wheelock," *Open Court*, XXXIV (Sept. 1920), 569; Simkins and Woody, *South Carolina during Reconstruction*, 125-26, 204,

Southern whites soon realized that an overwhelming majority of the freedmen would vote Republican. Most whites ceased their abortive attempt of 1867 to persuade the freedmen to cooperate with the Democratic party. They began to stage anti-Republican riots and to break up Republican meetings with increasing frequency in the spring and summer of 1867. The Democratic party reverted to its old belief that, in the words of the *New York Express*, "this is a Democratic government of white men, made for white men, and exclusively for white men."[26]

In Washington, meanwhile, the Johnson administration was taking steps to curtail the effectiveness of the Reconstruction Acts. Military commanders enforcing these Acts in the South had overruled the provisional state governments on many points and had issued orders to prevent the swearing of false oaths by former Confederates who hoped to qualify for voting. On June 20, 1867, Johnson issued a set of counter-orders prohibiting boards of registry from challenging a man's oath and directing military commanders to cooperate with existing state governments. If carried out these orders would have given the Johnson governments in the South a large measure of control over the reconstruction process. General Philip Sheridan declared that Johnson's orders opened "a broad macadamized road for perjury and fraud to travel on." Abolitionists praised Sheridan and renewed their demand for Johnson's impeachment. Republicans who had expected President Johnson to carry out the Reconstruction Acts in good faith were startled into convening Congress in July to pass a third Reconstruction Act to nullify the effect of the president's orders. Radicals urged Congress to impeach Johnson, but moderate counsels prevailed and the legislators confined themselves to passing a bill declaring that the existing state governments in the South were subject to the absolute authority of Congress and the military commanders.[27]

449, 464-68; Reuben Tomlinson to Ellen Collins, May 14, 1869, McKim Papers, Cornell; Tomlinson to E. D. Cheney, July 27, 1868, Cheney Papers, BPL; Gilbert Pillsbury to S. P. Chase, Sept. 24, 1867, Chase Papers, LC; *Liberator*, July 21, 1865; *N.A.S. Standard*, Aug. 29, Sept. 19, 1868; *Freedmen's Record*, IV (May 1868), 73.

[26] *New York Express*, quoted in *N.A.S. Standard*, July 6, 1867. See also the *Jackson* (Miss.) *Democrat*, quoted in *N.A.S. Standard*, Aug. 17, 1867; *New York Tribune*, May 18, June 20, 1867; and *Independent*, May 30, 1867.

[27] McKitrick, *Andrew Johnson and Reconstruction*, 493-94; *New York Tribune*, July 7, 11, 1867; *N.A.S. Standard*, June 29, Aug. 17, 24, 1867; *Independent*, June 27, July 4, 11, 1867.

In July 1867, President Johnson offered the post of commissioner of the Freedmen's Bureau to Frederick Douglass. One can only guess at the president's motives in making this offer. Perhaps he hoped to stifle the radical cry of impeachment by appointing a Negro to a prominent government position. He may have planned to wreck the Bureau by placing a Negro in charge of its operations, hoping that this would provoke many white officials to resign. At any rate Douglass, after pondering the offer, rejected it. He explained to friends that he was unwilling to "facilitate the removal of a man as just and good as General Howard and especially to place myself under any obligation to keep the peace with Andrew Johnson." Abolitionists applauded Douglass' decision. "The greatest black man in the nation," said Theodore Tilton, "did not consent to become the tool of the meanest white."[28] When Douglass refused, Johnson offered the job to John Mercer Langston, who also turned him down. Finally the president approached Robert Purvis. Purvis sought the advice of Wendell Phillips, who urged him to reject the offer. Nothing could make him happier than to see a Negro in such a high position, said Phillips, but he thought the president's offer "only a cunning trick. Johnson wishes just now to confuse & divide the loyal sentiment." Purvis accepted Phillips' advice and turned down the proposal. General Howard remained at the head of the Bureau.[29]

In August the president moved against the most important administrators of the Republican reconstruction policy. On August 12 he suspended Stanton and appointed General Grant as *ad interim* secretary of war. He followed this act by removing Generals Sheridan and Sickles from their commands of southern military districts and replacing them with conservative generals. Johnson's action gave a strong fillip to the impeachment drive. "It is now universally recognized that there will be no peace, no restoration, no business stability, till something is done to prevent Andrew Johnson from enthroning perpetual turmoil," declared the *Com-*

28 Benjamin Quarles, *Frederick Douglass* (Washington, 1948), 237-40; Wm. Slade to Douglass, July 29, Aug. 18, 1867, Douglass to Slade, Aug. 12, 1867, Douglass Papers, Anacostia; Douglass' statement quoted from Douglass to Tilton, Sept. 2, 1867, Tilton Papers, NYHS; Tilton's statement quoted in Quarles, *Douglass*, 239.

29 Bentley, *Freedmen's Bureau*, 196; Phillips to Purvis, Sept. 13, 1867, Weston Papers, BPL.

monwealth. Impeachment sentiment increased sharply among all segments of the Republican party in August and September.[30]

The approach of the important 1867 state elections temporarily eclipsed the drive for impeachment. Negro suffrage amendments were on the ballots in Ohio, Kansas, and Minnesota. Abolitionist lecturers canvassed Ohio and Kansas on behalf of the amendments, and the Republican parties in all three states officially endorsed Negro suffrage. But the voters rejected the amendments in every state. The issue of Negro suffrage also played an important part in the Pennsylvania and New York elections, both of which were won by the Democrats.[31] Abolitionists were dismayed by this renewed demonstration of northern race prejudice. "Deep & malignant & murderous is the hatred of the Negro" in Ohio, reported Henry Wright. Parker Pillsbury could hardly find words strong enough to express his disgust with northern people who supported Negro suffrage in the South but rejected it at home. "Our whole demeanor toward the southern states," he wrote, "is like that of the Pharisee toward the Publican."[32]

"I almost pity the Radicals," wrote one of President Johnson's supporters after the elections of 1867. "After giving ten states to the negroes, to keep the Democrats from getting them, they will have lost the rest. . . . Any party with an abolition head and a nigger tail will soon find itself with nothing left but the head and tail."[33] Moderate Republicans began whispering that the party must hold back on the Negro question, especially in the North, if it wished to remain in power. Abolitionists denounced this tendency toward conservatism. "The cowardly friends of a political party are more to be dreaded by it than its bravest foes," de-

[30] McKitrick, *Andrew Johnson and Reconstruction*, 494-98; *Commonwealth*, Aug. 17, 1867. See also Senator Richard Yates of Illinois to Anna Dickinson, Aug. 21, 1867, Dickinson Papers, LC; George Cheever to Henry Cheever, Aug. 28, 1867, Cheever Papers, AAS; *N.A.S. Standard*, Aug. 17, 1867; *New York Tribune*, Aug. 28, 1867; *Independent*, Sept. 19, 1867.

[31] *N.A.S. Standard*, Sept. 14, Oct. 12, Nov. 9, 1867; *New York Tribune*, Oct. 12, 1867; *Independent*, Oct. 17, 31, 1867; *Thirty-Fourth Annual Report of the Philadelphia Female Anti-Slavery Society* (Phila., 1868), 15-16.

[32] Wright to Garrison, Nov. 23, 1867, Garrison Papers, BPL; Pillsbury to Gerrit Smith, Nov. 27, 1867, Gerrit Smith Papers, SU. See also W. H. Furness to Sumner, Nov. 24, 1867, Sumner Papers, HU; and Parker Pillsbury, *Letter to a Radical Member of Congress*, Oct. 20, 1867, published letter, copy in Gerrit Smith Papers, SU.

[33] Quoted in Ira Brown, "Pennsylvania and the Rights of the Negro, 1865-1887," *Pennsylvania History*, XXVIII (Jan. 1961), 51.

clared Theodore Tilton in the *Independent.* "If the Republican party is not to stand for the negro's rights, then it has no better mission than the Democratic." Phillips maintained that the party's failure to take a bold, uncompromising stand on the questions of a national Negro suffrage amendment and impeachment was the reason for its electoral losses in 1867. The remedy for Republican weaknesses, according to Phillips, was more radicalism, not less. He urged adoption of three constitutional amendments to enfranchise the Negro in every state, guarantee a public school system in every state, and make national and state citizenship synonymous under the aegis of the federal government.[34]

Impeachment emerged as the main political issue during the 1867-68 session of Congress. Abolitionists circulated petitions demanding the removal of Johnson. On November 20 the House Judiciary Committee voted to recommend impeachment. Abolitionists hailed this action and urged Congress to do its duty. But Democratic gains in the 1867 elections had made Republican politicians wary. "We shall have burdens enough to carry in the next campaign," said Horace Greeley, "without making Mr. Johnson a martyr and carrying him also." The full House defeated the impeachment resolution on December 7.[35]

The impeachment question would have disappeared from politics after this vote had Johnson not chosen to make fresh assaults on Congress and its reconstruction policy. In his annual message the president excoriated the Reconstruction Acts and launched into a racist diatribe on the evils of Negro rule. On December 18 he publicly endorsed the actions of Winfield Hancock, a Democratic general who had replaced Sheridan and had issued orders asserting the supremacy of civil over military government in direct defiance of the Third Reconstruction Act. A few days later Johnson removed Generals Pope and Ord from command of southern military districts and replaced them with more conservative officers. Radicals writhed in anger as Johnson committed these provocative acts with impunity. "It is pitiful," wrote Frank

34 *Independent,* Nov. 14, Dec. 5, 1867; *N.A.S. Standard,* Sept. 21, Nov. 30, 1867.

35 *New York Tribune,* Dec. 9, 1867. See also McKitrick, *Andrew Johnson and Reconstruction,* 498-99; *N.A.S. Standard,* Sept. 28, Oct. 5, 26, Nov. 30, Dec. 7, 14, 21, 1867; *Independent,* Dec. 19, 1867.

Bird, "to see Congress floundering along, from one expedient to another, vainly endeavoring to tie the hands which they should have chopped off a year ago."[36]

On February 21 Johnson committed the act that finally caused his impeachment. Defying the Senate vote restoring Stanton to the War Department, the president dismissed Stanton and appointed Lorenzo Thomas secretary of war *ad interim*. Nearly the whole of the Republican party now clamored for impeachment. Construing the removal of Stanton as a breach of the Tenure of Office Act, the House on February 24 impeached Johnson. Abolitionists hailed the House vote with joy. Conviction of Johnson by the Senate, said the *Anti-Slavery Standard*, would mean "the emancipation of the Northern mind from the dominion of Southern, pro-slavery influence. It will end the 'Border State' policy in politics."[37]

National attention focused on the Senate, where for more than two months the trial of President Johnson proceeded amidst mounting drama and tension. Theodore Tilton, Gilbert Haven, Richard Hinton, Edmund Quincy, and other abolitionists descended on the capital to cover the trial for abolitionist and Republican newspapers. All of them served as lobbyists in behalf of impeachment. Tilton was especially active, flitting here and there, buttonholing senators in corridors and cloakrooms, urging upon them the necessity for the president's removal.[38] In reply to the skillful defense of Johnson by his lawyers, abolitionists and radicals asserted that impeachment should be construed as a *political* rather than as a narrowly legal process. Johnson should be removed, said Phillips, because of his persistent efforts to restore the rebel South to power, his attempts to frustrate the congressional plan of reconstruction, and his sanction of the murder and oppression of southern freedmen. "If the executive will not execute," wrote Elizur Wright, "there is no possible

[36] James D. Richardson, *Messages and Papers of the Presidents* (20 vols., Washington, 1897-1913), IX, 3762-63; McKitrick, *Andrew Johnson and Reconstruction*, 499-500; *N.A.S. Standard*, Jan. 11, 1868; *Commonwealth*, Jan. 11, 1868; Frank Bird to Sumner, Jan. 11, 1868, Sumner Papers, HU.

[37] McKitrick, *Andrew Johnson and Reconstruction*, 501-05; *N.A.S. Standard*, Feb. 29, 1868.

[38] *Zion's Herald*, Mar. 5, 26, Apr. 9, 1868; *New York Herald*, May 13, 1868; *Independent*, May 7, 1868; Howard K. Beale, ed., *The Diary of Gideon Welles* (3 vols., New York, 1960), III, 357.

reasonable remedy but to have the law-making power replace him with something that will execute."[39]

In March and April abolitionists expressed confidence that Johnson would be convicted. But as the date for the Senate vote approached, it became clear that several Republican senators considered impeachment a legal process and were unconvinced that Johnson had committed any impeachable acts. When the decisive vote was taken on May 16, seven Republicans voted with the Democrats and President Johnson was acquitted. Abolitionists were enraged. They excoriated the recalcitrant senators in bitter language. The New England Anti-Slavery Society resolved that in failing to convict Johnson "the Republican party records judgment against its own capacity, and justifies the Nation for distrusting its leadership." Wendell Phillips regarded the failure of impeachment as a sign of conservative resurgence. He urged radicals to gird themselves for a renewed struggle on behalf of justice and equality for the freedmen.[40]

In many ways the end of the impeachment struggle cleared the air. The Republican party began to close ranks in preparation for the presidential election of 1868. This election was crucial for the cause of Negro suffrage, but before turning to the campaign of 1868, it is necessary to consider two other measures that abolitionists deemed essential: education and land for the freedmen.

[39] *N.A.S. Standard*, Mar. 14, 1868; Wright's statement published in *Commonwealth*, Mar. 14, 1868.
[40] Resolution of New England Anti-Slavery Society published in *N.A.S. Standard*, June 6, 1868; Phillips' statement published in issue of May 23, 1868. See also *Independent*, May 21, 1868; *Commonwealth*, May 23, 1868; and Tilton to E. C. Stanton, May 28, 1868, Stanton Papers, LC.

XVII + EDUCATION AND CONFISCATION: 1865-1870

ABOLITIONISTS played an important part in the efforts to bring education and land to the freedmen. Garrison noted at the end of 1864 that emancipation would meet the southern Negroes "just where slavery leaves them—in need of everything that pertains to their physical, intellectual, and moral condition." Here was a vast field for philanthropic effort, and Garrison urged his fellow abolitionists to fulfill their obligations to the freed slaves. The *Anti-Slavery Standard* asserted that reconstruction of the South "must be social as well as political. . . . It must reach to the very groundwork of social order." The freedmen would have to be prepared for their new rights and responsibilities as citizens. "The duty of abolitionists to their clients will not cease with the technical abolition of slavery," said the *Standard*. "These [Freedmen's] Relief Associations prefigure the work that will remain to be done—the finishing of Emancipation and the perfecting of Reconstruction through Education."[1]

In 1864 an abolitionist army officer stationed in Louisiana issued an appeal for northern teachers to instruct the freedmen. He wanted "ABOLITIONISTS! dyed with the pure dye—men who dare face this *miserable, wheedling conservatism*, and *do* something to merit at least the prevalent epithet '*nigger on the brain.*'"[2] Of the several thousand northerners who went South to teach the freedmen during the war and reconstruction, a majority were probably abolitionists. Some teachers, of course, were motivated primarily by a desire for a change of climate, adventure, or by religious zeal, but most of them hoped to bear witness to their abolitionist faith by aiding the Negro in his transition to freedom. The correspondence of teachers was filled with references to their antislavery backgrounds. Several abolitionists devoted the rest of their lives to the southern Negro. Laura Towne, for example, founded the Penn School on St. Helena Island, South Carolina, in 1862 and remained there until

[1] *Liberator*, Dec. 30, 1864; *N.A.S. Standard*, Jan. 7, 1865.
[2] *American Missionary*, VIII (June 1864), 150.

her death in 1901. Sallie Holley and Caroline Putnam, old-line Garrisonian abolitionists from upstate New York, started a school for the freedmen at Lottsburgh, Virginia, in 1868. Miss Holley remained there until her death in 1893, and Miss Putnam was still instructing the Negroes of Lottsburgh in 1907. These examples of philanthropic longevity could be multiplied many times.[3]

Abolitionists predominated not only among the teachers of the freedmen but among the officers of the freedmen's aid societies as well. Professor Howard Swint found that of the 135 leading officials of the freedmen's societies, nearly half had been abolitionists, and many of the remainder had been active to a lesser degree in the antislavery movement. A few prominent abolitionists formed the backbone of the whole freedmen's aid movement. J. Miller McKim served as the corresponding secretary (chief executive officer) of the American Freedmen's Union Commission, which comprised all the secular freedmen's societies from 1866 to 1869. George Whipple and Lewis Tappan, secretary and treasurer respectively of the American Missionary Association, were the chief officials of this largest of the evangelical freedmen's aid societies. Levi Coffin was general agent of the Western Freedmen's Aid Commission. John W. Alvord was superintendent of education for the Freedmen's Bureau from 1865 to 1870. Reuben Tomlinson, H. R. Pease, and Edwin Wheelock served as state superintendents of education in South Carolina, Mississippi, and Texas during Reconstruction.[4]

[3] Rupert S. Holland, ed., *Letters and Diary of Laura M. Towne, Written from the Sea Islands of South Carolina, 1862-84* (Cambridge, Mass., 1912), xvi-xvii and passim; John White Chadwick, *Sallie Holley, A Life for Liberty* (New York, 1899); Caroline Putnam to William L. Garrison, Jr., May 23, 1907, Garrison Papers, sc. See also Henry Lee Swint, *The Northern Teacher in the South, 1862-1870* (Nashville, 1941), 35-56. The private correspondence of leading abolitionists, the antislavery newspapers, and the monthly journals of the various freedmen's aid societies contain uncounted hundreds of letters from abolitionists who had gone South to teach the freedmen.

[4] Swint, *Northern Teacher*, 26-32, 51n., 143-74; for McKim's activities, see his letterbooks as corresponding secretary of the American Freedmen's Aid Commission and the American Freedmen's Union Commission in the McKim Papers, Cornell; for the personnel of the A.M.A., see Richard B. Drake, "The American Missionary Association and the Southern Negro, 1861-1888," Ph.D. dissertation, Emory University, 1957, 78-98; Levi Coffin, *Reminiscences* (Cincinnati, 1880), 651-712; Charles Kassel, "Edwin Miller Wheelock," *Open Court*, xxxiv (Sept. 1920), 569.

Abolitionists were active at every level of the drive for education of the freedmen: organizing auxiliary societies, soliciting funds, lecturing, recruiting teachers, writing textbooks, and founding schools in the South. Samuel J. May devoted much of his time between 1863 and 1869 to organizing and administering the Syracuse Freedmen's Aid Society, an auxiliary of the New York association. His cousin Samuel May, Jr., formed an auxiliary of the New England Freedmen's Aid Society in Leicester, Massachusetts. Lydia Maria Child wrote a brief history of the Negro, entitled *The Freedmen's Book,* to dramatize the heroes of the race and inculcate honesty, courage, and morality in Negro children; this book was used as a primer and textbook in freedmen's schools. John G. Fee, one of the founders of Berea College, organized several schools, hospitals, and churches for the freedmen in his native Kentucky. As corresponding secretary of the New England Educational Commission for the Freedmen, a Baptist society, abolitionist Joseph Parker made several trips to the South and organized many freedmen's schools. Elected a bishop of the Methodist Episcopal Church in 1872, abolitionist Gilbert Haven was stationed in Atlanta for eight years, where he brought new energy to the work of the Methodist Freedmen's Aid Society and helped found Clark University. These are only a few examples of the activities of abolitionists at every level of the freedmen's aid movement.[5]

One instance of abolitionist organization of southern schools deserves special mention. In February 1865, Union troops marched into Charleston, accompanied by James Redpath, reporter for the *New York Tribune.* Colonel Woodford seized all school buildings and appointed Redpath superintendent of public

[5] G. B. Emerson, S. May, Jr., and T. J. Mumford, *Memoir of Samuel Joseph May* (New York, 1871), 229-30; Samuel J. May to J. Miller McKim, Jan. 28, 31, Feb. 1, 16, May 13, July 9, 20, 26, Aug. 15, 1866, July 18, Oct. 21, 1867, McKim Papers, Cornell; L. M. Child to James T. Fields, Aug. 23, 28, Sept. 3, 1865, Child Papers, Radcliffe Women's Archives; L. M. Child to Lewis Tappan, Jan. 1, 30, 1869, Tappan Papers, LC; John G. Fee, *Autobiography* (Chicago, 1891), 173-80; Joseph W. Parker, "Memoirs," typescript of MS supplied by Mrs. Perce J. Bentley, 106-10, 121-22, 128-34, 143-46; William H. Daniels, *Memorials of Gilbert Haven* (Boston, 1880), 183-84, 202-05. The Pennsylvania Society for the Abolition of Slavery, founded in 1775 by Benjamin Franklin and still in existence today, contributed money to 61 schools and colleges for the freedmen during Reconstruction. *Centennial Anniversary of the Pennsylvania Society for Promoting the Abolition of Slavery . . . April 14, 1875* (Philadelphia, 1875), 40.

instruction. Within ten days Redpath had secured teachers, text-books, and students. On March 4 he formally opened the schools to 1,200 freedmen and 300 white children. Negroes and whites were taught in the same building but segregated by classroom. Teachers were paid and textbooks supplied by northern freedmen's aid societies. Within a few weeks the children of Charleston were off the streets and in school. By the end of March there were 3,114 children of both races in the schools. Most of the teachers were natives of Charleston: 74 of the 83 teachers, including 25 Negroes. By the end of May there were more than 4,000 pupils studying under 34 northern and 68 native southern teachers in 9 day schools and 5 night schools. Redpath returned North in June, followed by the praises of Charlestonians, army officers, and abolitionists for his efficient reorganization of Charleston schools.[6]

Another abolitionist who accomplished a great deal as an educator and social worker among the freedmen was Josephine Griffing. During the war thousands of freedmen flocked into Washington. Appalled by the miserable living conditions of these people in disease-ridden slums, Mrs. Griffing became general agent of the National Freedmen's Relief Association of the District of Columbia in 1863. She distributed food and clothing and established vocational schools to teach new skills to freed men and women. In a period of two years—1865 to 1867—she found homes and employment in the North for more than 7,000 Washington Negroes. Thereafter she continued to send three or four hundred freedmen North every year for several years.[7]

---

[6] *Freedmen's Record*, i (April 1865), 61-64 (May 1865), 73 (July 1865), 110-11, 120; *Commonwealth*, Apr. 15, July 1, 1865; *N.A.S. Standard*, July 22, 29, 1865; *Liberator*, July 21, 1865; Luther P. Jackson, "The Educational Efforts of the Freedmen's Bureau and Freedmen's Aid Societies in South Carolina, 1862-1872," *Journal of Negro History*, viii (Jan. 1923), 19-20; Alrutheus A. Taylor, *The Negro in South Carolina during Reconstruction* (Washington, 1924), 85-86. With the opening of the fall term in 1865 the public school system in Charleston again came under the control of native white officials, who assigned all Negro children to the Morris Street School, where they were taught by southern whites. One of the best Negro schools in the city, however, was the Shaw Memorial Institute, named in honor of Colonel Robert Shaw, and sustained primarily by the Shaw family and their abolitionist friends until 1874, when it was incorporated into the public school system of the city. Taylor, *The Negro in South Carolina Reconstruction*, 86-89.

[7] E. C. Stanton et al., *History of Woman Suffrage* (6 vols., New York, 1881-1922), ii, 28-33; Josephine Griffing to Sumner, Nov. ?, 1864, Sumner Papers,

Despite her efforts the freedmen continued to pour into the District faster than she could find homes for them in the North. Unskilled and unemployed, these people became a grave social problem and their miserable hovels an eyesore and a danger to public health. Especially serious was the problem of aged or crippled freedmen, who had almost no hope of future rehabilitation. The task seemed hopeless, but Mrs. Griffing continued to work undauntedly: she distributed private and public relief, and visited Negroes in their homes. In 1865 she was appointed sub-assistant commissioner of the Freedmen's Bureau in the District of Columbia. When the Bureau proposed to reduce rations at the end of 1865 to avoid encouraging pauperism and idleness, she protested vigorously and gave several lectures publicizing the destitute condition of many freedmen in the capital. The aged and crippled Negroes could not support themselves, she declared, and the able-bodied men could not find work. Her lectures aroused considerable attention and controversy. Democrats cited the poverty and disease of Washington Negroes as proof that they had been better off in slavery. Some abolitionists were unhappy with Mrs. Griffing's disclosures, fearing that they would only confirm the popular image of the shiftless, helpless Negro. General Howard dismissed her from the Freedmen's Bureau because of her protests against Bureau policy. Yet Mrs. Griffing's portrayal of conditions in the District was essentially accurate, and the Bureau was compelled to renew the distribution of rations to needy freedmen.[8]

Mrs. Griffing continued to serve as a one-woman welfare agency for Washington Negroes until her death in 1872. She was on good terms with radical Republican leaders in Congress. Every year she appeared before congressional committees and tried to wheedle more money out of them for relief. She urged the creation of public works programs in Washington to alleviate unemploy-

---

HU; Memo. of Governor Buckingham of Connecticut, in Griffing Papers, CU; *N.A.S. Standard*, Sept. 1, 1866.

[8] George Bentley, *A History of the Freedmen's Bureau* (Phila., 1955), 77-78; Stanton et al., *History of Woman Suffrage*, II, 29, 33; Mrs. Griffing to E. B. Chace, Dec. 26, 1865, in Lillie B. C. Wyman and Arthur C. Wyman, *Elizabeth Buffum Chace* (2 vols., Boston, 1914), I, 285-86; Levi Coffin to McKim, Jan. 2, 1866, McKim to Coffin, Jan. 6, 1866, McKim Papers, Cornell; *Freedmen's Record*, I (Feb. 1865), 17-18; *N.A.S. Standard*, Jan. 27, 1866.

ment.[9] Mrs. Griffing remained a target of criticism from certain Republican quarters. In 1870 Horace Greeley charged that her activities among the freedmen had done them great injury. "They are an easy, worthless race, taking no thought for the morrow, and liking to lean on those who befriend them," Greeley told Mrs. Griffing. "Your course aggravates their weaknesses, when you should raise their ambition and stimulate them to self-reliance." In an angry reply, Mrs. Griffing pointed out that she helped only those who could not help themselves. She had found work for many of the able-bodied, and her relief efforts were directed toward "those broken-down aged slaves whom we have liberated in their declining years, when all their strength is gone, and for whom no home, family, friendship, or subsistence is furnished." If it was a "great injury" to help these people, then "there is no call for alms-house, hospital, home, or asylum in human society." Criticism such as Greeley's was exceptional, however. Most observers praised Mrs. Griffing for her herculean labors and steadfast humanitarianism. Senator Benjamin Wade told her in 1869, "I know of no person in America who has done so much for the cause of humanity for the last four years as you have done. Your disinterested labors have saved hundreds of poor human beings, not only [from] the greatest destitution and misery, but from actual starvation and death."[10]

Whether serving as organizers, administrators, teachers, or social workers, abolitionists were in the forefront of efforts to educate and rehabilitate the freedmen. Their contribution was recognized by a speaker at the National Education Association meeting in 1884: "Those very men, extremists, enthusiasts, 'fanatics,' who had formed the backbone of the abolition movement . . . became the dauntless leaders of an educational movement which was the natural sequel and supplement of their first crusade."[11]

✦

[9] Mrs. Griffing to Sumner, Feb. 12, 1867, Mar. 30, Apr. 10, 1869, Sumner Papers, HU; Mrs. Griffing to Gerrit Smith, Aug. 5, 12, 1869, Aug. 26, 1870, Mar. 13, 1871, Catharine Stebbins to Gerrit Smith, Aug. 17, 1870, Smith Papers, SU; Sumner to Mrs. Griffing, Apr. 2, 1868, July 27, Dec. 7, 1869, Mrs. Griffing to Lucretia Mott, Apr. 22, 1870, Griffing Papers, CU; *New York World*, Feb. 25, 1870; *National Standard*, Apr. 1, 1871.

[10] Horace Greeley to Griffing, Sept. 7, 1870, Griffing to Greeley, Sept. 12, 1870, Wade to Griffing, Nov. 12, 1869, Griffing Papers, CU.

[11] Quoted in Swint, *Northern Teacher*, 27.

The main purpose of freedmen's aid was to bring the rudiments of education to illiterate Negroes. "If the blacks are kept in ignorance they can be subjected to a system of serfdom," wrote J. Miller McKim. "If we enlighten them they are secure against the machinations of their old enemies—to which they will always be subject until educated." McKim proclaimed repeatedly that education was necessary to equip the freedmen for the rights and responsibilities of citizenship. "Democracy without the schoolmaster is an impossibility," he said. "Universal suffrage without universal education would be universal anarchy."[12] An element of cultural imperialism also entered into the thinking of some educators. The New England Freedmen's Aid Society announced in 1865 that "New England can furnish teachers enough . . . to make a New England of the whole South; God helping, we will not pause in our work until the free school system . . . has been established from Maryland to Florida, and all along the shores of the Gulf."[13]

The Freedmen's Bureau was an important partner of the freedmen's aid societies in the work of educating southern Negroes. The Bureau extended its benevolent protection over all educational activities in the South. It provided school buildings for the societies and transportation allowances for teachers. It systematized the record-keeping and reports of the societies. The state superintendents of education of the Bureau worked closely with officials and teachers of the freedmen's societies. General Oliver O. Howard, head of the Bureau, was in complete sympathy with the purposes of the aid societies and established cordial relations with their leaders. As a devoted Congregationalist Howard was particularly close to the leaders of the American Missionary Association. The A.M.A. also enjoyed the special friendship of John W. Alvord, superintendent of education of the Freedmen's Bureau, who had been associated with the evangelical wing of the abolitionist movement before the war.[14]

---

12 McKim to Arthur Albright, Oct. 19, 1866, McKim Papers, BPL; McKim to S. P. Chase, Oct. 15, 1866, Chase Papers, LC.

13 *Freedmen's Journal*, I (Jan. 1865), 3.

14 Bentley, *Freedmen's Bureau*, 172-76; Luther Jackson, "The Educational Efforts of the Freedmen's Bureau and Freedmen's Aid Societies in South Carolina," *op.cit.*, 13-15; McKim to Joseph Simpson, Feb. 28, 1866, McKim letterbooks, I, 400, McKim Papers, Cornell; McKim to Arthur Albright, Mar. 23, 1866, McKim Papers, BPL; Drake, "American Missionary Association," 37-43.

Under the leadership of J. Miller McKim, the regional secular freedmen's societies were merged into a loose national federation in the fall of 1865, known as the American Freedmen's Aid Commission (A.F.A.C.). Officials of the freedmen's associations were happy with the progress of their work in 1865-1866. Excluding night schools and Sunday schools, the societies operated a total of 975 schools with 1,405 teachers and 90,778 pupils during the school year of 1865-66. Of this total the A.F.A.C. supplied 760 teachers and instructed approximately 50,000 pupils. The A.M.A. sent 353 missionaries and teachers into the field who had more than 20,000 students under their charge. The remainder of the schools were operated by independent evangelical associations.[15]

Teachers of the freedmen were confronted by many difficulties. In the early years of freedom the Negroes moved about a great deal and the school population was highly transient. Attendance was irregular and seasonal because so many Negro children had to work in the fields at planting and harvest time. The children came from a cultural environment almost entirely devoid of intellectual stimulus. Many of them had never heard of the alphabet, geography, or arithmetic when they first came to school. Few of them knew their right hand from their left, or could tell the date of their birth. Most of them realized only vaguely that there was a world outside their own plantation or town. The only contact they had with such mysteries was during their few hours in school a few months of the year. Progress was slow under such circumstances, but there were compensating factors. The freedmen had an almost passionate desire to learn to read and write, and children laboriously taught their parents the alphabet and multiplication tables during their spare time. Teachers invariably testified that despite their disadvantages in background, training, and environment, Negro children learned to read almost as well and as rapidly as white children.[16]

[15] The story of the merger of the secular freedmen's aid societies can be traced in the correspondence of J. Miller McKim in his papers at Cornell; Julius H. Parmelee, "Freedmen's Aid Societies, 1861-1871," *Negro Education: A Study of the Private and Higher Schools for Colored People in the United States, U.S. Dept. of Interior; Bureau of Education Bulletin*, 1916, no. 38, pp. 269-71, 275, 289; and *American Freedman*, I (May 1866), 25-31 (Sept. 1866), 82 (Oct. 1866), 99.

[16] The statements in this paragraph are based upon a reading of hundreds of letters from teachers printed in the *American Freedman* and *Freedmen's Record* from 1865 to 1869.

The problems faced by the teacher in the classroom were often less severe than those confronting her in the community. Many southern whites did not take kindly to the idea of Yankee "schoolmarms" instructing their former slaves. Some southern communities accepted the inevitability of Negro education and cooperated with the northern teachers. In most places, however, the white people regarded the Yankee teachers as aliens come to instill ideas of political and social equality into the heads of Negroes. Some southerners considered education of the Negro a harmful waste of time. "To talk about educating this drudge is to talk without thinking," asserted the *Paducah* (Kentucky) *Herald*. "Either to 'educate,' or to teach him merely to read and write, is to ruin him as a laborer. Thousands of them have already been ruined by it."[17] Where the whites felt this way the teachers were sometimes insulted, beaten, and their schoolhouses burned. Southern contempt for the "nigger teacher," however, usually took the milder form of social ostracism. White teachers frequently found it impossible to get room and board in white southern homes, and native whites would deliberately snub the teachers socially.

Even in southern communities that favored Negro education the Yankee teachers were regarded with a certain amount of suspicion. In the spring of 1867 Anna Gardner, teacher of a freedmen's school in Charlottesville, Virginia, asked J. C. Southall, local newspaper editor and friend of Negro education, if he would print some diplomas for her school without charge. Southall replied that he would print them if he could be satisfied that the school confined itself to the ordinary rudiments of education. But he suspected that "you instruct them in politics and sociology; that you come among us not merely as an ordinary school teacher, but as a political missionary; that you communicate to the colored people ideas of social equality." Even if she did not actually teach these things in the classroom, "you may, by precept and example, inculcate ideas of social equality with the whites among the pupils of your school and the colored people generally." Such ideas were "mischievous, . . . tending to disturb the good feeling between the two races." Therefore Southall refused to print the diplomas. Anna Gardner sent him a blunt reply: "I teach *in school* and *out*, so far as my influence extends, the funda-

17 *Paducah Herald*, quoted in *Right Way*, June 23, 1866.

mental principles of 'politics' and 'sociology,' viz.:—'Whatsoever ye would that men should do to you, do ye even so unto them.' "
Anna Gardner's statement typified the attitude of many teachers, who did indeed practice "social equality"; and after the passage of Negro suffrage most of them taught Republican politics as well. Consequently relations between the Yankee teachers and a majority of southern whites remained somewhat strained as long as the schools existed.[18]

Another difficulty confronting the freedmen's aid enterprise was descriptions by newspaper correspondents, travelers, and so on, of the degraded, ignorant, and destitute condition of many freedmen. Such reports were gleefully picked up by the Democratic press and cited as proof of the Negro's worthlessness. In 1866 an official of the Freedmen's Bureau made a speech describing the freedmen as "ignorant, degraded, indolent, sensual, false, far below what I had supposed." The *London Times* published the speech. English friends of the freedmen wrote in alarm to J. Miller McKim telling him that such stories had a tendency in England to discourage contributions to freedmen's aid. McKim replied that the freedmen were indeed degraded. That was why they needed assistance and education. McKim told the British friends of the freedmen: "Of course the blacks are *to a degree* just what Major Lawrence represents them; and just what anyone of common sense must *a priori* know them to be. Among the *least* of slavery's evils are the manacles which it fastens on the limbs and the stripes which it inflicts on the backs of its victims. Our 'zeal' against it & in behalf of its injured subjects is kindled by the fact that its iron enters the soul—darkens the mind—dulls the intellect—perverts the affections—chokes the aspirations— and does every thing it can toward making the black man in fact what it has made him in law: a chattel. . . . The victims of the slave-system *are* 'degraded'; therefore it is that we labor to lift them up." The freedmen were actually less degraded than abolitionists had expected, said McKim. They had shown marked progress and gave every sign of susceptibility to improvement and education. The present backward condition of the freedmen,

---

[18] *Freedmen's Record*, III (Apr. 1867), 54. For a general discussion of the tensions between northern teachers and southern whites, see Swint, *Northern Teacher*, 77-142.

he concluded, should stimulate their friends to greater effort rather than cause them to despair for the future of the race.[19]

The freedmen's aid enterprise encountered hostility not only from its enemies but from those who should have been its friends. During the war Phillips and other abolitionists had criticized the aid societies for their paternalism (see Chapter VII). When at the end of the war the Garrison wing of the American Anti-Slavery Society suggested that abolitionists should dissolve their organizations and continue their work for the Negro in the freedmen's societies, Phillips renewed his criticism. He conceded that the freedmen's associations were "doing a good work," but it was a work of charity, an "old clothes movement" and "not the work of an Abolitionist." Frederick Douglass told J. Miller McKim:

"I have my doubts about these Freedmen's Societies. They may be a necessity of the hour and as such may be commended; but I fear everything looking to their permanence. The negro needs justice more than pity; liberty more than old clothes; rights more than training to enjoy them. Once give him equality before the law and special associations for his benefit may cease. He will then be comprehended as he ought to be, in all those schemes of benevolence, education and progress which apply to the masses of our Countrymen every where. In so far as these special efforts shall furnish an apology for excluding us from the general schemes of civilization so multitudinous in our country they will be an injury to the colored race. They will serve to keep up the very prejudices, which it is so desirable to banish from the country."[20]

McKim and other proponents of freedmen's aid resented these disparagements. McKim thought it more important to prepare the freedmen for the rights and duties of citizenship than to agitate for those rights in the abstract. "The Freedmen's movement . . . is not an eleemosynary movement; not an *old clothes* movement; not a movement merely to relieve physical want & teach little negroes to read," he declared. "It is a re-

[19] Arthur Albright to McKim, Feb. 16, 1866, McKim to Albright, Mar. 6, 1866, McKim letterbook, I, 445-49, McKim Papers, Cornell.

[20] *N.A.S. Standard*, May 6, 1865; *Liberator*, May 26, 1865; Douglass to McKim, May 2, 1865, McKim Papers, Cornell.

constructive movement. It is to reorganize Southern Society on a basis of impartial liberty. It is to remodel public opinion in regard to the black man by fitting him for [the responsible exercise of equal rights]. . . . It is a movement established and conducted in the interests of civilization."[21]

While the intramural abolitionist debate over the merits of freedmen's aid societies continued, an important development was taking place within the secular freedmen's associations. In November 1865, representatives of the A.F.A.C. and the American Union Commission met to discuss the possibility of merging the two organizations. The American Union Commission had been formed in 1864 to give aid to Unionist refugees, mostly whites, in the South. The leaders of this Commission and of the A.F.A.C. believed that they could prosecute their work more efficiently if their organizations were united. The merger was approved on January 31, 1866. The name of the new association was the American Freedmen's and Union Commission (the "and" was dropped in May 1866). The objectives of the new Commission were relief and education of blacks and whites alike in the wartorn South.[22]

Some of the auxiliary societies of the A.F.A.C. were opposed to the merger on the ground that it would divert too large a share of their limited resources to the education of southern whites. McKim worked hard to overcome this opposition. To a Pittsburgh abolitionist he wrote that "we can do more for the freedmen on the broad basis of man than of *freed* man or *black* man. We who go against class legislation & color distinctions—shall we legislate for a class—give preference to a color?" Was not the poor white southerner also a victim of slavery, McKim asked a Philadelphia abolitionist who opposed merger? "Shall we denounce President Johnson & his Congressional confreres for not legislating and administering the Government without respect to color, and yet ourselves . . . minister *with* regard to color?" McKim's arguments finally prevailed, and by May 1866, all the auxiliary societies had ratified the new constitution of the American Freedmen's Union Commission (A.F.U.C.). McKim became correspond-

21 McKim to Richard Webb, Mar. 27, 1865, Garrison Papers, BPL.
22 Ira Brown, "Lyman Abbot and Freedmen's Aid, 1865-1869," *Journal of Southern History*, xv (Feb. 1949), 23-28.

ing secretary of the new Commission, and Lyman Abbott, former secretary of the American Union Commission, became recording secretary of the merged organization. Abbott also edited the Commission's monthly journal, the *American Freedman*.[23]

The issue of school desegregation soon confronted the A.F.U.C. The Commission made its position on this question perfectly clear in the first issue of its monthly journal. "[We] insist . . . that both races shall enjoy the same rights, immunities, and opportunities," declared the *American Freedman*. "Our Commission is pledged to the maintenance of the doctrine of equal rights. . . . It took America three-quarters of a century of agitation and four years of war to learn the meaning of the word 'Liberty.' God grant to teach us by easier lessons the meaning of the words 'equal rights.' " The constitution of the A.F.U.C. declared that no person would be excluded from the Commission's schools because of race or color. The executive committee conceded that this integration policy "will produce difficulties in the South." Nevertheless integration was "inherently right" and the Commission would never "shut out a child from our schools because of his color."[24]

The constituent societies faithfully carried out the policy of desegregation. The New England Society, for example, instructed its teachers to admit white children "on precisely the same footing, and no other, with blacks; that is to say, they are to occupy the same rooms, recite in the same classes, and receive the same attention as the blacks. You cannot control public opinion outside of the school but, within its limits, you must secure entire respect from every pupil to every other."[25] The A.M.A. had always adhered to a desegregation policy, and most of the other evangelical societies did the same. In practice, however, few whites attended the freedmen's schools. Elizabeth Botume, a teacher in South Carolina, told of two white girls who came to her school

23 McKim to E. H. Irish, Feb. 8, 1866; McKim to Wm. H. Furness, Mar. 30, 1866; Samuel May, Jr., to McKim, Feb. 20, Mar. 5, 1866; Garrison to McKim, Mar. 31, 1866; McKim to F. J. Child, Dec. 9, 1865, McKim to Joseph Simpson, Feb. 16, 1866, McKim to Laura Towne, Feb. 21, Apr. 4, 1866, McKim to Reuben Tomlinson, Apr. 4, 1866, McKim letterbooks, I, 170-71, 328-29, 381, 458-60, 535-36, McKim Papers, Cornell; *American Freedman*, I (May 1866), 19-20.

24 *American Freedman*, I (April 1866), 2-3, 5-6.

25 *Freedmen's Record*, II (Mar. 1866), 37-38.

because there was no other school within a reasonable distance of their home. The children were happy, but after two months they suddenly stopped coming. Miss Botume visited their mother to learn the reason for their withdrawal. The mother "confessed the Southern white people had 'made so much fuss' because she allowed the children to go to a '*nigger school*,'" reported Miss Botume, that "she felt obliged to take them away." The mother told Miss Botume, "I would not care myself but the young men laugh at my husband. They tell him he must be pretty far gone and low down when he sends his children to a '*nigger school*.' That makes him mad, and he is vexed with me." To avoid family quarrels she withdrew the children. In the term ending June 30, 1867, there were 111,442 pupils in schools operated by the freedmen's societies, of whom only 1,348 were white.[26]

Abolitionists were delighted by the strong equal rights and integrationist position of the A.F.U.C. There was a noticeable decline in radical abolitionist criticism of the freedmen's aid movement in 1866. Several speakers at the annual meeting of the American Anti-Slavery Society praised the good work of the freedmen's associations, and the Society adopted a resolution expressing its gratitude to "the devoted, most efficient, and inexpressibly important labors" of the freedmen's teachers.[27]

But there was still some friction between the Phillips wing of abolitionism and the freedmen's aid societies. Both groups were competing for financial support from the same class of northern people. The competition for funds erupted into a major quarrel in 1867 over the issue of the Jackson bequest. When Francis Jackson died in 1861 he left a trust fund of $10,000 to the antislavery cause. The money did not become available until 1867, two years after the abolition of slavery. Both Garrison and Phillips were on the board of trustees of the Jackson fund, and a dispute arose between them over the disposition of the legacy. Phillips claimed the money for the American Anti-Slavery Society on the ground that the Society's campaign for Negro suffrage was a

26 Elizabeth Botume, *First Days Amongst the Contrabands* (Boston, 1893), 257-58; *Freedmen's Record*, III (Oct. 1867), 154.

27 *N.A.S. Standard*, May 12, 19, 1866. For several letters from abolitionists praising the stand of the freedmen's societies on school integration, see *American Freedman*, I (May 1866), 23-24.

direct continuation of the antislavery movement. Garrison wanted the $10,000 for the New England branch of the A.F.U.C., arguing with equal assurance that freedmen's aid was the logical heir of the abolitionist crusade. The two sides compromised in January 1867, and assigned half the legacy to freedmen's aid and half to the American Anti-Slavery Society. But when Congress passed the Reconstruction Acts two months later, Garrison changed his mind and claimed all the money for the freedmen again. The enactment of Negro suffrage, he maintained, completely obviated the need for an antislavery society. Phillips disagreed, and the board of trustees was unable to reach agreement on the disposition of the legacy. The matter went to the Massachusetts Supreme Court, which decided in Garrison's favor. Phillips was deeply angered by the decision and attacked Garrison and his supporters sharply in a series of *Standard* editorials. Garrison replied in kind. Abolitionists ranged themselves on either side of the quarrel and the whole affair became intensely bitter. Garrison and Phillips broke off personal and social relations for two years, and for a long time several of Phillips' old abolitionist friends passed him on the street without speaking. The upshot was a partial revival of the hostility of Phillips and some of his associates toward the freedmen's aid societies.[28]

✦

The A.F.U.C. began to break up almost as soon as it was formed. Religious factionalism was the main cause of its downfall. The American Missionary Association and other evangelical freedmen's aid societies required their teachers to be Christian missionaries as well as instructors. The evangelical associations believed that purification of the soul was as important as enlightenment of the mind. There was a sharp cleavage between the secular educational philosophy of the A.F.U.C. and the evangelical zeal of the A.M.A. This cleavage was essentially a continuation of the prewar rift between Garrisonian and evangelical abolitionists.

[28] The Garrison Papers and the Samuel May, Jr., Papers, BPL, contain a great deal of correspondence relating to this issue. See also *N.A.S. Standard*, July 20, Aug. 10, 24, 1867, Feb. 15, Mar. 14, June 13, 1868. Garrison and Phillips effected a personal reconciliation in the early 1870's, and the bitterness between other abolitionists gradually dissolved during the decade.

Garrisonians predominated among the abolitionist element in the A.F.U.C., and the leadership of the A.M.A. was the same as the leadership of the prewar evangelical abolitionists.

From the outset of the freedmen's aid movement there was competition between the secular societies and the A.M.A., especially in the matter of raising money in the North. In 1866-1867 the differences between the two groups came to a head. The A.M.A. declared that a freedman's education would not be complete unless he was "imbued with the principles of evangelical religion." Teachers of the A.F.U.C., on the other hand, were told that they were not "missionaries, nor preachers, nor exhorters" and instructed "not to inculcate doctrinal opinions or take part in sectarian propagandism of any kind." The A.F.U.C. accused the A.M.A. of conducting "parochial schools" and of placing proselytism above education. Such statements by leaders of the eastern wing of the A.F.U.C. precipitated a crisis in the organization. The western branches of the A.F.U.C. had always required their teachers to be practicing Christians. Angered by the aggressive secularism of the eastern leaders, the Cincinnati branch withdrew from the A.F.U.C. in 1866 and was absorbed by the A.M.A. It was followed by the Cleveland branch in 1867 and the Chicago branch in 1868.[29]

The result of these withdrawals was a sharp decrease in the strength of the A.F.U.C. The A.M.A. had several advantages in its competition with the secular societies. In the first place it was an older organization with well-established sources of income. As a missionary society it could rely on consistent church support while the A.F.U.C. was forced to depend on the North's short-lived philanthropic enthusiasm for education of the freedmen. Secondly, the A.M.A. enjoyed a greater degree of cooperation from the Freedmen's Bureau than did the secular societies. General Howard and the Reverend Alvord were devoted Congrega-

[29] The dispute between the secular and evangelical societies can be traced in *American Missionary*, x (Sept. 1866), 193-94 (Oct. 1866), 226-28, xi (Sept. 1867), 205; *Freedmen's Record*, iii (Jan. 1867), 1-2; *American Freedman*, i (Dec. 1866), 130-31 (Jan. 1867), 146-47, ii (April 1867), 194; Lewis Tappan to J. Sella Martin, July 3, 1865, Tappan to Levi Coffin, Jan. 30, 1865, Tappan letterbook, Tappan Papers, lc; McKim to Garrison, Mar. 29, 1866, McKim to Arthur Albright, Mar. 15, 1867, McKim to J. W. Alvord, Jan. 23, 1868, McKim Papers, Cornell; Swint, *Northern Teacher*, 37-40; and Drake, "American Missionary Association," 18-26.

tionalists. They sympathized with the A.M.A.'s philosophy of religious education. In many small ways the Freedmen's Bureau extended more assistance to the A.M.A. than to the secular societies, causing anger and frustration among some officials of the A.F.U.C. Lastly, A.M.A. teachers were often able to establish a closer rapport with the freedmen because their evangelical piety was more akin to the Negro's own religious experience than was the secularism of A.F.U.C. teachers.[30] The declining strength of the A.F.U.C. in relation to that of the A.M.A. is revealed by a glance at the statistics:

	1865-66	1866-67
A.F.U.C.		
Cash expended	$318,670.08	Cash and supplies: $250,662.52
Supplies shipped	$90,755.27	
Teachers in the field	760	Teachers in the field 494
A.M.A		
Cash expended	$271,586.78	Cash expended $334,500.00
Supplies shipped	$105,441.00	Supplies shipped $90,000.00
Teachers in the field	353	Teachers in the field 528

The expenditures and number of teachers of the A.F.U.C. continued to decline in subsequent years while those of the A.M.A. remained steady for the rest of the decade.[31]

The competition of evangelical associations was not the only reason for the decline of the A.F.U.C. From 1864-1866 a great many people contributed to freedmen's aid who were not deeply concerned about uplifting the Negro but who gave because it was the most "deserving" charity of those years. But in 1866 there was a slackening of popular interest in the movement. As early as 1865 one Gideonite commented on "the lethargy creeping over our community on this subject. . . . The feeling is somewhat general that the negro must make the most of his chances and pick up his a, b, c's as he can." All of the secular societies were forced to retrench during 1866-1867. The *American Freedman* noted in April 1867, that "the enthusiasm which accompanies a new movement, one especially which appealed so strongly to

[30] Drake, "American Missionary Association," 37-75; O. O. Howard to McKim, June 6, 1867, Samuel May, Jr., to McKim, July 22, 1870, McKim Papers, Cornell.

[31] *American Freedman*, I (Jan. 1867), 147, II (April 1867), 196; Parmelee, "Freedmen's Aid Societies," *op.cit.*, 275.

philanthropic and humane considerations as did this during the desolations of war, has somewhat passed away and left as its supporters only those who are attached to it by cardinal and well-considered principles."[32]

In 1868 the executive committee decided to dissolve the A.F.-U.C. The activities of the Commission had decreased to the point where the constituent societies could carry on the work more efficiently by themselves. Dissolution of the A.F.U.C. was accomplished in 1869. The New York and Pennsylvania societies disbanded in the same year. The only secular societies remaining in existence after 1869 were the Baltimore and New England associations. The Baltimore society was absorbed by the city's public school system in 1871. The New England society continued to support a few normal schools in the South until 1874, when it finally disbanded. The A.F.U.C. never fulfilled the grand hopes of its founders, but it accomplished a great deal for the education of southern freedmen. During their existence the secular freedmen's aid societies spent nearly $3,000,000 on southern education and brought the rudiments of learning to more than 150,000 freedmen.[33]

Most important of all, however, the freedmen's societies helped to lay the foundations of public education in the South. When the reconstructed state governments established their public school systems in the years 1868 to 1870, several of the freedmen's schools were taken over directly by the state boards of education. Many of the teachers of the South's new public schools had been educated by the northern freedmen's associations. In several southern states, officials of freedmen's aid societies drafted the public school legislation and served as the first superintendents of education. The public school system in the South was hardly

[32] E. S. Philbrick to Wm. C. Gannett, Oct. 15, 1865, in Elizabeth Pearson, ed., *Letters from Port Royal* (Boston, 1906), 317-18; *American Freedman*, II (Apr. 1867), 195. See also *Freedmen's Record*, II (Sept. 1866), 157-59, III (April 1867), 52 (May 1867), 69, IV (April 1868), 51; and Reuben Tomlinson to McKim, Sept. 24, 1866, McKim Papers, Cornell.

[33] Parmelee, "Freedmen's Aid Societies," *op.cit.*, 271-75, 292-96; Drake, "American Missionary Association," 275-76; McKim to Garrison, Dec. 2, 15, 1867, Feb. 1, 1868, Gerrit Smith to J. Miller McKim, Nov. 1, 1868, S. P. Chase to McKim, Nov. 6, 1868, Garrison Papers, BPL; McKim to Gerrit Smith, Nov. 6, 18, 1868, Smith Papers, SU; *Freedmen's Record*, IV (July 1868), 106-08 (Nov. 1868), 169; *American Freedman*, III (April 1869), 1-2.

in a flourishing condition when the A.F.U.C. disbanded in 1869, but the secular societies had run out of money, and making a virtue of necessity they proclaimed that the spread of public education in the South had ended the need for a northern freedmen's commission.[34]

The financial inability of the South to support an efficient public school system, however, and the takeover of several state governments by conservatives unfriendly to public education sparked a movement for federal aid to education in the early 1870's. In 1869 the new conservative government of Tennessee repealed the statewide compulsory school law, leaving the question of public education to the option of individual counties. All the state's public schools for Negroes except those in Memphis and Nashville soon closed down. Caroline Putnam, a veteran abolitionist teaching the freedmen in Lottsburgh, Virginia, reported in 1870 that Virginia's property tax for schools was unpopular with landowners. The new conservative governor had promised that the tax law would not be enforced. Caroline Putnam urged federal action to compel southern states to maintain a system of universal public education open to both races.[35] In 1870 Congressman George F. Hoar of Massachusetts introduced a bill to establish public schools by national authority in states that failed to do it themselves. Senator W. T. Willey of West Virginia sponsored a bill for the distribution of the proceeds of public land sales among the states to help finance public schools. Abolitionists gave their support to these measures, and both Houses at different times passed different versions of them, but the bills never came to final passage. Abolitionist hopes for an efficient public school system for both races in the South were doomed to disappointment.[36]

✦

During the war and early reconstruction years the freedmen's aid societies concentrated almost entirely on elementary educa-

[34] *Freedmen's Record*, IV (Oct. 1868), 155-56; *American Freedman*, III (April 1869), 2.

[35] Alrutheus A. Taylor, *The Negro in Tennessee, 1865-1880* (Washington, 1941), 182; *National Standard*, I (July 1870), 146-51.

[36] *National Standard*, Oct. 22, Nov. 19, Dec. 17, 1870, Jan. 7, Feb. 11, Mar. 11, Apr. 15, Oct. 28, 1871; George F. Hoar, *Autobiography of Seventy Years* (2 vols., New York, 1903), I, 265.

tion. This emphasis was designed to make literate a large body of people recently emancipated and soon to be enfranchised. But this policy proved very expensive, and did little more than dent the crust of southern illiteracy. At no time were more than 10 per cent of the freedmen of school age attending the societies' schools. Officials of the freedmen's associations realized by 1866 that the establishment of normal schools and colleges to train Negro teachers would be a more effective use of their limited resources. The movement toward normal schools came after the decline of the A.F.U.C. had set in, and the secular societies never supported more than six or eight small normal schools in the South. But the A.M.A. and other evangelical societies established a large number of normal schools and colleges. The A.M.A. was the pioneer in Negro higher education in the South. Between 1866 and 1869 the Association founded seven chartered institutions, all of which were called colleges, although they were at first little more than high schools: Berea College (founded in 1855 and reopened in 1866), Fisk University, Atlanta University, Hampton Institute, Talladega College, Tougaloo College, and Straight University. The A.M.A. also aided in the establishment of Howard University. Some of these schools are today among the best southern universities for Negroes. By 1876 the A.M.A. was also operating 14 nonchartered normal and high schools in the South. As early as 1869 there were 314 teachers trained in A.M.A. institutions teaching in southern schools. It was estimated in 1873 that graduates of A.M.A. normal schools and colleges were teaching 64,000 pupils in southern schools; by 1879 this number had risen to 150,000.[37]

The other denominational societies were not far behind the A.M.A. in founding institutions of higher learning for Negroes in the South. In 1879 there were 39 normal schools, colleges, and theological seminaries and 69 schools of lower grade supported by northern churches and missionary societies in the South. The various northern freedmen's aid and missionary societies and the Freedmen's Bureau spent more than $31,000,000 on southern edu-

[37] *Freedmen's Record*, iii (Jan. 1867), 2 (Oct. 1867), 143, iv (April 1868), 50-51; Augustus F. Beard, *Crusade of Brotherhood, A History of the American Missionary Association* (Boston, 1909), 100-04, 147-89; Drake, "American Missionary Association," 159-85.

cation from 1861 to 1893. This was nearly 30 per cent of the total amount expended for all Negro education in the South during those years. In 1888 of a total of 15,000 Negro teachers instructing more than 800,000 pupils in the South, 13,500 had been trained in schools supported by northern benevolence. The A.M.A. institutions alone had educated 7,000 teachers.[38] The freedmen's societies helped decrease the Negro illiteracy rate in the South from more than 90 per cent in 1861 to 81.1 per cent in 1870 and 70 per cent in 1880. Statistics do not tell the entire story of the contribution of freedmen's associations. Their influence penetrated every southern state, awakening the freedmen to the need for education and proving that the Negro was capable of higher learning. The southern Negro colleges founded by these societies have helped to produce the present generation of Negro leaders who are gradually changing the pattern of race relations in the South. Truly the abolitionist impulse, which motivated the original freedman's aid movement, has had a deep and lasting impact upon the southern Negro.

✦

Abolitionist efforts to win suffrage and education for the freedmen were partially successful. The same cannot be said of their attempts to obtain land for the emancipated Negroes. After the war many abolitionists stepped up their agitation for the confiscation and redistribution of large plantations. "The nominal freedom of the slaves . . . must be actually secured by the possession of land," wrote Edmund Quincy in April 1865. "If the monopoly of land be permitted to remain in the hands of the present rebel proprietors . . . the monopoly of labor might almost as well be given them, too."[39] Wendell Phillips, Anna Dickinson, Gerrit Smith, Lydia Maria Child, James Freeman Clarke, Thomas Wentworth Higginson, and many other abolitionists echoed these sentiments.

President Johnson's amnesty proclamation of May 29, 1865, dealt a sharp blow to radicals who hoped for wholesale confiscation. The proclamation restored political and property rights to most

[38] Harriet Beecher Stowe, "The Education of Freedmen," *North American Review,* cxxviii (June 1879), 605-15, and cxxix (July 1879), 81-94; Drake, "American Missionary Association," 185-205.

[39] *N.A.S. Standard,* Apr. 1, 1865.

rebels who would take an oath of allegiance. In subsequent months Johnson issued a large number of special pardons to men who had been exempted from the May 29 proclamation. Despite this setback, abolitionists continued to work for governmental action to secure land for the freedmen. They hoped for congressional reversal of Johnson's policy of property restoration, just as they hoped for congressional reversal of the rest of his reconstruction program. Several radical Republican leaders agreed with the abolitionists on this question. "We must see that the freedmen are established on the soil, and that they may become proprietors," wrote Charles Sumner. "From the beginning I have regarded confiscation only as ancillary to emancipation." In his famous speech at Lancaster, Pennsylvania, on September 6, 1865, Thaddeus Stevens advocated confiscation of the property of large southern landholders and the grant of 40 acres to each adult freedman. But most Republicans shied away from the radicalism of wholesale confiscation. Prospects for the adoption of Stevens' proposal or anything like it appeared dim in 1865.[40]

One of the anticipated functions of the Freedmen's Bureau was resettlement of freedmen on abandoned and confiscated land. Johnson's pardon and amnesty program, however, threatened to leave the Bureau with very little land for this purpose. In August 1865, Johnson issued a series of executive orders to General Howard instructing him to restore all confiscated property to former rebel owners except that which had already been sold under court decrees. These orders affected nearly all lands under Bureau control. The status of property along the South Atlantic coast assigned to the freedmen by Sherman's Order no. 15 (see Chapter XI) became a burning issue during the winter of 1865-1866. More than 40,000 freedmen lived on 485,000 acres with the "possessory titles" granted by Sherman's Order. In October 1865, Johnson sent General Howard to the sea islands to persuade the freedmen to return their farms to the pardoned owners. Howard had no taste for his mission, but like a good soldier he

---

[40] Sumner to John Bright, Mar. 13, 1865, in Edward L. Pierce, *Memoir and Letters of Charles Sumner* (4 vols., Boston, 1877-94), IV, 229; Fawn M. Brodie, *Thaddeus Stevens: Scourge of the South* (New York, 1959), 231-33. See also *Commonwealth*, June 10, 17, 1865; *Independent*, June 22, 1865; *Liberator*, June 23, Aug. 11, 1865; *N.A.S. Standard*, May 26, 1866; *New York Tribune*, Apr. 11, Sept. 11, 12, 1865.

carried out his superior's orders. He urged the freedmen quietly to abandon their farms and go back to work for their former masters.[41]

Freedmen on the sea islands could hardly believe their ears. "To turn us off from the land that the Government has allowed us to occupy, is nothing less than returning us to involuntary servitude," said one of them. "They will make freedom a curse to us, for we have no home, no land, no oath, no vote, and consequently no country."[42] Some of the Negroes vowed to defend their farms by force if necessary. Abolitionists summoned all their eloquence to denounce the government's action. "This villainous effort to rob loyal men for the benefit of ruffianly rebels whose hands are red with the blood of Northern soldiers, can succeed only through a breach of faith on the part of our government such as would be without parallel in history," declared the *Commonwealth*. The *Right Way* asked: "Shall our own, and all coming ages, brand us for the treachery of sacrificing our faithful friends to our and their enemies? GOD IN HIS MERCY SAVE US FROM SUCH PERFIDY AND SUCH IDIOCY." General Rufus Saxton, commissioner of the Freedmen's Bureau in South Carolina, refused to carry out the order dispossessing the Negroes of their land, and Johnson removed Saxton from office on January 15, 1866. Even after Saxton's removal the Freedmen's Bureau moved slowly, hoping that Congress would enact legislation nullifying the president's orders.[43]

In the end most of the freedmen were dispossessed. But the Freedmen's Bureau bill passed over Johnson's veto in July 1866, contained a provision for the lease of 20 acres of government-owned land on the sea islands to each dispossessed freedman with a six-year option to buy at $1.50 per acre. At the same time Congress passed the Southern Homestead Act, extending the principle of the homestead law of 1862 to the public lands of Alabama, Arkansas, Florida, Louisiana, and Mississippi. The

[41] Bentley, *Freedmen's Bureau*, 87-98; Edwin D. Hoffman, "From Slavery to Self-Reliance," *Journal of Negro History*, xli (January 1956), 20-24; *N.A.S. Standard*, Oct. 7, 1865.

[42] Quoted in *N.A.S. Standard*, Oct. 7, 1865.

[43] *Commonwealth*, Nov. 4, 1865; *Right Way*, Dec. 30, 1865; Bentley, *Freedmen's Bureau*, 98-101. See also *Liberator*, Nov. 17, Dec. 1, 15, 22, 1865; *Independent*, Dec. 7, 1865.

bill stipulated that until January 1, 1867, no one who had supported the Confederacy would be eligible for a homestead. This provision was intended to give the freedmen and Unionist whites first chance at the land. Abolitionists hoped for good results from the Southern Homestead Act, but their hopes were doomed to disappointment. Most of the lands opened for settlement were of inferior quality, and few freedmen had the necessary capital to buy tools and farm implements or to support themselves while they were trying to coax the first crop from the sandy soil. As a means of placing the freedmen on fertile land of their own, the Southern Homestead Act was a failure.[44]

Abolitionists soon discerned the inadequacy of the Homestead Act and renewed their demands for a program of confiscation and redistribution of southern plantations. An abolitionist traveler in the South reported in the fall of 1866 that the destitution of landless freedmen was appalling. He was alarmed by the nascent share-cropping and crop-lien systems that were taking root in the South. The Negroes "appear to have neither mind nor hope above their present condition, and will continue to work on from day to day, and from year to year, without more than enough to keep soul and body together," wrote the traveler. "When addressing their masters, they take off their hats, and speak in a hesitating, trembling manner, as though they were in the presence of a Superior Being." The freedman could never improve his status as long as he remained landless and penniless. "No other government ever ended a great rebellion before without confiscating the estates of principal rebels, and placing that mighty power, the landed interest, on its side."[45]

In the spring of 1867 abolitionists stepped up their agitation for confiscation, hoping to win public support for such a policy before the next session of Congress. The *Boston Commonwealth* published a series of militant editorials, some of them by Elizur

[44] Bentley, *Freedmen's Bureau*, 134, 144-46; Patrick W. Riddleberger, "George W. Julian: Abolitionist Land Reformer," *Agricultural History*, v (July 1955), 110; *Independent*, July 5, 1866; *Commonwealth*, July 14, 1866; *Right Way*, July 14, 1866; *N.A.S. Standard*, Dec. 18, 1869. See also Paul W. Gates, "Federal Land Policy in the South, 1866-1888," *Journal of Southern History*, vi (Aug. 1940), 304-10.

[45] Article by the Rev. John Savary in *N.A.S. Standard*, Nov. 3, 1866.

Wright, calling for expropriation. Wright chided "practical" Republican politicians who shrank from the radicalism of confiscation: "O ye mighty 'practical' men! don't you know—are you not sensible—does it not ever enter your noddles to suspect—that if you have thirty thousand disloyal nabobs to own more than half the land of the South, they, and nobody else, will *be* the South? That they laugh, now in their sleeves, and by-and-bye will laugh out of their sleeves, at your schoolma'ams and ballot-boxes? *They who own the real estate of a country control its vote.*"[46]

At the annual meeting of the American Anti-Slavery Society in May 1867, Phillips introduced a resolution urging agrarian reform in the South as "an act of justice" to the Negro. Several speakers supported the resolution. Higginson said that confiscation "is an essential part of abolition. To give to these people only freedom, without the land, is to give them only the mockery of freedom which the English or the Irish peasant has." Without land the Negro voter would be at the mercy of the planter, who could use economic coercion to dictate his vote. "The time will come," said Higginson, "when the nation must recognize that even political power does not confer safety upon a race of landless men." Phillips' resolution was adopted almost unanimously by the Society.[47] The New England Anti-Slavery Society passed a similar resolution three weeks later. In the following months Phillips hammered away relentlessly at the confiscation theme. "What we want to give the negro is what the masses must have or they are practically serfs, the world over," he declared. Confiscation during the French Revolution crippled the aristocracy; confiscation uprooted Toryism in the American Revolution. "Land is the usual basis of government," said Phillips; "the class that hold it must, in the long run, give tone and character to the Administration. It is manifestly suicidal, therefore, to leave it in the hands of the hostile party."[48]

But abolitionists were fighting a losing battle on the confiscation front. A majority of the Republican party was opposed to the measure. The *New York Times* thought that "the colored race is likely to be injured, rather than aided, by this sycophantic and

---

[46] *Commonwealth*, Mar. 23, 1867. See also *ibid.*, Mar. 30, Apr. 6, 1867.
[47] *N.A.S. Standard*, May 18, 25, 1867.
[48] *ibid.*, June 8, 15, 1867.

extravagant crusade on its behalf." The *Times* urged friends of the freedmen to teach the lessons of labor, patience, frugality, and virtue to the Negro rather than demand special favors for him. Horace Greeley thought the agitation for confiscation was "either knavery or madness. People who want farms work for them. The only class we know that takes other people's property because they want it is largely represented in Sing Sing."[49] The Democratic gains in the 1867 elections put a virtual end to the drive for confiscation. The mood of radicalism which might have sustained confiscation in 1866 or 1867 had passed away. There was no longer any chance (if indeed there ever had been) that Congress would pass a confiscation bill or any other wholesale measure to provide farms for the freedmen.

In 1869 abolitionists set forth a new plan to obtain land for the freedmen. Aaron M. Powell, editor of the *Anti-Slavery Standard*, drew up a petition urging Congress to create a federal land commission, to be composed of "well-known, disinterested friends of the freed people." The commission would be capitalized at $2,000,000 by the U.S. Treasury and empowered to buy up large tracts of available southern land for resale in small lots to the freedmen at low cost and on easy terms. The commission would also be authorized to make loans to the freedmen for transportation, tools, implements, building materials, and seed. Abolitionists circulated the petition widely in 1869-1870, obtaining thousands of signatures from southern freedmen as well as their northern sympathizers. A Tennessee congressman introduced a bill to create such a land commission, but it died in committee, the last monument to Congress's failure to place the freedmen in a position of economic viability.[50]

Abolitionists backed several private schemes to settle the freedmen on farms of their own. In 1865 a group of Boston and New York capitalists incorporated the "American Land Company and Agency," with Governor John Andrew as president. George L. Stearns was one of the largest stockholders in this company, whose purpose was to channel northern investment into the South to help rebuild the section's economy and settle as many freedmen as possible on land of their own. Andrew and Stearns rea-

---

[49] *New York Times*, June 1, Oct. 26, 1867; *New York Tribune*, June 20, 1867.
[50] *N.A.S. Standard*, Dec. 18, 25, 1869, Jan. 29, Feb. 5, 12, 26, Mar. 12, 1870.

soned that the war had left southern planters poor in everything except land. They planned to buy part of this land in order to provide the planters with enough capital to farm the remainder. The company could then resell some of its purchased property to the freedmen. Things went badly from the beginning, however. The company invested heavily in Tennessee cotton plantations, but crop failures in 1866 ate up most of the capital. Stearns' death in the spring of 1867 brought the enterprise to bankruptcy and failure.[51]

Not all of the private efforts to provide freedmen with land were failures. In 1865 John G. Fee, a Kentucky-born abolitionist and cofounder of Berea College, purchased 130 acres in central Kentucky and resold the land in small tracts to freedmen, who established a village on the property. In 1891 there were 42 families living in this village. Fee urged the American Missionary Association to go into the business of selling land to the freedmen. In 1868 the A.M.A. began purchasing plantations for resale to Negroes. On each tract of land the A.M.A. established a church and school, and several small agricultural villages grew up in the South around these A.M.A. centers. The A.F.U.C. also had a small fund for the purchase and resale of farms to the freedmen. In 1869 a group of Boston abolitionists and philanthropists purchased a plantation in Georgia and started a "Southern Industrial School and Labor Enterprise." William and Ellen Craft, a couple who had escaped from slavery before the war, went to Georgia to manage the enterprise. They were accompanied by Yankee farmers who taught the freedmen the latest methods of planting, seeding, plowing, and so on. The freedmen attended the vocational and agricultural school part of the day and worked in the fields the rest of the time. They were encouraged to save their wages to buy land for themselves. The Ku Klux Klan burned the crop and buildings of the plantation in 1871, but the Crafts rebuilt the school and carried on in Georgia until 1878, when they sold the plantation in small tracts to the freedmen and returned to Boston.[52]

[51] Henry G. Pearson, *The Life of John A. Andrew* (2 vols., Boston, 1904), II, 267-69; Frank P. Stearns, *The Life and Public Services of George Luther Stearns* (Phila., 1907), 352.

[52] John G. Fee, *Autobiography* (Chicago, 1891), 182-83; Drake, "American Missionary Association," 115-19; McKim to O. O. Howard, Nov. 27, 1866, Howard to McKim, Dec. 1, 1866, McKim Papers, Cornell; *N.A.S. Standard*, Nov. 6,

One of the most ambitious abolitionist efforts to secure land for the freedmen by private investment was a plan developed by Charles Stearns, an old-line Garrisonian from Springfield, Massachusetts. In 1854 Stearns had gone to Kansas to fight for freedom, and in 1860 he drifted west to Colorado Territory. He went to Georgia in May 1866, and purchased a 1,500-acre plantation near Augusta. He hoped to run the plantation for a few years on the cooperative principle and then sell it in small tracts to the freedmen who had worked for him.[53]

Stearns was filled with enthusiasm for his project when he first came South. He established night and Sunday schools to teach his laborers to read and write. Southern neighbors told him that he could never "manage the niggers" with kindness, but would be compelled to use force and punishment if he wanted to get any work out of them. Stearns hoped to prove his neighbors wrong. He substituted kindness, incentive bonuses, and moral suasion for insults and punishment. In a summary of his experiences written several lears later, Stearns admitted that the practical realities of the situation had soon modified his enthusiasm. The freedmen were inefficient workers and destroyed tools and implements by their carelessness. Stearns almost succumbed to disillusionment and despair several times. But he always rallied himself with the thought that slavery was a poor school for efficiency, honesty, or skill, and returned to work with renewed dedication. He later evaluated his experiment as a success. After six years the Negroes on his plantation were better educated, more honest, and more industrious than when he first came.[54]

Inability to pay off the mortgage on his plantation forced Stearns to postpone his plans to sell the land to his employees. In 1869 his creditors threatened to foreclose, and Stearns hurried to Boston to raise $6,000 to pay the mortgage. Samuel Sewall and Wendell Phillips listened sympathetically to Stearns' proposition. Sewall gave him a $1,000 loan, and Phillips and Sewall

---

20, 1869; L. M. Child to Elisa Scudder, Feb. 6, 1870, Child to Lucy Osgood, Feb. 14, 1870, Child Papers, Cornell; *Commonwealth*, Aug. 16, 1873; Garrison to Fanny Garrison Villard, June 14, 1878, Garrison Papers, BPL.

[53] Charles Stearns to Garrison, Jan. 21, 1863, in *Liberator*, Mar. 20, 1863; Stearns to Garrison, Mar. 27, 1865, in *Liberator*, Apr. 21, 1865; Charles Stearns, *The Black Man of the South, and the Rebels* (New York, 1872), 20-39.

[54] *ibid.*, 28, 49-54, 59-71, 115-16, 164, and passim.

helped him raise the remaining $5,000. He returned to Georgia and inaugurated his plan to sell the plantation in 25-acre lots to the Negroes. Only 20 freedmen were able to buy during the first year, and some of them soon fell behind on their payments. By the end of 1870 Stearns was in debt again and about ready to give up in despair. "I am certain I can never cultivate a farm successfully with the blacks as laborers," he wrote in his diary. "Nothing can be done without incessant and minute supervision of them, such as I am not able to give." He almost sold the plantation to one of his white neighbors, but his mother, who had come South to teach the freedmen, convinced him that to do so would be a breach of faith with the Negroes he had worked so hard to help. Stearns heeded her pleas. He stayed on for another year and began writing a book about his experiences in an effort to promote northern interest in the needs of the freedmen.[55]

In 1872 Stearns brought a group of 50 Massachusetts farmers and missionaries to his plantation to establish an agricultural and industrial colony. The Yankee farmers soon transformed the establishment into a model of efficiency and neatness. Most of the Negroes stayed on the plantation and tried to learn better methods of farming from the Yankees. Stearns returned to Boston to finish his book and to set on foot a project for northern purchase and resale of southern plantations to freedmen. In 1873 he organized a "Laborers' Homestead and Southern Emigration Society" with a planned capitalization of $50,000. Samuel Gridley Howe served as president, and Stearns, Phillips, and James Buffum (an abolitionist) acted as a three-man board of trustees. The Society purchased some property in Virginia to start their experiment. Stearns sent out hundreds of circulars urging capitalists to invest in his Society. Lands purchased by the trustees would be resold in 25-acre tracts on easy terms to freedmen and northern settlers. The Society planned also to make loans to the purchasers to enable them to buy tools, seed, and implements. Stearns had grandiose plans for his Society. He urged Congress to lend it $1,000,000 per year for ten years. Congress took no note of his appeal, however, and the panic of 1873 soon dried up Stearns'

[55] Stearns to Gerrit Smith, June 26, 1869, Smith Papers, su; *Commonwealth*, July 24, 1869; *N.A.S. Standard*, Sept. 25, Nov. 20, 1869; Stearns, *The Black Man of the South*, 154-55, 170, 258-75, 278-319; quotation from *ibid.*, p. 279.

meager sources of private capital. Apart from the Georgia plantation and the property in Virginia he had little to show for his efforts. He had established one agricultural colony and sold land to several dozen freedmen. It was a rather small ending to an ambitious beginning.[56]

In 1880 Frederick Douglass attributed the failure of Reconstruction to the refusal of Congress to provide the freedmen with an opportunity to obtain good land of their own. "Could the nation have been induced to listen to those stalwart Republicans, Thaddeus Stevens and Charles Sumner, some of the evils which we now suffer would have been averted," declared Douglass. "The negro would not today be on his knees, as he is, supplicating the old master class to give him leave to toil. . . . He would not now be swindled out of his hard earnings by money orders for wages with no money in them."[57] Many abolitionists still alive in 1880 would have agreed with Douglass. They had done their best to call attention to the necessity of land for the freedmen, but the nation was not sympathetic enough toward the plight of the Negro to provide any adequate means by which he could obtain land. As a result the Negroes remained economically a subordinate class, dependent upon white landowners or employers for their livelihood. The South was not "reconstructed" economically, and consequently the other measures of reconstruction rested upon an unstable foundation.

[56] *ibid.*, 319-25, 512-42; Stearns to Gerrit Smith, Feb. 17, 1873, Feb. 4, 11, 1874, Smith Papers, su; *Commonwealth*, June 27, Sept. 19, 1874; Stearns to Garrison, Dec. 12, 1876, Garrison Papers, bpl.

[57] Speech of Douglass at Elmira, New York, Aug. 1, 1880, copy in Douglass Papers, Anacostia.

XVIII ✦ THE CLIMAX OF THE CRU-
SADE: THE FIFTEENTH
AMENDMENT

THE presidential election of 1868 was crucial for the cause
of Negro suffrage: a Republican victory would insure continuation of the congressional reconstruction program; a Democratic triumph would probably foreshadow the overthrow of
radical reconstruction and the readmission of southern states
without Negro suffrage. It was almost inevitable that General
Grant, the nation's foremost military hero, would be the leading
contender for the presidency. Both the Republicans and the
Democrats realized that Grant would probably be the next president, and from 1865 to 1868 they jockeyed to win his political
affections.

As early as 1866 Wendell Phillips began trying to stop the
Republican swing toward Grant. Grant's Democratic affiliations
before the war, his conservative report on southern conditions
in 1865, and his accompaniment of President Johnson on the famous Swing Around the Circle campaign in 1866 caused radicals
to distrust him. As general of the army, Grant was gravitating
toward a radical concept of reconstruction in 1866-1867, but his
public silence left most observers uncertain of his views on politics.
During his lecture tour of 1866-67 Phillips repeatedly disparaged
Grant as a political leader. In these days of crisis, said Phillips,
the country could not afford an inarticulate president who probably lacked the brains to form his own political opinions. But
Phillips' unfavorable references to Grant were poorly received by
his audiences—an indication of the widespread popular support
for the taciturn general.[1]

Most abolitionists in 1867 concurred with Phillips' appraisal
of Grant. Many of them, like Phillips, had no particular alternative candidate in mind. But one group of radicals, led by Tilton
and Greeley, was definitely backing Chase for the Republican
nomination. The next president "ought to be a man with whom the

[1] *N.A.S. Standard*, Nov. 3, 1866, May 18, 25, June 15, 1867.

love of Liberty has been a life-long passion; with whom Political Equality is a cherished idea," declared Tilton. "He ought to be a man whose life has been identified with the great controversy of principles which ended in the overthrow of American Slavery; not a man who has been indifferent all his life long to the greatest moral movement of modern times." The *Independent* and the *New York Tribune* published frequent editorials favoring Chase in 1867.[2]

But political availability, not principle, was uppermost in the minds of most Republican leaders. By the summer of 1867 it was clear that Grant would be the Republican nominee unless some unforeseen event intervened. Radical leaders tried to quiet abolitionist fears of Grant's conservatism. "It looks now as if Gen. Grant would inevitably be the next President," Oliver Johnson informed Garrison in July 1867. "Such being the fact I am happy in being assured by Senator Wilson and others that he is in thorough sympathy with Congress in all that pertains to reconstruction and that he loathes and hates the whole Copperhead party."[3] But disturbing signs continued to disquiet the abolitionists. When Grant accepted the office of secretary of war *ad interim* after Johnson's ouster of Stanton in August 1867, the shock was felt all through the Republican party. Although Grant had advised against the suspension of Stanton and had protested the removal of General Sheridan from command of the Southwestern military district, many radicals believed that by accepting office under Johnson, Grant had made himself a tool of the president's attempt to overturn congressional reconstruction. "If Grant is a Republican, by what rule of party fidelity does he accept the office out of which Stanton has been turned simply for being a Republican?" asked Phillips. "To-day Grant is the staff which holds up the traitor President. Without him Johnson could neither stand nor walk."[4]

But Grant was still the Republican party's best hope to win the presidency. Republican leaders pointed out (truthfully) that Grant continued to enforce congressional reconstruction and that

[2] *Independent*, May 30, July 11, Oct. 24, 1867; *New York Tribune*, Apr. 12, 15, Nov. 7, 13, 22, Dec. 30, 1867. Quotation from *Independent*, May 30, 1867.
[3] Johnson to Garrison, July 29, 1867, Garrison Papers, BPL.
[4] *Independent*, Aug. 15, 29, Sept. 5, 1867; *N.A.S. Standard*, Aug. 3, 24, Sept. 7, 1867. Quotation from *ibid.*, Aug. 24, 1867.

his presence in the War Office probably prevented Johnson from further obstructionism. The *New York Tribune* and *Independent* were still backing Chase, and it was rumored that such radical leaders as Sumner and Julian were opposed to Grant's nomination. But a majority of the Republican party remained pledged to the general.[5]

Wendell Phillips, Anna Dickinson, and other abolitionists continued to criticize Grant during the winter of 1867-1868. He was "the great American riddle!" said Phillips. "Out of twenty millions of people who have watched him for six years, there is not one who knows his opinions."[6] But most abolitionists by this time realized that the general's nomination was inevitable. Grant's prompt relinquishment of the War Office when the Senate refused to concur in Stanton's suspension and the subsequent controversy between Johnson and Grant raised the latter's prestige in the eyes of many radicals. Chase's flirtation with the Democrats and his handling of Johnson's impeachment trial caused a collapse of the faltering Chase movement. Grant was nominated unanimously at the Republican convention in Chicago on May 21.[7]

Abolitionists hoped for endorsement by the Republican platform of a constitutional amendment to enact Negro suffrage. As early as December 1867, the Boston correspondent of the *New York Tribune* reported that Republicans in New England were determined "to see that the General shall be put upon a sound Republican platform. . . . Wendell Phillips, who has as great an influence on political affairs as any man can have who is outside of political organizations, is doing something by lectures to stimulate this feeling." Tilton wrote in April 1868, "Our demand, in case of General Grant's nomination, is, that as he is not popularly known to hold any political opinions, the platform on which he is to stand shall be unequivocally for Impartial Suffrage, North and South."[8]

5 *Commonwealth*, Aug. 31, Sept. 7, Nov. 16, 1867; *Independent*, Oct. 24, 1867; *New York Tribune*, Nov. 7, 13, 22, 1867; Edward L. Pierce, *Memoir and Letters of Charles Sumner* (4 vols., Boston, 1877-94), IV, 358; George Julian, *Political Recollections* (Chicago, 1884), 319.

6 *Commonwealth*, Nov. 9, 1867. See also *N.A.S. Standard*, Jan. 18, Feb. 1, 15, 29, 1868; *Independent*, Jan. 2, 16, 1868.

7 *Commonwealth*, Feb. 1, 8, 15, 1868; *Independent*, Mar. 12, 19, Apr. 16, May 28, 1868; *N.A.S. Standard*, Mar. 21, 1868.

8 *New York Tribune*, quoted in *N.A.S. Standard*, Dec. 7, 1867; *Independent*, Apr. 9, 1868. See also *N.A.S. Standard*, Jan. 25, Feb. 1, 1868.

In the spring of 1868, however, the voters of Michigan turned down a new constitution that contained Negro suffrage. At the same time the Democrats were victorious in Connecticut for the second straight year. Moderate Republicans interpreted these defeats as a popular repudiation of Negro suffrage in the North. "Discreditable as the fact may be, it is pretty evident that the enfranchisement of the colored race in the Northern States will have to wait," stated the *Springfield Republican.* "The more immediate interests of reconstruction might be jeopardized by forcing the issue at this juncture." The *New York Times* predicted that moderate Republicans would defeat radical attempts to insert a national Negro suffrage plank into the Republican platform. "Even Wendell Phillips will stand an excellent chance of being unceremoniously thrown overboard," said the *Times*, "when the Convention undertakes to construct a platform for States, not one of which has committed itself to the negro suffrage principle."[9]

Despite these signs of conservative opposition, radicals and abolitionists mounted an all-out drive for Republican commitment to national Negro suffrage. "No reconstruction at the South will be safe and enduring which does not give the negro a national guarantee that he shall not be deprived of the ballot under the shield of 'State Sovereignty,' " declared the *Anti-Slavery Standard.* "Nor should the invidious distinctions now made against the blacks in the North be long allowed to continue." Thomas Wentworth Higginson chided northerners for their hypocritical willingness "that the negro should be a man at the South, to spite the white man, but not . . . that he should be a man at the North, when it offends their prejudices." Tilton considered it "a mockery of justice to ordain negro suffrage in one-half the states and to forbid it in the other." The Republicans would not deserve to win if they refused justice to the northern Negro. "To dodge the issue, or to cover it out of sight under some meaningless generality, would be moral depravity and political folly."[10]

[9] *Springfield Republican*, quoted in *The Revolution*, Apr. 23, 1868; *New York Times*, quoted in *N.A.S. Standard*, Apr. 25, 1868.

[10] *N.A.S. Standard*, Apr. 18, 1868; Higginson quoted in *ibid.*, May 30, 1868; *Independent*, May 14, 1868.

Conservatism triumphed at Chicago in spite of the radicals' best efforts. The Republican platform proclaimed that Negro suffrage in the South "was demanded by every consideration of public safety, of gratitude, and of justice," while "the question of suffrage in all the loyal States properly belongs to the people of those States." Sumner considered this suffrage plank "foolish & contemptible. The Democrats will have a great opportunity in exposing its Janus-faced character." The *Anti-Slavery Standard* denounced the failure of the platform to endorse national Negro suffrage as a "criminal blunder," and the New England Anti-Slavery Society declared it "a practical surrender of the whole question." But Senator Henry Wilson told Aaron Powell, editor of the *Anti-Slavery Standard*, that the weak suffrage plank was necessary if the Republicans were to carry doubtful northern states. Wilson assured Powell that once the election was over, Congress would adopt a Fifteenth Amendment. Theodore Tilton denounced the "mean-spirited" suffrage resolution. But he did not despair. He recalled that in 1860 the Republican party had promised not to interfere with slavery in the states, but four years later the party pledged itself to universal emancipation. "In like manner," said Tilton, "the Republican platform of 1868 may hint or imply that the Federal Government has no right to interfere with suffrage in the Northern States," but after the election this plank would "fall to pieces by its own rottenness."[11]

In June 1868, Congress readmitted seven southern states to the Union upon the "fundamental condition" that their constitutional provisions for equal suffrage would never be repealed. Most abolitionists opposed readmission of the former Confederate states at this time. The New England Anti-Slavery Society predicted that the "fundamental condition" would prove unenforceable, and urged the delay of readmission until a Fifteenth Amendment guaranteeing equal suffrage and public schools in every state had been ratified. The *Anti-Slavery Standard* considered readmission "premature." "The conditions of self-government," said the *Standard*, "do not yet exist at the South. To at once readmit

11 *New York Tribune*, May 22, 1868, published the Republican platform; Sumner to Frank Bird, May 28, 1868, Bird Papers, HU; *N.A.S. Standard*, May 30, 1868; resolution of the New England Anti-Slavery Society published in *ibid.*, June 6, 1868; Henry Wilson's statement cited in *ibid.*, June 13, 1868; *Independent*, May 28, June 18, 1868.

the reconstructed States and withdraw direct Federal control, is to expose the South unnecessarily to renewed strife, violence and bloodshed." Phillips charged that the Republicans were restoring the southern states for the sole purpose of gaining their votes in the presidential election. "No one claims that they are ready or fit for places in Congress," declared Phillips. "But the Grant party needs them. We sink principle and risk the negro in order to elect Mr. Grant."[12]

Phillips continued to hammer away at the Republicans during the summer of 1868 until it appeared to some observers that he was absolutely opposed to Grant's election. "Its faults are legion," said Phillips of the Republican party. "Its defects glaring. It has never been loyal to a single principle." Grant was wholly inadequate. "Of the half dozen catch-words that the Nation has extorted from his lips, not one has any relation to Liberty. The mottoes he has lent to politics, or history, are such as a bull-dog might have growled forth."[13] But in *Standard* editorials of August 29 and September 26 Phillips made it clear that he desired Republican victory. He described the Republican party as "shuffling, evasive, unprincipled, corrupt, cowardly and mean, almost beyond the power of words to describe. Still a vote for Grant means the negro's suffrage recognized; a vote for Seymour [the Democratic candidate] means the negro disfranchised and another war." Bad as the Republican party was, it contained the only radical elements in the country and gave promise of future improvement. Some of Phillips' more radical followers criticized his support of the "shuffling, evasive, corrupt" Republican party. But the Republican press hailed Phillips' endorsement, and most abolitionists pitched in to help elect Grant.[14]

Phillips' aversion to the Democrats was not unfounded. That party nominated Horatio Seymour and Frank Blair on a platform that denounced the Reconstruction Acts as "usurpations, and unconstitutional, revolutionary, and void," and called for the readmission of southern states without Negro suffrage. The

---

[12] *U.S. Statutes at Large*, xv, 72-74; *N.A.S. Standard*, May 23, June 13, June 20, 1868.

[13] *N.A.S. Standard*, Aug. 29, Sept. 26, 1868.

[14] *Revolution*, Sept. 10, Oct. 8, 1868; S. B. Anthony to Anna Dickinson, Oct. 27, 1868, Dickinson Papers, LC; *Commonwealth*, Oct. 3, 1868; *Boston Advertiser*, Oct. 28, 1868.

Democrats pitched their campaign on a key of racism and violence. Frank Blair, the party's vice-presidential candidate, declared that "there is but one way to restore the Government and the Constitution, and that is for the President-elect to declare these acts null and void, compel the army to undo its usurpations at the South, disperse the carpet-bag State Governments, [and] allow the White people to reorganize their own governments."[15] Blair repeatedly referred to Negroes as "semi-barbarous blacks," "idle vagabonds," and "degraded men." One of Seymour's supporters, Brick Pomeroy of the La Crosse Democrat, declared that if the Democrats received a majority of white votes in the election they should "march to Washington . . . and take their seats, and reinaugurate the white men's government, in spite of man or devils. . . . If this brings bloodshed, then let blood flow!"[16]

One southern white man entered the campaign proclaiming his belief that "the noble Gothic race is the one that should inhabit this continent, and the only one. It is the kind of beings that must rule America; and not only America, but the whole earth."[17] Southern whites backed their words with action. The Ku Klux Klan and similar organizations stepped up their activities during the campaign. The Republican and abolitionist press publicized (and probably exaggerated) southern violence against the freedmen as examples of what the Negro's "best friends" would do if the Democrats won the election. Garrison in particular waved the bloody shirt. The purpose of the Democratic party, he wrote, was "to disfranchise the entire colored population and give them over to the tender mercies of their former owners, . . . who are never so jubilant as when burning negroes alive by a slow fire." In September the conservative majority of the Georgia legislature expelled its 32 Negro members and replaced them with whites, many of whom could not even qualify for office under the terms of the Fourteenth Amendment. Here was a concrete example, said abolitionists, of what would happen all over the South if the Democrats won in November.[18]

15 New York Tribune, July 10, 1868; Independent, July 16, 1868.

16 La Crosse Democrat, quoted in N.A.S. Standard, Mar. 7, 1868. See also N.A.S. Standard, July 11, 18, 25, Aug. 1, 29, 1868.

17 Norfolk Journal, quoted in N.A.S. Standard, Nov. 7, 1868.

18 Statement by Garrison published in Independent, Aug. 13, 1868. Garrison also wrote articles for ibid., Oct. 1, 15, 22, 29, 1868. For a discussion of the

Abolitionists welcomed Grant's election as a triumph of liberty and equal rights. But they did not rest content with electoral victory. In the winter of 1868-1869 radicals opened an intensive drive for a constitutional amendment to enact Negro suffrage nationally. The adoption of Negro suffrage by substantial majorities in Iowa and Minnesota in November 1868, gave an important fillip to the movement for a Fifteenth Amendment. Gilbert Haven expressed the prevailing feeling among abolitionists when he declared that the North could no longer deny justice to its own colored citizens while compelling the South to maintain equal rights. "It is the worst sore in the Southern heart to-day that they are required to receive what the North will not give itself," said Haven. "We have no moral right to impose an obligation on one part of the land which the rest will not accept. We can have no peace till this right is made national."[19]

Prominent Republican newspapers backed the drive for a Fifteenth Amendment. Several equal suffrage amendments were introduced in both Houses when Congress met in December 1868. These amendments fell into three general categories. The first type would have simply prohibited the states from denying the ballot on grounds of race, color, or previous condition. The second type of amendment would also have forbidden states to impose literacy, property, or nativity qualifications upon suffrage. The third class of amendment would have nationalized suffrage by giving the federal government complete control over voting rights in every state.[20]

Abolitionists favored, at least in theory, a broad amendment that would prohibit the imposition of literacy or property as well as racial qualifications upon the franchise. Richard Hinton declared that the form of amendment that forbade only racial disfranchisement "will not prevent any State adopting a property qualification, one of education, or any similar dodge."[21] But on

---

expulsion of Negro members from the Georgia legislature, see C. Mildred Thompson, *Reconstruction in Georgia* (New York, 1915), 211-16.

[19] *Zion's Herald*, Dec. 10, 1868. See also *Independent*, Nov. 5, 12, 19, 1868; *N.A.S. Standard*, Nov. 14, 21, Dec. 12, 1868.

[20] John M. Mathews, *Legislative and Judicial History of the Fifteenth Amendment* (Baltimore, 1909), 21-32.

[21] *N.A.S. Standard*, Dec. 12, 1868. See also *ibid.*, Nov. 21, 1868, Jan. 23, Feb. 6, 1869.

January 30, 1869, the House passed an amendment stipulating that "the right of any citizen of the United States to vote shall not be denied or abridged by the United States or any State by reason of race, color, or previous condition of servitude." The *Anti-Slavery Standard* protested that there was nothing in this amendment to prevent "future State application of unequal tests of education or property. Landless and almost without schools, [the freedmen] are at a great disadvantage, and there will be no stone left unturned by which to compass their political subjugation by the old ruling white class." Tilton also demanded protection of the freedmen against disfranchisement by literacy or property qualifications. Under the House-passed amendment, he wrote, "the Southern States may invent a dozen cunning schemes to defraud the negro of his franchise."[22]

Several senators agreed with Tilton, and on February 9 the Senate passed an amendment forbidding the denial of suffrage on grounds of "race, color, nativity, property, education, or creed." A storm of protest immediately arose from many Republicans who favored Negro suffrage. They argued that such a comprehensive amendment could never be ratified by the requisite number of states. Massachusetts and Connecticut required a literacy test, Rhode Island imposed a property qualification upon naturalized citizens, and the "nativity" provision would almost certainly run afoul of the anti-Chinese sentiment in California, Oregon, and Nevada. The *Boston Commonwealth* preferred "as an abstract proposition" the Senate version "because it makes suffrage less restricted than might possibly result from the House's limitation." But as a practical matter the *Commonwealth* favored the House amendment, for it seemed certain that the Senate version could not be ratified. The House-passed amendment was sufficient for present purposes, said the *Commonwealth*, "and if any one State, upon the adoption of the amendment, shall make invidious and unjust discriminations against any class of citizens, both Congress by appropriate legislation, and the Supreme Court by decisions in the spirit of the amendment, will remedy the wrong."[23]

22 *Cong. Globe*, 40 Cong., 3 Sess., 286, 742-45; *N.A.S. Standard*, Feb. 6, 1869; *Independent*, Feb. 11, 1869.

23 *Cong. Globe*, 40 Cong., 3 Sess., 1,044; Mathews, *Fifteenth Amendment*, 33-35; *Commonwealth*, Feb. 6, 13, 20, 1869.

The House refused to concur in the Senate amendment, and a deadlock ensued between the two Houses that threatened to prevent passage of any amendment at all before Congress adjourned on March 4. At this critical juncture Wendell Phillips published an important editorial in the *Anti-Slavery Standard*. In a statement that must have surprised nearly every reader, Phillips chastised the Senate for being too radical. The Fifteenth Amendment was confronted by "an emergency which calls for the most delicate handling," he wrote. The amendment passed by the House covered "all the ground that the people are ready to occupy." The Senate's attempt to prohibit educational, property, and nativity qualifications, said Phillips, "is utter lack of common sense, . . . a total forgetfulness of the commonest political prudence." Phillips urged Senate concurrence in the House amendment. "For the first time in our lives we beseech them to be a little more *politicians*—and a little less reformers." The editor of the *New York Times* blinked his eyes in amazement at Phillips' editorial. "The event is notable," said the *Times*. "That must have been rashness which elicits from the champion of all innovations a protest against its folly."[24]

Phillips' statement helped break the congressional deadlock and pave the way for Senate concurrence in the House version of the amendment. Congressman George Boutwell of Massachusetts, leader of the House forces supporting a Fifteenth Amendment, wrote Phillips a letter thanking him for his timely editorial. "That article saved the amendment," said Boutwell. "Its influence was immediate and potential. Men thought that if you, the extremest radical, could accept the House proposition they might safely do the same." Boutwell later told friends that without Phillips' editorial "the Fifteenth Amendment to the Constitution would have been lost in the Senate." Boutwell wrote in his memoirs that Phillips' "name and opinion settled the controversy."[25] It was one of the ironies of Reconstruction that the nation's greatest radical and equalitarian was partly responsible for adoption of a Fifteenth Amendment whose loopholes later allowed southern

[24] *N.A.S. Standard*, Feb. 20, 1869; *New York Times*, Feb. 19, 1869.

[25] Boutwell to Phillips, Mar. 13, 1870, printed in George S. Boutwell, *Reminiscences of Sixty Years in Public Affairs* (2 vols., New York, 1902), II, 48-50; *Commonwealth*, Apr. 30, 1870; Oliver Johnson, *William Lloyd Garrison and His Times* (2nd ed., Boston, 1885), 41; Boutwell, *Reminiscences*, II, 46.

states to disfranchise their Negroes. But Phillips and Boutwell were probably right in 1869. The Senate version could not have been ratified, and if Congress had not passed the simpler House amendment at that time there may not have been another opportunity for a Negro suffrage amendment for several decades. Phillips' editorial, therefore, was instrumental in creating a constitutional framework for Negro suffrage that might not have otherwise existed.

"What shall be said at the annual meeting of the American An[ti]-Slavery Society?" asked Frederick Douglass in April 1869. "There really seems not much to be said. Fifteenth amendment is on its [way to] passage, and is in a fair way to become a part of the organic law of the land." Many other people shared this belief that the antislavery movement no longer had any causes to agitate. Phillips and Tilton publicly declared that ratification of the Fifteenth Amendment would take the Negro question out of politics. Most abolitionists seemed to agree with this view, for the American Anti-Slavery Society resolved at its annual convention in May 1869, that the Fifteenth Amendment was "the capstone and completion of our movement; the fulfillment of our pledge to the Negro race; since it secures to them equal political rights with the white race, or, if any single right be still doubtful, places them in such circumstances that they can easily achieve it."[26]

But several delegates cautioned that the work of the abolitionists was not yet finished. Henry Wilson told the assembled crusaders that their mission would not be accomplished until the Negro was equal in fact as well as law. The convention resolved that social discrimination against Negroes "fully justifies the continued and earnest remonstrance of this Society." In one of his speeches to the meeting Phillips stated that "even with the ratification of the Fifteenth Amendment, our work is not done." As an organization the antislavery society could dissolve, but as individuals abolitionists must continue to work against segregation, discrimination, and inequality with every means at their command. There was a "continued obligation resting upon Abolitionists,

26 Frederick Douglass to Tilton, Apr. 24, 1869, autograph MS, PML; *N.A.S. Standard*, Mar. 27, 1869; *Independent*, Apr. 8, 1869; resolution of the American Anti-Slavery Society published in *N.A.S. Standard*, May 15, 1869.

individually, never to cease their individual and collateral work, in all the various forms in which a man can influence his times, to blot out the idea of race in the minds of the American people," said Phillips. "In regard to those great social forces which still continue in their influence to shape the future, our work is not done; we probably never shall live to see it done."[27]

By the end of 1869 the Fifteenth Amendment, capstone of the abolitionist crusade, appeared certain of ratification. Even in their rejoicing, however, abolitionists once again warned each other that they must not let down their guard. Despite the advances made since 1861, said John Sargent, the Negro did not yet enjoy "the fulness of those social rights, relations, and privileges . . . without which all this pretence of his freedom is but an idle sham and a tantalizing mockery." Lydia Maria Child said, "The passage of the Fifteenth Amendment will give a legal finish to the Anti-Slavery work," but the Amendment might "yet be so evaded, by some contrivance, that the colored population will in reality have no civil rights allowed them."[28] Wendell Phillips promised that dissolution of the antislavery societies would not be a signal for abolitionists to retire from their life's work. On the contrary, said Phillips, the *Anti-Slavery Standard* would be continued under the title *The Standard*. It would crusade for labor reform, women's rights, temperance, and racial equality. Aaron Powell called for renewed abolitionist dedication to equal social and economic rights for all men. Powell promised that "if not in the name of the *Anti-Slavery* Societies, then under some other —if not in the ANTI-SLAVERY STANDARD, then in a journal to be known simply as THE STANDARD, we shall press our demand earnestly and conscientiously until FREEDOM shall mean as much for the colored, as for the white people of America."[29]

The Fifteenth Amendment became part of the Constitution on March 30, 1870. This event touched off a general chorus of praise and tribute to the old abolitionists, especially Phillips. A correspondent of the *Troy* (New York) *Whig* wrote that "all the old epithets that used to defile [the abolitionists'] reputation have

[27] *N.A.S. Standard*, May 15, 22, 29, June 5, 1869.

[28] Sargent quoted in *N.A.S. Standard*, Nov. 27, 1869; Child quoted in *ibid.*, Dec. 25, 1869.

[29] *ibid.*, Feb. 5, 12, Mar. 12, 1870; Powell's statement quoted from *ibid.*, Feb. 5, 1870.

turned into trophies of their march, and are worn as wreaths of laurel. Yes, to have been an abolitionist is simply an honor now." Speaking for his race, Frederick Douglass praised Phillips as the foremost architect of the Fifteenth Amendment. "None have been more vigilant, clear-sighted, earnest, true and eloquent. Without office, without party, only a handful at his back, he has done more to lead and mould public opinion in favor of equal suffrage than any man I know of." And in a private letter Senator Henry Wilson declared: "More than to any other, more than to all others, the colored people owe it that they were not cheated out of their citizenship after emancipation, to Wendell Phillips."[30]

The executive committee of the American Anti-Slavery Society met and decided to dissolve the organization. The Society's constitution pledged its members to work for equal civil and political rights for Negroes. These rights had been attained, and the Society no longer had a formal reason for existence. Abolitionists gathered in New York on April 9, 1870, to disband their societies and commemorate the final victory of their organized crusade. The veteran agitators met in a festive mood. Congratulatory letters from dozens of politicians, journalists, and fellow reformers were read to the assemblage. Several abolitionists urged that the Society remain in existence to combat race prejudice, help the freedmen obtain land of their own, and agitate for strict enforcement of equal rights in the South. But Phillips, Douglass, and others maintained that these activities were outside the formal sphere of the Society. Abolitionists should remain vigilant, however, and carry on individually or in new organizations their work for the Negro. "Our long crusade for him is not therefore really and fully ended," said Phillips. "We may break up our ranks, but we may not yet dismiss our care nor lessen our interest. While this generation lasts it is probable the negro will need the special sympathy of his friends. The victim of cruel prejudice, of long disfranchisement, of accumulated wrongs, . . . he must long struggle under heavy disadvantages."[31]

30 *Troy Whig,* quoted in *Commonwealth,* Apr. 30, 1870; *New National Era,* May 5, 1870; Wilson to Sumner, Apr. 19, 1870, quoted in Carlos Martyn, *Wendell Phillips: The Agitator* (New York, 1890), 374.
31 *N.A.S. Standard,* Apr. 16, 1870.

On the day after the commemorative meeting, Aaron Powell and several other abolitionists organized the "National Reform League" as a successor of the American Anti-Slavery Society. The purpose of the League was to achieve desegregation of schools and public accommodations in the North, agitate for enforcement of equal rights in the South, and in general to watch over the welfare of the Negro.[32] Never very strong, the Reform League faded out of existence by 1872. For all practical purposes the *organizational* history of American abolitionism came to an end in 1870. As individuals most abolitionists remained active and vigilant in the cause of the Negro for the rest of their lives. But the militant antislavery crusade reached its climax and consummation in 1870, the year the Fifteenth Amendment was adopted.

✦

The abolitionists could look back with considerable satisfaction in 1870 upon the achievements of the past decade. Most of the measures they had originally advocated had been adopted: the immediate and universal abolition of slavery, the enlistment of Negro soldiers, government assistance for the education of freedmen, the creation of a Freedmen's Bureau, and the incorporation of the Negro's civil and political equality into the law of the land. Abolitionists themselves had been transformed by the crucible of war from troublesome fanatics to prophets honored in their own country.

But the next decade was to prove that many of the equalitarian achievements of the Civil War and Reconstruction were built on a foundation of sand. The freedom and equality of the Negro were based in part on the idealistic traditions of the abolitionist movement, but in greater part on the military and political exigencies of war and reconstruction. The North's conversion to emancipation and equal rights was primarily a conversion of expediency rather than one of conviction. The South was converted only by force. A policy based on "military necessity" may be abandoned when the necessity disappears, and this is what happened in the 1870's. It became expedient for northern

[32] *National Standard*, I (May 1870), 46-48, Apr. 29, May 13, 1871; Aaron Powell to George Julian, Feb. 24, 1871, Giddings-Julian Correspondence, LC; John K. Wildman to Sumner, Mar. 14, 1871, Sumner Papers, HU,

political and business interests to conciliate southern whites, and an end to federal enforcement of Negro equality in the South was the price of conciliation. The mass of northern people had never loved the Negro, were tired of the "everlasting negro question," and were glad to see the end of it.

A few abolitionists acquiesced in the northern abandonment of Reconstruction, but most of them protested strongly against it. Not many northerners, however, listened to their protests after 1875. Abolitionists were not slow to discern and deplore the North's return to apathy. It was startling "to realize how completely the antislavery struggle is forgotten by the people, and how even the terrible expenditure of blood and treasure, which followed it, is fast sinking into oblivion," wrote Lydia Maria Child in 1878. "The lamentable misfortune is that emancipation was not the result of a popular *moral sentiment*, but of a miserable 'military necessity.' It was not the 'fruit of righteousness,' and therefore it is not 'peace.' " Five years later Frederick Douglass declared that "as the war for the Union recedes into the misty shadows of the past, and the Negro is no longer needed to assault forts and stop rebel bullets, he is . . . of less importance. Peace with the old master class has been war to the Negro. As the one has risen, the other has fallen."[33]

Abolitionists had done their best to rally the conscience of the nation, but in the final analysis the nation refused to follow their leadership. Was this a "failure of the American abolitionists," as one historian has called it?[34] Perhaps. Such abolitionist techniques as incisive criticism, harsh language, and moral absolutism may have been ill-suited to the conversion of conscience. But in a larger sense, their failure was the failure of the American people, and the United States has yet to measure up to the ideals of the abolitionist crusade. The civil rights movement of today has a greater chance of permanent success than did its counterpart in the 1860's. But whatever success the contemporary movement finally does achieve will be built partly on the foundations laid down more than a century ago by the abolitionists. They

[33] Lydia Maria Child to George Julian, Sept. 28, 1878, Giddings-Julian Correspondence, LC; Philip S. Foner, ed., *The Life and Writings of Frederick Douglass* (4 vols., New York, 1950-55), IV, 355.

[34] Merton L. Dillon, "The Failure of the American Abolitionists," *Journal of Southern History*, XXV (May 1959), 159-77.

were the first "freedom riders," and their spirit still pervades the struggle for racial justice. The victories of Martin Luther King and his followers are, in a very real sense, victories of the abolitionist crusade.

BIBLIOGRAPHICAL ESSAY*

MANUSCRIPTS

The manuscript collections of individual abolitionists yielded rich results. The William Lloyd Garrison Papers, BPL, the largest and best organized collection of abolitionist letters in existence, contain the correspondence of a great many abolitionists besides Garrison's. The Garrison Family Papers, SC, include a large number of letters, clippings, and scrapbooks relating to the Garrison family. The William Lloyd Garrison Papers, NYHS, the Wendell Phillips Garrison Papers, HU, the Garrison Family Papers, RU, and the Fanny Garrison Villard Papers, HU, contain additional material of value.

The papers of many other Garrisonian abolitionists have been preserved. There are small collections of Susan B. Anthony's letters in the LC, NYHS, and SC. The Lydia Maria Child Papers, Cornell, contain many important letters from Mrs. Child to personal friends. Additional letters can be found in the Child-Whittier Correspondence, LC, the Child-Shaw Correspondence, NYPL, the Lydia and David Child Papers, BPL, the Child Papers, Radcliffe Women's Archives, and the Child Papers, Wayland (Mass.) Historical Society. The large collections of Moncure Conway Papers, CU, Anna Dickinson Papers, LC, and Sydney Howard Gay Papers, CU, are indispensable for an understanding of these three important Civil War figures. The J. Miller McKim Papers, Cornell, include letters from several abolitionists to McKim and letterbook copies of McKim's correspondence as secretary of the American Freedmen's Aid Commission and of the American Freedmen's Union Commission, 1865-68. The J. Miller McKim Papers, BPL, the J. Miller McKim Papers, NYPL, the McKim-Maloney-Garrison Papers, NYPL, and the Charles Follen McKim Papers, NYPL, contain additional material on the activities of McKim and his fellow abolitionists. The Samuel May, Jr., Papers, BPL, include a great deal of correspondence relating to the organizational aspects of the Garrisonian movement. The Samuel J. May Papers, BPL,

---

* For the sake of brevity the following abbreviations are used to designate the repositories of manuscript collections: AAS (The American Antiquarian Society, Worcester, Mass.); BPL (The Boston Public Library); CU (Columbia University Library); Cornell (Cornell University Library); HU (Houghton Library, Harvard University); LC (Library of Congress); MHS (Massachusetts Historical Society); NYHS (New York Historical Society); NYPL (New York Public Library); RU (Rochester University Library); SC (Smith College Library); SU (Syracuse University Library); VHS (Vermont Historical Society). The following abbreviations are used to designate periodicals: JNH (*Journal of Negro History*); JSH (*Journal of Southern History*); MVHR (*Mississippi Valley Historical Review*).

consist of letters from Samuel May, Jr., to his elder cousin, Samuel J. May. The Mary E. Estlin Papers, BPL, contain many letters from Garrisonian abolitionists to Mary Estlin, an English abolitionist. There are collections of the letters of Stephen S. Foster and Abby Kelley Foster in the AAS and the Worcester Historical Society. The Josephine S. Griffing Papers, CU, contain a small number of valuable letters relating to Mrs. Griffing's social welfare work among the freedmen of Washington. The small collections of Oliver Johnson Papers, VHS, Lucretia Mott Papers, SC, Wendell Phillips Papers, LC, Parker Pillsbury Papers, SC, the Quincy-Webb Correspondence, BPL, and the Edmund Quincy Papers, MHS, yielded some relevant information. The Elizabeth Cady Stanton Papers, LC, the Theodore Tilton Papers, NYHS, and the Weston Papers, BPL, include many important letters. The Records of the Board of Managers of the Massachusetts and New England Anti-Slavery Societies, bound MS volume, BPL, contain the minutes of the executive committee meetings of these two societies.

Non-Garrisonian abolitionists also diligently preserved their papers. The small collection of Francis W. Bird Papers, HU, contains several letters from Charles Sumner. The extensive Cheever Papers, AAS, include the letters and diaries of George and Henry Cheever, and many of the records of the Church Anti-Slavery Society. The James Freeman Clarke Papers, HU, and the Frederick Douglass Papers, Douglass Memorial Home, Anacostia Heights, Washington, D.C., were of limited value. The William Channing Gannett Papers, RU, include diaries, letters, and memoranda concerning Gannett's work among the Port Royal freedmen. The Thomas Wentworth Higginson Papers, HU, consist of diaries, journals, and scrapbooks as well as letters. The large collection of Samuel Gridley Howe Family Papers, HU, is restricted, and the author was able to consult only those letters to Howe from persons outside his family. The Sumner-Howe Correspondence, HU, contains letters from Charles Sumner to Samuel Gridley Howe. The Samuel Johnson Papers, Essex Institute, Salem, Mass., the Joshua Leavitt Papers, LC, the Loring Moody Papers, BPL, the John Pierpont Papers, Pierpont Morgan Library, the Franklin Sanborn Papers, Concord (Mass.) Public Library, and the Sanborn Papers, LC, were of minor value. The huge and well-indexed collection of Gerrit Smith Papers, SU, contains hundreds of letters from abolitionists during the 1860's. Two smaller collections of Gerrit Smith Papers are housed in the NYHS and the NYPL. The Lewis Tappan Papers, LC, contain letters to Tappan, journals, and letterbook copies of letters from Tappan. The William W. Thayer MS autobiography, LC, contains some interesting information on George L.

Stearns and the *Right Way*. The John G. Whittier Papers, Essex Institute, and the Whittier Papers, NYPL, were of limited importance. The Elizur Wright Papers, LC, include many relevant letters. The Miscellaneous Manuscript Collections of the LC, NYHS, and NYPL, and the Alfred Williams Anthony Autograph Collection, NYPL, contain several letters of abolitionists.

The papers of leading Republican politicians yielded considerable material relating to the abolitionists. The John A. Andrew Papers, MHS, and the large but unindexed collection of Benjamin Butler Papers, LC, were of limited importance. The Salmon P. Chase Papers, LC, on the other hand, are completely indexed, easy to use, and proved fruitful. The Joshua Giddings-George Julian Correspondence, LC, includes many letters from abolitionists to Julian. The Horace Greeley Papers, NYPL, and the Andrew Johnson Papers, LC, contain only a small number of abolitionist letters, but the Abraham Lincoln Papers (Robert Todd Lincoln Collection), LC, were unexpectedly rich in abolitionist materials. The Charles Sumner Papers, HU, include a very large number of important letters from abolitionists. The Thaddeus Stevens Papers, LC, and the Henry Wilson Papers, LC, were of limited value.

PUBLISHED CORRESPONDENCE, COLLECTED WRITINGS AND SPEECHES

Herbert Aptheker, ed., *Documentary History of the Negro People in the United States* (New York, 1951) contains many valuable items on the activities of Negro leaders during the 1860's. William H. Burleigh, *Poems by W. H. Burleigh. With a Sketch of His Life by Celia Burleigh* (New York, 1871) is useful for biographical information about this abolitionist poet. Jesse A. Marshall, ed., *The Private and Official Correspondence of Gen. Benjamin F. Butler during the Period of the Civil War* (5 vols., Norwood, Mass., 1917) includes several abolitionist letters. Lillie B. C. Wyman and Arthur Crawford Wyman, *Elizabeth Buffum Chace, 1806-1899* (2 vols., Boston, 1914) is especially valuable for its large number of letters from various abolitionists to Mrs. Chace. Harriet W. Sewall, ed., *Letters of Lydia Maria Child* (Boston, 1883) is poorly edited but helpful. Edward Everett Hale, ed., *James Freeman Clarke: Autobiography, Diary, and Correspondence* (Boston, 1891) is useful and informative. Philip S. Foner, *The Life and Writings of Frederick Douglass* (4 vols., New York, 1950-55) is invaluable. Vols. III and IV cover the period of the Civil War and Reconstruction. They contain private correspondence, speeches, and published writings. Ray Allen Billington, ed., *The Journal of Charlotte Forten* (New York, 1961 [1953]) is a superbly edited journal of a young northern Negro who came to the South Carolina sea islands to teach the freedmen. Sarah Hopper Emerson, *Life of Abby Hopper Gibbons, Told Chiefly Through Her Correspondence* (2 vols., New York, 1896-97) is a poorly organized but nevertheless valuable compilation. Gilbert Haven, *National Sermons, Speeches, and Letters on Slavery and Its War . . .* (Boston, 1869) sets forth the views of this radical, red-headed abolitionist clergyman. Laura E. Richards, ed., *Letters and Journals of Samuel Gridley Howe: The Servant of Humanity* (Boston, 1909) contains helpful information on the founding of the Emancipation League and the work of the American Freedmen's Inquiry Commission. John Jay, *Slavery and the War* (New York, 1868) is a collection of twenty-one pamphlets, speeches, and public letters by Jay during the war and early reconstruction years. Roy P. Basler, ed., *The Collected Works of Abraham Lincoln* (9 vols., New Brunswick, N.J.) contains information on Lincoln's relations with certain abolitionists. Elizabeth W. Pearson, ed., *Letters from Port Royal, Written at the Time of the Civil War* (Boston, 1906) is an indispensable source of information on the activities of the Gideonites. Wendell Phillips, *Speeches, Lectures, and Letters*, 1st Series (Boston, 1863) contains addresses by Phillips from 1837 to 1863. His *Speeches, Lectures, and Letters*, 2nd Series (Boston, 1891) includes speeches made from 1865 to 1881. By far the greater portion of Phillips' utterances on the Negro question, especially after 1863, are not published in these volumes. A. W. Stevens, ed., *Enfranchisement and Citizenship, Addresses and Papers of Edward L. Pierce* (Boston, 1896) includes several articles and reports by Pierce on freedmen's education. Mrs. William S. Robinson, ed., *"Warrington" Pen-Portraits: A Collection of . . . the Writings of William S. Robinson* (Boston, 1877) contains important excerpts from the diaries, letters, and articles of this Massachusetts free-soiler and abolitionist. Theodore Stanton and Harriot Stanton Blatch, *Elizabeth Cady Stanton, as Revealed in Her Letters, Diary, and Reminiscences* (2 vols., New York, 1922) includes many letters unavailable elsewhere. Gerrit Smith, *Speeches and Letters of Gerrit Smith . . . on the Rebellion* (2 vols. in 1, New York, 1864-65) contains Smith's wartime published letters and speeches from 1863-65. Charles Sumner, *The Works of Charles Sumner* (15 vols., Boston, 1870-73) include a considerable amount of material on Sumner's relations with abolitionists. Rupert S. Holland, ed., *Letters and Diary of Laura M. Towne, Written from the Sea Islands of South Carolina, 1862-84* (Cambridge, Mass., 1912) is useful for a portrayal of everyday life on the South Carolina sea islands. John Albree, ed., *Whittier Correspondence from Oakknoll* (Salem, Mass., 1911) contains several Whittier letters dealing with the issues of war and reconstruction.

John G. Whittier, *Anti-Slavery Poems: Songs of Labor and Reform* (vol. III of his *Poetical Works*, Riverside ed., Boston, 1888), and Whittier, *The Conflict with Slavery* (vol. III of his *Prose Works*, Riverside ed., Boston, 1889) contain Whittier's antislavery poems and prose writings from this period.

GOVERNMENT PUBLICATIONS AND ARCHIVES

The various issues of the *Congressional Globe, House Miscellaneous Documents, House Executive Documents, House Reports,* and the corresponding documents of the Senate were consulted where relevant. Edward McPherson, *The Political History of the United States of America during the Great Rebellion* (Washington, 1865), and *The Political History of the United States of America during the Period of Reconstruction* (Washington, 1871) contain reports, letters, orders, messages, public statements, and summaries of congressional action that are invaluable guides to the activities of the government. McPherson was clerk of the House of Representatives and had access to all government publications in the preparation of these volumes. James D. Richardson, ed., *The Messages and Papers of the Presidents* (20 vols., Washington, 1897-1913), and *The United States Statutes at Large* were also consulted. *War of the Rebellion: . . . Official Records of the Union and Confederate Armies* (128 vols., Washington, 1880-1901) contain a great deal of information on Negro soldiers and military administration of freedmen's affairs. *Special Report of the Commissioner of Education on the Condition and Improvement of Public Schools in the District of Columbia . . .* (Washington, D.C., 1871) is useful as a source of information about public education for Negroes in all the states as well as in the District of Columbia. Government publications and records concerning freedmen's education are overwhelming. They include several hundred linear feet of Freedmen's Bureau records in the National Archives, the annual reports of the commissioners and the superintendents of education of the Freedmen's Bureau, and various congressional and Treasury Department reports.

NEWSPAPERS

A. Abolitionist Newspapers

The *National Anti-Slavery Standard*, published weekly in New York, was the most important single source for this study. Oliver Johnson was editor-in-chief of the *Standard* until May 1865. Edmund Quincy was associate editor during the same period, and wrote most of the leading editorials. Parker Pillsbury and George W. Smalley took over as editors in May 1865. Smalley resigned early in 1866, and Pillsbury stepped down as editor soon afterward because of a disagreement with Phillips on the woman suffrage question. Aaron M. Powell succeeded Pillsbury as editor, and Phillips served as associate editor. Phillips wrote most of the leading editorials, and the paper was entirely under his influence after 1865. The *Standard's* circulation was never very large—it averaged less than 3,000 during the 1860's—but its influence was much greater than its circulation would indicate, especially after Phillips became associate editor. After the adoption of the Fifteenth Amendment in 1870 the *Standard* changed its name to *The National Standard*. At the beginning of 1872 it became a monthly instead of a weekly. The *National Standard* was merged with the *National Temperance Advocate* in 1873.

The *Liberator* was the most famous of all abolitionist newspapers. During the war Garrison wrote only about half of the weekly editorials. Charles K. Whipple and Samuel May, Jr., wrote most of the others and supervised much of the makeup work on the paper. Its circulation fluctuated between 2,500 and 3,000 during the war, but like the *Standard* its influence reached far beyond its circulation. Garrison terminated the *Liberator* at the end of 1865, exactly 35 years after he had begun publishing it.

For the early years of an important antislavery newspaper, see Louis Filler, "Liberalism, Anti-Slavery, and the Founders of the *Independent*," *New England Quarterly*, xxvii (Sept. 1954) 291-306. Under Theodore Tilton's editorship the *Independent*, published weekly in New York, was almost as much an abolitionist paper as the *Standard* or the *Liberator*. From the spring of 1863, when Tilton took over as editor, until the early 1870's the circulation of the *Independent* hovered around the 70,000 mark. In 1864-65 Wendell P. Garrison served as assistant editor of the *Independent*. Oliver Johnson was managing editor from 1865 through 1870. In addition, several abolitionists contributed regular or occasional columns to the *Independent*. Tilton resigned from the editorship at the end of 1870, winding up a brilliant eight-year career as editor of one of the most influential radical journals in the land.

The weekly *Boston Commonwealth* was founded in August 1862, as the semiofficial organ of the Emancipation League. It was financed at first primarily by George Stearns. Moncure Conway and Frank Sanborn served as dual editors of the *Commonwealth* until April 1863, when Conway went to England and Sanborn took over as editor-in-chief. The *Commonwealth* became the spokesman for the old John Brown abolitionists and radical Republicans of Massachusetts. Charles W. Slack became editor in October 1864, and continued in that position until his death in 1885. The circulation of the *Commonwealth* seldom rose higher than 5,000. Most of the time during Reconstruction the paper was less radical than the *Standard* or the *Independent*. Slack held several political offices in Massachusetts after the war, and he could not afford to be too far in advance of his party.

The *Principia* was a weekly paper edited in New York by William Goodell. It served as the semiofficial organ of the Radical Abolitionist party and the Church Anti-Slavery Society. Goodell was an uninspiring writer and the *Principia* a rather dull paper. Its circulation was small, and Goodell was forced to suspend publication temporarily several times during the war and scrape up more money to keep his paper going. The *Principia* was suspended permanently in 1866.

In Rochester Frederick Douglass published his own newspaper, *Douglass' Monthly*, until August 1863. The paper was the spokesman for northern Negroes and for the Douglass wing of the abolitionist movement. Another Negro newspaper was the *Anglo-African*, edited in New York by Robert Hamilton and James McCune Smith. The *Anglo-African* represented more narrowly than *Douglass' Monthly* the interests of northern Negroes, especially of New York City Negroes, and was a little bit out of the main current of abolitionism. The paper was suspended in 1865 after the death of Smith. I. Garland Penn, *The Afro-American Press and Its Editors* (Springfield, Mass., 1891) supplies background information on the personalities of the Negro press during the Civil War era.

In May 1861, James Redpath began publishing in Boston a weekly newspaper called *The Pine and Palm*, organ of Redpath's Haitian Emigration Bureau. The paper advocated traditional abolitionist doctrines plus voluntary emigration of American Negroes to Haiti. The *Pine and Palm* folded in October 1862, when the Haitian Emigration Bureau was dissolved.

In November 1865, George Stearns published the first issue of a Negro suffrage weekly newspaper called the *Right Way*, edited by Alpheus Crosby and William W. Thayer. Stearns financed the free distribution of 60,000 copies weekly until May 1866, when he began charging a subscription fee of $1 per year. Circulation promptly dropped to 30,000, where it remained until the paper was terminated after the passage of the first Reconstruction Act in March 1867.

The Revolution, a weekly newspaper published in New York, 1868-1870, and edited by E. C. Stanton and Parker Pillsbury, was the militant organ of the woman suffrage wing of the abolitionists.

Two religious journals edited by abolitionists during the 1860's were the *American Baptist*, a small Baptist weekly edited in New York by

Nathan Brown; and *Zion's Herald,* published in Boston as the official organ of the New England Methodist Conference. Gilbert Haven became editor of *Zion's Herald* in 1867, and continued in that post until 1872; this journal had a circulation of 16,000.

Most of the larger freedmen's aid societies published monthly or quarterly journals recording their activities and exhorting the faithful to contribute more money. The three most important such journals were the *American Missionary Magazine,* organ of the A.M.A., published monthly throughout the Civil War and Reconstruction; the *American Freedman,* monthly organ of the American Freedmen's Union Commission during its three-year existence, 1866-69; and *The Freedmen's Record,* organ of the New England Freedmen's Aid Society, published monthly from 1865-1868 and quarterly thereafter until it ceased publication in 1874.

B. Nonabolitionist Newspapers

The daily issues of the *New York Tribune* constituted one of the more important sources for this book. The *Tribune* published many speeches, letters, and articles by abolitionists, and occasionally printed news stories and editorials about antislavery leaders. From 1862 to 1866 the *Tribune* was, in part, an extension of the personality and ideas of its managing editor, Sydney Howard Gay. Gay resigned in 1866, but the *Tribune* continued to be a valuable source of information and opinion about radical activities after that time. Ralph Ray Fahrney, *Horace Greeley and the Tribune in the Civil War* (Cedar Rapids, Iowa, 1936), Harry W. Baehr, *The New York Tribune since the Civil War* (New York, 1936), and Glyndon G. Van Deusen, *Horace Greeley, Nineteenth Century Crusader* (Phila., 1953) furnish useful background information about the *Tribune.* Louis M. Starr, *Bohemian Brigade: Civil War Newsmen in Action* (New York, 1954) includes an excellent discussion of Gay's connection with the *Tribune.*

The *New York Times* was the most important single source for the opinions of moderate Republicans about the abolitionists and their ideas. The excellent index of the *Times* from 1863 onward made it possible to find many valuable editorial comments and news stories about the abolitionists and the radicals. Although generally aligning itself with moderate Republicans, the *Springfield Republican* carried a weekly column by William S. Robinson ("Warrington") throughout the entire Civil War and Reconstruction period, and Franklin Sanborn was a member of the *Republican's* editorial staff from 1868 to 1872.

Scattered issues of the following newspapers and periodicals were also consulted for information relating to the abolitionists: the *Boston Advertiser* (moderate Republican); the *Boston Courier* (Whiggish); the

Boston Herald (Democratic); the *Boston Journal* (Republican); the *Chicago Times* (Copperhead Democratic); the *Chicago Tribune* (Republican, tending to radicalism); the *Cincinnati Gazette* (Republican, leaning toward radicalism); the *Cleveland Leader* (Republican); the *Columbus Crisis* (Copperhead Democratic); the *Continental Monthly* (emancipationist); *Harper's Weekly* (Republican); the *Nation* (Republican); the *New York Evening Post* (moderate Republican); the *New York Herald* (maverick Democratic and independent); the *New York World* (Democratic); the *Philadelphia Press* (Republican); the *Washington Chronicle* (Republican); and the *Worcester Spy* (radical Republican).

PAMPHLETS, BROADSIDES, SPEECHES, BOOKS, AND OTHER
ABOLITIONIST PUBLICATIONS

The *Annual Reports* of the American Anti-Slavery Society for 1860 and 1861 (they were discontinued after 1861) contain information on the abolitionists' attitude toward the Republican party, the election of 1860, and the secession crisis. The *Proceedings of the American Anti-Slavery Society at Its Third Decade Anniversary Meeting in Philadelphia, December 3 and 4, 1863* (New York, 1864), includes much useful material on the abolitionists during the war. William Lloyd Garrison, *The Abolitionists, and Their Relation to the War* (*Pulpit and Rostrum*, nos. 26 and 27, New York, 1862), pp. 31-54; Wendell Phillips, *The Philosophy of the Abolition Movement* (New York, 1860); and Phillips, *The War for the Union* (New York, 1862) set forth the Garrisonian position toward the Republican party and the war. The *Annual Reports* of the Philadelphia Female Anti-Slavery Society, 1860-1869, provide a useful compendium of the year-by-year reaction of abolitionists to the events of the Civil War and Reconstruction.

Abolitionists' wartime pamphlets and books about West Indian emancipation are listed in footnote 2, Chapter VII of this book. The *Annual Reports* of the American Missionary Association, the New England Freedmen's Aid Society, the National Freedmen's Relief Association, and other freedmen's aid societies document the yearly activities in the field of freedmen's education.

The number of pamphlets, broadsides, printed letters and other published material produced by individual abolitionists during the Civil War and Reconstruction is immense. Gerrit Smith alone was the author of more than 40 broadsides and printed letters in the 1860's, which have been bound and deposited with the Gerrit Smith Papers, su. Speeches or sermons by such men as Wendell Phillips and George Cheever were frequently published in pamphlet form. For a useful although primitive bibliography of pamphlet material the reader is referred to John Russell Bartlett, *The Literature of the Rebellion* (Boston, 1866), which lists more than 6,000 titles, including hundreds of abolitionist items.

No effort will be made here to list every pamphlet or broadside consulted in the research for this book. Many of these items are cited in the footnotes. The following discussion will be confined to items of particular importance, interest, or relevance. John W. Alvord, *Letters from the South, Relating to the Condition of the Freedmen, addressed to Major General O. O. Howard* (Washington, 1870) were written while Alvord, superintendent of education for the Freedmen's Bureau, was on a tour of the South in 1869-1870. Two books by the Negro abolitionist, William Wells Brown—*The Black Man, His Antecedents, His Genius, and His Achievements* (Boston, 1863), and *The Rising Son* (Boston, 1874)— argue the case for the Negro's innate equality with the white man. David Lee Child, *Rights and Duties of the United States Relative to Slavery under the Laws of War* . . . (Boston, 1861) was an important exposition of the government's power over slavery in wartime. Three books by Moncure Conway presented moving pleas for emancipation and equal rights: *The Rejected Stone: or Insurrection vs. Resurrection in America* (Boston, 1861); *The Golden Hour* (Boston, 1862); and *Testimonies Concerning Slavery* (2nd ed., London, 1865). The Emancipation League published the replies to its questionnaire on the condition and needs of freedmen within Union lines in a pamphlet entitled *Facts Concerning the Freedmen, Their Capacity and Their Destiny* (Boston, 1863). William Channing Gannett, "The Freedmen at Port Royal," *North American Review*, CI (July 1865), 1-28 is an excellent article by a participant in the Port Royal experiment, setting forth soberly and incisively the difficulties and achievements of the freedmen's aid enterprise. Most of the chapters in Thomas Wentworth Higginson's classic *Army Life in a Black Regiment* (East Lansing, 1960, with an introduction by Howard Mumford Jones [1st ed., Boston, 1869]) had appeared as articles in the *Atlantic Monthly* from 1864 to 1867. Samuel Gridley Howe, *The Refugees from Slavery in Canada West* (Boston, 1864) is an interesting book growing out of Howe's research among Canadian Negroes for the Freedmen's Inquiry Commission. James Miller McKim, *The Freedmen of South Carolina* . . . (Phila., 1862) is a brief but shrewd appraisal of the possibilities of freedmen's education by one of the leading abolitionist workers in the cause. Mary Traill Spence Putnam, *Record of an Obscure Man* (Boston, 1861) argues eloquently for the nobility of the African race. Linda W. Slaughter, *The Freedmen of the South* (Cincinnati, 1869), by a teacher of the A.M.A., is polemical, zealous, but nevertheless useful.

Charles Stearns, *The Black Man of the South, and the Rebels* (New York, 1872), a very revealing book, recounts the experiences of an abolitionist who went South after the war with the intention of buying and reselling land to the freedmen. George L. Stearns published two pamphlets in 1865 containing speeches by Phillips, Douglass, William D. Kelley, Henry Ward Beecher, and others urging Negro suffrage and equal rights: *The Equality of All Men before the Law* (Boston, 1865); and *Universal Suffrage, and Complete Equality in Citizenship, The Safeguards of Democratic Institutions* (Boston, 1865). Harriet Beecher Stowe, "The Education of Freedmen," *North American Review*, cxxviii (June 1879), 605-15, cxxix (July 1879), 81-94 is a convenient and able summary of the record of the freedmen's aid societies. Theodore Tilton, *The Negro* (New York, 1863) is a poetic and moving statement of the essential equality of the Negro race. William Whiting, *The War Powers of the President, and the Legislative Powers of Congress in Relation to Rebellion, Treason, and Slavery* (1st ed., Boston, 1862), the foremost statement of the war power argument, went through 42 subsequent editions, with additions, revisions, and changes in title.

MEMOIRS, AUTOBIOGRAPHIES, AND REMINISCENCES

There is a plethora of memoirs by abolitionists and antislavery leaders. Most of them conceal more than they reveal. Only those that were helpful in the preparation of this study will be listed here.

Elizabeth Botume, *First Days Amongst the Contrabands* (Boston, 1893) is an excellent book of reminiscences written by one of the best teachers at Port Royal. William Wells Brown, *My Southern Home* (Boston, 1880) is the somewhat episodical and sensationalist autobiography of an ex-slave who became a leader in the abolitionist movement. James Freeman Clarke, *Anti-Slavery Days* (New York, 1884) is anecdotal in nature, but supplies an occasional insight of value. Levi Coffin, *Reminiscences* (Cincinnati, 1880) includes much useful information on Coffin's wartime efforts in behalf of freedmen's relief in the West. Moncure D. Conway, *Autobiography, Memoirs and Experiences* (2 vols., Boston, 1904) is important for an understanding of this southern-born abolitionist. Frederick Douglass, *Life and Times of Frederick Douglass* (Hartford, 1884) is somewhat disorganized, and less helpful than had been anticipated. James R. Gilmore, *Personal Recollections of Abraham Lincoln and the Civil War* (Boston, 1898) contains useful information on the *New York Tribune*, Sydney Gay, and the *Continental Monthly* during the war. Two books of autobiographical and biographical sketches by Thomas Wentworth Higginson—*Cheerful Yesterdays* (Boston, 1898) and *Contem-*

poraries (Boston, 1899)—include several chapters about the abolitionist movement and the Civil War. Oliver Johnson, *William Lloyd Garrison and His Times* (2nd ed., Boston, 1885) is a valuable account of the Garrisonians by one of Garrison's closest associates. George W. Julian, *Political Recollections, 1840 to 1872* (Chicago, 1884) provided some insights on the relation of abolitionists to radical Republicans. John Mercer Langston, *From the Virginia Plantation to the National Capital* (Hartford, 1894) is long-winded but useful. Samuel J. May, *Some Recollections of Our Anti-Slavery Conflict* (Boston, 1869) is a carefully written and important book, of limited value for the period after 1861. Joseph Whiting Parker, "Memoirs," typescript of MS written in 1880, supplied to the author by Parker's granddaughter, Mrs. Perce J. Bentley, is rambling and frequently inaccurate, but is nonetheless a valuable account of a Boston abolitionist who had lived in the South briefly before the war, and returned there after the war as a representative of New England Baptist freedmen's aid societies. George W. Smalley, *Anglo-American Memories*, 1st Series (London, 1911) contains a few anecdotes about Wendell Phillips. Lillie B. C. Wyman, *American Chivalry* (Boston, 1913) is also valuable for personal anecdotes about Phillips and other abolitionists.

BIOGRAPHIES

Henry Greenleaf Pearson, *The Life of John A. Andrew* (2 vols., Boston, 1904) is a comprehensive and valuable work containing much information about Andrew's antislavery career and his relations with the abolitionists. Ida H. Harper, *The Life and Work of Susan B. Anthony* (3 vols., Indianapolis, 1898-1908) prints several letters which are unavailable elsewhere. Alma Lutz, *Susan B. Anthony, Rebel, Crusader, Humanitarian* (Boston, 1959) is an accurate and readable biography, although sometimes overly sympathetic to Miss Anthony. Octavius B. Frothingham, *Memoir of William Henry Channing* (Boston, 1886) quotes liberally from Channing's diaries and letters. Robert M. York, *George B. Cheever, Religious and Social Reformer, 1807-1890* (Orono, Me., 1955) is informative and accurate. Mary Elizabeth Burtis, *Moncure Conway* (New Brunswick, N.J., 1952) is a readable but sometimes inaccurate biography. Frank A. Rollin, *Life and Public Services of Martin R. Delany* (Boston, 1868) is a eulogistic but useful study of a Negro abolitionist. Giraud Chester, *Embattled Maiden: The Life of Anna Dickinson* (New York, 1951) is well written and informative, although undocumented. It should be supplemented for the Civil War years by James Harvey Young, "Anna Elizabeth Dickinson and the Civil War: For and

Against Lincoln," MVHR, XXI (June 1944), 59-80. Benjamin Quarles, *Frederick Douglass* (Washington, 1948) is a sound and valuable biography. William H. Pease, "William Channing Gannett, A Social Biography," Ph.D. dissertation, University of Rochester, 1955 is a good study of one of the younger abolitionists who went to Port Royal in 1862.

Wendell P. Garrison and Francis J. Garrison, *William Lloyd Garrison* (4 vols., Boston, 1885-89), though marked by filial piety, is the basic source for an understanding of the Garrisonian abolitionist movement. The authors not only traced Garrison's life in great detail, but brought together and published excerpts from hundreds of his letters and editorials. Two recent biographies, Walter M. Merrill, *Against Wind and Tide: A Biography of William Lloyd Garrison* (Cambridge, Mass., 1963), and John L. Thomas, *The Liberator: William Lloyd Garrison* (Boston, 1963) supersede earlier studies of Garrison.

Catherine H. Birney, *The Grimké Sisters: Sarah and Angelina Grimké* . . . (Boston, 1885) is old but serviceable. William Haven Daniels, *Memorials of Gilbert Haven* (Boston, 1880) is eulogistic, but valuable because of the many letters which it publishes. Carl Wittke, *Against the Current, The Life of Karl Heinzen* (Chicago, 1945) is an important study of this little-known German-American abolitionist. Mary Thacher Higginson, *Thomas Wentworth Higginson* (Boston, 1914) is better than the usual family biography. It should be supplemented by Tilden Edelstein, "Strange Enthusiasm: Thomas Wentworth Higginson, 1823-1877," Ph.D. dissertation, Johns Hopkins University, 1961, and Anna Mary Wells, *Dear Preceptor, The Life and Times of Thomas Wentworth Higginson* (Boston, 1963). C. Carroll Hollis, "R. J. Hinton, Lincoln's Reluctant Biographer," *The Centennial Review of Arts & Sciences,* v (Winter 1961), 65-84 is an excellent biographical article, although unfortunately it is undocumented. John White Chadwick, *Sallie Holley, A Life for Liberty* (New York, 1899) is valuable for the many letters it prints. Harold Schwartz, *Samuel Gridley Howe: Social Reformer* (Cambridge, Mass., 1956) is accurate and helpful, but thin. Carol Brink, *Harps in the Wind: The Story of the Singing Hutchinsons* (New York, 1947) is an excellent biography of a family of musical abolitionists. Ira V. Brown, "Miller McKim and Pennsylvania Abolitionism," *Pennsylvania History,* xxx (January 1963), 56-72, presents a skeletal outline of McKim's career.

Irving H. Bartlett, *Wendell Phillips: Brahmin Radical* (Boston, 1961) is a first-rate piece of work and supersedes all earlier biographies of Phillips, including Oscar Sherwin's *Prophet of Liberty: The Life and Times of Wendell Phillips* (New York, 1958) which is poorly written, uncritical, and unoriginal. Richard Hofstadter, "Wendell Phillips: The Patrician as Agitator," in *The American Political Tradition and the*

Men Who Made It (Vintage ed., New York, 1958), 137-63 is a stimulating and suggestive essay.

Abe C. Ravitz, "John Pierpont: Portrait of a Nineteenth Century Reformer," Ph.D. dissertation, NYU, 1955, was moderately useful. Benjamin B. Hickok, "The Political and Literary Career of F. B. Sanborn," Ph.D. dissertation, Michigan State University, 1953, is disappointing on the Civil War and Reconstruction years. Octavius B. Frothingham, *Gerrit Smith* (New York, 1879) is valuable chiefly for the letters and writings of Smith which it publishes. A more complete study of Smith is Ralph Volney Harlow, *Gerrit Smith: Philanthropist and Reformer* (New York, 1939). Alma Lutz, *Created Equal: A Biography of Elizabeth Cady Stanton* (New York, 1940) is less satisfactory than the same author's study of Susan B. Anthony. Frank P. Stearns, *The Life and Public Services of George Luther Stearns* (Phila., 1907) is uncritical, but constitutes a vital source for an understanding of this important abolitionist, and prints many letters unavailable elsewhere. Larry Gara, "William Still and the Underground Railroad," *Pennsylvania History,* xxviii (Jan. 1961), 33-44 and Alberta S. Norwood, "Negro Welfare Work in Philadelphia, Especially as Illustrated by the Career of William Still," M.A. thesis, University of Pennsylvania, 1931, provide helpful information on this Philadelphia Negro abolitionist. Edward L. Pierce, *Memoir and Letters of Charles Sumner* (4 vols., Boston, 1877-94) is a detailed and eulogistic study, containing many Sumner letters. It has been largely superseded for the pre-Civil War period by David Donald, *Charles Sumner and the Coming of the Civil War* (New York, 1960). Benjamin Thomas, *Theodore Weld: Crusader for Freedom* (New Brunswick, N.J., 1950) is an excellent biography, treating fully Weld's return to the platform during the Civil War. A series of articles by Charles Kassel in *Open Court*, xxxiv (Sept. 1920), 564-69, xxxvii (Mar. 1923), 167-75, xxxviii (July 1924), 406-18, xxxix (Sept. 1925), 563-76, xli (Apr. 1927), 239-56, and xliii (Jan. 1929), 35-50 (Feb. 1929), 94-106 constitute the basic biographical sources for Edwin M. Wheelock, a New Hampshire abolitionist who lived in the South during and after the war. Samuel T. Pickard, *Life and Letters of John Greenleaf Whittier* (2 vols., New York, 1894) includes information on Whittier's wartime activities. Phillip Wright and Elizabeth Wright, *Elizur Wright: The Father of Life Insurance* (Chicago, 1937) is a rather disappointing study of this interesting abolitionist.

MONOGRAPHS, ARTICLES, AND OTHER WORKS

Several studies touch lightly upon the subject of the abolitionists and the Negro in the 1860's. William G. Cochrane, "Freedom without Equal-

ity: A Study of Northern Opinion and the Negro Issue, 1861-1870,"
Ph.D. dissertation, University of Minnesota, 1957, is superficial and thin,
but not without value. Two histories of the antislavery movement which
deal briefly with abolitionism in the early war years are Dwight L. Dumond, *Antislavery: The Crusade for Freedom in America* (Ann Arbor,
1961), a polemical and uncritical work; and Lawrence Lader, *The Bold
Brahmins: New England's War against Slavery, 1831-1863* (New York,
1961), which deals only with New England abolitionists and is inade-
quately researched. Benjamin Quarles, *The Negro in the Civil War* (Boston, 1953) is a readable and worthwhile study. The same author's *Lincoln
and the Negro* (New York, 1962) glosses over some of the anti-Lincoln
sentiment among radical Negroes, while William O. Douglas, *Mr. Lincoln and the Negroes: The Long Road to Equality* (New York, 1963)
is thin and not profound. Margaret Shortreed, "The Anti-Slavery Radicals, 1840-1868," *Past and Present*, no. 16 (Nov. 1959), 67-87 is a
Marxist interpretation of the revolutionary aspects of the antislavery
movement. Elizabeth Cady Stanton, Susan B. Anthony, and Matilda
Joslyn Gage, *History of Woman Suffrage* (6 vols., New York, 1881-1922),
vol. II, contains information on the activities of women abolitionists during the war and Reconstruction. Edith Ellen Ware, *Political Opinion in
Massachusetts during the Civil War and Reconstruction* (New York,
1916) and T. Harry Williams, *Lincoln and the Radicals* (Madison, Wis.,
1941) are important for an understanding of the political milieu in
which the abolitionists operated.

Most of the northern Protestant denominations included a number
of abolitionists among their leaders. The activities of these evangelicals
are touched upon in Chester F. Dunham, *The Attitude of the Northern
Clergy toward the South, 1860-1865* (Toledo, 1942); Ralph E. Morrow,
Northern Methodism and Reconstruction (East Lansing, 1956); William
Warren Sweet, *The Methodist Episcopal Church and the Civil War* (Cincinnati, 1912); and Lewis G. Vander Velde, *The Presbyterian Church
and the Federal Union, 1861-1869* (Cambridge, Mass., 1932).

The basic studies of the 1860 election are Emerson D. Fite, *The Presidential Campaign of 1860* (New York, 1911), which surveys all parties,
and Reinhard H. Luthin, *The First Lincoln Campaign* (Cambridge, Mass.,
1944), which concentrates primarily on the Republicans. Two excellent
studies of the North during the secession winter are David M. Potter,
Lincoln and His Party in the Secession Crisis (New Haven, 1942), and
Kenneth M. Stampp, *And the War Came: The North and the Secession
Crisis, 1860-61* (Baton Rouge, 1950), both of which mention briefly the
role of the abolitionists. Dwight L. Dumond, ed., *Southern Editorials on
Secession* (New York, 1931) and Howard C. Perkins, ed., *Northern*

Editorials on Secession (2 vols., New York, 1942) are valuable compilations of editorial opinion on the crisis. The Perkins volumes contain a great deal of material on the antiabolitionist attitudes of the northern conservative and Democratic press.

On the question of the Negro's racial potential, William S. Jenkins, *Pro-Slavery Thought in the Old South* (Chapel Hill, 1935), Guion G. Johnson, "A History of Racial Ideologies in the United States with Reference to the Negro," MS in the Schomburg Collection of the NYPL, Arthur Young Lloyd, *The Slavery Controversy, 1831-1860* (Chapel Hill, 1939), and William R. Stanton, *The Leopard's Spots: Scientific Attitudes Toward Race in America, 1815-59* (Chicago, 1960), provide the necessary background for an understanding of the abolitionists' attitude toward this issue. The anti-Negro, antiabolitionist sentiments of the northern workingman and Democrat are ably discussed in Williston Lofton, "Northern Labor and the Negro during the Civil War," JNH, xxxiv (July 1949), 251-73; Albon P. Man, Jr., "Labor Competition and the New York Draft Riots of 1863," JNH, xxxvi (1951), 375-405; and Emma L. Thornbrough, "The Race Issue in Indiana Politics during the Civil War," *Indiana Magazine of History*, xlvii (June 1951), 165-88. For a sample of the many studies of wartime efforts to colonize the Negro abroad, see footnote 4, Chapter VII of this book.

There are several able monographs and articles which deal with the freedmen's aid enterprise. Augustus F. Beard, *A Crusade of Brotherhood, A History of the American Missionary Association* (Boston, 1909), although old and eulogistic, is nevertheless valuable for an understanding of the A.M.A.'s work. George R. Bentley, *A History of the Freedmen's Bureau* (Phila., 1955) supersedes earlier studies of the Bureau, and contains helpful information on the relation of the Bureau to the freedmen's aid societies. Ira V. Brown, "Lyman Abbott and Freedmen's Aid, 1865-1869," JSH, xv (Feb. 1949) provides useful insights into the postwar activities of the freedmen's associations. Richard Bryant Drake, "The American Missionary Association and the Southern Negro, 1861-1888," Ph.D. dissertation, Emory University, 1957, is an excellent study, indispensable for an understanding of the A.M.A. Luther P. Jackson, "The Educational Efforts of the Freedmen's Bureau and Freedmen's Aid Societies in South Carolina, 1862-1872," JNH, viii (Jan. 1923), 1-40, is a thorough study, written from the Negro's point of view. Julius H. Parmelee, "Freedmen's Aid Societies, 1861-1871," in *Negro Education: A Study of the Private and Higher Schools for Colored People in the United States; U.S. Department of Interior, Bureau of Education Bulletin, 1916*, no. 38, pp. 268-95 (Washington, 1917), is crammed full of facts, and supplies a framework for the study of freedmen's education. William H. Pease, "Three Years Among the Freedmen: William C. Gannett and the Port Royal Experiment," JNH, XLII (Apr. 1957), 98-117 discusses the experiences of a young Gideonite. Willie L. Rose, "Rehearsal for Reconstruction: The Port Royal Experiment," Ph.D. dissertation, Johns Hopkins University, 1962, is an outstanding piece of work, indispensable for anyone interested in the Port Royal enterprise. This dissertation has recently been published by the Bobbs-Merrill Co. Henry Lee Swint, *The Northern Teacher in the South, 1862-1870* (Nashville, 1941), although marred by a slight pro-southern bias and a certain superficiality, remains required reading for anyone working in this field. Bell Wiley, *Southern Negroes, 1861-1865* (New Haven, 1938) contains a section on the transition of the Negro to freedom, written from the point of view of the southern white.

John Hope Franklin, *The Emancipation Proclamation* (New York, 1963) provides a detailed story of the formulation and execution of that historic edict. On the Negro as a soldier the standard work is Dudley T. Cornish, *The Sable Arm: Negro Troops in the Union Army, 1861-1865*. Cornish's excellent bibliography lists additional secondary material on Negro troops. Ira V. Brown, "Pennsylvania and the Rights of the Negro, 1865-1887," *Pennsylvania History,* XXVIII (Jan. 1961), 45-57, ably describes the efforts of abolitionists and Negroes to desegregate transportation facilities in Pennsylvania. Leon F. Litwack, *North of Slavery* (Chicago, 1961) is an excellent study of northern discrimination against the free Negro before the Civil War. John G. Sproat, "Blueprint for Radical Reconstruction," JSH, XXIII (Feb. 1957), 25-44, is an able article discussing the work of the American Freedmen's Inquiry Commission. Martin Abbott, "Free Land, Free Labor, and the Freedmen's Bureau," *Agricultural History,* XXX (1956), 150-56, portrays the efforts of the Bureau to settle freedmen upon land of their own. LaWanda Cox, "The Promise of Land for the Freedmen," MVHR, XLV (Dec. 1958), 413-40, is a very good article discussing the various wartime proposals for providing the freedmen with land. Edwin D. Hoffman, "From Slavery to Self-Reliance," JNH, XLI (Jan. 1956) recounts the fate of the freedmen who were assigned lands along the South Carolina, Georgia, and Florida coast under Sherman's Order no. 15. Patrick W. Riddleberger, "George W. Julian: Abolitionist Land Reformer," *Agricultural History,* V (July 1955), 108-15, summarizes Julian's efforts to obtain confiscation-homestead legislation for the freedmen.

Ruhl Jacob Bartlett, *John C. Frémont and the Republican Party* (Columbus, 1930) includes a helpful account of Frémont's candidacy for the presidency in 1864. William F. Zornow, *Lincoln and the Party Divided* (Norman, Okla., 1954) is the best general account of the election of 1864. Important works on Reconstruction include Howard K. Beale, *The Critical Year: A Study of Andrew Johnson and Reconstruction* (2nd ed., New York, 1958); LaWanda Cox and John H. Cox, *Politics, Principle, and Prejudice, 1865-1866* (New York, 1963); Leslie H. Fishel, Jr., "Northern Prejudice and Negro Suffrage, 1865-1870," JNH, XXXIX (Jan. 1954), 8-26; William B. Hesseltine, *Lincoln's Plan of Reconstruction* (Tuscaloosa, Ala., 1960); Joseph B. James, *The Framing of the Fourteenth Amendment* (Urbana, Ill., 1956); Charles H. McCarthy, *Lincoln's Plan of Reconstruction* (New York, 1901); and Eric L. McKitrick, *Andrew Johnson and Reconstruction* (Chicago, 1960). John G. Sproat, "Party of the Center: The Politics of Liberal Reform in Post-Civil War America," Ph.D. dissertation, U. of Cal., 1959, portrays the growing dissatisfaction of several liberals with Reconstruction after 1867. Jacobus Ten-Broek, *The Antislavery Origins of the Fourteenth Amendment* (Berkeley, 1951) gives the legal and legislative background of the equal protection and other important clauses of the Fourteenth Amendment. The standard work on the 1868 election is Charles H. Coleman, *The Election of 1868: the Democratic Effort to Regain Control* (New York, 1933), which deals primarily with the Democratic party. Republican activities are treated in William B. Hesseltine, *Ulysses S. Grant, Politician* (New York, 1935). John M. Mathews, *Legislative and Judicial History of the Fifteenth Amendment* (Baltimore, 1909) is old and inadequate. It should be supplemented by William Gillette, "The Power of the Ballot: the Politics of the Passage and Ratification of the Fifteenth Amendment," Ph.D. dissertation, Princeton University, 1963.

INDEX